THE INDIAN ADMINISTRATIVE YEAR BOOK
1990

OTHER BOOKS BY S. R. MAHESHWARI

Indian Administration
The Evolution of Indian Administration
The General Election in India
Public Administration (co-author)
Government Through Consultation
The Administrative Reforms Commission
Local Government in India
The Study of Public Administration (edited)
President's Rule in India
State Governments in India
Teaching of Public Administration in India (edited)
Public Administration in India: Management of Change
Open Government in India
Indian Parliamentary System
Administrative Reform in India
Electoral Politics in the National Metropolis
Comparative Government and Politics
Lok Prashasan (co-author)
Tulnatmak Rajniti
Bharat Mein Sthaniya Shasan
Political Development in India
Rural Development in India
The Civil Service in Great Britain
The Higher Civil Service in Japan
The Higher Civil Service in France
Administrative Reform (edited)
Administrative Federalism
Theories and Concepts in Public Administration
Education in Public Administration in India (edited)
Indian Political System (in press)

THE INDIAN ADMINISTRATIVE YEAR BOOK 1990

SHRIRAM MAHESHWARI
Professor of Political Science and Public Administration
Indian Institute of Public Administration
NEW DELHI

Completed under the auspices of
The Centre for Political and Administrative Studies

CONCEPT PUBLISHING COMPANY, NEW DELHI 110059

ISBN 81-7022-391-1

First Published 1992

Published and Printed by
Ashok Kumar Mittal
Concept Publishing Company
A/15-16, Commercial Block, Mohan Garden
NEW DELHI 110059

Lasertypeset by
Microtech Advance Printing Systems (Pvt.) Ltd.
H-13, Bali Nagar
NEW DELHI 110015

To

The Indian Institute of Public Administration:

You have occupied an immeasurably large part of my earthly existence

Though I know full well, I have been just a small cog in the Big Wheel

PREFACE

The present work admittedly is full of gaps, inadequacies, and shortcomings. It is but a product of a single individual's work completed within a strict time frame and amidst his other preoccupations and responsibilities.

Yet no one can deny or belittle the importance of an administrative year book. Indeed, a work of this nature is basic to sophisticated research and teaching and basic also to citizens' general understanding of the country's administrative system and practices. No less essential it is to civic education in the society.

For me at least, the *The Indian Administrative Year Book* marks the fulfilment of a dream, a dream dreamt for a long time. I have been talking about such a work for a long time, but the scale and volume of resources necessary for it prevented me from embarking upon it. At long last, I felt that a time has come when I should either myself undertake the challenge or observe silence, and talk about it no more. Challenges have somehow always tempted me. And the present work is the outcome.

A number of libraries in Delhi were helpful in the completion of this exercise, and I thank them. *The Times of India* Library was particularly kind as it made available its vast facilities, and I tender my sincere thanks to it. A work of this nature and scale could not have been complete without the advice, support and cooperation of a number of civil servants. Their number is too large to be identified here — nor may many like to be named. I particulary thank A.R. Bandopathyay, N. Mohanty and J.M. Phatak for readily extending their help whenever I approached them. One chapter of the manuscript was seen by P.K. Umashankar. T.N. Chaturvedi also went through a chapter. I thank them for their kindness.

Comments and suggestions for further improvement of the work are welcome from the readers as these would be valuable in preparing the next year's volume.

Navratra, 8 October 1991 SRM
156, Golf Links
New Delhi 110002

CONTENTS

1

THE ADMINISTRATIVE EVOLUTION OF THE GOVERNMENT OF INDIA

The origin of the present-day administrative system of the Government of India lies in the administration of the East India Company, a trading company chartered by England's Queen Elizabeth in 1600 (to be correct, the last day of the year 1599) which went into oblivion in 1857 when India's governance was finally taken over by the Crown (that is, British Parliament) in Great Britain. Under the Company, the provinces (or presidencies) came first, and the central government appeared much later — only in 1773 — when the British Government in London passed the Regulating Act of 1773. This Act is momentous: it laid down the skeleton of the governmental system of modern India: all subsequent enactments were basically in the nature of enlargements and amplifications on the core set up in 1773.

The Regulating Act of 1773, as already said, created for the first time a central, or what was then called "supreme", government, distinct from the provincial or presidency governments, thus clearly laying down the skeleton of the present governmental system in the country. It appointed a Governor-General at Fort William in Bengal, who was assisted by a council of four members and provided that "the whole civil and military government of the said presidency (of Fort William in Bengal), and also the ordering, management and government of all the territorial acquisitions and revenues in the kingdoms of Bengal, Bihar and Orissa, shall . . . be and are hereby vested in the said Governor-General and council. . . ." The Governor-General's council decided cases by majority (entailing the possibility of the Governor- General himself being overruled, which did happen sometime). The Governor-General and his council superintended and controlled the presidencies of Madras and Bombay in matters relating to war and peace with the princes. The Governor (or president) of each of the presidencies and his council were directed to "pay due obedience to such orders as they shall receive . . . from the Governor-General and council . . . and constantly and diligently to transmit to the said Governor-General and council advice and intelligence of all transactions and matters whatsoever that shall come to their knowledge relating to the government, revenues or interest of the Company". The Act also established a supreme court of judicature at Fort William, which consisted of a chief justice and three other judges.

The Governor-General's council discharged both executive and legislative functions, which remained united until 1833. The Charter Act of 1833 made, for the first time, a distinction between the executive and the legislative function of the Governor-General's council by providing for the addition of a law member to the latter when it sat to transact legislative work. To revert, there were three departments in the central government in the year 1774:

1. Public Department
2. Secret Department and
3. Revenue Department.

A number of new departments were created during the period 1773-1833.

The Charter Act of 1833 introduced several important changes in the country's public administration. The Governor-General of Bengal became the Governor-General of India. This functionary was also the Governor of Bengal. The Act of 1833 put an end to the trade activities of the East India Company, and from now onwards, the Company was left with only ruling responsibilities. The Act also entrusted the central government with the exclusive responsibility of legislation, and a Legislative Member was added to the Governor-General's council. Thirdly — and importantly — a beginning was made towards separation of the secretariat of the Government of India from that of the Government of Bengal. The Military Department, the Secret Department and the law functions emerged as the exclusive concern of the Government of India; but for the remaining functions the arrangement of a joint secretariat of the Government of India and that of Bengal continued.

A complete separation of the secretariat of the central government from that of Bengal was effected in 1843. In 1833, the central government was divided into the following departments even though some were under a separate secretariat and others under a joint one:

1. Military Department
2. Secret Department
3. General Department
4. Foreign Department
5. Finance Department
6. Political Department
7. Revenue Department
8. Judicial Department.

In 1843, the Government of India came to have its entirely separate secretariat, consisting of the following four departments:

1. Home Department (consisting of revenue, separate revenue, general, marine, judicial, legislative and ecclesiastical branches)
2. Foreign Department (consisting of political, foreign and secret branches)
3. Finance Department
4. Military Department.

Consequent upon the expansion of governmental functions, the machinery of public administration was expanding. In 1855, a new Public Works Department was set up to look after civil and military buildings, irrigation, communication including railways. The existing Military Board was considered superfluous and abolished. In 1857, the three universities of Bombay, Calcutta and Madras had been established, which necessitated the creation of a new Education Branch to look after "education". The Education Branch was located in the Home Department.

The Crown Takes Over

In 1857 occurred the armed uprising against the British, variously called the sepoy mutiny, the first war of Indian independence, etc. The uprising was crushed and the power of governance of India was fully assumed by the British Crown. This necessitated some apex level changes in the machinery of governance. The office of the Secretary of State for India was created to take over the functions of the East India Company's Court of Directors or the Board of Control. The Secretary of State for India was assisted by the Council of India and the council of Governor-General was designated as the "Council of the Governor-General of India". Other levels remained unchanged.

Government of India at the Time of the Royal Commission upon Decentralisation

The Government of India Act of 1858, which, as said earlier, abolished the control of the East India Company, placed the Government of India directly under the sovereign, acting through the Secretary of State for India. The Secretary of State for India, who was furnished by this Act with a council, had the power of giving orders to every officer in India, including the Governor-General and of directing all business relating to India that was transacted in the United Kingdom. Of these wide papers and duties many rested on his personal responsibility; others could be performed only in consultation with his council, and for some of these, mainly relating to financial matters, the concurrence of a majority of the members of the council was required.

All expenditure from Indian revenues, whether in India or elsewhere, was subject to the control of the Secretary of State in council who was required to lay the Indian budget annually before the British Parliament, with a report on the 'home accounts' by an independent auditor, and to submit therewith statement showing the 'moral and material' progress of India.

The Secretary of State was, in his turn, responsible to British Parliament. Parliamentary legislation had at one time or another, created the Government of India, authorised the establishment of the large provinces ruled by Lieutenant-Governors, and brought the presidency governments of Madras and Bombay into subordination to the Supreme Government of Fort William. From British Parliament, too, were derived the constitution and functions of the Indian and provincial legislatures, the high courts and the method of recruitment of the Indian Civil Service. Any material change in these, as a consequence, necessitated parliamentary sanction.

In the ordinary course, however, parliamentary legislation for India was confined to acts amending the political constitution, or empowering the Secretary of State to raise money by loan; nor did Parliament directly control the revenues of India, unless these were to be applied to military operations beyond the frontier. But the Indian budget had to be laid before the British Parliament annually; the Secretary of State, and the British cabinet, of which he was a member, were open to criticism, and if occasion arose, to censure, in either House of Parliament; while every member of either House had the right of interpellation on any matter relating to the administration of India.

The members of the executive council of the Governor-General were all appointed by the British Crown, on the advice of the Secretary of State, and while some of the ordinary members were drawn from the Indian Civil Service, others were appointed direct from Britain. The usual tenure of office of a member of the executive council of the Governor-General was five years.

The distribution of work among the various departments and the procedure regulating their mutual relations were laid down in 'rules of business', which were issued by the Governor-General (under the Indian Councils Act of 1861), and were supplemented by subsidiary regulations termed 'secretariat instructions'. Any important alteration in the rules of business required the concurrence of the Secretary of State.

In regard to his department, each member of executive council was largely in the position of a minister of state, and had the final voice in ordinary departmental matters. But any question of special importance, and any matter in which it was proposed to over-rule the views of a provincial (then called 'local') government was to be referred to the Governor-General. This latter provision acted as a safeguard against undue interference with the provincial government, but it necessarily threw a large amount of work on the Governoor-General. In the year 1907-8, no less than 21.7 per cent of the cases which arose in, or came up to, the home department, required submission to the Governor-General. The home department was, however, concerned with questions which were, in a special degree, subject to review by the head of the government, and that in other departments the percentage of the cases referred to the Governor-General was considerably less. Any matter originating in one department which also affected another was to be referred to the latter, and in the event of the departments not being able to agree, the case was referred to the Governor-General.

The members of executive council met periodically as a cabinet — ordinarily once a week — to discuss questions which the Governor-General desired to be put before them, or which a member, who had been over-ruled by the Governor-General, had asked to be referred to the council. The Secretary in the department primarily concerned with a council case attended the council meeting for the purpose of furnishing any information which could be required of him. If there was a difference of opinion in council the decision of the majority ordinarily prevailed, but the Governor-General could over-rule a majority of he considered that the matter was of such grave importance as to justify such a step.

Each department was in the subordinate charge of a secretary, whose position correspond very much to that of a permanent Under-Secretary of State in the United Kingdom, but with these differences: that the secretary, as above stated, was present at council meetings; that he attended on the Governor-General, usually once a week, and discussed with him all matters of importance arising in his department; that he had the right of bringing to the Governor-General's special notice any case in which he considered that the Governor-General's concurrence was to be obtained to action proposed by the departmental member of council; and that his tenure of office was usually limited to three years.

The Government of India had no civil service of its own, as distinct from that of the provincial governments. The Indian Civil Service was recruited for, and distributed among, the latter, and officers serving under the Government of India were borrowed from the provinces for longer or shorter periods. The ordinary tenure of office of a Government of India secretariat officer, drawn from the Indian Civil Service, was three years, after which time he generally reverted to his own province. An under-secretary might, however, return later on as a deputy secretary, and a deputy secretary as a secretary.

Until the enforcement of the Government of India Act 1919, the Government of India was responsible for everything done in the provinces but, all the same, it was required to discriminate between matters which were primarily within the scope of the provinces, where the central interference was to be of a very exceptional character, and matters in regard to which the central control was to be more detailed and constant. 'No definite steps towards the immediate attainment of this object appear, however, to have been taken, and the subsequent discrimination between the functions of the Imperial and the local governments, and the extent of the control normally exercised by the former over the latter, are the results of gradual administrative evolution.'

There were four departments in 1858: 1. Foreign, 2. Home, 3. Finance and 4. Military. The period starting from 1858 saw a steady increase in the functions of the Government of India. Necessarily, new departments were added. In 1869 a Legislative Department was established to look after the legal matters of the Government. In the year 1871, the Department of Revenue, Agriculture and Commerce was created, only to be abolished eight-year later. In 1881, however, it was re-established as the Department of Revenue and Agriculture. In 1905, the Department of Commerce and Industry was set up to deal with matters concerning industries and trade. The Railway Board was created in the same year and was placed under the Department of Commerce and Industry. In 1910, a Railways Department was created and the Railway Board was placed under it. The same year saw the clevation of the education branch of the Home Department into a separate Education Department. The nomenclatures of some other departments were changed around this time. The Military Department was redesignated as the Army Department and the Foreign Department was renamed as the Foreign and Political Department.

Landmark in Constitutional Evolution

Another landmark in the constitutional evolution in India was the passage of the Government of India Act, 1919. On 29 August 1917, the Secretary of State for India made the historic announcement of a responsible government for India. The immediate upshot of this declaration was the Government of India Act, 1919, which devolved definite responsibility on the provinces in many areas, thus altering significantly the pattern of relationship between the central government and the provinces. The subjects of education, medical administration, public health, local self-government, roads and buildings, agriculture, animal husbandry, cooperative societies, industries, excise, etc., were transferred to the control of ministers in the provinces.

Prior to the passage of the Government of India Act, 1919, the central government in India was really the government of the governments in India, supervising and directing the provincial governments in the entire field of administration. The Act of 1919 envisaged a vertical division of responsibility between the central government and the provinces. The workload of the central government ought to have shown some reduction. Contrary, however, to popular expectations, work in the central secretariat registered a remarkable increase during the period 1919-35. The political changes unleashed by the Government of India Act, 1919, resulted in a quickening of activities in various spheres, generating thereby new work in the central secretariat. Increasing intercourse with international organisations like the League of Nations and the International Labour Organisation (ILO) introduced an entirely new dimension in the functions of the central government. Besides, new subjects came to the fore in connection with broadcasting, civil aviation, public-service commission, etc. To make a long story short, the central secretariat found itself engaged in more work than ever in the past, which is reflected in the increasing number of both senior officers and clerical personnel employed in it. Not much change in the machinery of the government, however, occurred. In 1919, there were ten departments in the Government of India:

1. Home
2. Foreign and Political
3. Finance
4. Army
5. Public Works
6. Legislature
7. Revenue and Agriculture
8. Commerce and Industry
9. Railways and
10 Education.

Act of 1935 — Another Landmark

The next landmark in the administrative evolution was the enactment of the Government of India Act, 1935, which provided for a federal system entailing distribution of legislative powers between the Centre and the Provinces. While the provinces were conferred provincial autonomy dyarchy was introduced at the Centre. As is well known, the provisions of this Act of 1935 relating to the central government were not carried out.

The Act envisaged provincial autonomy in place of dyarchical system in vogue under the Government of India Act, 1919. The Wheeler Committee, called the Government of India Secretariat Committee (1936), sought to assess the impact of this change on the work load of the central government. It observed: "At first sight it would appear that the advent of provincial autonomy must mean a substantial curtailment of the work now devolving upon the Government of India, and it was with some initial surprise that we heard the unanimous testimony of the secretaries to that government that they did not anticipate any such degree of relief. We accordingly went through with these officers each item in the present distribution of business, and were forced eventually to the conclusion, unexpected as that might be, that in general their surmise was likely to be accurate. The work of defence, foreign and political, railway and ecclesiastical departments is obviously not affected by the inauguration of provincial autonomy, except that in the political department it will be increased now that all (princely) states are in direct relation with the Government of India (the intervention in some instances of a local government having been eliminated) and difficult and possibly protracted negotiations in connection with the federation are to be anticipated. . . . If this anticipation is correct, it follows that no great measure of relief to the Government of India is to be expected on this account". The number of departments in the central government remained at nine till 1937 when it was increased to twelve. The Foreign and Political Department was bifurcated into the External Affairs Department and the Political Department. The Department of Industries and Labour was divided into the Department of Labour and the Department of Communications. In 1938 the Army Department was re-designated as Defence Department.

A number of organisational changes took place during the Second World War. In 1939, a separate Department of Supply was created to look after provision of supplies. The Department of Co-ordination was created in the same year to deal with war legislation, particularly the Defence of India Act. In 1941, the Department of Information and Broadcasting was established to centralise the entire publicity and information machinery of the Government of India. In 1942, a new Defence Department was set up under an Indian Defence Member of the Governor-General's council and the old Defence Department was redesignated as the War Department. A Department of Food was also created in 1942, to look after the problem of food shortage in the country. In the same year, the Communications Department was bifurcated into the Department of Posts and Air and the Department of War Transport. In 1943, a Department of Industries and Civil Supplies was set up mainly to look after the exigencies created by the War.

Further reorganisation of the Departments was effected after the Second World War was over. This was understandable. Firstly, the two Military Departments, i.e., the War Department and the Defence Department, were merged to form the War Department, which was subsequently redesignated as the Defence Department. In 1945, the hitherto composite Department of Education, Health and Lands was trifurcated, resulting in the creation of the Departments of Education, Health and Agriculture. The Indian Overseas Section in the combined Department was also separated. It was entrusted with the additional work connected with the country's relationship with Burma and other British-ruled territories and was designated as the Department of Commonwealth Relations. The new department was, however, amalgamated with the Department of External Affairs in 1947, to form the Department of External Affairs and Commonwealth Relations. In 1946, the Department of Industries and Civil Supplies was combined with the Department of Supply to form the Department of Industries and Supplies. In the same year, the Department of Posts and Air was redesignated as the Communications Department and the Department of Labour was bifurcated to form the Department of Labour and the Department of Works, Mines and Power. A separate State Department was established in July 1947, to deal with matters relating to the princely states and in August 1947, there were the following 18 departments under the Government of India, which were redesignated as Ministries on 29 August 1947:

1. External Affairs and Commonwealth Relations
2. Defence
3. Finance
4. Home
5. States
6. Legislative (Law)
7. Commerce
8. Industries and Supplies
9. Railways
10. Transport
11. Communications
12. Labour
13. Agriculture
14. Food
15. Education
16. Health
17. Information and Broadcasting and
18. Works, Mines and Power.

Independence and After

All said and done, the public administration of the colonial rule had restricted functions which, moreover, were carried out on a modest scale. Independence of the country brought out qualitative changes in the concept and role of the state in India, with a far-reaching impact on the country's administration. Independent India was now boldly committed to the ideal of a welfare state, which meant considerable expansion of governmental activities.

In 1949, the government deputed Gopalaswamy Ayyangar, a senior civil servant and minister, to recommend a reorganisation of the administrative machinery though not much eventually came out of this effort. Ayyangar recommended that the central secretariat be divided into 28 departments to be accommodated in 20 ministries. This, he said,

> "does not mean that each ministry should always remain an independent portfolio. In fact, it would be an advantage to combine more than one ministry within the portfolio of one cabinet minister in a number of cases. It would also be an advantage to combine such an arrangement with the provision of assistance to the cabinet minister concerned through a minister of state, and even in exceptional cases more than one such minister".[1]

One can see the presence of "overlord" ministers in this recommendation, which was tried — and failed — in Great Britain during the Second World War. The Ayyangar suggestion was rejected by the cabinet in India.

Other important recommendations of this report related to the splitting of (i) the Ministry of Works, Mines and Power into two Ministries of Works, and of Mines (including Coal) and Power;[2] and (ii) of the Ministry of Industries and

Supply into two Ministries of Industries (including control of supplies and prices of industrial products, but excluding coal); and of Supply (proper) including disposals. Also, the report recommended the merger of the Department of Parliamentary Affairs in the Law Department on the ground that the former was not viable.[3]

The Constitution which India enacted in 1950 visualised new or vastly expanded functions for the Government. India embarked on planning in a systematic, organised way in the 1950s, which necessitated assumption of an entirely novel range of functions by the government. The belief that being a federation entailing division of functions between the centre and the state governments, the former's functions would remain curtailed was not proven correct. The functions of both the levels of the government increased in number, range and scale.

In February 1951, the existing Ministries of Commerce, Industries and Supply; Works, Mines and Power; and the Department of Scientific Research were merged to form three new ministries of:

1. Industry and Commerce
2. Works, Production and Supply
3. Natural Resources and Scientific Research.

Also, the Ministries of Food and Agricultural were merged into one ministry known as Food and Agriculture Ministry. The years to come saw greater economic development and industrialisation visualised in the country's Five Year Plans. In June 1952, the Ministry of Works, Production and Supply was bifurcated into the Ministry of Works, Housing and Supply and the Ministry of Production. In August of the same year, the Ministry of Irrigation and Power was created.

After the First General Election

In 1952, when the first general election had taken place, the central government comprised 20 ministries as under:

1. Ministry of Defence
2. Ministry of External Affairs and Commonwealth Relations
3. Ministry of Finance
4. Ministry of Home
5. Ministry of States
6. Ministry of Information and Broadcasting
7. Ministry of Law
8. Ministry of Food and Agriculture
9. Ministry of Education
10. Ministry of Health
11. Ministry of Commerce and Industry
12. Ministry of Labour
13. Ministry of Railways
14. Ministry of Transport
15. Ministry of Communications

16. Ministry of Works, Housing and Supply
17. Ministry of Production
18. Ministry of Irrigation and Power
19. Ministry of Relief and Rehabilitation and
20. Ministry of Parliamentary Affairs.

In August 1954, was created the Department of Atomic Energy and put directly under the Prime Minister. In 1955 a new Ministry of Iron and Steel was created and, two years later, the Ministry of Production was abolished. In September 1956, a new Ministry of Community Development emerged uncorporating the earlier Community Projects Administration. In August 1956, the Ministry of Commerce and Industry was bifurcated into two separate ministries:

1. Ministry of Commerce and Consumer Industry
2. Ministry of Heavy Industries.

In October 1956, the Ministry of Food and Agriculture was bifurcated into the Ministry of Food and the Ministry of Agriculture. The working of these two separated ministries prompted the states to pick up less scrupulous habits. Since states had to deal with two ministries, they found advantage in submitting two varying sets of production figures — lower figures to the Ministry of Agriculture, in hope of larger allotment of foodgrains; and higher figures to the Ministry of Food in the expectation of increased grants under the "Grow More Food" programmes. It was, therefore, an act of real politic to unite the two ministries. And, this happened in April 1957, when a major reorganisation of ministries was undertaken. The April 1957 reorganisation created two new ministries — Ministry of Steel, Mines and Fuel; and Ministry of Transport and Communications. The latter Ministry of Transport and Communications consisted of two departments — Transport, and Civil Aviation and Communications. A further change occurred in March 1958, after the death of the Education Minister, Abul Kalam Azad. The Ministry of Education and Scientific Research was split into the Ministry of Education and the Ministry of Scientific Research and Cultural Affairs. And this pattern of mergers of existing departments and carving of new ones continues till this day, and will not, one cannot help observe, come to an end.

In 1978 the central ministries increased to 54, as under:

1-5. *Ministry of Agriculture and Irrigation*
- i Department of Agriculture
- ii Department of Food
- iii Department of Rural Development
- iv Department of Agricultural Research and Education
- v Department of Irrigation

6-7. *Ministry of Commerce, Civil Supplies and Cooperation*
- i Department of Commerce
- ii Department of Civil Supplies and Cooperation

8. *Ministry of Communications*

9-11. *Ministry of Defence*
  i Department of Defence Production
  ii Department of Defence Supplies

12-13. *Ministry of Education and Social Welfare*
  i Department of Education
  ii Department of Social Welfare

14-15. *Ministry of Energy*
  i Department of Power
  ii Department of Coal

16. *Ministry of External Affairs*

17-20. *Ministry of Finance*
  i Department of Economic Affairs
  ii Department of Expenditure
  ii Department of Revenue

21-22. *Ministry of Health and Family Welfare*
  i Department of Health
  ii Department of Family Welfare

23-26. *Ministry of Home Affairs*
  i Department of Official Language
  ii Department of Personnel and Administrative
  iii Reforms

27-28. *Ministry of Industry*
  i Department of Industrial Development
  ii Department of Heavy Industry

29. *Ministry of Information and Broadcasting*

30. *Ministry of Labour*

31-33. *Ministry of Law, Justice and Company Affairs*
  i Department of Legal Affairs
  ii Department of Legislative
  iii Department of Company Affairs

34-35. *Ministry of Petroleum, Chemicals and Fertilisers*
  i Department of Petroleum
  ii Department of Chemical and Fertilisers

36-37. *Ministry of Planning*
  i Department of Statistics

38. *Ministry of Railways/Rail Board*

39. *Ministry of Shipping and Transport*

40-41. *Ministry of Steel and Mines*
   i Department of Steel
   ii Department of Mines

42-43. *Ministry of Supply and Rehabilitation*
   i Department of Rehabilitation
   ii Department of Supply

44. *Ministry of Tourism and Civil Aviation*

45. *Ministry of Works and Housing*

46. *Ministry of Atomic Energy*

47. *Department of Culture*

48. *Department of Electronics*

49. *Department of Parliamentary Affairs*

50. *Department of Science and Technology*

51. *Department of Space*

52. *Cabinet Secretariat*

53. *President's Secretariat*

54. *Prime Minister's Office*

The functions continued to expand. In 1987, the secretariat registered a further increase and consisted of 69 departments:

1-4. *Ministry of Agriculture*
   i Department of Agriculture and Cooperation
   ii Department of Agricultural Research and Education
   iii Department of Rural Development
   iv Department of Fertilisers

5-7. *Ministry of Commerce*
   i Department of Commerce
   ii Department of Textiles
   iii Department of Supply

8-9. *Ministry of Communications*
- i Department of Posts
- ii Department of Telecommunications

10-12. *Ministry of Defence*
- i Department of Defence
- ii Department of Defence Production and Supplies
- iii Department of Defence Research and Development

13-15. *Ministry of Energy*
- i Department of Coal
- ii Department of Power
- iii Department of Non-conventional Energy Sources

16-19. *Ministry of Home Affairs*
- i Department of Internal Security
- ii Department of States
- iii Department of Official Language
- iv Department of Home

20-24. *Ministry of Human Resource Development*
- i Department of Education
- ii Department of Youth Affairs and Sports
- iii Department of Women's Welfare
- iv Department of Arts
- v Department of Culture

25. *Ministry of Environment and Forests*
- i Department of Environment, Forests and Wild Life

26. *Ministry of External Affairs*

27-29. *Ministry of Finance*
- i Department of Economic Affairs
- ii Department of Expenditure
- iii Department of Revenue

30-31. *Ministry of Food and Civil Supplies*
- i Department of Food
- ii Department of Civil Supplies

32-33. *Ministry of Health and Family Welfare*
- i Department of Health
- ii Department of Family Welfare

34-37. *Ministry of Industry*
- i Department of Industrial Development
- ii Department of Company Affairs
- iii Department of Chemicals and Petrochemicals
- iv Department of Public Enterprises

38. *Ministry of Information and Broadcasting*

39. *Ministry of Labour*

40-42. *Ministry of Law and Justice*
- i Department of Legal
- ii Department of Legislative Department
- iii Department of Justice

43-44. *Ministry of Parliamentary Affairs and Tourism*
- i Department of Parliamentary Affairs
- ii Department of Tourism

45-48. *Ministry of Personnel, Public Grievances and Pensions*
- i Department of Personnel and Training
- ii Department of Administrative Reforms and Public
- iii Grievances
- iv Department of Pension and Pensioner's Welfare

49. *Ministry of Petroleum and Natural Gas*

50-51. *Ministry of Planning*
- i Department of Planning
- ii Department of Statistics

52. *Ministry of Programme Implementation*

53-54. *Ministry of Science and Technology*
- i Department of Science and Technology
- ii Department of Scientific and Industrial Research

55-56. *Ministry of Steel and Mines*
- i Department of Steel
- ii Department of Mines

57-59. *Ministry of Transport*
- i Department of Railways
- ii Department of Civil Aviation
- iii Department of Surface Transportation

60. *Ministry of Urban Development*

61. *Ministry of Water Resources*

62. *Ministry of Welfare*

63. *Department of Atomic Energy*

64. *Department of Electronics*

65. *Department of Ocean Development*

66. *Department of Space*

67. *Cabinet Secretariat*

68. *Prime Minister's Office*

69. *Planning Commission.*

Even when the labels continue unchanged the contents have materially altered. Today, despite the Central Constitution which entails division of functions between the two levels of the government the central government carries out no less than 2,000 functions. In the year 1990, the Government of India comprises 71 ministries and departments.

Ministries and Departments, 1990

1-4. *Ministry of Agriculture*
- i Department of Agriculture and Cooperation
- ii Department of Agricultural Research and Education
- iii Department of Rural Development
- iv Department of Fertilisers

5-6. *Ministry of Civil Aviation and Tourism*
- i Department of Civil Aviation
- ii Department of Tourism

7-8. *Ministry of Commerce*
- i Department of Commerce
- ii Department of Supply

9-10 *Ministry of Communications*
- i Department of Posts
- ii Department of Telecommunications

11-13. *Ministry of Defence*
- i Department of Defence
- ii Department of Defence Production and Supplies
- iii Department of Defence Research and Development

14-16. *Ministry of Energy*
- i Department of Coal
- ii Department of Power
- iii Department of Non-Conventional Energy Sources

17. *Ministry of Environment and Forests*
- i Department of Environment, Forests and Wild Life

18. *Ministry of External Affairs*

19-21. *Ministry of Finance*
- i Department of Economic Affairs
- ii Department of Expenditure
- iii Department of Revenue

22-23. *Ministry of Food and Civil Supplies*
- i Department of Food
- ii Department of Civil Supplies

24. *Ministry of Food Processing Industries*

25-26. *Ministry of Health and Family Welfare*
- i Department of Health
- ii Department of Family Welfare

27-30. *Ministry of Home Affairs*
- i Department of Internal Security
- ii Department of States
- iii Department of Official Language
- iv Department of Home

31-35. *Ministry of Human Resource Development*
- i Department of Education
- ii Department of Youth Affairs and Sports
- iii Department of Arts
- iv Department of Culture
- v Department of Women and Child Development

36-39. *Ministry of Industry*
- i Department of Industrial Development
- ii Department of Company Affairs
- iii Department of Chemicals and Petro-Chemicals
- iv Department of Public Enterprises

40. *Ministry of Information and Broadcasting*

41. *Ministry of Labour*

42-44. *Ministry of Law and Justice*
- i Department of Legal Affairs
- ii Department of Legislative
- iii Department of Justice

45. *Ministry of Parliamentary Affairs*

46-49. *Ministry of Personnel, Public Grievances and Pensions*
- i Department of Personnel and Training
- ii Department of Administrative Reforms and Public
- iii Grievances
- iv Department of Pension and Pensioners' Welfare

50. *Ministry of Petroleum and Natural Gas*

51-52. *Ministry of Planning*
- i Department of Planning
- ii Department of Statics

53. *Ministry of Programme Implementation*

54. *Ministry of Railways*

55-57. *Ministry of Science and Technology*
- i Department of Science and Technology
- ii Department of Scientific and Industrial Research
- iii Department of Biotechnology

58-59. *Ministry of Steel and Mines*
- i Department of Steel
- ii Department of Mines

60. *Ministry of Surface Transport*

61. *Ministry of Textiles*

62. *Ministry of Urban Development*

63. *Ministry of Water Resources*

64-71. *Ministry of Welfare*
- i Department of Atomic Energy
- ii Department of Electronics
- iii Department of Ocean Development
- iv Department of Space
- v Cabinet Secretariat
- vi President's Secretariat
- vii Prime Minister's Office
- viii Planning Commission

NOTES

1. Report on Reorganisation of the Machinery of Government, p.27.
2. *Ibid.*, p.13.
3. *Ibid.*

2

THE EVOLUTION OF CIVIL SERVICE IN INDIA

The civil service of independent India is a continuation of the civil service of the British colonial rule just as its public administration maintains continuity with the administrative system of the Raj. The British came to India as traders but in course of time emerged as rulers. The East India Company had received the charter of trade but by a quirk of destiny, emerged as a ruler of a country of continental dimensions. In 1858 the Company was abolished, and the ruling power was assumed by the British Crown. To the East India Company goes the credit of giving to the world the nomenclature of 'civil service'. The Company had its military personnel in India also; and the term 'civil service' was designed to distinguish its members from the military arm (and later the judiciary also).

The first members of the civil service were thus merchants and recruited in accordance with the practice of the times, which was the patronage system. Originally classified as 'Covenanted Civil Service' and 'Un-Covenanted Service', the former was exclusively European in its composition; and Indians could, generally, find entry only into the lower ranks of the lower service, namely the Un-covenanted Service, the mode of appointment in either category being patronage. The civil service of the day was in the beginning inefficient, lazy and corrupt with low awareness of the broader social purpose, but in course of time was purged of its weaknesses and emerged as a very efficient and dedicated one. In 1853, the British Government decided to do away with patronage and in its place, make an open competitive examination as the mode of public recruitment. The first open competitive examination was accordingly held in London in 1855. Earlier, in the mid-thirties, a decision was taken to introduce English as India's official language, which proved to be of profoundly historic significance for India. Indians with well-to-do socio-economic background began to learn English to prepare for a prestigious career under a secure regime. The resultant growing supply of English-educated youth led to a demand for employment of Indians, as was but to be expected, in the civil service.

While proclaiming, in 1858, the British Crown's direct assumption of rule over India from the hands of the East India Company, Queen Victoria, the reigning Sovereign, assured complete equality between Indians and Europeans, among others, in matters of public recruitment. The Royal assurance, however, remained virtually a dead letter, for the first-ever Indian was able to enter the Covenanted Civil Service as late as in 1864 — nine years after the commencement of the competitive examination. To undertake a long voyage to London, the centre of the examination, was not easy or practical for most

Indians; what is more, racial considerations were also not absolutely inoperative in matters of public recruitment.

Indian Civil Service

An account, howsoever brief, of the civil service in India must necessarily accord pride of place to the Indian Civil Service. If India was the jewel in the British Crown, the I.C.S., its sweetly abbreviated name, lent it lustre and fire. On when the Indian Civil Service was born there is little unanimity. Its birth may be traced to the year 1600 when the East India Company was established. Philip Woodruff, pseudonym of Philip Mason, himself a member of the I.C.S., ascribes the birth of this Service to the year 1769 when its members began to perform functions so characteristic of it and inseparable from its nomenclature.

Functionally, the year of origin of the Indian Civil Service was, according to this view, 1769. One could as well ascribe this Service's origin to the year 1855 when merit as judged through an open competitive examination was made the basis of recruitment to the I.C.S., thereby creating a level of efficiency whose other name became the I.C.S. The Macaulay Committee[1] Report (1854) provided the philosophy and base for this Service. Till 1892 what later came to be known as the Indian Civil Service bore the nomenclature of 'Indian Covenanted Civil Service.'[2] The Aitchison Commission on Public Service (1887) recommended the replacement of 'Indian Covenated Civil Service' by 'Imperial Civil Service' but the Secretary of State for India, the final authority to take decisions, preferred the nomenclature 'Indian Civil Service', the name which stayed ever since.

Statutory Civil Service

To provide avenues of public employment to suitable educated Indians, a separate civil service, called the Statutory Civil Service, was created in 1879. Nomination to the Statutory Civil Service was made by the provincial government subject to the approval of the Secretary of State for India. The selected person, moreover, was posted only within his own province. To make it an attractive service for Indians, one-sixth of the total number of the Indian Covenanted Civil Service posts were transferred to it. Even with the creation of the Statutory Civil Service, the educated Indians' demand for public employment did not much abate. The British Government in India reacted to this demand by setting up, in 1886 a committee designated as the Public Service Commission under the chairmanship of Sir C.U. Aitchison.

The Aitchison Commission and Civil Service

The Aitchison Report, published in 1887, recommended the admission of Indians, subject to their fitness, into the Indian Covenanted Civil Service but did not favour what Indians were demanding, namely the holding of the competitive examination simultaneously in India, arguing that this was not violative of Queen Victoria's royal proclamation. The basic objective of the British Government's public recruitment policy in India was to secure a public administration conducted on principles and by methods in harmony with the norms and standards of western civilisation. The competitive examination was, moreover, to bear a distinctively English character and was to be a test of English qualifications. This too pointed to the appropriateness of England being the centre of the examination. Also, western education in India was not equally or widely developed in India, both spatially and socially. The narrowly restricted provision for its dissemination in India was apt to favour only certain classes of people. Little purpose however was to be served when the intake was not to exceed six or so in a year: in the language of the Commission the mere holding of a competitive examination in India to select a handful of persons would rather create 'a large disappointed and thereby probably discontented class which would cause considerable embarrassment to the government'.[3] The Aitchison Commission made the Indian Covenanted Civil Service a *crops d'elite* by restricting its membership to what was absolutely necessary to fill the chief administrative positions of the government and such a number of smaller positions as was to ensure a complete course of training for junior civilians.

Another service, the Provincial Civil Service (or PCS), was to occupy the administrative posts released by the Indian Covenanted Civil Service, and was thus established in 1892, when the government announced action on the Report. The PCS was designed primarily to provide employment to educated Indians as part of the colonial pronouncement of 1858 favouring higher and more extensive employment in the civil service. This service was entirely for the locally recruited, and 'inferior' in power and status of the ICS. At the same time, a novel device of 'Listed Posts' was created to raise the stature of the Provincial Civil Service. 'Listed Posts' were the 'hived off' posts from the list of reserved posts for the I.C.S. included in the schedule of the Indian Civil Service Act of 1861. These were filled from amongst the members of the PCS on the basis of merit but were not transferred to and amalgamated with the latter service. Below the PCS was a third service comprising the lower administrative appointments above the ministerial grades, called the 'Subordinate Civil Service'.[4]

The civil service of the country, accordingly, came to be divided into three categories — Indian Civil Service, Provincial Civil Service, and the Subordinate Civil Service. The Statutory Civil Service was abolished in 1892. The superior posts were included in the indian Civil Service and the recruitment of it vested in the Secretary of State for India. The Aitchison Report has been a landmark in the evolution of civil services in India. The basic structure of the civil service in India had emerged, at least in its bare outline, in this Report. The Indian Covenanted Civil Service got designated as the indian Civil Service, or the I.C.S. Out of the Statutory Civil Service came the provincial civil service. The Uncovenanted services became the 'Subordinate Services'. In years to come new services were created. But the basic structure of the civil service in India remained altered.

The last years of the nineteenth century saw many changes in India, the more prominent being the political unification of the country, the centralisation of its government and the gradual assumption by it of new functions. In this process, new services were bound to be created and the existing ones strengthened. In the year 1892, the Indian Service of Engineers (Irrigation, Roads, and Buildings Branches) and the Indian Veterinary Service were created. Five years later, in 1897, the Indian Medical Service was constituted. No significant development took place for a few years. The years 1905-07 saw the formation of three new services, namely the Imperial Police (1905) the Indian Education Service (1906), and the Indian Agricultural Service (1907).

The British Declaration of 1917

The process of formation of such services, however, remained in abeyance in the years to come. The Indian national movement spearheaded by the Indian National Congress began demanding self-government. Later, the First Great War (1914-18) had a great reshuffling effect in many walks of life in India as in the larger world. The international equilibrium found itself substantially disturbed, particularly on the ideological plane, and this affected the political destiny of India too in a direct way. The British declaration of 20 August 1917 holding out the promise of a 'responsible government' in India opened a new chapter in the administrative (as in political) history of India. The Declaration acquired a legal base in the form of the Government of India Act, 1919, which introduced, for the first time in 1921, responsible government in a limited sphere at the provincial level through the device of 'transferred' subjects but under popular control. As a consequence, the central government ceased to be the sole government of the country even though constitutionally speaking, there was no departure from the existing unitary set up.

The Act of 1919 brought about significant change in the country's public administration. It created, for the first time, a vertical rather than a horizontal division of work in administration. It equipped the provinces with an independent sphere of administration in subjects like education, agriculture, medical, health, local government, roads and buildings, animal husbandry, cooperative societies etc. To the extent that the provincial governments were, for the first time, called upon to administer these subjects independently of the central government, the latter found itself released at least directly, from these responsibilities. This, therefore, nursed an expectation that the workload of the central government would decline as a result of the provincial government's assumption of functions in the 'nation-building' departments such as education, agriculture, public health etc. This, however, did not happen. The central government had now on to deal with a none too small volume of matters which the provinces began sending to it for advice or action. In other words, new work, mainly in the form of provincial references, was generated in the central government. Nor must one forget that India at the end of the First Great War (1914-18) though still a part of the British Empire, found itself more deeply involved in international matters. The League of Nations and the International Labour Organisation of which India was a member created new work in the Government of India. Moreover, as the transferred field in the provinces came under the control and direction of elected representatives of the people and as the latter were, expectedly, committed to the general welfare, the public expenditure on 'nation-building' departments began to increase as part of the ideology of the national movement. The technical departments in the provincial governments began to recruit more persons possessing expert knowledge in nation-building activities. These trends, to be sure, were not temporary, as they were to receive continual reinforcements in the years to come. With the emergence of two separate levels of governance, the provinces enjoying powers conferred by the Act itself, it was but logical for each level to possess and control its own civil service.

Indeed, the provincial civil service was already in existence since 1892. Its members were recruited in India and were given lower posts, the higher ones being reserved for the members of the Secretary of State for India's services.

In 1925, the Subordinate Civil Service was redesignated as the Junior Civil Service, and thus came to be recognised as a Provincial Service. What was unique in India was that in addition to the central services and the provincial services there was a set of services which was christened the 'All-India Services'.

The All-India Services

The term 'All-India Services' was first coined in 1918 by the Committee on Division of Functions under M.E. Gauntlett. Recruited and controlled by the secretary of State for India (hence also known as the Secretary of State's Services) the All-India Services were the following on the eve of the Government of India Act, 1919:

1. The Indian Civil Service
2. The Indian Police Service
3. The Indian Forest Service
4. The Indian Educational Service
5. The Indian Agricultural Service
6. The Indian Civil Veterinary Service
7. The Indian Forest Engineering Service
8. The Indian Medical Service
9. The Indian Service of Engineers.

Many services including the Indian Civil Service and the Indian Police Service continued to remain as before. But those which fell in the 'transferred' fields such as the Indian Educational Service, the Indian Agricultural Service, etc. were disbanded and replaced by the provincial services to which alone fresh recruitment was made. The existing members of the All-India Services, operating in the field of 'transferred' subjects continued to enjoy their usual privileges and facilities of All-India Services, but they were all wilting services. The fact is that the golden age of the All-India Services was over with the coming into enforcement of the Act of 1919 even though some of them were retained under the new dyarchical arrangements of governance. Especially, the Indian Civil Service and the Indian Police Service, the two security services, were retained under strong Indian protests. Nationalism in India was always sceptical of the All-India Services, and what appealed at that stage of political development was provincialisation of the services. The need for the country to retain these services is a belated, post-Independence phenomenon of Indian nationalism, and that too not favoured by the entire political spectrum.

Provincialisation of the services was both the declared British policy and the Indian nationalist demand. The British lent support to it for they were formally committed to a process of Indianisation of services within, of course, the framework of India as an integral part of the British Empire. The Islington Commission on the Public Services in India (1912-15) was the first to suggest a time-table of Indianisation: it fixed the ratio of Indians in the superior (that is, higher) civil services in the country. In 1919, the government announced its decision on the Islington Report; and the process of Indianisation became operative. The Lee Commission on the Superior Civil Services in India (1924) was the next move. The latter raised the scale and recommended a 50:50 cadre to be produced in the Indian Civil Service in about fifteen years. For the Indian Police Service, the Commission wanted half of the posts to be filled by Europeans and half by Indians. But not all Indians were to be recruited directly. White fifty Europeans were to be recruited directly, only thirty on the Indian side were to come from the open market, the remaining twenty to be promoted from the provincial service. In this way, the Indian Police Service was integrated with its provincial level partner. In sharp contrast, the Indian Civil Service did not have any feeder service. As regards the provincial services, it was expected that they would be manned by Indians.

Provincialisation of services accompanied by the emergence of responsible government in the field of transferred subjects brought the civil servants in the provinces and the politicians nearer each other which is a natural development in a democracy. To curb political patronage, the Government of India Act, 1919 provided for a public service commission responsible for recruitment of civil servants. The Lee Commission urged action on this constitutional provision 'without delay', regarding it as 'one of the cardinal features of our report and as forming an integral part of the whole structure of our proposals for the future of the (civil) services'.[5] The Central Public Service Commission was, accordingly, set up in 1926 with Sir Rose Barker, a senior member of the Home Civil Service, as its chairman, this choice being dictated by a desire to fashion the Commission after the traditions of the British Civil Service Commission. Public Service Commissions were later set up in the provinces. The Public Service Commission was viewed as the device to curb political patronage and to protect the civil services from the political influences to which they were now exposed, as well as to maintain reasonably high standards of recruitment in the civil service.

This new British policy of responsible government in India could not but disturb the morale of the European members and spoil the attractiveness of the Indian Civil Service for the bright graduates in Great Britain.[6] Though Lloyd George, the British Prime Minister, had at this time called the ICS 'the steel-frame', it did little to remove the fears regarding future career of the European members of the civil service as well of the potential candidates many, as a consequence, resigned and left India. In 1922, two hundred European members of the superior civil service sought premature retirement, the number increasing to 433 by the year 1927. Also, the bright university graduates were now somewhat unwilling to offer their services to India. To lure them to the civil service in India, some innovations outside the field of a written test were devised. All these administrative developments were taking place in midst of a mass political movement led by the Indian National Congress under the leadership of Mahatma Gandhi. The British, having perceived a threat to their career from the Indians now entering and about to enter the civil services, organised themselves into an association and so did the Indians. Inevitably, racialism crept into the public bureaucracy: at least to an extent.

The principal thrust of the reforms made under the British declaration of 1917 was, as has been made clear, in the direction of provincialisation of the services. In the process, the Secretary of State for India's hold over the superior services got loosened, and the gainers were the Government of India and the provinces, particularly the latter. The All-India Services were getting politically unacceptable and coming under the public criticism. While these services continued to operate under the ultimate control of the Secretary of State for India the central services came under the Government of India, and the latter's zone of authority expanded. The greatest gain, however, accrued to the provincial civil services and the subordinate services.

The functions of State began to increase under the Government of India Act, 1919 which inevitably led to an expansion of the central services as well as provincial services. In years to come, many new services, both central and provincial, were established to cope up with the increased functions. The greatest increase occurred, as was to be expected, in the sphere falling under the control of the provincial governments. At the same time, the combined forces of both democracy and development strengthened departmentalism in the public administration, creating, in the process, the problem of co-ordination at the field level. From now onwards, the district collector's writ could not be taken to run very smoothly consequent on the emergence of the politician-minister assertive of his control over the departmental hierarchy and of the specialists with their professional ego.

In the twenties the civil service in India stood classified into the following:

1. All-India Services
2. Central Civil Services
3. Provincial Services
4. Subordinate Services.

The members of the All-India Services owed their appointments to the Secretary of State for India who alone could terminate their services. The central civil services came under the control of the Government of India and were generally[7] recruited by it also. The provincial services fell under the appointing authority of the provinces. The subordinate services comprised minor administrative, executive and ministerial posts to which appointments were made by the provincial government concerned or an authority subordinate to it.

Government of India Act, 1935

The Constitution of 1919 was in its very conception a temporary one, paving way for the ultimate goal of a responsible government in India within the British Empire. The next constitution, the Government of India Act, 1935,[8] had had a long gestation period, visualising a federal form of government in India with the provinces enjoying an autonomous sphere of functions. Along with provincial autonomy, the Act set up a parliamentary form of government at the provincial level in which the executive was made accountable, within certain bounds, to the legislature. The provincial governments were inevitably to undergo re-structuring under the Act of 1935. With the inauguration of provincial autonomy in 1937, the popular ministries assumed power in the provinces, which affected the structure of public administration including the civil services. With the provision of federation under the act a review became necessary to find out whether the country's traditional integrated administrative system needed to be recast or not.

This needs some detailed discussion. Historically and operationally, Indian public administration right from the top to the village level has always remained unified, and even when the federalising process first began under the Act of 1919 (though formally not so designated) the integrated system of public administration was continued. As a result, the Government of India — in the sense of its headquarters organisation known as the secretariat — did not have a separate civil service of its own: it, as a rule, drew it policy-making and supervisory personnel from the provinces and the field services. A review was undertaken, consequent on the passage of the Act of 1935 with its feature of federalism, whether a bifurcation of civil service in India became desirable and even necessary.

The Maxwell Committee on Organisation and Procedure (1937) discussed the issue but recommended firm continuance of the existing tenure staffing of the central secretariat. According to it, a permanent civil service of the central government would verily be one without any direct touch with life in India which would be an inadequate preparation for the kind of work performed at the Centre. The background of many of the subjects with which the central government remains concerned cannot be understood unless officers dealing with them possess direct experience of working in the provinces, for it is at this level that effect of the policy made at the higher levels of governments are felt. A rotating civil service thus provides a valuable link between the Central and provincial governments. No less meaningful to the provincial government personnel is the insight into the outlook, method and even difficulties of the central government which a system of periodic inter-change provides.[9] Thus, the traditional method of staffing of the headquarters organisation of the Government of India continued.

But with the expanding functions of the central government under the new 1935 Constitution it discovered itself under mounting stress especially in regard to the recycling of officers. In 1937, a Finance-Commerce Pool, exempt from the traditional tenure system was constituted. The outbreak of the Second World War in 1939 in which India not only participated but also became an important Allies' centre for military operations in the East expanded suddenly and considerably the range and scale of governmental activities, leading to an expansion of the secretariat and necessitating appointment of a fairly large number of additional personnel. The result was that the Centre found itself indenting for a much larger number of officers from the provinces and at the same time showed a strong disposition not to revert them on the completion of their terms.

A sudden and substantial drop of the British element in the higher civil service in India occurred during this period even though the Joint Committee, whose Report formed the basis of the Government of India Act, 1935, put it on record that 'we are convinced that India for a long time to come will not be able to dispense with a strong British element in the Services'.[10] For the ICS it was accepted that the British proportion should be one-half. In practice, the arrangement was that part of the Indian half was to be recruited by examination in India and the remaining vacancies by examination in Britain. In 1936 the vacancies for the ICS were 20 and for the Home Service 33. The first 20 places on the joint list went to British candidates of whom not one accepted the ICS. In fact, none of the 20 candidates who could secure any home appointment elected for the ICS. More than that, of the 12 British candidates who were not high enough for the Home Service, but high enough for the ICS, 10 refused the latter service.[11]

The declining fortunes of the All-India Services have already been pointed out while discussing the impact of the Constitution of 1919 on the civil services. The Constitution of 1935 though based on provincial autonomy did not do away completely with them. The Indian Civil Service, the Indian Police and the Indian Medical Service (Civil) were retained, the first two being the security services and the last named to cater to the medical requirements of the European civil servants. Competitive examinations had begun to be held in India also.

Mention has already been made of the Central Public Service Commission set up in 1926. This commission, indeed, set the pattern of the scheme embodied in the Government of India Act, 1935, which provided for the setting up of a federal public service commission at the central level and a provincial public service commission for each province. They were set up by 1937 when the 1935 Act became operative. The federal public service commission was made responsible for conducting examinations for appointment to the civil services of the central government or the federation. Similarly, the provincial public service commission, closely patterned after the federal one, was holding competitive examinations for filling the vacancies in the provincial services.

In 1937, the popular ministries were formed in the provinces amidst a widespread national movement for Independence. Before the Constitution of 1935 could settle down to its normal level of functioning, the Second World War broke out drawing India into the global conflict on the side of the Allied Powers. The Congress ministries resigned on ideological ground leaving the task of governing in the hands of the career bureaucracy. Under the pressure of Second World War, public administration in India had to take up new functions to cope up with the new requirements. An expansion of the machinery of administration thus took place at various levels of governance. A sudden demand for additional public personnel could be met only by relaxing the usual standards of recruitment. As many war-time activities were viewed as temporary, the persons recruited were kept temporary. Recruitment to the All-India Services stopped from July 1942 because of extremely unsettled conditions. Even when the end of the Second World War was in sight recruitment in London was not resumed as meanwhile the political situation in India had changed drastically. In 1947, India won its Independence but the country was partitioned along communal lines. As part of the partition plan, the public personnel were also given the option of service in either of the newly created countries or retirement with generously planned pensionary benefits.

On the eve of Independence the civil service under the central government consisted of the following:

1. All-India Services
2. Central Services—Class I
3. Central Services—Class II
4. Subordinate Service[12]
5. Inferior Service.[13]

The Central Services (Class I) were th[illegible]llowing:

1. Indian Audit and Accounts Service
2. Central Engineering Service
3. Central Electrical Engineering Service
4. Imperial Customs Service
5. Superior Telegraph Engineering and Wireless Branches of the Indian Posts and Telegraphs Department.
6. Indian Posts and Telegraph Service
7. Geological Survey of India
8. Indian Meteorological Service
9. Mines Department
10. Archaeological Department
11. Zoological Survey of India
12. Indian Ecclesiastical Establishment
13. Medical Research Department (including Indian Medical Service)
14. Central Revenues Chemical Service
15. Bengal Pilot Service
16. Income-Tax Service
17. Mercantile Marine Training Ship Service
18. Imperial Secretariat Service
19. General Central Service
20. Railway Inspectorate Service
21. Indian Railway Service of Engineers
22. Transportation (Traffic) and Commercial Departments
23. Transportation (Power) and Mechanical Engineering Departments
24. Indian Railway Accounts Service.

Civil Service Since Independence

Independence in 1947 was bound to usher in profound and far-reaching changes in the country's civil service. The functions of the civil service were surely expanding particularly since the First Great War (1914-18), but this expansion was slow, and certainly not in the nature of a quantum jump. Historically speaking, the predominant concern of the civil service in India was regulatory and maintenance and whatever in developmental and promotional fields was undertaken was certainly not a part of the central thrust of the raj. The second basic concern of the civil service under the colonial rule was to entrust as a matter of deliberate policy strategically sensitive positions in the government to the British officers: they alone could be trusted to ensure a rule which respected the metropolitan interests over everything else.

With the exit of the British from India, the colonial objectives of governance ceased to be either valid or sufficient in themselves. The civil service in Independent India is necessarily obliged to function within the ordering framework of the Constitution of 1950. From a remotely governed country, India emerged as a democracy of the parliamentary type based on a system of periodic election held on adult franchise. Secondly, India is a union of States, the Constitution making both the centre and the constituent states ('provinces') autonomous in their respective areas of operation. This implies an autonomous civil service also. Thirdly, irrespective of levels or political complexions, the government in the country is irrevocably committed to the directive principles of state policy enshrined in the constitution itself, which direct it actively to work for the economic and social well-being of the people. This brings about a qualitative change in the role and place of public administration including the civil service in the Indian society.

Yet, independent India did not re-create its administering instrumentalities consequent on its tryst with destiny. On the contrary the public administration including the civil service rooted in the colonial culture was not only retained but also utilised for the carrying out of new tasks natural under a new order. This is all the more surprising because the nationalist leadership was consistently critical of the colonial administrative system and emphasised its radical reform.

How was it that public administration including its civil service with such a colonial track record was not reformed when the opportunity presented itself in 1947. This is one of the puzzles of modern Indian administrative history, and no conclusive or easy answer can be given — or even accepted. Perhaps, the true explanation behind the retention in independent India of the colonially designed administration including the civil service lies in the style in which India won its Independence. Once Great Britain decided, after the end of the Second World War, to get out of India, a constitutional process was firmly set into motion to complete the process. This was called 'transfer of power' characterised by the closest and fullest adherence to constitutionalism and legality, and further facilitated by an abundant presence of goodwill on both the sides, symbolised by the Mountbattens. The style of India gaining its Independence from Great Britain through a process of legislation created a kind of social climate with all emphasis on legality and propriety. Everything was done in accordance with laws, rules and regulations. The behaviour of the civil service too smoothened the transition of power and must have been endearing to the top leadership. At any rate, the pressure of work demanded using the machinery optimally: its reform could wait until the return of normal times. Not only this. India went a step forward to provide safeguards to the civil service. The Interim government under Jawaharlal Nehru initiated negotiations with London on guarantees to be given to the former Secretary of State for India's Services. India, on its own, had agreed to respect the existing rights of all members of these Services, whether European or Indian if they were willing to continue and were retained by the successor government. Members of the All-India Services were also given a joint guarantee by the central and provincial governments in India protecting their existing rights as well as terms and conditions of service. In short, the whole accent at the time was on strong continuity with the past. In such a climate, a radical change in public administration stood completely ruled out.

Whether it was wise on the part of the national leadership to keep the inherited administrative system going without much amendment is a rather debatable issue. The decision not to make any radical change certainly allowed the new political leadership to take full advantage of the old system. The new state had a pool of experienced public personnel to keep the administrative system in operation. When the transfer of power took place in 1947, Indian public personnel with 12 to 25 years' experience were available in reasonably large numbers—in over three quarters of their pre-war strength. This was a fortunate circumstance. Very fortunate also was the fact that since the mid-twenties, direct recruitment of high quality had begun to be made in India not only to the Indian Civil Service but also to the central service as well as the civil services of provinces. As a result, a small but significant reserve of high quality personnel had been accumulated, which could be and was drawn upon when, with Independence, challenges of nation-making state building and development faced India. At the same time, an opportunity for revamping the country's civil service to suit new goals and aspirations was missed. It ought to be remembered that systemic administrative reform is easy to carry out at a time of intense political change, and the period following independence was perhaps the most opportune one for such as exercise.

What is more, a nearly complete reversal of the nationalist attitude towards some bureaucratic institutions of the land also took place. The Indian political leadership, one may recall, was consistently critical of the All-India Services and openly demanded their disbandment. But when the Secretary of India for State announced, in 1946, the British Government's decision not to make future recruitment to them the Indian leadership suddenly began to solicit them and activated itself to retain these services.

Indian Reaction at the Time of Independence

The Interim central government was quick to convene a provincial premiers' conference in October 1946 to consider the question of replacement of the Indian Civil Service and the Indian Police. This conference met on 21 and 22 October 1946 under the chairmanship of Vallabhbhai Patel, the Home Member in the Interim Government. Patel made a plea for an 'All-India Administrative Service'. The arguments advanced for this were the obvious importance of maintaining the highest possible standard of efficiency, of giving the civil service 'experience . . . at the centre leading to efficiency, and administrative experience of the district, of serving as a liaison between the provinces and the (central) government', and of introducing, both in the provinces and in the centre, 'a progressive and wide outlook and freshness and vigour of administration.'[14] Patel secured acceptance of his proposal for the All-India Administrative Service as well as for a second All-India Service, namely the Indian Police Service. All this was a magnificent victory for the centre and, more truly, a personal triumph for Vallabhbhai Patel. Indeed, Patel may rightly be acknowledged as the father off All-India Services. His task was probably rendered less arduous by the Muslim League's initial abstention from the Interim central government. The Muslim League one may recall, joined the central government after the provincial premiers' conference had finished its deliberations. The first competitive examination for recruitment to the IAS was held in July 1947. The event is important in more than one way. The IAS emerged as a successor service to the Indian Civil Service. The constitution of this Service demonstrated that the all-India character of the ICS could be adopted to the changed circumstances in the country. About the same time, personnel earlier selected to the Indian Civil Service but actually not appointed in that Service were also diverted to the IAS. By the middle of 1948 officers selected on the basis of their war records were also appointed to the IAS.

Central Secretariat Service

One of the earliest measures which the central government initiated soon after Independence was the re-organisation of the Central Secretariat Service. The Central Secretariat Service, as designed, consisted of four grades in descending order: under secretary, superintendent, assistant superintendent and assistant. The Imperial Secretariat Service was never permitted to reach above the level of assistant secretary, a level below the under-secretary. The Central Secretariat Service, on the other hand, was designed with a much higher reach. It recruited the first line supervisors in the central secretariat but entry into the top grade was open, through promotion, to the clerical level personnel also.

As the officers of the Central Secretariat Service were to assume higher responsibilities, it was necessary to recruit them from a keener and stiffer competitive examination and appoint them at a higher level where they could after proper training and experience be suitable to assume higher responsibilities. The Central Secretariat Service is recruited from the combined civil services examination conducted by the Union Public Service Commission. It must be emphasised, the central secretariat has as a rule avoided giving itself a corps of permanent officers, and thus viewed, the constitution of a permanent officer class in the secretariat in the form of the Central Secretariat Service went against the grain of the country's administrative philosophy, namely that those engaged in policy-making must possess direct and first-hand experience of administration. Accordingly, in a bid to integrate it with the overall philosophy it was made an essential feature of the Central Secretariat Service to systematically expose its members to a minimum period of work in the field of enable them to acquire practical experience of executive administration. When the scheme for the Central Secretariat Services was being finalised a provision was accordingly made for 'training deputation' under state government.

Creation of New All-India Services

The central government has been making conspicuous efforts at the creation of new All-India Services, and it is but appropriate to turn one's attention to them even if in the process chronological discipline does not get fully observed.

Both the historical past and the constitutional feasibility of creating new All-India Services have been tempting the central government to create more of them in new spheres of activities. The existence of as many as nine such services in the past provided the contents of the centre's dream, and action was initiated to realise the latter. Besides, the constitution holds out a possibility of creating new All-India Services, which itself tempts the centre to action. The demand has often arisen from other sources also. For instance, these services have been viewed (see the States Reorganisation Commission, 1953-55) as a check on the separatist trends in the country, posing a threat to national integrity.

In the sixties, social turmoil in many part of country was steadily increasing to curb which the government convened, in August 1961, the chief ministers' conference to formulate an effective strategy of action. The chief ministers' deliberations covered many areas but significant is their recommendation for the creation of three new All-India Services.

1. The Indian Services of Engineers (Irrigation, Power, Building and Roads).
2. The Indian Forest Service.
3. The Indian Medical and Health Service.

The centre was in fact waiting for such an opportunity and thus reinforced, it initiated the necessary constitutional action in the winter session of the Indian Parliament. On 6 December 1961, the Rajya Sabha adopted a resolution in favour of these three services.[15] The advantages claimed by the centre for All-India Services are principally three.[16]

1. These services ensure a uniform and high standard of recruitment and training of officers.
2. The rotation of officers between the centre and the states and the inter-change of experience is beneficial to both the centre and the states.
3. These services develop an all India outlook.

The necessary legislation for the creation of All-India Services in the field of engineering, forestry and medicine was passed by Parliament on 6 September 1963. This involved an amendment of the All-India Services Act, 1951. As a result, section 2A was inserted into the Act of 1951, making provision for these three new services.

This was a distinct victory of the centre and a notable event in the history of the All-India Services. Even official orders were issued announcing the constituting of the Indian Medical and Health Service; and basic rules regarding recruitment and cadre management were notified in the *Gazette of India*. All this, however, was being done without taking into account the state governments' susceptibilities. Several state governments, not without reason, were opposed to the proposed services which compelled the centre to go slow.

However, in the mid-sixties the centre looked buoyant and was poised for further moves. The immediate success gained in the enactment of the legislation itself reinforced its confidence in regard to extended deployment of All-India Services. At any rate, this success emboldened the centre to initiate bolder moves. The centre, in 1965, initiated the move for the creation of two more All-India Services, namely the Indian Agricultural Service and the Indian Educational Service (General Education, Technical Education).[17] The resolution was eventually passed by the Rajya Sabha, which was but expected in view of the majority of the Congress Party in the House.

In the winter session of 1965 of the Parliament the government introduced the All-India Services (Amendment) Bill, 1965[18] to set up the Indian Agricultural Services and the Indian Educational Service (General Education, Technical Education). The bill, however, lapsed as the Lok Sabha was in the meantime dissolved.

Meanwhile, the Indian Forest Services was formally constituted on 1 July 1966, and initially it consisted of officers all selected from the State Forest Service. The first examination for direct recruitment to the Service was conducted by the Union Public Service Commission in September 1967.[19] The general election held in 1967 radically changed the political complexion of India, for the hitherto ruling party, the Congress, suffered defeat in several states and could form its government at the centre with a much reduced majority. The new political equilibrium was not auspicious for the All-India Services. The non-Congress parties came into power in as many as nine states out of the then total of seventeen states. These states did not hide their unreserved disapproval of the scheme. Thus, the plan of three new services in the fields of forestry, engineering and health to be supplemented by two others in education and agriculture appeared to have been shelved with the disappearance of the single party dominance in the country. What is really of interest is that the All-India Services were discovered to be not very welcome not only to some non-Congress state governments but also to some Congress-ruled ones.

When the Janata Party came into power at the centre in 1977 it abandoned the proposal for the setting up of the remaining two services in view of the several state governments' resistance to them. The Congress (I) Party, came into power at the centre in 1980, and again revived the move stating 'the proposal' that was earlier dropped was now under the consideration of the government'.[20] Rajiv Gandhi's government, however, preferred no action. Nor did the National Front coming into power in December 1989 move to promote these services in view of its constituent parties' consistent opposition.

The Commission on Centre-state Relations, commonly known as the Sarkaria Commission (1988), is the latest to have examined the institution of All-India Services in the context of India's centre-state relations. It recommended a further strengthening of these services with greater emphasis on selection, training, placement etc. and on more regular consultation between the centre and the states on matters relating to the management of these services. It recommended the creation of All-India Services in fields of engineering, medicine, and education, and even lent its support to constituting such services in other sectors like agriculture, cooperation, industry etc.[21] The Sarkaria formula envisages a much larger and fuller role for All-India Services.

The crucial question however is: will the state governments withdraw their opposition and see the Sarkaria virtues in them exactly the way the latter sees them? The states under the rule of non-Congress political parties are openly vociferous in their opposition to them. Basically, the issue of whether to have new All-India Services or not has become one of patronage. Ostensibly, the centre musters its plea for All-India Services on the criteria of administrative efficiency but control over a service inevitably gives it a silent but very effective tool of manipulation and pressure and it is this capacity which tends to arouse the state governments' fear ~~for~~ them. And they are not completely unjustified and mistaken for nursing such fears. The Congress government at the centre has not always successfully resisted the temptation of using the accredited tools and agencies of Indian federalism for short-term partisan ends. An abuse of the institution of governors of the states is widely known. This being the track record of the Congress at the centre, times are not very propitious for the creation of new All-India Services even though they may be warmly recommended by a high-powered commission like the Commission on Centre-State Relations (the Sarkaria Commission). Emphasis should be to run the existing All-India Services along purely professional lines so that these services evolve in course of time a distinct personality of their own and become an institution which begins to be sought after in the society for its own absolutely professionally motivated behaviour.

The Constitution irrevocably pledges the nation to the ideals enshrined in the preamble, the directive principles of state policy, the fundamental rights and fundamental duties. The era of socio-economic planning began in the fifties in a systematic way with the First Five Year Plan. The government had necessarily to take up new or additional responsibilities in social, economic or cultural fields, which necessitated creation of new organisations and expansion of the existing ones. The challenges of nation-making and state-building had to be met by the state, and in the process administrative machinery and personnel too expanded. Fresh recruitment of personnel became necessary to man these new positions. Within a decade of India's Independence, many new civil services came into existence, notable among them being (in addition to the Central Secretariat Service) the Central Health Service, the Central Legal Service and the Central Information Service. These were soon joined by the Indian Economic Service and the Indian Statistical Service. New services were getting organised to cope with the increasing work-load. By the year 1971, thirty organised services came into existence. The number increased to forty-nine in 1984 and fifty three in 1990. These are listed below:

Civil Service recruited through Civil Services (Non-Technical) Examination

1. Indian Administrative Service[22]
2. Indian Foreign Service
3. Indian Police Service[23]
4. Indian P & T Accounts and Finance Service
5. Indian Audit and Accounts Service
6. Indian Customs and Central Excise Service
7. Indian Defence Accounts Service
8. Indian Revenue Service
9. Indian Ordnance Factories Service
10. Indian Postal Service
11. Indian Civil Accounts Service
12. Indian Railway Traffic Service
13. Indian Railway Accounts Service
14. Indian Railway Personnel Service
15. Indian Defence Estates Service
16. Indian Information Service
17. Central Trade Service
18. Central Secretariat Service
19. Railway Board Secretariat Service
20. Armed Forces Headquarters Civil Service
21. Customs' Appraisers' Service

Service Recruited through the Engineering Service Examination

1. Indian Telecommunication Service
2. Indian Railway Service of Electrical Engineers
3. Indian Railway Service of Signal Engineers
4. Indian Railway Service of Mechanical Engineers

5. Indian Railway Service of Engineers
6. Indian Railway Stores Service
7. Military Engineering Service
8. Indian Naval Armament Service
9. Indian Ordnance Factories Service (Technical)
10. Central Power Engineering Service
11. Indian Inspection Service
12. Indian Supply Service
13. Central Electrical and Mechanical Engineering Service
14. Central Engineering Service
15. Central Water Engineering Service
16. Central Engineering Service (Roads)
17. Indian Broadcasting (Engs.) Service
18. Border Roads Engineering Service
19. Overseas Communication Service

Services Recruited through the Combined Medical Services Examination

20. Railway Medical Service
21. Central Health Service
22. Indian Ordnance Factories Health Service

Other Services Recruited through UPSC

23. Indian Forest Service[24]
24. Indian Cost Accounts Service
25. Indian Economic Service
26. Indian Statistical Service
27. Defence Research and Development Service
28. Defence Aeronautical Quality Assurance Service
29. Defence Quality Assurance Service
30. Central Legal Service
31. Company Law Board Service
32. Indian Salt Service

The number many look large but many services are small in size. The Indian Salt Service has a total membership of but 11. The Central Legal Service has 70 posts within its cadre. Only twenty-nine services have a cadre strength of more than 500. The Indian Economic Service and the Indian Statistical Service have 600 and 560 members respectively. All the engineering services taken together have a strength of about 10,000. In other words the engineering personnel constitute 15 per cent of the higher civil servants (Group A) in India where as the non-technical central services personnel recruited through the combined civil service examination number 9000 which is 13.4 per cent of the higher civil servants.

The IAS, the premier leadership service of the land, had an authorised strength of 1188 in the year 1951 which rose of 5047 in 1984. Table 2.1 below provides the authorised strength, state-wise, of the IAS for the year 1951, when the planning process first began in India. The seven five year plans plus a couple of annual plans which India has more or less successfully completed since the fifties have led to a vast increase in the number of personnel. Most states have undergone boundary changes consequent on the states' reorganisation undertaken on a massive scale in 1955, but also subsequently in 1960, 1961, 1966, 1971 and 1975. As a result, many states of 1951 no longer exist in their original size or even nomenclature. Yet Table 2.1 giving comparative figures for 1951 and 1984 may carry some interest.

TABLE 2.1: **Indian Administrative Service — Authorised Strength**

Year 1951		*Year 1984*	
Assam	42	Assam	186
		Nagaland	44
Bihar	96	Bihar	356
Bombay	110	Maharashtra	318
		Gujarat	195
Madhya Pradesh	73	Madhya Pradesh	361
Vindhya Pradesh	24		
Madhya Bharat	36		
Madras	151	Tamil Nadu	288
Hyderabad	72	Andhra Pradesh	312
Orissa	71	Orissa	199
Punjab	48	Punjab	180
Pepsu	21	Haryana	179
Uttar Pradesh	190	Uttar Pradesh	500
West Bengal	98	West Bengal	281

The Second, Third and Fourth Pay Commissions set up by the central government and reporting in 1959, 1973 and 1986 respectively have given the figures for civil services for the years 1957, 1971 and 1984. On the basis of the data culled from these three reports Table 2.2 has been prepared giving class-wise (or group-wise) break-up of the numbers.

TABLE 2.2: **Size of the Civil Service**

	Year 1957	Percentage of the total	Year 1971	Percentage of the total	Year 1984	Percentage of the total
Class I	10400	0.6	34100	1.2	68000	1.8
Class II	19300	1.1	46100	1.6	80000	2.1
Class III	728800	42.0	1545000	52.1	2286800	48.0
Class IV	978400	56.3	1337500	45.1	1330900	35.4
Total	1736900	100.0	296270	100.0	3765700	100.0

Though the central level civil service is 3.76 million strong, the number of personnel in managerial cadres is but 68,000 which comes to 1.8 per cent of the total number. What is more, a not too small number of them have been in the service only for a few years and are yet occupying rather junior positions in their respective hierarchies, thus outside the orbit of policy-making responsibilities. Besides, this number includes personnel of technical services also. A bulk of them are engaged in jobs of an executive nature and thus are not directly engaged in policy-making. In short, it is a small class of about 30,000 or so which may be said to constitute the managerial class directly involved in public policy-making and reviewing functions in the central government. They occupy leadership positions in the government and their decisions impinge on a large number of people with varying degrees of gravity.

It is necessary at this stage to mention that India has adopted the rank position, and not the 'duties' one which obtains in countries such as the U.S.A. and Canada. The basis of the classification in India is the rank and personal status of the incumbent rather than the precise duties inhering in the post. The civil service is classified into 'Groups' (or classes) as well as services. There are, in descending order, four groups — Group A, Group B, Group C and Group D, corresponding to differences in the responsibility of the work performed and the qualifications required. Group A and Group B include personnel performing higher administrative and executive responsibilities in the government. Group C includes clerical personnel. Group D, the lowest in the hierarchy, includes peons, orderlies, sweepers etc. Another way of classification is into services. Civil servants in India are recruited to distinct services. Thus recruited, they continue to be members of the particular service, and hold their posts by virtue of their membership of a particular service. The central government has two categories of higher civil services: (i) All-India Services, and (ii) Central Civil Services. Of 68000 higher civil servants, as many as 31,825 are grouped in services other than the three All-India Services. In 1984, the IAS had an authorised strength of 5047, the IPS of 2679 and the Indian Forest Service of 2006.

The Changing Concerns of Civil Services

The dominant concern of the political leadership following Independence was to rehabilitate the battered civil service of the land and to tone up its operational efficiency. This exercise was essential to ensure that it was fit for the emerging functions of state-building and development. A large number the European and Muslim officers left India in 1947; and filling up of these vacancies was a major unpostponable task before the new government soon after Independence. Decisions were quickly taken to constitute two new All-India Services and to set them going. The earliest concern in regard to the civil services was thus principally structural — to launch new civil services, to undertake fresh public recruitment to them, to formulate and standardise rules and regulations relating to them, etc. This was the period when India had launched its First Five Year Plan which, one may note, made public administration its instrument of execution.

A shift of priority was discerned when the civil services were in the midst of implementing of the Second Five Year Plan (1956-61). The Second Plan, it is important to recall, was industry-oriented and emphasised, above all, self-reliance and self-sufficiency. This strategy led to a spawning of a vast network of regulatory administration in India: the government sought to develop and regulate private sector industries through an extensive control mechanism in the form of permits and licences. The emerging inter-face between the industry and government including the civil service was not without its perils. The sixties was a period characterised by growing corruption in public administration in India. The environment at this time was getting thick with rumours about widespread corruption in the country's politico-administrative system. More particularly, Punjab's contro- versial chief minister, Sardar Pratap Singh Kairon, was publicly criticised for indulging in corruption and thus himself encouraging it. India's first Prime Minister Jawaharlal Nehru's political stature had declined around this time directly as a result of Indo-China armed conflict in 1962. Reluctant Nehru announced constitution of the S.R. Das Commission of Inquiry to look into charges of corruption against Pratap Singh Kairon. Soon thereafter, the Indian Parliament set up the committee on Prevention of Corruption under the chairmanship of K. Santhanam to examine corruption in the public administration and suggest action. Both the Das Report on Kairon and the Santhanam Report forcefully confirmed the popular misgivings. Integrity in the civil service was discovered to be low and corruption began to arouse widespread concern in the society.

The initial reaction of disbelief, even shock at corruption in the civil service has, over the years, given way to a more or less pathetic acceptance of the malady. The earlier phase of public wailing and breast-beating over corruption has thus passed over, and more and more people are, willingly or unwillingly, acquiescing into it, viewing it as but an integral part of the contemporary life-style. For sometime, therefore, corruption in the country's civil services has ceased to be the dominant theme for public debate and discussion. At the same time, political projections directly or indirectly impinging on the lives and activities of the civil servants have been assuming a level of seriousness causing national concern.

There is, in the meanwhile, yet another shift of priority on the part of the policy-makers. Since the seventies, the government feels more and more concerned about citizen satisfaction in administration. An examination of the annual reports of India's central personnel agency, namely the Ministry (earlier, Department) of Personnel discloses that for some time for policy-makers are giving more thought to redressal of grievances of the citizens, responsive administration, decentralisation and accountability in administration.

At the same time, one may also notice a growing emphasis on the introduction of what may be called modern management' in the country's civil services. Since 1984, in-service training of middle and senior level personnel has emerged as the single most significant function of the central personnel agency. In service training for the IAS has been made compulsory, and every member including even the cabinet secretary must attend a prescribed training programme in a year. Emphasis on in-service training has, however, declined since 1989. Similarly, computers have entered the government in a big way and its knowledge on the part of civil servants is getting widely insisted upon.

NOTES

1. Its full nomenclature was the Committee on consideration of the Subject of the Examination of Candidates for the Civil Service of the East India Company.
2. Its members signed a covenant with the Company detailing their obligations and privileges. Hence called 'Covenanted'.
3. *Report of the Public Service Commission*, (Sir C.U. Aitchison), 1886-87, p.49.
4. *Ibid.*, p.70.
5. *Report of the Royal Commission on the Superior Civil Services in India*, London, H.M.S.O., 1924, p.16.
6. *Parliamentary Debates*, House of Commons, Fifth Series, Vol. 157, 1922, col. 1513.
7. Some central services continued to be recruited by the Secretary of State for India. An example is the Imperial Customs Service.
8. It must be mentioned that only a part of the Act — the constitutional provisions relating to the provinces — came into operation and the contemplated federation could for a variety of reasons never formally come into effect in India.
9. *Report of the Committee on Organisation and Procedure*, 1937, pp.19-20.
10. *Report of the Joint Committee on Indian Constitutional Reform*, Vol. I (Part 1), London, HMSO, 1934, para 275.
11. Government of India, Home Department (Establishment) F. 21/4/36-Ests., 1936.
12. The subordinate Services comprised clerks, assistants, stenographers, typists etc.
13. The Inferior Service included record sorlirs, *Jamadars, daffadars, daftaries*, peons, farashes, chowkidars etc.
14. Government of India, Home Department, File No. 45/3/46-Ests(R), para 7.
15. One must more that the resolution by the upper chamber is constitutionally obligatory for the creation of All-India services.
16. Ministry of Home Affairs: *Report 1961-62*, p.4.
17. *Parliamentary Debates: Rajya Sabha Official Report*, Vol. II, No. 26, 26 March 1985, Col. 4782.
18. Ministry of Home Affairs: *Report 1965-66*, p.1.
19. *Ibid. Annual Report, 1967-68*, p.1.
20. Department of Personnel and Administrative Reforms: *Annual Report 1981-82*, p.38.
21. *The Report of the Commission of Centre-State Relations* Part-I, pp. 219-31.
22. It is an All-India Service.
23. *Ibid.*
24. *Ibid.*

3

THE 1989 GENERAL ELECTION AND AFTER

The Ninth General Election was held on 22, 24 and 26 November 1989. The party position which emerged in the November 1989 General Election ousted the ruling Congress(I) Party of Rajiv Gandhi but did not give clear majority to any party. The party position in the 529 seat Lok Sabha was as follows:

Congress(I)	192
Janata Dal	141
Telugu Desam	2
Bhartiya Janata Party	88
Communist Party of India (Marxist)	32
Community Party of India (CPI)	12
Independent and Others	58
Congress(S)	1
Unfilled	3
Total	529

The Congress(I) Party suffered a defeat in the northern states although it staged a come-back in nearly all the southern states. The south voted differently from the north.

The Bhartiya Janata Party was perhaps the single largest gainer, securing 88 seats in the Lok Sabha. The Ninth Lok Sabha election was also the bloodiest and most violent of elections held so far. It was marked by criminalisation of politics. It was the most expensive too. Political parties are reported to have spent almost Rs. 12 crores on advertising through the mainline newspapers between 20 October and 25 November 1989, out of which Rs. 10 crores are said to have been spent by the Congress(I) alone. An escalation in the campaign expenditure caused concern to the champions of democracy in the country. Further, it could be said that the 1989 election was a kind of referendum on Rajiv Gandhi. All political parties, except of course the Congress(I), had trained their guns on him. To add to this was the obvious rampant corruption encompassing even the top levels in the government. The electorate withdrew its confidence in him.

The Congress(I) losing the general election in 1989 was an event of historic significance. The Titan who ruled continuously since 1947 except for a brief period of 1977-79 fell, securing less than 200 seats in the 529-members Lok Sabha, the Lower House of Indian Parliament. This fall from power was all the more remarkable for barely five years back the Party had secured more than two-thirds majority in the Lok Sabha, and in terms of votes scared, even ashamed, Rajiv's grandfather who could never get as many votes even during the heyday of his popularity.

On 29 November, Rajiv Gandhi submitted his resignation from the office of Prime Minister thus paving the way for the new party making processes. This ended the five tumultuous years which began with his dizzy popularity. The dissolution of the Lok Sabha was quickly followed by the government resignation. On 1 December 1989, Vishwanath Pratap Singh was elected leader of the Janata Dal Parliamentary Board. On 2 December, he was sworn in as India's Prime Minister to succeed Rajiv Gandhi.

The long stay in power of the Congress had its own disadvantages, and one certainly was politicisation of the higher or top-level bureaucracy. As the Congress(I) keeps coming into power both at the centre and in the states, the higher civil servants, especially of the two All-India Services — IAS and IPS — come in contact with the politicians at an early age while serving in the districts, and a sort of personalised relationship, as is not natural develops between them and this continues in later years also. Occasions for knowing each other inevitably multiply. Some of the civil servants do their work honestly and professionally. But some get too close to individual ministers and when the latter leave, they are placed in a state of anxiety and fear.

Vishwanath Pratap Singh, after assuming office of Prime Minister, assured the nation that no witch-hunting or radical changes in the central bureaucracy would be undertaken by the new government. This assurance of course, ran counter to the then prevailing practice under which top-level posts like secretaries, secret agency officials, governors, members of the Planning Commission, etc., enjoyed no defined tenure and used to go at the will of the political chief executive. Many who identified themselves too deeply either with the previous Prime Minister Rajiv Gandhi, or with individual ministers or with the even ruling party were themselves to blame for they were no longer professional. Similarly, investigating agencies like the Central Bureau began to exist for the then party in power* instead, suggest a brief quota from the paper — it has its own effect. So is the case with the police and the income-tax. Some officials cross the boundary between politics and civil service. With the new government coming into power many bureaucratic heads, rolled and prominently on the "hit list" were those who broke the well-established code of neutrality, and committed themselves to the previous regime.

Some changes of the secretaries are routine — to fill up vacancies. Retirement is a process of a career bureaucracy, and a number of senior civil servants retired regularly, creating vacancies as secretaries, additional secretaries and joint secretaries. these have to be filled up. But not all changes can he also explained.

* See *The Tribune*, 14 December 1989

4

PARTY MANIFESTOES

A party manifesto is a formal announcement of what a political party pledges to do when it is put into power by the electorate. All political parties routinely issue their respective manifestoes to persuade the voter about what they proclaim to do if and when returned to power. But experience shows that manifestoes cannot claim much sanctity. Some political analysts even regard them as frauds periodically committed on the people. One may not agree with such extreme views howsoever limited be their practical value. Even at their worst, they constitute the standard against which parties' performance may be viewed by the voters at the time of choosing the new party. In the 1989 general election as on previous occasions all political parties issued their manifestoes. As the National Front constituted the government after the election, it is proposed to begin with its own declaration. The National Front's manifesto was the distillation of efforts of as many as 13 sub-committees which had been set up soon after the announcement of the election. The National Front made several promises falling within public administration. It promised to make the Planning Commission a statutory body and to reactivate the National Development Council in which the states were to be given a much larger voice in policy matters. The National Front sought to devolve larger functions and finances on to the states, thus standing for a fair measure of decentralisation. It expressed its anguish over rising corruption in public administration and expressed its determination to curb corruption, track down the kickbacks in the Bofors and other deals and further, to revitalize the constitutional institutions. It promised to liberate Doordarshan and All India Radio — the two powerful instruments of "disinformation" — and make them autonomous public corporations. It criticised the systematic abuse of the office of Governor and sought to make this functionary constitutionally accountable. It promised to bar the Chief Justice of India, the Lok Pal, the Lokayukta and the Chief Election Commissioner from holding any public office after their retirement. It promised to set up the National Security Council to undertake a comprehensive perspective plan on national defence.

The Congress(I) Party, which held power at the centre continuously since 1947 except for a short period 1977-79 in its 1989 manifesto promised power to the people, implying a dose of decentralisation. On corruption, the party's manifesto said "We must squarely tackle the problem of corruption. It is most oppressive at the grassroots, at the interface where the bulk of our people and the machinery of government meet." Its contention was that the single most important cause of inefficiency and corruption was the absence of locally-elected and locally-resident representatives directly responsible to the people for the ending of corruption.

The Communist Party of India (Marxist) [CPI(M)] indicted the government on "corruption, jobbery and nepotism" and reiterated its resolve to put an end to these evils. It called for restructuring of the centre-state, fiscal and political relations. The party described the Panchayati and Nagarpalika Bills introduced in Parliament in 1988 as part of Rajiv Gandhi's bid to establish control over local bodies and further erode the powers of the States. It was committed to "genuine decentralisation". It expressed its concern at the "growing erosion of the federal character of the Constitution and concentration of power at the centre". It stood for more powers to the states and in the process all arbitrary Central intervention through Governors was to be ended.

The Bhartiya Janata Party (BJP) held that roots of all corruption lay in political corruption, and promised to inquire into all cases of corruption in the foreign deals if voted to power. It promised to cleanse public life asserting: "The Party recognises the urgency of evolving effective mechanism to break the unholy nexus between the corrupt bureaucrat, the corrupt businessman and the corrupt politicians." Apart from inquiring into all cases of corruption in foreign deals including the defence deals, the BJP promised to bring the Prime Minister and chief ministers under the purview of Lok Pal and Lokayuktas and make all ministers declare their assets every year. The party assured that it would create an atmosphere of austerity and simplicity in life and work for the streamlining of procedures and rules and rationalising of the country's tax structure. It favoured the creation of smaller states so that they are economically and administratively viable. It supported statehood for Delhi and Ladakh; and creation of separate States of "Uttaranchal" and "Vananchal" in U.P. and Bihar respectively. It promised to set up an inter-State Council under Article 263 of the Constitution to settle inter-state and centre-state disputes. The BJP sought to limit the number of ministers to 10 per cent of the total number of legislators. The Minorities Commission is to be converted into a Human Rights Commission to take care of the just rights of all individuals, groups and communities.

It would be seen from the preceding that all political parties cover more or less common areas and show a broad unanimity as regards remedial measures. They bemoan widespread corruption, recommend the institution of Lok Pal and Lokayukta, support decentralisation and want reformed centre state relations.

In what follows are reproduced the election manifestoes (Annexures A to E) of the national parties, in the hope that a reader may be curious to know which party has promises what. As the National Front formed the government at the centre after the general election held in November 1989, it would be particularly interesting to watch its behaviour and orientation when in power.

ANNEXURE A

THE BHARATIYA JANATA PARTY ELECTION MANIFESTO General Election, 1989

INTRODUCTION

The Bharatiya Janata Party is wedded to the Unity and Integrity of India. It stands for Law and Order — for Justice, Social and Economic and for Security, Internal and External. It is committed to the uplift of the poor and the downtrodden. But BJP is sorry to note that the Rajiv Government has disappointed the country on all these counts.

India today is in the grip of a serious multidimensional crisis of unprecedented proportions. The national mood is not just of cynicism but of mounting disgust and rage, not unmixed with sorrow, at the steady deterioration in public morality at the topmost leadership level. The people feel sad that through an accident of history this great country should have been saddled with a coterie of small men who are not only incompetent and corrupt, but who lack a sense of commitment to the nation, its democratic institutions and cultural traditions.

Evidence is mounting that the Prime Minister, whose personal probity is now in serious doubt, has not only been bending words but telling lies, distorting facts, changing versions, elbowing out ministers of integrity and unabashedly misleading the Parliament and the Nation even on crucial issues of national defence and security. The men at the top are not only without integrity but also without shame. In any other country, such a government would have resigned long ago. But it is continuing in office and trying to subvert the democratic process by resorting to fascist methods, including mugging of the press, instigation of communal riots and subversion of the judiciary.

Stark failure faces the country on all fronts. Accords have ended up in bloody discords. The Rajiv regime is bathed in blood and muck from head to foot, from Punjab to Assam and from Kashmir to Sri Lanka. Everything Rajiv Gandhi touches ends up in a bloody mess. A man who waded to his office through the blood-soaked streets of Delhi will be leaving behind a gory legacy. This country is not safe in the hands of such a man or such a party. How can men who lack integrity themselves, and are not above looting the country, defend the country and protect its integrity and honour?

The power and prestige of great institutions like the Parliament, the Army and the Judiciary have been eroded; the press has been repeatedly threatened and harassed; and the electronic media have been prostituted. The directive principles of State policy have been forgotten; the Mandal Report on the welfare of backward classes has been pigeonholed; and never before has Indian womanhood suffered insult and assault as during the last five years.

By negativing the Supreme Court judgment in the Shahabano case, the government has put a premium on communalism and obscurantism. And by recognising Urdu as second official language in Uttar Pradesh on election eve, it has shown more interest in Muslim votes than in Urdu language. In the process it has only given the country so many corpses. By not allowing the rebuilding of the Ram Janma Mandir in Ayodhya, on the lines of Somnath Mandir built by the Government of India in 1948, it has allowed tensions to rise, and gravely strained social harmony.

About the situation on the economic front, the less said the better. During the last five years, prices have doubled and in many cases trebled; unemployment has soared by leaps and bounds and national debt increased three times. And all this while the country has been thrown open for plunder by foreign interests who are taking out more from the country than they ever put in. The country has paid out more to foreigners in the last five years than the entire debt of farmers which the government refuses to write off.

In this enveloping darkness, the Bharatiya Janata Party stands as a beacon of light. It is wedded to *Desh* and *Dharma, Samata* and *Samanvay*. It stands for justice — social and economic — for all, for the *Kisan* and the *Jawan*, for the young and the old, for the poor and the downtrodden, for women and children, irrespective of class, creed or gender. It also stands for law and order particularly moral order, for without such an order, the country cannot endure and flourish.

BJP rejects both exploitative capitalism and suppressive communism. Its approach to life and society, as expounded by our late Pt. Deendayal Upadhyay, is integrative and holistic. It books upon the farmer in the field and the worker in the factory as two mighty wheels of our modern *Rashtra-rath*. It believes that the nation cannot progress until those who have remained at the bottom of the social pile for centuries are helped to elevate themselves and join the mainstream on a footing of equality.

BJP believes in positive secularism which, according to our constitution-makers, means *Sarva-Dharma-Sama-Bhava* and which does not connote an irreligious state. It certainly does not mean rejection of our history and cultural heritage, the very foundations of this great nation. The BJP stands for "*Justice for All and Appeasement of None*".

This is what we are and this is what we aim to do. *Come and join us* in the great enterprise of nation-building, in taking this country to great heights of prosperity and glory. Following is the programme which the BJP offers to the people for taking India to its destiny — a modern, peaceful and prosperous nation on the road to an exciting future.

I

NATIONAL UNITY AND NATIONAL INTEGRATION

India is one country, and all Indians irrespective of caste, creed or language are one people, one nation.

The idea of a theocratic state is an anathema to Indian mind and the BJP believes that State in India has always been a civil institution which respects all religions equally and makes no discrimination between one citizen and the other on the grounds of language, gender, caste or religion.

It is the duty of the State to guarantee justice and security to all minorities — linguistic, religious or ethnic. The BJP considers that it is also imperative for national integration that minorities do not develop a minority complex.

Indian Constitution is quasi-federal. It envisages strong States with a strong Centre. The BJP believes in maintaining a balance between the two as visualised in our Constitution.

The BJP also recognises that regional imbalances have developed in some States because of their size. The party stands for the formation of smaller States which are economically and administratively viable. The BJP will:

1. Support and strengthen State Governments and not destabilise and topple them;
2. Give the States a fairer share of Central revenues and increase the financial powers of the States;
3. Constitute an Inter-State Council under Article 263 to settle all Inter-State and State-Centre disputes;
4. Appoint State Governors in consultation with State Governments;
5. Limit the number of ministers to 10 per cent of legislators;
6. Guarantee to all minorities, linguistic and religious, peace and security, and full opportunities for progress and development;
7. Delete the temporary Article 370 of the Constitution and scrap the 59th Amendment of the Constitution;
8. Appoint a Commission to examine the various personal laws in vogue in the country — Hindu Law, Muslim Law, Christian Law, Parsi Law, Civil Law etc. and to identify the fair and equitable ingredients in these laws, prepare a draft with a view to evolve a consensus for a uniform Civil Code;
9. Appoint a Commission to examine the Constitution of India for making it an effective instrument for containing centrifugal tendencies;
10. Grant statehood to the Union Territory of Delhi, create Separate States of Uttaranchal in U.P. and Vananchal in Bihar, give the status of Union Territory to Laddakh; and
11. Maintain a National Register of Citizens.

Human Rights Commission

BJP will widen the scope of the present Minorities Commission and convert it into a Human Rights Commission to take care of the just rights of all individuals, groups and communities.

Fair Elections

Free and fair elections are *sine qua non* of a democratic polity. The BJP believes that elections must be held regularly and very fairly. The BJP will:

1. Introduce compulsory voting for all citizens;
2. Arrange for public funding of elections;
3. Ban the company donations;

4. Introduce Identity Cards for voters;
5. Use electronic voting machines in all elections;
6. Give the right of Postal Ballot to Indian citizens living abroad;
7. Strengthen the independence of the Election Commission by making expenditure incurred on the Commission as a charge on the Consolidated Fund of India, as is provided in the case of Comptroller and Auditor General and Supreme Court and High Court judges, and by providing the Commission with an independent infrastructure;
8. Hold State and Central elections simultaneously every five years;
9. Examine the feasibility of introducing the List system to elections;
10. Have party accounts publicly audited;
11. To prevent abuse of governmental power by the ruling party give legal teeth to the Code of Conduct framed by the Election Commission; violation of the Code shall be made a corrupt practice under the Law;
12. Empower Election Commission to monitor all political and election coverage by the Doordarshan and the Akashvani and ensure that these media are not abused; and
13. Include in the limitative ceiling of election expenses all expenditure incurred by the candidate, his election agent, his party and supporters.

Clean Public Life

Cleansing of the public life will receive BJP's top priority. The party holds that the roots of all corruption lie in political corruption. The party recognises the urgency of evolving effective mechanism to break the unholy nexus between the corrupt bureaucrat, corrupt businessmen and the corrupt politician. The BJP is determined to fight corruption at all levels and will specifically adopt the following measures:

1. It will enquire into all cases of corruption in the foreign deals (including the defence deals) by various ministries and departments of the Government and punish the guilty.
2. It will enact a law, and create institutions of Lokpal and Lokayukta bringing the P.M. and the Chief Minister also under its purview.
3. Streamline procedures and rules relating to purchase, awarding contracts etc. in government and public sector undertakings, and also the discretionary powers of political authorities.
4. Rationalise and streamline the tax structure, providing for sufficient incentives to savings and avoiding harassment to honest tax-payers and to avoid generation of black money.
5. Require all Ministers to make an annual declaration of assets.
6. Review and update the existing laws, administrative procedures and powers for detecting the corrupt practices and for speedily punishing the guilty.
7. Create an atmosphere of austerity and simplicity by enforcing strictly the norms of expenditure in government departments.

The North East

The entire North Eastern region is in ferment. The *BJP* holds, the central government squarely responsible for the neglect of the North Eastern Region and its unsatisfactory economic development and consequent exploitation by the foreign Missionaries.

The BJP would take following steps to meet the alarming situation in the North East:

1. Setting up of the barbed wire fencing along the Indo-Bangladesh border;
2. Detection of infiltrators and deletion of their names from the voters list on a war footing. Steps will be taken for their deportation;
3. Issue identity cards to all citizens in border States;
4. Creating a special cell for identification of the landed properties acquired by infiltrators, such property will be confiscated;
5. Repealing the Foreign Contribution (Regulation) Act. Foreign contributions will be totally banned. No private organisation, religious, social or any other will be allowed to receive any foreign contributions — in cash or kind;
6. Abolishing the Innerline permit system in all the North Eastern States;
7. Safeguarding the interests of refugees;
8. Taking effective steps for an honourable return of the Chakmas to Bangladesh;
9. Ensuring no further division of Assam; and
10. Implementing a sub-plan for the economic development of the Tribals.

Punjab

The BJP holds the Congress(I) squarely responsible for what is happening in Punjab. Punjab situation continues to deteriorate not because of any lack of power with the government. The government is possessing enormous powers but lacks a policy and a will to act.

The BJP has always been striving for maintaining social harmony in Punjab. Several party leaders including the State BJP President and other colleagues have laid down their lives in this cause.

The BJP would strive for a fair and peaceful solution of the Punjab problem. It would adopt the following approach for containing terrorism in Punjab:

1. Creation of a security belt all along the Western borders with Pakistan without delay;
2. Secure the assistance of Army to help the civil administration in the Mand area, if need be;
3. Strengthen the intelligence apparatus;
4. Punishing those who were responsible for the killings of innocents in Delhi and elsewhere after the assassination of Mrs. Gandhi;
5. Adequately compensating the victims of violence; and
6. Review the structural changes in the economy of Punjab and to remove the distortions.

Jammu and Kashmir and the Western Sector

The BJP views with concern the recent developments in the State of Jammu and Kashmir and the continued discrimination against the people of Jammu. The rabid communal and pro-Pakistan elements are spearheading a massive hate India campaign in Kashmir valley and the entire region is engulfed by widespread terrorism. The unabated infiltration and smuggling all along the western border needs to be effectively curbed. The BJP suggests that:

1. Effective and immediate measures to weed out the foreigners from Jammu and Kashmir, Rajasthan and Gujarat be taken;
2. Border with Pakistan should be effectively guarded by creating a security belt to stop infiltration of trained terrorists and smuggling of arms and ammunition, narcotics and other contraband commodities; and
3. A Regional Council for Jammu be formed so that regional imbalances in development be removed.

Law and Order and Protection of Weaker Sections

The BJP views with alarm the rise of social violence in the country. This includes communal violence, atrocities on scheduled castes and tribals, and criminal assaults on women. The BJP believes that the weaker sections need an effective protection from atrocities and the Party is committed to the security of life, limb, property and honour of all citizens. In case of a serious eruption of violence, the BJP commends that:

1. A judicial inquiry will always be held;
2. The inquiry report will be published;
3. Those guilty of incitement to violence or dereliction of duty will be punished;
4. All not sufferers will be suitably compensated and rehabilitated;
5. An indepth socio-economic study of riot-prone areas to take effective steps for riot-prevention will be conducted;
6. The Police Force be transformed into an efficient and impartial instrument of law and order, through modernisation programme and better service conditions; and
7. Political meddling in police work be stopped and a machinery for redressal of Police/People's grievances be created.

Justice and Judicial Reforms

The BJP believes that without an independent judiciary, it is impossible to have the Rule of Law. Also the judicial system should be speedy, inexpensive and just. The BJP would undertake the following measures to restore the independence, integrity and efficiency of the judicial system:

1. Take effective measures to provide free legal aid to the poor and specially the scheduled castes and tribes and gradual abolition of the Court-fees;
2. Simplify the legal procedures and increase the number of judges so that

majority of the cases are disposed of within one year;
3. Provide mobile courts for the rural areas and set up Nyaya Panchayats with judicial powers;
4. Offer better service conditions and emoluments to judges at all levels;
5. The Chief Justice of India should have the final say in the appointment of the High Court and Supreme Court Judges to be recommended by an independent body;
6. Raise the retirement age of judges to 65, give them full pension equal to their salary, prohibit them from holding any office after retirement;
7. Appoint a Commission for suggesting an overhaul of the Judicial System which is under serious stress;
8. Appoint special courts for different categories of cases so that pending cases in various High Courts and Supreme Court are cleared within one year; and
9. Introduce social security measures like provident fund and group insurance schemes for the advocates.

Decentralisation of Power and Panchayati Raj

The Panchayat System formed the bedrock of the democratic functioning of the Indian Social System since the Vedic period. Mahatma Gandhi and Jay Prakash Narayan were strong votaries of local self-government. The Jana Sangh under the leadership of Pt. Deendayal Upadhyay had always canvassed for the Constitutional status of the Panchayats and Municipal boards.

The BJP believes in decentralisation of power and strengthening of democracy at the grass roots.

The party ensures a Constitutional status to the Panchayats and other local self-institution and assured share of resources so that they do not depend upon discretionary grants.

The BJP will neither impose Panchayats from above nor will use them to bypass the State Governments.

II

NATIONAL ECONOMY

The Indian economy is presently going through an acute crisis. In fact it has been stagnating since the last ten years and more so since 1985. The per capita availability of the items of staple diet of the nation, in these years has gone down. The nation is more undernourished today than it was few years ago. As a result of wrong plan priorities, the country is producing more colour TV sets, but not enough steel, more computers but not enough power, more fancy cars but not enough buses, more superfine fabrics but not enough cheaper varieties of *dhoties* and *saries*. The result of this lopsided elitist sense of priorities, combined with corruption and profligacy, is that today there are more people looking for jobs than ever before, more landless farmers than ever before, more illiterates than ever before. The consumer is groaning under the burden of back-breaking prices. There is more sorrow than happiness, more poverty than wealth.

The BJP hold the ruling party squarely responsible for deliberately neglecting the agriculture sector in pursuit of mythical modernisation.

Forty years ago, the disparity between the farmer and his counterpart in other sectors was not very large. Today it is one to three; soon, it will be one to four. A country that treats its farmers with contempt is bound to remain mired in poverty, as India is. The Country is again resorting to imports of foodgrains after so many years, which in itself is a tell-tale commentary on the mess that has been made on the farm front, in fact, in respect of the entire economy. Thanks to the wrong policies of our rulers over the years, thousands of crores of rupees from the rural poor have been transferred to the urban rich, resulting in a colossal rural indebtedness. The BJP will reverse all these ugly trends and give the country a humane economy. It will take all steps necessary to achieve full employment, maximise production stabilise prices and eradicate poverty and rural indebtedness. For this BJP offers the following programme:

Agriculture

In the opinion of the BJP the speedy development of the agriculture and rural sector is the key to India's prosperity. The party recognises that more than 65 per cent of Indian farmers are poor, they need capital and subsidised inputs for their rapid growth. The *Kisan* will continue to flaunder in poverty unless the burden of people depending upon agriculture is reduced. A network of agro-industrial complexes in the rural areas is the real answer to the problems of poverty of the Indian peasantry. The party is committed to implement its Charter of Rights of *Kisan*. The BJP offers a new deal to the farmers and it will:

1. Write off the debts of the farmers, agricultural labourers and rural artisans;
2. Allocate sixty per cent of the plant money, both Central and State, for rural development, agricultural and allied services;
3. Ensure remunerative prices to the farmers, computed after taking into consideration all the parameters like cost of inputs and living index etc.;
4. Ensure minimum wages to farm labour;
5. Maintain parity of prices between agricultural and inoustrial produce;
6. Remove all restrictions on the movement of agricultural produce throughout the country;
7. Arrange abundant and regular supply of water and energy;
8. Introduce crop and cattle insurance schemes which would guarantee adequate compensation in case of crop failure, damage or loss due to natural calamities or outbreak of epidemics in cattle; also update the age old famine code;
9. Provide market value compensation in one instalment in case of land acquisition and rehabilitation of the uprooted in the process;
10. Issue Pass Books to *Kisans* and implement the land laws;
11. Reclaim all wasteland and give special attention to dry farming;
12. Speedily complete the on-going big irrigation projects, take up thousands of small and minor irrigation projects, organise efficient flood management and relief;
13. Encourage the cultivation of pulses, oil-seeds, fruits, nuts, and other cash crops;

14. Protect the traditional rights on village forests and Nistar Land;
15. Speedily provide the minimum civic facilities like drinking water, roads and other means of communication, public health and hygiene;
16. Organise the purchase operations through a wide and efficient network so as to ensure that all farmers and particularly the small farmers realise the guaranteed price and are not forced to make a distress sale; and
17. Restructuring the Agriculture Cost and Price Commission so that two-thirds of tis members are drawn from those engaged in farming.

Cow Protection and Animal Husbandry

The BJP notes with concern that in spite of the clear provision of the Constitution in Article 48 and the Supreme Court's emphasis that cow protection is a constitutional mandate and slaughter of cows is not enjoined in any religion including Muslim religion, complete prohibition of cow slaughter has yet not been introduced in various States of India, specially in West Bengal and Kerala.

The BJP recognises the fact the from times immemorial Cow-protection has remained one of the basic tenets of Indian culture and it is on the patient back of the cow and its progeny that the entire structure of the Indian agriculture rests. Over seventy million animals are employed in the farming operations in Indian villages, more than eighty per cent rural transport requirements are met by the bullocks. Cow and its progeny continue to be the major source of power, manure and fuel including bio-gas. Cow is also an effective protection against environmental degradations.

The BJP regretfully observes that about three million cows are slaughtered every year and most of them for export. The party would put a total ban on the slaughter of the cows. It will:

1. Amend the Article 48 of the Constitution to include bulls, and bullocks, and to prohibit State-trading in slaughter of cows; to ensure that no-one has a fundamental right of trade or business to slaughter cows; and to incorporate the subject of Cow-protection in the concurrent list;
2. Implement a policy of Go-Samvardhan or development of cow and cattle breeding including the improvement of Sheep and Goat breeds to bring about a white revolution in the country; and
3. Provide tax exemption to the income of Gashalas and Pinjarapoles.

Industry

The BJP's industrial policy flows from the following principles :

1. *Self-reliance*: The Party's industrial policy would be strongly nationalistic in approach and content.

   The party, would like to keep multinationals out of the field of consumer industries. The party regards self-reliance as an overriding component in our external economic relations, including the import of technology and capital
2. *Decentralisation*: The party stands for political as well as economic democracy, so that the benefits of economic development go to the

smallest man. The party believes that for this decentralisation of economic power, presently concentrated in the hands of the State or of big business, is necessary. Primacy for agriculture and agro-based industries, *Swadeshi* and importance to the small and medium scale sector in industry are commitments that flow from this.

3. *Modernisation*: BJP will harness new technologies to the changing requirements of the country, and build India as a modern and progressive nation. But it will not allow technology to degrade man as just another input in Gross National Product. Man will be the main focus of our developmental policies.
4. *Daridra Narayan Sewa*: Consistent with the above three elements, the party will aim at securing to every Indian citizen minimum conditions of material welfare in terms of food, raiment, shelter, health and education.

The party will leave no stone unturned in carrying jobs to the people. Generation of employment will be a major component of BJP's industrial policy.

BJP will encourage and improve industry all-round. We will:

1. Make the public sector productive and profitable; its management will be professionalised and a Central service called the "Indian Management Service" will be formed to select train and allocate the professional managers to these units;
2. Demarcate the spheres of multinational corporations, big-scale industry, small-scale industry and cottage industry;
3. Ensure that the existing patent laws safeguarding Indian national interests remain intact under external pressure;
4. Cut down the plethora of controls which presently exist, and which breed corruption and dampen enterprises, and maintain only such of these restrictions as are necessary for social justice;
5. Foster the spirit of *Swadeshi*;
6. Reserve more and more consumer items to small-scale and cottage sectors;
7. Make credit more cheaply available to small-scale industry;
8. Modernise industrial plants; and ensure fuller utilisation of capacity;
9. Promote agro-based industries;
10. Encourage Research and Development to play a live role in industrial growth;
11. Require businessmen to consider themselves as trustees of the public good;
12. Publicly honour excellence in industry and commerce; and
13. Provide tax and non-tax incentives to companies for making permanent workers share-holders out of a part of their gross profit.

National Textile Policy

The BJP recognises the need to have an integrated textile policy and would ensure protection to handloom and cottage sectors of textile industry. To this end the party will demarcate the role of each of the Sectors viz. organised sector or mills, powerloom and handloom sectors, and Khadi and cottage industries. The Party would ensure cheap clothing to the poor and national and international market to various sectors. The handloom sector would receive adequate protection. The interests of cotton growers would also be duly safeguarded.

Taxation

BJP would adopt firm and bold measures to prevent generation of black-money. It will:

1. Rationalise and simplify the entire tax structure. The highest rate of income-tax shall be 40 per cent;
2. Raise the present exemption limit of income-tax to Rs. 30,000; and introduce differential slab system and lower rates for fixed income groups;
3. Abolish octroi duty and require the State Governments to make good the loss of Municipalities;
4. Abolish Sales Tax and require the Centre to make good the loss of State Governments;
5. Exempt all savings and investments in approved organisations (including non-government institutions) from Wealth-tax and Estate duty;
6. Share Corporation tax revenues with the States;
7. Take stringent measures against the smugglers and other economic offenders; and
8. Keep a strict watch on the operations of foreign banks.

Foreign Assets

The BJP will enact and strictly enforce a suitable legislation so as to require all Indian citizens to disclose their foreign assets including secret and undeclared bank accounts. The Party will take all measures including signing treaties for unearthing Indian unaccounted money in foreign countries.

1. Encourage the growth of small local banks, duly supervised and guaranteed by the Reserve Bank of India.
2. Take drastic action against tax-evasion but would motivate people for savings and protect the honest tax-payer from harassment.
3. Pursue a policy of balanced-budget for the country and will discontinue the present practice of huge deficits in the national budget.
4. Impose statutory ceilings on deficits in budget and debts of the government.
5. Convert RBI into an autonomous institution, responsible to the Parliament for regulating the monetary policies of the government.

Prices

BJP will maintain price stability by efficient management of production and supplies, and by rooting out corruption, which is a major contributory factor for price rise. With this view the party will evolve a well co-ordinated wages, prices and profits policy. The BJP will:

1. Appoint a Price Commission to regulate the prices of manufactured goods both in private and public sectors;
2. Fully and promptly neutralise any rise in prices by increased DA in both private and public sectors and in private and Government service, including Central, State and local government;
3. Open more fair price shops in towns and villages, existing arrangements will be streamlined; and
4. Make not only grains, sugar and kerosene, but also pulses, cooking oil and soap and such sundry articles of everyday use available at these shops.

Consumer Protection

The BJP is of the opinion that there must be a co-relation between cost of production, price and profit. Nobody should be permitted to pocket super-profits. The party also recognises the need to enforce strict measures of quality control and price regulation. With this view the BJP will:

1. Build a powerful consumer movement and formulate a price and profit policy for industrially manufactured goods;
2. Make statutory provision for declaring cost of production of industrially manufactured goods;
3. Ensure a reasonable rate of interest on the deposits by a consumer for registering his demand for cars, scooters, installation of telephones, gas, electric connections etc.; and
4. Enforce the Consumer Protection Act, 1986, specially by constituting consumers' courts in all the districts.

Labour

BJP believes in healthy trade unionism. It will:

1. Rationalise and simplify Labour Laws;
2. Pecognise unions on the basis of secret ballot;
3. Introduce worker participation from the Shop Floor to the Board Room in all public sector projects, public limited companies and foreign companies operating in India;
4. Protect workers against inflation; and
5. Make laws and evolve an effective mechanism to protect the labour from occupational health hazards arising from industries like asbestos, cement, slate, mica, chemicals, textiles.

Full Employment and Right to Work

BJP recognises the citizen's Fundamental Right to work and will incorporate it in the Constitution. All our economic policies—whether it is small dams or cottage industry, house construction or road building—will boost employment. In addition we will:

1. Introduce Employment Guarantee Scheme throughout the country;
2. Provide Pensions for the aged poor;
3. Establish techno-economic project formulation bureaus in all districts and blocks for speedy launching of various full employment schemes with a special emphasis to cover the poor under-employed; and
4. Announce a work guarantee scheme as soon as the full employment plan for the block is approved.

Energy

There is acute energy crisis in India particularly in the villages which have remained without any dependable sources of energy even after forty-two years of Independence. This situation will have to be tackled on a war-footing. BJP will:

1. Intensify efforts to find more oil, coal and natural gas reserves;
2. Improve the working of power plants which are now functioning at less than 50 per cent of capacity;
3. Stop the massive theft of electric power;
4. Introduce power-efficient, energy-saving devices in homes and factories;
5. Increase forest cover from the present 19 per cent of land to the desired 33 per cent; and
6. Encourage wind, water, bio-gas and solar power generation.

Justice to the Poor

For accelerating the process of distributive justice the following policy measures will be under taken:

1. The surplus land already identified (about 5.5 million acres) shall be distributed to the landless within a maximum period of 3 years;
2. All tillers of the land shall be given title deeds, on the basis of quick, on-the-spot inquiries by competent authorities. The report regarding the progress made in this connection would be placed on the floor of the Assembly every year for approval;
3. Block level committees and tribunals with 50 per cent representation from tenants and landless labour would be appointed to implement land ceiling and tenancy reforms;
4. Legislative measures for the protection of unorganised rural worker would be introduced;
5. The share of small and marginal farmers landless workers and artisans in institutional credit will be raised up to 50 per cent under a time-bound programme;
6. *Antyodaya* Schemes covering every development block would be launched; and
7. The big industrial houses will be required to spend a portion of their wealth for the rural welfare every year.

III

THE PEOPLE

The Indian people are nation's greatest assets. They are the real instruments of transforming the country and building its future. The BJP is fully conscious of their manifold problems and is committed to redress their sufferings. It offers the following programme for different sections of Indian citizens.

Rural Folk

The BJP recognises that rural poor has to be provided or subsidised a set of social services and an infrastructure for their speedy development. The BJP will:

1. Launch Schemes to supply ample and clean drinking water to each village, all problem villages to be covered in five years;
2. Energise every village;
3. Connect the villages through all-weather *pucca* roads;
4. Provide comfortable mass transit;
5. Implement schemes to offer health and family planning knowledge supplies and services;
6. Undertake a massive drive for literacy and continuous non-formal education to transmit professional knowledge, and to raise the consciousness to the poor about current injustices, and their rights;
7. Provide sanitation (with increasingly mechanised and covered waste and sewage haulage, disposal and recycling); and
8. Implement Housing Schemes for the poor.

Salariat

The BJP fully appreciates the problems of the government employees and the salaried class, now crushed between fixed income and rising prices. It will:

1. Link salaries in private services also to cost of living index; include minimum housing standard in computing minimum wages;
2. Provide residential accommodation to all government employees and encourage employers to build houses for staff;
3. Progressively introduce triple benefit schemes in private services, private sector and public sector;
4. Lower Life Insurance premia; and
5. Increase the return on Provident Fund deposits.

Senior Citizens and Pensioners

The Party recognises the need to nave a National Policy for Senior Citizens. In the opinion of the BJP the pensioners are the most hard-pressed in the fixed income group. BJP will:

1. Have a National Pension Policy to secure social and economic justice to all citizens including senior citizens;
2. Replace the 1971 Pension Act by a new law, more in tune with the changed social security concepts;
3. Launch Schemes to utilise the talents and expertise of the Senior Citizens;
4. Grant pensioners DA relief on the same scale as to serving employees;
5. Introduce lower income-tax rates for pensioners and ensure higher rates of interest of senior citizens on investment in certain approved schemes;
6. Re-fix pensions as and when pay scales are revised; and
7. Grant travel concessions to pensioners and Senior Citizens.

Ex-Servicemen

The BJP holds that the plight of the ex-servicemen has suffered at the hands of the Rajiv Government.

The BJP would work towards a purposeful resolution of their problems and is committed to implementing the following proposals:

1. One rank, one pension;
2. Guaranteed avenues of employment up to the age of 58;
3. Necessary changes in the agricultural and urban land tenancy laws so as to ensure proprietory rights of servicemen;
4. To bring the welfare of ex-servicemen on the Concurrent List in the Constitution; and
5. Strengthen District Sainik Boards.

Sindhi Speaking People

The BJP recognises the valuable contributions made by the Sindhi speaking people for enriching the Indian society. The party also assures the Sindhi Community of protection and promotion of their identity, culture, language, and literature and fulfilment of constitutional guarantees enshrined in Article 350A and 350B of the Constitution of India.

The Party would also give them due representation in various spheres of social and political life.

Women

The BJP will:

1. Take measures to remove gender discrimination and give equal status to the women in society; ban the determination of sex of a child in embryonic stage;
2. Make registration of marriages compulsory — like births and deaths to prevent child marriages;
3. Make the wife equal co-sharer in the husband's wealth and income;
4. Initiate schemes to provide economic opportunities for women, provide more facilities in technical and vocational training by starting ITIs and

Polytechnics specially for women;

5. Take stringent measures against employers who discriminate against women workers on the ground of marital status, age or family responsibility, in order to save themselves the responsibility of providing maternity benefit, creche facilities etc.;
6. Launch a special drive to improve the educational status for women. More women's universities will be opened;
7. Reserve up to 30 per cent certain categories of jobs for women;
8. Treat burning injuries as attempt to murder and dowry deaths as murder under section 302 IPC;
9. Provide smokeless *Chulhas* at concessional rates to village women; and
10. Build hostels for single women working in the cities.

Youths

The BJP has a special appeal to the youth of India. The Party recognises the tremendous potential in them and calls upon them to join great endeavour of national reconstruction. The BJP in accordance with a National Youth Policy, will:

1. Device mechanism for the participation of youths in the complementation of the poverty alleviation programmes;
2. Ensure participation of youths in literacy drive, conservation of environment, Land Army etc;
3. Mobilise youths for fighting social evils like untouchability, dowry, superstitions, casteism, etc. and develop a scientific outlook in them;
4. Encourage the spirit of adventurism in the youths; and
5. Inculcate in them a sense of pride for their glorious heritage and a will to transform India into a modern, progressive, prosperous and front rank nation.

Scheduled Castes and Scheduled Tribes

The BJP stands for all such measures which will bring the SC and ST people on par with the rest of the society, not in terms of economic status alone but on broad spectrum of social life giving them a rightful place of honour to live with a sense of belonging. The BJP will:

1. Enforce laws against untouchability and atrocities very stringently and set up mobile or special courts to try cases of atrocities against SC and ST;
2. Atrocity prone villages will be identified and steps will be taken to safeguard the life, honour and property of the scheduled castes and tribes;
3. A massive campaign to eradicate untouchability will be launched;
4. Full allocation and utilisation of funds under special component plan in proportion to SC population will be ensured;
5. A national level financial agency on the lines of NABARD to cater the credit needs of SC/ST will be set up;

6. Ensure greater participation of SC/ST is small, cottage and rural industries;
7. Launch vigorous schemes during VII Five Year Plan coinciding with Dr. Ambedkar's centenary to raise SCs and STs families above poverty line;
8. Implement the reservation policy for SC and ST by resorting to special recruitment drives so as to fill their quota within the shortest possible time;
9. Put an end to the carrying of night soil as headload and introduce modern technique for disposal. Also take steps for effective rehabilitation;
10. Separate heads of account for SC/ST expenditure will be maintained by the Central and the State Governments;
11. A befitting memorial to Dr. B.R. Ambedkar will be established in Delhi during his centenary year;
12. Evolve a new forest policy based on a partnership between the forest tribals and the forest authorities;
13. Frame policies which protect tribals from exploitation, and indebtedness, and enable them to grow in accordance with their own genius;
14. Remove the impediments in the speedy development of Tribal and Hill areas and settle the pending claims for grant of permanent *pattas* to the tribals by amending the Forest Conservation Act (1986);
15. Amend the laws relating to the collection and marketing of the minor forest produce to protect the economic interests of the ST;
16. Convert all forest villages into revenue villages; and
17. Formulate a sub-plan for the economic development of the Scheduled Tribes.

Reservation Policy

In the opinion of the BJP the question of reservation has to be viewed with an open mind free from all prejudices of any kind. For this BJP commends:

1. Reservation should be continued for the scheduled castes and scheduled tribes as before;
2. Reservation should also be made for other backward classes broadly on the basis of the Mandal Commission Report, with preference to be given to the poor among these very classes; and
3. As poverty is an important contributory factor for backwardness, reservation should also be provided for members of the other castes on the basis of their economic condition.

Physically Handicapped

The BJP accepts the rehabilitation of the physically handicapped persons as a component of Social Welfare. The party will:

1. Make a detailed survey and prepare a register of disabled persons in each district;
2. Open centres to train the disabled for appropriate vocations;
3. Give tax benefits to those industries, firms, and organisations who either absorb the disabled or provide limbs and other artefacts for their use;

4. Provide marketing and other infrastructural facilities for the items manufactured by the disabled; and
5. Will pay cash awards and other incentives to those handicapped who excel in any field of life.

Destitutes

The BJP recognises the need for providing the destitute homes and orphanages and this would form an important component of Social Welfare Schemes. Institutions providing such facilities would be given tax relief.

IV

QUALITY OF LIFE

Man does not live by bread alone. He must also have health and housing, education and sports, and above all a happy environment.

Housing and Town Development

The BJP recognises the right to shelter by all citizens of India. The party would evolve a National Housing Policy based on the minimum housing standards for the urban and the rural poor. In this direction the Party will:

1. Take measures for providing minimum area of land for housing to each family at cheaper rates;
2. Expand and strengthen housing co-operatives, and encourage trusts and other establishments for building houses to be rented or sold;
3. Improve the basic civil amenities in towns and pay special attention to the problems of slums to improve their habitats;
4. Develop small and medium townships to prevent over-crowding of metropolitan towns;
5. Progressively develop all urban centres as garden cities;
6. Rationalise Housing and Rent Control laws; and
7. Double the number of houses now built annually by various State Housing Boards.

Education

The party views with concern that with the rising cost of education, the existing socio-economic disparities will be perpetuated in the field of education. The BJP believes in equalisation of educational opportunities and build up a system worthy of the genius of our heritage and the undoubted capacities of our youth. Towards this end, we will:

1. Implement Articles 45 of the Constitution to give free education to all children in the 6-14 age group, evolve a new strategy for a teacher-oriented expansion programme for this;
2. Launch an Adult Literacy Programme;

3. Give education a vocational and technical content, establish a complex of agro-industrial polytechnics in each district;
4. Introduce compulsory moral instruction, that will be non-denominational but character-building;
5. Supply subsidised text-books and writing materials, develop book-banks in the educational institutions;
6. Ensure academic freedom and the autonomy of universities, raise the emoluments and status of teachers;
7. Make the Universities and colleges adopt localities and villages and help them in their overall development;
8. Delink jobs from degrees;
9. Progressively increase the allocation for education till it reaches the six per cent of the GNP; and
10. Associate students' unions with the management of student welfare programmes.

Language

The BJP supports the principle that people have a right to be educated and run their administration in their own language. The BJP will:

1. Implement the three language formula and make adequate arrangements for language teaching so that persons knowing different Indian languages are available in each region;
2. Speedily implement the recommendations of the Parliamentary Committee on Official language;
3. Take necessary administrative steps that candidates can appear with Hindi medium in all Competitive Examinations and/or interviews for recruitment in all central services, and admissions to national institution like IITs and AIIMS;
4. Remove all impediments in pursuing higher education and research through Hindi or other Indian languages;
5. Promote the study of Sanskrit language as the storehouse of ancient Indian wisdom and restore its position in the three languages formula;
6. Assist the development of those Indian languages which are neither State languages nor regional languages, but have contributed to the enrichment of Indian culture; and
7. Include Nepali in the Eighth Schedule of the Constitution.

Health and Nutrition

Health care to all citizens is the primary duty of the State. A majority of children born in families below poverty line are under-nourished and show sign of mental retardation chiefly due to protein deficiency. BJP, therefore, considers hygiene, sanitation and nutrition as more important than medicines and hospitals. We will:

1. Along with Allopathy, recognise and promote Ayurveda and Siddha, Unani and Homoeopathy, Chromopathy and Nature Cure — and in general

encourage holistic healing;

2. Supply free milk and nutrition to children in primary schools, and give every child an annual physical check-up;
3. Improve the present district civil hospitals, and set up similar hospitals at taluka level;
4. Give every village a Health Care Centre to take particular care of expectant mothers and provide them with adequate nourishment;
5. Have a Mobile Dispensary in each taluka;
6. Build more and better public latrines, particularly for women in villages;
7. Organise Eye Camps, and camps for other serious ailments in various areas;
8. Implement Hathi Committee Report on Pharmaceuticals and make essential medicines available cheap to the people;
9. Implement a programme to control and eradicate the communicable diseases; and
10. Take effective measures against drug addiction and alcoholism.

Science and Technology

The BJP believes that Science and Technology (ST) should be allowed to play its due role to transform India into a prosperous, modern and enlightened society. The party would unhesitatingly apply appropriate scientific and technological methods for increasing productivity, eradicating poverty, hunger and disease and to provide meaningful employment along with the basic amenities of life to the vast percentage of population living below the poverty line. The party holds that science is not merely harnessing nature for material wealth but is as well liberating and enriching mind and enlarging the human spirit. The BJP would use science in the service of the poor and would develop technology with a human face.

The party is equally concerned about the rising trends of brain drain. The BJP will:

1. Foster a scientific temper among the people;
2. Use Science and Technology for increasing productivity and generating employment;
3. Implement a vigorous programme of science education and research for improving quality of life;
4. Establish a network of Centres for Application of Science and Technology to Rural Areas, implement lab to land programmes and develop a strong low cost agro-industrial base;
5. Put new life in National Laboratories, develop them as centres of excellence in applied research;
6. Direct these laboratories to evolve Appropriate Technology for Indian needs;
7. Accelerate the production of scientific literature in regional languages and evolve a national terminology for science and technology; and
8. Create the right working conditions, for our best brains to remain here and serve the country and not migrate to other lands.

Sports

The BJP will give all encouragement to sports and put India on the Olympic map of the world. We will:

1. Evolve a new dynamic national sports policy aiming at bringing 10 per cent population on the playgrounds and winning medals in Olympic and other international competitions;
2. Provide play fields in schools, colleges, universities, rural areas and open sports complexes in all districts with modern equipments under a time bound programme;
3. Provide coaching, training, diet, and other, facilities to our sports persons at par with those available to the sports persons of advanced countries;
4. Ensure job security for sportsmen and admission to the colleges and technical courses; and
5. Respect the Olympic charter and autonomy of the sports bodies and will prohibit governmentalisation of sports.

Family Welfare and Population Policy

The BJP recognises the growing concern of the people about the dangers of a demographic explosion and distortions created by the mishandling of the population control programmes by the Congress (I) government. The BJP is committed to the policy of responsible parenthood and believes that population control programme should be given top priority while formulating national plans. It expects all sections of Indian Community to full participate in these programmes. The BJP will:

1. Strive for creating a national consensus for adopting a National Population Policy and if necessary to take suitable legislative measures for it;
2. Make Family Planning information and facilities available to the people. Involve all voluntary, social and cultural organisations in creating an awareness for adopting family planning as a way of life.
3. Perform Vasectomy and Tubectomy operations free, and encourage all methods including herbal and biorhythmic;
4. Help childless couples with medical assistance to have a child;
5. Integrate the family planning programme with other community welfare programmes; and
6. Pursue vigorously for the voluntary adoption of the "two children" norm and evolve a system of incentives and disincentives for achieving the long term demographic goals.

Environment

The BJP attaches high priority to stop the degradation of environment. In the opinion of the BJP, the rapid depletion of natural resources, risks of green house effect, the destruction of tropical rain-forests, and the hazards of dumping of industrial waste and discharge of highly toxic materials in air and water are matters of global concern and world opinion has to be alerted against them. International efforts are needed to save the planet. Preservation of environment has been an integral part of Indian way of life. We look upon India as *Bharat Mata* and a holy land. Our land, air, waters, our hills, forests, flora and fauna are all sacred to us. We will keep them neat, clean and intact. We will:

1. Formulate a National Resources Management Policy and adopt a holistic approach in planning;
2. Require anti-pollution devices to be installed to process and clean up industrial and Municipal effluents before the same are discharged into our rivers;
3. Keep a strict watch on chemical fertilisers and insecticides for any poisoning of the soil;
4. Improve auto exhausts to prevent the fouling of the air;
5. Ćurb the aggression of noise in the cities;
6. Undertake a massive afforestation programme;
7. While protecting the traditional rights of *Vanavasis,* we will require the planting of three trees for every single tree that is cut by anybody for any reason;
8. Make environmental concerns an integral part of education; and
9. Take special care in import of technology and promote research for developing indigenous pollution free technology.

Culture

The BJP believes in preserving and propagating the cultural values which have kept India united through the ages. It will:

1. Conserve the ancient heritage of India and make people feel proud about it;
2. Promote India values of life through cultural centres;
3. Acquaint people with the glorious traditions and achievements of ancient Indian genius in the fields of science, technology, medicine, agriculture etc.;
4. Wage a relentless war against superstitions and outmoded customs; and
5. Emphasise on culture as a dynamic and synthetic process.

Arts

Arts is the essence of life. BJP will encourage all art forms. It will make the various arts, part of Education, Production and Life.

To promote theatre, BJP will, as a rule, exempt all theatrical performances from entertainment tax.

The BJP will encourage folk art in various fields.

Films

BJP recognises the great role of cinema entertainment, education and national integration. BJP will:

1. Have, in addition to 'A' and 'U' Films, 'Q' that is Quality films, which will be exempt from entertainment taxes;
2. Have special theatres in metropolitan centres to screen art films and other Quality films; and
3. Implement the recommendations of the Karanth Committee on National Film Policy.

Tourism

The BJP recognises the importance of tourism as an instrument of national integration, international understanding and employment generation. India abounds in natural beauty and charming tourist centres, which have fascinated people from far distant quarters. It will:

1. Promote tourism both national and international as an industry and give incentives to those who take it as a profession;
2. Will evolve a policy of integrating tourism and marketing of handicrafts and other art works;
3. Take a scheme of training tourist guides and opening tourist homes and information centres; and
4. Provide infrastructural facilities like sites for building dormitories at subsidised rates and network of communication channels.

Mass Media

The BJP reaffirms its commitments to the freedom of thought and expression. We will:

1. Make freedom of the Press an explicit Fundamental Right, and not just an implied one derived from the citizen's right to Freedom of Expression;
2. Encourage the growth of the Press by abolishing the duty on newsprint and the tax on newspaper advertising;
3. Revive the 'Prasar Bharati Bill' of 1979, which sought to convert AIR and Doordarshan into an autonomous corporation, *sui generis*. The Corporation would have greater autonomy than that enjoyed by BBC today;
4. Review the Official Secrets Act in so far as it obstructs the Right to Know and enact a Freedom of Information Law; and
5. Implement the P.C. Joshi Report on TV software to improve the quality of TV programmes.

V

NATIONAL SECURITY

The BJP holds that National security is a primary responsibility of State. Security of the nation is an integrated whole: an amalgam of the internal, the economic, the social, the political, the military and the diplomatic. The BJP will, therefore, resolve the social and political turmoil in strategically sensitive border States like

Jammu & Kashmir, Punjab, North East and Assam. Indian diplomacy can assist in the protection of our national interests only if it is guided by a purposeful foreign policy.

Foreign Policy

The conduct of diplomacy by the Rajiv Government has left India's foreign policy in tatters. Never has the country faced so much animosity from so many of our neighbours, as today. It is BJP's view that the challenges, we face in the field of external relations, arise from a re-assertion of the altered importance of non-alignment, as a concept, in a rapidly transforming world. It is our view that increasingly, we should give emphasis to foreign economic policy under the time-proved concept of non-alignment. It is vital to move the world towards a greater and more effective North-South and South-South Co-operation.

The BJP has stood for, and is committed to mutually beneficial aim of good bilateral relation with all our neighbours and a strengthening of SAARC. We stand for a normalisation of relations with China, with due safeguards for Tibet, proper recognition of India's national interests and honourable solution of the border dispute. We would work for a comprehensive package of settlement of all outstanding matters with Pakistan and a widening of the people-to-people relations between our two countries. We would work for an early withdrawal of IPKF from Sri Lanka. With Nepal BJP would seek the re-establishment of harmonious relations based on the concept of interdependent growth.

The BJP stands for a foreign policy committed to world peace, disarmament and a non-exploitative new international economic order. The Party will:

1. Work towards re-imparting dynamism to the non-aligned movement;
2. Pursue a policy of peace, friendship and co-operation with neighbouring countries;
3. Reject the domination of super-power interest in South Asia and the Indian Ocean.
4. Work towards the establishment of a regional common market by strengthening South Asian Regional Conference;
5. Work for the establishment of a new international economic order, take initiative for trade and monetary reform, North-South dialogue with emphasis on enhanced South-South Co-operation;
6. Continued efforts for the world-wide rejection of apartheid; and
7. Continuously work towards the solution of problems of people of Indian origin living abroad.

Defence

Defence preparedness has suffered grievously in the hands of Rajiv Government gripped as it is, by ad-hocism and by corruption surrounding defence procurements. This has brought to a standstill all policy-making and implementation within the Defence Ministry. The other great harm that Rajiv Government has caused to the country is excessive misemployment in an adventurous manner, of the Indian Armed Forces on Political roles or on militarily unattainable tasks. This has caused a very serious lowering of the morale of our Armed Forces, and hence of its total combat effectiveness. BJP wishes to caution the nation against the extremely harmful consequences if such a situation is permitted to continue.

The BJP would work actively towards reviving the morale of the Armed Forces, giving a solemn assurance that the Indian Armed Forces, the Army, the Navy and the Air Force, would not lack either in equipment or in the necessary wherewithals to execute their responsibilities.

The BJP will exert for:

1. Optimum defence preparedness including production of nuclear bombs and delivery systems;
2. Diversification of sources of supply of defence hardware, continued emphasis on maximising indegenous production, self-reliance and Defence Research and Development;
3. Greater public accountability of defence expenditure;
4. Enhancement of Indian Navy's capability;
5. Identification, and elimination of, foreign lobbies associated with defence weapons procurement and contracts; and
6. Improve service conditions in the Armed Forces so as to make careers in the Army, Navy and Air Force more attractive to the best talent in the country.

This then is the programme which the BJP pledges to implement under the inspiring leadership of Shri A.B. Vajpayee and Shri L.K. Advani. The dedicated cadres of the party, headed by these brilliant leaders of impeccable record of clean public life and selfless service to the nation, are committed to usher in a new political culture. In the opinion of the BJP a critical moment of history has arrived for India. The country cannot afford to miss this moment of history, this opportunity to throw out the last vestige of the dynastic rule mainly responsible for this country's ruination.

The BJP on its part has left no stone unturned in its efforts to put up a determined and united electoral battle and has unhesitatingly sacrificed its party interests whenever national interests so demanded. The Bharatiya Janata Party calls upon the people to join in its struggle for a value based polity and throw out this corrupt and incompetent government.

ANNEXURE B

THE COMMUNIST PARTY OF INDIA (CPI) ELECTION MANIFESTO General Election, 1989

The ninth general election to the Lok Sabha and five State assemblies takes places in an extremely critical situation in the country.

The nation faces a grave peril to its unity and integrity and to its democratic institutions. Never before since Independence was the threat to the country's secular-democratic set up so serious. The communal-divisive forces have launched a vicious offensive.

Five years of the Rajiv Gandhi government have brought the country to a sorry pass. The government's pandering to communalism is undermining national unity. Its economic policies have heaped more misery on the people with 50 per cent of the people forced to live below poverty line.

Its rule is marked by increasing corruption at various levels, particularly in high places, even in the circles close to the prime minister. The exposures in the Bofors deal are a telling commentary on the shameful conduct of the rulers of this country who cheat the people and make money from kickbacks.

There has been considerable erosion of democratic institutions and democratic values under the rule of the Congress (I). Even Parliament has been denigrated under the Rajiv Gandhi.

A ruling party like the Congress (I) which has not even held elections in its own party for nearly two decades can hardly have any respect for country's democratic institutions.

The Sarkaria Commission's report has been shelved. Even the unexceptionable recommendations like testing the strength of the government on the floor of the house, not to appoint ex-politicians as governors and in case of dissolution of the house fresh elections must be held within three months, have not been accepted.

Growing violence in political life, criminalisation and communalisation of politics now pose a most serious threat to Indian democracy.

To pull the country back from this serious situation and to give a purposeful turn to its socio-economic development and to its political life is a task of paramount importance. All the secular-democratic forces, all patriotic Indians, all men and women of goodwill have to join hands at this critical juncture to ensure that the Rajiv Gandhi government is defeated and a government better than this one is formed as a result of this election.

The CPI will do its best towards the realisation of this aim.

Communal Menace

Today the country is faced with the menacing spectre of a communal holocaust.

In the name of Ram Janam Bhoomi-Babri Masjid issue unprecedented communal violence has been unleashed all over the Hindi heartland and Gujarat.

Because of the pandering which the Rajiv Gandhi government had done to the religious fundamentalists of both sides (on one side in the Shah Bano case and on the other breaking open the locks of the Ayodhya complex), communal forces have gained new leverage during the last few years.

Even after the elections have been announced, the RSS-BJP-VHP combine is going ahead with the *Shila Pujan* in preparation for laying the foundation-stone for the Ram temple at the site of the Babri Masjid. Home Minister Buta Singh's understanding with the VHP at Lucknow has encouraged it (VHP) to carry out its dangerous designs.

The BJP is the only political party which is not prepared to accept the Allahabad High Court verdict for maintenance of the *status quo*. The BJP is cynically playing the communal card to reap electoral harvest. It is totally unmindful of how it would profoundly damage the inter-communal relations in the long run. Such open playing of the Hindu card has never happened before and has already vitiated the communal atmosphere to a dangerous degree.

The aggressive communalists are also campaigning for establishing "Hindu Rashtra" for abolition of the Minorities Commission and for scrapping of article 370 of the Constitution (which gives a special status within the Indian Union to the State of Jammu and Kashmir).

Those who talk of establishing the "Hindu Rashtra" will surely disrupt the unity of our country. They are only helping the advocates of Sikh Raj in Punjab and Islamic Raj in Kashmir. "Hindu Rashtra" will ultimately lead to disintegration of our motherland.

The CPI expresses happiness that in the face of the communal danger, anti-communal forces in various parties and liberal professions are raising their voice in defence of the secular values and traditions.

Faced with such a forbidding danger to the unity and integrity of the country, Prime Minister Rajiv Gandhi has not taken any serious steps to counter the communal menace and to build up a mass campaign against communalism and in defence of secularism. Despite repeated demands, he has not cared to call a meeting of the national integration council (NIC).

He has not even bothered about implementation of the decisions of the Srinagar meeting of the NIC (1968), one of which was of hold the district magistrate and district superintendent of police responsible for communal peace. The Congress (I) continues its alliance with the Muslim League.

The Congress (I) government's failure to act at all against the vicious communal forces, its failure to honour its promise of creating a composite police force, particularly in the northern States and in Gujarat and Maharashtra, have caused much damage to the cause of communal harmony and national unity.

The CPI, along with other left and secular forces, is in the forefront of the nationwide struggle against the divisive-communal forces, to defend communal amity and integrity of the country and its secular set up. To that end, the Communist Party of India's planned march to Ayodhya on November 9, along with the CPI (M), is an important landmark.

The Communist Party of India fervently appeals to all the secular forces of the country to join hands to save the unity of the country and its secular traditions. They must take a firm stand that the religious places of any religion would not be demolished to build that of another religion, that the *status quo* of every religious place as on August 15, 1947 would be maintained.

Punjab

The depredations of the Khalistani terrorists helped by foreign powers continue to fester Punjab. The Rajiv Gandhi government does nothing for a political solution of the Punjab problem and to evolve a consensus with political parties in the spirit of the Punjab accord. Instead, it seeks of find allies among some sections of the terrorists. It refuses to combine administrative measures with a mass political campaign so as to isolate the terrorists. Certain police excesses also provide grist to the mill of the extremists.

It does nothing to reactivate the administrative system, including the judicial system. It refuses to take action against the organisers of anti-Sikh riots of 1984 in Delhi and other places. Some opposition leaders adopt a position which can only help the terrorists.

The CPI and the CPI (M) are in the forefront in the struggle against the terrorists. Our comrades are laying down their lives for the sacred cause of national unity. We promise to continue this battle and are prepared to make more sacrifices for it. We appeal to all political parties to rise above partisan politics and help to evolve a national consensus on this issue.

Kashmir

The situation in Kashmir is getting increasingly serious. the pro-Pak elements and secessionists are on the rampage. Over the years the Congress rulers have been complicating the Kashmir situation. The communal elements in the country like the BJP have added fuel to the fire by launching attacks on Article 370.

The Congress rulers have always wanted yesmen to rule Kashmir. Installation of G. M. Shah after dismissing the elected government of Dr. Farooq Abdullah in 1984 is one such example.

The electoral process in the state has almost always been eroded through rigging, undermining the confidence of the people in elections and hurting the Kashmiri sentiment. The pro-Pak elements have taken advantage of it to mislead the young generation. It has now become an uphill task for the patriotic forces in Kashmir. There is need to look at the problem with sympathy and to make a determined effort to wean away the Kashmiri youth. A series of measures—political, administrative and economic—will have to be taken.

Ethnic Problems

In the recent period the ethnic problem (Jharkhand, Bodos, Ladakhis, etc.) have assumed new dimension. The tribals long suppressed are demanding a share in the national cake. Our party takes a positive and sympathetic view of the problem. However, the Rajiv Gandhi government uses this problem also for its own partisan politics, sometimes to complicate matters for non-Congress (I) state governments.

The CPI stands for accepting the legitimate demands of the various tribal areas—from statehood to regional and district councils, depending on the concrete situation.

The CPI appeals to all the patriotic forces to join hands in a spirit of humility and dedication to evolve a national consensus in the fight against communalism and casteism to protect secularism and to solve the Punjab and Kashmir problems, as well as the ethnic problem of the various tribal groups. National unity has to be protected. Let us get rid of narrow-minded politics and considerations of short-term political gains. The country comes first and everything else after.

Economy

The Rajiv Gandhi government's policies have brought Indian economy to a critical juncture as demonstrated in constantly rising prices, growing unemployment, mounting debts and deficit budgets. While the common man suffers, the monopoly capitalists are having a field day. As compared to 1982, the assets of big capitalists have increased ten times.

(a) The most dramatic indication of this was the sudden jump in sugar prices, a 100 per cent rise in September 1989. The Rajiv Gandhi government promised to bring them down to Rs. 9.50 a kg in place of the Rs. 6.50 a kg prevailing in August 1989, but it has not been able to do even that. The sugar barons have made hundreds of crores of rupees of extra profit, part of it for the Congress fund.

But it is not only sugar prices that have spiralled: prices of every item of consumption of the common man have moved up in a steep manner in the last five years.

The wholesale price index has gone up from 338.4 (Base 1970-71 as 100) in March 1985 to 467.8 in September 1989. The rise in the consumer price index is from 582 (base: 1960 as 100) in March 1985 to 848 in July 1989.

The Rajiv Gandhi government refuses to build up a powerful countrywide public distribution system and to fix a margin of profit to control prices.

The cost of production of all products and the cost audit report of industrial undertakings must be publicly announced through the Bureau of Industrial Costs and Prices, so that consumers are fully informed about the real price and a check can be kept on prices.

No wonder people are groaning about difficulty in making both ends meet.

(b) The rising number of the jobless is adding to the overall poverty of the people. The number of unemployed with the employment exchanges has touched the 33 million figure. When Rajiv Gandhi assumed power, the number was placed at 23 million.

Thousands are also being pushed into the ranks of the jobless through modernisation, mechanisation, computerisation, etc. to increase the profits of the capitalists. As many as 180,000 factories are lying closed. As much as Rs. 5,000 crore of bank funds are tied up in sick units and will probably have to be written off as bad debts. There is no national policy on this issue, i.e., how to strike a balance between modernisation and providing of jobs.

All the poverty alleviation programmes did nothing to improve the employment situation. Rajiv Gandhi has now played an election gimmick by combining all of them together and renaming it as Jawahar Rozgar Yojana. This is not going to reduce the ranks of the jobless and neither will its urban counterpart announced just on the eve of the election.

(c) Rajiv Gandhi's years as prime minister have seen the quantum jump in deficit-financing, now averaging around Rs. 10,000 crore. This is one of the reasons why prices are spiralling.

The years have also seen the burgeoining of India's debt burden, both external and internal. External debt is now placed at Rs. 90,000 crore to Rs. 100,000 crore, though the government is seeking to pass off a lower figure. Internal debt is estimated to have reached the figure of Rs. 150,000 crore. Debt servicing itself is costing more than Rs. 10,000 crore annually.

(d) The dramatic increase in the debt burden is the result of the Rajiv Gandhi government's policy of refusing to raise resources internally by taxing the capitalists and the rich, and instead relying on borrowings. This is another aspect of the policy of liberalisation which the government is following along with the open-door to the transnational companies. Between 1985 and 1988 the number of foreign collaborations increased by 3,386. Their total number today is 15,000.

Since it is not only high technology but also luxury consumer goods that are being imported, the country's balanced economic growth based on self-reliance is not being helped.

Elitist Education System

Rajiv Gandhi has given up the aim of cent per cent literacy and universal primary education envisaged in the Constitution. Instead, he has brought a new fangled elitist educational system called Navodaya Schools in which hand-picked students are given in-house education and reared as a special chosen class. If this policy continues, India will continue to be the country with the biggest illiterate people—rather a strange way of going into the 21st century!

Undermining Public Sector

The Rajiv Gandhi government is trying to undermine the public sector. Public sector units have been sought to be sold away to the private sector like the Scooters India Ltd. and the Bharat Electronics Ltd. unit in Maharashtra. There is a concerted attempt at privatisation and even works like road building and rail track maintenance are being handed over to contractors. Privatisation of even defence production is favoured.

Planning has been downgraded, with the decision-making on projects shifted from the Planning Commission and the Yojana Bhavan to the prime minister's office.

Anti-Working Class Policies

The Rajiv Gandhi government pursues an anti-working class policy. Black laws of ESMA, NSA and even anti-terrorists act have been used against the workers in their struggles. The government even tried to enact a new anti-working class law. But the attempt was defeated because of the united stand displayed by the working class.

The worst sufferers of government's anti-working class policies are the millions of unorganised workers in small-scale industries, whose rights to a minimum wage, provident fund and social security are being denied. They have to struggle hard to secure even paltry concessions.

However, workers and employees in largescale units have secured benefits through their struggles, despite repression.

The Communist Party of India, as the party of the working people, determinedly leads the fight for the legitimate rights and demands of the working class.

Raw Deal for Peasants

Peasants have not fared any better, particularly the small and marginal farmers. Due to the short-sighted policies of the government a serious crisis has gripped the agrarian economy. Poor growth rate, frequent fluctuations in production and glaring regional and inter-regional inequalities are the features of agrarian scene.

Alternating floods and droughts have hit agriculture badly, making large sections of the peasants paupers in several areas. The repeated promise of a comprehensive crop insurance scheme has not been fulfilled. Over and above, the government consistently refuse to fix remunerative prices for peasants' produces. The Kisan Sabha led by our party fights for the peasants' demands and will continue to do so.

Land Reforms

Land reforms have been put in deep freeze by Congress (I) state governments. Land concentration continues as 2.4 per cent holdings (large) own 24.6 per cent of the land. At the other end, 75 per cent of the landholdings are below two hectares each. The number of landless and land poor is ever growing and overcrowding agriculture. With the free market economy, there is also increasing grip of monopolies and transnationals on the rural market.

Only the left-democratic front government of Kerala and the left front government of West Bengal have done creditable work in carrying out land reforms.

The CPI has conducted bitter land occupation struggles, particularly in Bihar, Andhra Pradesh and U.P. One of our major demands is the grant of *pattas*.

Agricultural Workers

Agricultural workers continue to suffer from the worst forms of exploitation, social oppression and atrocities. Unemployment and under-employment, low wages failure of the government to implement even the very low minimum wages, immerse them in deep poverty. Wherever they organise and launch struggle for better wages, landlords and their armed senas attack them. The police and administration collude with the landlords or themselves launch attack on them. Except in Kerala and West Bengal, there is at present no law to protect the interests of the agricultural workers.

Harijans and Adivasis

Harijans and adivasis continue to be victims of landlord terror and social boycott despite the untouchability abolition law. They are also victims of police atrocities and barbarism. According to the Commissioner for scheduled castes and scheduled tribes, on an average 500 of them are being killed every year. In 1988 alone, 564 harijans and 160 adivasis were killed. As many as 1,406 harijans were seriously injured and so were 311 adivasis.

As many as 727 harijan and 285 adivasi women were victims of rape in the same year. A new feature is that adivasi and harijan women are victims of gangrape by men in uniform. The record of Congress (I) ruled states in this respect (Bihar, U.P.) is indeed shameful.

Crimes Against Women

Despite the fact that the government provided for stricter laws in crimes against women, there is no reduction in these. Women increasingly are victims of rape, dowry killings, police mayhem.

Sati was abolished one and a half century ago by the British rulers. But under Rajiv Gandhi regime *sati* has made a comeback (Roop Kanwar case in Rajasthan). Even this year the Congress (I) government in Rajasthan did not prevent *sati* celebrations in several places. Some of the opposition leaders also collude with the religious obscurantists in the revival of the barbarous practice of sati.

In the name of "power to the people", Rajiv Gandhi brought the panchayati raj and nagarpalika bills, providing for 30 per cent reservation for women. But he has nothing to provide social and economic equality for women. Unless thorough-going social reforms are carried out, according equal status to women in the society, in jobs, in the economy, no representation in panchayat is going to improve the status of women. The Communist Party of India is firm champion of the rights of women for their social, political and economic equality.

The situation demands a broad-based movement for social reforms, against social oppression of women, scheduled castes, scheduled tribes if the country has to move forward.

Centre-State Relations

Though the government appointed the Sarkaria Commission to go into the question of centre-state relations, even the moderate recommendations of the commission have not been accepted by the government, leave alone implementing them. The suggestion to set up an inter-state council is not being implemented.

Every effort is made by Rajiv Gandhi to usurp even the existing powers enjoyed by the states, thereby making a mockery of the slogan of decentralisation of powers as was revealed in the case of panchayati raj and Nagarpalika bills which were sought to be used to deprive the states of some of the existing powers. It adopts a discriminatory policy towards non-Congress (I) state governments. The need for restructuring of centre-state relations on a democratic basis has assumed urgent importance.

Downgrading Democratic Institutions

While concentrating power and decision-making in his own hands, Rajiv Gandhi has also downgraded Parliament, lowered its standards, flouted its conventions. The crassest example of devaluing Parliament was, when the opposition demanded his presence in the house to explain his position following the report of the Comptroller and Auditor General (CAG) on the Bofors gun deal, his refusal to present himself in the two houses for days together. A recent example of flouting the conventions of Parliament was the refusal to nominate an opposition member as chairman of the public accounts committee.

Corruption in High Places

The latest revelations on the Bofors gun deal—the report of the Comptroller and Auditor General, *The Hindu* disclosures and the interview of General K. Sundarji—have dramatically shown how corruption flourishes in high places under Rajiv Gandhi government.

In fact, the finger of accusation is uncomfortably pointing to circles close to the prime minister himself, his having been the defence minister when the Bofors deal was struck. Right from the first exposure by the Swedish media up to the latest *Hindu* reports. Rajiv Gandhi's has been a stand of evasion, lies and bland denials. All this forced the opposition in the Lok Sabha to resign in protest and seek people's mandate.

Left-Secular-Democratic Alternative: Need of the Hour

The Communist Party of India is fighting the election to defeat Rajiv Gandhi government, to isolate the communal forces like the BJP and the Muslim League and to strengthen the representation of left, democratic and secular forces and for a government which is better than Rajiv Gandhi's.

The Communist Party of India is striving for a national alternative based on the unity of programme left, secular and democratic forces and pursuing the following:

1. Defence of national unity and integrity, maintenance of communal harmony and safeguarding secular-democratic set-up; against mis-use of religious places for disruptive and communal activities;
2. The Commonest Party of India is proud of the role it has played in the post-Independence period in strengthening India's anti-imperialist foreign policy, which has raised India's prestige in world politics. We must continue and strengthen the country's policy of peace, anti-imperialism and non-alignment, of friendship and cooperation with the Soviet Union and other countries of the socialist world and anti-imperialist regimes; improvement of our relations with our neighbours, including China;

— Firms stand against neocolonialism, apartheid and exploitation by transnational corporations; support to national-liberation struggles of the peoples of Palestine; Namibia, South Africa and Western Sahara;

— Restructuring of international economic relations on an equitable and just basis;

3. Restructuring centre-state relations to expand the powers of the states and provide them with adequate financial resources; limiting the use of Article 356 of the Constitution to exceptional situations; the fate of every state government to be decided on the floor of the house;
4. Curbs on monopoly houses and transnational giants; nationalisation of sugar, textile, jute and vanaspati industries and foreign trade;
5. Protection and encouragement of small-scale industry support and encouragement for cottage industry and artisans;
6. State takeover of wholesale trade in foodgrains, strengthening and widening the public distribution system covering all essential commodities, absorbing small traders and shopkeepers in the system;
7. Need-based minimum wage for low-paid factory workers, toddy tappers, handloom, bidi and building workers social security for this category, dearness allowance to fully neutralise rise in prices, against wage freeze, lock-outs, closures and lay-off in factories, full trade union rights to all workers and government employees, effective workers' participation in management of public sector units; pension schemes for all workers and employees;
8. Guaranteed remunerative prices for peasants' produces, comprehensive crop insurance scheme, cheap and guaranteed credit and inputs; write off loans taken by small peasants from government institutions as well as from money lenders;
9. Radical land reforms, distribution of surplus and government lands to the landless and poor peasants, immediate grant of *pattas* by the government, fair wages for agricultural workers and comprehensive legislation to protect their rights; employment guarantee scheme for rural workers;
10. Planned and independent development of national economy, ensuring dominant position of the public sector, mobilisation of resources for planning by taxing the rich, including the rural rich;
11. Crash programme for economic and cultural development in Jammu and Kashmir and north-eastern states and other backward regions;
12. People's housing policy, guarantee of free house-sites to the rural and urban poor, provision of cheap housing for the low income groups; curbing speculation in land prices in urban areas, big and small.
13. The right to employment to be included in the fundamental rights in the Constitution; employment programmes for rural workers and educated youth, unemployment allowance for the jobless;.
14. Comprehensive policy for youth, including adequate facilities for cultural and sports activities;
15. Implementation of compulsory primary education; midday meals for children in primary schools; free education up to the secondary stage; stipends and hostel facilities for students from low income groups and for girls; time-bound programmes for abolition of illiteracy and providing

adequate funds to fulfil this aim;

16. Special vocational training programmes for women, creches in all workplaces where women are employed in significant numbers;
17. Effective measures to put an end to injustices and atrocities against women, equal wage, status and opportunities for women including the right to parental property; reservation of women in panchayats and other local bodies;
18. Scrapping the elitist Navodaya schools system, radical reorganisation of the education system to make it vocation-oriented;
19. An extensive free health programme;
20. Old age pension;
21. Safeguarding the rights of Muslims and other religious minorities, ban on communal and obscurantist propaganda, strengthening the unity and integrity of the country by firm adherence to the principles of secularism; secularisation of the system of education;
22. Inclusion of all India languages in VIII schedule, protection and promotion of Urdu in states where sizeable numbers of people have Urdu as their mother tongue, adequate facilities for promotion of Sindhi;
23. Introduction of the system of proportional representation in elections; effective reforms in the electoral system to eliminate money and muscle power;
24. Effective steps for the protection of the rights of Harijans and Adivasis, stringent action against instances of social boycott; reservation of scheduled castes and scheduled tribes in panchayats and other local bodies;
25. The legitimate demands of army jawans in regard to their working conditions as well as demands of ex-servicemen to be sympathetically considered;
26. Effective steps for the elimination of corruption, including permanent judicial machinery for enquiring into allegations of corruption against ministers and public men holding high positions, including chief ministers and prime ministers; Kerala model can be adopted.

    — All legislators, MPs, MLAs, ministers and high officials must disclose their assets and place them before Parliament and Assemblies;

27. Effective steps for the protection of environment; of air and water against constant pollution; noise control particularly in big cities, largescale programme of afforestation;
28. Building up of national water grid for proper utilisation of national water resources, also evolve a policy for domestic fuel;
29. For a national policy for urban decongestion and helping the slum dwellers;
30. Repeal of all undemocratic statutes including ESMA and NSA; enlarging democratic and civil rights of the people and extending support to civil rights organisations who seek to protect civil liberties;
31. Reform of the judicial system; justice should be easily available to the common people and should be inexpensive;
32. Strengthening the Parliamentary democratic system, restoration of

democratic traditions and conventions;

33. The Rajiv Gandhi government has totally and shamelessly abused the electronic mass media, TV and radio for partisan ends and to hurl slanders against opposition. This must stop. The electronic mass media must be controlled by an autonomous corporation with constant supervision by an all-party Parliamentary committee.

The Communist Party of India fervently appeals to the people to vote for our party on the basis of the above programme. In the constituencies where the CPI is not fighting the party would appeal to vote for other left, democratic and secular candidates of the opposition who alone can be depended upon to voice the will of the people in Parliament. The coming days are crucial for the future of our country and our people.

The nation needs a healing touch and the country a new healthy orientation in all spheres—social, economic and political.

Only a left-democratic-secular alternative can guarantee the realisation of this goal.

ANNEXURE C

THE COMMUNIST PARTY OF INDIA (MARXIST) ELECTION MANIFESTO General Election, 1989

In November this year the people of India will elect a new Lok Sabha and decide who should rule the country and how, for the next five years. The Communist Party of India (Marxist) calls upon the people to express their sovereign will, taking into consideration the events of the last five years.

The five years of Congress(I) rule are full of betrayal of hopes, of the interests of the nation, years of growing national disintegration and growing incapacity to check it, and above all years of immense immiserisation of our people, who were expecting some relief from the unbearable conditions.

They have been years of growing emergence of authoritarian rule, rising roughshod over the democratic rights of the common man, of growing dependence of India's economy on Western imperialist aid with attendant dangers. And, finally, they have been years of widespread corruption in the administration touching the highest echelons of the government including the Prime Minister, corruption in connection with vital defence deals.

How do matters stand today under Rajiv Gandhi's five years' rule in relation to the all-important question of national unity?

Congress(I) Rule : Danger to National Unity

Every year of the Congress(I)'s misrule under the Rajiv government has accelerated the challenge of the secessionist and disruptive forces raising the threat of destabilisation and disintegration.

For years now the secessionist threat in Punjab remains uncontrolled with innocent people paying with their lives. Every day a new blow is struck against national unity by the foreign financed Khalistanis, and the government, in its bankruptcy and its opportunism, sees no other way than that of placing Punjab under Emergency rule, denying the people of Punjab an elected government to fight the menace.

The secessionist threat has now extended to Kashmir. There the separatist elements raise Pakistani flag at their will, organise violence and bomb attacks, and lose no occasion to dishonour the days of national importance, and the government looks on.

The situation in the North Eastern region again is full of dangers with the central government's RAW organisation being used for inciting the Bodo agitation. In Tripura the Congress(I) party and the Rajiv government have played a treacherous role by rigging the elections and removing the CPI(M) ministry which held together the tribals and non-tribals in solid unity to defend the integrity of the country.

In the Hindi heartland, the Babri Masjid/Ramjanmabhoomi dispute threatens to unleash communal riots with the Rajiv Gandhi government and the Congress(I) party playing the role of a cheering spectator and with the BJP-RSS-VHP spreading the most vicious anti-Muslim poison.

If the situation is allowed to deteriorate further, it will inflict permanent damage on Indian unity weakening the country for years. The Rajiv Gandhi government has proved to be a government of national disintegration and disunity.

Congress(I) Opportunism

The Khalistanis would have been put in their place and Punjab would have been returned to normalcy if the Rajiv government had not gone back on the Rajiv-Longowal Accord, betrayed the promise to release the Jodhpur detenus, and punished the organisers of anti-Sikh orgy of murders in Delhi after the assassination of Indira Gandhi.

The ruling party and its government further betrayed national interests to win the Haryana elections, sacked the Barnala government and imposed President's Rule on Punjab and saddled the state with a permanent state of Emergency rule. This has alienated the great mass of the Punjabi people, the patriotic peasantry with the fighting traditions against every kind of injustice. It was this force that was to be roused to wage an effective fight against the secessionists. But the Rajiv government is afraid of this very force.

The Congress(I) party which even now has a substantial following in the state is guilty of cowardly behaviour. A leadership corroded by selfishness and self-aggrandisement, is unwilling to take an risk and mobilise its following in the fight against the secessionists. It plays the same role in Uttar Pradesh where again, it can pit its following against the communal forces. But relying to cash on the Hindu sentiments on the Ramjanmabhoomi issue in the elections, it betrays the people and allows the communal challenge to spread. In Kerala, the Congress(I) joins hands with the Muslim League to fight the Left and Democratic Front. The Congress(I) is totally unworthy of the trust of the people.

Active Fight of the CPI(M)

The CPI(M) does not believe in only criticising the Rajiv government and the Congress(I) party. It carries on an active fight among the people for national unity against secessionist, communal and other divisive forces. It considers that the communal and secessionist challenges cannot be reduced to a law and order question alone. They constitute political and ideological attacks on national unity and have to be fought as such with the initiative of the masses.

The CPI(M) is therefore in the forefront of the fight against the communal forces. In Punjab, along with the CPI, when all bourgeois parties have collapsed, its cadres and members of mass organisations are waging a heroic fight for unity, organising the people and facing the bullets of the terrorists. Long is the list of the martyrs. But the struggle inspires their family members also to take their place and carry on the fight.

In Uttar Pradesh, the CPI(M) and the CPI are already intervening to organise mass opinion and resist the fanaticism of the VHP-RSS-BJP combine which fans riots by organising 'Shilapoojan' processions.

In West Bengal where for years the CPI(M) and the Left have maintained and stabilised communal amity, the Left Front Ministry is able to take a firm stand against provocative '*Shilapoojan*' processions and warn the communal forces from both sides. In Kerala, the CPI(M)-led Left and Democratic Front Ministry, supported by the mass organisations, is waging a relentless fight against the RSS, Muslim League and other disruptive forces. The CPI(M) considers that the continuous united action of the masses is the only guarantee of winning the battle for unity. The CPI(M) calls upon all secular opposition parties, all patriotic forces to give up the role of spectators and critics, and unleash the initiative of the patriotic masses to fight the communal and other disruptors.

The Dual Character

The CPI(M) calls upon the electorate to remember the dual character of the election struggle. It must defeat the Rajiv Gandhi government and the Congress(I). It must isolate the communal forces from the people, eliminate the influence of communal appeal and defeat the game of disruption. The election must result not only in ousting the Congress(I) from power but in emergence of an India united and capable of defeating all disruptive challenges.

The Communist Party of India (Marxist) calls upon all secular opposition parties to keep in view this double obligation to our people and direct the election struggle so that a new government, firmly based on national unity and capable of dealing with communal challenges, emerges from the struggle.

Concern for Minority

The CPI(M) expresses deep sympathy with the minority Muslim masses who are the worst victims of communal fanaticism and governmental oppression during the riots. The CPI(M) will never forget the massacre of the Malliana Muslims for which has Congress(I) government neither made any amends nor punished the guilty. The CPI(M) has always stood for the protection of minority rights, full freedom of conscience, and equality of opportunity. It considers protection of minority rights as the acid test of democracy. The CPI(M) stands for equality of all languages and rightful place for Urdu.

The CPI(M) at the same time calls upon the minority masses to realise that the fight for the minority rights and equality to be successful, has to be carried on in cooperation with the democratic and class forces who are fighting the injustices and inequities of the bourgeois-landlord rule. The bourgeois-landlord rulers are incapable or protecting the democratic rights of the minority. It is only the common fight of all sections of the masses that will deliver the minority from the injustices of the present regime.

The minority communal leaders and the fundamentalists never think in terms of the common struggle of the Hindu and Muslim masses against the Congress(I) regime. They encourage and maintain the communal divisions among the masses which keep the toilers divided and help the Congress(I) regime.

On the Babri Masjid/Ramjanmabhoomi dispute the CPI(M) is of the firm opinion that it should be settled through a court verdict. This is the only way such explosive disputes in society can be settled. Pending the court verdict there should be no agitation and procession which are likely to break communal peace.

Whither Self-Reliance

The Indian people will come into their own only if their economy is self-reliant and they are able to control it and direct it. During the years of the Congress(I) rule, and especially under the new economic policy of the Rajiv government, Indian economy, its direction and policy are more and more being influenced by the directives and conditionalities of the World Bank and the IMF from whom India is borrowing heavily.

More and more, internal policies—exchange rate of rupee, food subsidies, prices, policies regarding sick and closed industries, and public sector—are being influenced by the World Bank with the Indian people threatened with the danger of losing their control over economy.

Besides conditionalities like imports liberalisations, greater openings to foreign capital are having prejudicial effects on Indian industry. Many industrial concerns are closing because of foreign competition and aggravating the unemployment problem.

India's helpless dependence on foreign borrowings is now emboldening the U.S. imperialists to insist that India accept its demands for intellectual property rights, open the Indian market for goods, capital and services, and allow the U.S. free run for penetrating every aspect of Indian economy.

The burden of foreign debt has grown. Every year India has to pay a huge amount in debt payments. Every year repayment and interest charges on loans absorb a greater part of the new borrowings.

High Prices and Massive Unemployment

While the prices of the common necessities of life continue to rise, the Indian peasant does not get a remunerative price for his produce. In the years of bumper harvest, food prices for the common man do not decline but continue to increase. The continuous rise in the prices of the necessities of life has led to tremendous deprivation of the people, throwing millions to abject poverty and enforced starvation.

Never before in India were so many millions undergoing starvation after days of hard labour. The recent price rises coming on top of earlier price increases, have broken the back of the people, with almost every article like sugar, foodgrains, edible oil, tea going beyond the reach of the people. The public distribution system has collapsed and the people are at the mercy of black-marketeers and the ruling party profiteers.

Workers in Distress

Hunger, starvation, unemployment, closed factories and mills have been the blessings of the Congress(I) rule. Three crores of unemployed in cities, ten crores in the rural areas, two lakh concerns closed or sick with no provision of unemployment relief except in a few states, no right to work—this is the gift of the bourgeois-landlord government, the Congress(I) government of Rajiv Gandhi.

Lakhs of industrial workers are on the streets. Under the textile policy of the government, the textile mill, handloom and jute workers are getting ruined. The handloom and powerloom workers had never witnessed such distressing days. The ruination of traditional industries like coir continues, and tens of thousands are out of job.

Bleak Prospects for Youth

The voting age has been lowered to 18 years and lakhs of young people will be exercising their vote for the first time. What are the prospects for a young person under the present dispensation? The youth coming from workers' and peasants' families find that there is hardly any opportunity for them for doing productive work and contributing to the progress of society. Increasing rural unemployment is driving lakhs of young people from the villages to the cities where at best they get temporary employment in unorganised industries and are paid miserable wages. A large number of them are forced to seek employment in questionable trades and have often to be at the service of smugglers and other anti-socials.

For the educated youth of the country also the prospects are extremely bleak. More than four million men and women graduates and undergraduates including engineers, doctors and others are seeking fruitful employment. India under the Congress(I) does not require their services, their skills, their urge to do useful work for our people. Thousands of them are leaving the country and forced to place their skills and education at the service of other countries and people, and the modernisation and computerisation drive launched under the Rajiv government is everyday narrowing employment opportunities for them.

The right to work and unemployment benefit alone can relieve the distressing situation facing the country.

The Rajiv government accepts no responsibility to check this growing chaos. The government refuses to take over and run sick industries. The World Bank demands that the government money should not be spent on reviving sick concerns. The Rajiv government, therefore, is denotifying the taken-over mills and adding to the chaos. Further, the Rajiv government's policy of modernisation and computerisation of industry, adopted in the name of increasing the competitive capacity of Indian industries, is again throwing out thousands of workers and employees out of job.

There can be no relief from the anarchy unless the Rajiv government is thrown out and the policies are reversed.

Raw Deal for the Peasants

The talk of land reforms and distribution of land to the landless has disappeared from the Congress(I) vocabulary despite extreme concentration of land and unheard of exploitation of the agricultural labour and poor peasants at the hands of the landlords. The Rajiv government has refused to implement the recommendations of the Rural Labour Committee for a Central legislation for agricultural labour. Landlords are allowed to organise armed bands to terrorise the Scheduled Castes and agricultural workers who dare to oppose their exploitation or demand wage increase. Their women-folk are molested and raped as in Bihar. Their homes are burnt and men murdered in collusion with the police.

Surrender to Multinationals

The public sector built with the aid of the Soviet Union and other socialist countries, which offered a basis for building an independent economy, is being liquidated and the economy is being handed over to Indian private capital. Foreign multinationals are being given more freedom to penetrate our economy. This is a dangerous trend. The surrender of the government to the multinational Union Carbide, on the question of compensation to the Bhopal gas victims, shows the inability of the government to control the growing influence of the multinationals.

Monstrous Burdens on the People

Life has been made a burden and a curse by continuous robbery of the hard-earned income of the common man through devaluation of the rupee. The rupee's present purchasing capacity is now only 12 paise. Deficit budgets again cut the purchasing power through high prices and, finally, the monstrous burden of increased taxation amounting to thousands of crores of rupees, again defraud the people. Over and above this, the rural masses get fleeced through extortionate payments on its huge accummulated debt. What chance has a hard-working honest man before this entire arsenal of robbery by the bourgeois-landlord government.

Intimidation by Anti-Socials

The ordinary Indian possesses no right excepting the right to vote. Deeply affected by corruption, jobbery and nepotism Congress(I) rule has become a curse for the common people in India. Under the Congress(I) rule the common man has no protection against the police, against the criminals and men of influence working in league with the police.

The stories of rape by policemen and murders in police custody continue to multiply. Barring transfer or temporary suspension hardly anything is done to bring the guilty offenders to book.

Even in the country's capital there is a common complaint that officers in-charge of police stations often refuse to register complaints against criminals and persons with social pull with the ruling party and leave the ordinary citizens totally defenceless against intimidation and encroachment on their rights.

The bastis, the slums of the big cities, the localities in the periphery of big towns are ruled by anti-socials in league with the police. This parallel government functions openly and people live in terror of anti-socials. In Congress(I) ruled States, honest and bold journalists and correspondents who expose the misdeeds of the police and anti-socials run the risk of threat to their lives. Every effort is being made to subordinate the judiciary to meet the needs of the ruling party and the judiciary appears to be increasingly yielding under this pressure.

Authoritarian Onslaughts

All democratic rights of the people are under constant attack. The 59th Amendment Act which hangs the sword of Emergency over the country, the use of ESMA, NSA and Preventive Detention Act are frequently used against workers' strikes and other mass movements. The falsification of Tripura elections and the establishment of a terror regime there underlines the growing trend towards authoritarianism under the Congress(I) rule. A vote for the Congress(I) is an invitation to engulf the country under a cruel authoritarian rule.

Attacks on Scheduled Castes and Tribes

The Congress(I) talks about protecting the weaker sections but its record of the last five years has been one of cruel attacks and total absence of protection against the atrocities of the landlords. In rural areas the Scheduled Castes and Scheduled Tribes are subjected to murderous attacks by the police and landlord goondas. Gang-rape of women by these agencies is a frequent phenomenon and the Congress(I) government looks on; nobody is punished.

Atrocities on Women

Atrocities on women continue to multiply. Dowry deaths are increasing. The Congress(I) government is unable to prevent forcible burning of women in the name of Sati. In government services and educational institutions, sexual harassment by higher officials, denial of equal pay and promotion are rampant.

On the eve of elections the Congress(I) government now offers 30 per cent reservation for women in panchayats. The Scheduled Castes and Scheduled Tribes whose homes have been burnt, whose women have been raped, are now being wooed by the offer of filling up of vacancies in reserved posts in government services. It seems that these vacancies were deliberately allowed to be accumulated over the years so that they can be used for electoral advantage. This is adding insult to injury.

Protect Tribal Interests

The tribal areas of the country are in great ferment, even revolt, against the miserable conditions imposed on them, their backwardness and the devastating effects of the capitalist path which have led to deprivation, and made them strangers in their own land. The situation is worst in the Congress(I) ruled States of Orissa, Bihar and M.P. In Madhya Pradesh, the tribals are virtually bonded labourers. Immediate intervention of the democratic forces is necessary to change the situation. Immediately it is a necessary to have autonomy in the compact areas where there is a tribal majority within the state to ensure full powers to them, to protect their living conditions and cultural and linguistic identity.

Capitalist Path : Basic Problem

All these are not the result of Rajiv Gandhi's rule alone. They are the evil results of the capitalist path pursued by the Congress(I) for the last 40 years. The capitalist path can produce no other results. While making a determined effort to oust the Congress(I) from power, unless the people, also decide to develop sufficient strength to get rid of the capitalist path, the basic problems cannot be solved.

Education

No wonder alongwith a crashing economy and rising unemployment the country's educational system shows signs of growing collapse. A nation which cannot ensure two meals for its people cannot afford the luxury of widespread education and end to illiteracy. Progress in primary education has slowed down. Education at higher levels has become more and more costly taking it beyond the reach of the ordinary people. And now the Rajiv government has embarked upon a plan of promoting and encouraging elitist education confined to narrow upper sections in accordance with the needs of the computerised industry. The elitist education policy is the reflection of the social reality of the economy at the service of the private capitalists and monopolists.

Centre-State Relations

The CPI(M) demands an immediate end to discrimination against the Left Front ministries and other non-Congress(I) ministries. It took years for the Rajiv government to sanction the Haldia Petrochemicals Project and the sanction came only on the eve of elections.

The last five years have witnessed a growing erosion of the federal character of the Constitution and concentration of power at the centre undermining the functioning of democracy in the states and providing a fertile ground for the rise of regional feelings. The Congress(I) at the centre makes blatant use of the Centrally appointed Governors to interfere in the states' administration. Elected governments are arbitrarily dismissed, the latest example being the dismissal of the Janata Dal's Karnataka ministry. More and more concentration of financial power in the hands of the centre is making the states abjectly dependent on the central government. For stopping the process of disintegration it is necessary that more powers are transferred to the states and all arbitrary Central intervention through Governors is ended. A strong centre which is necessary for India is possible only if it is backed by strong states armed with sufficient powers to carry out their tasks without fear of intervention from the centre.

Corruption Scandals

In addition to the crimes and evils of the capitalist path, the Rajiv government has made its own contribution. No previous government of the Congress(I) was surrounded by so many corruption scandals shaking the faith of the common man in the administration and the entire system.

The Bofors gun scandal, H.D.W. submarine and other scandals have cost the country hundreds of crores of rupees. The submarine deal, besides, involves the defence security of the nation. The Bofors scandal is the biggest and most important and with the new facts coming out every day Rajiv and his Cabinet colleagues stand tarred and condemned.

Any person with the faintest attachment to parliamentary norms would have resigned. These norms demand resignation when there is reasonable suspicion in the minds of the people. Backed by an unprecedented and sychophantic majority, Rajiv Gandhi has refused to step down, even refused to face the Parliament. The Members of the parliamentary majority in defending Rajiv Gandhi have acted as feudal retainers of the Prime Minister and betrayed the national interest for the sake of personal interest. The entire lot along with Rajiv Gandhi must be given quit orders in the elections, declaring them to be unworthy of the trust of the nation.

Strengthen Policy of Non-Alignment

While calling for the immediate ouster of Rajiv Gandhi and Congress(I), the CPI(M) calls upon the people to realise that there are constant conspiracies against our country to erode its independence, to destabilise and subjugate our country. The U.S. imperialists with their ambition of global domination seek to bring us in the orbit of their influence utilising our foreign borrowings, continuing internal strifes and financing anti-national elements.

It is known that behind the attacks of the Khalistani terrorists in Punjab stands the training and financing of U.S. imperialists done through the military intelligence clique of Pakistan. The Rajiv government though sometimes talks about destabilising efforts from abroad, it refuses to pin down the USA the main abettor of the Khalistani disruptors because of its dependence on World Bank loans.

Those countries and governments which have succumbed to USA's pressures, given up their independent foreign policy have virtually become subservient to the U.S. dictates. The people in these countries have lost all democratic rights with military dictatorship ruling over them. Pakistan, for instance, has been under military dictatorship for a major part of the period since independence and even now the military clique supported by the U.S. is powerful.

India has been saved this fate because of our country's foreign policy of non-alignment based on opposition to imperialism, opposition to war and support for peace, support for all liberation struggles and friendship with socialist countries. But for this our country would have shared the same fate as Pakistan or other countries which have aligned themselves with the USA. We have been able to hold on our own because of precious economic and defence help from the Soviet Union and the Socialist countries. The Indo-Soviet Treaty of Friendship and Cooperation has been the biggest support for independence in foreign affairs.

The entire people of India must support and strengthen our policy of non-alignment. The CPI(M) vigorously supports the four decades old policy of non-alignment and calls for its strengthening. Vigorous support from the people will remove the fear of vacillations and compromise by any government. The people must make the foreign policy their special concern, support and strengthen it.

This is all the more necessary because the reactionary communal forces in India like the BJP and RSS denigrate this policy and in the name of genuine non-alignment demanded a tilt towards U.S. imperialists. This is nothing but undermining non-alignment and India's foreign policy. The country must be warned against it. While fighting to defeat the Congress(I) the people must defeat all the attempts to destabilise our foreign policy.

The CPI(M) calls upon all patriotic forces, all Left and secular opposition parties to firmly support and strengthen the policy of non-alignment.

Congress(I) Manoeuvres Exposed

The CPI(M) calls upon all patriotic, democratic and progressive forces to unite in the election struggle and give battle to the Congress(I). The Congress(I) though growingly isolated from the people, has still a big base. It is desperately trying to improve its position by offering new package of reforms.

In their electoral appeal the Congress(I) party and Rajiv Gandhi are laying great stress on the Panchayat and Nagarpalika Bills and the two Rozgar Yojanas. They present the two Bills as symbolising their desire to transfer power to the people, as a genuine attempt for decentralisation of power and attack the opposition parties for defeating the Bills.

The CPI(M) and the Left parties stand for genuine decentralisation and transfer of power to the local bodies. In West Bengal, under the Left Front Ministry headed by the CPI(M), there is more decentralisation of power accompanied by more democratic and active functioning of the panchayats. This has been rendered possible because apart from the powers given to the panchayats, the mass of peasants and agricultural workers are in a position to defeat the hold of the vested interests over the panchayats.

But the Panchayati Raj and Nagarpalika Bills of the Congress(I) are not genuine measures to transfer more powers to these bodies. They are an attempt to establish the overlordship of the central government over these institutions making them helplessly dependent on the central government. They are simultaneously an attempt to erode the powers of the state governments breaking the links between them and the panchayats. The main purpose of the amendment was to appropriate for the centre the powers of the states.

Besides, it is clear that by mere supply of funds, the panchayats can neither be run democratically nor effectively. There is no chance for real power to be exercised by ordinary members of the panchayat unless the grip of the vested interests over them, the domination of the upper strata is eliminated. But for this there is no possibility in the Congress(I) ruled states.

The CPI(M) stands for reservation for women and Scheduled Castes and Tribes and for spending larger amounts of the panchayat funds for the benefit of the Scheduled Castes and Scheduled Tribes. It also is of the opinion that many measures for relief of the Scheduled Castes and Scheduled Tribes which have been announced in the past have not been implemented just because of the grip of vested interests over the panchayats. Unless there are guarantees about the implementation of all such legislation they become nothing but a pious wish. Besides, the attack on the powers of the states and the overlordship of the centre means increased centralisation of power and not decentralisation. It is clear that under the guise of Panchayati Raj, the Congress(I) seeks to concentrate more power at the centre and undermine the federal structure.

The Congress(I) is also advertising the Jawahar Rozgar Yojana and Nehru Rozgar Yojana. The unemployment problem both in rural and urban areas has become extremely acute and every genuine measure of relief is to be welcomed. But the Congress(I) and the Rajiv government are making fantastic claims about the two Yojanas to mislead the electorate. The Jawahar Rozgar Yojana is advertised as providing at least 100 days work for at least one member per family. In reality, it can at best provide a few days work for a few people and nothing else. This also will be possible only if a greater part of the allotted money is not misappropriated. According to Rajiv Gandhi himself out of every rupee sanctioned for the welfare of the people only 15 paise reach them. And there is no reason to believe that things have materially changed because of the new Yojanas. Besides, in every election year, the promise of one job for a family is made and never fulfilled. The Jawahar Rozgar Yojana is nothing but a combination of several earlier schemes and the claims made on behalf of the Nehru Rozgar Yojana are also exaggerated.

The two Yojanas and other packages form the main plank of the Congress(I) election propaganda. The Congress(I) propaganda is really a callous attempt to exploit the urgent needs and the hopes of the suffering millions for electoral purposes.

Vote for Left and Secular Forces

To combat Congress(I) claims, it is necessary to unite all the Left and democratic and secular forces and all sections of the fighting masses.

The CPI(M) considers that united stand and common understanding between the Left parties and the secular opposition parties represented by the National Front and Janata Dal and isolating all communal parties like the BJP will ensure the defeat and the rout of the Congress(I) and at the same time protect national unity.

This combination is the biggest and most powerful combination today. It embraces the States of West Bengal and Kerala where Left-led ministries headed by the CPI(M) lead the people. It embraces several states headed by non-Congress(I) governments where the secular opposition parties lead the people and wide sections in other states. Its strength was seen in the August 30th Bandh when the entire country responded to the demand for Rajiv Gandhi's resignation. Consolidating and strengthening this understanding, leading the people to victory against Congress(I) and defeating the forces of national disintegration is the common task of all. The CPI(M) calls upon all sections of the people, irrespective of religion and caste affiliations, to vote for the candidates of this combination and inflict a decisive defeat on the Congress(I).

The CPI(M) places before the entire people the work of the two Left-led governments headed by it as earnest of its resolve to defend the common man and the unity of the country. Despite the limitations of the existing Constitution and the limited powers of the state governments, the two governments have done everything possible to defend the common man and his rights.

They have refused to use any extraordinary legislation like Preventive Detention Act against those who oppose the government. They have refused to use the police against the legitimate struggles of the working class and the agrarian masses and other toiling sections, and have thrown the weight of their governments on the side of the fighting people. In spite of several limitations of resources, they have introduced unemployment relief, pension for agricultural workers and several other measures giving relief to the common man. More land has been distributed in West Bengal among peasants than anywhere else. The atrocities on weaker section in the two states have been virtually eliminated, the weaker sections being fully assured of protection by the state. In both West Bengal and Kerala, panchayats are fully active, functioning democratically and creating a new urge among peasant masses to collectively move forward. Above all the two governments backed by the masses have decisively intervened to protect national unity and defeat the forces of communalism and disunity. Their actions during the outbreak of communal conflict have completely assured the minority of safety and security and increased their confidence in the democratic institutions.

Strengthen CPI(M) and Left

The CPI(M) calls upon the electorate to vote enthusiastically for the candidates for the CPI(M) and Left parties who have shown themselves as consistent defenders of the interests of the masses against Congress(I) policies and defenders of national unity against Congress(I) opportunism. The success of Left candidates and the increased strength of the CPI(M) and the Left in the new Lok Sabha constitute an essential element to strengthen the forces of national unity and shift the balance of forces in favour of the common people.

The CPI(M) calls upon all Left parties to strengthen Left unity which has played an important role in shaping the trend of opposition politics. The initiative which the united Left has taken on several issues of national importance, its persistent fight against compromise with the divisive forces, its readiness to cooperate with all others on democratic issues and fight against corruption and above all its independent activities among the fighting people have all served to direct the discontent against the Congress(I) into a healthy democratic channel. It is absolutely essential for future progress that this unity is further strengthened in the course of the election struggle and the importance of the initiative and contribution of the Left parties is clearly seen by the masses.

Programme of Demands

Taking into consideration the critical situation facing the country, the CPI(M) puts before the people the following programme of demands to be achieved so that the electoral struggle ends in the strengthening of the democratic forces, national unity and justice to the suffering masses:

1. Defeat of the Congress(I) party and ouster of the Rajiv government and in its place the election of a government of people's choice, based on the support of secular opposition parties and the Left parties.
2. Fight against the authoritarian drive of the Congress(I) government,

defence of democratic rights and their expansion, withdrawal of all repressive legislations like NSA, ESMA.

3. Restructuring of centre-state relations with more powers to the states. Support to the democratic and progressive policies of the Left-led governments and support to the progressive measures of non-Congress(I) governments.
4. Reversal of the Rajiv government's economic policy, fight for the independence of the economy, resistance to the U.S. pressures and demands, fight against massacre of jobs in the name of promoting advanced technology.
5. Immediate nationalisation of jute and cotton textile industries, immediate relief to powerloom and handloom workers, take over and nationalisation of sick and closed concerns and introduction of workers' participation with equal status in management in all concerns to run the country's industries efficiently. Protective legislation for unorganised workers.
6. Urgent steps to check the growth of monopolies; check the growing penetration of multinationals.
7. Measures against high prices, high taxation on the common people; for state trading in foodgrains and for effective functioning of public distribution system.
8. Implementation of land reforms and distribution of land; correction of land records; enactment of comprehensive Central legislation to protect the rights of agricultural workers in relation to wages, living conditions and social benefits; cancellation of debts of the impoverished rural masses; remunerative prices for the peasants' produce; adequate irrigation facilities and implementation of the irrigation projects awaiting the assent of the central government.
9. Urgent measures to promote employment in the urban and rural areas; provision for statutory legislation to provide unemployment benefit to the unemployed; right to work to be embodied in the Constitution as a fundamental right; one rank, one pension for ex-servicemen; upgrading pensions of all categories in consonance with the cost of living.
10. Defence of national unity against secessionists, communal and divisive forces by mobilising the people against attempts at destabilisation by external agencies; appeal to all to stop agitation on the Babri Masjid-Ramjanmabhoomi issue and accept the verdict of the court; actively fight those who rouse communal passions on this issue.
11. Defence of all minority rights and implementation of provisions in the Constitution. Demand full protection to the minority during riots.
12. Fight against atrocities and crimes against women. End of feudal disabilities, the implementation of legal and constitutional rights guaranteed under the Constitution; end of discrimination in pay, recruitment and promotion, expanded employment opportunities and proper working conditions for all sections of working women, provision of social security for women agricultural workers and women in unorganised industry, equal right of women to property and other rights, reservation for women in panchayats and local bodies.
13. Fight against atrocities on Scheduled Castes and Scheduled Tribes, disbandment of armed senas of the landlords and guarantee for adequate

protection. Protection of tribal lands, cultures and languages; Autonomy for compact continuous and tribal majority areas in states where necessary.

14. Universal primary education and eradication of illiteracy; for free education up to secondary level; fight against the elitist and anti-people essence of the new education policy of Rajiv Gandhi.
15. Housing to be accorded the status of a basic right for all citizens. Housing schemes for the urban and rural poor must be an urgent priority. Drinking water to all villages has to be ensured.
16. Defence of non-alignment, world peace, support to the people of neighbouring countries for democratic rights, friendship with socialist and non-aligned countries.

ANNEXURE D

INDIAN NATIONAL CONGRESS (I) ELECTION MANIFESTO General Election, 1989

I

THE MANIFESTO

In its long and distinguished history of service and sacrifice for the people of India, the Congress has consistently returned to the people to seek their support for its policies and programmes. Nearly always, the people have given to the Congress their abundant affection and support because they know that tho congress is one with the people, that the Congress has no aim other than the uplift of the weak, the poor and the deprived, and that the Congress embodies the vision of the great leaders of Indian thought and action, notably Mahatma Gandhi, Pandit Jawaharlal Nehru and Shrimati Indira Gandhi. The Congress approaches the people once again to renew the mandate which the people of India gave it in 1984. The Congress does so with pride and humility.

The Congress is proud that it has had the privilege to lead the people of this ancient country in their historic endeavour to eradicate poverty and build a strong, prosperous and modern India. It is the kisans and khet mazdoors of India who have raised agricultural production to unprecedented heights. It is the industrial workers and the entrepreneurs who have established new landmarks in industrial growth. It is the scientists of India who have filled us with confidence and hope by successfully demonstrating the capabilities of Indian science and technology through *Prithvi* and *Agni*. There has been all round progress in every sphere of national activity. In foreign policy, the cardinal tenants of Non-alignment have stood the test of a rapidly changing international scene and new configurations and equations of power. The triumph of Non-alignment and of India's vision of sustained peace through peaceful co-existence has proved once again the wisdom of the founders of our Republic. We say, therefore, that these five years have been years of purposeful and steady advance, of promises redeemed, of pledges kept.

The Congress approaches the people with humility because while it mirrors their aspirations, it always learns from them. The people of India, in their infinite variety, in their tumultuous emotions and in their yearning for change with stability are the true teachers of the Congress. The Congress is deeply aware that although much has been accomplished in these five years, much remains to be done. The Congress recognizes that the people are impatient. They want more rapid progress. They desire the pace of socio-economic transformation to be accelerated. They ask for more rigorous commitment to social justice in all its diverse manifestations. These are lessons the Congress has learnt. These lessons are deeply imprinted in the consciousness of the leadership of the Congress Party and its rank and file.

Great and challenging tasks beckon us, and because the tasks are great and challenging, we approach the people with a sense of humility.

Let us look back at the years that have gone by since the Congress took office under the leadership of Shri Rajiv Gandhi.

Five years, ago, the country stood at the crossroads. Indiraji had fallen martyr to the bullets of assassins who wanted to shatter the unity of the country, wreck its integrity and end its centuries-long traditions of secularism. Behind the assassins was a larger conspiracy aimed at dismembering India.

Five years later, the nightmare of November 1984 has receded into a distant historical past. No longer does the nation ask itself anxiously what the future holds. No longer does the nation wonder apprehensively whether India has a future at all.

When this government took office, there was terrorism, treachery, and rampant fundamentalism in Punjab. In the North East, there was armed insurrection in Mizoram and Tripura. In Assam, an unrelenting students' agitation. At the helm of the nation was a young Prime Minister.

The Prime Minister, the Congress Party and the Congress government have passed every test to which they have been subjected.

In the North-East, armed insurrection have given way to peace and democracy—democracy rejuvenated by two Assembly elections each in Mizoram and Nagaland, and a most successful Assembly election in Tripura. In Assam, the agitators of earlier years are today integral to the nation's democratic mainstream. In Darjeeling, a difficult and dangerous problems was resolved by the Prime Minister sticking unflinchingly to the path of minority rights, economic development for backward regions, and respect for the ethnic and cultural identity of minorities. The Darjeeling Hills have been retained within the State of West Bengal. The integrity of the Union of India has been strengthened.

In Punjab, the threat of secession has been pushed back, the links with the foreign backers of these forces have been weakened, the challenges of fundamentalism has been met, and the glorious traditions of secularism have been upheld. The people of Punjab have refused to succumb to the provocations of the communalists. Sikh and Hindu, Christian and Muslim, all the people of Punjab have stood together shoulder to shoulder in a magnificent display of unflinching courage, deep patriotism and determined secularism. The sanctity of the Golden Temple and other places of worship has been restored, religious rituals are no longer conducted under the looming menace of stenguns and rifles, *granthis* no longer live in the shadow of assassins. The ideological followers of separatism have been exposed as nothing better than smugglers, drug-runners, hired gunmen and common criminals. At the same time, development has continued unabated and Punjab continues to hold its pride of place as India's foremost agricultural state and one of the fastest growing industrial economies, far ahead of most others in the level of per capita income and the rate of growth. But terrorism has still not been finally crushed. The

Congress shall continue the battle against terrorism with courage, grit and determination. A political solution will be found with the participation and cooperation of all the people and political parties of Punjab who eschew violence, affirm their loyalty to the Constitution, and accept the democratic way of life.

In the last five yeas, the country, under the leadership of the Congress Party, has made enormous economic and social progress:

* we have achieved the highest long-term rate of growth in the economic history of post-Independence India
* we have so successfully faced up to the challenge in 1987 of one of the most severe droughts to afflict our country that, for the first time ever, the economy registered a positive rate of growth even in a year of almost unprecedented drought
* foodgrains production has attained a new record, as has the output of most other agricultural crops
* all poverty alleviation programmes have been revamped and rationalised to contribute as quickly and efficiently as possible to the major national task of eradicating poverty. In the ten years that have passed since the end of Janata rule, the proportion of our population living below the poverty line has dropped from nearly a half to well under a third of the population. There is no rest for the Congress till poverty is completely eradicated
* the Jawahar Rozgar Yojana and the Nehru Rozgar Yojana have been launched, to bring employment and the opportunity for self-employment to the doorstep of those in search of work
* industry is growing at a rate comparable to the highest in the world, with a new accent on higher productivity, lower costs, better quality and technological upgradation. Industry is now acquiring the self-confidence to respond most encouragingly to government's emphasis on competitiveness, fist, within the domestic economy and, in due course, in the international economy.
* remarkable progress has been made in bringing the public sector into its own: SAIL alone has converted its earlier losses of a crore of rupees a day into a profit of a crore of rupees a day. The first shore-based and the only integrated steel plant in the south at Visakhapatnam is being commissioned.
* infrastructure (mostly in the pubic sector)—power, the railway, cargo handling at seaports and airports, banking and insurance, the airlines, shipping lines and road transport—have never before returned as outstanding a performance as in the last five years
* exports are booming: a virtual doubling of exports over the last five years, reinforcing our self-reliance as also our capacity to service debt and keep the machinery of economic growth well-lubricated with needed imports of inputs and technology. Our creditworthiness in international banking circles is among the highest in the world
* the capital market is buoyant: the thrift of the Indian people is finding highly remunerative avenues of investment

* the New Education Policy has transformed the country's educational future, especially by making the best education in the country available through the Navodaya Vidyalayas to all boys and girls of talent, however poor their families might be or however remote the village of hamlet they inhabit
* the vote for all young men and women who have crossed the age of eighteen, so as to ensure the involvement of youth in the building of the nation as also to ensure that the nation responds to the demands and aspirations of its young men and women
* the Technology Mission which are tackling the most acute problems of the poor: drinking water, immunisation, illiteracy, flood control, edible oil, milk production, telecommunications, and the like
* the National Perspective Plan for Women, to empower women and enable them to be recognised, regarded and rewarded in a measure commensurate with their role in nation building
* the extension of reservations and various special schemes for the advancement of the Scheduled Caste and Scheduled Tribes and other weaker of backward sections of society
* the sacred Ganga is being cleaned. At the great Kumbh Mela in Allahabad, crores of pilgrims dipped themselves in waters which are both spiritually pure and now physically clean
* scientific and technological achievement of a high order, not only in agriculture and industry but also in frontier areas of biotechnology, medicine, astronomy and telecommunications
* concentrated attention on the defence of the country. Our brave young jawan are now equipped with nothing less than the best. Prithvi and Agni have shown the country and the world that India is second to none in promoting self-reliance for the defence of the Motherland
* fidelity to the principles and philosophy of Non-alignment, combined with new initiatives in foreign policy that have made us respected in our neighbourhood, honoured in the world, and looked up to by the international community as the standard bearers of a new international order that will take the world beyond nuclear weapons and anchor international relations in nonviolence, peaceful coexistence, sovereign equality and democracy among nations.

Towering above all, in its scope and sweep, is the revolutionary legislation to enshrine democracy in the Panchayats and Nagarpalikas in the Constitution.

Panchayati Raj goes back to the earliest beginning of our history and constitutes the basic foundation of our democratic institutions. In its modern setting, Panchayati Raj was envisaged by Mahatma Gandhi as the very condition of dignity and self-respect for the vast masses of our people living in India's seven lakh villages. To Pandit Jawaharlal Nehru, Panchayati Raj was the essential pre-condition for radical change in rural society: political, social, economic and technological.

Under the dynamic leadership of Shri Rajiv Gandhi, the Congress has taken this decisive step to accord Constitutional status to Panchayati Raj institutions in the countryside and to Nagarpalikas in the rapidly growing urban settlements. This is not a mere legal and constitutional exercise. In a profound political sense, it is the completion of the democratic structure of India. It is a measure that will unleash the creative energies of our talented people at all levels by transferring to them control over their own density.

Ours was a conscientious endeavour to strengthen the foundations of our democracy at the grassroots through the Panchayati Raj and Nagarpalika Bills. These Bills would have assured elections every five years to all Panchayati Raj institutions and Nagarpalikas. They would have stopped the practice of arbitrary suspensions and arbitrary extensions. They would guaranteed elected representation in all Panchayats and Nagarpalikas through reserved constituencies for scheduled castes and scheduled tribes in proportion to their population and 30 per cent of the seats for women. They would have involved the people directly in planning for development and in the implementation of development projects. They would have stopped the practice of planning from above and stated a process of planning from the grassroots. The social justice component of development would have been integrated into the planning process itself because no plan for economic development would have been validated unless its social justice component had been spelt out. Primacy to social justice as the distinctive characteristic of grassroots planning would have been built into the system by the Bills' provision to ensure proportionate representation for the scheduled castes and scheduled tribes and 30 per cent seats for women in the District Planning Committee that will finalise the district plan. The Bills also provide, for the first time in the history of economic planning in the country, for a very close nexus to be established between the rural economy and the urban economy at the district level. No longer would young men and women from rural and semi-rural India have to travel to the teeming slums of the large metropolitan cities. They would have found work and opportunity in the burgeoning urban settlements of their own districts.

Above all, the vast gap which at present exists between the 83 crore people of India and their 5500 representatives in Parliament and the State Assemblies would have been closed by building a grassroots tier of democracy that would have brought in something like 20 lakh elected representatives, chosen by the people and responsible to them in the very same village and *mohallas* where the people live. The common people of India would no longer have needed to use the intermediation of the power brokers to reach centres of authority in state capitals and the national capital. The solution to their everyday problems would have been found at a distance no further than the Panchayat Ghar or the local Ward Office of the Nagarpalika.

No single step would have done more to rid the suffering people of India of corruption, inefficiency and neglect than the Panchayati Raj and Nagarpalika Bills.

This endeavour has been temporarily thwarted by 83 members of the Opposition in the Rajya Sabha. The Congress now takes the issue to the 83 crore people of India. Democracy is the people's right. This election is, above all, a struggle between the Congress, which wants to give POWER TO THE PEOPLE, and the Opposition, which wants to continue the regime of POWER TO THE POWERBROKERS.

The Congress affirms before the people of India its pledge to:

* bring back to Parliament the Panchayati Raj and Nagarpalika Bills, which

will usher in the most significant 'systemic transformation in the country's polity since the Constitution was brought into force forty years ago and involve the people in the development process, thus accelerating growth for all

* revamp the cooperative movement to make it the dynamic economic counterpart of political democracy at the grassroots through Panchayats and Nagarpalikas
* sweeping judicial reforms to ensure quick and inexpensive justice, especially to the poor, the weak and the deprived
* a rational, well-planned and well-managed path of urbanisation, so that the present overcrowding of the large urban concentration gives way to an even spread of urban settlements, throughout the country, which will enhance prosperity in every district, bring industry and infrastructure to the doorstep of rural India, provide employment and higher income, as also training and skills-upgradation, to rural and semi-urban youth, and lead to attractive, well-run townships instead of the squalor of the slums of our present day cities. The upgradation of slums and the provision of basic urban amenities to all such settlement will be a high priority
* the Indira Mahila Yojana will be launched for the emancipation of women and their economic and social advancement
* a sensitive, people-oriented administrator will be provided that delivers programmes to the people with efficiency, compassion and understanding.

The Congress makes this pledge in the month of November 1989.

It was in this month a hundred years ago that our nation was blessed with the birth of Jawaharlal Nehru.

In a sense, it is but coincidence that these elections are being held in the very month of Panditji's birth centenary.

But, in another and more profound sense, these elections are a tribute to the democracy which Jawaharlal Nehru planted in the soil of India and nurtured with loving care to its full bloom.

These elections are a reaffirmation of our conviction that, as Panditji said, the independence of the country must translate into freedom for out people, the freedom to choose their own government without let or hindrance, a government not of rulers of the country but of servants of the people.

These elections are a reflection of our determination, as a people and as a nation to remain true to the high ideals of Democracy, Secularism, Socialism and Nonalignment which were so dear to Jawaharlal Nehru's heart.

During the tenure of this government, the Congress had the proud privilege of celebrating its centenary. For over a hundred years, the Congress has been in the vanguard of he Freedom Movement and the building of modern India. It is a Party whose ideology and principles derive from the quintessence of over eight thousand years of Indian civilisation. Through the struggle for Independence, scores of dedicated freedom fighters and other giant intellectuals pondered deeply over the India of their vision.

Out of that vision has emerged the ideology of the Congress Party. Out of that dream have emerged the principles of the Congress Party. Out of that endeavour have emerged the policies of the Congress Party. Out of that experience have emerged the programmes of the Congress Party.

When the Congress Party stands before the country, it stands by more than a century of he finest thoughts of the noblest men and women this country has produced in a hundred years.

It is from these great souls that the Congress-and the country has learned the abiding political significance of India's traditional ethical principles of Truth and Nonviolence, compassion and tolerance, and the oneness of humanity: *vasudhaiva kutumbakam.*

These are the great souls who have given the Congress—and the country—the four great pillars of our modern nationhood: Democracy, Secularism, Socialism and Nonalignment.

And it is from their ideology and principles that Panditji, Indiraji and the other architects of independent India drew the great programmes of the Congress:

* independence of thought and action in the face of external challenges to our freedom and internal subversion of our integrity
* democracy, to translate independence for the nation into freedom for the individual
* *vibhinnata mein ekta*—national integration, to preserve the emotional unity of the country while celebrating its glorious diversity
* *sarva dharma sambhaava*—equal respect for all religions — so that the great spiritual tradition of our country, which are the source of all that is noble and wonderful about out land, are conserved even while community is assured of honour, security, opportunity and full participation as equal members in the life of the nation, but politics remaining unmixed with religion
* planned development to eradicate poverty, promote progress, protect our economic sovereignty, and restore India to its traditional primacy in the comity of nations
* self-reliance, a key component of which is the public sector, to equip the country to forestall the domination of our economy by the major economic powers
* agriculture as the highest national priority
* booming industrial development, especially industrialisation which brings progress to backward areas
* special attention to the weaker sections, especially the scheduled castes and scheduled tribes
* education, employment, opportunity—and the vote—for youth
* Justice to all, especially to the poor, the weak and the deprived
* equality of status, honour and opportunity to the women of India so that our mothers and sisters take their place alongside the menfolk in the building of a great India.

The heritage to which the Congress is heir has been both conserved and strengthened by the Congress government and its leader, Shri Rajiv Gandhi, the symbol of continuity with change.

DEMOCRACY is founded in our Constitution, embodied in our institutions, imprinted in the hearts and minds of our people. With the announcement of the Ninth General Elections, the country maintains its continuous tradition of being the world's largest democracy.

Our democratic institutions have stood the test of time. Nevertheless, the challenges that confront our democratic institutions are formidable. Speedy progress has to be achieved. Freedom of discussion and dissent have to go hand in hand with the acceleration of the processes of growth and development. This is not an easy task. The Congress will address itself to the question of how democratic institutions at every level can be strengthened to provide for cohesive decision-making vital for the progress of the nation. The Congress Party pledges itself to upholding and strengthening the norms and values of a democratic, plural society.

The Congress is committed to the freedom of the press as the essential and indispensable component of our democracy. Without a free press and a free flow of information there can be no democracy.

The print media in India is almost entirely in the private sector. Newspaper owners and their editors determine the values they deem to be newsworthy and base the flow of information to the public on the basis of these values.

Radio and TV have to serve the purpose of informing the general public, especially the millions of poor with little or no capacity to read and write, of the great events affecting the destiny of the nation and the lives of our people.

To this end, the electronic media will continue to be owned by government. However, with a view to ensuring functional autonomy, high professionalism and the right mix of entertainment, information, news and views, Akashvani and Doordarshan will be converted into corporations.

SECULARISM is the bedrock of our nationhood, the core of our value system, the distilled essence of thousands years of co-existence among religions, arising out of our adherence to Truth and Non-violence, tolerance and compassion, and the concept of one humanity. Secularism is the manifestation of our unity in diversity, of our celebration of the glorious diversity of our nation. Secularism is the outcome of our long tradition of self-confident interaction with all that is of the best in other civilisations and other cultures, of the cross-fertilisation of our heritage with the heritage of others, of the synthesis which, over thousands of years, has characterised the evolution of our society and our nation. Secularism in India does not mean anti-religion or irreligion. It means *sarva dharma sambhaava* — equal respect for all religions, as much the religion of the majority as of the minorities, with full freedom of worship and freedom of propagation for the individual. But the state has no religion and forbids any discrimination or favour to any of its citizens on grounds of religion. Religion and politics must be separated.

An India that is not secular cannot survive.

One of the major issues in these elections is the future of secularism. The Congress has fought communalism everywhere. Congress workers have laid down their lives to protect the composite culture of India. The Congress reiterates its full commitment to secularism and its determination to continue the struggle, in cooperation with like-minded forces, to eradicate all communalism from the body politic.

Despite all the nefarious efforts of the terrorists and secessionists to provoke communal rioting within and outside Punjab, the people and government have stood firm against any recurrence of such riots. The Congress has refused to compromise, or arrive at any kind of accommodation, with the forces of communalism and fundamentalism.

The sensitive issue of the Ram Janam Bhoomi-Babri Masjid needs to be looked at from the broader perspective of maintenance of communal harmony and good will. The case is before a bench of the Allahabad High Court and both sides are parties to the case. The Congress is committed to maintaining communal peace and tranquillity. It appeals to the patriotic sense of all the people to maintain peace and to foster understanding and amity between different communities.

The deeper cause underlying the communal situation is the desperate attempt of communal forces and their opportunistic political allies to undermine the secular heritage of the country. For the Congress, there can be no diluting its secular ideals. While communal forces have been relentlessly engaged in fomenting hatred and bitterness between different communities, the Congress has never wavered in its determination to combat the forces of communalism and sectarianism. Neither the Congress nor the country can ever forget that we have lost two of the most previous lives of India at the altar of secularism: Mahatma Gandhi and Indira Gandhi.

SOCIALISM is enshrined in our Constitution and is the foundation of our economic policies. Our socialism is neither dogmatic nor borrowed from abroad. It is an authentic Indian ideology, deriving from the experience of our history and the realities of our society. Our socialism is characterised by the priority being accorded to the poorest, the weakest, the neediest and the most deprived. Our highest national objective is the eradication of poverty. We believe not just in growth but in growth with social justice. We are unflinching in our commitment to national self-reliance. Our main instrument of economic and social advancement is planned development to safeguard our economic sovereignty, promote self-reliant growth, ensure equity in reaping the fruits of development, and to take the nation forward to the vanguard of human civilisation. That is the position which India continuously occupied till the onset of colonialism. That is the position of which we intend to restore the glory and fortunes of our country.

The Congress remains firm in its commitment to socialism. We declare categorically that the unrestricted play of market forces, of the freedom for private selfishness and private greed, is not the path for India. The State in India must continue to intervene to enable those who are poor and have no access to productive assets to play a meaningful role in the national economy. The poor cannot be left at the mercy of market forces. To usher in a society where economic and social disparities have been minimised remains our basic goal. This objective can be accomplished only if the growth processes in the Indian economy are moved on to a much higher trajectory. In the ultimate analysis, it is only the growth of productive forces that will resolve the social dilemma of poverty and inequality. As Jawaharlal Nehru never tired to reminding us, unless we create wealth in abundant measure, there will be little to distribute. Therefore, the Congress is committed to strengthening the productive forces in our society. Simultaneously, the crusade against poverty and the drive for preferential treatment for the scheduled castes and scheduled tribes, the weaker sections, the backward classes and the minorities, must continue. The Congress pledges that the Eighth Plan will be based on a development strategy which will be formulated to create a social and economic environment in which growth and development will mean opportunities for all. In the last five years, much has already happened in this direction. The nation is moving forward with a sense of robust confidence. But more decisive intervention on the part of the state is required.

In accomplishing these tasks, we accord primacy to the public sector, which has captured the commanding heights of the economy, pioneered the entry into new areas of industrialisation, opened up backward regions, provided the engine for technological development and generally set the tone for industrialisation in the country.

The public sector is an integral part of the socialistic pattern of society visualised by Pandit Jawaharlal Nehru. Indiraji built on the foundations he laid. With the nationalisation of banks, the financial system of the country was directly linked to the national task of poverty alleviation. Under Shri Rajiv Gandhi's leadership, the public sector has continued to grow with redoubled vigour. Massive investments have been made in the period 1984-89 in the public sector. Profits generated by public sector undertakings have attained unprecedented records. New policies to strengthen the functional autonomy of the public sector have been introduced and a new work culture, based on accountability and the achievement of results, has come to permeate the consciousness of the workers and management. The public sector, revitalised and fired with a new sense of mission, is spearheading India's drive to emerge as a leading industrial nation. The Congress will continue to rely upon the public sector as a major instrument of industrialisation, of technological modernisation and of broadening the base of knowledge and skills throughout the country. The Congress holds fast to the belief that efficiency, competitiveness, quality improvement, cost reduction and generation of surpluses are capable of achievement by the public enterprises, provided workers and managements are given the right policy environment and a clear and precise mandate.

A major plank in the strategy for growth with social justice will be a qualitatively new emphasis on employment. Industrial policy, foreign trade policy, fiscal policy and agricultural policy will be redesigned to foster the rapid growth of employment and self-employment. Imperatives of modernisation and technological advance will be harmonised with those of employment opportunities for millions and millions of youth in the countryside and in the urban areas. This will require a marshalling of resources on a scale not seen before in our history. It will also require a careful husbanding of such resources for the social good. The people are impatient. They will not wait indefinitely for the promise of plenty. They want something here and now. This is what the Congress will endeavour to realise in the Eighth Plan. The country is in a position today to do this because its growth prospects rest on solid foundations.

NONALIGNMENT is the unique contribution of Panditji, the Congress and India to world peace, world cooperation and, indeed, world survival. The path of Nonalignment is based on the basic values of India's civilisation. It derives from the ideology and principles of our Freedom Movement. It is now the basic foreign policy doctrine of nearly two-thirds of the countries of the world. It is a policy that is looked up to not only by vast sections of the people of the developed nations but also, increasingly, by their leaderships. That is the measure of the extent to which Shri Rajiv Gandhi's Congress government has raised the prestige and standing of India.

India offers her friendship and cooperation to all in the quest for a peaceful world which will have banished the spectre of nuclear holocaust, which will have realised the peaceful co-existence of diverse social and political systems, and which will have replaced glaring dichotomies of affluence and destitution by a more cooperative sharing of global resources. This new paradigm of international relations has flowed from the policy of Nonalignment. India is at the forefront of global concerns for peace, disarmament and development. The Six-Nation, Five-Continent initiative on disarmament, the Africa Fund, the Gorbachev-Rajiv Gandhi Delhi Declaration of 1986, the global Action Plan for time-bound total disarmament, the Planet Protection Fund — all these constitute new milestones in India's dynamic approach to international affairs.

With our neighbours, India has opened new avenues of peace and cooperation. The Prime Minister's historic visit to China, in December, 1988, heralded a new era of peace and cooperation between Asia's two largest countries. With Pakistan, a new beginning has been made consequent on the restoration of democracy in that country. In Sri Lanka, the historic agreement of July 1987 has contributed to the preservation of the unity and integrity of Sri Lanka and to the protection of the legitimate political interests of the Tamil minority. India's role in SAARC illustrates our commitment to regional cooperation and to friendship and amity with all neighbouring countries.

We are living through a period of profound change in international relations. For the first time in forty years, the major nuclear powers are seriously engaged in dialogue to reduce nuclear arsenals and defuse tensions around the world. Prime Minister Rajiv Gandhi has been the foremost of all Nonaligned statesmen in defining the role of Nonalignment in the changing international situation. He has urged that neither sustained peace nor sustainable development are possible until the mindset that seeks dominance is replaced by a mindset that bases its worldview on the basic values of India's civilisation. It is essential, he has said, for the world to learn from the Indian experience of unity in diversity, of relations between peoples, countries, ideologies and points-of-view being based on Truth and non-violence, tolerance and compassion, one world and one humanity. The world listens with respect to India under the leadership of Shri Rajiv Gandhi.

In 1984, the people of India accorded an overwhelming, unprecedented mandate to Shri Rajiv Gandhi:

* because he represented continuity with the quintessential values of our unbroken legacy
* because he championed the cause of change to bring justice to our people, prosperity to our nation, respect and regard for India in the world and, indeed, survival with honour in this nuclear age for humanity itself
* and because he symbolised reform in politics and ethics in government.

There has been continuity with past principles but change in their application to evolving circumstances. A mind that stands still is a dead heart in a dead body. Today's India is young, vibrant and innovative. It is an India that thinks ahead. What India thinks today, the world will think tomorrow. In the world of ideas, India is already in the forefront of the world community. In but a few years from now, India will be returned to the position of glory it has held through most of history, a great India, a noble India, an India venerated not so much for its military muscle or economic powers but for its ethical, moral and spiritual values, its thoughts and its ideas.

To bring cleanliness into politics, the Congress government has secured the passage through Parliament of two revolutionary pieces of legislation:

* the Anti-Defection Act
* amendments to the Representation of the People Act to forestall the candidature for elections to the State Assemblies or Parliament of criminals and those who indulge in atrocities against scheduled castes and scheduled tribes and offenses under the laws relating to sati and dowry.

We must squarely tackle the problem of corruption. It is most oppressive at the grassroots, at the interface where the bulk of our people and the machinery of government meet.

The single most important cause of inefficiency and corruption is the absence of locally-elected and locally-resident representatives directly responsible to the people for the ending of corruption. The Panchayati Raj and Nagarpalika Bills would have debarred the participation in local government of criminals and their ilk and all those guilty of atrocities against Scheduled Castes, Scheduled Tribes and offenses under the laws relating to sati and dowry. The Bills would have empowered the people to unleash their elected representatives against the perpetrators of corruption. The people would have been able to hold their elected representatives responsible for forestalling and rectifying corruption.

Tragically, 83 members of the Opposition in the Rajya Sabha have prevented the Panchayati Raj and Nagarpalika Bills from becoming the law of the land. In doing this, they have, wittingly or unwittingly, collaborated with the forces of corruption and injustice.

The people recognise this. The people will give the Congress Party a renewed mandate to bring about the profound systemic change which will give substance to the Congress promise of clean politics and clean government.

Where do we go from here? In which direction do we move? What is the context of the continuing struggle for India's socio-economic transformation? What is the kind of future we would like to shape? What obstacles do we face and how shall they be overcome? These are the critical issues before the people as they decide to cast their votes. To answer these questions one must have a vision of india, a vision that derives from the enduring values of our ancient civilisation and from the contemporary striving of our people for a just and humane society.

It is only if we chart our path in the clear and steady light of the principles which guided Mahatma Gandhi, Pandit Jawaharlal Nehru and Smt. Indira Gandhi that we shall take the high road in national integration, unity, progress, self-reliance and the elimination of poverty.

There are other voices, there are other interests. These are the voices of feudalism, of casteism, of regression to narrow sectarian, communal, chauvinistic patterns of social life. These are the voices that reject the glorious accomplishments of 40 years of independence. These are the voices of despair. They are reproductions in new form of the blind anti-Congressism for which the country had to pay a heavy price from 1977 to 1979. The self-same false prophets, the self-same false gods have re-appeared again to give birth to new illusions. Expediency has once again come to be regarded as a supreme political value.

Crass opportunism is once again being employed as a weapon to smother the growth and development of India. Communalists and secularists, reactionaries and progressives, nationalists and narrow-minded bigots sit together and dream of power.

This is the broad political picture of India today: On the one side, a national movement based on a century-old ideology. On the other, a congeries of disparate groups, bound together by nothing but hatred of the Congress and an overweening lust for power. A political party that brought freedom to India and has carried India forward for most of the last 40 years, which has transformed India into a major economic force, which has raised India's prestige in the international community, which has defended India's unity and integrity and which has realised for the people of India a considerable measure of progress for the eradication of poverty and injustice, is being opposed by individuals and groups whose sole claim to public recognition is their consistent penchant for character assassination, their backward-looking social and economic views, which include the suppression of women and exploitation of the weaker sections such as scheduled castes and scheduled tribes and landless labour, their dogmatic opposition to industrialisation and modernisation, their total non-comprehension of the vast changes taking place in the international arena, and their stubborn refusal to understand the aspirations of the people for playing a decisive role in designing and implementing programmes for their own development and welfare.

Shall India march forward into the closing decade of the 20th century with its perspectives firmly fixed on modernisation and social justice, or will India be thrown back to the political wasteland of negativism where no roots of progress grow?

These elections are about the road that tomorrow's India will take: forward to the twenty first century or backward to mediaeval obscurantism?

During the last five years, there have been many challenges to the leadership and mandate of the Congress Party. Challenge is inherent in politics. The capacity to stand up to challenge is the litmus test of leadership.

The country remembers how the Janata government crumbled at the first signs of challenge.

The country also remembers how, in the last five years, the Congress Party and its leader have stood firm in the face of every challenge. IT remembers how the Prime Minister, with courage and conviction, has stood up to treachery within his ranks, attempts at assassination, calumny against himself and his family, and a dastardly attempt to subvert the Constitution. In Parliament, the Congress has preserved democracy, debate, and dialogue while the Opposition has disrupted the proceedings and, eventually, simply run away from the House. Outside Parliament, the Congress has stood steadfast against violence in the streets and hatred being carried to every home and hearth.

A Party that aspires to office must have the capacity to govern. It must have the capacity to serve. It must have the capacity to keep itself together — and the country together. It must have the capacity to fulfil its mandate.

The Congress is the only Party which can do so.

The Congress comes before the electorate as a Party of both performance and promise. The Congress has ended the darkness that enveloped the country when Indiraji was martyred. It has ensured the unity, integrity, security and independence of the country through five difficult years. The Party has taken the country forward at the fastest pace ever in the direction of economic growth and technological advancement. The Congress has given the country unprecedented agricultural, industrial and infrastructural development. We have firmly focussed on the eradication of poverty and the welfare and uplift of the weak. The Congress government has defended the country and upheld the nation's honour in the world.

All this has been possible because the Congress has been able to preserve:

* the stability of the Party
* the stability of its leadership
* the stability of its government.

Both performance and promise will be in jeopardy if the country falls into the hands of the jumble of conflicting interests and unprincipled opportunists who today constitute the Opposition.

There can be no progress under a motely collection of parties who do not know where they want to take the country. There can be no progress under a political leadership that pulls in a dozen different directions. There can be no progress under a government that is so caught up in the struggle for survival that it has no time or energy for governance.

It has taken ten years of Congress government to pull the country out of the abyss into which the three-year debacle of Janata rule had pushed our country.

The people of India say: Never again.

The people of India know that the Congress alone is the beacon of hope that lights the path to the future.

II

RETROSPECT AND PROSPECT 1984-89 — 1989-94

A. Scheduled Castes and Scheduled Tribes

The welfare of scheduled castes and scheduled tribes has been an article of faith with the Congress. Since 1985, the Congress government has taken the following steps:

* reservations for scheduled castes and scheduled tribes in Parliament and the Assemblies, as well as employment, which was to expire in 1990, is being extended by another ten years
* no post reserved for SC/ST communities will be de-reserved
* a special recruitment drive has been launched to fill all vacancies of SC/ST posts in central government, banks, insurance companies, public sector enterprises and the Delhi Administration. About 45,000 SC/ST

candidates have been so recruited in less than six months time

* over Rs. 110 crores has already been sanctioned for setting up the new Dr. Ambedkar University, Lucknow
* a national Commission for SC/STs has been established. Disciplinary mechanisms have been put in place to enforce guarantees
* the landmark scheduled castes and scheduled tribes (Prevention of Atrocities) Act has been passed this year to check atrocities on SCs/STs
* a scheme of providing remedial and special coaching for the upgradation of the merit of SC/ST students has been started. Pre-matric scholarships have been introduced to benefit 1.3 million students in 1988/89. Hostels for SC/ST girls have been constructed
* a National Scheduled Caste and Scheduled Tribe Finance and Development Corporation, with an authorised capital of Rs. 75 crores, has been established to develop and assist schemes of employment generation for SC/ST communities
* the One Million Wells Scheme was launched in 1988 to provide open irrigation wells to small and marginal farmers belonging to the SC/ST communities
* the Indira Awas Yojna was introduced in 1985-86 to provide dwelling units to SC/ST communities. About 4.3 lakh housing units have been completed so far
* the Kutirjyoti Scheme was launched in 1988-89 to extend single-point light connections to Harijan and Adivasi families. 50 lakh families have been covered in 1988-89
* a Tribal Cooperative Marketing Development Federation has been set up as a multi-state cooperative society to provide remunerative prices to the tribals for minor forest produce. On account of market intervention, increased earnings to tribals have been ensured in 10 items of minor forest and tribal produce
* a special line of credit of Rs. 100 crores has been opened through cooperative and commercial banks exclusively for SC/ST farmers
* mobile teams have been set up to enforce the Protection of Civil Rights Act which makes untouchability illegal.

Future programmes for Harijan and Adivasi welfare will consolidate the large number of initiatives already taken. In addition, programmes will be designed for specific occupation groups. Schemes under agriculture and irrigation will be given priority. Scavenging will be eradicated in the next five years and the affected people effectively rehabilitated. The training of scheduled caste and scheduled tribe communities in modern skills and technology will be strengthened.

B. Women

Programme for women and children have received an unprecedented boost in the last five years.

For the first time, a major exercise was initiated to prepare a detailed perspective plan for the social, economic and political advancement of women, both in the organised sector and of self-employed women. In the last five years, the Congress government has taken the following initiatives:

* the Integrated Child Development Services (ICDS) have been expanded considerably to provide nutrition to over 12 million children and pregnant and nursing mothers in 2200 blocks of the country. Over 300,000 women have been employed in Anganwadi workers and helpers
* the Universal Immunisation Programme was launched in 1985 to protect all pregnant women against tetanus and all infants against DPT, Polio, TB and measles. Simple techniques for the control of diarrhoeal diseases have been propagated in 300 districts
* Women's Development Corporations have been established in different states to initiate and manage economic programmes for upliftment of women
* the Improved *Chulha* Programme has been introduced to reduce drudgery for women and improve their kitchen work environment. The programme has reached around 2 million rural families in the past five years
* the Integrated Rural Energy Programme has been launched in 200 blocks all over the country to use alternative energy for meeting the cooking, heating and lighting needs of rural women.

The Congress government is committed to reserving 30 per cent of the representation in local self-government bodies for women. It is committed to pushing through schemes aimed at distributing assets like land and house sites jointly or singly in the names of women. Already, a commissioner of women's rights is in place to coordinate the initiation of timely action in case of atrocities on women.

The Indira Mahila Yojana is under preparation. The basic philosophy of the Indira Mahila Yojana is that the problems of women, especially of poor women in rural areas, should be approached holistically instead of being split into several separate and disparate components. Women must, first of all, be made conscious of their rights and, simultaneously, empowered to exercise their rights. Conscientisation and empowerment must grow together. The economic strength of women must lie at the core of the programme, so that women acquire the skills and mental orientation to become economically strong, and the assets and access to credit, inputs and marketing to ensure adequate rewards for their efforts. Special attention is needed for their health and nutrition, including the health and nutrition of their children. The education of girls and adult education for women is the key to raising their levels of awareness and status in the family and society at large. The Indira Mahila Yojana will bring together, rationalize and further augment all that has been done, is being done and will be done to ensure respect, recognition and reward for women commensurate with their great and indispensable contribution to the building of our nation.

There is then the dimension of legislation to underpin the social progress of women. In the last five years, the Congress government has:

* banned the practice, propagation, celebration and glorification of *sati* and endowed extraordinary powers to state government and district officials to end this evil practice

* strengthened the legal provisions in respect of offences relating to dowry
* amended the Criminal Procedure Code and other penal legislation to place the onus for proving innocence on the bridegroom and his family in cases of suspected dowry deaths
* introduced major changes in the Act dealing with the suppression of immoral traffic to protest and rehabilitate the unfortunate women who are compelled by circumstances to fall into this dreadful profession
* banned the indecent representation of women on posters, advertisements, hoardings etc.

C. Minorities

Secularism is the essence of the Congress creed. The Congress has lost two of the most valuable lives of India at the altar of secularism: Mahatma Gandhi and Indira Gandhi. These lives have not been sacrificed in vain.

The Congress government has taken a number of steps to promote the interests and fulfill the aspirations of minorities. These include:

* establishing ten community polytechnics in minority concentration areas to extend vocational and technical education
* setting up the Maulana Azad Education Foundation to promote and accelerate the pace of education among Muslims. 1700 candidates have benefitted from special coaching schemes run by UGC among minority communities in 20 universities and 14 degree colleges
* giving special consideration to minorities in the recruitment of police personnel
* creating special courts specifically earmarked to try communal offences
* launching social security and special welfare schemes to enable artisans from minority groups to construct houses and to protect them from middlemen. two lakh weavers have already been benefited
* simplifying procedures for emigration of workers to Middle East countries. Group clearances to recruiting agencies are being provided on the same day and systems to safeguard interests of people working overseas are being strengthened.

The Congress government rededicates itself to furthering the economic and social development of minority groups. The Prime Minister has been personally monitoring the implementation of Indiraji's 15-Point Programme drawn up for the welfare of minorities. The spread of education and the development of entrepreneurship in the minority groups will be a special area of attention in the next five years.

D. Youth

The Congress government's faith in the youth of the country is reflected in its decision to lower the voting age from 21 to 18, as well as strengthening and enlarging the Nehru Yuvak Kendras.

The Nehru Yuvak Kendras have established contact with over 50,000 youth clubs in the country. These clubs are presently implementing anti-poverty programmes, running adult education centres and promoting national integration by holding youth camps and sporting and adventure activities.

In the next five years the Congress government is committed to identifying one youth club in every village which could be a powerful instrument for social change. Special efforts to involve youth from scheduled caste/tribe communities will be made.

The Congress government will also institute several awards and means of recognising the contributions made by youth in constructive work.

E. Kisans and Khet Mazdoors

The highest national priority is agriculture. The kisan and the khet mazdoor are in the vanguard of the Congress Party's plans for the economic advancement of India.

The Congress government has:

* invested Rs. 5500 crores annually in agriculture and irrigation since 1985, as compared to Rs. 3500 crores per year during the previous give years
* not changed the prices of fertiliser since 1981, despite increases in the cost of production of fertiliser. In 1988/89, fertilizer prices actually fell by Rs. 9 per bag of urea. The subsidy borne by the central government providing fertiliser to the kisan has increased from Rs. 900 crores in 1981 to Rs. 3000 crores in 1988/89
* doubled the credit supply to farmers to Rs. 11,000 crores over the past five years. 75 per cent of this credit goes to small and marginal farmers
* reduced the interest rate on crop loans for small farmers from 12.5 per cent in 1984 to 10 per cent in 1989
* introduced a crop insurance scheme in 1985. Loans taken by farmers affected by drought have been rescheduled
* supplied farmers power at 18 paise per unit which costs 80 paise per unit to generate and supply
* increased support prices by 28 per cent for paddy, 27 per cent for wheat and 38 per cent for groundnut over the past five years
* provided a big thrust to oilseed production by price support and marketing arrangements and the introduction of improved seed varieties. This is benefitting 35 million small and marginal farmers cultivating oilseeds on rainfed lands
* launched a National Watershed Development Programme for Rainfed Agriculture in 1986 for the benefit of poor farmers in rainfed areas. The programme is being implemented in 99 districts
* proposed the setting up of a National Agriculture Credit Relief Fund to provide credit on a sytic basis to farmers affected by drought and other natural calamities. Reliefs will include the rescheduling of loans, waivers of interest and also the writing off of principal in specified circumstances.

The drought of 1987-88 was the most severe of this century. 267 districts, two and a half lakh villages, 285 million people and 168 million cattle were affected. To fight the drought:

* the Prime Minister established a Cabinet Committee on Drought which prepared an Action Plan for Drought Management which was circulated to state governments for implementation
* the central government sanctioned over Rs. 1200 crores to fight the drought, of which Rs. 360 crores was for Rajasthan, Rs. 250 crores was earmarked for Gujarat, and Rs. 150 crores for Uttar Pradesh
* 17 high powered drilling rigs were deployed in drought affected areas. Rigs and drilling equipment were purchased for speeding up drinking water programmes
* fodder banks were established to provide relief to cattle. Paddy straw was transported from Punjab to Rajasthan and Gujarat
* an additional outlay of over Rs. 100 crores was made in 1987/88 for executing irrigation projects in 14 affected areas. Special programmes were put through for the energisation of 1.5 lakh pumpsets
* fresh finance was provided through NABARD for second sowing and for converting short term loans into medium term loans in drought affected areas. 75 lakh tonnes of foodgrains were distributed to workers engaged in relief works.

For the first time, village panchayats were involved in tackling drought by making their own plans and executing them. The result of these steps was that the drought was managed without having to take the begging bowl to foreign countries, without compromising our self-reliance and without putting our economic sovereignty in jeopardy. Indeed, for the first time in its economic history the nation recorded a positive rate of growth even in a year of severe drought.

Last month, the Congress government introduced a comprehensive programme for increasing farm incomes. This will form the basis of the farm strategy in the Eighth Plan. Major elements of the package are:

* modification in the formulae for the determination of the cost of production in fixing support prices to reflect costs incurred by farmers more realistically
* expansion in the number of procurement centres so that every farmer will have access to a procurement centre within 10 km of his farm or village
* rural godowns and cold storage facilities to be expanded for the benefit of small farmers
* facilities for pass-books and agriculture credit cards to be further extended to enable easy drawal of loans from banks
* a major programme for updating land records, recording the rights of tenants and sharecroppers and increasing the accessibility of landowners to the record of their rights
* more efficient use of irrigation water and land by ensuring the supply of water to canal projects, reclaiming 5 lakh ha per year of *usar/barani* lands, taking up a massive programme of construction of 10 lakh irrigation wells per year and expanding the watershed programme to cover 50 lakh ha in the next five years
* a substantial expansion in the production of quality seeds for a number of foodgrain crops

* diversification of agriculture by promoting horticulture, and agro-exports. Special steps will be taken to assist small producers
* a massive thrust to food processing and other agroprocessing, to increase the incomes of farmers, augment employment opportunities in rural areas, diversify the rural economy and bring industrialisation to agricultural areas.

The Congress government is committed to a policy that will add value to agricultural produce and that will create new markets for farm output. Technological, organisational and marketing support will be provided to strengthen food processing and agro based industries.

F. Labour

The interests of labour have always been safe in the hands of Congress governments. The Congress Party is proud of the fact that the number of mandays lost due to industrial disputes has been the least in the recent past. Indeed, it is a sad commentary on the Congress Party's opponents that over half the mandays lost in India is in one state that is ruled by a party claiming to represent workers interests.

The Congress government established a National Commission on Rural Labour to study the problems faced by rural labour in detail and to suggest measures to improve their well-being. Specific programmes will be drawn up based on the report of this Commission. Already social security schemes for weaker sections like landless labour, handloom workers and rickshaw pullers have been launched by the LIC. The initial corpus in Rs. 100 crores and the insurance is at subsidised rates.

The Congress government will introduce a pension scheme for all workers in the organised sector so that the gratuity and part of the provident fund will be available in a lump sum and part would be converted into a pension fund to provide continuous monthly income.

We also propose to introduce a family pension scheme for the widow or the dependents of the worker in case of his death while in service.

The Congress government will also work towards introducing specified social security schemes for workers in the unorganised sector to provide for medical treatment, maternity benefit as well as old age pension.

The Congress government is committed to increasing workers' participation in management. We will actively promote the formation of worker's cooperatives to turn around sick companies.

Stock of public sector companies will be sold to workers on a preferential basis. As far as possible, representation of workers or of labour would be ensured at the Board level.

The Congress steadtfastly believes that labour should not just bear the pains of growth but should also enjoy its gains in just measure. We will seek a national consensus on issues like the linkage between wage and productivity, on the desirability of reducing the multiplicity of unions and on allowing managements to deal directly with labour without outside intervention.

The Congress Party recognises the inevitability of technological change. Labour will be equipped and made ready for this by extensive training and skill development programmes.

G. Backward Classes

The Congress has always enjoyed the full support of backward classes. It is fully committed to their welfare and all round progress.

Special programmes will be instituted to support the professional activities and occupations of the backward classes through the provision of better technologies, more generous financial assistance and better marketing. Educational concessions, including scholarships and other schemes of academic improvement, will be extended from the primary to the university level to students belonging to the backward classes.

H. Jawans

The Congress recalls are slogan given to the nation by Prime Minister Lal Bahadur Shastri at a time of grave national crisis: Jai Jawan Jai Kisan.

For those servicemen who are protecting our borders at great personal cost and sacrifice, no effort has been spared to provide the best and the most modern equipment.

Between 1984 and 1989, a new generation of missiles to protect our borders and enhance our defence capabilities — *Prithivi, Trishul, Agni* — has been developed. Only five countries in the world have this capability.

In the last five years, fighter aircraft, aircraft carriers, sub-marines and helicopters of increased mobility, accuracy, firepower and better communications have been inducted in the defence forces. Equipment for the 1990s is being developed in India so that we are not at the mercy of foreign powers.

But equipment is not all.

Welfare measures for armed forces personnel have been enhanced. A pension *adalat* scheme has been introduced for redressing grievances.

A resettlement organisation covering the entire country and going down to the district level, has been established. These are now 29 Rajya Sainik Boards and 282 Zilla Sainik Boards in the state and union territories, to look after the resettlement and welfare of ex-servicemen.

The Congress government has taken steps to encourage ex-servicemen to take up self-employment ventures. A scheme for the self-employment of ex-servicemen was introduced in 1987 to provide term loans and seed capital assistance for small industrial ventures and transport services. Another scheme was started in 1988 to provide loans for agriculture and allied activities.

The Congress government has augmented facilities in military hospitals for use by ex-servicemen. It has also decided to meet 50 per cent of the cost of augmenting facilities in civil hospitals.

The Congress government will continue its efforts to involve ex-servicemen closely in development programmes and schemes, like literacy and afforestation. This resource will be mobilised to far greater extent because it is a disciplined, trained and motivated manpower. Ex-servicemen's cooperatives will be encouraged to manage development activity in specific areas.

I. New Economic Initiatives

The last five years have witnessed a new growth momentum induced by changes in policy and procedures. The growth performance of the Indian economy has been unprecedented. The growth rate of the economy during 1985-1989 has been the highest ever recorded in Indian history.

* Emphasis in economic policy has been on efficiency and increasing competition. Without competition, it will be difficult to be efficient. Money locked in inefficient units only means slower job creation and less money for other welfare programmes.
* A new Textiles Policy was announced in the 1985. Since then per capita consumption of cloth has increased by 7 per cent production of cloth by about 8 per cent, overall employment by 25 per cent and export by over 100 per cent. New items have been reserved for production by handlooms.
* A new Drugs Policy was announced in 1986. This has ensured availability of medicines at reasonable prices which are among the lowest in the world. Prices of about 68 medicines reduced by 5 per cent.
* A small Industry Development Fund was set up in 1986 with a corpus of Rs. 2500 crores to coordinate assistance to small industry sector. In addition, a National Equity Fund has been set up to provide equity support to tiny and small units.
* Growth in industrial output since 1985 has been over 8.5 per cent per year, compared to 4.5 per cent in 1970s and 6 per cent in early 1980s. Shortages of most industrial goods and commodities like cement, 2-wheelers, steel, aluminium, commercial vehicles, etc. have been tackled successfully.
* There is now greater dispersal of industrial activity. Share of traditionally backward regions in industrial output and investments has gone up substantially over the past five years.
* A focus is being provided to employmentoriented industries like electronics, plastic processing, agro-processing, sericulture, leather etc.
* Modernisation programmes to retool Indian industries have been initiated in steel and machinery sectors. This will result in reduction of costs. Textile Modernisation Fund and Jute Modernisation Fund set up to manage revival of he two traditional industries.
* Exports are essential to earn foreign exchange for the oil, kerosene, diesel, fertilisers, steel, edible oil and machinery we have to import. Record performance of exports over past three years have been induced by major policy changes.
* Volume of exports has grown by approximately 10 per cent per annum over the period 1986-89, whereas global average is around 6.4 per cent.
* Growth areas of exports are largely in industries that are labour-intensive like gems and jewellery, leather, textiles, siik and handicrafts. Chemicals and engineering goods are other important export areas.

The Congress government will consolidate the gains made so far. It will give a further push to accelerating growth in the economy. The growth performance during the last five years will enable us to set our sights even higher and plan for a 6 per cent rate of growth in the next five years. Our policies on redistributive justice become meaningful only when the Indian economy is growing vibrantly.

Policies will be adopted to further spur production, efficiency and competitiveness. Indian industry will gradually be exposed to competition from outside. This will ultimately benefit the Indian consumer in urban and rural areas.

Industries that produce goods consumed by our farmers, workers and professionals will be modernised to bring down prices and make a large range of such goods accessible to increasing sections of the population.

The Congress government will continue the export thrust provided in the recent past. This will create not only more prosperity at home but also create many more new jobs.

The Congress government will provide a new impetus to the growth to village and small industry. It will endeavour to provide modern technological and professional marketing support to this section of industry. New growth centres will be developed.

Suitable strategies will be evolved to restructure old industries in a manner that the interest of workers is not just protected but is also enhanced.

The Congress government will continue with the policy of removing bureaucratic control on the economy and industry so that our entrepreneurs can concentrate on generating wealth and jobs. State control will be used strategically and selectively where it is most needed. The Indian economy has now the strength and maturity to absorb foreign investment and technology in critical areas without a compromise on the objective of self-reliance.

J. Tax Reform

The Congress government is committed to bringing about further reform on both the direct and indirect tax front. In the last five years much has been accomplished.

* Sweeping reforms of the tax system have been undertaken. Direct tax rates have been reduced to check large-scale evasion. Personal income tax collections increased by an unprecedented 30 per cent in 1985-86. Subsequent increases have proceeded from this higher base.
* Excise taxation has been simplified and rationalised through the MODVAT system which minimises undesirable cascading effects and also makes clear as to which commodities and which sections of society are bearing the burden of taxation.
* Articles of mass consumption are kept free of taxation to reduce prices to consumers. Examples are footwear, life-saving drugs, handloom yarn, soaps etc.
* A major reform of the tax administration machinery has been undertaken to reduce harassment of tax assesses. Action against tax evaders has been stepped up.
* The capital market is booming. This has given many new opportunities to people to invest their saving in productive areas. Protection of small

investors has been ensured through the establishment of new institutions and introduction of new guidelines.

The Congress government pledges to continue the process of tax reform with a carrot and stick approach. Tax evaders will not be spared and shown any leniency, while the entire gamut of laws and regulations is reviewed to make them simpler and more transparent.

K. Industry

Congress policies have already produced an acceleration in Indian industry, with industrial growth averaging over 8 per cent in the first four years of the Seventh Plan.

A new package for industrialising backward areas has been taken up for implementation. A Small Industry Development Bank has been set up to develop and modernise Khadi and Village Industries.

Now the Congress will:

* Consolidate the gains achieved in the past four years and give a further push to accelerating the rate of growth of the industrial sector through policies aimed at increasing the production efficiency and competitive strength of Indian industry;
* Make a sustained effort to improve the international competitiveness of Indian industry in general and in selected areas aim at world class standards of quality, productivity and cost;
* Give a special thrust to the development of agro-based industry which would provide assured market linkages between the process of agricultural diversification, on the one hand, and growing urban markets, on the other;
* Develop a number of new growth centres, with balanced investment in basic infrastructure, with a view to encouraging greater regional dispersal in industry by developing new, viable industrial growth poles in hitherto undeveloped areas;
* Continue to provide strong support to the small scale sector so that it flourishes in an environment conducive to economic efficiency and continuous technological upgradation;
* Evolve suitable strategies for restructuring older industries to ensue that they are able to adjust to changes in demand patterns and technology with minimum economic disruption;
* Giver top priority to developing export capability in a wide range of industries so as to ensure that the industrial sector earns the foreign exchange needed to finance industrial expansion and modernisation.

L. Infrastructure

After a period of poor performance of infrastructure, particularly during the period 1977-79, the last five years have witnessed a remarkable performance in the infrastructure sector. Sound infrastructure is the key to sustaining and accelerating growth.

The Plant Load Factor (PLF) of power stations, which is an index of efficiency was 55 per cent in 1988-89, as compared to less than 4 per cent in 1979-80. There has been a steady increase in the PLF in the last five years.

Steel production which showed a negative growth of 1 per cent in the first four years of the 1980s, grew by 7 per cent per year in the last four years. Similarly the growth in fertilizer production averaged most 14 per cent per year during 1985-89 as compared to 8 per cent during 1980-84.

The efficiency of the railway system in the last five years has been a noteworthy feature. Rail freight movement has grown by 6 per cent during 1985-89, as compared to 2 per cent during 1980-84.

One hundred and ninety new long-distance and 225 new suburban trains were added. The entire fleet of sleeper coaches is being provided with cushioned berths.

Two hundred new halt stations have been opened, predominantly in rural areas. Rail Yatri Niwas has been opened in New Delhi and Howrah to provide better and convenient facilities to passengers. Delays in rail reservations have been significantly reduced and in many places eliminated.

Further efforts will be taken to provide for more comfortable and safer rail travel.

The Motor Vehicles Act has been amended to simplify and liberalise procedures. Learner's licence is now valid throughout the country. Multiplicity of permits has been avoided and the scheme of national permits has been streamlined. In the last five years, the production of commercial vehicles has gone up substantially and more fuel-efficient vehicles have been introduced.

The Congress government will accord top priority to the development of rural roads to open up backward areas and accelerate their socio-economic development.

Special emphasis will be placed on extending the availability cooking gas and on improving the reliability of power supply. A programme for electrifying houses in rural areas will be taken up Schemes for augmenting fuelwood supply will be expanded.

The Congress government believes that telecommunication vital for socio-economic development. In the next five years, the reliability of the telephone network will be improved in a major way through the use of new technology.

Every panchayat will be provided with a phone facility and even telephone with an STD facility.

Telephones cannot be the privilege of only a few. Accessibility for all to telecom services will be promoted through public call offices that function well.

A time-bound programmes for modernising the postal system will be taken up. By 1992, it will be ensured that all telegrams will be delivered within 12 hours.

M. Employment Opportunities

The Congress government will pursue an employment-oriented development strategy in the years ahead. It will promote sustainable self-employment opportunities. Unemployment among the educated will be tackled specifically. The base for training and skill upgradation will be expanded.

The Congress government has taken bold steps to eliminate unemployment in the country. These set the stage for a concerted effort to making the right to work a practical reality in the next five years:

* the path-breaking Jawahar Rozgar Yojna has already been introduced to provide guaranteed employment of 100 days to 1 person in each of the 44 million poor rural families in villages. Implementation, for the first time, is directly through Village Panchayats, each of whom will get Rs. 80,000 — Rs. 1 lakh in 1989-90. 80 per cent of the funds are being provided by central government.
* a Rs. 650 crore Nehru Rozgar Yojna has also been introduced to provide 1 million jobs to urban poor in towns and cities. Eighty per cent of the funds are being provided by central government.
* in agriculture, the spread of new technology to traditionally backward regions of East UP, Bihar, Orissa and West Bengal has been accelerated. In addition, new avenues for generating employment like in food processing, dairying, fisheries, poultry, are being supported actively.
* A new package for industrialising backward areas has been introduced. A small Industry Development Bank has been set up and steps taken to strengthen and expand the activities of the Khadi and Village Industries Commission (KVIC).
* Steps have been taken to ensure that employment exchanges provide quicker and more efficient service to job seekers.

The Congress government is committed to making the Eighth Plan a plan for productive employment. Public investment will be reoriented to catalysing the growth and expansion of employment-intensive economic activities. The Jawahar and Nehru Rozgar Yojanas will be implemented with vigour and adequate funds will be provided to facilitate this.

N. Cooperatives

The Congress will undertake a major programme to revamp the cooperative system in the country structurally and financially and:

* Ensure regular and timely elections to all Cooperative Societies and provide for special representation for SC/ST and women members;
* Restrict the powers of the government to superseded Cooperative Societies;
* Professionalise the management of Cooperative Societies;
* Strengthen and make primary Cooperative societies viable by converting them into multi-purpose societies and increasing their financial powers and responsibilities;
* Reduce regional imbalances in the development of Cooperatives and accelerate the development of the cooperative movement in hilly and tribal areas;
* Take special steps to meet the credit need of small and marginal farmers, especially those belonging to SC/ST communities, through the cooperative system ; and

* Actively encourage the increased participation of cooperatives in agro/food processing and their diversification into non-traditional activities.

O. Public Distribution System

The Congress government is committed to providing food security to those who need it most. Its record in the last five years on this score speaks for itself.

* 3400 additional fair price shops have been opened during 1985-1989, against a target of about 20,000 additional fair price shops to be set up.
* During the drought years of 1987 and 1988 about 16 million tonnes of rice and 13 million tonnes of wheat were supplied to fair price shops compared to 11 million tonnes of rice and 6 million tonnes of wheat during 1984 and 1985.
* 57 million people in tribal areas are receiving 2 million tonnes of rice and wheat annually at specially subsidised (below fair price shop) rates since 1985.

The Congress government believes in a poor-oriented public distribution system (PDS). It will redouble its efforts to augment food production in poor regions of the country, provide entitlements to vulnerable groups including the aged and organise an effective PDS for supply of essential commodities to them.

A rural PDS will be integrated with income-generating programmes in the poverty pockets of the country. The use of employment programmes to improve the nutritional status of people by giving a part of wages in foodgrains will be continued.

P. Drinking Water

The achievement in the last five years in providing safe drinking water to villages has been truly spectacular. 165,000 villages were identified in 1985 as not having easy access to any potable water source. 162,000 of these villages have been provided with at least one safe source of drinking water. The remaining three thousand village will be covered next year.

The tools of modern science and technology were pressed into service to provide water where no source existed before. With the help of new technology, water sources were identified in 13000 villages where no clean and safe source could be identified over the last forty years.

Major programmes to provide clean water have been taken up. A programme to eradicate guineaworm was launched in Maharashtra, Rajasthan, Gujarat and Karnataka. By 1991, as a result of these efforts guineaworm would have been totally eradicated.

Similarly, programmes to remove excess iron, excess fluoride and excess salt have been launched. By 1995, every district will have a water testing facility which people can use to check the quality of water they use.

The Congress government will continue the high priority accorded to rural drinking water schemes. It will encourage panchayats and local-level organisations to be responsible for the maintenance of assets like handpumps.

It will continue to assure sustained access to potable water to socially disadvantaged sections in rural communities.

The Congress government will mount a concerted campaign to tackle the special problem of urban water supply and sanitation.

Q. Housing

The Congress government is committed to providing shelter to all by 1995. It has already initiated a number of steps to expand the supply of housing.

- A National Housing policy was announced in 1988. This is an expression of our determination to provide a house to every family.
- A National Housing Bank has been established to expand the availability of funds for housing, particularly low-income housing. Three new housing finance corporations were set up in 1988.
- almost 3.5 million landless families have been provided house sites in rural areas and 1.6 million given construction assistance.
- 7.6 million slum dwellers have benefited from environment improvement of urban slums. In 1985, on the occasion of the Congress Centenary celebrations in Bombay, the Prime Minister sanctioned Rs. 100 crores of the improvement of slums in Bombay.
- a new scheme has been launched to provide shelter and sanitation, including toilet facilities to pavement dwellers in Calcutta, Madras, and Hyderabad.
- a new scheme has been launched to meet the housing needs of single, working women in urban areas, as also widows and families headed by women.
- Thirty eight building centres are functioning all over the country for ensuring easy access to standardised building materials and components and for imparting training to unemployment youth, artisans and small contractors, 53 more centres are being established.
- a new scheme has been implemented for increasing resources for housing. The National Housing Bank has introduced a scheme through the scheduled banks for the mobilisation of saving guaranteed loans from banks. A Home Loan Account Scheme has been introduced to facilitate construction of houses by those who have deposits with any scheduled bank.

The Congress government will increase the access of low-income groups to institutional finance for housing. In particular, the urban poor will be provided adequate funds to repair, redevelop or augment their homes.

The Congress government will address itself to strengthening legislation to facilities improvement programmes in squatter settlements, upgrading slums in built-up areas, speedier acquisition of private lands under slums and grant of tenure to residents of improved slums.

A major programme to improve the quality of biomass material used in rural housing will be taken up.

A review of land policy in urban areas will be carried out to ensure adequate supply of serviced land for housing to all classes of people at affordable prices and as close to their places of work as possible. Private profiteering in land in and around urban areas will be checked.

R. Science and Technology

The Congress leadership considers science and technology not as an end in itself but as a means to an end — the solution of the urgent and challenging problems of the people, particularly in rural India.

In the last five years a whole new approach to the application of science and technology has been put into practice. This approach stresses the systematic mobilisation of science and technology to tackle pressing socio-economic concerns.

Science and technology is now being used to locate and drill for water sources, instead of depending on *ad hoc* measures. We are now more successful in drilling for water. These methods will be extended.

Science and technology is being used to eliminate delays in railway booking so that millions of passengers can get instant reservations. Such areas where the application of modern technology can have a large impact on consumer-welfare will be extended.

Science and technology is now being used to produce new vaccines in the country to protect mothers and children, from tetanus, polio, measles and other diseases. New advances in technology are making available more potent vaccines and drugs to control disease. These will be systematically harnessed.

Science and technology is being used, in an experimental way to update land records to free millions of landowners from the clutches of local revenue officials, the Congress government stands committed to updating all land records in the next five years and ensuring their easy accessibility.

Science and technology will be used to improve the nutritional status of our livestock and to improve milk yields from cows and buffaloes.

The Congress government is committed to extending the range of application of science and technology in areas that are of direct interest to people.

It will be used to upgrade tools used by rural artisans like weavers, leather workers, carpenters and women handicraft workers.

It will be used to develop and deliver low-cost building materials.

It will be used to develop technologies for dryland farming and for quick and cheap reclamation of land.

The Congress Party will initiate a people's movement for science, for making people aware of what science and technology can do to improve the quality of their lives and for spreading science education.

Science and technology will be used to promote the goals of decentralisation, openness, efficiency and social justice that the Congress Party has always stood for.

Science institution will be made to work together on specific problems affecting the lives of millions, instead of working in isolation and divorced from societal concerns. They will be given full autonomy and flexibility.

S. Environment

In 1972, Indiraji has stated that poverty is the worst pollutant. This has formed the basis for the sustained campaign mounted by the Congress government to eliminate poverty. The Congress leadership believes that environmental issues in India must go beyond protecting tigers and establishing wildlife sanctuaries. It also believes that environmental concerns affect all of us and need to be fully integrated into development activity. Development has to be sustainable, if it is to be efficient and equitable.

The Congress leadership's commitment to provide clean air, water and living environment to our people is reflected in the programme launched to clean the sacred Ganga. 260 schemes have been launched in 27 cities extending from Hardwar to Calcutta. These schemes include interception and diversion of waste water, construction of sewage treatment plants and river quality monitoring. For the first time, 1.5 crore pilgrims bathed in water free from sewage at Allahabad during the 1988 *Kumbh Mela*.

Based on the success achieved in cleaning the Ganga, the Congress government will have action plans formulated for cleaning the Kaveri, Narmada, Yamuna and Swarna-Rekha rivers.

Poor people generally cultivate degraded lands. It is in recognition of this nexus that a major programme for the development of wastelands was launched along with the cleaning of the Ganga in 1985.

The wastelands development programme has succeeded in establishing a large number of decentralised people's nurseries to enhance the participation of local communities in afforestation,

The wastelands programme will be strengthened to provide for greater involvement of people and for meeting the fuelwood, fodder and small timber requirements of the poor in the most cost-effective manner.

The Congress government has tightened the Forest Conservation Act. This has had far-reaching effects in dramatically reducing the amount of forest land diverted for non-forestry purposes. No development project now gets cleared without detailed environmental assessment, including the impact on local communities. This is forcing a new conservation ethic on industry.

A major piece of legislation, almost unique in the world of its scope and detail enacted by the Congress government was the Environmental Protection Act of 1986. The Act is a charter for clean air and water. It will be implemented with determination.

A unique feature of the Seventh Five Year plan has been the introduction of specific area development programme. Special location-specific schemes have been undertaken in hill, desert and drought-prone areas, western ghats and two island territories. The Congress government is committed to strengthening and expanding such programmes during the next five years.

T. Education

Among the very first commitments which the Congress Party under Rajiv Gandhi made at the 1984 election was to bring a new education policy, forward-looking and based on the principle of equal opportunity for all, cultivation of excellence at all levels and the capability to cope with the requirements of rapid change in the coming years.

This commitment was implemented in full. Under the New Education Policy adopted by Parliament in 1986 and endorsed by the National Development Council.

* The central plan outlay for education has more than doubled to over Rs. 800 crores annually.
* Operation Blackboard has been launched to provide minimum learning facilities in all primary schools. 2.5 lakh schools have been covered. Non-formal education facilities have been significantly expanded.
* 256 Navodaya Vidyalayas are now functioning to provide secondary education opportunities to gifted and talented rural children. Present enrollment is over 34,000, 80 per cent of whom are from rural India and 30 per cent belong to SC/ST communities. Another feature is the cross mobilisation of students from Hindi speaking to non Hindi speaking areas (e.g. Haryana to Maharashtra) that will lead to national integration.
* A National Mission on Adult Literacy has been launched. Mass mobilisation and campaign strategies have been put into operation in many states, including Gujarat, Rajasthan, Tamil Nadu and Karnataka.
* An innovative programme called the Mahila Samakhya has been launched in .2000 villages in Gujarat, UP and Karnataka of empower women through education and provide a forum for collective self expression.

The Congress Party firmly reiterates its resolve to ensue that the Navodaya Vidyalayas live up to their promise. This concept of Navodaya Vidyalayas, completely funded by the Central government, has brought higher secondary education of the highest quality of the most talented children in rural and semi-urban India absolutely free of cost for the very first time. This single measure has the potential of boosting the poorest of children with real promise to the highest positions the nation can offer in all spheres of activity.

The Congress Party is fully committed to the universalisation of elementary education. All facilities will be provided for making this possible in the quickest period.

Special incentives will be provided to retain girls and children belonging to SC/ST and minority communities in school.

Non-formal educational programmes will be strengthened to enable children who are compelled not to attend school to have easy access to high quality education free of cost.

The Congress government will vigorously pursue the implementation of he mission to eradicated illiteracy, particularly among women by 1995. Literacy programmes will be totally revamped to enable a far greater involvement of voluntary agencies and by making the programmes relevant to local situation and conditions.

U. Health and Family Welfare

The Congress leadership and the Party is committed to extending primary health care facilities and improving the quality of service provided. The focus will be on women and children.

The Congress government pioneered the introduction of a family welfare programme that emphasises voluntary birth control.

We will vigorously pursue the implementation of women's welfare programmes which encourage smaller families and the spacing of children. Special incentives will be provided for the education and maintenance of the girl child.

We stand committed to the goal of eradicating all communicable diseases by the year 2000. National programmes to control TB, malaria and leprosy will be revitalised.

The service conditions of the doctors and health workers at all levels will be improved and their work environment modernised.

A major public health problem still prevalent in the country is malnutrition arising mainly out of lack of access to food. Employment programmes with a food-for-work component will be used imaginatively to increase the nutritional status of vulnerable sections of society.

The Congress government will ensure that the Eighth Plan will treat nutrition as a priority sector.

V. Social Legislation

The Congress government is committed to enacting social legislation to provide legal support for social change. Since 1985, an impressive array of legislation has been enacted.

* a National Child Labour Policy was framed to free millions of children from drudgery and exploitation and provide education, health and nutrition at their places of work to improve their lot
* the Maternity Benefit Act was amended in 1988 so that women employees who have worked for 80 days are eligible for the benefit as against 160 days earlier. Rates for medical bonus have been increased ten times
* the Dowry Prohibition (Amendment) Act was passed in 1986 to make laws more stringent in relation to offenses pertaining to dowry
* the Consumer Protection Act was passed in 1986 to protect consumers from unfair trade practice and to provide for simple, speedy and inexpensive redressal of grievances. A National Consumer Redressal Commission, with corresponding forums in states and districts, has been established.
* the Legal Services Authorities Act was passed in 1987 to give effect to Article 39 of the Constitution by establishing legal services authorities to provide free and competent legal services to weaker sections of society
* 2400 *Lok Adalats* have been held so far to settle 1 million cases. Free legal aid has been provided law courts to 1 million poor people in 1985-89, against 38 lakhs in 1980-84; 50 per cent of these belongs to SC/ST communities and backward classes
* for the first time, minimum wage legislation has been extended to cover drought and famine relief works
* legislation to protect the interests of the disabled is under consideration. Since 1984, about 25,000 physically handicapped persons have found employment through special employment exchanges

* a Group Insurance Scheme and maternity benefit scheme have been introduced for bidi and mine workers
* a National Welfare Fund for fishermen has been set up for providing amenities and infrastructural facilities in fishing villages. A Group Insurance Scheme has also been introduced to provide accident cover to active fishermen.

Party workers will take the lead in ensuring that critical pieces of legislation, like those relating to minimum wages and the minimum age at marriage are made known to people and implemented effectively. Social action groups and activists will be closely involved in spreading awareness of law and the people's rights.

W. Justice for All

The Congress government has brought power to the people. We will now bring justice to the people.

We will convert our courts of litigation into temples of justice. Placing power in the hands of people is an essential first step. It will be complemented by ready access to quick and inexpensive justice.

Cumbersome procedures lead to long delays. Justice delayed is justice denied. The simplification of laws is a first priority.

The heavy backlog of cases will be cleared in the quickest manner and shortest period possible. Far more powers will be given to the Nyaya Panchayats so that litigation which can be resolved at the village level is resolved at that level. We will extend the concept of Nyaya Panchayats to urban areas as well.

Lok Adalats will be made more pervasive. Public interest litigation will be sanctified by law. The Congress government will also bring about systemic changes to ensure inexpensive justice. Equality in the eyes of the law must translate into equal opportunity to seek the protection of the law. Speedy justice itself will reduce the cost of litigation. In addition, the cost of litigation will be brought within reach of all those who seek justice in the law.

X. Foreign Policy Initiatives

Under the Congress government of Shri Rajiv Gandhi:

* the major military powers that earlier scoffed at the principles and philosophy of Nonalignment are now beginning to see the world through Indian eyes
* one of the world's great superpowers, the Soviet Union, has affirmed its adherence to the traditional Indian principle of Nonviolence through the Delhi Declaration signed in November 1986 between Prime Minister Rajiv Gandhi and the Soviet President, Mikhail Sergeyevich Gorbachev
* immediately after the Delhi Declaration was signed, the negotiations between the Soviet Union and the United States of America commenced which led to the INF Treaty, the first-ever agreement on eliminating an entire class of nuclear weapons

* The Prime Minister presented to the United Nations at its Special Session on Disarmament in June 1988 an Action Plan for the complete elimination of nuclear weapons within the next 20 years and the establishment of a new world order based on nonviolence, tolerance, the sovereign democratic equality of all nations, and the oneness of humanity, to sustain a world beyond nuclear weapons. The Action Plan has received acclaim every where as a major contribution to world survival
* Prime Minister Rajiv Gandhi has also unveiled a proposal for the establishment of a Planet Protection Fund, which has caught the imagination of people and statesmen all over the world. The proposal is based on a recognition of the fact that development can be sustained only if the environment is protected. But the protection of the environment costs a great deal of money and it is, therefore, only proper that the developing countries of the world be assisted in their efforts to conserve the environment. The Planet Protection Fund would be the realisation of Indiraji's vision, articulated first in her renowned inaugural address to the UN Conference on Environment at Stockholm in 1972 that the problems of the environment are global problems which must be resolved by global cooperation
* India and the Congress Party have relentlessly crusaded against the evil of apartheid in South Africa. In this, the Prime Minister has carried forward the struggle started by Mahatma Gandhi in South Africa nearly a century ago, a struggle which deeply influenced our own national destiny. For it was in South Africa that Mahatma Gandhi began his experiments with the revolutionary new political technique of satyagraha, or nonviolent resistance to oppression and untruth. Prime Minister Rajiv Gandhi's proposal for an AFRICA Fund (Action For Resisting Invasion, Colonialism & Apartheid) was unanimously accepted at the 1986 Harare Summit of the Nonalignment Movement and Rajivji himself was elected Chairman of the Fund, a mandate that was renewed at the recent Summit in Belgrade. The Fund has brought together nations and organisations from the East and the West, the North and South on a common platform to fight for human rights and human dignity for all the people of South Africa
* in our neighbourhood, India's prestige is at a new height:
* with china, the Prime Minister's historic visit to that country in December 1988 heralded a new era of peace and cooperation between Asia's who greatest countries, notwithstanding the difficult negotiations that lie ahead in resolving the border issue
* in Pakistan, the restoration of democracy promises a new beginning. Meanwhile, we remain ever vigilant in Siachen and other sensitive areas along the border.
* in Sri Lanka, the historic Agreement of July 1987 has contributed to preserving the unity and integrity of Sri Lanka, while meeting our deep security concerns and ensuring the devolution of adequate political, financial and administrative powers to the Regional Councils. The genocide of the Tamils has been forestalled and democracy for the Sri Lankan Tamils ensured by protecting them from non-democratic elements within their own ranks. The noble jawans of the IPKF are to be congratulated on a difficult job extremely well done

* there are problems with Bangladesh, many deriving from the mistakes made by the Janata government over the augmenting and sharing of the Ganga waters, but these can be resolved with goodwill on both sides
* with Nepal the origin of the present problem can be traced to the confused Janata regime where the then Prime Minister over-ruled the advice of his Foreign Minister and ordered the merging of the Treaties on Trade and Transit. A solution is being worked out
* our smallest neighbours, Maldives and Bhutan, are among out closest friends. Their trust in our intentions, and their goodwill towards us, give the lie to the false allegations that are sometimes made of India's hegemonistic ambitions. We week friendship and cooperation with our neighbours, not dominance.

The Congress reaffirms its commitment to Nonalignment to pursue the objective of peace, disarmament and environmentally sustainable development. India, under the Congress, will:

* Promote traditional ties of friendship with all of India's neighbours and deepen exchanges in the political, economic and cultural fields with them. It will give direction and substance to SAARC through economic cooperation and the promotion of people-to-people contacts
* explore new opportunities for strengthening India's friendly and cooperative relations with the USSR and other socialist countries in the context of the significant political and economic changes taking place in those countries
* enlarge the area of mutual understanding and cooperation with the United States and achieve a further improvement in bilateral relations
* follow up on Prime Minister Rajiv Gandhi's historic visit to China by further deepening the process of normalisation of relations with that country
* follow up on the positive atmosphere in the improvement of relations with Pakistan which has come about after the advent of democracy in that country
* maintain the growing momentum of ties forged between India and Japan in the political, economic and cultural fields
* continue efforts to work with all concerned to ensure a sovereign, independent and Nonaligned Afghanistan
* continue India's active participation in efforts to promote a peaceful solution to the Kampuchean problem while ensuring that no opportunity is given to the Khmer Rouge to return to its genocidal practices of the past
* support the legitimate demand for a Palestinian homeland
* continue moral and material support for the elimination of apartheid in South Africa
* mobilize international opinion in support of the forces struggling to restore peace, stability and racial equality and harmony in Fiji
* vigorously pursue the "Action Plan for Ushering in a Nuclear Weapon-Free and Non-Violent World" launched in the United nations by Prime Minister Rajiv Gandhi in 1988
* safeguard and promote India's interests in the process of European integration, scheduled for 1992, by forging closer political and economic

ties with all the countries of the European Communities.

* pursue India's recent initiatives for the resumption of the North-South dialogue and the intensification of South-South cooperation
* play an active and leading role in cooperative international action to save the world's deteriorating environment and mobilize support for Prime Minister Rajiv Gandhi's recent initiative for establishing a "Planet Protection Fund", and above all
* safeguard India's security and territorial integrity by maintaining the country's defence preparedness at a level where it is capable of effectively meeting any threat of external aggression or domestic destabilisation linked to Inimical external forces.

Y. Voluntary Agencies

The Congress government is committed to encouraging and supporting spontaneous people's organisation and social action groups working to further the aims of social justice and removal of inequalities.

In the last five years a serious effort has been made to involve voluntary agencies and grassroot organisations in areas like literacy. Water and sanitation, wastelands development and health.

The Congress Party reiterates its conviction that such efforts need to be supported and expanded because it promotes self-respect among people and reduces the dependency of communities on government, thus making them self-reliant.

Specific areas like awareness generation and organising the rural poor and the socially vulnerable to fight for their rights will be given sharper focus to enable voluntary organisations to be effective.

Z. Responsive Administration

The commitment of the Congress leadership to provide a responsive administration was reflected in the Prime Minister's very first broadcast to nation in January 1985. subsequently, this item was included in the 20 point programme, to highlight its importance and enable regular monitoring at the highest level.

The systematic answer to the problem of responsive administration lies in making administration at the grassroot both responsive and responsible. This systemic transformation constitutes the heart of the Panchayati Raj and Nagarpalika Bills. The Opposition has stalled these Bills in the Rajya Sabha.

Meanwhile, a machinery was set up in 1988 to make redress for public grievances effective 85 per cent of the cases examined so far have been settled in favour of people. A large number of these cases had been pending for between 2 to 15 years.

For the first time, the Prime Minister had held detailed meetings with Collectors/DMs to impress on them the need to have administration at local level on the side of the poor, the dispossessed, weaker sections and the under privileged.

The Congress government has been pushing for greater openness in development programmes.

For the first time at the instance of the Congress leadership, names of villages where water has been provided has been made public to enable public scrutiny. The establishment of village-level committees has been deliberately encouraged to put pressure on government functionaries to be accountable in areas like water supply, education and health.

The Congress Party reaffirms its resolve to strive for an open government, for a responsive administration at all levels.

It will take all steps needed to extend and expand the machinery for the quick redressal of public grievances and will encourage the social audit of development programmes.

It will bring about far-reaching administrative reform so that public service institutions serve the public better.

It will make it easier for all people to obtain ration cards as a matter of right and in a matter of hours.

It will make it easier for landowners to acquire, in the shortest period possible a copy of the record of rights to their property. It will make it easier for people to deal with public utilities like telephone departments, electricity companies and banks.

The Congress Party will bring about major administrative reform. It will reduce the size and scope of government so as to enable a greater reliance on the resourcefulness, initiative and innovativeness of people themselves.

The Congress government will initiate a major programme to revamp the cooperative system in the country structurally and financially. It will ensue that political and bureaucratic interference is minimised and cooperatives are run on professional lines.

The Congress Party is convinced of the need to usher in a new work culture and environment in all institutions. The Party will set a new example to demonstrate an approach to openness, responsiveness, informality and compassion. The Party will be reorganised and restructured along these lines to make it a more potent weapon of change.

Steps have been taken in the last five years to instill this culture in the bureaucracy through massive training programmes. These will be continued and expanded. District administration will be given more powers to introduce this work culture at the block and village levels.

As our population grows younger, existing organisation and administrative structures will need to change with the times to promote creativity and innovativeness.

Performance and not patronage has to be the guiding principal as part of the new work culture.

Team work and collective effort, rather than individual initiatives, will be encouraged.

ANNEXURE E

NATIONAL FRONT ELECTION MANIFESTO GENERAL ELECTION, 1989

STATE OF THE NATION

Appalling poverty, glaring inequality and growing destitution of large numbers have rendered India weak and demoralised. The people are discontented and disheartened. Escalating conflicts and an increasing resort to violence engulf large areas in the country. In several places mafia gangs and anti-social elements are fully in control.

Today's India witnesses corruption at the highest level in government and administration: an irresolute government unable to resolve conflicts and maintain even minimal law and order; spiralling prices and man-made scarcities; a currency shrinking in value and a mounting load of foreign debt.

The nation is in a whirlpool of crises — crisis of confidence, crisis of character and crisis of leadership — a fallout of the policies pursued by successive Congress (I) governments and particularly by the Rajiv Gandhi government in the last five years.

The Rajiv Gandhi governments, which came into power on a sympathy wave and promised a "Clean government", has scaled new heights in corruption and inefficiency.

Rajiv Gandhi's path to power was marked by the violent deaths of thousands of innocent men, women and children in Delhi and elsewhere in the country. Punjab is now a boiling cauldron. What is worse, the spectre of violence has now spread to several other parts of the country. Not a day has passed since his coming to power when scores of innocent citizens have not been massacred in various parts of the country. The communal virus has now assumed the proportions of an epidemic. Atrocities on Scheduled Castes, Scheduled Tribes, and other weaker sections, as well as women, have multiplied.

Our foreign policy, once lauded for defusing tensions elsewhere in the world, has now led to embittered relations even with friendly neighbours like Nepal, Bangladesh and Sri Lanka.

Collusion between an unprincipled government and the unbridled bit business has resulted in the prices of essential commodities such as foodgrains, sugar, tea and edible oils sky rocketing at the expense of both the producer and the consumer.

Unemployment of both the educated and the unlettered has reached new heights. Despite tall claims about the elitist New Education policy, the number of illiterates has been increasing and the quality of education deteriorating.

The ruling party, while talking of stability has itself proved to be the biggest destabilising factor. Divisive forces have been encouraged in sensitive areas to gain short-term partisan ends. The Rajiv Gandhi government, has caused incalculable harm to the institutions of the Republic like the Presidency, the parliament, the judiciary, the CAG and the press. Overnight changes of his own Chief Ministers, frequent Cabinet reshuffles and ceaseless attempts to remove non-Congress(I) governments by foul means, disprove his claim of providing a stable government. The one-party rule at the Centre has been reduced to one-man rule destroying inner party democracy and that one-man rule has proved intolerably incompetent and notoriously corrupt. Bofors, corruption and Rajiv Gandhi are now synonyms. Other brazen scandals such as submarine kickbacks, wasteful expenditure on Westland helicopters etc. and illegal foreign accounts of proxies of Rajiv Gandhi have rocked our democratic policy to its foundations and endangered the country's security. With conclusive evidence of the involvement of the Prime Minister and his aides in the coverup of the kickbacks, Rajiv Gandhi has made himself vulnerable to international blackmail. The en-masse resignation of all the opposition MPs from the Lok Sabha, a momentous Bharat Bandh and the rejection of the phoney decentralisation bills symbolise the people's protest against the government's failures and perversions.

It is against this background that the people of India have been craving for an alternative to the discredited Congress(I). The National Front is a response to this call of our people. The parties that comprise the National Front are deeply committed to the philosophy of national unity, democracy, socialism, secularism and federalism.

In contrast to the Congress(I) misrule, the governments run by the constituents of the National Front have provided dynamic administration, both in the spheres of development and law and order. Genuine decentralisation of powers to Panchayati Raj institutions, social welfare measures to benefit the weaker sections and women and benefits to farmers, as well as clean and efficient administration, are the outstanding achievements of the National Front Constituent party governments.

To resurrect the nation out of the morass and despondency in which it finds itself today and build a new India, the National Front is offering in this manifesto, a concrete programme and pledges to implement it with all sincerity.

The record of our performance encourages the National Front to approach the people of India with confidence and conviction. We stand united to fulfil our pledge to the nation.

II

OUR RESOLVE

The National Front is committed to upholding the nation's honour and democratic values, promoting the ideal of secularism and ushering a new social and economic order based on equality and justice.

Democratic Rights

We declare our resolve to restore and extend the democratic rights of our people.

Corruption

The National Front stands firmly for dismantling the nexus between politicians and vested interests and to eradicate the all-pervasive corruption. It will track down the kickback funds generated in Bofors and other deals and slashed away in foreign banks. The funds will be restored to the nation and the guilty will be punished.

Electoral Reforms

Comprehensive Electoral reforms to curb money and muscle power will be urgently introduced.

Parliamentary Democracy

The Front is pledged to revitalise the parliamentary institutions and to make them accountable to the people. The National Front will defend and strengthen, through appropriate reforms, the independence of judiciary and institutions like the C&AG and the Election Commission.

True Federalism

The National Front is committed to true federalism, and will reverse the over-centralisation brought about by the ruling party. Not only will the states benefit by decentralisation of powers from the Centre, but there will be a corresponding and simultaneous devolution of power to the districts, the taluks, tahsils the mandals and the Panchayats, on the basis of a national consensus.

National Reconciliation

Conflict, violence and confrontation have divided and hurt the nation during the last five years. This must end. A climate of tolerance and fraternity among all social groups must grow. Reconciliation through dialogue is the need of the hour. It shall be our foremost endeavour to bring about national reconciliation and provide the healing touch.

Equality and Justice

The National Front stands for a fair deal for all the people, particularly for marginalised and oppressed groups — the scheduled castes, the scheduled tribes and other weaker sections, the bonded labour, the marginal farmers and the artisans.

Minorities

Religious and ethnic minorities will have the fullest protection in pursuing their modes of worship, following their personal laws and developing their institutions. Communal disturbances shall be prevented and firmly put down, when they occur. Educational and employment opportunities for the minorities will receive special attention.

Women's Participation

Our success in national reconstruction will depend on the equal participation and involvement of women. The Front will, accordingly, give special attention to ensure this.

Youth

Youth will be involved in national reconstruction and special schemes will be devised to ensure employment and their all round development.

Minimum Needs

Through a major programme of employment generation and asset creation, the National Front will achieve its declared goal of fulfilling the essential minimum need of the people.

Right to Work

"Right to Work" will be included in the Fundamental Rights guaranteed by the Constitution.

Rural Economy

The National Front will evolve a set of long overdue policies for the benefit of the neglected farming community and the rural society. Not less than 50 per cent of the investible resources will be deployed for the development of rural economy. Farmers will be assured of guaranteed remunerative prices for their produce, a countrywide network of godowns and warehouses, remission of debts, provision of cheap credit, removal of unreasonable restrictions on movement of agricultural produce, crop insurance, security in land holding and strict implementation of land reforms and improved access to water resources.

Labour Welfare

Minimum wages and social security will be guaranteed to agricultural labour as also to all workers in the unorganised sectors of the economy. As for the industrial sector, the National Front will introduce progressive labour laws and promote workers' participation in the management of industries to create conditions in which industrial democracy could flourish. A rational wage policy will be formulated.

Foreign Debt

The National Front shall restore to the nation its dignity and confidence by achieving self-reliance in the economy. The National Front's policies will be directed towards freeing the country from indiscriminate and highly expensive technologies, the humiliating burden of fast escalating foreign debt and the abject dependence on multi-national corporations.

Open Government

The National Front commits itself to full freedom of the media, autonomous corporations for television and ratio and elimination of practices that lead to direct and indirect arm-twisting of the Press. People's right to information shall be guaranteed through Constitutional Provisions.

Our Vision

We envision an awakened India, free from poverty, ignorance and exploitation, with total involvement of millions in the struggle for national reconstruction.

The Pledge

We pledge not merely a replacement of one set of rulers by the other, but an alternative model of governance, based on federalism and decentralisation institutional accountability, economic equality and social justice, human rights, freedom of communication and access to information for all citizens, and a responsive and responsible administration and through all this ensure the dignity of both the individual citizen and the nation.

III

POLITICAL TASKS

Union-State Relations

We firmly believe that genuine federalism along can broaden and deepen the bonds of unity and integrity of our great nation. The National Front believes that the strengthening of the states need not be at the expense of the Union and will, on the other hand, enable the Union to discharge its responsibilities more effectively.

The states ought to enjoy genuine autonomy — political, legislative, economic, fiscal and administrative — without submitting themselves to the indignity of becoming supplicants before the Centre, with a begging bowl.

Successive attempts have been made by the Union Government, under Rajiv Gandhi, to encroach upon the autonomy of the states.

The National Front will undertake a comprehensive review of Union-State relations, in consultation with all Chief Ministers and having regard to the reports of the Commissions and Committees on the subject and the representations made to them by the states and political parties. On this basis, it will strengthen the federal nature of the Indian polity so as to make it responsive to the aspirations of the people living in various states.

The National Front is Committed to:

— establish an Inter-State Council under Article 263 of the Constitution;
— activate the National Development Council in order to achieve and maintain a national consensus on all issues relating to planning and development. The Planning Commission will be given a Constitutional status and will function as an executive arm of the National Development Council;
— not to misuse for political purposes, Article 356 relating to the dismissal of State governments. Legislative Assemblies — not Raj Bhavans — will be the forum for testing the strength of the duly elected Ministries in the states;
— ensure that Governors are not used as agents of the party in power in the Centre. The National Front will ensure Constitutional accountability of the Governor by bringing in necessary amendments to the Constitution. The role, powers and functions of the Governors, as also whether any alternative arrangements can be made, will be examined, and
— to devolve adequate financial and administrative powers to states to enable them to discharge their responsibilities to the people.

Panchayat Raj

The National Front is committed to promote a genuine devolution of powers, functions and resources to Panchayati Raj Institutions enabling the fullest participation of the people in the developmental process. The discredited attempts made by Rajiv government to bypass the states, through legislative measures in the name of decentralisation will be replaced by genuine decentralisation based on a national consensus.

The National Front will provide a legal guarantee to ensure regular elections to Panchayati Raj Institutions. It will secure, with the cooperation of the states, adequate representations in these bodies for Scheduled Castes, Scheduled Tribes, Backward classes and Women and devolution of financial and administrative powers.

Curbing Corruption

Corruption not only demoralises the people but also robs the poor as plan priorities and delivery to target groups are distorted. The National Front reiterates its firm conviction that with the transformation of the administrative set-up corruption will also be curbed. An institution of Lok Pal will be created at the Centre and Lok Ayuktas will be introduced in states and strengthened where they exist. The purview of the Lok Pal and Lok Ayukta will be expanded to include the highest political offices in the country. It will also be laid down that the Lok Pal, Lok Ayuktas, the Comptroller and Auditor General (C&AG), the Chief Election Commissioner and the Chief Justice of India will hold no public office after retirement. All elected representatives to legislatures and Zilla Parishads will be required to periodically declare their assets and incomes for scrutiny by an appropriate authority.

Independence of Judiciary

Nothing has hurt the rule of law and the provision of a just and humane framework of governance as the present government's attempt to compromise an independent judiciary. The National Front government will take steps to restore the independence of the judiciary.

Steps will be taken to speed the process of law. The powers of the Executive to influence the appointments and transfers of judges will be eliminated. A high-level judicial commission will be entrusted with these powers. The number of judges will be constantly reviewed, and *ad hoc* appointments will also be sanctioned to clear the huge backlog of pending cases expeditiously. The system of Nyaya Panchayats and Lok Adalats in settling cases by mutual discussion will be strengthened and extended. Free legal aid to the poor will be made a reality.

Electoral Reforms

The Indian state cannot be rejuvenated and made to play its appointed role in social transformation unless it also steps in to combat the growing nexus between the big money, mafias and the politicians. The National Front will urgently implement the long-pending proposals for public financing of elections to reduce money power, regular audit of party funds and observance by political parties of the rules framed by their respective Constitutions. Contrary to the existing practice, the Election Commission will be appointed in consultation with the Opposition. System of multi-purpose photo-identity cards will be introduced. Measures for expeditious disposal of election disputes, holding of bye-elections on time and fresh delimitation will be undertaken. To ensure a continuous inflow of new blood dynamism, devotion, dedication and sacrifice into the arena of public life and service the National Front will introduce the principle that legislators at the Centre and state level are barred from holding any elected office at the district or the lower levels. Suitable changes will be made in the Anti-Defection Law to prevent its misuse.

Civil Liberties

Civil liberties and human rights will be protected and strengthened. The 59th Amendment to the Constitution, the Posts and Telegraphs (Amendment) Bill, and the other laws violative of civil liberties shall be withdrawn. Undertrials shall be safeguarded from harassment. Institution of Executive Magistrates, wherever they exist, shall be dispensed with. The U.N. Conventions against torture and those relating to prisoners and refugees shall be ratified and adopted. Suitable prison reforms will be undertaken on a systematic basis.

Protection of Rights of Minorities

Religious minorities will enjoy the fullest protection and opportunity to pursue their modes of worship and their religious beliefs and practices, and develop their institutions, whether religious, cultural, educational or welfare-oriented. Complete non-interference will be observed in their personal laws, their cultural advancement and fulfilment of their distinctive cultural identities.

The tragic recurrence of communal riots during the last five years has gained momentum in the Congress(I) states, killing large number of people in places like Kota, Badayun and Indore. Communal riots shall be strongly put down by effective prohibition of incitement of communal passions and by pursuing appropriate recruitment policies in police services and by creating mixed anti-riot force so as to ensure totally impartial conduct from them. Full compensation to victims of communal and caste riots will be provided. Action will be taken against officers who fail to control riots. Special courts will be constituted to try cases relating to communal and caste riots. Justice will be done to the victims of November 1984 riots in Delhi and elsewhere and those responsible will be punished.

The Minority Commission will be given statutory status.

In order to remove unemployment and economic backwardness among the minorities, the government would take, *inter alia*, the following steps:

1. Setting up Minorities Financial Corporations,
2. Representation for minorities on various recruitment committees and boards.
3. Encouragement for establishment of technical and polytechnic institutions by minorities.
4. Preservation of the minority character of the educational institutions guaranteed under the Constitution.

Right to Information

A participatory democracy requires an enlightened and informed electorate. Instead of sustaining and enlarging this basic postulate of our freedom struggle, the Rajiv Gandhi government has choked Radio and TV with partisan and personal propaganda, prevented dissemination of facts and outraged the nation's sense of fairness.

It has also done its worst to harass and pressurise the print media from time to time. Legislative measures were attempted to gag the Press and to end its freedom. A vigilant public opinion did not permit these measures to succeed. The Rajiv government has increased the newsprint prices and massively burdened the economies of newspapers. The National Front commits itself to remove all such impediments. Excise duty on newsprint will be reduced and restrictions on import of newsprint removed.

On of the first acts of the National Front government will be to liberate the electronic media from the governmental stranglehold and convert them into autonomous corporations.

The National Front government will, by *amending the Constitution, ensure the citizen's right to information.* With this in mind, the Official Secrets Act will be suitably amended.

Solutions to Political Problems

Punjab

The National Front government will immediately take steps to resolve the

Punjab tangle. Laws that violate civil liberties will be reviewed. All those prisoners against whom there are no specific charges will be released. Wide-ranging discussions will be held, without preconditions, with leaders of various sections of the people for a political solution to the Punjab problem. A round-table Conference will be convened for this purpose. Elections to the Punjab Assembly will be held expeditiously. Discussions between Punjab, Haryana and Rajasthan for settlement of disputes will be organised.

Assam

In respect of Assam, full and expeditious implementation of the Assam Accord shall be ensured. Utmost care will be taken to ensure that there is no injustice or harassment to genuine Indian citizens. The National Front government shall not allow any further division of Assam and the tribal problem will be settled through dialogue and negotiations.

Regional Aspirations

Regional aspirations of the submerged groups residing in such underdeveloped areas as the eastern tribal belt call for fulfilment by appropriate measures. Equally legitimate is the demand for the application of the 6th Schedule of the Constitution of India to some districts in the North Eastern States such as Manipur.

Ram Janam Bhoomi/Babri Masjid Issue

The Babri Masjid-Ram Janam Bhoomi controversy has become a matter of grave anxiety to the people of the country. The Union Government by its inaction and sometimes by deliberate instigation by the Congress(I) state government, has allowed this sore to fester. It is the firm belief of the National Front that the controversy can be settled through negotiations, based upon mutual understanding.

The National Front feels that the Babri Masjid should not be demolished. At the same time, the Hindu sentiments to have a temple dedicated to Lord Rama should be respected.

The National Front feels that an amicable settlement on the above lines can be found. No precipitate action should be taken by any group pending such settlement or a decision by the Court.

Responsive Administrative Structure

The present administrative system, with its in-built colonial hangover, needs a radical overhaul. A new administrative structure, with new systems, procedures and tools, to promote a new work culture has to be built-up. Administration should be responsive to the needs of the common man and be an effective instrument to achieve radical socio-economic transformation. This would end the alienation between the rulers and the ruled and give a new orientation to the role of the civil servant. Honest civil servants at all levels will be protected from harassment and highhandedness. Serious efforts will be made to eliminate red-tape and simplify procedures.

IV

ECONOMIC TASKS

Poverty Eradication

Of all the problems facing India none is as stark as poverty. It is a national disgrace that after four decades of independence, and implementation of seven five years plans, more than two-thirds of the population remain illiterate, ill-fed, ill-clothed, ill-housed and in poor health, while the rich roll in extravagance, leading an ostentatious life.

The absolute number of the poor in the country today exceeds the total population of India at the time of Independence. More than one-third of the rural population is unable to find productive and gainful work for most of the year. In the urban areas over 35 million people are on the live register as unemployed - a tenfold increase since 1952. The disparities between the top 10 per cent and bottom 30 per cent of the population have, meanwhile, widened menacingly.

Concentration of wealth, assets and incomes, which has created increasingly steep disparities, shall be reduced to a minimum by introducing structural changes, with a strong political will. Growing disparities in incomes and wealth have led to shocking distortions in planned economic development, created vicious circles of poverty, ignorance and squalour and condemned large sections of Indians to dehumanised living. These disparities will be brought down by dispersal of ownership, whether in industry, commerce or trade, and ceiling on urban property and land or agricultural estates and land holdings as well as incomes. Rationalisation of direct and indirect taxation will be the other measure towards this end. While reiterating its commitment to planning, the National Front shall use it as an instrument for widening the social base of the economy by expanding the purchasing power of the people and extending the benefit of development to the masses rather than a small class of people and by reducing the regional and sectoral imbalance. The National Front reiterates its belief that without the double process of simultaneous lowering of the ceiling and lifting of the floor, it will never be possible to remove poverty and narrow disparities, whether economic or social.

Right to Work

The National Front believes that every citizen has the right to productive and gainful work in order to live meaningfully and with dignity. The social and economic policy of the National Front will be geared to the realisation of the "Right to Work" as a fundamental right of the citizens of India.

We have to find productive work for the people, at wages that are commensurate with human needs and dignity. It is well within our means to generate socially productive employment on a scale necessary to convert the right to work into a reality. As a first step, new Employment Guarantee Schemes will be introduced all over the country. To realise conditions of full employment an alternative strategy of social and economic development will be followed which accords primacy to development of agriculture and allied occupations, with investment on building up infrastructure of essential physical and social services in villages and towns. Production of basic consumer goods will be reserved for cottage and small industries.

Wrong Policies

The National Front believes that mass unemployment, poverty, inequality, ignorance and ill-health are the noncommitant of wrong socio-economic policies pursued by the entrenched ruling elite during the last forty-two years. All these ailments have aggravated in the eighties, more particularly in the last four-five years, when the so-called capital and import-intensive high-tech modernisation of the economy has been attempted to be imposed recklessly and mindlessly.

Investment on the People

The National Front's policy of socio-economic development will centre round the people, their right to productive and gainful work and eradication of mass poverty. Priority will be given to direct investment on the people, that is, on the provision of basic needs: education, nutrition, health, drinking water, housing, sanitation and easy access to items of essential consumption at subsidised prices. These will enable the people to make their full contribution to the advancement of our socio-economic, political and cultural life.

Agriculture

Land and labour are our most precious assets and their prosperity is correlated. This crucial sector of our economy has not only been neglected for too long but also exploited by an in-built structural disadvantage. The National Front is committed to correct this distortion. It will be our highest policy objective to ensure that the enormous potential of these resources are realised and the corresponding benefits are enjoyed by those who had so far been deprived.

Land Reforms

The National Front will revise the existing laws to bring about equitable distribution of land and other natural resources like water and make the tiller of the land its owner. An land reform laws shall be included in the Ninth Schedule of the Constitution.

Land Tribunals will be appointed to look into and settle cases of benami transfers of land. Surplus land will be distributed among the landless people belonging to scheduled castes and scheduled tribes.

Two-thirds of our cultivable land is still dependent on rain and large areas, which are potentially cultivable, have remained as wastelands. Priority will be given to provide protective irrigation in the entire rain-fed agricultural areas.

Research in agriculture, animal husbandry, food processing, etc., shall be oriented to make smaller holdings and dry farming economically viable. Emphasis will be on integrative and versatile technology inputs for the small farmer and neglected areas.

Inputs and Remunerative Prices

Remunerative prices to the cultivator and provision of all input for agriculture at fair prices will be guaranteed. The prices will be fixed on the basis of real cost of farming by the Agricultural Prices and Costs Commission, which will be strengthened with effective participation of farmers. All prices will be announced before the sowing season. A guarantee that no rural lands are acquired at deferred prices for profiteering by private colonisers or the state and reservation of agro-based industries, including food processing and processing of minor forest produce for cooperative and small scale sector in the rural areas, will guide the agrarian strategy of the National Front.

Marketing Committees, constituted by farmers, will be given liberal credit, transport and warehousing facilities. Elected Karshak Parishads (Farmers' Forums) will be organised at State, District and Block levels to take up programmes benefiting the farmers. These will be developed into true representative bodies of the farmers.

Export and import of agricultural commodities will be guided by a Commodities Management Board, with effective representation for farmers and consumers, so that the prices of farm produce are not affected adversely. Farmers will be ensured regular supply of inputs and liberal credit facilities.

Crop Insurance

Cultivators will be further protected by insurance of crops and cattle against natural or man-made calamities; an assurance against distress sales by providing godowns; removal of zonal restrictions on the movement of agricultural produce; and a guarantee that the state will purchase crops at assured prices to break market manipulations.

Consolidation of land holdings will be taken up and completed expeditiously. Holdings of marginal farmers will be grouped into separate blocks for special treatment to increase productivity. The system of levying fixed service charges on irrigation and electricity will be reviewed to make them fair and just and power will be supplied to farmers at cheaper rate.

Loans up to Rs. 10,000 of small, marginal and landless cultivators and artisans, as on 2 October 1989, will be written off. NABARD will provide loans to farmers at concessional rate of interest through cooperative banks.

Natural Resources and Environment

Since independence, we have witnessed India rapidly deteriorate from one of the world's richest naturally endowed nations to a progressively growing waste land. During this period the country lost almost half of the forests which provided the people's daily needs of food, fodder, fuel, timber, herbs, medicines, fibre, fruits and a variety of other essential utility items. Another consequences of deforestation is the severe depletion of groundwater resources.

With the majority of the countrymen still being poor, the degradation of the environment is leading to the degradation of the resource base on which alone the basic needs of people can be met.

To stop the degradation and the consequent forced rural exodus, the National Front will make the regeneration of the nation's recourse base a priority area of the State Policy.

The National Front government will ensue strict implementation of the pollution control laws.

Water Management

The National Front firmly believes that the stability of our national life is totally do the stability of our water systems. Primary importance will be given to ensuring long term water stability through (1) harvesting rain water in catchment areas, thereby effectively controlling floods and restoring the perennial character of Indian rivers and augmenting groundwater recharge, (2) conserving water use in both agriculture and industry and (3) strict protection of water-system from pollution by industry, civic authorities, etc.

The irrigation policies of the National Front government will be based on a rational water-management approach, of developing tiny water-sheds and the sub-basins, fulfilling the needs of the local population, while effectivity controlling floods and also ensuring the riparian rights of the downstream people. Priority in irrigation will be given to minor and medium projects.

Formation of a national grid to optimise utilisation of water resources will be pursued.

The potential of river Brahmaputra shall be harnessed through long term measures to combat floods and generate power.

The National Front government will find an expeditious solution to Inter-State water disputes in a fair and equitable manner.

Industrialisation

In the industrial sphere present policies are biased towards large sized, capital-intensive urban-based industries. Even the small-scale industries, which have prospered in recent years, have largely been ancillaries of urban-oriented service industries. Their potential for creation of additional employment has been limited and the commodities they produce meet mainly the requirements of affluent sections. Simultaneously, a large number of small-scale and village industries, which have for centuries provided gainful employment to men and women in all parts of the country, have been woefully neglected. Millions of jobs in these industries have been sacrificed to satisfy the captains of industries in the large-scale private-sector as is evident from the government's National Textile Policy of 1985, encouragement of harvestor combines and other labour displacing machinery in various sectors. The impact of these policies have been very severe on some of the poorest states like Bihar and Uttar Pradesh.

The National Front government will promote industrial development in such a way as to maximise employment. The emphasis will be on producing wage goods and services required for consumption by the mass of our people. Agro-processing industries, industries based on the craft of rural artisans, village industries of particular benefit to women and rural households will receive full support by way of credit, extension service, supply of inputs, marketing organisation etc. Manufacture of items of mass consumption, which can be produced by the cottage and small-scale industries, will be reserved for these centres.

In respect of infrastructure and capital goods industries we shall modify the conditions and parameters to ensure efficiency in the utilisation of investment and relevance to national priorities in end-use. The commanding position will continue to be occupied by the public sector — which will be made more managerially efficient and less dominated by the bureaucracy. Infrastructure development will again be oriented to the better distribution of goods, services and benefits.

The strategy of development pursued so far, and more brazenly in the eighties, has made the country increasingly subservient to foreign capital in order to satisfy the demand pattern of the affluent 10 per cent population. In the name of technological upgradation, the liberalised import of capital goods and turnkey projects has blocked indigenous enterprise for the development of industries on a self-reliant basis, including such vital industries as transport, steel, chemicals, power and engineering. In addition, Indian big business and transnational corporations have been allowed, on an increasing scale, to manufacture all kinds of consumer goods, including foods and toiletery in which the small producers are efficient and viable. The so-called latest and sophisticated technologies have been imported without taking into consideration their impact on employment. Indiscriminate automation and thoughtless computerisation has been resorted to, thereby allocating scarce capital resources for labour displacement and increasing the country's dependence on foreign capital. The impact of this on indigenous R & D and meaningful deployment of Indian Scientists and Technologists has been most deleterious and utilisation of their talents has been on the decline.

Research and Development

Our Science and Technology Policy will aim at strengthening Research and Development substantially. Indigenous technology will be developed to provide for a strong base of self-reliance and cut in import of foreign technology. It will be directed towards import substitution, development of modernised and appropriate technology and promotion of organic agricultural techniques. Non-conventional and renewable energy creation and utilisation will be one of our major objectives. The National Front has abundant faith in the capabilities of the scientific and technological community of the country, that it can shoulder these tasks magnificently.

Public Sector and Private Enterprise

The Public sector shall be freed from excessive bureaucratisation, inefficiency and underutilisation of capacity, while the private corporate sector shall be freed from the rigours of unnecessary and excessive controls. The National Front shall strengthen both these sectors so that they can reduce the role of multinationals in Indian economy, subserve the needs of agriculture, develop and provide appropriate technology for cottage and small scale sector, activate import substitution and push up exports in a big way in order to achieve the goal of national self-reliance. The National Front shall make all necessary adjustments in taxation and credit policies to ensure that they achieve these goals and also respond to the growing market in the rural sector, which will be the obvious consequence of the altered strategy of economic development.

Indebtedness

The Congress(I) policy of dependence on foreign technology has resulted in rapid and stupendous increase in foreign debt which has already exceeded Rs. 100,000 crores.

The burden of internal debt too has reached a menacing level of Rs. 200,000 crores so that interest payments have already become the most important component of non-plan expenditure of the government. The country is fast heading towards bankruptcy and debt trap.

The National Front will alter these policies and resist the pressures which have led to such an excessive debt burden. There will be severe and effective controls on deficit financing.

Fiscal Policies and Monetary Controls

Our fiscal policy needs drastic change. A long-term fiscal policy for both direct and indirect taxation will be formulated to increase revenue and curb corruption. It will also be ensured that there is a steady rise in the ratio of direct to indirect taxes.

Black Money

Effective administrative and economic measures will be taken to curb tax evasion, unearth black money and check its generation at source.

Tax Relief to Middle Income Group

To provide relief to middle income groups, the exemption limit for income-tax will be raised.

Licensing Policy

Adhocism in licensing is at the root of all commercial corruption. Long-term licensing policies will be announced for various sectors of industry and the entire procedure will be freed from both political favouritism and bureaucratic arbitrariness.

Institutional Finance

The public financial institutions shall be required to reorient their investment and credit policies in favour of the poor and the downtrodden groups such as cultivators and artisans, agro-industries and small and medium sector industries.

Suitable mechanism through financial institutions will be worked out to enable workers acquire shares in industrial enterprises in which they are employed.

Company Law Amendment

Company Law will be suitably amended to curb malpractices indulged in by private corporate sector, particularly family managements.

Sales Tax

The Present system of Sales Tax will be rationalised.

Import-Export Policy

The National Front is determined to plug every loophole in the import-export rules and policies which has enabled the anti-social and corrupt elements in industry or government to hoard illegal money in foreign banks. All such money shall be brought back.

FERA and MRTP

FERA and MRTP Acts shall be strengthened to ensure that opportunities for expansion are not misused for creating monopolies. Violations of FERA or MRTP shall not be counternanced and provisions of these Acts will be suitably strengthened and strictly enforced.

Ostentatious and elitist consumption, luxurious living, and five-star culture shall be checked by appropriate fiscal policies and other measures.

Arresting Price Rise

The annual double digit rate of inflation and spiralling prices of essential commodities during the 6th and 7th Plan periods have affected the common man adversely and jeopardised the entire development process. The worst hit are the rural poor as is obvious from the escalation in the cost of living index for the agricultural labour. The National Front considers price stability as crucial for removal of poverty and steady growth of economy.

Abnormal price rise will be checked by firm control on deficit financing and inflation, strict enforcement of financial discipline, austerity in public expenditure and progressive reduction in non-developmental expenditure. The public distribution system will be strengthened and expanded to cover all the vulnerable sections of the society so that cereals, sugar, edible oils, standard cloth and other daily household needs are supplied at fair prices. Stringent action shall be taken against hoarders and blackmarketeers. Consumer protection and cooperative marketing will be encouraged.

Labour Policy

The workers in factories will be made effective partners in management at plant and shop levels so that their willing cooperation in increasing production can be secured and conditions of industrial peace and democracy can be promoted.

The repressive and obnoxious features of the industrial relations laws will be replaced by more democratic and rational provisions. Article 311 of the Constitution will be restored to its original position to ensure against arbitrary dismisal of government servants. Recognition of trade unions on the basis of workers' support will be determined by secret ballot.

The National Front promises regularisation of casual labour in various government departments and public undertakings, having regard to the length of their continuous service. Delays, arbitrariness and circumventions shall not be allowed to hamper conciliation and arbitration in collective bargaining. The Indian Labour Conference will be activated to help create harmonious industrial relations and increase productivity.

For the workers in the unorganised sectors of the economy, including construction workers, appropriate legislation will be undertaken to ensure security against arbitrary removal, provision of fair wages, maternity benefits, safety and adequate accident compensation, creches for infants and social security in old age.

V

SOCIAL TASKS

Scheduled Castes, Scheduled Tribes and Backward Classes

The National Front is committed to removal of social inequality in all forms.

Implementation of reservation policy will be made effective in government, public and private sector industrial undertakings, banking institutions, etc., by resorting to special recruitment drives so as to fulfil their quotas within the shortest possible time.

The Scheduled Castes and Scheduled Tribes Commission will be armed with statutory powers.

Preferential opportunities and concessions will be ensured to scheduled castes, even after they embrace Buddhism, in view of the fact that they continue to suffer from social disability.

Special courts will be constituted to try cases concerning atrocities against scheduled castes and scheduled tribes and the violation of "Protection of Civil Rights Act".

Steps shall be taken to fight all vestiges of untouchability and social disabilities. Propagation of untouchability shall be severely dealt with.

The tribals' interests will be fully protected and various hardships and evictions, which they face owing to ill-conceived forest laws and arbitrary actions of forest officials, will be removed. Their customary laws will be respected and observed. Wherever tribal lands have been occupied by others, without survey operations being held, these will be restored after conducting survey operations. Their special needs will be attended to in the formulations and execution of forest policies and they will be made active participants in the process of massive afforestation.

The socially and educationally backward classes will be given special opportunities and substantial reservations in employment education and public offices.

The recommendations of the Mandal Commission will be implemented expeditiously.

Fishermen

Non-mechanised fishing will be protected from exploitation by mechanised fishing. Credit facilities and excise duty concessions will be given to small fishermen.

Equal Status for Women

Women, constituting half the population, shall be enabled to live with self-respect and free from oppression and indignity. The basis for the social policy of the National Front shall be to guarantee women equality with men before law and to discourage and ultimately eliminate all those practices which militate against equality of the sexes. It will make India a signatory to the U.N. Convention on Women's Rights and ensure that its policies and programmes for women flow from its charter.

A statutory All India Commission on Women will be appointed to monitor and accelerate the process of equal representation for women, to enforce all legislation for women's rights, including labour laws, and to check discrimination in all spheres.

The National Front will take all steps to enable women to fully participate in the development process. It will plan for the creation of jobs on a massive scale for women, particularly in the agrarian sector through agro-industries. Special vocational training institutions shall be set up for women to encourage self-employment, as well as to increase their eligibility for recruitment in industrial enterprises and offices. There will be 30 per cent reservation for women in government jobs, with preference to the destitute, widowed, divorced, deserted and to women heads of households. The private sector will be encouraged to employ more women. The principle of equal pay for equal or similar work will be upheld. Funds for special employment generating sectors more conductive to women's employment shall be specially earmarked and augmented.

A Maternity Fund will be created to benefit needy pregnant women, including the self-employed for the first two deliveries. Maternity health and child care will be included in the minimum needs programme.

There will be special emphasis on women's education.

The National Front commits to provide public latrines (*Sulabh Sauchalayas*) for the use of women in all villages in the next five years. Smokeless Chulhas will be subsidised and made available on a large scale to reduce drudging of women in the kitchens.

A review will be undertaken of all social legislation concerning marriage, divorce, maintenance, custody, adoption, inheritance etc. in consultation with women's organisations and all concerned communities, enact new legislation to give women equal rights in all these matters. Strict punishment will be given to those who violate laws meant to protect women's rights and abate crimes like *Sati* or dowry murders. All forms of harassment and violence against women will be strictly punished.

Suitable enactments will be undertaken to confer equal rights for women in the parental properties.

The National Front believes that no woman should go shelterless. Women-headed households and destitute women shall be given priority in allotment of housing loans. Housing sites allotted by the government will be jointly registered in the name of husband and wife. Land distributed under land reforms schemes will be jointly registered. More shelter homes will be opened for destitute women and they shall be given vocational training and rehabilitated. More women's hostels with provision to accommodate children, will be provided.

Depiction of women in any form of obscenity and indignity will be banned through stringent legislation. Participation of women's organisations to monitor this will be sought. Media will be used to more positive image of women.

The Old and the Handicapped

The old, the destitute and the physically handicapped will be specially looked after by providing them social security. Old age pensions will be guaranteed to all persons above the age of 60 years, who might otherwise be left uncared for and vulnerable, and they will be provided with cereals at subsidised rates and minimum cloth requirement. All the pensioners drawing Rs. 500 or below per month will also be made eligible for these benefits.

Education

The National Front will accord the greatest importance to raising the level of national investment in education. It will be the endeavour of the National Front government to raise the investment to the level of 6 per cent of the national income as the Kothari Commission had recommended. The effort will be to achieve this target by the end of 1995.

Universalisation of elementary education will receive the urgent attention of the National Front government. It will be our endeavour to achieve compulsory universalisation of elementary education for children up to the age of 14 by the end of 1995. All children will be imparted elementary education in their mother tongue.

Vocational education at secondary stage needs to be restructured on a large to make education employment-oriented. The National Front government will take necessary and early steps to forge interactive linkages between productive establishments outside the schools. Such vocationalisation of education will be linked to self-employment in agriculture and industry thereby enabling the young to earn while they learn.

The National Front believes that all children should have access to the same standard and type of education. The National Front government will rectify elitist aberrations in the educational system.

It will abolish capitation fee and other distortions in our educational system. The New Education Policy, introduced by the present government, has failed to serve the purpose and will therefore, be reviewed and revised.

The National Front will endeavour to help bring a new spirit to our campuses of higher education and foster the growth of research and innovative thinking. It will also give a vigorous push to adult education.

The National Front considers education of the minorities, both religious and linguistic, and of women to be a national responsibility and will take vigorous steps to see that the constraints on their educational progress are removed, as early as possible, through planned and concerted action.

Language Policy

Use of regional languages in administration at state level and education at all levels shall be promoted. Pandit Nehru's assurance regarding language policy will be implemented and all efforts will be taken to promote Indian languages. Gujral Committee's recommenda- tions on Urdu will be implemented. The Eighth Schedule will be extended to respond to the urges of other linguistic groups.

Art and Culture

The National Front government will take steps to democratically evolve a national Cultural Policy through encouragement of and respect for different cultural identities and their manifestations. But, the present government has been promoting 'Sarkari Culture' with great fanfare.

The National Front government will promote classical and folk traditions in arts, crafts, music, theatre, dance etc., and encourage them through traditional institutions and schools, which evolved and sustained them for hundreds of years. Expensive and ostentatious centrally-sponsored festivals and synthetic utsavs will be abandoned in favour of a multitude of local initiatives and talents.

Schemes for giving financial support to artists will be reviewed and strengthened so as to encourage them in their creative pursuits.

A comprehensive National Cultural Policy will be formulated.

Health and Family Welfare

It is evident that there has been a serious breakdown in health services in the country. Even the nation's capital has recently witnessed out-break of Cholera and Gastroenteritis epidemics. Preventive, promotive and rehabilitative strategies have failed. Likewise, there has been a serious failure in providing services to the weaker sections, specially in remote rural areas.

The National Front will give utmost priority to remedy this sordid state of affairs. Implementation of the Alma Ata Declaration which assures Health for all by 2000 A.D., will be the major plank of our policy on health and family welfare. Specially it would mean:

a. Promoting community self-reliance,
b. Strengthening social control over health services, and
c. Improving health status by strengthening water supply, environment sanitation, nutrition, employment, housing etc.

While population control will be brought about be a resolute multi-pronged endeavour, the National Front believes that development is the best contraceptive. The present target approach in family planning will be revised to promote and popularise use of contraceptive methods, as well as provide suitable incentives and disincentives. The problem of population growth will be tackled by making various efforts to create conditions where a small family becomes meaningful to the people. The focus will be on reduction in infant mortality, women's education and employment. The National Front will endeavour to bring down the rate of population growth from 2.1 per cent to 1.2 per cent by 2000 A.D.

The National Front will encourage and strengthen indigenous systems of medicine like Ayurveda and Siddha, Unani, Homeopathy and Nature Cure. Research and Educational facilities and employment opportunities in these systems of medicines will be promoted.

Occupational health hazard is a serious area of concern. The National Front government will see to it that disasters like the Bhopal Gas tragedy are not repeated in future. The rehabilitation of Bhopal Gas victims will be treated as a national responsibility.

The drug policy will be revised in line with the recommendations of the Hathi Committee. The reduction in the prices of life-saving drugs and their availability are also part of the National Front's health policy.

Housing as a Right

The National Front will endeavour to develop housing and public transport on a large scale to meet the growing needs of the urban population. The focus of urban development will be shifted from the four metropolises and a score of big cities to thousands of small medium towns. The National Front will introduce a new levy on the urban rich to develop slums into liveable shelters. Environmental considerations will be accorded priority in all urban and rural landscaping.

Cooperative ownership in urban housing will be promoted on a large scale to ensure shelter for all. Special schemes will be launched to provide the rural poor with adequate housing within the next five years. Developed house sites will also be provided to the poor in urban areas. Footh-path dwellers will be provided shelters.

Ex-serviceman

The National Front reaffirms its commitment to the principle of "one-rank-one pension" for ex-servicemen. The welfare of ex-servicemen, hitherto the exclusive responsibility of state governments, will be made a joint concern of central and state governments, with effective monitoring. Steps will be taken to provide meaningful post-retirement employment to defence personnel.

Youth

Many of the ills that we are suffering from have their genesis in the decline of national character, intellectual degeneration and the disappearance of a sense of discipline. To rejuvenate the society with influx of dedicated youth, special emphasis will be laid on moral and physical education of the young, alongwith their intellectual evolution. Time-tested programmes of N.C.C., N.S.S., participation in literacy campaign, Bharat Scouts and Guides, etc. shall be given added impetus.

Special efforts will be made to promote sports and games among the youth and enhance the prestige and honour of India in the national and international sports and games. Schemes will be developed to catch the young with potential, talent and train them in sports and co-curricular activities.

To promote self-employment among the educated and skilled youth, a low interest loan of Rs. 50,000 will be provided, along with a scheme for training in appropriate trades and crafts and necessary infrastructural support.

VI

FOREIGN POLICY

The National Front's foreign policy is based on India's traditional values and beliefs, enshrined in the concepts of non-alignment and on the changing realities of the international scene — the world's gradual transition from conflict and confrontation to dialogue, mutual understanding and peaceful cooperation.

India can play its legitimate role in the changing world only by adopting a comprehensive foreign policy which integrates diplomacy, defence, economic and cultural policies as well as technological cooperation.

National Front's foreign policy will reject any manipulation from outside. It will strengthen global peace initiatives, the process of nuclear disarmament adopted by USSR and USA, and will strive for similar limitations to be placed on conventional and chemical weapons. The National Front will pursue the policy of non-alignment and strengthen the non-alignment movement. The NAM will be persuaded to play a more active role in advancement of South-South Cooperation and to diffuse regional tensions. In a spirits of cooperation and mutuality of interests the role of SAARC will be strengthened and furthered. It will also strengthen the positive role of the U.N.

The establishment of New International Economic and Information Orders will be fully supported. It expresses full solidarity with anti-colonial and anti-apartheid struggles, and supports the Palestinians' right of self-determination, the Namibians' struggle for independence, Nicaragua's fight against outside interference, the struggle of the Saharwi nationalists and the South African people's struggle against the racist regime.

The National Front government will take bold and creative initiatives to weave a new pattern of cooperative relationship with the neighbours. India's friendship with her traditional friends in South, South East Asia and West Asia will be further strengthened. The National Front will strive to secure the safety and security of the Tamils in Sri Lanka and promote lasting peace and amity amongst all sections of population in that country. It shall restore our friendly relations with Sri Lanka by withdrawing the Indian Peace Keeping Force.

With Nepal, negotiations will be started on all issues of contention to find an amicable solution. The National Front will help strengthen the economy of Nepal and honour her self-respect. The National Front will offer to Pakistan mutual withdrawal of VISA restrictions and promotion of bilateral commerce and trade.

The National Front recognises the value of traditional friendship between

India and USSR and will strive to further strengthen it while making all efforts to improve friendly relations with USA and other western countries. The National Front believes that normalisation of Sino-Indian relations is in the interests of both countries and will make efforts to improve and expand them without sacrificing national interests.

National Security

The security of the Nation has been gravely endangered by the Rajiv Gandhi government and made vulnerable to outside pressures. Total absence of a national security doctrine, *ad hoc* decision making, and easy resort to importing arms, often for extraneous considerations and kickbacks, have all adversely affected the nation's security.

The assessment of external threats to the security of the country should be based on a careful study of the strategic environment. Instead, it has been tailored to the ruling party's immediate needs to gain support for itself. Defence and Diplomacy, which are two sides of the same coin, continue to be pursued in an irrational and arbitrary manner by the present government. Moreover, they are implemented independently of each other, creating confusion all around.

The National Front holds that it is necessary to evolve an overall security doctrine for India, which will be convincingly peace-oriented. The doctrine would take a total view of defence rather than a fractured service by service approach, which is the case at present and would give a central place to self-reliance in defence matters.

Towards this end, the National Front government will establish a NATIONAL SECURITY COUNCIL under the chairmanship of the Prime Minister. The National Security Council will help evolve a consensus on our foreign and defence policies and coordinate with various Ministries and Departments connected with national security.

Nuclear Policy

While committing itself to the peaceful uses of nuclear energy India cannot ignore the proximity of nuclear weapon and non-nuclear weapon powers in the region and must take that into account in evolving her security doctrine and it must keep its options open. The National Front government will work for removal of the discriminatory clauses of the NPT.

IN CONCLUSION

The National Front reiterates its commitment to the policies and programmes spelt out in this manifesto. Burdened by the price rise, hurt by violence, fractured by communalism and shamed by corruption at the top, the nation longs for relief. At last, the hour of change has struck. It is for the people of India to ring it in with their votes.

5

THE SURVEY, 1990

1990, which is covered in the present volume, is an year which stands apart from most previous years and is distinguished for events and happenings of no ordinary nature or dimension in Independent India's political and administrative history. This was the year when the central government discovered itself placed under the control of a political party other than the Congress. True, the earlier period 1977-79 had seen the rule by a non-Congress Party, but the latter was generally viewed as an exception rather than a rule, as an aberration or temporary aberration. The political scenario in 1989 was qualitatively different. The Congress at this time stood like an ageing organisation under indecisive political leadership, riddled with corruption, internal intrigues, cliques, factions. If it did not split it was because the Party still preferred clinging to a voter-winning personality which in its eye Rajiv Gandhi looked like at the time though this was being increasingly disproved.

In 1989 election, the Congress, which barely five years ago, commanded nearly three-fourths majority in the Lok Sabha and got votes which even Jawaharlal Nehru's Congress could not win during the height of that charismatic leader's popularity. In 1989 election the same Congress (I) uneviable figure of 200 in a house of 542 members. The government was formed by the National Front, a coalition comprising Janata Dal, Telegu Desam Party, Dravid Munnetra Kazgam (DMK), Congress(S), Assam Gana Parishad, which had emerged as the second largest party in the Lok Sabha. For the first time in Independent India, a coalition government was constituted at the centre. The National Front under Vishwanath Pratap Singh was a minority government.

As regards the minority government, it was the second occasion of its kind, the first one being the Indira Gandhi's government after the famous split in 1969. The minority National Front was supported from outside by two parties of plainly dissimilar orientations, namely the Bharatiya Janata Party and the Left Front consisting of the Communist Party of India (Marxist), Forward Bloc, Revolutionary Socialist Party. The year saw two governments, both being minority ones. The first, V.P. Singh led National Front, as said earlier, was a coalition also, making it vulnerable and fragile. It fell in November 1990; and a break-away group, calling itself as the Janata Dal Socialist commanding the support of less than 60 MPs formed the government. It was supported from outside by the Congress (I) — a strange spectacle of the Janata Dal (S) with 54 MPs in it, all defecting from the parent Janata Dal, running the Government of India with the support, from outside of another much, much bigger party. The second minority government was even more vulnerable: that the Congress was using the group of defectors as a cover-up and twisting the latter's tail should be a safe guess.

Almost as a rule, a coalition in India provides for the office of a deputy prime ministership (or deputy chief ministership) even though the Constitution of India is absolutely silent on it. The Administrative Reforms Commission (1966-70), had recommended the setting up of a deputy prime minister in India to relieve the political chief of part of his undoubtedly enormous workload and to facilitate better co-ordination among central ministries. But the recommendation was not accepted — and wisely. The final view taken was that a deputy prime minister's appointment should be left to the prime minister of the day. This has merit. In a sound political and administrative system, number two post should as a rule remain vacant, with no one earmarked for it. A deputy prime minister becomes, naturally, an aspirant for the top post, which must be avoided, and which is all the same embarrassing to the prime minister. At any rate, the appointment of a deputy prime minister ought to be left to the prime minister who is to take the decision, depending on his own perception and capabilities. Coming to India, the year 1990 was an year characterised by the presence on the political scene a deputy prime minister, and a lot of time was necessarily spent in sorting out inter-personal problems.

A word on the coalitional government in India seems necessary. The general perception of a coalitional government in India is not very positive, such a view being conditioned largely, by the British perception, articulated in the observation 'Britain is not in line with coalitions'. This is not a very rational view. The Congress Party was a leviathan, and when it suffered an electoral defeat, the space vacated cannot — and could not be — filled by another single party. Party building is, among others, an intricate time-consuming process, and thus viewed a coalition alone could replace the Congress — at any rate at the present stage of India's political development.

Equally necessary it is to reflect on the legitimacy of a minority government — an aspect on which the Constitution again is absolutely silent. In a way, minority-ism is virtually inherent in the principle of voting adopted in India under which the candidate obtaining the largest number of votes cast is declared elected even though he might have obtained a minority of the total votes in the constituency. In this sense of the number of votes in a constituency, all governments right since the commencements of the Constitution have been minority oneness.

Even under the present principle of voting the government of Indira Gandhi after the split in the Congress in 1961 was a minority one surviving with the parliamentary support of the Communist Party and the AIDMK. Most conspicuously, the year 1990 has been a year of minority governments; both the V.P. Singh government and the succeeding Chandra Shekhar government have been minority ones.

In this age of popular sovereignty and more so in a country where ultimate power ostensible resides in 'we, the people of India', all governments have to behave in a most circumsect manner ever conscious of limitedness of their mandate, constitutionality of their administrative behaviour and supremacy of law of rule. A minority government by its very definition has not been explicitly mandated by the people to rule, its legitimacy being, always open to challenge. In other words, it must resist initiating itself in areas which do not command society's near unanimity and which instead are of controversial nature. It must not launch itself on issues which have not been sufficiently debated in the society, leading to an emergence of common agreement on the course of action. If controversy persists the matter may be shelved and should be taken up after the general election.

It is not merely sufficient for a minority government, more so a minority behind it. A minority regime is by shorn of majority support; and it is malicious on its part to talk about legislative backing. Even a majority democratic government in a democracy must as a principle steer clear of moved which may divide the society, and particularly a minority government, particularly, must conduct itself with utter humility and circumspection. A developing society like India is replete with problems on which nearly complete unanimity prevails in the society and the party in power shall not find itself briefless if it is pleased to act sincerely and efficiently in such areas.

One may be excused to dilate on the political philosophy of a modern government in the foregoing, but its justification lies in the fact that the year 1990 was the year of minority government, and in future also it form of government, may get repeated.

The question of accountability becomes apt in the light of the events of 1990. As already stressed, a minority government by its very definition enjoys but a level of legitimacy. The minority National Front government under V.P. Singh was being propped up as a result of support assured by the Bharatiya Janata Party and the Leftist Front. On 23 September the BJP announced the withdrawal of its support, and with this the National Front government ought to have immediately resigned or faced dismissal. Instead, it sought an unnecessarily long time to convene the Lok Sabha session to prove — or confirm — its minority. The interval was long enough to tempt it to indulge in horse-trading, which is a bane of Indian politics. A minority government ought not to be allowed grace period.

Importance of Election Manifesto

The year under review is bound to be remembered to the apparently high level of importance which the ruling National Front attached to its election manifesto. Indeed, it was perhaps for the first time in India's political history that an election manifesto received such serious sustained attention by its political party regardless of whether it was prepared thoughtfully or otherwise. In the eyes of the National Front, the election manifesto appeared as a most revered document which could even supersede or trespass the Constitution of India in case of seeming conflict between the two. It is common knowledge that an election manifesto in India is prepared hurriedly and hastily, and is hardly carefully read by its party's own leadership before its finalisation. No political party is equipped with a research wing worth the name. What therefore go in India into a manifesto are the board wishes and intentions of the party. Nor do the members of the public care to read it. It is also notable that the election speeches made by various parties are free wheeling and unrestricted and oblivious of the manifesto contents. The opening preamble of the National Front manifesto does not care even once to refer to the high priority deserved by the Mandal Report on Backward Classes. 'Our Pledge', the Chapter II of the manifesto, is equally conspicuous by absence of any priority mention of the Mandal prescription. One should take the case of Janata Dal. For V.P. Singh, the Bofors political corruption and Rajiv Gandhi's alleged misdeeds were the favourite topics of public debate. At any rate, no one would dare assert that its leaders were loudly and vociferously advocating the Party resolve to implement the Mandal Report. Yet when the Party formed the government despite being in minority began to swear by its the Mandal report. Apropos of this, for the first time, an election manifesto acquired primacy of attention, and the public lesson is that parties must explain their respective manifestos to the voters so that the latter know what they are exactly voting for, and why.

The importance which the National Front apparently attached to the election manifesto may not, however, bear a very close scrutiny. To give but one example, the election manifesto contained not a single word on or about Dr. B.R. Ambedkar (1890-1958) the chairman of the Drafting Committee of the Constitution. Suddenly, the Party discovered its obligation towards the Constitution's chief architect, celebrated his birth anniversary with great pomp and show. All this suited the National Front politically. According to the widely circulated speculation, Vishwa Nath Pratap Singh, the Prime Minister, wanted to outwit his former Deputy Prime Minister Devi Lal, and to neutralise the latter, Singh turned to Mandal and used his report to beat him. The claim, therefore, that the election manifesto constituted the National Front's basic text is empirically not sustainable. If certain proposals contained in the manifesto were given closer attention it was primarily because these were politically paying. V.P. Singh's chief concern is — and was — to create vote-bank or banks in his favour.

Upper Age for Civil Service Recruitment

The earliest administrative change announced by the National Front was early in January itself, this relating to raising the upper age of entry in the higher civil service in India by two years to 28 years. The fixing of the lower and upper ages for appearing at the competitive examination has been publicly debated ever since the adoption of open competition for public recruitment in 1854. These years are purported broadly to correspond with the college leaving years of British youth. When the upper age of 23 was prescribed for the competitive examination for the Indian Civil Service, the Indian public opinion criticised it, insisting on a higher upper age, the plea being the late start of education in India. The demand for raising the upper age to 28 in India is made by the champions of the rural lobby. The argument adduced is that education in rural areas and in lower income group families start late with the inevitable result that the rural youth completes his graduation at a somewhat higher age, necessitating a modification in the upper age for entry. It may perhaps he in the higher interest of the society to keep the entry age at 21-28 years, and what is equally important, not to temper with it from time to time.

In a way, chance-restriction and age restriction may look to be counter-productive from the larger perspective of social and natural justice. A society like India which is unequal stands divided into what may be called 'early starters' and 'late starters' from the stand point of education. Boys in villages and towns begin their education late which puts them at a distinct disadvantage when compared with the clientele of English medium schools. In short, rural based persons including ones from low income group families are generally late starters in education and need more time than the students of English medium school to become ready for the base for the higher civil service examination. The age, moreover, must not be altered too frequently. Moreover, frequent change in the age-limit introduces an element of uncertainty in the minds of students and makes a non-sense of career-planning on their part.

A more, it seems, was afoot to revert to the earlier administrative arrangement of six-day week thus making Saturday also as a working day. This had been the rule in the Government of India until 1985. In that year, Rajiv Gandhi's government switched over to a five-day week, opening public offices half an hour earlier and closing them half-an-hour later. It was argued that two full holidays would keep the public officials refreshed and energetic, which would raise administrative productivity — at any rate is would not go down simply because of the extra hour of work put in everyday. Putting administrative India on a five-day week was an ill-thought out move. Work-culture in the public administration has already not been very high in India. Punctuality in public offices is more honoured in the breach than in observance. Public functionaries in the government do not view the five-day week as re-arrangement of the working system. It is a common sight to see public functionaries especially those at the lower levels of administration trekking down to their office leisurely although the time clock has already chimed ten, and equally, it is difficult to find them at their seat after 4.30 p.m. That the citizens the tax-payers — are inconvenienced as a result is anybody's guess. But a united civil service resistance to the move in favour of six-day week was sufficient to silence the V.P. Singh government. A *status quo* in the matter prevails. An arrangement which is advantageous to the public officials becomes self-perpetuating in India as any move towards reform is bound to provoke stiff resistance and opposition.

Job Reservation

If the year 1990 is to be viewed as the year of V.P. Singh's National Front government, the latter is to be remembered for its job reservation policy for the backward castes: twenty seven per cent of the jobs in the central government and public undertakings were reserved for them. This has been the year 1990s most controversial decision and for a long long time to come V.P. Singh is to be praised or denounced, lauded or condemned for the reservation. At one stroke, Vishwanath Pratap Singh released and institutionalised forces in the society which would keep India frequented. This frequentation is bound to be most dangerous, based as it is on other than caste, the classic bane of the Indian society. Earlier, V.P. Singh announced the government's decision to confer on the neo-Buddhists in India all the benefits available to the scheduled castes in the country. If we include — as we must — 15 per cent reserved for scheduled castes and $7^1/_2$ per cent for scheduled tribes. The total percentage jobs for goes to 49.5 per cent with this announcement.

Job reservation announced by the minority V.P. Singh government raises several questions but brief mention may be made of two here. And a cultured society must find satisfactory answers. It is difficult to recall any other public issue which has aroused so much social controversy even bordering on acute acrimony as the Mandal scheme of job reservation. The Mandal Report has vertically divided the society in India. What is more, the cleavages thus created are neither temporary nor shortlived. The issue is about the extent to which a government in a democracy could go in the matter of making public policies. Democracy implies a level of sensitivity to the other views even though it entrusts the task of governance to a particular party based on majority — or to any other minority in a minority government. Democracy has its boundaries, setting a definite limit to the rulers' options and choices. In India, the V.P. government has shown stubbornly inflexible attitude on the Mandal Report even though the opposition to it is widespread and still. A government elected for a five-year term has little moral right to fetter and handicap the society indefinitely by its myopic actions. In other words, the society will have to devise ways of obliging a government to evolve and internalise norms of understanding politeness and circumspection. Controlling the arrogance and obstinacy of the politician is a major problem for the society.

Coming to Babasaheb Bhimrao Ramji Ambedkar, a few comments sure are not entirely impertitent in *The Survey*. An undoubtedly great son of India, Babasaheb as he is addressed today by some politicians, called as 'Dr. Ambedkar' during his life time, has been steadily gaining in his stature and ranking for quite sometime, but it is the year 1990, the National Front's year, which may also be viewed as Babasaheb's year, par excellence. Ambedkar's birthday was declared as a public holiday; his portrait was unveiled in the Central Hall of Parliament. Public places were named after him. Even the setting up of a university was announced in 1990. His crowning glory was reached in 1990 when he was decorated with the country's highest civilian award, the Bharat Ratna. the meteoric posthumous rise of Dr. B.R. Ambedkar proves that it is not enough to render distinguished service to the society, a perquisite of political and consequently social recognition in the contemporary India is the clout one gathers. That modern India is re-writing its history is a proof of how India is redigging its past to politically suite the present. Perhaps, every age.

The award of Bharat Ratna warrants a couple of comments here. How far back in history may one travel for decorational purposes? What are the criteria for award-giving? Bharat Ratna is too serious an issue to be left entirely to the government at the moment in power, much less to a coalition or minority? Should states of the Union of India have no say — as at present — in the matter of conferment? Should not the decision-making process on matters like such award giving he made more broad-based? Is not respectability of the award dependent on keeping it scarce? One should look at the following table to draw his own inference:

Bharat Ratna Awardees

1. C. Rajagopalachari	1954
2. S. Radhakrishnan	1954
3. C.V. Raman	1954
4. Jawaharlal Nehru	1955
5. Bhagwan Das	1955
6. M. Vishweswariya	1955
7. Gobindballabh Pant	1958
8. D.K. Karve	1958

9.	B.C. Roy	1961
10.	P.D. Tandon	1961
11.	Rajendra Prasad	1962
12.	Zakir Hussain	1963
13.	P.V. Kane	1963
14.	Lal Bahadur Shastri[P]	1966
15.	Mrs. Indira Gandhi	1971
16.	V.V. Giri	1975
17.	K. Kamaraj[P]	1976
18.	Mother Teresa	1980
19.	Vinoba Bhave	1983
20.	Khan Abdul Gaffar Khan	1987
21.	M.G. Ramachandran[P]	1988
22.	B.R. Ambedkar[P]	1990
23.	Dr. Nelson Mandela	1990

P—*Posthumous*

The foregoing should be the fit point of departure for making a brief comment on Mahatma Gandhi. The year 1990 was the first year since Independence which spoke the least about the man lovingly called 'Bapu' during his lifetime and 'Father of the Nation' since then. Mahatma Gandhi was encyclopaedic in the range of his activities, and whatever he took up he went into minutest details following up by an action plan. He presided over the Indian social scene for so long that others, in comparison, would truly be regarded as but bearers of the torch blazed by that rearest of the rare. For sometime, a trend was a foot to contain the Mahatma and the space thus seized was getting earmarked to others. Today, Gandhi is losing 'territory' after 'territory', and others are made to thrive at his expense. What is the true role of a historian in such a social context? Is there is a need for a historian of the historians especially when history is running the risk of degenerating into a mouth-piece of contemporary politics.

In June 1990, a not very common event happened: a sitting judge of the High Court, anticipating his transfer to another High Court, resigned in the wake of widespread rumour of corruption charges against him. It was being alleged that a serving judge of the Bombay High Court had his involvement with a woman who was exercising undue influence on his judicial responsibilities. The purpose of writing about this particular case is to reflect on the contemporary judicial behaviour. Administrative corruption is an old subject in India. One also talks about corruption among legislators and parliamentarians including ministers. Judiciary has for long escaped public criticism. Yet many responsible commentators argue albeit privately that lower and middle level seats of judiciary have remained succumbed to corruption for a long time, and if firm remedial measures are not immediately launched even the higher levels of the judiciary may attract adverse criticism. Clearly more marked and pronounced is the legislative deterioration. India's legislative chambers, even at the central level, are becoming less and less serious bodies to discuss national concerns, issues and interests and take the society forward. Wastage of legislative time and resources need cause concern to the society.

Corruption in public life including India's public administration was the dominant symphony of the political music of the preceding years, more so of 1989. This certainly helped the divided opposition parties to come together, and even turn the public opinion against Rajiv Gandhi's Congress (I). But once the National Front was put into power at the centre even though the voters' verdict was neither totally affirmative or negative, the National Front government under V.P. Singh initiated measures to probe into the scandals associated with the previous regime. Not only that practically nothing of use came to be known. The year 1990 was conspicuous by absence of graphic accounts of corruption. This does not indicate or imply the India has effectively solved this problem. For a large section corruption is now virtually accepted as a way of life: so why wailing and breast-beating. Corruption exists in the public bureaucracy at practically all levels and in nearly all spheres of life though it is patently unfair to point everybody in the higher civil service with the same brush. Things came to such a pass that Vinod Pande, the cabinet secretary felt it necessary to issue a circular to the secretaries in March 1990.

Explaining that "it has become necessary to reiterate the obvious because some unfortunate patterns of behaviour have become persistent", Vinod Pande has listed out various actions of government servants which are "reprehensible".

— Undesirable contact with businessmen of whatever nationality.

— Acceptance of lavish and frequent hospitality from businessmen/individuals having official dealings and hosting of lavish entertainment at public expense.

— Consumption of alcoholic drinks in public places.

— Sexual harassment of women officials.

— Misuse of vehicles, telephones, accommodation and other facilities owned by government or PSUs (public sector undertakings).

— Planning stories in the press for furthering private interests or to spread misinformation.

— Acceptance of expensive gifts from individual companies, including foreigners and/or distribution of such items to others at public expense.

— Accepting hospitality from foreigners unless essential in the course of official work.

— Retaining government accommodation beyond authorised period in disregard of government directives.

— Frequent socialisation leading to an impression that some individuals/companies have greater access or influence with the government than others.

— Purchase of shares of companies out of quotas reserved for friends and associates of directors of companies.

This extraordinary letter from the seniormost bureaucrat in the country has gone on to say that "while violation of conduct rules in such cases has always been an offence, serious efforts to enforce them may not always have been taken in the past". Urging the secretaries to "take serious note of violations of this nature and ensure that government servants follow the prescribed code of conduct both in letter and spirit". Vinod Pande has said "apart from disciplinary action in serious cases, such misconduct on the part of officers would necessarily form an important input in decisions regarding their promotions, placements, empanelment for central staffing assignments, etc."

The purpose of this two-pages letter dated 15 March 1990 is to emphasise that "a sense of service to the people should not only be observed by government servants, but also seen to be observed". Senior officers have both to set an example by personal conduct and also to ensure that officers working with them do not deviate from the letter and spirit of the conduct rules. In the same vein, Vinod Pande has written: "The substance and style of functioning of civil servants at all levels must reflect the socio-economic realities of the country and the concerns of the government".

The Survey is silent on many events, otherwise significant of 1990; it does not refer to the Ramjanma Bhoomi-Babri Masjid dispute. It does not give a detailed day-to-day mention of terrorist activities in Kashmir, Punjab and Assam. International events have been kept out of account even though an occurrence like the Iraq-Kuwait crisis; it does not given an exhaustive much less comprehensive account of the terrorism which is today a great menace in several parts including Kashmir, Punjab, Assam, Andhra Pradesh etc. Nor does it refer to the Ramjanma Bhoomi-Babri Masjid dispute. One thing however must be pointed out. The large scale violation of basic human rights committed with unashamed impunity by Uttar Pradesh Chief Minister Mulayam Singh Yadav against a massive chunk of humanity at Ayodhya is a commentary on how thin and superficial is the ruling political leadership's commitment to democracy and human values. Equally, the silence of the champions of human rights movement in India, never tired of talking about 'state terrorism', what was a wanton loosening of police atrocities on the defenceless pilgrims at Ayodhya is both agonising and puzzling.

6

THE ADMINISTRATIVE DIARY, 1990

JANUARY 1990

1 January 1990

The Prime Minister said that the National Front government would present its agricultural policy document before the Budget session of the Parliament.

— A citizen writes about the police:

"I was driving with my wife and her parents when the vehicle began shaking with a horrible, rattling sound. I stopped at the junction of the IIT taxi stand. Unfortunately, the stand was deserted. I was looking around for help when I spotted a traffic police van parked near by. At my wife's coaxin', I went to them for help in changing the tyre. Without any hesitation, the three men in the van, No. DDV 2680, came to my rescue, helping to change the tyre in minutes. When we all profusely thanked them, the proudly said, it was their duty to help (*The Times of India*, 1 January 1990).

— Senior IAS and IPS officers in Madhya Pradesh (M.P.) now expect more promotion avenues. The exit of P. Chidambaram from the government has brought new hope among the senior bureaucrats. Their promotion avenues had been blocked in M.P. following last year's decision of the central government to have non-cadre posts only equivalent to the cadre posts. In IAS there are two Cadre posts and in IPS only one.
The IAS officers of 1959 batch have become secretaries in the government of India but in Madhya Pradesh over a dozen senior officers have been waiting in the wings to get the scale of Rs. 8,000 p.m. (secretary's pay). As far as IPS is concerned, the situation is no better. In several states, IPS officers of even the 1960 batch have become Directors General of Police. But not in M.P.

— The new government is committed to confer the constitutional right to work on the adult citizens.

— The National Front government announced a timebound action plan envisaging right to work, land reforms, a long-term fiscal policy, new support price for agricultural crops, judicial reforms, special programmes for the urban poor, a commission on women, a new three-year import-export policy and amendment of the Official Secrets Act to ensure citizens' right to information and special measures for the minorities.

— The various Ministries have been asked to work out detailed plans for the implementation of these objectives.

— The Delhi Transport Undertaking Mazdoor Sangharsh Samiti, which backed the Janata Dal in the recent Lok Sabha poll, is planning to organize a demonstration on 5 January to protest against the humiliating terms on which the Delhi Transport Corporation says it is ready to take back the workers dismissed during the March 1988, strike.

— The Central Bureau of Investigation (CBI) will from this year onwards focus more on areas of corruption and misconduct by public servants that directly affect the common man. This was disclosed by the Bureau today.

— The Central Board of Film Certification has been transferred to the Ministry of Information and Broadcasting from the Ministry of Human Resource Development. The Information and Broadcasting Ministry thus becomes the nodal agency for matters relating to films.

— The following is the text of the Action Plan released by the government today:

The manifesto of the National Front has presented a concrete programme of action. Ministries and departments have been requested to identify priority areas of action for implementation in a time-bound manner. The first set of points on which the action is under way is listed below. Ministries and departments will prepare comprehensive and detailed action plans on these and other items and announce them separately. Implementation of the action plans will be a matter of highest priority and will be closely monitored.

An outlay of at least 50 per cent of investible resources in the agricultural and rural sectors of the economy will be ensured starting with the Annual Plan for 1990-91.

In order to give farmers a remunerative price for their produce, the following changes are being made in the method of computing support prices:

(i) Introduce a formula for adjusting support prices for inflation from the date of announcement to the time of market.

(ii) Labour will be costed on the basis of actual wages paid or minimum wages, whichever is higher, instead of the present system where it is costed on the basis of actual wages paid when there are lower than the minimum wages.

(iii) Include an element of managerial or entrepreneurial labour in the family labour input and cost this labour at a higher rate than agricultural labour.

The Ministry of Agriculture will appoint an expert committee to recommend ways of implementing these changes and their recommendations will be taken into account in fixing support price for the next kharif season.

"The right to work" will be made a fundamental right and the necessary Bill for amending the Constitution will be introduced in the forthcoming Budget session. An Employment Guarantee Scheme will be implemented progressively.

A comprehensive Constitutional Amendment Bill on Panchayati Raj will be prepared and introduced during the Budget session of Parliament, after discussion with the chief ministers.

Land reforms: The government places the highest importance on land reforms. All land reforms legislation will be incorporated in the Ninth Schedule to the Constitution. Land reforms will continue to be an agenda in the proposed Inter-State Council. A meeting of the chief ministers will be held by April 1990 to finalise a programme of land reform implementation.

A scheme for debt relief up to Rs. 10,000 to small, marginal and landless cultivators and artisans will be finalised during the forthcoming Budget session.

A long-term fiscal policy will be presented during the budget session.

The government is committed to curbing ostentatious and elitist consumption and the measures required in this regard will be taken early.

With a view to pushing up export in a big way and plugging loopholes in the import-export rules and simplifying the procedures:

(i) A new three-year import-export policy will be announced on 1 April 1990.
(ii) Simplified pre-shipment documentation will be finalised and announced on 1 March 1990.
(iii) Export policy will encourage the exports of items with high net foreign exchange content.

The Ministry of Defence shall appoint a committee to examine modalities for implementing a scheme for realising the National Front's commitment to the principle of "one rank one pension" for ex-servicemen. The committee will submit its report by 31 March 1990.

A National Security Council under the chairmanship of the Prime Minister will be set up by April 1990.

Electoral Reforms: A comprehensive Bill on electoral reforms will be introduced in the budget session of Parliament.

A high level Judicial Commission will be set up for appointments and transfers of judges. The necessary Constitutional Amendment Bill is proposed to be introduced in the Budget session. A Bill to amend the Legal Services Authorities Act will be introduced in the budget session with a view to strengthening *Lok Adalats* and legal aid programmes. A Bill for setting up an autonomous corporation for TV and radio has already been introduced on 29 December 1989. It is proposed to have the Bill enacted after a national debate during the Budget session. The government will, by amending the Constitution, guarantee the 'right to information' as a fundamental right. The Bill for the purpose will be introduced during the Budget session. New Bills will be brought in during the Budget session to amend the Indian Post Office Act and the Indian Telegraph Act, ensuring that the citizen's right to privacy is respected. The Indian Post Office (Amendment) Bill, 1986, will be withdrawn. The National Integration Council for reviewing issues relating to national integration, and to make recommendations thereon will be reconstituted. A meeting of chief ministers to consider this matter will be held in January 1990. The proposal in this regard will be finalised thereafter and the first meeting of the Council convened before April 1990.

An amendment of the Official Secrets Act to ensure the citizen's right to information will be carried out. A Bill for this purpose will be introduced in the Budget session.

An Inter-State Council will be set up after the forthcoming elections to the legislative Assemblies of the states. The process of eliciting views of the state governments on the nature of duties to be performed by the Inter-State Council, and its organisation and procedures, will be started straight-away.

Special measures under the 15-Point Programme for minorities will be formulated during the Budget session of Parliament to ensure for minorities adequate implementation of development programmes, representation in employment, enhanced availability of credit and increased facilities for technical education. A committee will be set up before the end of January 1990 to examine the recommendations of the Gujral Committee.

A scheme to ensure that special courts are promptly set up for expeditious disposal of cases relating to caste and communal riots and atrocities will be finalised before March 1990.

The Prevention of Atrocities Act for prevention of atrocities against members of the scheduled castes and scheduled tribes, which is still to be notified, will be made effective by 31 January 1990, after a meeting with state governments.

A cabinet committee will be set up in January 1990 for consideration of the recommendations of the Second Backward Classes Commission (Mandal Commission).

Promotion of workers' participation in the management of industries will be given high priority. A national seminar is being organised for this purpose during January 1990 and further steps will be worked out by the end of February 1990. Necessary legislation will be brought up during the Budge session of Parliament.

A new Industrial Relations Bill will be brought forward during the monsoon session of Parliament, and necessary consultations with all the interests will be completed before the end of May 1990.

Substantial expansion of the existing programmes serving the urban poor will be undertaken from April 1990. These will include:

(i) Provision of basic services and facilities in slums, with particular attention to the needs of women and children.

(ii) A significantly stepped up scheme for providing night shelter for pavement dwellers in major cities; it is hoped to benefit about one lakh persons during 1990-91.

(iii) A comprehensive national housing policy for different sections of society, with specific programmes directed towards the poor, and improving the housing finance system, to be finalised during the Budget session of Parliament.

(iv) Liberation and rehabilitation of scavengers in medium and small towns according to a time-bound programme covering 500 towns annually.

A master plan for providing a net-work of warehouses and godowns, both in public and co-operative sectors, for the entire country will be drawn up by 31 March 1990 to insure farmers against distress sale.

A long-term policy on licensing of sugar mills will be announced by 31 March 1990 to eliminate political favouritism and bureaucratic arbitrariness.

The science and technology programmes will be reviewed to provide emphasis on the needs of rural society especially in the areas of poverty alleviation, water management and land use.

A review of our environmental policy and laws, specially as they effect the tribal population, will be undertaken to ensure that our twin objectives of protection of tribal interests and protection of our environment are pursued in a harmonious manner, by April 1990.

2 January 1990

— The Election Commission again became a one-man body consequent on the President of India's removal of two election commissioners — S.S. Dhanoa (an ex-IAS officer) and V. Seigell (an ex-IPS officer) — who had been appointed on 16 October 1989 by the Congress Ministry. The decision to convert the Election Commission into a single-member body was taken by the cabinet after the Attorney-General's opinion on the matter was elicited.

— Some State Governors appointed by the previous Congress government are soon to be changed.

— A statistics expert in the USA has estimated that in 180 years, non-hispanic Whites in the USA will lose their majority status and will be equal in numbers to the blacks.

— The anti-reservationists in M.P. have threatened to contest all the 320 seats in the M.P. Vidhan Sabha election if its 7-point charter of demands is not accepted:

1. No reservations for the wards of persons who have gained the benefit of the reservation facility.
2. Economic-based reservation.

3. One-time reservation benefit for one person.
4. No reservation during the promotion stage.
5. Declaration of this year as Arakshan Mukti Varsha.
6. Reduction in the percentage of reservation.
7. Reservation for minorities.

— Bimal Jain took over as the new finance secretary, replacing Gopi Arora. Soon after taking charge, he held a meeting with senior officials of the ministry to review the trends in the revenue and expenditure of the central government. Gopi Arora replaces Jalan as the executive director of the International Monetary Fund in Washington, D.C.

5 January 1990

— Rajendra Sekhar, IPS, presently Director-General of Police, Rajasthan, has been appointed Director of the Central Bureau of Investigation.

— The Minister for Information and Broadcasting, P. Upendra, has allayed fears that bureaucrats would control the new set-up for the electronic media, saying:

> "There will be no bureaucrat on the Board except for an Information and Broadcasting official who will act as a postman between the Board and Parliament. Even this post will be temporary."

— The central government today constituted a five-member committee headed by C.H. Hanumanthaiya to undertake a review of the methodology of determining support prices for the farm produce.

A committee to look into various issued relating to the granting of status of industry to agriculture.

6 January 1990

— The government of Bihar transferred three senior officers of commissioner's rank, notwithstanding the directives of the Election Commission to the contrary.

— Prime Minister V.P. Singh today, in a letter to the President of India, has suggested that the latter should return the Controversial Indian Post Office (Amendment) Bill, 1986, to the Houses of Parliament with a message requesting that they reconsider the Bill, especially Clause 16.

Clause 16 conferred power on authorities specified there in to intercept postal articles in certain cases. There had been widespread concern at the time of adoption of the Bill that the section would seriously interfere with the citizens' right to privacy. The National Front in its manifesto had assured the nation that this Act would be amended if it came into power.

A copy of the opinion of the former Attorney-General of India, K. Parasarthi, who also felt that the proposed section (Clause 16, which was to amend section 26 of the Indian Post Office Act) would be unconstitutional was also forwarded by the Prime Minister to the President.

The Bill has been awaiting the President's assent since it was forwarded to the then President of India, Giani Zail Singh, who left the controversial matter to be handled by his successor.

The President had suggested that the opinion of the Attorney-General of India should be obtained. Accordingly, the Attorney-General of India was consulted on the constitutional and legal validity of the various provisions contained in the Bill.

— Devi Lal, Deputy Prime Minister, assured a group of students that efforts would be made to raise the upper age limit from 26 to 30 for the Civil Service Examination and increase the number of chances to appear for it. The same students met the Prime Minister, V.P. Singh, over the issue but expressed dissatisfaction at not being assured that some action would be taken immediately.

7 January 1990

— The elected house of the Municipal Corporation of Delhi has been dissolved. The order, the third in the civic body's 32-year history, was issued today by the central government.

Unlike the two previous occasions, the powers of the House will not be exercised by the Municipal Commissioner but by the Delhi administrations chief secretary.

— The National Capital Region project has not taken off primarily because of inadequate financial provisions by the central government, the Balakrishnan (Sarkaria) Committee on reorganisation of the Delhi set-up, has observed in its report.

8 January 1990

— The Seminar on Labour Participation in Management starts at New Delhi.

9 January 1990

— Prime Minister to meet public between 3.30 and 4.30 p.m. on all working days at his residence.

— Seventy-nine J&K police officials have been transferred with effect from today. They have been transferred keeping in view the deteriorating law and order situation in the state. Police officials between the rank of assistant sub-inspector rank are in the transfer list.

— Ajit Singh, Minister of Industry, has written to the home minister suggesting that the upper age limit for candidates competing for civil services should be raised to 30 years. Also, candidates should be allowed five attempts instead of the present three. He, in his letter, pointed out that the students coming from rural and backward areas in the country are experiencing severe limitations and constraints in competing for their due share of jobs in the government and public sector undertakings.

— Raj Kumar Bhargawa was appointed chief secretary in Uttar Pradesh bypassing the claims of several senior officials.

— The chief minister of Bihar, Jagannath Mishra, sprang a surprise by telling Press reporters that the government would not abide by the Election Commission's directives and refuted the charge that article 324 of the Constitution was being violated in the process of effecting large-scale transfers.

The Election Commission had taken exception to the large-scale transfers and postings of senior IAS and IPS officials and had directed the state government last month to stop the process.

Mishra was of the view that the government was within its rights to transfer officials till the date the election was notified. He maintained that transfers were ordered in the interest of the people and not with an eye to the elections.

8 January 1990

— President R. Venkataraman has returned the controversial Indian Post Offices (Amendment) Bill to Parliament for reconsideration. The Bill seeks to confer power on specified authorities to intercept postal articles. Former President Giani Zail Singh did not give assent to the Bill. Mr Venkataraman got various aspects of the measure examined and sought the opinion of the Attorney-General who said that the legislation was unconstitutional.

— Prime Minister V.P. Singh had written to the President on 6 January urging him to return the Bill to Parliament for reconsideration. Venkataraman in his reply today intimated the Prime Minister that he had acceded to this request. The Postal Bill has been returned to Rajya Sabha chairman S.D. Sharma with the request that the Houses of Parliament may reconsider the Bill, especially Clause 16.

— The Sarkaria Committee report on Reorganisation of Delhi's set-up has recommended setting up separate municipalities in various areas of the Capital on the basis of population and other relevant factors in place of the Municipal Corporation of Delhi monolith.

9 January 1990

— The Congress (I) Party forms the Ministry in Goa.

— The All-Party Meeting on Electoral Reform convened by the National Front government decided to set up a committee to suggest poll reforms.

10 January 1990

— Disturbed over the reports of transfer of officials, the Election Commission today asked the Bihar government to explain the transfer of senior officials in the state in violation of the Commission's ban since last month in view of the coming Assembly election.

— The Lokayukta Act of Andhra Pradesh is to cover the Chief Minister too. Also, all ministers are to disclose their assets to the Speaker and these would also be released to the Press.

— Differences between Chief Minister S.C. Shukla, Principal home secretary Nirmala Buch and Director-General of Police P.D. Malviya are brewing over the implementation of certain transfer orders. The latter two are not carrying out certain transfer orders in the police department.

— The centre is considering re-introducing the six-day week system for all offices throughout the country by the end of this month.

The five-day week was first introduced on 3 June 1985, and the working day was made longer by an hour to make up for the lost hours on Saturday, the additional holiday. Under the five-day week, the ministries work from 9.00 a.m. to 5.00 p.m. with a half-hour lunch break. The attached and subordinate offices observe 10.00 a.m. to 6.00 p.m. schedule with a half-hour lunch break.

11 January 1990

— The proposed reintroduction of the six-day week by the central government in its offices by this month-end is most likely to be resented by its women employees who had found the five-day system a great relief.

The five-day working week had been introduced by the previous government in June 1985, less than six months after assumption of its office. The move was hailed as a major administrative reform aimed at achieving higher efficiency and greater staff satisfaction.

The Congress-I government had conducted a couple of surveys to estimated the impact of the new system in one of these exercises, the government had found that women were particularly relieved as the six-day week meant heavy strain on them what with responsibilities to cope at home and office both.

The working women with young children particularly welcome the new system as they could now devote much more attention to the young ones who specially needed their mothers' care.

Although the Union Cabinet is learnt to have discussed the issue and opinion the new government favours reintroduction of the earlier system though a final decision is yet to be taken.

The government may have to hold discussions with the staff of the Joint Consultative Machinery as the JCM was consulted when the new system was introduced. It may not be easy for the government to bypass the JCM in such a matter as this non-statutory body is consulted on issues concerning the staff with a view to promote harmonious relations.

The administrative reforms were high on the "priority" of the Rajiv Gandhi government. After the consultations, the five-day week was introduced on 3 June 1985. It was felt the change would "improve efficiency". It was stated that the employees would work for $37^1/_2$ hours per week as before.

The new system which gave an extra holiday on Saturday was to provide "opportunity to the government servants to go out on excursions during weekends with their families, besides encouraging cultural and other recreational activities all of which are expected to improve their physical and mental health and consequently improve productivity and efficiency".

An early survey by the Department of Administrative Reforms and Public Grievances with respect to some ministries and departments did not indicate any all in work output in terms of quantity and quality after the introduction of the system.

The previous government held the view that the five-day system had been accepted well and there was no need to revert to the old system.

At one time an offer was made to reduce the working hours subject to matching curtailment of holidays or regular leave but the proposal was turned down by the staff of the JCM.

The new government is learnt to have consulted various ministries and departments on the issue and felt that the objectives for which the five-day week was introduced had not been achieved.

Should the government go in finally for the six-day week, it is likely to "invoke" the discipline "clause" as the conduct of the employees for not staying on duty during the fixed hours could be interpreted as a neglect of normal discipline.

13 January 1990

— Dr Karan Singh has resigned as Indian Ambassador to the United States after a five-month tenure, on the advice of the V.P. Singh government.

— General V.N. Sharma, the Chief of the Army Staff, has said that he increasing trends towards utilisation of the army for assistance to civil authorities could have adverse effects on training and operational preparedness particularly if these were for prolonged durations.

14 January 1990

— General K.V. Krishan Rao, Governor of Jammu & Kashmir, has resigned.

— India and Maldives have agreed in principle to abolish the visa system for travel between the two countries to become the first SAARC member-states to take such a step.

— The government has decided to drastically curtail procedural formalities in exports.

15 January 1990

— Sam Patroda will continue to be the chairman of the Telecom Commission though he has been divested of his position as Adviser to the Prime Minister on technology missions.

— The long-awaited one-time road tax payment scheme doing away with the yearly payment and bringing relief to lakhs of private vehicle owners will come into effect in Delhi from 9 February 1990.

— The Bihar government today agreed to the Election Commission's suggestion not to transfer any officials connected with the elections till the Assembly polls are over.

— Railway Minister George Fernandes today dissolved all the Zonal Railway Users Consultative Councils, the Divisional Railway Users Consultative Committees and the National Railway Users Consultative Council.

16 January 1990

— President R. Venkataraman called upon all Governors to resign their posts in the light of changed political circumstances.

18 January 1990

— Elections for the state legislatures of Arunachal Pradesh, Bihar, Gujarat, Himachal Pradesh, Madhya Pradesh, Maharashtra, Orissa and Rajasthan and the Union Territory of Pondicherry will be held on 27 February 1990.

19 January 1990

— The central government decided to bracket Neo-Buddhists with the Scheduled Castes, if they belonged to the Scheduled Castes before converting to Buddhism.

20 January 1990

— The refusal of the top civil servants to order appointment of the new Director-General of Police has developed into an unprecedented situation in Madhya Pradesh. The senior civil servants — chief secretary R.S. Khanna and principal home secretary Nirmala Buch — are understood to have refused to comply with the orders of chief minister Shyama Charan Shukla for the appointment of a new director-general of Police in place of the present DGP, P.D. Malviya. P.D. Malviya does not order large-scale transfer of police officials on political promptings, especially on the eve of Assembly elections.

— Noted nuclear scientist Raja Ramana was inducted into the Central Council of Ministers as the Minister of State for Science.

— A Cabinet committee under the chairmanship of Prime Minister V.P. Singh has been set up to give a new thrust to the 15-Point Programme for the welfare of the minorities. It has identified 41 minority concentration districts in India for intensive welfare programmes.

22 January 1990

— The Central Bureau of Investigation has registered a criminal case in respect of allegations of corruption in the Bofors gun contract with India. Win Chadha and G.P. Hinduja are among the 14 accused mentioned in the first information report.

25 January 1990

— T.N. Chaturvedi, Comptroller and Auditor-General of India is awarded Padma Vibhushan by the Government of India.

— Officers of the public sector undertakings following the central dearness allowance pattern based on the High Power Pay Committee recommendations will resort to country-wide strike from 30 January 1990, if the government does not correct the anomalies in the pay revision.

27 January 1990

— Bad external debt of $ 50 billion complicated by short-term borrowing could compel India to turn to the International Monetary Fund (IMF), according to I.G. Patel, former Governor of the Reserve Bank of India.

— The National Front government is under heavy pressures on the appointment of new Governors. This is one of the reasons why even seven days after the present Governors sent in their resignations on demand from the President the new appointments have not be made. The constituents of the ruling coalition and the two parties supporting it from outside want their own men to be appointed.

— The Central Administrative Tribunal has quashed the orders of termination of services of a senior IAS officer of the M.P. cadre, V.P. Seth.

28 January 1990

— The V.P. Singh government is firm on farm loans waiver and the beginning is to be made in the coming Budget session (March 1990).

30 January 1990

— H.D. Pillai, Additional Commissioner of Police (Security), suspended from service on the charge of alleged dereliction of duty in the Indira Gandhi assassination case.

— The Registrar-General of Census Commission, Government of India, has in his letter to the M.P. chief secretary, R.S. Khanna, expressed concern over changes in the administrative units of the state on the eve of the Census operations. The Census operations in 1990-91 will be seriously jeopardised if such changes in the boundaries of the administrative units are effected at this stage, he has warned. This came in the wake of the violation of the directive from the central Home Ministry that after October 1989, no changes in the administrative units should be made till June 1991.

— Six new tahsils of Madhya Pradesh — Gurur (Durg), Ranapur (Jhabua), Ambagarh (Rajnandgaon), Barghat (Seoni), Tildo (Raipur) and Chorai (Chhindwara) — have been set up in the last three months to please the political bosses in view of the Assembly election.

FEBRUARY 1990

1 February 1990

— President of India to-night replaced Governors of 13 states and one union territory, and shifted Nurul Hasan from Orissa to West Bengal. Among those who have been left untouched are the Governors of Tamil Nadu (P.C. Alexander), Goa (Khurshid Alam Khan), Karnataka (P. Venkatasubbiah) and Nagaland (Gopal Singh).

— D.P. Chattopadhyaya, an ex-Congressman, Yagya Dutta Sharma, BJP leader, and Telugu Desam Rajya Sabha MP whose term has just ended, Satyanarayana Reddy are among the new Governors. The appointments are as follows:

1. D.P. Chattopadhyaya	Rajasthan
2. Yagya Dutta Sharma	Orissa
3. B. Satyanarayana Reddy	U.P.
4. Yunus Saleem (former Minister of State for Railways)	Bihar
5. C. Subramaniam	Maharashtra
6. Kunwar Mehmood Ali	M.P.
7. Krishna Kant	A.P.
8. Raghunath Reddy	Tripura
9. B. Rachaiah, Janata leader of Karnataka	H.P.
10. Admiral R.H. Tahiliani	Sikkim
11. Dhanik Lal Mandal (Janata leader)	Haryana
12. Sarup Singh	Kerala
13. Swaraj Kaushal	Mizoram

— The Punjab government orders transfers affecting six IAS officers.

— In selecting Governors, the two guidelines adopted have been to ensure that no retired judges of the High Courts or the Supreme Court are included and that no one who has been defeated in the recent elections gets a gubernatorial assignment.

— The Home Minister, Mufti Mohammad Sayeed said, he had discussed the Governors appointments with the respective chief ministers.

— The National Front government since coming to power has appointed Jagmohan as the Governor of Jammu and Kashmir, N.K. Mukerji as Governor of Punjab. Air Chief Marshal (Retd.) Arjun Singh was appointed as Lt.-Governor of Delhi

2 February 1990

— Sixty officers of the Delhi Administration subordinate services cadres have been promoted to the city civil service. This number is a record of a sort. The promotions have been made to the Delhi and Andaman and Nicobar Islands Civil Service (DANICS). The DANICS is the Class B officer service of the union territory, the feeder one of the IAS. Today's promotions are a result of two-year old judgments of the Supreme Court and the Central Administrative Tribunal: the seniority list of more than 10,000 employees had to be redone.

3 February 1990

— The security arrangements for Rajiv Gandhi, the former Prime Minister, have been scaled down. The Gandhi family is now provided with four bullet-proof cars, one for each member of the family, along with a pilot car and four escort cars, all bullet proof. This was about one-third or one-fourth of what he had as Prime Minister.

— Since the Special Protection Group (SPG) had been set up under an Act of Parliament for the protection and security of the Prime Minister, its job now was in relation to V.P. Singh. The safari clad SPG men who were seen around Rajiv Gandhi are now to be replaced by the Black Cat commandos of the National Security Guards (NSG)

— A 100-Member new National Integration Council was announced today with V.P. Singh as its chairman. It has about 20 members more than the last one.

4 February 1990

— The Comptroller and Auditor-General of India T.N. Chaturvedi, has called for constitutional immunity against personal attacks on his office on the lines of the privileges enjoyed by the courts and the legislatures.

— Prime Minister V.P. Singh said in a public meeting that an inter-state council would be established after the assembly elections due in nine states in February itself.

5 February 1990

— About 125 security personnel are deployed to protect Rajiv Gandhi, the former Prime Minister.

— A big shake-up in the Doordarshan set up began today when the portfolios of four top Mandi House (headquarters) officials were re-allocated.

— The Delhi Administration has set up a Department of Urban Improvement for a properly balanced and integrated development of all parts of Delhi.

— The deputy chairman of the Planning Commission, Ramkrishna Hegde today called for changing the priorities of planning to focus on development of the human being. If planning is not relevant to the well being of the poorest of the poor, then it has no meaning at all, he said.

7 February 1990

— The government constituted an advisory committee with Bhanu Pratap Singh as its chairman to examine the proposal about declaring agriculture as an industry. The terms of reference of the committee is to review the present policies and programmes for the promotion of agricultural development in the country especially with a view to generating export surpluses, and to examine the feasibility of declaring agriculture as an industry.

— Vice-President S.D. Sharma urged the IAS probationers today to keep the common man in mind despite pressures that may come from diverse quarters—and create better living conditions for him. In a democratic set up, the right to take decisions ultimately rests with the elected representatives of the people. The civil servants have a duty to tender their advice after carefully weighing all the pros and cons and keeping in view the wider interests of the common men. The fast pace of economic and sociological changes, resulting from industrialisation and technological advances, had made society quite complex, making the job of the civil servants very challenging, particularly in a welfare state.

Earlier in 1990, the Election Commission of India suggested the creation of an all-India service to conduct the periodical democratic exercise of the people choosing their rulers.

— A committee of ministers has been constituted to oversee the economic development of the north-eastern region, Home Minister, Mufti Mohammad Sayeed being its chairman. A committee of this nature was first constituted in 1980 and it provided a forum for interaction between chief ministers of north eastern states and the various ministries of the central government.

— Politicisation of the judiciary must stop, the Bar Council of Delhi warned the National Front government today. The Bar Council's chairman protested against the recent appointments of the government law officers and public counsel including the Attorney General of India, the Solicitor General and the Additional Solicitor General of India, on "political grounds".

9 February 1990

— Under the government's drive to wipe out corruption from public administration in U.P. 14 officers from the irrigation department including two superintending engineers, ten executive engineers and two assistant engineers.

— The security arrangement for the former Prime Minister Rajiv Gandhi has been reinforced following a review by the Prime Minister V.P. Singh. The annual expenditure on Gandhi's security how is Rs 1 crore, Rs.25 lakh more than what are earlier incurred. Rajiv Gandhi is now entitled to take two or if necessary three personal security officers when going out of the capital. It was also decided to transfer some of the persons from SPG to Rajiv Gandhi's security by transferring these persons to the Delhi Police. The selection of these persons has been left to Gandhi

— Prime Minister V.P. Singh exhorted the IAS probationers to stand by the socially deprived and afford him justice and fair deal without yielding to pressures from politicians and money-power.

10 February 1990

— A massive backlog of cases characterizes the country's courts. The *lok adalat* system is a useful and viable alternative for speedy and inexpensive justice.

— Prime Minister V.P. Singh has directed that his photographs should not be displayed in any central government office. The earlier practice of putting up photographs of national leaders like Mahatma Gandhi and President will, however, be continued.

— The Punjab government has ordered a top level inquiry into the alleged charges of corruption amounting to several lakhs against a senior IAS officer due to retire shortly. The charges levelled against the senior official included that he had been paid amounts ranging from Rs. 50,000 to Rs. 3 lakh through a former chairman of the Backward Classes Financial Corporation by about two dozen provincial civil services officers and the managing director of the PEPSU Roadways Transport Corporation for postings, reinstatements and out of turn promotions.

— The Congress (I) had spent Rs. 17 crore on its election campaign advertisements during the last 1984 Lok Sabha elections. These included advertisements showing crocodiles, snakes, tigers and other animals to depict the state of affairs in the then opposition. The big-money advertising of the Congress(I) reminded one of the kind commonly seen in American politics.

— The Central Bureau of Investigation (CBI) is going ahead with the investigations into the Rs. 18 crore Czech pistol deal. The first information report in a Delhi Court on 10 April 1988 against Arun Nehru, the minister for internal security in the Rajiv Gandhi government and a civil servant D. P. Singal the then additional secretary in the Ministry of Home Affairs.

— B. Satya Narayan Reddy took oath as the Governor of Uttar Pradesh.

12 February 1990

— The country is likely to see the establishment of the first environment courts shortly, the Environment Minister Maneka Gandhi said today.

14 February 1990

— Indian Airlines Airbus 320 crashed at Bangalore killing 89 passengers.

15 February 1990

— Prime Minister V.P. Singh has asked his colleagues not to accept any donations for the campaign in the coming elections to the state assemblies.

16 February 1990

— R. Prasad, managing director-cum-chairman of the Indian Airlines tendered his resignation on moral grounds following the crash of a newly acquired Airbus 320 at Bangalore on 14 February 1990.

17 February 1990

— A former director-general of police and a former state excise commissioner have jumped into the election fray in M.P. H.M. Joshi, the former DGP, is the candidate of the anti-reservationists from the Bhopal south assembly constituency. D.S. Tomar, a former state excise commissioner, is the Janata Dal candidate from Gwalior.

— The states of Haryana and Ohio in the USA will have a sister state relationship shortly, said Richard Feteste, Governor of Ohio. The exchange of knowledge, skills and research in agriculture and agro-processing industry would be the cornerstone of the special relationship.

18 February 1990

— All the 14 Airbus 320 planes grounded pending a high level enquiry by a committee.

— The Supreme Court told Rajasthan chief secretary V.B.L. Mathur that his plea that his appearance in the state High Court in answer to a contempt petition will humiliate him is "misconceived" and directed him to appear before the high court. The latter had directed him to appear on a notice of contempt for non-compliance with its promotion of police officer K. K. Singh.

— Several thousand employees of Bharat Heavy Electricals Ltd are on a two-day strike demanding implementation of pay revision due since 1986.

21 February 1990

— The opposition United Legislature Front will form the government in Meghalaya. It secured 32 seats, six more than the Congress(I) tally of 26 in the final result announced today.

— The upper age limit for the civil service examination has been raised to 31 years for 1990 only. From 1991 onwards thus it will be 28 years.

— Maulana Syed Abdulah Bukhari Imam of Jama Masjid has extended his poll support to the Janata Dal. He said, in view of the present situation, Prime Minister V.P. Singh's efforts to get the construction of the proposed Ram Mandir at Ayodhya postponed and the statements and announcements of the U.P. Chief Minister in this regard, it would be proper and fair that secular forces be strengthened by supporting the Janata Dal.

22 February 1990

— The central government has decided to introduce a Bill during the Parliament's budget session to amend the Ninth Schedule of the Constitution, to protect 55 land reform laws passed by states from being challenged in the courts.

23 February 1990

— The Central Secretariat Service Direct Recruit Assistants' Association organised a demonstration, on 22 February, of secretariat and additional offices employees to express resentment against the undue delay by the government in the redressal of their grievance, that is grant of the pay scale of Rs.1640-2900 to assistant stenographers of secretariat and allied offices.

— Former Prime Minister Rajiv Gandhi today alleged that the security personnel provided to him by the National Front government are not geared to respond to the situation in demand.

26 February 1990

— The government has constituted a new panel of honorary advisers which would interact closely with the Planning Commission on a regular basis to take stock of developments and would suggest policy options and programme strategies.

The panel consists of nine members: Acharya Ramamurthy, D.T. Lakdawala, K.N. Raj, K.S. Krishnaswamy, V. Kurien, Amulya Reddy, Veena Majumdar, V.A. Pai Panandikar and V.P. Rudrappa.

27 February 1990

— At least 85 persons were killed, 80 of them in Bihar alone, and more than 250 injured as violence marred the Assembly elections in the eight states and the union territory of Pondicherry that went to the polls today.

— Abid Hussain, a member of the Planning Commission till recently, is made India's Ambassador to the USA in place of Dr. Karan Singh.

MARCH 1990

3 March 1990

— The Congress (I) won in Arunachal Pradesh. The Janata Dal emerges as the single largest party in Bihar and Gujarat. The Bhartiya Janata Party won in Rajasthan, Madhya Pradesh and Himachal Pradesh.

— Prime Minister V.P. Singh is understood to have indicated that he was keen to quit as the President of the Janata Dal under the one-man one-post convention.

5 March 1990

— The Central Bureau of Investigation today registered criminal cases against six accused in the Rs. 465 crore HDW submarine deal (December 1981) in which kickbacks to the tune of Rs. 69 crore were alleged to have been paid to middlemen. These included S.S. Sidhu and S.K. Bhatnagar both former additional secretaries. The FIR gives the name of the businessman Gopichand Hinduja also as an accused.

— Increasing politicisation of lending institutions and credit programmes ostensibly for sub-serving political objectives have been progressively undermining the credit disciplines in recent times, reports a government appointed committee chaired by A.M. Khusro. Considering the deterinitic effects such trends have on the functioning of agricultural credit system the committee suggested 'the need for creating the necessary political will and observance of a code of ethics so as to induce non-interference in the functioning of credit agencies'.

6 March 1990

— The Communist Party of India (Marxist) has made an allegation that the Darjeeling Gorkha Council has been misusing development funds placed at its disposed.

7 March 1990

— The central government has decided to set up an Inter-State Council, visualised under article 263 of the Constitution to inquire into inter-state disputes and investigate subjects of inter-state or centre-state interest.

8 March 1990

— Deputy chairman, Planning Commission, Ramkrishna Hedge said that the 'New National Front' government is committed to make the right to work as a constitutional right.

— The centre has selected 250 out of 400 districts for possible replication of the 100 per cent literacy experiment successfully attempted in Ernakulam District of Kerala. The significance of the Ernakulam experiment was that it was a totally people's movement with 20,000 trainers who spread literacy doing the work as volunteers and the people providing the other requirements through contribution.

— The decision of the state government to improve the service conditions of the West Bengal Civil Service (Executive) cadre in pursuance of the recommendations of the Third Pay Commission has upset the state cadre of the IAS. A delegation of IAS officers lately met the finance minister and the chief secretary and tried to impress upon them that the acceptance of the recommendations would "undermine their authority in the state administration" since the WBCS officers are supposed to work "under them", according to sources in Calcutta.

Frustrated in their attempt to convince the minister, a section of IAS officers has launched a campaign to embarrass the government in a round about way. Inquiries reveal that some recently-promoted IAS officers, under the guidance of direct recruits, have petitioned the chief secretary for their reversion to the WBCS cadre. It is learnt that they are smarting under the grouse that they would be receiving less pay and holding diminished position than senior WBCS officers following the latest government decision.

10 March 1990

— Laloo Prasad Yadav, leader of the Bihar Janata Dal Legislative Party, was sworn in as the chief minister of the state.

— The central government has issued letters to 51 army deserters who had left their posts during Bluestar Operation offering them to join the Central Industrial Security Force as part of the move to rehabilitate them subject to physical interest.

— George Fernandes, the Railway Minister, is also look after the Jammu and Kashmir affairs.

11 March 1990

— The Delhi Police ordered a major reshuffle of officials of the rank of police inspectors and SHO.

12 March 1990

— The government today announced its decision to accept all the major recommendations made by the Ninth Finance Commission.

13 March 1990

— Indian pupils are winning a handsdown battle of brains in British classrooms which a leading education expert described as staggering and depressing for white parents. It was disclosed in a research data compiled by the Inner London Education Authority.

15 March 1990

— Over 2.61 lakh persons are in the waiting list for telephone connections under various categories in Delhi as on 1 February 1990, the Communication Minister, K.P. Unnikrishnan, said.

— Terrorists in Punjab have issued a *dictat* banning teaching of Hindi in schools and restraining the lady teachers from sporting "bindi" and applying lipsticks.

— The total number of Sri Lankan refugees in India at present is 93,481 of these 5,262 are living in relief camps and the rest are on their own.

16 March 1990

— The three-and-a-half-month old National Front government today received a big jolt when Devi Lal resigned from the post of Deputy Prime Minister in the Union Cabinet. He said, he has not left the Party where he heads the Central Parliamentary Board.

— The pre-Budget Economic Survey, 1989-90 calls for growth with equity, rapid export growth and reduction in external debt payment deficit.

18 March 1990

— Devi Lal withdraws his resignation.

19 March 1990

— The overall growth rate of population of the scheduled castes/tribes as per the 1981 census is higher than the growth rate of total population in the country.

— The total expenditure on police will be of the order of Rs. 1,552,83 crores against Rs. 1,382 crores provided in the budget for the year 1989-90. The increase has been allowed in cases of Central Reserve Police, Border Security Force, Indo-Tibetan Border Police, Central Industrial Security Force and Assam Rifles.

20 March 1990

— The government will spend Rs. 1,200 crores during 1989-90 in providing pension to 10 lakh ex-servicemen. This was told in a parliamentary reply.

21 March 1990

— The coordination committee of the West Bengal government employees, a CPI(M) outfit, announced that it would launch a movement against any public servant if he was found to be habitually late in coming to office, negligent in attending to his duties and dishonest in his job.

— The government had spent Rs. 7,91,40,139 on the security of the Prime Minister during 1989-90.

22 March 1990

— March 22 is India's New Year's Day according to the official calendar. This calendar was introduced from March 1956 after a study of all available calendars. However, neither the President nor the Prime Minister has thought it fit to greet the people on the occasion of the New Year. The official calendar is known as the Sakar Era and is one of the most scientific and accurate calendars: it is even more accurate than the Gregorian (or Christian calendar) which suffers from at least a dozen defects.

— Devi Lal has resigned from the chairmanship of the cabinet committee set up to go into the Mandal Commission's recommendations on reservations for backward castes.

— A Dinner was hosted today by the Madhya Pradesh IAS Association to the entire Sunderlal Patwa cabinet. This was the first time since the inception of the state that such a dinner was hosted by the Association.

23 March 1990

— There are about 32 lakh slum dwellers in Delhi, according to the Town and Country Planning Organisation.

— The central government has raised the upper age for admission to the Indian Forest Service from 26 to 28 years and to increase the number of permissible attempts from three to four. For the year 1990, the upper age limit is up to 31 years.

— India, according to Nani A. Palkhiwala, is facing a "grave financial crisis" and a time has come for Parliament to assert forthwith its authority under article 292 of the Constitution to limit government borrowings, both internal and external.

24 March 1990

— A new controversy has been generated in the IAS cadre in Madhya

Pradesh. 'Who is supreme, secretary or the principal secretary?' this is in nut-shell the reason of debate in the corridors of power.

A few principal secretaries have sought to know the answer from the government as to who is the administrative head of the Secretariat Department in those departments which have principal secretaries as well as secretaries — is the principal secretary or the secretary?

Mr. N.S. Sethi, principal secretary, Forest and Cooperative Department has written a letter to the state chief secretary saying 'both the officers can not be deemed to be the heads of the Secretary Department: only one can be so. The head of the Secretariat Department has to held responsible for monitoring of the activities of the department, coordination, providing the department necessary direction and guidance and administrative leadership.

He was of the view that this role cannot be performed by two officers and the government must therefore clearly decide as to who shall perform this pivotal role.

In fact, the problem has arisen due to the fact that Madhya Pradesh has more officers functioning as secretary or principal secretary than what the requirement was. There are about 21 officers of the rank of principal secretary.

The principal secretaries were of the view that as a matter of policy, the more senior super-time scale officers should not normally bee placed under principal secretaries and to the extent possible junior secretary level officer should only be posted to assist the principal secretaries as the senior officers feel that they should function in an independent capacity and they also have sufficient expertise, experience and competence to handle at the departments independently.

The principal secretaries have also a demand that they should be authorised to write the annual confidential reports of the secretaries as also of other secretariat officers working under them. 'This way, it will ensure effective coordination and functioning of the departments', they have pleaded with the state government.

At present, there are three kinds of arrangements in the state secretariat. Under one, the departments are entirely under officers of the level of secretaries (super-time scale officers), under the second kind departments are under officers of the level of principal secretaries (above super-time scale) only and the third category is the one in which officers of the principal secretary's grade as well as secretary level officers have been posted.

In a note to the government, it has been stated that the principal secretaries have to be deemed to be the administrative heads of the secretariat departments and held squarely responsible for the proper functioning of the departments under their control. Secretary-level officers in these departments if provided should be considered as additional help for the transaction of business of the department.

"Since the matter is important and already some ambiguity and ambivalence has arisen, the matter should be referred to the senior secretaries committee", principal secretaries have demanded.

25 March 1990

— A number of MPs in their speeches on the Railway Budget for 1990-91 have demanded the creation of the post of member (Stores) in the Railway Board in order to streamline of and bring in efficiency in the materials management of India's largest public undertaking. Store constitute as high as 45 per cent of Railway's working expenses, being of the order of Rs. 4,300 crores in 1988-89.

26 March 1990

— Most of the one lakh members of the minority community in Kashmir valley have left and migrated to either Jammu or other parts of India.

— An estimated 29.2 per cent of India's population lived below the poverty-line in 1987-88, according to a parliamentary reply by V.P. Singh.
The percentage of population below poverty-line has been declining during the last decade. In 1977-78, the percentage was 48.3 which came into 29.2 in 1987-88.

— The number of educated unemployed persons aged 15 years and above was 3.7 million in 1988.

— The governments in Goa and in Meghalaya have fallen. These ministries belonged to the Congress (I).

— The Uttar Pradesh government has banned the use of English in all its offices from today and all official work is now to be done only in Hindi.

27 March 1990

— The Progressive Democratic Front ministry with Churchill Alemao as chief minister was sworn in at Panaji, Goa.

28 March 1990

— The Constitution (Sixty-fourth Amendment) Bill has been passed by the Rajya Sabha enabling extension of President's rule in Punjab by six more months. The Bill is to go to the Lok Sabha for its clearance.

— There is no proposal under the consideration of the government to abolish the Commissioner of Police system in Delhi.

— The Controller and Auditor General of India (CAG) has berated the Maharashtra Antibiotics and Pharmaceuticals Ltd. for utilising its installed capacity up to 33 per cent. The drug firm has also delayed commissioning several of its plants.

29 March 1990

— Replying to the Rajya Sabha question, the government said that its policy is to undertake judgment of the personal laws minority communities themselves for training a common civil code for all Indian citizens.

— The number of branches of 28 public sector banks in rural areas in 1985 was 29,837 which increased to 33,640 in 1989.

— An estimated 13.3 million people had benefited from the Integrated Rural Development Programme (IRDP), the Lok Sabha was informed.

30 March 1990

— The Constitution (Sixty-fourth Amendment) Bill seeking to extending Presidents Rule in Punjab by another six months fell through in the Lok Sabha because the requisite number of members were not present at the introduction stage.

— The Interval of one rupee, measured as reciprocal of consumer price index for industrial workers (base 1982 = 100) amounted to 60.2 paise in March 1989, and 65.4 paise in March 1988, the Finance Minister informed the Lok Sabha.

31 March 1990

— Prime Minister Vishwanath Pratap Singh today announced that the government had decided to honour posthumously Bhimrao Ramji Ambedkar with the country's highest award, the "Bharat Ratna". The announcement was made at a national Conference on the problems of the scheduled castes and tribes at Vigyan Bhawan. R. Venkataraman had given his consent for the proposal. Also, Ambedkar's portrait is to be unveiled in the Central Hall of Parliament.

— The All-India Central Committee of Pensioners Association today pressed its demand for formulation of the national pension policy to ensure social security for senior citizens, housing and medicare for them.

APRIL 1990

1 April 1990

— Portugal has taken a 'final decision' to return to India gold ornaments taken from Goan banks during the liberation of Goa in 1961. The gold is estimated at some $2.5 million (USA) at current prices.

— The first phase of the 1991 census begins today with the launching of preliminary house listing operations in Goa, Himachal Pradesh, Orissa, Chandigarh and the Andamans.

Before a census of the population is taken, it is essential to locate and identify all places that are occupied or are likely to be occupied. The house listing operations serve this purpose and in addition, provide data on the purpose for which each house is used and the number of persons residing there.

— The social forestry programmes have failed to make much headway despite occasional success stories because these have degenerated from people's programmes to mere a government scheme. This is what participants at a recent workshop on forestry have felt. Particularly, tribals who have a symbiotic relationship with forests have been kept at the periphery of decision-making on forestry scheme.

2 April 1990

— Prime Minister Vishwanath Pratap Singh today held an informed meeting with the leaders of the main political parties in Parliament to discuss the course of action to be followed for getting the Constitution (Sixty-Fourth Amendment) Bill passed by both Houses of Parliament in time. The Bill seeks extension of President's Rule in Punjab by six months.

— Political wranglings by the BJP and the CPM have been delaying the final selection of the Vice-Chancellor of Delhi University.

— Use of Hindi has been made compulsory in all the offices of Madhya Pradesh government.

3 April 1990

— T.U. Vijayasekharan, secretary in the Department of Coal, has been appointed as the Chief Vigilance Commissioner in place of C.G. Somaiya who has taken over as the Comptroller and Auditor-General of India.

— The government removed two associates of Sam G. Patroda, chairman of the Telecommunication Commission, G.B. Meemamsi, Executive Director and Dr. Mahajan, Director of the Centre for Development of Telematics (CDT) replacing with persons known to be critical of the CDT's claim.

4 April 1990

— The government reintroduced in the Lok Sabha the Constitution Amendment Bill seeking extension of the President's rule in Punjab by another six months. Earlier, the home minister secured the approval of the house for waiving Rule 338 of the Lok Sabha. Under this Rule, no legislation which is substantially identical to the one on which the House has already given a decision, can be introduced in the same session.

— The were 64.4 million agricultural labourers in the country including 8.9 million marginal farmers. The number of female agricultural labourers was 28.5 million which constituted 44.85 per cent of the total female workers. This was disclosed by the government while replying to a parliamentary question.

— The government has rejected the plea of the public sector undertakings' employees that they should be governed by the central government dearness allowance. The central public sector enterprises thus continue to be governed by the existing industrial dearness allowance formula.

5 April 1990

— The Constitution Amendment Bill seeking to extend President's Rule in Punjab by six months from 11 May 1990 was passed by the Lok Sabha today.

— The Janata Dal leader Chandra Shekhar has alleged that his telephones had been tapped and so were the phones of 27 other politicians.

6 April 1990

— The Central Bureau of Investigation took up 76 cases for investigation during February 1990 in which 93 public servants including 57 gazetted officers were involved.

— The Rajasthan government today transferred 24 senior IAS officers and one IPS officer.

7 April 1990

— Kidnapping, extortions and killings are virtually the order of the day in Assam where the United Liberation Front of Assam (ULFA) is having a free run of the place.

9 April 1990

— The Indian Telephones Act and the Post Office Act should be amended to impose certain limitations on the government's powers to invade an individual's privacy. This was observed by L.K. Advani.

— The right to work when incorporated as a fundamental right will ensure minimum incomes to the unemployed poor.

10 April 1990

— Terrorists in Kashmir killed the HMT general manager H.L. Khera, Vice-Chancellor of Kashmir University Masheer-ul-Haq and his private secretary Abdul Ghani.

— The total investment in the central public sector enterprises was Rs. 85,563.78 crore in 1989.

12 April 1990

— The Election Commission has called for an explanation from the Haryana government on the transfer of officials from Meham, Darba Kalan and Ambala cantonment assembly constituencies. These transfers are in violation of the model code of conduct.

— The Reserve Bank of India has prepared a multi-point plan to curb inflation. There is disproportionate and persistent growth in money supply with the public. In 1989-90 the overall monetary expansion was as high as 19.4 per cent.

— Delhi has 104 police stations and 45 police posts in Delhi.

— The portrait of Bhimrao Ramji Ambedkar was unveiled in the Central Hall of Parliament by Prime Minister V.P. Singh.

— The number of post offices in India was in 1989 was 1,47,102 out of which 1,30,838 were in rural areas and 16,264 in the urban area.

14 April 1990

— Dr Bhimrao Ramji Ambedkar was bestowed the country's high civilian award of Bharat Ratna on his birth centenary. On 31 March the government had announced the conferring of the award.

— Prime Minister V.P. Singh announced the intention of the National Front government to include all the laws geared towards social justice in the Ninth Schedule of the Constitution so that these are not reviewed by the judiciary.

— The National Capital Region Planing Cell for the sub-region of Delhi will soon start functioning.

— V.P. Singh has insisted on his cabinet colleagues to take all administrative decisions themselves, thus reducing the workload on the Prime Minister's office. He lays stress on decentralisation of authority, the start being made with the Prime Minister's office.

— National Bank for Agriculture and Rural Development, the apex level financial institution in the country, has set up district level offices.

— The year 1990-91 has been declared a year of social justice as a tribute to Dr. Balasaheb Bhimrao Ramji Ambedkar. This was announced by the Prime Minister V.P. Singh. The Prime Minister said in the public meting that a Bill has been introduced in Parliament which has sought for neo-Buddhists the same benefits which are accorded to the scheduled and scheduled tribes.

15 April 1990

— The V.P. Singh ministry is to be expanded very shortly. This is to reduce heavy workload on some ministers.

16 April 1990

— Vigyan Bhawan was virtually destroyed in a fire today. The fire broke out minutes after a conference of Inspectors General of Police and Directors-general of Police ended.

— About 100 persons were burnt alive in train fire near Patna.

— Industry Minister Ajit Singh stated that the government would not go in for further nationalisation of sick industrial units. As much as Rs. 6000 crore of bank credit is presently locked in some 160,000 industrial sick units in the country.

17 April 1990

— A high power committee is to enquire into all the incidents of fire that took place in Delhi yesterday.

— A major administrative shake-up has occurred in Punjab with transfer of 18 senior IAS officers.

— Fire Services need to be strengthened. The inadequacy of the fire services was disclosed in the recent fires.

18 April 1990

— Progress was made in the tripartite meeting held in Delhi today to resolve the Bodo problem of Assam when the representatives of the Bodo movement agreed to formation of an eight-member committee to study the problem of Bodos. Membership of the committee contains representatives of the centre, the government of Assam and the Bodos.

— Job guarantee plan is under the study of the Government of India.

— Cancer patients in India number 1.5 to 2 million. Almost half a million new cases occur every year.

19 April 1990

— The Sixty-sixth Amendment Bill was introduced by the government in the Lok Sabha today seeking to incorporate all the acts passed by the states and amendments to laws pertaining to land reforms in the Ninth Scheduled of the Constitution thereby giving them immunity from legal challenge.

— The consensus approach of V.P. Singh in cabinet expansion has created problems in completing the process. V.P. Singh has asked some of the cabinet ministers to send a list of names whom they consider a good choice.

21 April 1990

— Prime Minister Vishwanath Pratap Singh expanded his four month old council of ministers by inducting 13 ministers of state and 5 deputy ministers taking the strength to 40. Their portfolios were not announced.

22 April 1990

— Portfolios of the 18 new ministers inducted into the union council of ministers would be announced tomorrow.

23 April 1990

— Lt-General Sunith Frances Rodrigines is to be the next chief of the Army Staff.

— The Committee of Ministers for Economic Development of North-Eastern Region has been reconstituted with the Union Home minister as chairman. The Finance Minister, the deputy chairman of Planning Commission and union ministers from the north-eastern regions are members of the committee.

— The National Water Development Agency (NWDA) an organisation under the Ministry of Water Resources, is undertaking studies for inter-basin transfer of river waters and is completing studies on five of the proposed 17 water transfer links in Peninsular India, Mahanadi and Godavari rivers.

24 April 1990

— The Director-General of the Central Public Works Department has submitted to the Urban Development Ministry Secretary the departmental report on the fire in Vigyan Bhawan recently.

— Asset-wise, the Birlas top the twenty largest business houses in India. The Tatas top in terms of both turn-over and profits before tax. The Lok Sabha was informed today in a parliamentary reply.

25 April 1990

— Delhi has an estimated 10,000 beggars.

— Bombay will hereafter be known as 'Mumbai' instead of Bombay in Hindi in the proceedings and records of the Lok Sabha.

— The North-Eastern Council, so crucial for the economic development of the seven north eastern states, is without a chairman for nearly a year.

26 April 1990

— The process of replacing most of the governors appointed by the Rajiv Gandhi government was completed today with R. Venkataraman, President, appointing five new governors and accepting the resignations of three. D.P. Thakur is to be the Governor of Assam, Mahipal Shastri of Gujarat, Bhanu Pratap Singh of Karnataka, M.M. Thomas of Nagaland and Madhukar Dighe of Meghalaya.

27 April 1990

— Differences at the highest level in the government and pressure from the IAS cadre in the state service has forced the Kerala government to go back on its decision to suspend a Harijan IAS official of the general education department.

The chief minister had directed the administration to place under suspension pending inquiry, Mr S. Subbaya deputy secretary in the general education department for alleged dereliction of duty. He was charged with failing to secure in time a budgetary allocation of Rs. 87 lakhs for the education department from the PWD. This amount was meant for construction of school buildings under the Central Operation Blackboard Scheme. The IAS official was the coordinator of the project.

Mr Subbaya was charged with not monitoring and following up with the disbursing department the papers on the subject leading to the amount lapsing at the end of the financial year on 31 March. The file in question was reportedly put before the PWD on 22 March, leaving them less than a week for processing and disbursement. Two junior officials of the PWD, an assistant administrative officer and a finance officer were also ordered by the government to be placed under suspension along with the IAS officer.

But the chief minister's decision, taken at the instance of the Education Minister, Mr K. Chandrasekharan, is learnt to have met with strong opposition from a section of the state Cabinet and senior IAS officials in the state. The minister in charge of Scheduled Caste and Scheduled Tribe Development, Mr P.K. Raghavan, was reportedly among those who strongly criticised the suspension move. Some of the leaders of the IAS officers association are also reported to have found the government decision improper.

Mr Chandrasekharan who had initiated the government action, when contacted refused to comment on the developments. "No formal orders on the matter have so far been issued", he told ENS. As for the lapse of the allocated funds for construction of school buildings under the Operation Blackboard Scheme, he said the government would order an inquiry into it.

Mr Subbaya, when contacted said that he had not received any order of suspension till late in the evening on Wednesday. He also reserved his comments on the charge of dereliction of duty that had been levelled against him.

— Kiran Bedi, IPS, has been transferred to Mizoram. She was inducted by the Wadhwa Commission which probed into the incident involving the lawyers and the police in 1988.

28 April 1990

— Non-plan expenditure of the centre has been increasing continuously for the past 10 years.

30 April 1990

— The Christian Dalit Liberation Movement, Vellore has made an appeal that Indian Christians of Scheduled Caste Origin (CSCOs) be granted constitutional recognition as scheduled castes. The two day seminar submitted a memorandum to the Prime Minister, saying 'Their conversion to Christianity has not changed for the better their social and economic status and they remain as backward and handicapped as their fellow dalits in other religions.'

— The Delhi Janata Dal demanded major changes in the Delhi Development Authority (DDA) to improve its functioning. 'The DDA has become a den of corruption'. It was alleged that the DDA had acquired 1.13 lakh acres of land but it has taken possession of 50,000 acres only. 'Some DDA officials were minting money in land deals.'

— The Central Minister for Environment Maneka Gandhi told the Lok Sabha that 30 million hectares of forests area have no tree cover in the country.

— To mark the 100th anniversary of Labour Day, the government of India declared 1 May 1990 as a public holiday.

MAY 1990

1 May 1990

— Angami Zapu Phizo, the legendary figure of Nagaland and chief of the Nagaland Nationalist Council (MNC), died at London at the age of 83. Phizo spearheaded an armed hostility demanding seccession of Nagaland from India. He went into exile in December 1957.

— In Karnataka the ruling Congress (I) Party re-established its popularity in the state by capturing nearly 50 per cent of the 226 local bodies and *mandals*.

2 May 1990

— Rashid Masood, the minister, told in the Lok Sabha that there were 25,87,464 leprosy patients on record in the country.

3 May 1990

— As on 30 March 1990, against the actual strength of 25 judges, there are few scheduled castes judges in the Supreme Court of India. On the same date, against the actual strength of 377 judges/additional judges there were nine judges belonging to scheduled castes and three judges to the scheduled tribes in various High Courts. There was one woman judge in the Supreme Court and 11 women judges out of 377 judges in various High Courts.

— The Madhya Pradesh IAS association has resented chief minister Sunderlal Patwa's remarks at a press conference castigating the conduct of same IAS officers.

A delegation of the Association led by its president met the state chief secretary R.P. Kapoor to express their concern over the remarks. A note was also submitted to the chief secretary.

Sunder Lal Patwa had given a strong warning to the IAS officers for seeking intervention of their Association for personal matters. He had also asked the chief secretary to convey his displeasure to those officers who had gone to the association.

4 May 1990

— The Lok Sabha was told that in 1989-90 the number of foreign tourists visiting India was 17,65,079. This included nationals of Pakistan and Bangladesh.

7 May 1990

— The health minister while replying a parliamentary question said, the life expectancy in India is 58.1 years for males and 59.1 for females. This was 32.09 and 31.37 years for male and female respectively in 1941, and 32.45 and 31.66 for male and female respectively in 1951.

— Former Chief Justice of India P.N. Bhagwati suggested that an independent judicial commission be constituted to control the judiciary and impart justice between the government and public. At present, the legislature and the executive control the judiciary and as such it is not independent. The proposed judicial commission should have powers to investigate charges levelled against judges, should appoint them and even remove the corrupt if any.

10 May 1990

— The total expenditure likely to be incurred on the 1990-91 census in the country is Rs. 110.94 crores. The Minister of State for Home told the Lok Sabha in a parliamentary reply.

— Kuldip Nayar, the Indian High Commissioner in England, has criticised the bureaucracy in India which he feels is 'frightfully large and considers its business to retard business' 'We are one of the most rule-ridden governments, frustratingly slow. Petty regulations going back to the Raj have cost us millions of pounds'.

11 May 1990

— The total internal debt and other internal habilities of the government of India outstanding at the end of March 1990, was estimated at Rs. 2,38,096 crores.
The rate of inflation for the first quarter of 1990 was 8.2 per cent in 1990.

12 May 1990

— The Haryana government decided to build administrative-cum-judicial complexes at every district headquarters on the pattern of Gurgaon mini-secretariat. The mini-secretariat will be helpful for over one million population of the district where the public will be able to visit administrative and judicial offices in the same complex.

— The splinter group of the Congress(J) today formally merged with the Congress(S), a constituent of the National Front at the centre. The Congress (J), founded and headed by Jagjivan Ram had already merged with the Congress-I in 1987.

13 May 1990

— The Union Minister for Labour and Social Welfare Ram Vilas Paswan said, the central cabinet would take a decision on the Mandal Commission recommendations for backward classes within a week.

14 May 1990

— Nearly 11 people die against every 1,000 births in India, the Rajya Sabha was told.

15 May 1990

— A 14-member two-tier Nagaland ministry was installed in Kohima headed by leader of the Nagaland People's Council (NPC) K.L. Chisi, with the help of a 12-member Congress-I splinter group

— The Comptroller and Auditor-General of India has severally criticised the working of the Amnesty Scheme for repentant tax-payers introduced in 1985. The scheme can not be regarded as a success. It certainly had enabled recalcitrant tax-payers to launder large amounts of their black money into white, as evident from the fact that even though the government could collect only Rs. 458 crores from over 20 lakh returns of income tax/ wealth-tax, the scheme enabled conversion of income-wealth aggregating to Rs. 10,778 crores.

16 May 1990

— Nearly five lakh *Anganwadi* helpers and workers throughout the country demand better wages.

— The Delhi Transport Corporation suffers a loss of Rs. 1.76 per kilometre.

— The percentage of women farm labour in the country excluding Assam is 37.42 according to 1981 census, Lok Sabha was told in a parliamentary reply.

17 May 1990

— The Comptroller and Auditor-General of India has pulled up the agriculture ministry for the manners in which the ambitious Jawahar Rojgar Yojna was implemented without adequate funds and for failing to adhere to the prescribed criteria for release of central assistance to states under the programme. The total resources of Rs. 2,623.08 crores provided for the programme in 1989-90 were inadequate to achieve its objectives and could sustain employment for hardly 21 days on an average to one member of each rural family living below poverty line.

The Nehru Rojgar Yojna was launched on 9 April 1989 by merging the National Rural Employment Programme (NREP) and the Rural Landless

Employment Guarantee Programme (RLEGP). The main objective of the programme was to generate additional employment for the unemployed and under-employed in rural areas, with expenditure to be shared between the centre and states on an 80 : 20 basis.

This is disclosed in the CAG's report presented to the Lok Sabha on 17 May 1990.

— Instances of considerable delays ranging up to 62 months in allotment to government servants of units vacated by earlier occupants and up to 17 months for newly constructed units have been highlighted by the Comptroller and Auditor-General of India. A large number of *ad hoc* allotments were being made and 48 per cent of the total allotment in Type V in 1988 was on an 'out of turn' basis.

— The total waiting list in the country for telephones as on 31 March 1990, in 17.14 lakh.

20 May 1990

— Over 500 leaders and activists of various political parties including former ministers and legislators have fled the trouble-torn valley of Kashmir in the wake of threats by terrorists. They have shifted to Jammu where they were living in government buildings including MLA's Hostel under tight security.

— In its audit report presented to Parliament the Comptroller and Auditor General of India has pointed out that the Central Health Scheme (CHS), which started with 16 allopathic dispensaries covering 2.23 lakh people in Delhi in 1954, has been extended to 16 states with 221 allopathic dispensaries and 13 allopathic clinics and 71 units of the Indian system of medicines.

The annual expenditure on the scheme had increased from Rs. 29.63 crores in 1984-85 to Rs. 55.20 crores in 1988-89 and the average cost per card holder had increased from Rs. 375 to Rs. 650. But the amount spent on medicines was proportionately less. In Delhi, the average annual expenditure on medicines per beneficiary was Rs. 9 in Sriniwaspuri and Rs. 65 in North Avenue, a high-salary area. The contribution from the beneficiaries covered just 13 per cent of the recurring expenditure.

Several shortcomings were noticed in the working of the CHS. The criteria for opening dispensaries were not observed. In Delhi, the number of families attached to a dispensary varied from 1,547 (President's Estate) to 17,432 (Kingsway Camp). The dispensaries were working a single six-hour shift, though it had resulted in inconvenience to the beneficiaries. The deployment of medical and paramedical staff did not conform to the sanctioned strength resulting in uneven workload. Fifty per cent of the doctors whose work was test-checked, attended to 50 patients against the norm of 75 patients a day.

— The former Chief Minister of Haryana, Bansi Lal, launched his 'non-political organisation' Haryana Vikas Manch at Rohtak, the Jat heartland.

21 May 1990

— In a parliamentary reply, the Prime Minister told the Lok Sabha that there was no proposal to give any weightage to rural candidates as compared to urban candidate appearing in written test and interview for recruitment to government jobs.

22 May 1990

— The Madhya Pradash IAS association hosted a dinner on 22 May 1990, to the entire Sunder Lal Patwa cabinet at Bhopal. This is for the first time since the inception of the state that such a dinner is being organised by the association.

— Om Prakash Chautala, son of Devi Lal and Haryana's chief minister, resigned from the chief ministership of Haryana when the Janata Dal leadership asked him to step down from office in view of the violent killings that preceded the recent counter-manding of the Meham by-election.

— Prime Minister V.P. Singh told the Rajya Sabha in a parliamentary reply that there was no proposal to give at least 2/3 promotions to each and every government servant in his entire career.

— Three of the 19 Daulphin Helicopters in the Pawan Hans fleet are grounded for want of spares. All the 19 Westland helicopters in the Pawan Hans fleet are grounded on instructions from the central government.

— The Comptroller and Auditor-General of India has severely criticised frequent cancellation of flights by Air-India, loss of income on account of endorsement of tickets to other airlines and charging low charter price for VIP flights.

23 May 1990

— In 1986 India had the fourth highest rate of road accidents in the world, the Central Surface Transport Minister told the Rajya Sabha.

— There were 1,197 islands including islets, reefs and isolated rocks under Indian jurisdiction in the Bay of Bengal, the Arabian Sea, the Andaman Sea and the Lakshadweep Sea. Of these, 48 are inhabited, the Rajya Sabha was told in a parliamentary reply.

25 May 1990

— Jagmohan, Governor of Jammu and Kashmir, resigned his post. He was replaced by Girish Saxena.

— The number of *jhuggies* spread all over Delhi is estimated to be around 2.27 lakh, the Urban Development Minister told the Rajya Sabha.

— The Rajya Sabha was told in a parliamentary reply that as many as 171 mills and factories were lying closed in 1989 affecting 4,701 workers. The reasons for closure include financial stringency, shortage of raw materials, power etc., breakdown of machinery and lack of demand for products.

— Total investment made by Non-Resident Indians (NRIs) in the country including bank deposits amounted to Rs. 19,000 crores in 1989.

27 May 1990

— If it is tough for women in the developing countries, it is tougher in the Third World. The Human Development Report published for the United Nations Development Fund shows that the Third World women have less of everything—except suffering.

— Female children in developing countries get less food, less health care and less education. In some countries more girl babies die before their fifth birth day than boys. Adult women get less education, less professional training and less pay even when they work longer hours than men. Families in India's rural Punjab spend more than twice as much on the medical care of male infants than on female infants. Spending on clothing is 40 per cent higher for boys than for girls.

28 May 1990

— President of India R. Venkataraman has forwarded to Attorney-General Soli Sarabjee a memorandum of complaints received by him from several members of the Bombay High Court bar against Justice S.K. Desai, the senior most judge of the Bombay High Court after the Chief Justice of India. The memorandum containing the allegations against Justice Desai has been forwarded to the President by the Governor of Maharashtra, who in turn received it from the Advocate-General.

— The Comptroller and Auditor-General of India (CAG) has roundly criticised the Municipal Corporation of Delhi for excessive spending over income in its general wing and other lapses in the Corporation's Water Supply and Sewage Disposal Undertaking and the Electricity Supply Undertaking.

29 May 1990

— Prime Minister V.P. Singh told the Rajya Sabha in a parliamentary reply that there were roughly 17 lakh retired central government employees in receipt of pension. The budget estimate for 1990 provides for Rs. 3104 crore for meeting expenditure on pension and other retirement benefits.

30 May 1990

— The chairman of the Rajya Sabha will be entitled to a daily allowance at the same rate as is applicable to the Speaker of the Lok Sabha under a Bill introduced in the Lok Sabha today. The Bill also exempts the daily allowance from income-tax. Thus, he is entitled to a daily allowance during the whole of his term at the rate of Rs. 150 per day. This involves an annual expenditure of Rs. 54,000 from the Consolidated Fund of India.

— The Constitution (Sixty-fifth Amendment) Bill 1990 was passed to give statutory status to the Commission for Scheduled Castes and Tribes. The Constitution (Sixty-Sixth Amendment) Bill was passed to include land reform in the Ninth Schedule of the Constitution to repulse judicial intervention.

31 May 1990

— The government announced the new industrial policy which aims at promotion of small-scale and agro-based industries and changes in procedures for industrial approvals.

The policy tabled in the Lok Sabha by the industry minister, Ajit Singh, raises the investment ceiling in plant and machinery to small-scale industries to Rs. 60 lakh from the present Rs. 35 lakh. Correspondingly, for ancillary units, the investment ceiling has been raised to Rs. 75 lakh from the present Rs. 45 lakh.

The policy gives licensing exemption for all new units up to an investment of Rs. 25 crore in fixed assets in non-backward areas and Rs. 75 crore in centrally notified backward areas. Cent per cent export-oriented units and units set up in export processing zones are also being delicensed under the scheme up to an investment of Rs. 75 crore. In order to enable small-scale industries play an important role in the total export effort, the small units which undertake to export 30 per cent of their annual production by the third year would be permitted to step up their investment in plant and machinery to Rs. 75 lakh.

Investment ceiling for tiny units has been increased to Rs. five lakh from the present Rs. two lakh. However, with regard to their location, the population limit of 50,000 as per the 1981 Census would continue to apply.

For the import of capital goods, the entrepreneur would have entitlement to import up to a landed value of 30 per cent of the total value of plant and machinery required for the unit.

For imports of raw materials and components, imports would be permissible up to a landed value of 30 per cent of the ex-factory value of annual production.

Keeping in view the need to attract effective inflow of technology, investment up to 40 per cent of equity would be allowed on an automatic basis. In such proposals also, the landed value of imported capital goods should not exceed 30 per cent of value of plant an machinery.

A new scheme of central investment subsidy, exclusively for the small-scale sector in rural and backward areas capable of generating higher level of employment at lower capital cost, would be implemented.

With a view to improving the competitiveness of the products manufactured in the small-scale sector, programmes for modernisation and upgradation of technology would be implemented.

A number of technology centres, tool rooms, process and product development centres and testing centres, would be set up under the umbrella of an apex technology development centre in the Small Industries Development Organisation.

The new policy envisages that the existing regime of fiscal concessions would be reviewed both to provide sustained support to the units in the small-scale sector and to remove the disincentives for their graduation and further growth.

Attempt would be made to expand the list of 836 items reserved for exclusive manufacture in the small-scale sector. Encroachment and violation by large-scale units into areas reserved for the small-scale sector would be effectively dealt with.

One of the major tasks of SIDBI and other commercial banks and financial institutions would be to channel need-based, higher flow of credit, both by way of term loans and working capital, to the tiny and rural industries.

The policy attempts to reorient industrial growth to serve the objective of employment generation, dispersal of industry in the rural areas, and to enhance the contribution of small-scale industries to exports.

Under the new policy, import of technology would be allowed without obtaining any clearance from the government, provided that royalty payment did not exceed five per cent on domestic sales and eight per cent on exports. If lump sum payment was involved in the import of technology, the proposal would require government clearance, but a decision would be communicated to the entrepreneur within a period of 3 days.

An exercise will be undertaken to identify locations in rural areas endowed with adequate power supply and intensive campaigns will be launched to attract suitable entrepreneurs, provided all other inputs and foster small-scale and tiny industries. Similarly, industries which are not energy-intensive will be identified for proliferation in rural areas where power supply is presently a constraint. In order to widen the entrepreneurial base, the government would lay particular emphasis on training of women and youth under the entrepreneurial development programme. A special cell would be established in SIDO and state directorates of industries to assist women entrepreneurs. Bureaucratic controls will be reduced so that unnecessary interference is eliminated. Further, procedures will be simplified and paper work cut down. In order to assist the large number of artisans engaged in the rural and cottage industries, the activities of the KVIC and KVI boards will be expanded, and these organisations will be strengthened to discharge the responsibility more effectively. Special marketing organisations at the centre and state levels shall be created to assist rural artisans, besides, providing concessional credit, training facilities and free consultancy. The industrial policy will promote projects which are organised in close cooperation on the basis of joint ownership. Growers will be encouraged to set up processing units within the framework of cooperative societies or similar institutional framework. Agro-processing industry will receive high priority in credit allocation from the financial institutions. In order to bring the best technology available to these industries, technology approvals will be given within 30 days of presentation to the secretariat for industrial approvals in the department of industrial development.

— The minister for environment and forests who has been lying low so far, has achieved a coup in the ministry that he has divested Maneka Gandhi of virtually all major responsibilities. The senior minister has pulled rank and taken over the responsibilities of the new forest policy which is on the anvil, the national wasteland development board, environment appraisal and clearance of all projects, administration of the newly set up National Fund for Afforestation and umpteen other responsibilities of this important ministry handling some of the most sensitive issues of development. For a whole month, there has been a silent struggle going on in the ministry on the distribution of work. Maneka Gandhi was keen to push through some of the major programmes she had initiated and was seen by industrialists as well as political adversaries as being almost inflexibly committed to environment. There was a great deal of speculation when Routray was moved from health to environment and forests last month. It was seen as a victory for those trying to dampen her enthusiasm.

But the high profile minister of state continued to battle on, attracting as many brickbats as plaudits. The circular "in supersession of all previous orders on the subject and in exercise of the powers under Rule 3 of the government (transaction of business rules) "by the minister for environment and forests has, however, with immediate effect, limited the cases to be disposed of by Maneka Gandhi to 17 heads. These responsibilities concern wildlife. Delhi Zoo, administration of centrally-sponsored schemes relating to protection of wildlife, programme of depolluting Delhi, greening of Haryana, and administration of three Acts concerning water and air pollution. Maneka Gandhi has, however, been given full responsibility for appointment, transfer and taking disciplinary action against group B category of non-gazetted officers. She can grant study leave to group B officers and institute awards and medals for outstanding work in forestry and wildlife. Implementation of Hindi and answering of all starred and unstarred questions and laying of papers in the Rajya Sabha has also been entrusted to her. The National Zoo Authority, which Maneka Gandhi is supposed to be responsible for, does not even exist and there are no centrally-sponsored schemes relating to protection of wildlife. The programme of depolluting Delhi is really the responsibility of the chief secretary of Delhi and that of greening Haryana that of its chief minister. The three water and air pollution control acts would really be governed by the Environment Protection Act. For a policy decision to be taken by the cabinet or a cabinet committee in these cases too, they will have to be put up by the minister of state to the cabinet minister. In exercise of his powers, Routray has already revoked the cancellation order issued by his minister of state to the government of Orissa on the transfer of prime forest land for the construction of a hotel. J.B. Patnaik, the former chief minister of the state, had, in contravention of the Forest Act, transferred land in the Konarak forest area to Oberoi group of hotels. Maneka Gandhi had cancelled this allotment.

— The Constitution (Seventy-second Amendment) Bill, 1990 providing full statehood for the union territory of Delhi was introduced in the Lok Sabha.

— The Lok Sabha passed a Bill seeking to rise the monthly salary of the President of India (from Rs. 15,000 to Rs. 20,000 and the pension of the ex-President to Rs. 10,000 per month.

— The government introduced a Bill in the Lok Sabha seeking to bring the salary, pension and other service conditions of the Chief Election Commissioner on a par with that of a judge of the Supreme Court and the Comptroller and Auditor-General of India.

JUNE 1990

1 June 1990

— The Punjab Governor Nirmal Kumar Mukarji has tendered his resignation to the President. He submitted his resignation on 31 May at the instance of the Home Minister Mufti Mohammed Sayeed. The latter directed him to submit his resignation. Immediately afterwards Mukarji wrote a two line resignation letter in his own hand-writing which was then sent through a specially emissary to Shimla where the President, R. Venkataraman, is currently holidaying.

— The deputy chairman of the Rajya Sabha Nazma Heptulla administered a reprimand to K.K. Tewary, former Central Minister, for making derogatory remarks against the chairman, Dr. Shankar Dayal Sharma. The text of the reprimand is:

> 'K.K. Tewary — this House has deplored the grave act of misdemeanour for which you bear responsibility in committing contempt of this House. The House is pained that the citizens of India should ever have been so at fault and apparently be unrepentent thereafter.
>
> This House therefore reprimands you and a more severe penalty is not administered only in the hope that through introspection you should realise the seriousness of your misdemeanour towards this House and to the sacred system of parliamentary democracy.
>
> I now direct you to withdraw.'

— The Third Backward Classes Commission, headed by O. Chinnappa Reddy, retired Supreme Court Judge, in its report to the Karnataka government, has restricted the reservations in favour of Other Backward Classes to 38 per cent as against the existing *ad hoc* reservation of 50 per cent for purposes of articles 15(4) and 16(4) of the Constitution.

The report, which was considered by the Veerendra Patil cabinet today, has suggested that the reservations under both the articles of the Constitution should be common. The commission has also taken away 32 specified castes from the list of the Other Backward Classes.

A cabinet sub-committee, under the chairmanship of the chief minister, is being constituted to scrutinise the report. The report would also be placed before the state legislature which is to begin its extended Budget session on 4 June.

The Law and Parliamentary Affairs Minister, Veerappa Moily, told a press conference that the Karnataka government would be earnest in implementing the commission's recommendations, after they are processed by the cabinet sub-committee. He asserted that the present government would not be "dishonest" as the previous government, a reference to the Hegde government's decision not to accept the Second

Backward Classes Commission's report.

After rejecting the Second Backward Classes Commission's report, the Hegde government evolved its own *ad hoc* scheme of reservation pending the report of the Third Commission it appointed under the chairmanship of Chinnappa Reddy. The one-man Third Commission submitted its report to the present government on 7 April.

Under the Hegde government's *ad hoc* scheme of reservations, nearly 92 per cent of the total population of the state had been brought under the Backward Classes and fitted into the reservation framework. The Venkataswamy Commission (Second Commission) had pegged the reservation quota to a rockbottom of 27 per cent on the basis of its finding that 33 per cent of the total population could be classed as Backward (apart from the 18 per cent constitutional reservation for the Scheduled Castes and the Scheduled Tribes). The first Backward Classes Commission headed by L.G. Havanur, had recommended 32 per cent reservation on the basis that 45 per cent of the total population was backward (it was later revised to 50 per cent by the Deveraj Urs government).

The main differences between the recommendations of the Third Backward Classes Commission and the reservation policy for backward classes as its exists under the present *ad hoc* scheme are: under the existing policy, except persons belonging to Group A, the backwardness in respect of all other categories is based on the caste-cum-means test, linked to profession/income-tax and sales tax payment/extent of land holding, etc. under the existing policy. Group A consists of denotified and nomadic tribes who are considered as backward, without reference to their incomes. Even these groups will fall within the indirect means test of profession-tax payment/land holding as formulated by the latest Commission.

The Commission, among other things, has divided the socially and the educationally backward classes into three categories. Categories I and II consist of caste/ community/religious/tribal groups identified by it on the basis of the comparative backwardness of the community as well as the size of the community, bearing in mind that some of the castes, etc. and groups were either so extremely backward or so small in number that they could not possibly hope to compete with the larger groups. Fifty-three such groups have been listed together with 14 such groups in the second category. The third category consists of occupational groups sans caste/community/religious/ tribal identification and those are in the nature of agricultural labourers, etc.

The reservations are for category I — 5 per cent, category II — 28 per cent, and category III is 5 per cent.

According to the bar put by the commission, no one will be entitled to the benefit of reservation, either under article 15(4) or article 16(4) if either of his parents is a Class I or Class II government officer or holds an equivalent post in a public sector undertaking or is employed under a private employer and draws a salary which is not less than that of a Class II officer; either of his parents is a professional-doctor, lawyer, chartered accountant, dental surgeon, engineer or architect, both of his parents are

Mixed Response: The news of the setting up of the tribunal elicited a mixed response.

The Tamil Nadu chief minister, M. Karunanidhi, welcomed the constitution of the tribunal.

The Karnataka law minister, M. Veerappa Moily, however said the National Front government at the centre had 'totally betrayed', the interests of the people of Karnataka by appointing the Cauvery tribunal.

Reacting sharply to the appointment of a three-member tribunal to settle the Cauvery dispute he said the action particularly when the review petition of the state government was pending before the Supreme Court, was highly 'condemnable'.

He said the changing attitude of the Prime Minister, V.P. Singh, on the issue on different occasions exposed his 'indifferent attitude', towards national issues.

The Karnataka chief minister, Veerendra Patil, today expressed surprise over the 'hurry', in which the union government had appointed the tribunal, but hoped that the state would get 'justice'.

Reacting to the appointment of the tribunal, Patil said despite Karnataka's request to the centre to solve the issue through negotiation, the appointment showed that the centre was in a hurry. 'If they wanted they could have approached the Supreme Court for the extension of time before the deadline', he pointed out.

'The National Front government's appointment of a tribunal to solve the Cauvery water dispute is a planned move and a political conspiracy' against Karnataka's farmers, the Congress leader, K.N. Nage Gowda, MLC, said in Bangalore today.

3 June 1990

— The World Bank has for India proposed a series of reforms to reduce fiscal deficits, increase efficiency and competitiveness of industry and overcome the serious imbalances in balance of payment.

This year's report of the bank of Indian economy, 'trends, issues and options', provides a review of the growth performance in the Seventh Plan and highlights the problems confronting the policy-makers. It will go before the India consortium meeting in Paris on 18 and 19 June.

With an average growth of 5.2 per cent in the 1980s, the bank says, a more dynamic economy should emerge in the 90s, but growing fiscal and balance of payments deficits pose 'the most serious threat to the economy'.

In the Seventh Plan period, agriculture staged a recovery on the strength of excellent crops in 1988-89 and 1989-90, industrial growth was faster than in the 1960s and 1970s and exports grew in volume by ten per cent annually in the last four years, 'largely dispelling the pressimism about exports that had gripped India since independence'.

Dealing with the macro-economic imbalance, the report says that rapidly increasing government consumption enlarged the public sector deficit to about 8.9 per cent of GDP. This was more than what could be accommodated by the rising private sector saving surplus. Excessive domestic aggregate demand spilled over into the balance of payments, financed by foreign savings and resulted in upward pressure on prices. Government's internal and external debt accumulated rapidly.

The bank notes the concern of Indian policy-makers at the high growth rates of the 1980s tending to be concentrated in capital and import-intensive industrial sectors and not generating the expected level of employment. Such a pattern of growth might be depleting the country's scarce capital and foreign exchange resources and not contributing to close the gap between the rich and poor.

Despite the excellent export performance, the current account deficit last year is estimated at 3.3 per cent of GDP ($ 7.7 billion exclusive of interest on NRI bank deposits). Industrial production also suffered a setback in 1989-90 with declines in output of phosphate fertiliser, steel and cement. Overall, the economy grew by 4.6 per cent.

In view of an uncomfortably low level of reserves and domestic price pressures, the report says, India needs to move promptly to restore balance to its economy.

On fiscal reforms, the report calls for compression of government consumption expenditure through limitations on growth of employment in government, and of wage and salary rates, limiting food and fertiliser subsidies and other subsidies provided implicitly (electricity, higher education and financial services offered at below cost rates).

The report calls for increased resources generation by public enterprises to ensure at least a three per cent return on invested capital so as to increase public savings. Coal India and the state electricity boards should be able to reduce claims on the budget for investment resources.

The tax structure should be rid of distortions like 'generous deductions and exemptions', built into the system of direct taxes and accelerated depreciation allowance in the corporate tax structure.

— Orissa's council of ministers has a blend of the rich and the poor, going by the list of their property statements formally released by the chief minister, Biju Patnaik, on 1 June 1990.

The richest of them all is the minister of state for industries, Dilip Ray, whose family assets, including those of his wife, his widowed mother and sons, total Rs. 65 lakh.

At the other end of the spectrum is the minister of state for labour and employment, Prafulla Samal, who is by far the poorest of the lot. He does not have any landed property of his own nor does he have any bank account.

The chief minister has shown a net wealth of Rs. 4.26 lakh after deducting the liabilities from the value of his property and bank balances.

The release of the property lists is in keeping with the assurance given by the Janata Dal before the elections. The chief minister has called upon the press and the public to point out if there are any discrepancies in the lists.

A close scrutiny of the lists reveal some curious details about the ministers' assets. For instance, the minister of state for food and civil supplies, Prasanna Acharya, says his wife received about 15 *tolas* of gold ornaments from her parents in 'the shape of dowry presentations'. The irrigation minister, Bijoy Mohapatra, includes in his list 'gold ornaments of my wife amounting to Rs. 30,000 which she brought during marriage'.

— The Tamil Nadu chief minister and DMK president, M. Karunanidhi, started his day at midnight by cutting a six-foot tall birthday cake. The ruling party chief is 67 today. His party made elaborate arrangements to celebrate the occasion.

Everything about the three-day celebrations was on a grand scale. The organisers printed invitation cards in the form of a 10-page booklet — one page of every function. Mega-cutouts of Kalainger Karunanidhi towered over welcome-arches put up on the roads leading the DMK party headquarters — Anna Arivalayam — and Panagal Park at T. Nagar, where a public meeting was held this evening as a grand finale to the celebrations. The birthday cake was in the shape of the five-storeyed Arivalayam building.

A panel discussion on the achievements of the Karunanidhi government, a photographic exhibition and a *kavi sammelan* were the highlights of the birthday celebrations that started on 1 June. Among the special invites were the chief ministers of Assam, Orissa and Pondicherry, four Union ministers and the Telugu Desam Party chief N.T. Rama Rao.

The vice-president, Shankar Dayal Sharma, sent a message greeting to Karunanidhi on his sixty-seventh birthday. The governor, Surjit Singh Barnala, called on him and presented a bouquet. The Union finance minister, Madhu Dandavate, on a visit to the city yesterday to address the Tamil Nadu Chamber of Commerce, took time off to drop in at Kalaivanar Arangam, where Karunanidhi was attending the *kavi sammelan*. Dandavate, spoke of his admiration for Karunanidhi's courage in imposing the Emergency.

The public meeting at Panagal Park this evening marked the end of three-day programme. The meeting was addressed, among others, by Rama Rao, the visiting ministers and representatives of the DMK-led alliance partners — the CPI, the CPM, the Janata Dal and the Tamil Nadu Muslim League (Latheef).

In a message to his partymen Karunanidhi said they were the source of his strength. The party cadres, who stood by him all along, had given him the courage to go through the ordeals he faced in his public life. The DMK chief observed that he had no ill feeling towards his critics. Nor was he perturbed by those who thrived on attacking him.

The DMK chief, in recent weeks, had been criticised even by his party allies for the stand he took against the IPKF. Karunanidhi's boycott of the public reception given to the IPKF on its return from Sri Lanka evoked sharp reaction from many quarters. Karunanidhi, rattled by persistent reports regarding LTTE presence in Tamil Nadu, has vehemently refuted the charge saying that it was levelled by those seeking to drive a wedge between the DMK government and the centre.

— The Constitution (Scheduled Castes) Orders (Amendment) Act, 1990 was passed by Parliament on 9 May 1990 extending the benefits of reservation in services to the neo-Buddhists. The Bill received the President's assent on 3 June 1990

4 June 1990

— The central government today announced the issue of four loans totalling Rs. 2,000 crore.

— The President of the Federation of Indian Chambers of Commerce and Industry (FICCI), Raunaq Singh, today, exhorted the business community to take up pollution control measures in 'right earnestness' and to treat environment as an integral part of the corporate strategy. 'A new culture has to be built which should address itself to environment content of a product or a technology before it has been or put to use'.

— The Bank Employees Federation of India today decided to observe a full day strike on 12 July. They put forward their demand: 'restructure pay scales, revise dearness allowance, grant pension, pay bonus for all and halt further computerisation and others'.

5 June 1990

— A national government at the centre is favoured by the Prime Minister, V.P. Singh. The national government is to include all political parties: a national consensus on issues would be positive for the people.

Brain drain from premier Indian institutes is on the rise and so is the number of students who commit suicide. T.N. Kaul, former Ambassador to Soviet Union, said today.

— The World Bank loan for a 400 kV transmission ring around the Capital, to ensure more and quality electricity supply, is unlikely to come through, it is learnt.

The World Bank is understood to have informally conveyed this to the Union energy ministry about a week ago. The Rs. 60 million loan, suspended in early 1989, is linked to the Delhi Electric Supply Undertaking's (DESU) financial health. DESU had agreed to take action to earn a surplus of three per cent on fixed capital assets by 1990-91 — essentially necessitating a revision in tariff.

The Delhi Electric Supply Committee even gave the green signal for this in October last but the tariff hike has not come through. And, since the supersession of the corporation, the buck has been passed back and forth between the Delhi Administration and the ministry.

The ministry, it is learnt, is likely to send a letter to the Delhi Administration within the next few days, asking it to arrange funds on its own by approaching the Planning Commission.

In August last, it may be recalled, the cabinet committee on economic affairs had partially approved DESU's financial recovery plan, to which the loan is linked. It waived the Rs. 1,100 crore owed by DESU to the

Badarpur power station, which is controlled by the National Thermal Power Corporation, and, approved the conversion of principal amount of loan — Rs. 1,000 crore — into perpetual loan. After March 1989, 50 per cent of the amount would attract interest.

8 June 1990

— Virendra Verma, Janata Dal member of Rajya Sabha, has been appointed Governor of Punjab.

— The Union Law Minister, Dinesh Goswami, today explained that the transfer of two Judges — Justice P.S. Mishra of the Patna High Court and Justice S.K. Desai of the Bombay High Court — had been done on the recommendation of the Chief Justice of India and that the government had no hand in it.

Addressing a press conference here today. Goswami said the government had only processed the recommendations made by the Chief Justice and had not initiated any transfer orders on its own. 'The executive would go strictly by the recommendations of the Chief Justice', the minister said, adding, 'no proposal for transfer of any judge will be initiated from my table'.

A controversy has arisen over the transfer of Justice Mishra, who was moved from the Patna High Court to the Madras High Court. There had been some protests about his transfer and the Madras High Court bar had even dubbed it as 'vindictive'.

Justice Desai's transfer order has also become controversial as the recommendation has come in the wake of serious corruption charges being levelled against the judge.

In the case of Justice Mishra, the minister said, the recommendation to transfer him had actually been made last June during the tenure of the former Chief Justice. The recommendation was made again in August but was not processed by the government immediately. When the National Front government came to power, Goswami said, it decided not to act on this proposal but sent it back to the new Chief Justice for his remarks. The transfer, he said, was processed by the government only after it received his recommendation on 21 April.

Similarly, in the case of Justice Desai, Goswami said, 'the government would only process the proposal of the Chief Justice, confirming that a recommendation to this effect has been made. Unless there was any valid reason, the government would not reject the recommendations of the Chief Justice. The transfers were not punitive, he added.

Regarding the future transfer of judges, Goswami said the government had introduced a Bill in the Lok Sabha on the setting up of a National Judicial Commission, which would recommend all appointments and transfers of judges.'

— A conflict between the legislature and the judiciary appears to be surfacing in Orissa with members of the state legislative assembly criticising the decision of the Central Administrative Tribunal (CAT) to grant a stay on the disclosure of property statements of officials to a house committee of the assembly.

Cutting across party lines, several members of the assembly today argued that the CAT had committed a breach of privilege of the House by granting the stay.

Moving a privilege notice in the assembly, Prasanna Pal of the Janata Dal demanded that the tribunal be censured for 'interfering in the business of this house'. Several members from both treasury and opposition benches shared his views. The speaker reserved his ruling.

Only yesterday, a house committee, inquiring into the illegal acquisition of property by persons holding public office, had created a storm in the assembly when it stated that its investigations had been hampered because the property statements of government officials had not been made available to it.

Presenting its interim report to the assembly, the committee chairman, Ashok Das, MLA, said despite several reminders, the chief secretary had not provided the required statements to the committee on the plea that they were secret documents.

The chief secretary, who appeared before the committee on 21 May, is said to have held that the property statements of the officials kept in sealed covers in pursuance of the Orissa government servants conduct rules could only be opened and used by the authorities prescribed under the said rules.

Das, however, contended that the committee duly constituted by the assembly had the powers to send for persons, papers and records. He also said that there was 'no reason to entertain any doubt over the jurisdiction of the committee in calling for the property statements of officers because its disclosure does not in any way jeopardise the safety and security of the state'.

The Central Administrative Tribunal, meanwhile, is reported to have issued an interim order to the chief secretary staying the handing over the property statements to the house committee till 19 June, while admitting a writ petition filed by the secretary of the IAS officers' association.

The issue was raised today by Arun Dey (CPI) who demanded a discussion on the matter which concerned the privilege and the immunity of the legislature. He said that under the Constitution, the functioning of the Parliament and state legislatures did not come under the purview of courts.

Bhagabat Behera of the Augmta Dal wanted a notice of breach of privilege to be served on the chief secretary and the secretary of the IAS Officers' Association which had filed a petition before the CAT.

The former chief minister, Nandini Satpathy (Congress), supported the step taken by the house committee to investigate cases of illegal acquisition of wealth and said that 'those in public life cannot escape scrutiny'.

The BJP member, B.K. Deo, also criticised the CAT for its stay. He said that the house committee was a fact-finding committee set by the assembly to cleanse public life and it should be allowed to carry out its investigations.

— Justice S.K. Desai today resigned his judgeship of the Bombay High Court amidst charges of corruption, after 20 years on the bench.

The controversial judge took the unprecedented step after he was informed at around noon that he had been transferred to the Kerala High Court as puisne judge. The telephonic message said he would cease to be a judge of the Bombay High Court from noon tomorrow. Justice Desai submitted his resignation to the Chief Justice, Chittatosh Mookerjee, a few hours later. It was to be forwarded to the President of India by courier at 5.30 p.m. so as to reach him before noon tomorrow. It is believed that this is the first time in the post-independence history of the higher judiciary that a judge has resigned following corruption charges.

Lawyers at the court realised that something was in the offing when an employee from the chief justice's office interrupted the court of the judicial head to convey a message. Mookerjee immediately rose and went to his chamber. He then called Justice Desai and communicated to him the message from Delhi that he had been transferred.

The news spread throughout the court in no time and the emotionally stirred judge confirmed to press persons who rushed to his chamber that he had been shifted. He indicated that he would have something important to say at around 3.45 p.m. It is reliably understood that the judge had decided in advance that he would resign if he were transferred.

Despite recurrent rumours over the last few years that there was interference in some cases before the judge, his popularity among sections of the bar was evident today. A team of lawyers came to meet Justice Desai and said he could be unanimously accepted as being among the best legal minds in the country.

The judge spoke at length to the press, once after he got the news of his transfer and later when he sent in his resignation, which merely said that he had quit with immediate effect. The resignation becomes valid when it reaches the president.

A composed Justice Desai said he was saddened by the transfer order due to which he had to quit, just over four months before he was to have retired on 27 October. He said he had asked the Chief Justice of India, who is believed to have recommended his transfer, that he wanted to meet him in Delhi at his own cost to explain his point of view.

That did not happen, he said, and added that the transfer order was not fair since it gave him no chance to rebutt the charges against him.

He felt he had to resign since 'it was not a question of manoeuvering but of doing what was right'. Justice Desai said the decision to transfer him had been taken some time ago.

The Judge, speaking about the future, said he would take it easy for some time after which he would 'do some work'. He added that he would take the advice of legal experts with regard to those who had made scandalous allegations against him.

Justice Desai said charges that he was corrupt and that he was intimate with a woman, Ms Thelma Menezes, who allegedly interfered in the functioning of the court, were a mystery to him. He expressed surprise over the animus shown towards him by some persons. He was particularly pained by the letters written by the advocate-general, Arvind Bobde, to the governor, C. Subramaniam, over Justice M. P. Kenta's fast. The letter listed serious charges against him.

The judge also accused a section of the press for his present predicament. He reiterated his demand for an inquiry either by the Chief Justice of Bombay or the Attorney-General of India. Commenting on the 'loss of confidence' resolutions sought to be passed against him, the judge said they were 'totally unfair'.

9 June 1990

— Improving access to housing finance, setting up of special institutions both at the national and state levels for increasing the flow of funds for providing serviced land, increasing investments and amendment of the Urban Land Ceiling Act are among the highlights of the draft housing policy released here today.

— The Minister for Environment and Forests, Nilamani Routray, says there is no question of 'clipping Maneka Gandhi's wings' because she had herself 'insisted upon' a division of the ministry's work.

Besides, the cabinet secretary, V.C. Pande, requested all the ministries on 16 May to distribute work between the respective cabinet ministers and ministers of state, Routray said in an interview.

'I was in fact the last one to carry out the distribution because I personally preferred working jointly (with Maneka Gandhi) in all the matters'. Routray added.

He recalled that one of his earliest orders (dated 8 May) after his transfer to the environment ministry was that all the files should come to him through the minister of state.

Then why does Gandhi appear to be upset with the division made on 30 May? In a sarcastic reaction in the press, she said: 'If Nilamoni Routray thinks he can take care of the whole of India's environmental problems, except the Delhi Zoo, he is most welcome'.

When this was pointed out to Routray, he said: 'I don't want to be sarcastic like her. That is here view. All I can say is I have given her 40 per cent of the responsibilities. You may compare this with other ministries. There are ministers of state who have just 10 to 15 per cent'. But Gandhi, despite her commitment and dynamism, is alleged to have been left with rather innocuous powers. 'No, no, that is also a great misconception. Take for instance, the three water and air pollution laws I have put under her charge. There are some 4,000 cases being prosecuted under these laws, which were strengthened as recently as in 1988. Whereas there are only 92 cases under the Environment Protection Act, which I have kept with myself'. Routray said.

Does he plan to make any policy changes? 'No, we really have no policy differences. I stand by the policy pronouncements made when V.P. Singh himself was holding the environment portfolio. . . . But for some reason the press has been trying to make out that there have been drastic changes since I took over. Worse, they are trying to bolster their claim by making false charges.

'One report said I had revoked Ms Gandhi's order against the construction of a hotel in the Konark forest. We issued a contradiction saying the cancellation order still stands. Another report talks of yet another hotel project I am supposed to have cleared in the forest near Khajuraho. This is a worse fabrication because the ministry has received no such proposal in the first place. So the question of Gandhi having refused permission does not arise, much less that of the new cabinet minister having reversed her action'.

While Routray claims to have no policy differences with Ms Gandhi, he has obliquely admitted that he disagrees with her style of functioning.

Referring to the Narmada controversy, he said Ms Gandhi had suggested to him that they should boycott a meeting convened by the water resources ministry to discuss the issue with the chief ministers concerned. Her reason was that the water resources ministry was disregarding environmental factors involved in the issue.

'Now how can a government function if one ministry boycotts another? And how can a problem be solved if you are not willing to discuss it? So I did attend the meeting and I did so without compromising my ministry's stand. I can say my approach has succeeded because Manubhai Kotadia (minister for water resources development) had in writing accepted all our pre-conditions for the environmental clearance of the project,' Routray said.

Regarding the general debate on 'big dams vs small dams'. Routray said he was not averse to the construction of big dams as well so long as they fulfilled all the environmental criteria. When it was pointed out that big dams are said to induce earthquakes, he insisted that only those that are located in high seismic zones are hazardous.

Does it then mean he will not allow the Tehri dam? 'Let me clarify that the fate of a national project like it is decided by the cabinet, not just the environment ministry. Out environmental appraisal committee has already submitted a report opposing the project. This report is now being studied by a committee appointed by the cabinet secretariat. After this committee gives its opinion, the matter will be finalised by the cabinet,' Routray explained.

Though he insists that the Baliapal issue will also be decided by the entire cabinet, Routray takes a very keen interest because of his personal association with it. Going into various intricacies of the proposed missile test range in his home state of Orissa, he said he knew so much about it because he had been part of the movement against it.

But surprisingly, the minister for environment and forests has never heard of Kaiga, let alone the controversy about locating a nuclear power station in that Karnataka village. He even claimed that 'to the best of my knowledge' the environment ministry did not have any file on the subject.

Routray had an even more surprising observation to make about some radical proposals publicised by Ms Gandhi: Environmental courts, solar energy commission, national river authority and national fund for afforestation.

'I have not come across any written proposal on any of them. She may have talked about them with the press but no attempt seems to have been made to translate her words into action', he said.

11 June 1990

— While broadly supporting the proposal to accord constitutional status to Panchayati Raj institutions, reserving seats for women and weaker section and making supersession of local bodies difficult, the state chief ministers, who met in Delhi, could not arrive at a consensus on some crucial issues like the mode of holding elections and disqualification of members. Opinions also differed on the centre's proposal to set up state-level finance commissions to monitor finances of these institutions. The concept of gram sabha (body of all electorates of a village) being the supreme basic wing of the rural democratic set up received general approval.

Significantly, the West Bengal chief minister, Jyoti Basu, who had serious reservations about the Panchayati Raj Amendment Bill circulated by the previous Rajiv government, gave his nod to the fresh proposals. The Gujarat chief minister, Chimanbhai Patel, who had also been a staunch opponent of the idea of 'centralising' the Panchayati Raj system through a constitutional amendment, also seemed to have relented. The Maharashtra government, however, welcomed the proposal to accord constitutional status to the Panchayati Raj bodies if 'representative character of these institutions in maintained'.

Inaugurating the two-day conference of state chief ministers, the Prime Minister, V.P. Singh, pointed out that the National Front government's proposals sought to provide a constitutional mandate to Panchayati Raj bodies to make sure that their basic framework was beyond the intervention of political leadership or bureaucracy. Model guidelines were also being issued to facilitate amendment of laws by state governments. The proposed measures were far more flexible.

According to an official spokesman, the fresh proposals differed vastly from the earlier ones and gave a greater choice to state governments to modify the system. While the previous government wanted panchayat elections to be conducted by the Election Commission, the suggestion now is to let the states set up their own election commissions for this purpose. The states have also been given the option to appoint finance commissions to supervise the financial aspects of panchayats, against the former proposal of handing over this task to the auditor-general. Similarly, the present move is not rigid about a three-tier structure for the panchayati raj system.

However, it is intended to make gram sabha as the main instrument of grass-root democracy. Constituted by all persons registered in electoral rolls of a village, the gram sabha may exercise such powers in relation to panchayats as the state legislature may provide for.

Besides the panchayati raj, the agenda before the conference includes strengthening of urban local bodies, revision of agrarian laws for effective implementation of land reforms and urban land and property reforms.

Though most chief ministers who participated in the deliberations today stressed the need for paying greater attention to urban local bodies and urban land reforms, the main focus remained on the rural sector. All the speakers, including the Prime Minister and other central ministers, expressed dissatisfaction over the implementation of land reforms.

Even, while conceding failure on the land reforms front, the Deputy Prime Minister, Devi Lal made a statement stressing that 'a similar concern' had not been shown towards 'more far reaching inequities that exist and have developed over the years in respect of ownership of land in urban areas'. He pointed out that about 55 per cent of vacant urban land in Bombay was owned by 91 individuals.

He said land in urban areas had emerged as a source of abnormal profits and was being used for speculative purposes which was generally not the case in rural areas. He suggested that value of both land and buildings be taken into account and the ceiling limits be determined on the basis of the entire value of the property. There was need to establish some correspondence between the ceiling limits on agricultural holdings and for urban land and property.

In his inaugural address, the Prime Minister deviated from the test to suggest that, like the poverty line, there should be an upper line for richness. '*Lok Garibi Rekha ke upar rahein aur Amiri Rekha ke neechey rahein*', he said (People should live above the poverty line and below the richness line).

Pointing out that formal courts and conventional judicial procedures were too slow and complex to be of benefit to rural people, V.P. Singh suggested the setting up of 'nyaya panchayats' to provide speedy and inexpensive justice to villagers.

He announced that, based on the consensus, a constitutional amendment Bill would be introduced in the next session of Parliament. A larger set of issues, including the core provisions proposed for inclusion in the Constitution and other aspects, such as social control and Nyaya Panchayats, had been specifically identified in the set of model guidelines on Panchayati Raj institutions. He expressed the hope that states would adopt these guidelines and incorporate them in their legislation. He also said the government proposed to bring forward a Constitution amendment Bill to include a new provision dealing with urban local bodies.

Singh posed a question to the chief ministers, ministers and officials whether it was fair on their part to occupy large bungalows built on urban land? "We should ask ourselves where should the urban ceiling start? If we opt for smaller houses, it will be a good moral message to the country that we mean business", he said.

The urban development minister, Murasoli Maran, told the chief ministers that the agenda for urban bodies was the same as for village panchayats — regular election through state election commissions, reservation of seats for women and persons belonging to the scheduled castes and scheduled tribes, and state finance commissions for periodic review of finances of local bodies.

Stressing the need for strengthening urban local bodies as effective instruments of local self-government, Maran said the Constitution should enable the states to bring about the necessary measures without in any way harming the federal character.

Addressing the conference, the Bihar chief minister, Lalu Prasad said, persons involved in the misuse or misappropriation of public funds should be disqualified for membership to the panchayati raj institutions.

Prasad said the provisions in the Constitution at present with regard to the panchayati raj institutions were insufficient and for that reason these institutions had not grown to acquire the required strength.

13 June 1990

— Cecil Noronha, Karnataka's home commissioner till recently, took over as Vice-chairman of Delhi Development Authority. He is thus the chief executive head of DDA. He is an IAS officer of the 1962 batch.

— After their success with prepoll predictions during the 1989 Lok Sabha and 1990 State Assembly Elections, Indian election experts are now looking for swing zones to make even more accurate forecasts.

"Swing" and "split" factors together with what pollsters call Index of Opposition Unity (IOU) spell the outcome of an election, says a new book on elections. So far national swing zones — or homogeneous areas which react the same way to a national swing in their voting behaviour — have eluded Indian pollsters. But they have discerned interesting patterns at the state level. Feeding past pattern of electoral behaviour into computers, election experts have divided most states into at least three distinct zones, according to the book *Forty Years of the World's Largest Democracy*. These groups constitute traditional Congress strongholds, areas which have generally voted non-Congress parties, and the constituencies which sway with electoral "winds" and "waves". The book also describes how psephologists were able to just hit the bull's eye with their pre-poll prediction in the November 1989 Lok Sabha and February 1990 assembly elections. Election experts look for patterns and trends in the way Indians have voted over the last 38 years, hold opinion polls in carefully selected constituencies, and then translate the data into seats, says the book. This is done by some complex calculations based on what they call the "cube law", the "Index of Opposition Unity" (IOU), and the "lying factor". Several studies have shown that in two-party systems the seats won by a party are usually "in proportion to the cube of the percentage of votes polled by the party". By this "cube law" a party getting say 52 per cent of the popular vote may corner over 78 per cent of the seats and a swing of two per cent in favour of a party may give it eight per cent more seats. In India too, one witnesses the phenomenon of the winning party getting a much larger share of seats. But notwithstanding this similarity of disproportions, the "cube law" in its original form does not seem to work in India. It one treats the winning party and a combination of the losing parties as two parties, the law would give the opposition parties a majority, as the Congress, or for that matter the Janata Party in 1977, has never won the national election with the support of a majority of national voters.

But a modified version of the cube law seems to work in the Indian type multi-party systems. This involves a marriage with another concept evolved to translate a multi-party situation into a two-party one — the concept of the Index of Opposition Unity (IOU). Psephologists define IOU as the proportion of votes polled by the largest opposition party to the total opposition vote. In a two-party situation, the IOU would be one and a split in opposition votes would lower the IOU. Seat adjustments and understanding between various anti-Congress parties at the time of the November 1989 Lok Sabha elections raised the IOU to 0.8951 — which was somewhat akin to visual one-to-one straight contests between the Congress and its opponents in nine out of every 10 constituencies. By the time of the February 1990 elections, the IOU had fallen to 0.7, denoting some fragmentation in the ranks of anti-Congress parties and resulting in fewer straight contests. The modified cube law multiplies the total vote of opposition or lower parties by the IOU and then assigns this proportion of votes to an "ideal" second party to calculate the number of seat that may be won by the losing parties together.

— Augmenting edible oil supply through imports, strict enforcement of weekly sale quota of sugar mills, punishment for the diversion of kerosene for adulterating diesel and stepping up vigilance against hoarding are among the measures proposed by the government to bring down prices of essential items.

The Prime Minister, V.P. Singh, who reviewed the overall price situation in a meeting with the cabinet committee on prices yesterday, directed the State Trading Corporation (STC) to ensure sufficient stocking of edible oils for supply through the public distribution system (PDS). It was pointed out in the meeting that arrangements had already been made for the import of adequate quantity of edible oil to meet the deficit during the lean season. The government was confident that the prices of tea and cement would fall soon. The industry ministry has been asked to take "firm measures" for bringing down the price of salt by boosting production to meet increasing industrial demand. The meeting was attended by the Deputy Prime Minister, Devi Lal, the finance minister, Prof. Madhu Dandavate, the commerce minister, Arun Nehru, the food and civil supplies minister, Nathu Ram Mirdha and the industry minister, Ajit Singh besides senior officials. A government spokesman claimed that the rise in wholesale prices was only 0.9 per cent this year in the four months preceding the week ending on 26 May. This was marginally lower than the one per cent rise in the corresponding period last year. In 1988, however, the increase was only 0.3 per cent.

It was pointed out in meeting that sugar availability in 1990 would be adequate to meet the demand as the domestic production was expected to be a record 106 lakh tonnes. Emphasis was nevertheless laid on enforcement of the weekly sale target of a minimum of 20 per cent of the monthly free sale quota of each mill. The quantity remaining undespatched out of the month would be treated as levy sugar and used in subsequent months for distribution through the PDS.

The step takes to increase the availability of edible oil included reduction of stock limits, increase of bank margins, dehoarding operations, larger issues through public distribution system and substantial increase in the supply of one kilogram poly pouches.

It was decided in the meeting that blending of oil by the approved agencies including oilseeds growers' cooperative federations. would be expedited. The National Diary Development Board (NDDB) was authorised to undertake judicious market intervention measures with imported and domestic oil procured by it. The review of the tea situation revealed that the offerings of tea in domestic auctions had gone up and there had been a noticeable decrease in auction prices. It was decided to ask manufacturers to increase supplies of economy tea packs. It was hoped that tea prices would come down in the retail market thanks to bright crop prospects.

After a series of meetings with the government, the cement industry had agreed to roll back cement prices to the level obtaining in March 1990. The Prime Minister expressed the desire that this commitment be fulfilled. The industry ministry had been asked to do the needful. Adulteration of kerosene with diesel has been a major factor in kerosene diversion. V.P. Singh directed that kerosene control order be promulgated in all states, incorporating the provision for punishment to prevent adulteration. The increase in salt prices following iodisation and packing was considered to be on the high side and not commensurate with the cost of iodisation. The Prime Minister, therefore, asked the industry ministry to take steps to increase production to bring down prices. The enforcement and vigilance organisations under the civil supplies department in all states have also been instructed to keep strict vigil over hoarders and anti-social elements to curb hoarding and black-marketeering.

— The scheme for waivering farm loans is facing rough weather with nearly all the states expressing their inability to meet their share of the financial burden.

The cost of the scheme which was estimated at Rs. 2,842 crore, has gone up by another Rs. 282 crore following the decision to extend the scheme to even those who have borrowed more than Rs. 10,000.

The centre's original proposal was that it would meet 100 per cent of the cost so far as the loans taken from the nationalised banks were concerned, but the state governments would have to reimburse the state cooperative and land development banks for writing off the loans.

This was strongly opposed by Maharashtra and Gujarat which argued that they were being penalised for having a strong cooperative movement. Following their representation the centre agreed to beer 50 per cent of the states' share of the cost.

The state chief ministers who met the Prime Minister in the connection have said that because of their budgetary constraints they would not be able to meet more than 10 per cent of their share of the burden. While no decision has been taken on the issue, the finance minister, Madhu Dandavate, told the Forum of Financial Writers last night that the government was considering if the Reserve Bank of India could give an overdraft to National Bank for Agriculture and Rural Development (NABARD) to write off the loans from cooperative and land development banks. The finance minister agreed that in effect this would imply the RBI giving overdrafts to the state governments. He said the state government would be required to clear the amount within two to three years. Dandavate was present at the chief minister's meeting with the Prime Minister. The finance minister admitted that since the announcement of the farm loan waiver scheme, recovery rate of loans in the farm sector has dropped sharply. He, however, assured that the government would not allow the credibility of the banking system to erode.

Dandavate said the promise of waiving the loans was put in the election manifesto of the National Front without studying its financial implications. Asked if there was a guarantee that such a promise would not be repeated every five years before the polls. Dandavate said there could be some justification of the scheme as the farm prices have been unremunerative. Since the agriculture prices commission would examine the cost structure and recommend remunerative prices, there would be no possibility of the loan waiver scheme being repeated in future. What if the opposition parties made such promises to get rural votes, the finance minister was asked. "It is up to them," he said. The budget for 1990-91 has provided Rs. 1,000 crore for the scheme but with the states refusing to meet the cost more money has to be found. At the same time, the finance minister reiterated that he would make all efforts to contain the deficit within the budgetary estimate of Rs. 7,206 crore. He would also like to get a law enacted under the article 292 of the Constitution to put a ceiling on both internal and external borrowings.

14 June 1990

— In an attempt to re-orient the Public Distribution System (PDS) in the country, the central government proposes to make the poor the main beneficiaries of the programme. The Planning Commission has proposed that from April next allocation of cereals from the central pool would be made to states on the basis of the number of people below the poverty line, according to Ela Bhatt, member of the Planning Commission.

— The price of land allotments to the cooperative group housing societies in "Dwaraka" (Papankalan), has been cut by Rs. 400 sq. m. Allotments will be made within the next three months to approximately 400 such societies.

The Delhi Administration has done this in response to public protest at last year's trebling of land prices from about Rs. 450 square metre (fixed in 1985-86) to Rs. 1375 square metre. The new square metre rate of land allotted by the Delhi Development Authority (DDA) to cooperative group housing societies, will be Rs. 975 for "Dwaraka", Rs. 950 for north and west Delhi and Rs. 925 for trans-Yamuna land. These rates will apply till 31 March next after which they may be revised.

Besides "Dwaraka" (meant to house 11 lakh, when finished) the other ongoing housing project is at Narela (extreme north Delhi). Allotments of land will begin right away — only to cooperative group housing societies — in both. Around 300 housing societies are expected to get land by end-September at "Dwaraka" and another 100 at Narela. "Dwaraka" has finally been cleared by the city's Urban Art Commission, the official aesthetic watchdog.

These housing societies were formed recently under the DDA's "Avas Saakar Yojana". This scheme was meant for those who had registered with the DDA in 1979 for a house. Of the approximately 1.7 lakh who did so that year, the DDA has still to give houses to about 73000. Last year, DDA offered those waiting an opportunity — if they could get together and form cooperative group housing societies, these would get first priority in land allotments. Those who chose not to would remain on the DDA rolls with no conditions changed, the commitments made to them would stay.

Many took up the DDA offer. They will be cleared first in the new allotments. After them, follow those registered in 1983.

Around 1400 societies had applied to the office of the registrar, cooperative group housing societies. The registrar asked them to finalise their members and then began verifying their credentials. He has, so far, cleared 917 of these; their lists have been sent to the DDA.

These 917 societies, plus the others of 1983 who will be cleared in due course, will get their turn after the 1979-Awas Saakar groups have been served. Allotment will follow the "first come, first served" principle. This means the seniority list of societies with the DDA based on when the registrar of cooperative societies cleared them, will be followed.

Has water and electricity for these to-be-allotted societies been arranged or not? The answer, so far, the Delhi Administration's soothing assurances aside, is a clear no. Delhi is short of water for current needs itself. However, the bright spot is an imminent agreement with Haryana to give Delhi an additional 100 million gallons of water a day. Set against this, rising consumption and shortages apart, is the requirement for "Dwaraka" alone, when completed — 80 million gallons a day of water (MGD). The massive Rohini housing scheme (another 11 lakh people when completed) is already short of water. It ideally needs about 50 MGD, but the municipal corporation says they were never consulted about this. They aren't giving much more than a fifth of that amount. Everyone's pinning hopes on water agreements with neighbouring states — Haryana right now. Delhi's annual population influx might be about two lakh but it depends on neighbouring states for every drop of water it currently takes or hopes to take, from the Yamuna or elsewhere.

15 June 1990

A piquant political situation has developed today in Nagaland after the chief minister, K.L. Chishi, challenged the speaker, T.N. Ngulie's authority to convene the emergency session of the assembly on 19 June for the trial of strength.

Chishi said that the speaker had convened the session without taking the governor M.M. Thomas' concurrence.

The Raj Bhavan sources, meanwhile, when contracted, denied that the governor had summoned an emergency session of the assembly.

This was, however, contradicted by the speaker who said the governor had already sent a note regarding the emergency session to the chief minister. He said that the decision had been taken only after a meeting with the governor.

The state capital witnessed hectic political activities with the rival groups trying to get the support of legislators.

Supporters of Vamuzo, leader of the Joint Legislature Party of the Joint Legislature Party (JLP), comprising the Nagaland Peoples Council (NPC) and the Congress, have been camping in a hotel for the past three days.

Chishi held frequent meetings with his supporters and ministers. He reiterated that most of the NPC MLAs, who had withdrawn their support earlier, had decided to back him during the trial of strength on Tuesday.

Meanwhile, the finance and higher education minister, Chubatemjenao, who had resigned from the ministry on 13 June, withdrew his resignation today.

16 June 1990

— In the startling abdication of ministerial responsibility and rejection of the established norms of cabinet functioning, the Deputy Prime Minister. Devi Lal, went against his own ministry during the chief minister's meetings on 11 and 12 June. He renounced not only the official papers prepared for the meeting and circulated under his own signature, but practically disowned the officials of his department when they were subjected to virulent attacks.

The course that the conference was allowed to take was such that it was apparent that the government's commitment to land reforms and the National Front's promise in its election manifesto were a mere eye-wash. In spite of invoking a blatantly populist concept of *amiri rekha* (line of affluence), even the Prime Minister, V.P. Singh, departed from his prepared concluding speech to go along with the anti-land reforms views by pro-rich farmer chief ministers. He, too, stated that there was no need for further legislative action in this regard when the agenda papers prepared for the conference with his approval say quite the opposite.

The distance between the leaders' public posture and their real views on issues of poverty alleviation became apparent when a concerted attack was launched on the secretary of the department of rural development and other officials who on the behest of the Deputy Prime Minister had prepared the official notes for the chief ministers' meeting and had followed the letter and spirit of the deliberations in the earlier meetings of revenue ministers.

The attack was launched by Veerendra Verma whose presence in the chief ministers' meeting was itself odd. Verma was then merely governor-designate of Punjab and had not taken the oath of office. Nevertheless, he was allowed to be present and initiate a personal tirade against the rural development secretary, the redoubtable S.R. Sankaran, and the joint secretary, K.B. Saxena, who are both known for their pro-poor records and strict action against various law-breaking mafia. In the manner of Pontius Pilate, the Deputy Prime Minister washed his hands off the affair and allowed his subordinate officials to be attacked.

The gravemen of Verma's charge was that land reforms were

unnecessary and that they were being promoted only by bureaucrats who had no knowledge of ground realities. Verma was supported by several chief ministers who departed from their prepared speeches, which were proland reforms, and articulated the real concerns which revolved round the protection of those who grossly violate the laws of the land in this regard.

Chimanbhai Patel, whose government has announced its intention of changing the definition of "personal cultivation" and thereby encouraging the violation of land laws in Gujarat, joined the attack. Sunderlal Patwa spoke in defence of absentee landlordism. Sharad Pawar said that whatever needed to be done in terms of land reforms had already been accomplished in Maharashtra. Even Biju Patnaik, who keeps a populist posture intact and whose government in Orissa had prescribed a low land ceiling, spoke against the government's proposals.

Indeed the anti-land reforms approach cut across party lines and went against the election manifestoes of the National Front, Congress and the BJP. The West Bengal chief minister, Jyoti Basu, and the revenue minister, Benoy Choudhri, were of course predictably for land reforms. But of the others, very few even cared to make appropriate noises.

Interestingly, while Mulayam Singh Yadav's UP government took a positive stand the strongest support for the measures came from Lalloo Prasad Yadav, chief minister of Bihar, who even asked the assembled chief ministers to resign if they were not able to implement laws which were pro-poor.

The chief minister's conference on land reforms, which was taking place after 18 long years in spite of public professions of different governments in this regard, was hijacked by the more amiable discussions on panchayati raj. There too, reporting on the deliberations, the official spokesperson committed a faux pas by claiming that the Karnataka panchayat system had provisions for the right of recall, which in fact is not true.

In all, the conference was a disaster, marked by the articulation of an abysmal lack of political will even as the Prime Minister in particular unleashed his now familiar populist rhetoric. The demoralisation caused by the Prime Minister and the Deputy Prime Minister among serious-minded officials is such that some of them have been pushed towards submitting their resignations. The cabinet secretary is reported to have tried to do some "damage control", but the response of the top leaders of the government to their own electoral promises does not inspire confidence among a large segment of officials who are appalled by the distance between public posturing and actual action.

— The Delhi Administration will make sales tax assessment easier for traders whose gross turnover does not exceed Rs. 6 lakhs annually.

The new scheme, to take effect from 1 August, is called "Simplified tax assessment according to returns of traders" (START). Essentially, it calls for "trust in traders", since the annual statement filed by the dealer will be the basis for assessment. Officials will help in filing the returns, and give an acknowledgement-cum-assessment order on the spot. One in 10 of these forms will be randomly taken for a detailed scrutiny.

About three in five of the more than lakh registered dealers are likely to benefit, says the city's Lieutenant-Governor, Arjan Singh. With some exceptions, new dealers, for instance, cannot take advantage of the scheme in their first year of assessment. Neither can those for whom it will be the last year of assessment. Or, if there have been he adverse comments against any dealer in the past three years, he will be out, too. And, of course, those blacklisted — some 500 — cannot even seek fresh registration.

The aim, as Arjan Singh put it, is to reduce the department's work and enable it to concentrate on the "big fish". Two, to lessen harassment of traders.

What if traders try to hoodwink the authorities? Those filing false declarations can be booked under the law, reply officials. Plus the post-assessment scrutiny up to 10 per cent of the cases.

Self-assessment for 1986-87, 1987-88 and 1988-89 must be filed by 1 October and for 1989-90 by 30 November. Then on, the yearly last date for filing returns will be 30 November.

Seven in every 10 rupees earned by the Delhi administration comes from sales tax — nearly Rs. 600 crores out of a total income of Rs. 860 crores in the last year. In the past five years, the number of dealers registered with the department has risen from 1.7 lakhs to 2.1 lakhs; that is, by 8,000 each year.

Despite this, confessed the Lieutenant-Governor, the administration is only getting half of what it should from sales tax. People, added officials, should insist on the case memo with buying and know the tax rates for various items so they are not fooled. A public education campaign is to be launched about this.

18 June 1990

— The CPM headed Left Front has swept the prestigious Calcutta Municipal Corporation (CMC) polls with a two-thirds majority, substantially improving its position of five years ago when it had a razor-thin majority of one.

In the elections, concluded on 17 June CPM has won 71 seats out of the 141-member CMC, improving its position from 50 members in the previous election. The Congress has won 37 seats, thus losing ground since it had 66 seats in the earlier corporation. The BJP has failed to make an impact just as it failed in the elections to the 74 municipalities in West Bengal in May this year. It has retained two seats.

Result began pouring in late last night and by then it had become clear that the CPM led Left Front had succeeded in wresting the initiative from the Congress which had hoped to stage a come back in Calcutta, following its performance in the municipality elections in the state.

CPM leaders said that the victory was decisive and inevitable despite the propaganda by the Congress over the breakdown of law and order in the state in the context of the Bantala lynching episode in which two persons lost their lives. In the recently concluded parliamentary elections. CPM leaders pointed out, the party had improved its strength in Calcutta having conceded only two seats in central Calcutta to the Congress out of the five within the corporation area. The Janata Dal, which fielded four candidates, and the Congress (S) which fielded one, have been pushed aside in the tussle between the Congress and the Left Front for supremacy over Calcutta.

The events of 17 June suggest that the concentration of the Congress was in central Calcutta and the Left Front was equally determined to oust it from its traditional strongholds. There was large-scale violence in central Calcutta and at Garden. Reach to the south west of the city. Intimidation, threats, bombs and jamming of polling booths were widespread in the battle for capturing the CMC. In other parts of the city, polling was smooth and there was no indication of the kind of rigging alleged by the Congress. The concentration of goons used to subvert the democratic process of elections was mainly in central Calcutta and at Garden Reach.

Sailen Dasgupta, secretary, state CPM, said here today that rigging was localised in central Calcutta and at Garden Reach. He said that sporadic incidents of rigging did occur in three or four wards of central Calcutta and the Congress was responsible for the violence at Garden Reach, ward No. 135, where repolling has been ordered for June 19.

Even before the commencement of the elections on 17 June, there was considerable tension in central Calcutta and the Congress had informally stated that it anticipated large-scale violence on poll day. The *modus operandi*, according to Congress and eye witness accounts, indicated that when voters crowded the polling booths, the queues were suspiciously slow moving. As the queue of voters grew longer and impatient, there were threats, allegedly from CPM goons, to turn back, without casting their votes. After that there was a virtual hail of bombs which ensured that voters in central Calcutta stayed away from the polling booths.

Polling agents complained of intimidation and presiding officers looked on helpless according to eye witness accounts while gangs of hoodlums invaded the polling booths and stamped ballot papers. Congress and BJP polling agents said that revolvers were used to make them leave the polling booths in central Calcutta. The gangs of hoodlums, allegedly unleashed by CPM on polling day in central Calcutta, moved about without fear of police action. Graphic photographs have been published of hoodlums running down roads armed with revolvers and bombs in the presence of policemen. These photographs substantiate the Congress charge that the police were actively conniving with the hoodlums to do their dirty work.

19 June 1990

— The rains are slated to be good this monsoon, the weatherman has predicted, raising hopes of a bumper harvest for the second year in succession. But the bounty of the rain god will not reach all consumers of rice or wheat.

Especially the poorer among them will find foodgrains, which constitute the single largest item of mass consumption, excruciatingly dear because the government has ordained that prices must go up with an increase in supply.

It has raised the issue price of rice by a whacking Rs. 45 per quintal or 45 paise per kg. In ration shops all over the country, the price of rice will be 15 to 17 per cent more, depending on whether the buyer takes the common or the superfine variety.

In the open market, from which many among the poor, get their supplies along with the affluent, prices will be even higher. This is not only because the next harvest is four months away but, as in the case of wheat, the inferior quality of rationed supplies drives the consumer to the market.

To the third of the rural population that is landless, who buy the grain they eat must be added other rural segments that are dependent on the market for foodgrains. These are the small farmers whose land holdings yield far less than their requirement of year-round consumption.

The objective of a foodgrain pricing policy that hurts the urban and rural poor has not been explained by the government. Three months ago, it had effected a hike of a like order in wheat prices. Following the increase in the price of rationed wheat last April, prices have firmed up in the open market.

The Left parties in West Bengal had protested against the rise in prices of wheat rations last April. It is an open question whether the increased prices of rationed rice will raise the political temperature of this section of the supporters of the National Front government at the centre.

One consequence of the regime of high cereal prices will be to build up stocks of foodgrains in government godowns. Public stocks, essential to meet scarcities, had dropped in 1988-89, the year following the drought. The build-up of foodgrains stocks will reflect as before the surplus from under-consumption. Another consequence will be to raise the costs of employment schemes which the government operates to mitigate under-employment in the countryside. With foodgrains on which the poor spend most of their income, getting dearer, employment guarantee wages will have to be raised. That will make a hole in the centre's budget, if expenditure on employment generation is not curtailed. Besides, states like Andhra Pradesh, and Tamil Nadu, which operate special subsidised schemes for supplying rice to the poor and school children will be additionally burdened by the high cost of supplies of centrally procured grain.

The increase in issue prices which determine prices in ration shops was preceded by a hike in procurement prices paid to the farmer. The government's policy is to put farmers who produce surplus grains in clover, ostensibly to ensure that foodgrain production rises rapidly in the Eighth Plan. This means that foodgrain prices, will be raised every year, perhaps as steeply as has been done this year.

What the government has not cared to explain is how much is the price incentive that farmers need to produce more, even though an official committee has worked out a methodology for working out costs.

A new phenomenon is the costing methodology the government adopts in ordering administered price increases. The cost now includes wages to agricultural labour, not what is actually paid but the higher statutory wage rates the states prescribe without the political will to enforce them.

Statutory wages are thus used not to protect agricultural labour but to support profiteering by farm entrepreneurs. Orissa, for example, to well above the prevailing wage rates.

The cascading effect of the policy of appeasing farmers may soon give rise to serious inflation. Higher foodgrain prices will increase dearness allowance payments in industry and the entire organised sector. As not only foodgrain prices but other agricultural prices are to be jacked up, industrial prices will have to be raised to cover higher input prices.

The government is ignoring these dangers in appeasing the surplus farmers who dominate agriculture in Punjab, Haryana, Western U.P., parts of Rajasthan, Andhra Pradesh and in green revolution pockets elsewhere in the country.

Farmers are given subsidised supplies of high cost fertilisers. They get soft rates for electricity and irrigated water. This casts a strain on central and state budgets which are in the red.

The extra payment by way of farm price incentive gets translated into a foodgrain subsidy to the consumer. It is the size of the latter that the government is seeking to keep under control through a pricing arrangement that dispropotionately burdens the poor. And all this in a year when the rains will add to farmer's bounty without extra effort.

June 20 1990

— Some unions of the electricity department, calling themselves the DESU Employees United Front, began a week-long programme of gate meetings to highlight the need to fill up all vacant posts and revise pay scales, among other things. The front consists of four unions: DESU Sub-station Technical Staff Association, DESU Association, DESU Technical Employees Association, DESU Cable Jointer Employees and DESU Time-keepers Association. At the gate meetings, held outside offices in Rohini and Lawrence Road, it was pointed out that the officer-worker relation is increasingly tilted in favour of the former. Fill up the 10,000 vacant posts, they demand. Their other demands: jobs for dependent of employees who have served 20 years, generation incentive to all employees rather than to those in selected departments, better promotion avenues, more *ex gratia* payment, revision of scales and upgradation of posts, free electricity and medical aid for staff. They also was the compensation amount for accidents on duty raised: Rs. 5 lakh in case of death and Rs. 1 lakh in case of injury.

It is only the weather and the thought of the citizens misery that is binding them to a peaceful agitation, they say. Warning, however, that if the "autocratic, vindictive" management fails to listen, they will feel free to resort to demonstrations, hunger-strike and a strike.

— In a significant decision the government announced that from 1 July this additional instalments of dearness allowance (DA) to central government employees drawing over Rs. 3,500 per month will not be paid in cash. It would instead be credited to their provident fund (PF) accounts. This decision has apparently been taken in view of the increasing liquidity in the economy. Any further increase, it is feared, would lead to increased inflationary tendencies. With the government having accepted the recommendations of the fourth pay commission, two instalments of DA are being released to government employees in cash payable from July 1 and January 1, based on the price increase above the 12 monthly index average of 608 (base 1960 = 100).

— Advocates of the Bombay High Court created history today by passing resolution of "complete lack of confidence" in four judges of the Court, namely Justice V.S. Kotwal, Justice Sharad Manohar, Justice G.H. Guttal and Justice M.P. Kenia. In an atmosphere surcharged with emotion and tension, the large meeting urged the four judges by an overwhelming majority to resign as permanent judges of the court. The lawyers resolved that till such time as they resigned, no member of the appellate side bar would appear before them. This is the first time in the post-independence history of Indian judiciary and also the first time in the over 125-year history of the Bombay High Court that such resolutions have been passed. Realising the gravity of the occasion, the Western India Advocates' Association (WIAA) meeting was held in solemnity except for occasions when a few speakers urged some other action than the passing of the resolutions. The boycott of the courts of the four judges becomes effective from tomorrow itself.

About 350 advocates, who constitute, the active strength of the appellate bar, were present at the meeting. Over 240 lawyers had signed the requisitions calling for today's meeting, which is believed to be a record. The Bombay Bar Association, the original side body of lawyers at the court, will meet tomorrow to consider resolutions against Justice Kotwal, Justice Manohar and Justice Gutal. Given the clear opinion of the appellate side expressed in the voting today, there will be no difficulty for the original side to endorse the three resolutions against the judges. The bombay city civil and sessions court is also likely to hold a meeting tomorrow. However, the lawyers made it clear that in their subjective judgement, the judges had decided judicial matters on extraneous considerations. The speakers confessed that they did not have concrete evidence to establish any charge against the four judicial officers. But experience spread over years had convinced the lawyers that their integrity and impartiality were suspect. Briefing newsmen later, the WIAA president, Bal Apte, said if impeachment proceedings were initiated against the four, the advocates as collective body would be able to raise substantial material against the judges. He, however, clarified that neither he personally nor the association had any evidence at the moment.

22 June 1990

Just before leaving for the Maldives, the Prime Minister, V.P. Singh, instructed his Press adviser to inform Maneka Gandhi, the state minister for environment and forests, that the division of work between the two warring ministers had been returned to the *status quo ante*.

Now, as earlier, the executive orders would be given by Maneka Gandhi and the policy decisions would be taken by Nilamani Routray but only after Maneka Gandhi sent up the file to him. This was how the ministry was functioning when the Prime Minister used to head the ministry.

The Prime Minister's decision, which has been due for three weeks now, however, had not reached Routray, the minister.

The cabinet secretariat and the Prime Minister's office are not aware of any order under which all work relating to the ministry of environment is to be again routed through Maneka Gandhi.

The Prime Minister's intervention, undoing Routray's circular of 30 May, divesting Maneka Gandhi of all powers may, however, have come too late to undo all the damage of the period of confusion. The squabble between the two ministers split the ministry's bureaucrats down the line leading to the reopening and clearance of some cases that were once considered closed. However, Routray flatly denies this.

Mahesh Prasad, the secretary, environment and forests, who is currently abroad, and Maneka Gandhi have not been talking terms. Prasad's IAS colleagues were impressed by Maneka Gandhi's drive when she was solely in charge of environment and forests. But aware of the discord at the top, were nervous about expressing their loyalties or seeing too much of the junior minister. Maneka Gandhi's aggressiveness and sharp tongue did not help matters either. Caught in the crossfire, some old hands and environmentally committed officers are now looking for cover. Take the case of Bisht, the deputy director for wildlife preservation, who has sought a transfer back to his parent cadre, West Bengal. Bisht was asked by the additional I-G, wildlife, to go to Jaipur to check information received by the ministry that the real Munna went to the Festival of India in Paris, was not in Delhi Zoo but in Jaipur. Bisht came back with information that would have helped ministry in the Supreme Court case about the *Delhi Zoo* vs *Munna*. But, instead of getting a pat on his back, Bisht was pulled for going without the permission of the secretary.

With Mrs Maneka Gandhi sidelined and Routray still finding his bearings, it is the cause of environment that has been suffering. Political heavy weights from other ministries, whether commerce, energy or tourism, have been taking advantage of the impasse.

The manner in which the tourism and hotel lobby has won the battle on construction along the beaches has shocked environmentalists. It is seen as a reversal of the steps taken by the ministry earlier this year to curb pollution of the beaches through indiscriminate construction.

The fragile 70-km beach of Goa, it is feared, will be vandalised. According to the agreement between Arun Nehru and Routray the no-construction limit has been relaxed from 500 metres to 200 metres on beaches all over the country. In Goa the environment and forest ministry had come down heavily on a group of hotels that violated even the 200 metres stipulation (which was already there for Goa). Significantly the hotels were all owned by influential and affluent groups like the Dalmia resorts, Leela Penta and Taj. The latter had 27 cottages within the 200 m barrier and the environment ministry had issued demolition notices. The tourism minister of Goa, Churchill Alemao, has also put up a proposal for a five-star hotel in violation of the 200 metre guideline. He is now asking for relaxation up to 90 metres.

Routray said, however, that the committee of secretaries had taken the decision to decrease the 500 metres limit to 200 metres in January this year and the agreement between him and Arun Nehru was only a ratification of that decision.

Fears are also being expressed that NOCIL's plan for major expansion of its project in Bombay may go through. Routray indicated that there was such a proposal but no decision had been taken. Routray, however, said the ministry was receiving a lot of flak from chief ministers that various projects were being help up by the ministry. Development work cannot be held up, he said.

Proposals for export of frog legs are being raised again in the commerce ministry though their export was banned some years ago on studies by the ministry of environment and forests that the indiscriminate killing of frogs was disturbing the ecology and increasing agricultural pests.

The difference between the ministers had led to a decision to return to the UNDP a Cessna aircraft and a helicopter given to the forest department for spotting fires and preventing their spread. It is believed that Routray wanted to use the aircraft to visit Shimla and was told it could be used only for fire-fighting work. Maneka Gandhi, who used it for her "greening Haryana" programme was hoping to use it extensively for aerial seeding. A colossal Rs. 140 crore has been budgeted for the Haryana greening operation and without an aircraft the programme would suffer.

The senior minister's argument is that Rs. 15 lakh is being spent on maintenance of the aircraft and on the staff for it. The money can be better spent on actual forestry work. Routray said no decision had been taken to return the aircraft and other vehicles as yet. On the Prime Minister's request to the Ministry to review its decision on the setting up of the Adirapally hydroelectric project on 104 hectares of forest land, Routray said it was the prerogative of the Prime Minister to take the final decision. Ironically enough while a final decision on the safety of Tehri dam is pending following certain disclosures made by an expert, The Tehri Hydel Development Corporation is going ahead with a massive programme of constructing the coffer dam. This is contrary to the decision that no work on the coffer dam will be taken up till the environment and safety issues are fully resolved on the basis of a cabinet decision. The charge against the ministry is that it is sitting back without a whimper of protest.

— The World Bank, it is learnt, has given the Delhi Electric Supply Undertaking a week more to come up with a "satisfactory" financial recovery programme. Otherwise, it says in a telex, it will cancel the $60 million loan for a 400 kV transmission ring around the Capital to ensure more electric supply. No need to panic, contend some. It is not the first such deadline, they say, adding that the bank has already been asked to keep the loan pending for a month and reconsider the issue. The telex, it is understood, is pretty clear that unless the bank receives the recovery programme by 30 June, cancellation will follow.

As it is, the loan, linked to DESU's financial health, has been suspended since January 1989. And, has helped up the 400 kV project, considered vital if the Delhi system is not to collapse within the next couple of years.

Chances of the loan coming through have been considered bleak by officials. For, as part of the mid-eighties agreement, DESU was to earn a surplus of three per cent on fixed capital assets by 1990-91 — essentially necessitating a raise in rates.

This has not come through the bank, saying it is aware of DESU's efforts in this regard, is not satisfied.

Hope for revival of the loan came last August, when the cabinet committee on economic affairs partially approved DESU's financial recovery plan. It cancelled the Rs. 1,100 crore owed by DESU to the Badarpur power station, controlled by the National Thermal Power Corporation. And, waived repayment of the principal on the Rs. 1,000 crore DESU owed the centre; it was the major part of DESU's debts. Plus, interest would be charged on only half the borrowed amount. That was the first part. The second, a hike in rates, was not approved at the time. The final restructuring, it was said than, would be done in six months. Following this, the municipal corporation's electric supply committee even gave the green signal for a tariff hike last October. It authorised DESU's general manager to do what necessary to earn the three per cent surplus. That would, it was indicated, entail a tariff hike. Though no hike was affected, after the supersession of the corporation earlier this year, the buck has been oscillating between the Delhi administration and Union energy ministry.

— The Prime Minister, V.P. Singh, the Deputy Prime Minister, Devi Lal, the Finance Minister, Madhu Dandavate, the Home Minister, Mufti Mohammed Sayeed, besides several other important ministers, together accounting for more than half the strength of the 19-member Union Cabinet, were out of the Capital today, visiting foreign countries on goodwill mission, or relaxing in chosen retreats within the country.

The absence of such a large number of ministers at the same time from the Capital is rather unusual. While the Prime Minister is away on a three-day visit to Maldive islands, the Deputy Prime Minister is recuperating at a health farm in Karnataka. The home minister proceeded on a 13-day trip to Morocco, Tunisia and several other countries to build bridges of goodwill, leaving the charge of running one of the most important ministries in the hands of Subodh Kant Sahay, minister of state for home. The minister for commerce and tourism, Arun Nehru, accompanied the Prime Minister.

While the finance minister was expected to return tomorrow, inquiries about the programme of the railway minister, George Fernandes, who is in Calcutta, drew a blank.

23 June 1990

— The Planning Commission's approach to Eighth Plan — that the emphasis should be on the content of development rather than on the growth rate *per se* — has found support in the Human Development Report (1990) brought out by the United Nations Development Programme (UNDP). The report provides a new Human Development Index (HDI) to measure development and offers a new strategy to meet human needs. To be published annually for the UNDP, the report quantifies the human condition and ranks countries by their success in meeting human needs. The HDI consists of three components: The first is the average life expectancy which speaks of health-care delivery. The second is literacy which not only helps people to get and keep jobs but to understand their surroundings and culture. And finally, purchasing power — per capita income adjusted to account for national differences in exchange rates, tariffs and tradable goods — demonstrates the relative ability to buy commodities and meet basic needs.

Prepared under the guidance of Dr Mahbubul Haq, former finance and planning minister of Pakistan who is now special advisor to the UNDP administrator, the HDI report formulated by a team of UNDP experts and a panel of consultants. Among them are such distinguished economists and development professionals as Gustav Ranis, Amartya K. Sen, Frances Stewart, Keith Friffin, Paul Streeten and Meghnad Desai. According to the latest UNDP publication, *World Development*, the report reveals startling results when countries' development is measured on the basis of HDI. Even ccuntries with low per capita Gross National Product (GNP) have ranked high on the Human Development Index, meaning that the longevity of their people is high, literacy is widespread, and the people have enough purchasing power to rise above poverty. Life does not begin at $ 11,000, the average per capita income in the industrialised world", the report says, implying that respectable levels of human development are possible even at fairly modest levels of income.

Among the low human development countries, India with a Human Development Index of .439 ranks above Pakistan but below seven other countries. These are Madagascar, Papua New Guinea, Kampuchea, Cameroon, Kenya, Zambia and Morocco. China, with HDI of .716, has been placed in medium human development countries, while Costa Rica has received the highest HDI ranking among the poorer countries with HDI of .916. Costa Rica has a life expectancy of 75 years, a literacy rate of 93 per cent, and an average adjusted real income of $ 3,760. Among the high human development countries. Japan tops with the HDI of .996 followed by Sweden with .987. On the basis of the data for life expectancy in 1987, and literacy in 1985, the report finds that average life expectancy in Japan was 78 years, and adult literacy, 99 per cent. The report poses several key questions and provides answers. Does a government care more about economic development alone or about health care and education as well? Does it spend more money on armaments than in education? Do women share in the wealth and responsibilities of a nation?

Startling Answers: The answers to these questions have revealed startling facts. For instance, it has been found that 25 developing countries spend more on the military than on education and health and that developing countries have eight times more soldiers than physicians.

The report suggests restructuring budget priorities but warns that it will require tremendous political courage.

— One by one, some of our most significant monuments are being demolished. Last year, it was Bahadur Shah Zaffar's *tahsil* in Mehrauli, a noteworthy example of late Mughal architecture. In April 1990, it was the historic Kotwali in Chandni Chowk, the only symbol of Sikh resistance, apart from Gurdwara Rakabganj, to the oppressive rule of Aurangzeb. And now it is the turn of Bhagirath Palace, also located in Chandni Chowk. Needless to say, all three will give way to highrise commercial buildings that will notch up a tidy sum for its owners. The Conservation Society of Delhi and INTACH tried their utmost to prevent the Kotwali and Bahadur Shah Zafar's *tahsil* from being axed. But such is the complex private ownership pattern of many of these historical monuments that the government would have to amend many of its existing laws to prevent such a step from being taken Bhagirath Palace, presently the main wholesale market for electrical goods and medical appliances, is a case in point. Prior to independence, it was known as Begum Samru's palace and consisted of a gracious old building with a high-roofed verandah supported by massive corinthian pillars. It had two flights of semi-curving steps leading up to a verandah, which have now been taken over by a number of tea-stalls and *panwallahs*, and tiny shops selling a variety of goods.

The palace was built in the 1840s by Begum Samru, a colourful personality of her time who led a chequered rags-to-riches life. After independence, it was bought by Lala Bhagirath Mal, and presently houses the Central Bank. Subsequently, allege members of the Delhi Conservation Society, the ownership changed hands several times over and is presently in the hands of a consortium of developers who insist they are well within their rights to apply to the Delhi Municipal Corporation to demolish the structure and reconstruct a new building. Architects in the Capital feel Bhagirath Palace has considerable architectural significance, as it is one of the best examples of colonial building constructed at a time when Europe was experiencing a revival of classical Greco-Roman architecture. The British believed that the Indian climate was suited to a style with huge columns and porticos that gave adequate space for a free movement of light and shade. Later structures gave way to the Gothic style. All three buildings — Zafar's *tahsil*, the Kotwali and Bhagirath Palace — were listed by INTACH under their list of historically important monuments. Unfortunately, even though this list has been circulated to different government departments such as the Delhi Development Authority and the Delhi Urban Arts Commission, it has no legal sanctity.

It would not be inappropriate to mention that at the turn of this century, the historian Zaffar Hassan, also a senior official at the Archaeological Survey of India, had prepared a list of 1400 important monuments in the Capital. From amongst these 170 are presently under the care of the ASI, while another 100 are being looked after by Delhi Administration.

24 June 1990

— The union cabinet is to discuss an approach paper to economic planning that argues for reduction in the degree of protection to Indian industry, opening up to foreign investment to globalise the economy, devaluing the rupee by 20 per cent over the next five-year period, and abandoning the National Front's promise of right to work.

These and other proposals are contained in a documented entitled "towards restructuring of industrial trade and fiscal policies", reportedly prepared by Montek Singh Ahluwalia, a special secretary in the Prime Minister's office and an ex-World Bank employee. The document which seems to represent a counter approach paper to planning was discussed by the committee of secretaries to the government of India on 13 and 14 June barely four days before the National Development Council met and approved the approach paper to the eighth Five-Year Plan. Senior government officials believe that if the policies argued for in the above document are adopted by the government, the NDC's efforts would then seem to be sheer waste, in retrospect. "This document runs counter to the ideology of the approach paper to eighth Five-Year Plan", said one senior official.

At least, a couple of secretaries to the government have already voiced their objection to the policy framework listed in the document originating from the Prime Minister's office, claiming that this was what several multilateral lending institutions like the World Bank and the IME wanted India to do. Senior bureaucrats are of the view that if the government wants to "liberalise" the economy, it should then bring out a White Paper on the subject rather than trying to push the policy through, without a public debate.

The main recommendations of the policy document being pushed through are reduction in the degree of protection to the Indian industry, opening up to foreign investment to globalise the economy, a 20 per cent depreciation in the rupee over a five-year period, increasing the administered prices of rice, sugar steel, electricity and railway freight, linking central assistance to states to conditionalities imposed by the centre, increasing fertiliser prices reviewing implementation of the one-rank one-pension scheme promised by the National Front government, keeping additional central assistance to the states to a minimum limiting access to the public distribution system to only those families where the head of the household earns below Rs. 2,000 per month, cutting back in government staff, virtual abandonment of the right-to-work promise of the government, productivity-linked wage negotiations, raising MRTP limit from Rs. 100 crore to 500 crore, and reducing duty levels on raw materials, components and capital goods to 30 to 40 per cent by 1994-95. All these changes are contemplated over a five-year period.

According to senior government officials, there is an uncanny resemblance between this policy document and the World Bank thinking on India. Although they admit that there are some similarities in a few areas between this document and the Eighth Plan approach paper, such as in the approach to public sector reform, these sources say that while the Plan approach paper lays emphasis on employment, this document's primary concern is macro-economic balance even if that slows down economic growth. "This is the standard IMF line", said one official.

In opening up the economy to foreign investment, the document argues that India needs to rethink its approach to foreign investment as the changing world economic situation has already led to such rethinking in most of the developing countries and even in the socialist world. Foreign investment is seen as playing a key role in industrial modernisation by providing additional financial resources on terms that would be advantageous over commercial borrowing, providing access to technology on a continual basis, providing a link to the global marketing network, and providing inputs of management styles and methods. The document argues that the government should bring out lists of industries where 40 per cent and 51 per cent foreign ownership would be allowed automatically. !t also argues that initiative should be taken by the government to give a signal to foreign investors that they are welcome in India by attracting some high-visibility cases of investment from abroad. In the case of reducing the degree of protection, the document argues that the level of protection in India is very high compared to most other developing countries and that this limits India's ability to penetrate export markets. The document argues for a clear policy decision to reduce the average level of protection over the next five years to a level around 30 to 40 per cent. This would mean reducing the duty on capital goods by half and cutting the duty on intermediate goods import even more.

On the promise of right-to-work, the document says that till the resource position improves, the government should not take on any new obligations involving a heavy drain on resources. It, therefore, advices caution on the proposal of right to work being included in the constitution. The additional cost of implementing the proposal of right to work is estimated the paper was later disowned by the Prime Minister's Office to be Rs. 9,000 crore per year.

— The President has issued a notification formally constituting an inter-state council headed by the Prime Minister as recommended by the Sarkaria Commission on centre-state relations, reports UNI. Besides the Prime Minister, six cabinet ministers, to be nominated, and chief ministers of all states and union territories will constitute the council, set up as a forum for dialogue to ensure better coordination between the Centre and states. Official sources said the chief secretaries of states and Union territories had been intimated about the presidential notification. A permanent secretariat is to be set up for the day-to-day functioning of the council. The process of activating the council is being accelerated as its first meeting is to be held any time after 20 July in Bangalore, as suggested by the Karnataka chief minister, Veerendra Patil.

With the formation of the counci!, the National Front government has fulfilled another commitment spelt out in its manifesto which promised to restore the federal character of the national polity by establishing an inter-state council under article 263 of the Constitution.

Article 263 states that if at any time it appears to the President that the public interests would be served by the establishment of a council charged with the duty of:

(a) inquiring into or advising upon disputes which may have arisen between states;
(b) investigating and discussing subjects in which some or all the states, or the Union and one or more of the states, have a common interest, or
(c) making recommendations upon any such subject and, in particular, recommendations for the better coordination of policy and action with respect to that subject.

It shall be lawful for the President by order to establish such a council, and to define the nature of the duties to be performed by it and its organisation and procedure.

The Sarkaria Commission has recommended the establishment of the council under article 263 as a permanent body and that it deal with subjects other than socio-economic development.

In this context, the commission has also suggested amending of the law relating to inter-state river tribunals to ensure that the award becomes effective within five years — unless extended by the centre — and should have the same force as a decree of the Supreme Court.

25 June 1990

— The Prime Minister's office (PMO) clarified that it had not prepared a document which ran counter to the Planning Commission's approach paper on the 8th Plan.

What had been reported in the Press, an official spokesman said, was one of the many papers received by the core group of secretaries. The group, comprising secretaries to economic ministries, discuss, in routine course, various aspects of the country's economy.

The impression sought to be created that the PMO had prepared special economic proposals on planning, was wrong, the spokesman said.

— In a major administrative shake-up, the government has transferred and promoted eleven top officials.

Bhaskar Ghose, additional secretary in the cabinet secretariat, has been appointed secretary in the Department of Culture and Art. Ghose, who was Director General of Doordarshan and later additional secretary in the Information and Broadcasting Ministry before being shifted to the cabinet secretariat, succeeds Veeraraghavan, who has retired.

Ramakant Rath, of the Orissa cadre, has been made secretary in the Department of Food.

N.R. Ranganathan, additional secretary, Insurance, in the Ministry of Economic Affairs, has been promoted as special secretary, Insurance.

N. Vittal, additional secretary, Department of Atomic Energy, will be the new secretary of the Department of Electronics. He replaces R. rajamani who has been made chairman of the Committee for Advancement of People Action and Rural Technology (CAPART).

S.V. Giri, additional secretary in the Department of Agriculture and Cooperation, has been promoted to the rank of special secretary.

B.K. Goswami, Director General of Tourism, has been shifted as secretary, Department of Official Languages.

K.K. Mathur, additional secretary, Department of Power, has been promoted as special secretary in the same department.

V. Krishnan of Karnataka cadre has been appointed special Commissioner of scheduled caste and scheduled tribe.

Usha Vora, additional secretary in the Department of mines, has been appointed officer on special duty in the rank of secretary in the National Commission for Women.

A.K. Saikia of Assam cadre has been made Adviser in the Planning Commission in the rank of secretary — PTI.

26 June 1990

— Over Rs. 1 crore worth illegal assets were unearthed by the CBI in country-wide raids, under its anti-corruption drive today. Cases against 20 top government officials have been registered. They include officials belonging to the public sector undertakings and the nationalised banks. The searches were still going on in at least 70 places and more recoveries were expected, said a senior spokesman of the CBI. While six of these cases relate to possession of assets disproportionate to the income and 10 relate to the abuse of official position in endowing undue favour to private parties and four relate to charges of cheating, forgery and other irregularities. Two senior officials, a director of finance and director of marketing of the Hindustan Insecticides, were charged with making un-sanctioned trips to West Germany and Geneva, while they had officially gone to Brazil. The were also charged with under invoicing in their negotiations with M/s Helms AG.

Investigation revealed that the board of directors of the Hindustan Times, had rejected his underinvoicing, which provided the insecticide at $ 6.6 per kg to the West German firm as against $ 7.5 per kg the current price of insecticide in the world market. The CBI was trying to find the kickbacks accruing to them for this deal the official said Back in Delhi one ITDC official was bound having made a considerable of money by granting contract for the expansion of Hotel Ashok in Jaipur to private firms.

Similarly the chairman, the managing director, the chief finance manager, and the deputy general manager of the Rashtriya Fertilizers. Bombay were charged of buying 20 special type of packing machines at a higher price without floating any tender. While the lowest bidder was offering it for Rs. 80,000 they bought the 20 machines for Rs. 1,50,000 a piece, the spokesman disclosed.

In another case the chairman and managing director of Bharat Petroleum and Electricals refused to give the Tatas the contract for consultancy for a project at Butcher Island near Bombay. Instead, the consultancy was given to the highest bidder without giving any reasons for rejecting other tenders. The loss accrued to over Rs. 50 lakh to the BPE in this case, the CBI spokesman disclosed.

The seizure made from the ITDC official included Rs. 5,15,000 in NSC bonds. besides houses in Gurgaon, Chandigarh and Alaknanda in Delhi and also a plot in Sainik farm.

— The acceleration of domestic and external liberalisation has been put back on the policy agenda by the paper on industry and trade the mandarins in the Prime Minister's office have readied for the Union cabinet. The planners did not quite grapple with the issue of modernising industry and boosting India's export competitiveness in their approach to the Eighth Plan. They focused on creating jobs in agriculture and industry and opted for larger allocation of resources for rural development and for promoting labour-intensive industry. Liberalisation was treated as a fringe issue, though they did not oppose it. The gap has been filled by the paper finished a few days before the National Development Council (NDC) adopted the Planning Commission's approach to the Eighth Plan. Its proposals have, as was to be expected, touched off a controversy.

The core proposals of the paper, prepared by Montek Singh Ahluwalia, special secretary, and cleared by a committee of secretaries, seek to hike the MRTP investment exemption limit from Rs. 100 crore to Rs. 500 crore and the automatic approval limit for foreign equity control from 40 per cent to 51 per cent in specified industries. Though the MRTP hike appears to be startling, the proposal is hardly inconsistent with the plan approach. After noting the entrepreneurial ability and capacity to mobilise resources on a large scale, the planners, too, had argued the case for greater private sector "involvement" or "participation" in areas hitherto largely in the public sector.

This is a clear recognition in the approach paper of the need to let the private sector go in for mega investments. For this, the path is to be cleared by raising the MRTP ceiling. To be consistent with the Eighth Plan approach, however, care will have to be taken to ensure that large investments do not go into "non-priority" areas, though 'employment need not be the primary consideration" if technological innovation, energy efficiency and cost-effectiveness are achieved.

The planners recognised that foreign capital "also has a role to play as a medium for bringing in better technology", though according to them, the inflow was unlikely to be large in relation to the size of the balance of payments gap. They assigned to imported technology an "important role" in the modernisation of industry and raising its efficiency. The proposed 51 per cent limit for automatic approval of foreign equity control is supportive of this view. The planners favoured exposing domestic producers to external competition, especially in segments where there is a "high degree of concentration in ownership or monopolistic market structure". This means, besides liberalised entry of foreign capital, a reduction in import duties, precisely what is recommended in the Ahluwalia paper which wants duties to be brought down to the 30 to 40 per cent range against over 90 per cent at present.

The liberalisation of foreign investment proposed in the Ahluwalia paper is a counterpart of its proposal to hike the MRTP exemption limit. And, for competition to be meaningful, import duties have to be brought down. This will keep the threat of external competition alive for both domestic and foreign industry in the country.

Logically, again, it follows that the rupee must be depreciated. For three reasons: to protect government revenues following a reduction in customs duties, to avoid, giving an excessive fillip to imports, by restoring their rupee cost, and to boost rupee receipts of the exporter from India. The triple objectives require depreciation of the rupee. If it is to be modest, the domestic rate of inflation will have to register a significant slow down. This is in line with the thinking of the planners who have called for "supportive exchange rate and demand management". The Ahluwalia paper calls for a four per cent annual depreciation on the assumption that domestic inflation will drop to five per cent. However, the latter is contrary to the experience of the past two decades.

The control of inflation will mean, *inter alia*, rationalisation of government expenditure and administered prices. The Eighth Plan approach wanted a reorientation of the policy on subsidies to curb government expenditure. In particular, it wanted a re-examination of the policy of providing irrigation, electricity, higher general education and other public services "much below cost". The Ahluwalia paper calls for an increase in the administered prices of rice, sugar, fertilisers, steel and electricity. It wants to focus rationed supplies to targeted income groups, that is households where their heads have an income of less than Rs. 2,000 per month.

On all these basic points, the paper's suggestions are in consonance with the planners' approach. This is true even of its advocacy of limiting the "right to work" which would cost an estimated Rs. 9,000 crore annually. According to the Eighth Plan approach, the challenge of "right to work" cannot be met with government resources which are under pressure. Conditions should therefore be created to make "the local population in each village contribute to development resources". The measures and the bureaucrats have placed before the cabinet flesh out the approach of the planners. One cannot, however, be wholly sure if this has been done in keeping with the spirit of the Eighth Plan approach. This is because the planners have not spelt out where they stand on self-reliance or on the resources to be made available for investment, including infrastructure for foreign private capital. The omission contrasts with the forceful stand taken on rural development and small-scale industry.

The planners did make points, however. First, "the thrust of liberalisation should also shift towards improving the technology and efficiency of the intermediate and capital goods industries, increasing the competitiveness of domestic industry over a wider range than at present, and building the base for greater self-reliance". Second, the government should review "all proposals for new, large investments with the aim of working out a phased programme in consonance with the new priorities in and the multiple demands on investment requirements". But they did not outline even the contours of a strategy consistent with these two overriding considerations. The lacuna is hardly surprising in a plan that does not prescribe the perspective of which it is a part. This may explain why the government has initiated moves for defining working premises.

But the Ahluwalia paper is silent about the implications of its proposals for the country's balance of payments, industrial structure, inter-sectoral balances, employment, investment allocation or inflation. Like the coming Eighth Plan, this paper, too, is steeped in the ambiance of non-planning created by Yojana Bhavan.

27 June 1990

— The Prime Minister, V.P. Singh, has asked the states to strengthen the law and order machinery to check the atrocities on scheduled castes and scheduled tribes as the spate of crimes against them has not shown any sign of abatement in the last three years.

In a letter written to the chief ministers, Singh said the scheduled castes and scheduled tribes continue to be the target so much that there was no decline in the crimes against them. More than 14,000 cases of crimes against the scheduled castes and about 3,000 cases against scheduled tribes had been reported every year.

While expressing concern over the continued atrocity on these sections of society, Singh said, "We cannot allow the perpetrators of these crimes to continue to break laws and practice inhuman violence and get away with it all".

Reiterating the government's resolve to solve the socio-economic problems of the weak and the downtrodden, the Prime Minister said the chief ministers should visit the places where such atrocities had been committed to galvanise the administration to take prompt action against the culprits and ensure rehabilitative measures to the victims. "No law and no orders will have sufficient impact unless the entire administration perceives from its actual experience that the chief minister of the state is totally and uncompromisingly against any kind of atrocity against the scheduled castes and scheduled tribes. This perception would also be a great deterrent to those who benefit by the exploitation of the scheduled castes and scheduled tribes. This has to be buttressed by strong action, the moment any atrocity or crime takes place", he said in the letter. The Prime Minister also suggested setting up of special courts to try cases of atrocities and crimes against these sections. Strict implementation of land reforms, inclusion of SC/ST members in tribunals to settle land disputes and adopting suitable socio-economic measures are among other suggestions made by the Prime Minister to fulfil the government's commitment to uplift these sections. He also sought the cooperation of the chief ministers in ensuring social and economic justice to them.

— The first international environmental fund is expected to be launched here with the UK today committing its contribution for the three-year budget that may range from $ 160 million to $ 240 million. The latter sum has been projected for the fund if India and China decide to join the Montreal

Protocol on chemicals that deplete the ozone layer. The British Prime Minister, Margaret Thatcher, told an international environment conference that the UK would give $ 9 million for the action plan to halt ozone depletion. The amount would be increased to $ 15 million if major consuming countries like China and India join the Montreal Protocol to save the ozone layer from chemical damage. Thatcher whose environmental concerns have been growing, of late, pleaded for extending the scope of the Montreal Protocol to cover other substances such as carbon tetrachloride and methyl chloroform which also caused similar damage. She said "We need to speed up action and set ourselves higher targets and shorter deadlines for reducing and eventually eliminating CFC's and halons. Environment ministers from nearly 100 countries today began discussion that are intended to tighten the montreal Protocol to prevent the destruction of the ozone layer which will have serious consequences on human, animal and plant life. Two recorded serious consequences of this are an increase in the incidence of blindness and of skin cancer. Among the participating countries, only 60 are signatories to the protocol.

India and China, among others, have not signed the protocol, Maneka Gandhi, India's minister of state for environment and forest, said on the eve of the meeting that India's stand depended on an offer of adequate money for the fund to help developing countries and assurances to them of transfer of technology which would facilitate their switching from the existing harmful chemicals. Developing countries were interested in protecting global environment but because of their other more urgent problems, their priorities could not be the same as those of developed countries.

The problem is being sought to be tackled by strengthening the Montreal Protocol of 1987 which set targets for phasing out of chloro fluouro carbons (CFC's), the chemicals used by refrigeration and packing industries and in aerosole cans. These chemicals deplete the ozone layer which in turn permits an increase in damaging ultra violent radiation to reach the earth's surface. The Montreal Protocol turned out to be far too inadequate pace of phasing out as envisaged in the protocol was too slow and also because several third world countries did not join it.

These third world countries have maintained that it is the developed countries which mainly benefited all these years by using cheap CFCs and have harmed the global environment and now if they wanted developing countries to restrain themselves from following the same course they should assist the third world. Developing countries, even though they produce only a small proportion of the world output of chloro fluouro-carbons, need massive assistance to switch over to new technologies and to less harmful substitutes. This led to the proposal for the international fund but there are still contentions issues about the mechanism of administering the fund and assurances on technology transfer to be sorted out by the conference even after a week-long meeting of the officials who prepared for the ministerial meeting. There are differences over the phase-out year also as Norway, Sweden and Finland have proposed that CFCs should be phased out by 1997, with reductions of 50 per cent by 1993 and 85 per cent by 1995. The US, Japan and the Soviet Union want a phase out by the year 2000, though the European Community is prepared to settle for an earlier date. Scientists and environmentalist groups demand a faster phase out and according to one estimate even if the conference agreed to phase out CFCs by the year 2000, it would still be leading to a depletion of up to 25 per cent in the stratospheric ozone layer in the northern hemisphere and even higher levels of thinning in the southern hemisphere. A spokesman of Greenpeace said on the eve of the ministerial conference that even the second current attempt at the protocol will, in its present form, fail to protect the ozone layer. The hole in the Antarctic ozone layer will continue to increase, a hole may appear over the Arctic and global ozone depletion will continue to occur, with unforeseeable consequences for the health of the planet and the life upon it. According to Greenpeace, the 1990 Montreal Protocol, if not modified, will allow the production of an extra 50 per cent of the substances that have so far depleted the ozone layer. It will allow the production of ozone depleters for another 50 years and it will permit the production of CFC 'substitutes' that are immensely powerful greenhouse gases.

28 June 1990

— Compensation for train passengers in case of death or injury in mishaps has been doubled in the new Railway Act that comes into effect from 1 June. The Act also provides for stringent punishment for offences concerning railways. The liability of the railways for death and injury to passenger due to an accident has been increased from the present limit of Rs. 1 lakh to Rs. 2 lakh. The liability for scheduled injuries has also been doubled. This will now range between Rs. 16,000 and Rs. 2 lakh. For the purpose of claiming compensation dependents have been redefined to include among other the parents in the case of a minor. A railway employee on duty can now receive compensation at par with passengers. This Act repeals the Indian Railway Act, 1890, which had become disjointed due to several amendments made from time to time. Under the new Act a person carrying dangerous goods through the railways could be given a prison term for three years or fined up to Rs. 1,000 or both. Passengers misusing the alarm chain pulling facility on trains would be imprisoned for one year or fined up to Rs. 1,000, or both, with a minimum fine of Rs. 500 for the first offence under the new Act. The penalty for the transfer of a reserved ticket is imprisonment up to three months or fine up to Rs. 500 or both. The penalty for unauthorised purchase and sale of railway tickets or reserved accommodation is three years imprisonment or fine up to Rs. 10,000, or both, in addition to forfeiture of tickets. The Act has also simplified the procedure for payment of compensation for damages caused to private property in the case of construction or maintenance of railways. It has also been made obligatory for the railways to give open delivery of a booked consignment where it arrives in a damaged condition.

— The progress of all public sector enterprises in the country is being watched and special monthly reports on each would be submitted to the Prime Minister, V.P. Singh, according to the Union Minister of state for planning and programme implementation, B. Govardhan. The minister said that of the 239 public sector enterprises in the country at present. One hundred were running well and some 47 were in a very bad state. The remaining were 'not bad', he said. Singh was keen that production should touch a new high and that poverty should be eliminated through increased production and clean administration, the minister said.

— This isn't just brain drain. It's an intellectual calamity. Twenty highly qualified and established engineers from C-DoT have left or are planning to leave the country in sheer disgust following the controversy which has enveloped the organisation after the change of government. Most of the engineers, who have been with C-DoT since its inception, are headed for the United States — some to join companies like Harris, etc., and others to study. The twenty engineers who have deserted C-DoT constitute about ten per cent of the cream of engineering talent who form the core of the outfit. The minister for communication, Janeshwar Mishra, seems blissfully unaware of the tragedy and expressed surprise at the development when approached by this correspondent. He was, however, quick to acknowledge that the development is unfortunate. "We will try to hold back the engineers and if any plan of action is drawn up to keep them back, it will have my full support", he promised. "We will try to come out with some incentive scheme or something like that to dissuade people from leaving", he added. All the engineers who have left were deeply involved with various aspects of C-DoTs development work. Software, which constitutes over 60 per cent of the modern switching system, seems to be the major loser as most of the engineers were working on that aspect. This includes the development of the operating system, administration software, call processing software, etc. Others were involved with the hardware design for the main automatic exchange, trouble management system, field trials at certain installations and even CCITT-7 (common channel signalling system-7). CCITT-7 is a vehicle for ISDN (integrated systems digital network). ISDN is the in-thing in the communication world these days for business communications. Most engineers felt demoralised as the controversy surrounding C-DoT refuses to die down. "I have waited months hoping that things will improve, but to no avail", said an engineer, who is making plans to leave for the United States. Many feel that the government, despite the change of minister, has not done its bit to defuse the crisis. The new minister has merely expressed his desire to undo the wrong done to the 'institution', but has not so far backed his words with action. Some are demotivated because they are not sure whether what they develop will ever be manufactured. "Where is the motivation if what we develop does not get productionised?", lamented one. The engineers claim that things have come to a virtual standstill at C-DoT after the blow-out in January. Several others have offers from various foreign companies. Only, they appear to have a little more patience than the ones who have already left. They say they would like to wait for some more time to see if the dust settles down before deciding to seek cleaner, if not fresher, pastures. In just one instance, Sandeep Gupta, a young engineer, was all set to move to the United Kingdom, but has been persuaded to stay back for another couple of months in the hope that things will improve. Says Gupta, 'My heart is still in C-DoT, though my head is already outside'.

30 June 1990

— The deputy finance minister, Anil Shastri, today disclosed his assets in order to 'uphold value systems and norms in public life'.

Shastri said in a signed statement here that he was disclosing his assets and those of his wife and three children keeping in line with his 'conviction' and in his bid to restore certain values and codes of conduct in the larger interest of the country.

According to the details of his disclosure as on 31 March 1990, Shastri owned two houses one in Bangalore purchased in 1984 and another in Shahpura, Madhya Pradesh, purchased in 1986. The two immovable properties were bought from respective state housing Boards in instalments and were valued at Rs. 3.86 lakh. His movable property included two vehicles — a 1964 model Fiát and a 1985 model Maruti. His bank deposits totalled about Rs. 1.45 lakh. The bank deposits of his wife, Mrs. Manju Shastri, totalled about Rs. 2.5 lakh. The bank deposits are in joint names. Her disclosures included 45 tolas of gold ornaments on 31 March 1990. Shastri's three minor children Adarsh, Lagan and Mudit, together have bank deposits of about Rs. 1.32 lakh.

JULY 1990

1 July 1990

— Ramakrishna Hegde resigned as deputy chairman of the Rlanning Commission. He said, he resigned to enable the V.P. Singh government, to take its own decision on the Kuldeep Singh Commission's Report on the alleged land allotment in Bangalore when he was the chief minister of Karnataka.

The Kuldeep Singh Commission said the persistence with which the proposal of land allocation was followed, the role played by an important relation of Hegde in the deal and the fact that the proposed builders namely Lakhandewala and Co. were quite close to Hegde clinches the charge against him.

— The disclosure of names of 31 IAS officials in the Bihar Vidhan Sabha against whom vigilance inquiries are pending has put the department in a tight spot as it is known that about half a dozen of these officials have either been exonerated of their charges or are in the process of being exonerated. The officials whose names have been deleted from the list by the order of the chief minister, Laloo Prasad Yadav, include U.K. Sinha, B.B. Sahay and Mahendra Singh. The allegations of corruption were levelled against the three officials in the case of Nishant Construction Corporation (Surya Apartments) but the then chief minister. Bhagwat Jha Azad, after examining the matter and on the recommendation of the then chief secretary, Arun Pathak, had closed the file. According to informed sources, Azad had directed the departments concerned that "No further inquiries against these officials was necessary as the charges were minor and had nothing to do with corruption".

But surprisingly, the vigilance department, in response to a question of Shanti Devi (JD), furnished the old list which contained the names of these officials that the parliamentary affairs minister, Raghunath Jha read in the Vidhan Sabha at the directive of the chief minister.

The vigilance department had mentioned in the file that the names should not be disclosed as this would hamper its proceedings. Surprisingly, these officials had not asked to clarify their position through any show-cause notice.

Further, the list which was read in the Vdhan Sabha has omitted the name of Vishram Prasad, IAS, who was suspended on charges of corruption about two years ago. The sources said the name of U. K. Sinha should not have been in the list as he, in his capacity as the chief executive officer of the Patna Municipal Corporation (PMC), had opposed the move of the government to settle the land with Nishant Construction Corporation. According to these sources, Sinha at the meeting of the standing committee of the corporation on 10 January 1985, had mentioned that if "the land is settled, this will amount to selling land to an encroacher and giving recognition to the encroacher". But the standing committee decided to recommend to the PMC the settling of the land with Nishant Construction Corporation. After it was decided by the standing committee, the promoters of Surya Apartments deposited a cheque of Rs. 2,03,625 for over one "katha" of land on which they had encroached. Sinha, however, returned the cheque to the promoters on the ground that the decision of the standing committee had to be ratified by the full meeting of the PMC and then approved by the government before being settled.

The sources said that after Sinha returned the cheque, he was transferred to Giridih on 11 May 1985. Several months later, the proposal for settling the land was accepted by a majority vote at the meeting of the councillors on 30 September 1985. The promoters submitted a fresh cheque to the PMC on 16 October which was accepted by the then chief executive officer. The sources wondered how Sinha could be held responsible for the deal which did not take place during his regime?

— There is a mammoth 14-lakh army of health and anganwadi workers deployed in rural India whose wages alone cost the exchequer a whopping Rs. 333 crores in 1989. But the welfare revolution envisaged has remained a pipe dream.

When the statistics of grassroot workers are matched with the number of villages it comes to two functionaries per village. In addition, there are adult educators, "sathins" or village women working for women's upliftment in some states. In 1989-90 over Rs. 543 crores was spent on some 50 schemes for women and children. The question that is worrying planners who want to make the welfare dream a reality is where and why have their grandiose plans gone away. According to a paper prepared by the Planning Commission member, Ela Bhatt, and circulated among her colleagues, for the restructuring of the rural land social welfare network in the Eighth Plan, funds as well as activities of the grassroot workers are spread out thinly or distributed unevenly and the benefits do not reach the poor. "Each service today is being delivered through different schemes and each scheme is formulated, administered and implemented separately by different departments and ministries working through different functionaries." Ela Bhatt's paper is considered significant because it is probably for the first time that a serious effort is being made to analyse the reasons for India's inability to deliver the welfare utopia promised in the plan papers.

The paper proposes the convergence of village-level welfare facilities for effective delivery of mother and child care services is considered vital for improving the quality of life in rural areas. The army of functionaries are rendered ineffective because each worker sees his or her work to be limited to a specific task, whether it is immunisation, women's development or education. Grassroot workers also tend to concentrate on target achievement, whether it is for family planning or immunisation, and neglect other responsibilities. Besides, there is duplication of effort, particularly in health education and nutrition programmes run by the department of women and child as well as the department of education and social welfare. It has also been found that some functionaries are so overburdened that they are unable to do the job properly. The anganwadi worker has to maintain 20 registers and ends up concentrating on nutrition. Medical and para-medical staff are so busy in family planning work that the visits to the anganwadis are irregular. Referal services, too, are not provided efficiently. A recent study of 327 anganwadis in Rajasthan showed that none of the anganwadi workers had directly referred any case of illness to the hospitals. Ela Bhatt has argued for convergence of services through one body so that people do not waste time and effort running from functionary to functionary. Funds for the convergence of these services has also been suggested. There would be one conduit for delivery of the services and one body to receive services and funds at the grassroots. Ela Bhatt also emphasises that beneficiaries must have a say in the implementation of the programmes. Technical and supervisory assistance is to be provided by the centre through a local voluntary or professional organisation. The pooled funds, it has been suggested, should be released in an "united manner" to the block or the implementing agency so that there is freedom in choosing programmes according to local needs and capabilities. In most cases the village panchayat is expected to be the implementing agency. Elected representatives living in the villages are found to be more accountable than elected representatives at the higher level. Where panchayats have lost the confidence of the people, particularly weaker sections and women, the implementing agency could be a mahila mandal, a village level corporation or association. Ela Bhatt has emphasised the need to keep the programme and services above party politics. For facilitating as well as selecting the appropriate implementing agency, a core group or committee has been suggested at the national level. The ministries and departments would have to work through the selected agency, taking care to keep a low profile. Ela Bhatt stresses that the thrust should be on achievement of final objectives through effective performance rather than evaluation of quantitative targets. Health, mother and child care programmes can succeed only when people themselves have a hand in the design and implementation of the schemes and not when it is thrust from above. However, the success of the converged services will depend on the strength of the panchayati raj system and the cooperation of the voluntary agencies. Ela Bhatt's paper traces the high infant mortality rate (99 in 1987 as against 33 in Sri Lanka—also a low income country), high maternal mortality (500 as against 90 in Sri Lanka) and dismal literacy level of 24.8 per cent for women to the schemes and welfare measure not having the desired impact. Similarly, population control measures have achieved only "limited success" despite the large work force for family welfare. At the present growth rate, the population is expected to cross the 1010 million by the year 2000.

2 July 1990

— The government has ordered an immediate cut of 10 per cent in the financial allocation of all the ministries on an across-the-board basis. This is to bring down the deficit. The two pronged plan of the government is to bring down the deficit by improving revenue collection and reducing public expenditure.

— Credit cards (plastic money as they are known) may substantially replace travellers cheques by the end of the century, according to senior bank officials.

3 July 1990

— The government has decided to reduce the foreign travel budget of the ministries by 20 per cent in the current financial year.

— The vigilance department in Madhya Pradesh today lodged an FIR against two IAS officers R.S. Tiwari, secretary in the Public Health Engineering Department and Ramringar Singh ex-director of prime education for their negligence in criminal conspiracy, cheating and corrupt practices. They are alleged to be involved in misappropriation of about Rs. 2 crore under the Operation Blackboard.

4 July 1990

— V.P. Singh, the Prime Minister, has accepted Ramakrishna Hegde's resignation.

5 July 1990

— In Madhya Pradesh the BJP government seems to have broken all previous records in transfers: 40,000 to 50,000 government employees have so far been transferred to make the new regime's impact felt. Finance Department sources said the state exchequer would have to bear a burden of Rs. 50 to 100 crore on the transfers. Never in the past — not even during the tenures of Arjun Singh and Moti Lal Vora, have such large numbers of transfers taken place, the sources confirmed. Although the state government has lifted the ban on transfers till 30 June, no end of transfers is in sight. Local newspapers have been publishing transfer lists — like examination results — sometimes covering two full pages. The transfers cover all classes of staff — from class one officers to class four employees. This is the first time that even chaprasis have not been spared from being transferred. Most of the transfers, have been effected at the district and tehsil levels done at the behest of the local MLAs and party workers. Mostly, the employees transferred were having connections with Congress-I leaders. The maximum transfers have been done in the Education Department followed by Health, Revenue and Police. The number of transfers in other departments like Public Health Engineering, Forest and Tribal Welfare is also quite large. In 1986, the state government had announced a transfer policy, making it clear that all the officers and other employees with a stay of three years would be transferred. The new government has thrown that policy to the winds. It is widely known that chief secretary R. P. Kapoor is the key adviser to the chief minister in transfer matters. "The chief secretary appears to be more powerful than the chief minister", a top party functionary told this correspondent. The state government began the spate of transfers with the IAS officers. At least half a dozen lists of the transferred IAS officers have so far been released and two or three more lists are expected this month. Some secretaries and managing directors of Corporations are to be changed. As far as the IPS is concerned, the transfers could not take place because of the change in the portfolio of Home Minister Shitla Sahai. DIGs and IGs have been waiting for their transfers for the last three months, whereas 37 of the total 46 district superintendents of police have been changed. Interestingly, two IGs — Pratap Singh and D. K. Arya, who have returned to the parent state from deputation, have been sitting idle for the last several days. However, one thing which deserves admiration is the disappearance of the 'brokers' engaged in the transfer business, which had become an industry without investment during the Congress regime.

— People in Rajasthan above the age of 70 and living below the poverty line will now get enhanced pension at the rate of Rs. 100 a month. Under the present scheme those above 60 years of age are drawing old-age pension at the rate of Rs. 60 a month.

— India continues to lead as the country with the largest irrigated areas in the world though the eighties have witnessed a gradual showing down of investments an irrigation. John R. Hennessy, an international expert, said. India with 56 million hectares and drainage topped the list for irrigation, followed by China with 47 million hectares, the USA with 27 million hectares and the Soviet Union with 21 million hectares.

6 July 1990

— Jammu and Kashmir Governor Girish Chandra Saxena today promulgated the Armed Forces (Jammu-Kashmir) Special Power Ordinance, 1990. This empowers the armed forces to carry out searches and destroy hideouts of militants in the entire Kashmir valley and a 20-km belt from the line of actual control in the border districts of Poonch and Rajouri in Jammu region.

Jammu and Kashmir is already under Governor's Rule since 19 January 1990, after the resignation of the Congress-National Conference coalition under Farooq Abdullah in protest against the appointment of Jagmohan as Governor. From 19 July 1990, the state of Jammu and Kashmir will be placed under President's rule.

— The previous Congress-I government in Orissa has come under severe criticism from the Comptroller and Auditor General of India (CAG) for making "inflated claims" on drought relief with central assistance and for utilising huge amounts of it in non-affected areas in clear violation of central guidelines.

In its latest report laid in the Orissa Assembly, the CAG said though the state government reported the expenditure for 1987-88 as Rs. 52.86 crore against the centrally fixed ceiling of Rs. 59.61 crore, the actual expenditure as reported by units was only Rs. 38.16 crore. The government was given extension up to June 1988 to make use of the unutilised assistance to the extent of Rs. 6.29 crore on employment generation in the drought-hit areas, and on fodder cultivation. However, a substantial amount of the assistance remained unutilised, it said. The CAG report said that contrary to specific central instructions that no contractor should be engaged for employment generation works, these were executed through contractors for irrigation and drinking water supply schemes. Out of Rs. 10.57 crore placed with the Orissa Lift Irrigation Corporation (OLIC) to take up modernisation of field channels and construction of lift irrigation projects in districts, it spent only Rs. 2.80 crore till the end of March 1988, which worked out to 27 per cent. While Rs. 7.77 crore remained unutilised with the corporation, Rs. 81.85 lakh of the Rs. 2.80 crore remained unspent with the executing agencies. "Most surprisingly" the expenditure included Rs. 31 lakh paid to the Orissa State Electricity Board for replacement of conductors which did not form a part of the employment generation component, the CAG stated. During 1987-88, all the 13 districts were declared drought-affected, and the districts of Bolangir, Kalahandi, Genjam, Koraput and Phulbani were worst affected. However, Cuttack district was given the highest share of funds (Rs. 2.15 crore), though it was not one of the worst affected districts, the report said.

Contrary to central instructions that the feeding programme implemented under drought relief with central assistance should not cover Integrated Child Development Service (ICDS) blocks, huge amounts were spent on ICDS blocks in Cuttack and Koraput districts. Besides, 15 blocks not declared as drought-affected were covered under the programme, the report revealed. The centre approved Rs. 43 crore for the employment generation scheme for 1987-88. However, the Orissa government spent only Rs. 27.02 crore but reported an expenditure of Rs. 36.45 crore, it said. The CAG noted that the Orissa government was required to send the list of works executed under the employment generation scheme to the ministries of Finance and Agriculture, but this was not done. Neither was any monitoring or evaluation study undertaken by the government to assess the community assets created out of relief funds.

9 July 1990

— Thirty people including 13 militants and three Central Reserve Police Force were killed in the Kashmir valley.

— Terrorists gun down 41 persons in Punjab.

10 July 1990

— Akali Dal (B) leader and former Finance Minister Balwant Singh and 16 other persons were shot down in Punjab.

— Twenty-six persons were killed in Srinagar by terrorists.

— The Central Bureau of Investigation in the month of May 1990, took up 95 cases in which 134 public officers were involved. The number includes 84 gazetted officers.

11 July 1990

— The Ministry of Environment at the behest of Maneka Gandhi prepared a draft Bill envisaging a three-tier machinery comprising the National Environment Commission, the National Environment Court and the State Environment Court for speedy payment of compensation for the damage done to the people by polluting industries and polluters. The draft Bill was an abortive attempt having been turned down by her Cabinet Minister Nilamani Routray. Maneka Gandhi angered by this act resigned.

— Exactly after 51 days, Om Prakash Chautala today bounced back to political power as chief minister of Haryana.

— The Kuldeep Singh Commission has concluded in its report that the former Karnataka chief minister, Ramakrishna Hedge, is guilty of abetting the commission of a fraud by the Bombay builder, Siraj Lokhandwala, through a non-existent organisation called the Non-Resident Indian Housing Association (Karnataka) Pvt. Ltd. This was evident from the copy of the Commission's report placed in the library of Parliament by the government today. The four major conclusions that the Commission headed by Justice Kuldeep Singh of the Supreme Court of India in regard to Hegde are:

* The decision of the Bangalore Development Authority, dated 3 July 1987, approving the allotment of 110 acres of land in the name of NRIHA (K) was to the knowledge of Hegde.
* It was further to the knowledge of Hegde that the NRIHA(K) was a non-existent body and that it was a false front set up by Lokhandwala to grab the multi-crore NRIs housing project.
* In spite of Hegde's knowledge that the NRIHA(K) was a false front behind which Lokhandwala was operating, he did not take any action to stop the fraud being perpetrated. By deliberate inaction on his part Hegde abetted the commission of the fraud by Lokhandwala.
* There is no material before the commission to show that the fact of fabrication interpolation of official records by Lokhandwala and Reddy (Dr H. G. V. Reddy, the then chairman of the Bangalore Development Authority) was to the knowledge of Hegde.

The findings of the Commission about the son-in-law of Hegde, Manohar Lal Nichani, are even more damning for the "value-based politics" that Hegde has been claiming to practice. The Commission noted that from the scrutiny of the material before it and after carefully examining the facts and circumstances its conclusion was "that Nichani used his influence as son-in-law of the chief minister to help Lokhandwala procure the 110 acres NRIs housing project from the Bangalore Development Authority. Reddy, at Nichani's behest, went out of the way and extended undue favours to Lokhandwala in securing the said project". About Nichani's behaviour before the commission, Justice Kuldip Singh has observed: "I minutely watched his demeanour in the witness box. He gave the impression of a determined liar. He showed no regard for truth. He told deliberate lies even in respect of patent facts. He threw the oath to the winds and perjured with impunity". How was the fraud committed by Lokhandwala, in the words of Commission: "The project involved more than 100 crores of rupees and as such was attractive for any private builder. It was a goldmine promising an easy profit of 20/30 crores. The project could only by allotted to a group of NRIs of Karnataka origin. Lokhandwala as such could not have got the project. He, therefore, created a bogus NRI association and named it NRIHA(K). The Bangalore Development Authority approved the allotment in the name of the NRIHA(K). Lokhnadwala's effort was to grab the project and make 20/30 crores. Lokhandwala was a friend of Manohar Lal Nichani, the son-in-law of Hegde. Lokhandwala was also personally known to Hegde." And further, that "Hegde was fully aware that the NRIHA(K) was a creation of Lokhandwala to achieve his personal ends."

What should have Hegde done to keep his head above water? According to Justice Kuldip Singh: In a situation like that Hegde should have taken stern action to stop the fraud from being perpetrated. The resolution of the Bangalore Development Authority (selecting NRIHA(K) for the project and allotting it 110 acres of land) should have been cancelled and follow-up action taken against the officers/officials concerned. A chief minister of the state is the custodian of public interests. It is his duty to guard and protect the public interest with a vigilant eye. A multi-crore project was being manoeuvred by fraudulent means under the nose of the chief minister and no action was taken at all. Instead of taking prompt action, Hegde kept silent while Lokhandwala went on with the project and took various steps for its execution. It was the duty of Hegde to act positively." The Commission has found that the Bangalore Development Authority modified its own rules at the behest of the then chief minister, Hegde, to make a bulk allotment of 110 acres of land to the NRIHA (K). It knew that the land was not meant for merely constructing the houses for the members of the NRIHA (K) which was registered as a private limited company and residential buildings would have to be sold to non-members, that some of the land being allotted to the NRIHA (K) was designated as green-belt land the authority had not redesignated its use at the time of allotting it to the NRIHA (K), that Rs. 55 lakhs had been remitted to the Bangalore Development Authority from Dubai and no attempt seemed to have been made to find out whether it was laundered money or sent by genuine NRIs, that the NRIHA (K) had been allowed to take possession of the land and build a boundary wall and several permanent structures on the land even when the government had not fully cleared this and that Lokhandwala had begun the sale of the proposed houses internationally. The really damning evidence against Hegde that the Commission found was in the proceedings of a meeting held in the chief minister's chamber on 14 December 1987. They made it evident that Hegde took active interest in the allotment of land to the fake NRI company and was in fact told that the company had taken possession of the land and begun work at the site. It is evident from the record of the proceedings of the meeting that the land which was actually allotted to the fake NRI group was already being bought by the Greater Bangalore House Building Society. This information was given by the minister for Bangalore development. At this, the commissioner of the Bangalore Development Authority intervened to say that the authority had handed over the land to the NRIHA (K) for group housing and that work had already begun on it. Then "the chief minister, after some discussion stated that the society (the Greater Bangalore House Building Cooperative Society) be given alternate land".

That Hegde was kept informed of the progress of the project is evident also from the deposition of H. G. V. Reddy, the chairman of the Bangalore Development Authority. When Reddy was asked how often he kept the chief minister informed of the NRI housing project, he replied, "occasionally. Whenever, there used to be meetings, he used to inquire about the progress." Asked whether he was aware of what was happening to the project, Reddy replied, "yes. He was aware." Hegde's role in changing the rules to allot the land in bulk to the fake NRI company is also evident from Reddy's deposition. The counsel for the commission asked Reddy: "After this allotment was made in favour of the NRI association, the authorities found that the existing rules do not provide for bulk allotment and therefore this required to be amended. Is it a fact?" Reddy replied: "Correct. Actually at the instance of the chief minister these rules were drafted and processed through our legal department and sent to the government for approval. It is still pending with the government."

13 July 1990

— The re-induction of Om Prakash Chautala as Haryana's chief minister has been perceived as an unashamed violation of all norms of democratic behaviour and moral values in public life. As a result, the National Front government is plunged in a crisis. Three ministers - Arun Nehru, Arif Mohammad Khan and Sat Pal Malik resigned in protest.

— Maneka Gandhi's resignation is not accepted by V.P. Singh who asks her to continue as minister.

14 July 1990

— V.P. Singh sent in his resignation from the office of Prime Ministership to the Janata Dal President S.R. Bommai, asking the party to elect a new leader to succeed him. This follows Om Prakash Chautala's re-induction as Haryana's chief minister.

— Six more ministers at the centre submitted their resignations to V.P. Singh in protest against the re-induction of Om Prakash Chautala as the chief minister of Haryana.

16 July 1990

— Haryana chief minister Om Prakash Chautala accepted the Janata Dal Political Affairs Committee's decision and accordingly resigned from the chief minister office unconditionally. Devi Lal earlier laid down a condition that if Chautala must go so must four ministers — Arun Nehru, Arif Mohammad Khan, I.K. Gujral and Satpal Malik — who had publicly protested against Chautala's reinstatement.

— The two-day convention of the Indian Revenue Service concluded today urging the government to provide them better service conditions. It recommended elevation of the status of the Central Board of Direct Taxes making it a department of direct taxes.

17 July 1990

— V.P. Singh refuses to accept the resignations earlier submitted by four ministers.

— Hukum Singh was sworn in as Haryana's chief minister in place of Om Prakash Chautala.

18 July 1990

— The new chief minister of Haryana said: " Devi Lal and Om Prakash will be the super chief ministers whereas I would be much below the status of a dummy chief minister."

— 37 Pak-trained terrorists were killed and 18 others arrested in the Kashmir valley.

— President's Rule was imposed on Jammu & Kashmir with effect from tonight — after the expiry of Governor's Rule.

— A secretary in the M. P. government, B. K. Taimini, refused to cancel some transfer orders of public servants issued by chief minister Sunderlal Patwa.

— A committee of the Bihar Assembly will inquire into the irregularities committed by the IAS officers Cooperative Housing Society in the state capital, Speaker Ghulam Sarvar announced in the House today. The committee is being constituted at the instance of the government. Uproarious scenes were witnessed in the House during the question hour when ruling party and opposition members exchanged remarks, displayed frayed tempers and cast aspersions on each other. The uproar followed the refusal of Building Construction Minister Ilyas Hussain to institute an inquiry into the violation of the terms and conditions by these officers in the construction of their houses at Shrikrishna Nagar here. Dissatisfied at the minister's reply to a short-notice question of Kumud Ranjan Jha (Cong-I), members of the CPI, headed by their leader Ramendra Kumar, supported the Congress-I on the demand. Enraged by the "evasive reply" of the minister, all the Congress-I members rose in protest. This drew a similar protest from the ruling party members. Heated exchanges followed. Jha alleged that the government had been favouring the officers who were given the government land for building houses. The officers had violated the terms and conditions of the allotment. At this point most of the Congress-I members stormed into the well of the House and rushed to the podium to lodge their complaint with the Speaker. When it became difficult for the Speaker to restore order, Parliamentary Affairs Minister, Raghunath Jha, intervened and cast aspersions on the Congress-I members who were in the government when these officers were allotted land. However, the Speaker said the present government could not evade its responsibility. The Minister for Parliamentary Affairs then conceded that the terms and conditions had been violated by the members of the society. Irregularities also had been committed. He suggested to the Speaker to constitute a committee of the House to inquire into these irregularities. The Speaker immediately announced that the committee would be constituted within two days. Earlier, the Building Construction Minister had said that 18 houses had been constructed in the colony. This was challenged by the questioner, who claimed that of the 24 members of the society 20 had constructed their houses. Except two, all the houses had been rented out while these officers had been occupying government flats, creating housing problems for other officers. The Jharkhand Mukti Morcha (JMM) member Suraj Mandal and the BJP members too expressed their annoyance over the delay in the decision of the assurances committee of the House in regard to filling up the vacant posts against reservations for scheduled castes and tribes. The members rapped the government when the Building Construction Minister replied that the question of Mandal had been pending before the committee.

The Minister of State for Minor Irrigation, Bhola Prasad Toofani, while replying to short-notice question of Upendra Prasad Verma (JD), denied Verma's claim that over Rs. 300 crore had been spent without creating any additional irrigation potential.

The House again witnessed angry exchanges when the Building Construction Minister said that of the 42 districts 33 had been neglected by the previous government in regard to the sanction of roads. Nine districts had been allotted over 540 km roads for construction, two districts—Gaya and Jehanabad—alone had been allotted 240 km roads.

The Speaker upheld the government's decision to review the decisions of the previous government.

19 July 1990

— Supreme Court Judge V. Ramaswamy, against whom investigations are pending on audit reports alleging financial irregularities during his tenure as Chief Justice, of the Punjab and Haryana High Court will be on leave for six weeks in the first instance.

20 July 1990

— The multi-edition Swadesh, the mouth-piece of the BJP, is very critical of the BJP-run Patwa government in regard to its mass transfer policy in the state.

21 July 1990

— Khushwant Singh, the well-known writer, says in his column "With Malice Towards One and All" in *The Hindustan Times*.

Castrating the bureaucracy: One lesson politicians — not famous for foresight or patriotism — will not learn is that mucking about with the bureaucracy is the surest way of reducing it to importance and bringing the business of governance to a sticky halt. The Congress Party in power did it; the National Front government continues to do the same: sack, suspend, or transfer officers they don't like and replace them with their cronies. One case of scandalous misuse of ministerial power to denigrate a senior bureaucrat to accommodate a political ally concerns Suresh Kapur, till recently chairman of the Hindustan Vegetable Oils Corporation which has nine factories producing edible oils, vanaspati and breakfast foods. I have written about him earlier and do so again because I know of his achievements. And he is a friend.

Kapur took over as chairman of the company in 1985 when it was on the verge of bankruptcy with its accounts several crores in the red. The then Minister of Food and Civil Supplies had asked for Rs. 25 crores to rehabilitate it. Within a year Kapur turned it into a highly lucrative enterprise netting a profit of Rs. 13 crores per year. The company has not looked back since then and is listed seventh among the 206 public sector companies. Kapur came to be highly rated amongst managers for efficiency and integrity.

The government changed. The new minister, Nathu Ram Mirdha was happy with Kapur's performance. However, the Minister of State, Ram Poojan Patel (ironically) elected from Pandit Nehru's constituency) wanted his own man, a politico, to be chairman of the company. All manners of utterly frivolous charges were trumped up against Kapur, his subordinates were asked to tender evidence against him, an invitation to attend a six-week commercial course at Harvard was cancelled a few hours before his flight was to take off. His contract for service extended first by a month was reduced to a fortnight. Every attempt was made to humiliate him and force him to quite. He has quit.

It is time the Prime Minister puts his foot down firmly on colleagues who go out of their way to meddle with the bureaucracy and so destroy the most important pillar of the administration.'

— Because of the differences between the cabinet secretary and the chairman of the Public Enterprises Selection Board on the issue of selecting new chief executives of Air-India and Indian Airlines, the two posts remain unfilled.

24 July 1990

— Punjab Governor, Virendra Verma today termed Operation Bluestar held in 1984 as the Himalayan blunder of the then central government.

25 July 1990

— Thousands of families of Hindus and Sikhs have left the Kashmir valley to seek shelter in other parts of India.

— The Ministry of Information and Broadcasting has decided to close down its Research and Reference Division which has been in existence for the last three decades.

26 July 1990

— The Chief Justice of India, Sabyasachi Mukherjee, has written to all the chief justices of the High Courts seeking their views on constituting an intra-judiciary machinery to look into allegations of corruption against judges.

The letters despatched on 18 July seek the chief justices' views on what kind of allegations should be looked into by the proposed machinery and what should be the status of the person making the allegations against a judge. The chief justices are scheduled to meet here on 30 and 31 August.

Earlier, at their annual conference the chief justices had opposed framing of any formal code of conduct. The Chief Justice has suggested holding a discussion on the issue on an alternative scheme during the two-day conference. The straightforward letter appears to be a fallout of the massive public outcry against increasing corruption in the judiciary. The proposed machinery, if it gets the approval, would investigate the conduct or misconduct of any member of the judiciary either *suo motu* or on an allegation made against him which gains public credence. The Chief Justice has also urged them to have the views of maximum number of judges on the proposal since the matter "concerns us all". Along with the Chief Justice's letter, tentative draft proposals earlier sent by the bar association to former Chief Justice R. S. Pathak have also been annexed. The bar association had said in the draft proposals that "the times has come to consider measures short of impeachment which would, without undermining the independence of the judiciary, help retain public confidence in the High Courts". The bar association has suggested holding of a judicial conference of all the judges of the High Courts and the Supreme Court to find out certain "self-cleansing measures". The conference may also approve an informal committee consisting of some judges of the Supreme Court to investigate the complaints against the High Court Judges. The Chief Justices of the High Courts should also be *ad hoc* members of the proposed committee. The lawyers memorandum has suggested a "polite inquiry" by the concerned judge. It would help obviate suspicion. Where suspicions appear to be well-founded, a private "chat" by the committee with the judge concerned, might prove helpful, the memorandum said adding that such a committee may also consider allegations against the subordinate judiciary.

27 July 1990

— The Home Ministry's orders transferring 11 top officials of the Delhi Administration out of Delhi has sent a shock wave among the IAS officers of the Union Territory Cadre. There is resentment among the officers also over the ministry not following its own transfer rules and precedents. The practice in the past had been that those officers who are to retire after three or four years are not transferred. In the present shake-up, at least two officers are over 55 years, the retirement age is 58. Interestingly, who have not been in Delhi for five or more years have been transferred. One of the "victims of the ire of the Home Ministry is an officer who has already done hard station posting, and has been in Delhi for less than five years". The chief secretary, Delhi Administration, has been asked to relieve all the officers immediately without waiting for their replacements. Six of the 11 officers are being sent to Arunachal Pradesh. They are Labour Commissioner D. K. Spolia, Excise Commissioner V. Madan, Registrar, Cooperatives K. S. Mehra, Director, Social Welfare D. R. Nafri, Commissioner (Lands), Delhi Development Authority Rakesh Behari, special secretary Land and Building K. K. Bhasin, who is out of the country. Ashok Bakshi, joint secretary Medical, and B. Prasad, Director, Training and Technical Education have been transferred to Andamans. Savitri Kashyap, Director, Delhi Energy Development Agency is to go to Goa and Naini Jisheelan is likely to go Lakashdweep. I. J. Talwar, Director, Agricultural Marketing Board and another officers S. N. Sahai have also been transferred. Some of the officers on the transferred list had taken over new department only a few days ago, Madan and Behari. Replacement for the officers transferred are likely to be drawn from UT cadre, who are coming back to Delhi from their outstation postings. They are S.P. Singh, R.K. Srivastav, and J.K. Dadoo, all from Arunachal. Ravi Malik from the Andamans and N. Sathyavathy and Archana Arora from Arunachal

28 July 1990

— Highlighting the need for structural change in the Indian polity, Vasant Sathe, former minister at the centre, recommended change over to the presidential form of government. Other recommendations included reorganisation of states, amendment of electoral laws to give statutory recognition and status to political parties in the Constitution.

30 July 1990

— V.P. Singh asks Deputy Prime Minister Devi Lal to explain his allegations of corruption against Arun Nehru, Commerce Minister and Arif Mohammad Khan, Energy and Civil Aviation Minister.

— Transfer of several hundred doctors and nurses in M. P. had led to a rift between Health Minister and his secretary B. K. Taimini. The Health Minister told the chief minister that he was misguided by Taimini in transfer matters which brought a lot of flak for the BJP government. The minister Prakash Singh said that Taimini was a favourite of the former chief minister Shyama Charan Shukla.

— Twenty-one persons including 14 militants are killed in the Kashmir valley.

— Expressing disappointment over the country's achievements in the farm sector, the highpowered committee on agricultural policies and programmes, headed by the Karnataka Governor, Bhanu Pratap Singh, has recommended that agriculture be provided the same facilities and incentives as are available to industry.

The series of measures suggested by the committee in its report presented to the Deputy Prime Minister Devi Lal, here today also include launching a new, cost-effective food security system, mechanisation of small farms, amending land ceiling laws and greater attention to minor irrigation rather than major and medium irrigation projects.

It has suggested a target of doubling agricultural production in the next 15 years, at an average annual growth rate of 4.7 per cent. This would need doubling of the present rate of capital formation in the farm sector.

Describing the stress on rapid industrialisation as "misplaced", the committee has said that the wrong development strategies, flowing from unrealistic policies, had ignored many ground realities. Despite the natural advantage Indian agriculture enjoyed, the country remained out of the world's most backward nations, not producing even two-fifths of its potential. "Agriculturists have become worse off in real terms than they were before the Green Revolution. The Indian village continues to be unlivable, devoid of basic amenities of life—good schools, hospitals, dependable power supply and transport facilities," the committee says.

Besides going into the policies and programmes, this committee was asked to study the question of providing industrial status to agriculture. It has concluded that so long as agriculture is given the same facilities and incentives as are available to industry, and similar norms, standards and criteria are applied to both in fixation of prices and provision of budgetary support, credit, power transport and export facilities, it is immaterial whether any formal status is given to agriculture or not. "However, if bias against agriculture cannot be shed without giving it the formal status of industry, then certainly it should be given that status", the report says.

Expressing concern over the 25 per cent of the cultivable land having remained unutilised, the committee has suggested that state governments be persuaded to amend their agricultural and ceiling Acts. The new legislations should provide that anyone who brings under productive cultivation any piece of culturable land, which had been lying barren and uncultivated for long, will be allowed to retain 50 per cent of the reclaimed land, exempted from the ceiling Act. He should be asked to surrender the remaining 50 per cent for redistribution among the landless. It suggests that consolidation of holdings should completed by the end of the Eighth Plan. This is essential as the modernisation of even small farms cannot begin if it remains scattered in small bits all over the village. It has also suggested that the Land Acquisition Act, 1894, be amended to prevent acquisition of farmer's good agricultural land, rendering him landless and violating his right to pursue his avocation. A "greening the country" campaign should be launched immediately under which village panchayat and government land be leased to landless, other individuals, cooperatives or corporations for forestry purposes.

The committee has favoured mechanisation of small farms to minimise the drudgery of cultivators and improve the efficiency of inputs. This would leave spare time with the farmers to take up income-augmenting supplementary enterprises like dairying, goat-keeping, sericulture, etc.

In the case of irrigation, the committee felt that the expenditure on major and medium projects be limited, for the time being, to only completion of the on-going works. Greater attention should be paid to minor irrigation, especially in the eastern states. The committee has strongly recommended that the credit needs of the farmers be met fully. Realising that it would not be possible to provide all the services needed for all the cash crops or enterprises, the panel has suggested that specific enterprises be selected for particular areas and all the desired services be made available there.

Suggesting an alternative food security system, the committee has stated that besides being cost-effective, it has to be less harmful to the poor. The three-pronged system aims at:

* Restoring farmer's freedom to sell his produce without let or hindrance so long as open market prices remain within a price band, the lower and upper limits to be called "support" and "intervention" prices which, in turn, should be fixed to maintain a balance between prices received and prices paid by farmers;
* Promoting direct producer-consumer links;
* Providing food aid directly to the genuinely poor.

Stressing the need for reorienting farm research, the committee has suggested that more attention be paid to animal husbandry, horticulture, fishery and sericulture — all of which can generate more income for small farmers. Dryland agriculture also merits greater attention than it had received in the past. Farm research centres needed to be increased. Transfer of technology, through model small farmers, be made the direct responsibility of research centres.

31 July 1990

— U.P. government abolishes octroi in the state from 1 August 1990.

The Municipal governments are likely to incur an annual loss of Rs. 100 crores, which will be compensated by increasing surcharge on sales tax. With the abolition of octroi, the staff engaged in the realisation of this tax will not be retrenched and their services will be utilised in other works of the municipalities.

AUGUST 1990

1 August 1990

— Prime Minister Vishwanath Pratap Singh dropped Devi Lal from Oabinet. Devi Lal, Deputy Prime Minister in the National Front government, was dismissed by the President of India following his refusal to substantiate his allegations against Commerce Minister Arun Nehru and Energy Minister Arif Mohammad Khan and to make amends for his derogatory references to his cabinet colleagues and to Prime Minister himself in a Press interview.

7 August 1990

— A 27 per cent reservation for the backward castes in the Central government services and public undertakings was announced by Prime Minister V.P. Singh in Parliament today.

Making a *suo motu* statement in both the Houses on the government's decisions on the report of the Mandal Commission dealing with the backward classes, V.P. Singh said that such reservation of jobs for the socially and educationally backward classes (SEBC) was being made for the first time since Independence. The reservation quota had gone up to 49.5 per cent with this announcement. Of this, 15 per cent was for the scheduled castes and 7.5 per cent for the scheduled tribes.

9 August 1990

— Announcement of job reservation has been swiftly followed by undignant protests in the country.

— The anti-reservation stir took a violent turn in Bihar following the announcement made by Prime Minister V.P. Singh to provide 27 per cent job reservation for the backward classes.

— As many as 1,08,379 cases were pending before the Supreme Court of India as on 30 June 1990, the Rajya Sabha was told in a parliamentary reply.

— The ruling National Front government is prepared to amend the Constitution of India to reserve 40 per cent seats in Parliament and the State Assemblies for the poor if there is a consensus among the political parties. This was announced by Prime Minister V.P. Singh in the Rajya Sabha.

He also said he would take note of the suggestion to declare the whole Muslim and Christian community as backward.

— The Lok Sabha passed the Bill to constitute a National Commission for Women.

10 August 1990

— The anti-reservation stir spreads in Bihar. The agitation overtakes Delhi also.

— The Rajya Sabha was told that the number of total job-seekers on the live registers of the employment exchanges was 30 million.

— The total amount of domestic and external debt outstanding against India on 30 March 1990, is estimated at Rs. 2,38,096 crores and Rs. 80,132 crores respectively. The amount of interest payment during 1989-90 on domestic and external debts is estimated to be Rs. 16,226 crores and Rs. 3,559 crores.

— The Supreme Court of India has declared that the policy of reservation in favour of the scheduled castes and scheduled tribes officers is applicable even in the case of promotion within the officers' cadre.

13 August 1990

— The anti-reservation stir spreads to U.P. and Delhi Students burn their degrees in Delhi.

— Ram Vilas Paswan, the minister, said that the centre would introduce a Bill in the current session of Parliament proposing three per cent reservation for the physically handicapped and the blind in the government and public sector undertakings.

14 August 1990

— Anti-reservation stir intensifies. Paswan is firm on reservation of jobs.

15 August 1990

— Prophet Mohammed's birthday has been declared by the government as a public holiday in India. The announcement was made by the Prime Minister in his Independence Day speech.

— Prime Minister V.P. Singh said in his Independence Day speech that while the backward classes constitute 52 per cent of the population they had only 14.5 per cent share in government jobs. "Their share was as low as 4.5 per cent in Class I jobs", he said.

— Prime Minister V.P. Singh in his Independence Day speech reiterated the resolve of the National Front government to protect the rights of the poor and vulnerable who over the years had suffered neglect and discrimination. He defended job reservation for the backward castes. He also announced setting up of development boards for backward areas of Vidarbha, Marathwada and Konkan.

— The government has constituted seven sub-committees to help finalise programmes and schemes for celebrating the birth anniversary of Dr B.R. Ambedkar.

— There has been a massive inflow of funds into the country from prominent Gulf cities following growing tension between the United States and Iraq over Kuwait's invasion.

16 August 1990

— The government has decided that whenever a selection committee exists or has to be set up for making recruitment to 10 or more vacancies in Group C or D posts, it shall be mandatory to have one member belonging to the scheduled castes and scheduled tribes and from minority community on them.

— The government told the Lok Sabha that a Constitution Amendment Bill seeking to revitalise Panchayati Raj institutions is likely to be introduced during the current session of Parliament.

17 August 1990

— Christians of the scheduled caste origin demanded their inclusion in the scheduled caste list and the resultant extension of privileges and reservations as their exclusion for the last 40 years is an act of discrimination based on religion.

— Among the private members' Bills introduced in the Rajya Sabha was a Constitution Amendment Bill seeking to provide constitutional immunity to the Comptroller and Auditor-General of India and his office.

— The BJP and the Left Parties call for economic criterion for reservation policy for government jobs.

18 August 1990

— The anti-reservation stir spreads to the South with students courting arrest in Andhra Pradesh while protesters blocked traffic in several cities in Rajasthan and set fire to a railway compartment.

— The government decided to limit extravagance in public spending. No expenditure proposal beyond the sanctioned budget is to be allowed unless the method of financing is clearly indicated.

— The government issued an executive order reserving 27 per cent of vacancies in civil posts and services under for socially and educationally backward classes as recommended by the Mandal Commission.

20 August 1990

— The anti-reservation agitation spreads to several parts of U.P. compelling closing down of educational institutions.

— The government proposed to set up a National Security Council under the chairmanship of the Prime Minister to consider all aspects of national security in a fully coordinated manner.

— The government is grilled over *Khula Manch*, a "Meet the Minister" programme on the Doordarshan.

21 August 1990

— The National Forum of Teachers called upon Prime Minister V.P. Singh to withhold the decision to make 27 per cent reservations for backward classes in government jobs till the government conducted a dialogue with the various sections in society.

— The Kashmiri migrants protest against the failure of the National Front government to restore peace in the trouble-torn Kashmir valley and provide them succour to lead a normal life.

22 August 1990

— The government today raised the excise duty on motor cars by 10 per cent *ad valorem* as part of its package of measures to reduce consumption of petroleum products in the wake of the Gulf crisis. The Finance Minister also announced a reduction in the rate of depreciation from the present rate of 33.33 per cent to 20 per cent in respect of cars.

— Twelve of the 21 participants in the *Khula Manch* programme with George Fernandes have in two separate letters to the Information and Broadcasting Minister, P. Upendra, protested about the manner in which the programme was conducted.

— School-children join the anti-Mandal agitation.

— Doordarshan earned a gross revenue of Rs. 210.13 crores from commercial advertisement and sponsorship of programmes in 1989-90.

23 August 1990

— Anti-Mandal agitation spreads. Students in Delhi form a human chain around Parliament.

— An inter-ministerial task force has been set up to suggest firm proposals on the proposed right to information and related matters. This was told to the Lok Sabha in a parliamentary reply.

— The *Khula Manch* programme of Doordarshan has been criticised.

— The Lok Sabha debate on the Prasar Bharati Bill for autonomy to radio and television took an unexpected turn with political parties on both sides of the House agreeing to discuss the suggested amendments in an all-party meeting before voting on the Bill on 26 August 1990.

— Simranjit Singh Mann, former president of the Akali Dal (Mann), has resigned from the Lok Sabha.

— Private vehicle owners in Delhi have to obtain "pollution under control" certificates by January 1991, the Lok Sabha was informed in a parliamentary reply.

— As many as 157 high-rise building constructed in India prior to 1983 do not have adequate in-built fire safety measure.

— There has been an increase in cases of dacoity, attempts to murder, kidnapping, abduction and rape in 1989 and 1990 in Delhi. This was disclosed in a parliamentary reply.

— The internal debt of India was Rs. 96,505 crores at the end of 1989.

24 August 1990

— The fortnight-old anti-reservation stir turned violent with student-police clashes in the Capital. The agitating students included a large number of girls.

— The Master Plan for Delhi, which comes into force this month, envisages planned growth of the city with various urban activities like housing, transport, employment centres and recreation to cater to a population of 12.8 million by the year 2001.

25 August 1990

— School students took to the streets today, and registered their protest against the Mandal Commission report by indulging in large-scale vandalism throughout Delhi. The Bharatiya Janata Party urges the government to talk to the students.

— Simranjit Singh Mann withdraws his resignation from the Lok Sabha.

26 August 1990

— The cabinet Committee on Political Affairs (CCP) today mooted a proposal for reservation of 5 to 10 per cent posts in government services and public sector undertakings for the economically backward sections of society. Together with 15 per cent reservations for the scheduled castes and 7.5 per cent for the scheduled tribes, the 27 per cent suggested by the Mandal Commission amount to 49.5 per cent reservations in central government services. The new 5 to 10 per cent additional reservations will be on the basis of economic criteria.

— Ram Vilas Paswan and Sharad Yadav gave a call to the backward communities to "hit the streets and give a fitting reply" to anti-reservationists while addressing a Janata Dal rally held at Boat Club, Delhi.

27 August 1990

— The anti-reservation bandh disrupted normal life in Delhi causing massive traffic dislocations and other cessation of business activity.

— The anti-Mandal agitation already gripping the northern states spreads to Gujarat.

— The Haryana cabinet today decided to raise the upper age limit for entry into government service from 30 years to 35 years to mitigate the hardship of educated unemployed youth.

28 August 1990

— Two senior ministers in the Union Cabinet have cautioned V.P. Singh on the issue of implementation of the Mandal Commission.

— Medical doctors in Delhi join anti-reservation demonstrations.

— The Mahila Janata Dal today urged the government that out of the total reserved quota made for the backward classes, a certain percentage must be set aside for women.

— The upper age limit for recruitment for the IAS and allied services in the 1990 examination has been raised from 26 to 31 years. From 1991 examination onwards, it will be 28 years.

29 August 1990

— There is a growing demand within the ruling Janata Dal for reconsideration of the Mandal Commission recommendations.

30 August 1990

— The Prasar Bharati Bill has been passed by the Lok Sabha today. This Bill was passed unanimously.

— An all-party meeting is being convened on 3 September to discuss the issue of reservations in government jobs.

31 August 1990

— The Bharatiya Janata Party observed that reservation in government jobs should under no circumstance exceed 50 per cent, as prescribed by the Supreme Court of India.

— The V.P. Singh government told the Rajya Sabha in a parliamentary reply that wherever Muslim communities are included in both the state list and the Mandal Commission list, they would get the benefit of 27 per cent reservation announced by the government for socially backward classes.

SEPTEMBER 1990

2 September 1990

— The BJP opposed any move by the V.P. Singh government to grant reservation to minorities. L.K. Advani said that any such move would invite "unwanted second partition" of the country.

3 September 1990

— The expression "amiri rekha" or the line of richness has been defined to convey the idea that savings devoted to unproductive assets are a waste of resources and accumulation of unproductive wealth is undesirable. This was disclosed in the Lok Sabha in a parliamentary reply.

— The number of unemployed doctors was 27,286 in 1988. This was the number registered with the employment exchanges in the states and union territories.

— The V.P. Singh government appointed a 21 member committee of National Front MPs to consider the various issues connected with the proposal to enshrine the right to work as a fundamental right in the Constitution of India.

5 September 1990

— The number of girl child labour in the country is estimated to be about 7.6 million. This number was given in a parliamentary reply.

6 September 1990

— The Parliament approved the Prasar Bharati Bill (Broadcasting Corporation of India) to give antonomy to the electronic media.

14 September 1990

— The Congress Working Committee (I) alleged that the National Front government under V.P. Singh while sorting out its internal problems had plunged the nation into four unnecessary civil confrontations: on caste, communal, language and rural-urban. The need of the hour is, the CWC(I) declared, "a united national response to these challenges".

— The President of India gave its assent to the Prasar Bharati Bill (Broadcasting Corporation of India) Bill, 1990, thereby clearing the decks for the setting up of an autonomous corporation to manage the radio and television network. At present, the government controls the radio and television network in India.

— Faced with the burgeoning budget deficit, the government today announced a cut of 10 per cent in government expenditure to be incurred in the remaining months in the current financial year out of the sanctioned budget for 1990-91.

— Caste clashes continue, anti-reservation stir deepens.

15 September 1990

— Anti-reservation stir continues.

— Prime Minister V.P. Singh stated that the reservation of 27 per cent of the vacancies in all services under the Government of India and public sector shall not be applied in subsequent promotions in these departments.

— The Chief Election Commissioner shall now enjoy the status of a Supreme Court Judge.

16 September 1990

— The armed forces, science and technology, space, atomic energy and educational institutions will be exempted from the 27 per cent reservation for the socially and educationally backward classes.

— Anti-reservation violence continues in the states.

17 September 1990

— Anti-reservation violence continues.

18 September 1990

— Anti-reservation violence continues.

— Jawaharlal Nehru, India's first Prime Minister, was strongly against any kind of reservation, mainly in public services and promotions, based on caste. He favoured providing opportunities for good education and "help" on economic considerations and not on caste, but opposed reservation in jobs which might kill efficiency. These views are recorded in the letter he wrote to the chief ministers on 27 June 1961. This is disclosed in the fifth volume of Jawaharlal Nehru's letters to chief ministers, covering 1958-1964. He pointed out the necessity of our getting out of the old habit of reservations and particular privileges being given to "this caste or that group".

— The Ali Sardar Jafri Committee, which was set up to examine the recommendation of the Gujral Committee on the Promotion of Urdu submitted its Report to the Ministry of Human Resource Development.

— The World Bank's Annual Report 1990 puts India's GNP at U.S. $ 340 and China's GNP at $330 for fiscal years 1988-90.

19 September 1990

— A student tries to immolate himself to protest against Mandalisation of the civil services.

— Student agitation continues.

— Anti-Mandal students continue their agitation.

— One-fifth of the electricity power generated in India is lost during transmission and distribution, says a publication.

20 September 1990

— Anti-Mandal students continue their agitation.

21 September 1990

— Farmers in Delhi, Haryana, Bihar, U.P. and Rajasthan oppose job quota.

22 September 1990

— The Anti-Mandal agitation spreads to the Hindi belt. Situation worsens in the states.

23 September 1990

— Anti-Mandal agitation continues.

24 September 1990

— Anti-Mandal agitation continues.

25 September 1990

— Anti-Mandal agitation continues.

26 September 1990

— Anti-Mandal agitation continues.

27 September 1990

— Anti-Mandal agitation continues.

28 September 1990

— Over 100 professors urged Prime Minister V.P. Singh to give up his rigid stance and suspend implementation of the Mandal Report.

— Anti-Mandal agitation deepens.

29 September 1990

— Dissidence within the ruling Janata Dal has grown over the reservation issue. V.P. Singh comes under attack by MPs belonging to the Chandra Shekhar and Devi Lal camps.

— There are 117.82 lakh children and 22.71 lakh mothers receiving supplementary nutrition and 64.36 lakh children attending pre-school education under the Integrated Child Development Scheme (ICDS) which completes 15 years of its implementation on 2 October 1990.

— 3 October 1990, declared a government holiday on account of the birthday of Prophet Mohammad.

30 September 1990

— Prime Minister V.P. Singh today won a fresh vote of confidence from the National Front when a resolution reaffirming full faith in his leadership was adopted by an overwhelming majority at a meeting of the National Front Parliamentary Party. The resolution also authorised the Prime Minister to go ahead with the implementation of the Mandal Commission recommendations.

— The anti-reservation stir claimed at least seven more lines while army was called out in Una (Himachal Pradesh) as protests against the Mandal Commission report continued to disrupt life in several parts of northern India.

— Talks with the anti-reservationists are deadlocked.

— Devi Lal, former Deputy Prime Minister, sent his resignation from the Lok Sabha to Janata Dal President S.R. Bommai.

— As the row over the number of backward communities listed by the Mandal Commission continues, a just-concluded study by the Anthropological Survey of India (ASI) had identified 1,051 backward classes in the country.

(The Mandal Commission has listed more than 3,000 communities as socially and educationally backward). The objective of the project, launched in 1985, was, of course, different from that of the Mandal Commission. It was to generate brief descriptive anthropological profile of all communities of India, the impact of change and development process on them and the linkage that brings them together. The study, free from political overtones, is expected to enrich knowledge on the sociological pattern of the country. Explaining the necessity of such a project, the director-general of ASI, K.S. Singh, said in an interview that there existed a wide information gap about a very large number of communities in India, or the information that was there was scanty and needed to be updated.

The Project was also in accordance with the objective of ASI which has been pursuing bio-cultural researches among different population groups since its inception 45 years ago, Singh said. The ASI's objective had been redefined in the policy resolution adopted in 1985 which committed it to the survey of "the human surface of India", he added. The ASI has been able to identify, locate and write on 4,384 communities, including scheduled castes (443), scheduled tribes (426), backward classes (1,051), and other communities. "We have been able to prepare probably the most comprehensive lists of communities with all their ramifications such as subgroups, divisions, clans, lineages, surnames and titles", Singh said. The ASI is releasing its data called "People of India" tomorrow for scrutiny and further discussion. As the data is still being analysed it will not be appropriate to mention any findings conclusively, he added. However, a few trends in the analysis of the data could be shared tentatively, Singh said.

* The study revels the strength and continuity of regional identities which go back to the prehistoric times, in terms of morphological and genetic characteristics of populations, language and literature, material culture, food habits, rituals, folklore, local forms of religion, fairs and festivals etc. These regional identifies are primarily secular, according to the study. The communities, no matter how ranked they are, share the regional space and ethos. This explains why about 80-90 per cent of the communities of India are within the boundaries of Indian states and union territories, which were reorganise on the basis of language. These are thus linguistic-cultural and social identities, largely homogeneous. Only about 10 per cent of communities are spread over more than one state or adjoining area of states. They consist of traders, merchants, artisans, minorities and so on. There are few communities which do not consider themselves migrants. Every community recalls its migration in its folklore and history, set off by famines, wars, political considerations and sheer necessity.

The whole of India is a *kshetra* and an Indian is a migrant par excellence. The immigrants accepted regional ethos. Their role in promoting the development of regional languages and literature, building economy is well-known, the study emphasises. Caste and *Jati* have now become rigid in their "political" role, but they have been dynamic entities when seen in the historical context, and in contemporaneous terms of a caste's perception of itself, its role, its relationship with others and with environment. There has been a good deal of occupational mobility and change in spite of continuity. Segments of a community have moved away from traditional moorings or a section of a community has given up its traditional occupation, and or adopted a new technology. Almost all communities of India have felt the impact of change and development, of market and technology. There is an all-pervasive sense of Indianness often elusive and indefinable but ever present. In the words of Jawaharlal

Nehru, Indianness has been a matter of feeling, a dream, a vision, an emotion. In terms of prosaic anthropological concepts, it represents sharing of ethos and environment, a way of life and a world of rituals and fairs and festivals with their local meanings, of interaction in many ways, says the study. Singh said that the ASI prepared a list of all communities based on the lists of scheduled castes and scheduled tribes drawn up by the centre, of backward classes drawn up by the commissions in state governments and at the centre, and of other communities mentioned in the earlier ethnographic surveys. He said the project covered the whole country bringing within the ambit such parts of the country that had not been ethnographically surveyed earlier or where the survey had been perfunctory.

— Text of Devi Lal's letter:

My dear Mr Bommai,

I am writing this letter with deep distress and heartfelt anguish over the way our young boys and girls, even in their early teens, are sacrificing their dear lives by self-immolation, consuming poison or otherwise. These young hopes of the future have taken to this extreme step by one hurried and unplanned decision of our government of implementing the recommendations of the Mandal Commission report. I am led to believe that no proper discussion was held either in the cabinet or the party or with the supporting parties of our minority government before the announcement. The undue haste and abandoning the process of consensus in deciding such a momentous issue is the very root cause of the whole problem today. This has even led to the Press to impute motives to the sincerity of the government in implementing the recommendations of the Mandal Commission report: and even the so-called friends of the government in the Press reacted critically to the decision.

Let me make it clear at the very outset that I am not, repeat not, opposed to the upliftment of our unfortunate brothers and sisters belonging to the backward communities. I, in fact, started my political career with a protest against the treatment meted out to one of the members of the backward community.

I continued the struggle for their welfare throughout my life along with leaders like Karpoori Thakur of the depressed classes and backward communities. I, as a member of the drafting committee of the Janata Dal election manifesto fully understood the implications of including the demand in the manifesto and had also stated so in the Lok Sabha. I am not therefore, opposed to the idea of the Mandal Commission Recommendations but am opposed to the style, timing and the manner of announcing the acceptance of the recommendations and the mishandling of the whole issue.

The announcement of the acceptance of the recommendations on 7 August, was an abortive attempt to scuttle the chances of the success of 9 August rally at Boat Club.

Some of the members of the government seems to have thought, and accordingly misadvised the Prime Minister, that the announcement with one stroke will take away a major chunk of my sympathisers and friends away from me, and the rally shall collapse, little knowing that the announcement will also immediately divide the whole society into two factions — the pro-Mandalites and the anti-Mandalites. Thus, preparing a ground for the civil war in every village, every town, every mohalla and every street. The fire was further fanned by two cabinet ministers by an open call to their sympathisers to come on the streets and fight their opponents. It is unheard of in the history of our country, nay of any country. The cabinet ministers have instigated a section of the people to take to the streets to silence those expressing their grievances.

No government can afford to divide its own people just to carry its views across. All my efforts to request the Prime Minister to dissuade one of his cabinet colleagues from going to Jaipur and addressing the meeting there came to a naught. The visit further deteriorated conditions there and the minister had to face the public wrath.

I expected the Prime Minister to rise above the petty personal prejudices and to give a healing touch by opening a dialogue with the agitating students and try to remove their misconceptions. However, his broadcast to the nation on 26 September, fell far short of the expectations of the young students. He on the one hand stuck to his early stand of not diluting the recommendations and even talked of his resignation. And on the other invited the students for discussion with an "open mind".

This duplicity, coupled with insensitivity of the government to the problem of the children have further estranged them and in spite of the proper channel for the dialogue with the agitating students being opened, creating an impasse. The young lives are being lost, the property worth millions is being destroyed, the law and order situation has collapsed, the credibility of the government to govern has been shattered, and it has failed even to provide drinking water to a population of 80 lakh in the Capital. All this because a decision was taken at a wrong moment and without taking the consensus of all concerned.

I am a loyal and disciplined worker of the party and have contributed my little bit in the formation of the party and also of the government. I have been keeping my silence all these days because of the party discipline and also, that any move on my part may not be misunderstood and mis-interpreted. But the time comes when the inner voice of your conscience compels you to rise above your party affiliations and your personal whims and prejudices. The time, I feel, is now. Though it is very sad for me to part company especially from the friends in the government, which has come into being by my efforts, still I cannot support the government, which is so insensitive to the cries of the dying children and is leading the country to Balkanisation and the society to fragmentation. I have, therefore, decided to relinquish my membership of the Lok Sabha. I am enclosing my resignation with the request that the same may be forwarded to the Speaker of the Lok Sabha for acceptance with immediate effect.

With regards.

Yours sincerely,
(Devi Lal)

OCTOBER 1990

1 October 1990

— Justice Ranganath Mishra, acting Chief Justice, has been appointed as the Chief Justice of India.

— The Supreme Court of India stayed the 13 August, notification for the implementation of Mandal Commission recommendations overruling the government's opposition.

A five-judge Constitution Bench headed by the acting Chief Justice Ranganath Mishra, however, held that the identification of the castes shall continue. "Until the matter is heard — and we expect it to be finished before the end of the year — no further steps should be taken. No other steps to implement the order of 13 August, shall be taken", the judges held.

The Court also advanced to 25 October, from 6 November the hearing of the main case challenging the 27 per cent job reservation policy for the backward classes.

Attorney-General Soli Sorabjee had urged the court to reaffirm its order of 21 September not to modify the 13 August notification. Grant of stay due to the agitation would set a wrong precedent, he said, "If the Court grants stay on the grounds of self-immolations and suicides, it will be a self-immolation of this institution", Sorabjee said. Sorabji was replying to the arguments of K.K. Venugopal who had moved the petition for stay on the Mandal Commission recommendations on behalf of the Supreme Court Bar Association. Venugopal had sought stay to prevent further bloodshed, self-immolation bids and suicides by the anti-reservation agitators.

In its four-page order, the Constitution Bench observed that the earlier order relating to the recruitment of doctors by the Union Public Service Commission was "left unaffected as the question of reservation shall not arise until after the written examination". Besides Justice Mishra, the Bench comprised Justice K.N. Singh, Justice M.H. Kania, Justice Kuldip Singh and Justice P.B. Sawant. The Court reiterated that the legitimate interest of every backward class shall be appropriately protected. "We make it further clear that the order made today is only a clarification of the order made on September 21 bringing out the real purport", it said. The Bench also recorded the statement of the Attorney-General that the prevailing benefits of reservation for the handicapped have not been affected by the government order. The five judges said that they expected that the law and order situation shall immediately improve and both the parties would take "our appeal seriously and restore peace so that the hearing of the matter can be taken up by this court in an appropriate atmosphere" on 25 October. The judges said that in the 21 September order, a three-judge Bench had indicated that the decision to implement three aspects of the Mandal Commission recommendations was "a political one and ordinarily the court would not interfere with such a decision". Quoting the Attorney-General that identification of castes would take about two to three months, the court said it was not in dispute that until such identification was made no further steps for conferring benefits contained in the government's order of 13 August could at all be worked out. "Till the end of November there would be no occasion for proceeding with the implementation of the government order excepting identification of the castes to be benefited", the court said. Venugopal referred to the sudden intensification of the anti-reservation agitation and claimed that so far 56 people had been killed including 36 in police firing and 20 in self-immolations. At least 294 people had been injured during the agitation, he said.

2 October 1990

— Anti-quota agitation led by students grips Northern India. Self-immolation continues.

3 October 1990

— Eighty MPs including 13 union ministers have signed a memorandum urging Prime Minister V.P. Singh to include Jats, "certain sections" of Marathas and some other communities Kurmis of M.P., Mehtars in U.P., Meos in Rajasthan and Haryana, Jats of U.P., Rajasthan, Haryana, Punjab and Delhi, Muslim Gujjars of Jammu & Kashmir, Sirvis, Yadavas and Sainis of Haryana and Rajasthan, etc., in the list of backward classes and extend the job reservation facility to them.

— Anti-Mandal agitation continues, claiming more lives.

4 October 1990

— North India continues to be in the grip of anti-Mandal agitation.

— Parliament passed the Constitution (76th Amendment) Bill, clearing the decks for extension of President's Rule in Punjab for six more months.

5 October 1990

— The anti-reservation agitation continues and many people are killed.

— The Chandra Shekhar-Devi Lal camp kept up the pressure on V.P. Singh when 29 Party MPs urged him to resign since "we have failed completely to give this country an alternative mode of government as promised in our manifesto".

6 October 1990

— The anti-quota stir claims more lives.

— Justice Ranganath Mishra is sworn is as the Chief Justice of India.

7 October 1990

— The anti-reservation agitation continues.

8 October 1990

— More suicides in anti-quota stir.

— The Steel secretary, R. Venkatanarayan, has been shifted from the Ministry much against the wishes of Steel Minister Dinesh Goswami. The decision was taken by cabinet secretary, Vinod Pandey. According to official sources, the cabinet secretary has been gunning for Venkatanarayan for quite some time now and the controversy over the Commerce Ministry's proposal to export 10 lakh tonnes of iron ore to Japan provided the cabinet secretary with a chance to shift him. Venkatanarayan opposed the export proposal.

There were rumours that Venkatanarayan would resign from the service. But sources in the Steel Ministry maintain that he would be joining the powerful finance corporation tomorrow. He has already handed over charge to the new Steel secretary. Venkatanarayan belongs to the U.P. cadre of the IAS.

10 October 1990

— President's rule in proclaimed in Karnataka.

— The Inter-State Council recently constituted held its first one-day meeting today.

— A sub-committee of the inter-state council will be set up to consider all aspects of Centre-state relations and a Bill on levy of consignment tax will be introduced in the winter session of Parliament, report agencies.

This was agreed to at a day-long meeting of the recently constituted Inter-state Council here, presided over by the Prime Minister V.P. Singh. Winding up the first meeting, the Prime Minister said that the sub-committee would come up with concrete suggestions on 247 recommendations of the Sarkaria Commission on Centre-state relations. At today's meeting, chief ministers of various state had given their comments on most of the recommendations. The sub-committee will also come up with policy packages in areas where precise formulations could be made, Singh said.

The chief ministers of Karnataka and Andhra Pradesh did not attend the meeting in which five Union ministers participated. Addressing the meeting, the Prime Minister called upon the state governments to hasten the process of setting up special courts, to speed up deterrent action against tax evaders.

Mr Singh indicated that the progress made in setting up these courts was not satisfactory.

He said hardly 11 states had responded to the Centre's request in this regard by setting up 13 courts. Stating that these were "wholly inadequate" considering the intensity of the problem. Mr Singh appealed to the state governments to set more such courts in larger numbers as soon as possible.

He also requested high courts to nominate competent judicial officers to these courts and give them an opportunity to specialise in complex tax laws.

V.P. Signh maintained that though there were adequate penal provision in our fiscal laws desired deterrence could not be achieved in view of the enormous delays in disposing of cases against economic offenders.

It was unlikely that these important cases would get the desired attention unless special courts were set up for the purpose. Further economic laws were complex and required specialised knowledge.

The need of the hour was to curb tax evasion and improve its administration in the context of the government efforts to tone up resource mobilisation, he said.

Referring to the long-pending decision on levy of consignment tax, the Prime Minister cautioned against the possibility of the levy adding to inflationary pressures.

He said the government should avoid the "cascading effect" of such levies especially in the case of essential commodities and vital inputs for the economy. The Centre while working out the proposal for the levy had taken care to ensure that the revenue interests of the states were fully protected.

V.P. Singh appealed to the chief ministers to approve the Centre's proposal in this regard so that it could take steps to bring forward a legislation to impose this long awaited levy at the earliest opportunity.

He said the government had promoted a wide-ranging discussion in the Sarkaria Commission report since its receipt two years ago to arrive at a national consensus on the action to be taken.

He said 21 states had already sent in their comments to the home ministry for follow-up action, and the concerned Union ministries had examined the relevant recommendations in consultation with state governments.

Speaking at the meeting, the home minister, Mufti Mohammad Sayeed, said the whole question of Centre-state relations should be "viewed from a larger perspective, the total good of the country".

11 October 1990

— The National Development Council (NDC) at its meeting, shelved a decision on the implementation of right to work, a major election promise of the ruling National Front.

The NDC approved the modified Gadgil Formula, which reduces the weightage for population in the central assistance to states from 60 per cent to 55 per cent. The meeting decided to appoint a committee to go into all the details and prepare a "practical formula" for implementation of right to work. Briefing newspersons, an official spokesman said the consensus at the meeting was that the resource availability and work potential should be looked at carefully before deciding to implement the right to work. The scheme can be implemented only in a phased manner. The proposed committee would have representatives from states, Planning Commission and the Central government. The Centre also agreed in principle to transfer centrally-sponsored schemes to states. The Prime Minister, V.P. Singh, made it clear that the transfer should not be from New Delhi to state capitals but should go down to the grassroots level. Under the existing Gadgil Formula, five per cent weightage was given to taxation. This weightage in future will be for fiscal management.

The modified Gadgil Formula approved by the NDC, was summed up by the finance minister, Prof Madhu Dandavate. There will be no change in the funds required for centrally-aided schemes. There will be separate funds for special areas programmes such as hill area, tribal area and border area. From the balance, 30 per cent will go to special category states inclusive of northeastern council. It was decided to appoint a committee to suggest a solution to the financial problems of the special category states. Assam and Jammu and Kashmir will get grant and loan in the ratio of 90:10 as against the present pattern of 30 per cent grant and 70 per cent loan. This step was hailed by the chief minister of Assam. Mr Prafulla Kumar Mahanta, and said this would bring about a big transformation in the pace of economic development of Assam. The balance would be distributed among the non-special category states giving 55 per cent weightage for population. The Prime Minister warned of the grave implications of the Gulf crisis in the meeting and said the country's import bill on account of petroleum could jump by Rs. 4000 crore to Rs. 5000 crore annually. In his opening remarks at the meeting, the Prime Minister said the time had come when the problems created by the Gulf crisis "could no longer be swept, under the carpet. We have to make sacrifices now. Otherwise, we will be engulfed by the Gulf crisis". He asked the chief minister to explain to the people in their states the gravity of the situation "which is not of our own making but which has been thrust upon us". Giving reasons for the abnormal increase in the country's import bill, the Prime Minister said the cost of a barrel of crude had increase from $ 15 to $ 30 in September due to the Gulf crisis. The latest price per barrel was $ 35. And it may go on increasing further. "We cannot say exactly what will be the size of the import bill if the crisis continues for long", he added. The Prime Minister said while fighting this "calamity" we have to ensure that its impact on the core sector of our economy is marginal. "We have to observe fiscal discipline of the kind not witnessed in this country before. We have to expand our exports. Not only the Centre, but the whole nation should be involved infighting this crisis", the Prime Minister said. Dwelling on the same theme, Dandavate, spoke of the meetings of various aid-giving agencies of IMF in Washington which he had attended recently. "It has become apparent that no special assistance for countries like India, such as the oil facility of 1974, is likely to be put in place. We have to take measures to reduce consumption and imports of oil, which we can no longer afford. The times ahead are going to be hard and call for sacrifices from us all". The Prime Minister also spoke at length on the problems relating to statutory guarantee for the right to work and the Central assistance for financing the states' plans. He said the Gadgil Formula, which governed allocation to states on the basis of population, per capita income, fiscal management and resource mobilisation efforts through taxation, needed modification for it did not ensure equitable growth. For instance, smaller states with a better rate of growth and taxation effort got disproportionately more than the larger states like Rajasthan or Madhya Pradesh.

In future, among other things, geographical area of states besides social indicators like infant mortality rate, quality of life and such other factors should determine allocations for states from the Central kitty, the Prime Minister suggested. He said the new yardsticks would not involve any drastic changes, but give some additional benefits to relatively weaker states in the North-Eat or in hilly regions elsewhere. In al, the proposed changes in the formula for government assistance would result in about seven per cent increase or decrease in fund allocations to different states. The Prime Minister said that earlier the tax effort by states used to be the dominant factor in determining size and magnitude of assistance. Now the government would like the emphasis to shift on fiscal management. States which manage their finances better should enjoy certain amount of weightage in preferring claims for Central allocations for execution of their plans. Dealing with the growing demand for statutory guarantee for the right to work, the Prime Minister said it could not be conceded straightway for it had serious implication for the economy. First, the available employment opportunities likely to be created would not be enough to meet this demand. The constitutional guarantee for the right to work would imply that this would be justifiable. This is a proposition which no government could accept, considering the economic constraints the country was faced with.

However, the government's efforts will be directed to achieving this goal. According to present indications and projections, there will be jobs for all in the country by 2000 AD provided there is three per cent annual increase in the number of employment opportunities.

- The two-day strike by the officers of public sector undertakings began today, totally paralyzing the operations in the oil sector, disrupted production in fertilizer companies and forced Indian Airlines to ground more than 50 per cent of its flights.

- The Baroda-based Indian Petrochemicals Corporation Ltd. (IPCL) was shut down to avoid any major shortcoming due to absence of supervisory staff.

The officers have gone strike demanding a settlement of the Dearness Allowance (DA) issue.

Power Sector: Power generation by National Thermal Power Corporation (NTPC) was not seriously affected except for minor fluctuations recorded by the gas-based and Auriya in UP. The Madras Fertilisers Ltd and the Bongaigaon Refinery and Petrochemicals Ltd were not affected. All the units under the Steel Authority of India Ltd (SAIL) too worked normally. According to an official spokesman, the strike was near total in ONGC while Oil India's operations continued unaffected. Of the 13,000 executives in the fertiliser sector over 80 per cent were on strike and of the 37,000 executives in the oil sector over 90 per cent did not turn up for work.

The official spokesman hinted at disciplinary proceedings against the striking officials. Marketing operations of all oil companies, except Bharat Petroleum, were affected. There was no major disruption in the flight schedules of Air India (IA) as they were lifting fuel from other countries. The disruption in the flights of IA, if any, was mainly due to the unavailability of fuel. Of the 12 refineries, 11 were shut down. The operation of pipelines also came to a halt. However, the Gas Authority of India Ltd (GAIL) has been maintaining supplies to power plants. It claims that it is in a position to supply gas to the three fertiliser plants the HBJ pipeline.

The official spokesman declined to make an estimate of the likely production loss.

12 October 1990

— The anti-reservation stir continues and seven persons die while protesting.

— Four Border Security Force personnel are among 8 persons killed in the Kashmir valley.

14 October 1990

— The Government of India has decided to honour Nelson Mandela, the African nationalist leader, with Bharat Ratna.

— The anti-reservation stir continues.

15 October 1990

— Five more die in the quota stir.

16 October 1990

— Nelson Mandela, is conferred Bharat Ratna.

— More persons die in anti-reservation stir.

17 October 1990

— The Bharatiya Janata Party has warned that it would withdraw its support to the minority V.P. Singh government in case the Somnath Ayodhya Rath Yatra was disrupted in Bihar or Uttar Pradesh.

— President's Rule is revoked in Karnataka exactly a week after its imposition.

— The anti-reservation stir makes the Diwali a dull affair: a large number of houses remained unilluminated to voice popular protest.

18 October 1990

— Anti-reservation stir continues.

19 October 1990

— Anti-reservation stir continues.

21 October 1990

— College students would have to render compulsory national service of one year to get a degree under a proposal for inclusion in the new National Youth Policy, now being formulated. The service could in the form of three months' residence in rural/backward areas and other states plus mine months of several other forms of national service — attachment to industrial units, slum clearance. etc — official sources say. The prime focus would be on the involvement of the youth in the national literacy mission. The residence in villages could be at the rate of one month per year of college plus the equivalent of nine months of service spread over three years of college life. The government is also likely to consider the idea of having a national guards scheme to create a cadre of dedicated, motivated and committed youth activists in rural areas, the sources say. On the compulsory national service, a notable feature that is to be considered is whether the total of 12 months may be compressed within the existing three-year college course of whether it could be part of a four-year course. The expenditure and modalities would also have to be considered and evolved, the sources point out. National guards, at the rate of one per village in the first instance, would be voluntary pioneers who would bring awareness among the rural population and help them assert their rights and understand their responsibilities and role in national development. The national guards will also act as the nodal point of contact between youth councils at the appropriate levels and the rural mass, in ventilating their grievances as well as in implementing various youth programmes effectively. The national guards will be in the age group of 18-30 years and will be deployed for a period of two to three years at a stretch. They will be subjected to an appropriate orientation/training course each year The national guards will be purely volunteers and will not receive payment of any kind, it is being pointed out

The current national youth policy was tabled before Parliament in the winter of 1988 but there has been no significant change in direction or step-up in activities concerning and affecting the youth since the formulation of that policy, the sources point out. The National Front government, which came to power a year later, has already declared its intention to formulate a new youth policy giving thrusts to the promotion of national unity and integrity, development of a sense of respect for the constitution as well creation of awareness about the country's great historic cultural heritage. Among the other objectives of the new policy are preservation and revitalisation of democracy and secularism, fostering a sense of commitment to fight injustice and inequalities in society, development of correct attitudes towards character building, promotion of a spirit of respect and tolerance for others' points of view, formulation, as far as possible, of an education system based on equality and unversality and making the youth aware of burning national and international issues. A preliminary all-party, all-India conference of youth leaders in January this year considered these objectives. This was followed by a national conference of youth leaders in May to elicit the opinion of the youth themselves. The suggestions which emerged from these meets would be given weight while formulating the new policy, the sources say. A significant suggestion was the implementation of the three-languages formula. This would greatly enhance the understanding of each other in different regions of the country, it is being pointed out. The new youth policy, which the government intended to announce on the Independence Day this year, will probably be unfolded before the year is out, perhaps during the winter session of Parliament, according to informed sources.

22 October 1990

— The National Front-BJP ties have reached a fresh point of ruptures.

— The Central Bureau of Investigation has filed a criminal case against a joint Chief Controller of Imports and Exports for cheating a nationalised bank to the tune of Rs. 1.58 crores.

— L.K. Advani, the BJP leader, was arrested at Samastipur in Bihar by the Laloo Prasad Yadav government when he was continuing with his "rath yatra" in connection with the Ramjanmabhumi issue.

23 October 1990

— The 10-month-old National Front government under V.P. Singh was plunged into its deepest crisis following the Bhartiya Janata Party's withdrawal of support to it. L.K. Advani was arrested in Bihar.

V.P. Singh, however, did not tender his resignation. He said, he would prove his majority on the floor of the Lok Sabha. The date of the "floor test" has not yet been announced.

24 October 1990

— V.P. Singh has been asked by the President, R. Venkataraman, to prove his majority on 7November, — fifteen days after the BJP announced the withdrawal of its support to the National Front government.

25 October 1990

— The stay granted by the Supreme Court against the implementation of the Mandal Commission report will continue until a final decision by the Supreme Court on the Constitutional validity of the National Front government's notification to reserve 27 per cent jobs for the OBCs.

A five-judge Constitution Bench head by the chief Justice. Ranganath Misra, declined to vacate the stay granted by the court on 1 October. The Court also rejected a plea by the noted lawyer, Ram Jethmalani, to implead all the political parties as necessary parties in about 40 petitions challenging the validity of the government's notification to implement the controversial report leading to suicide by several protesting students. The Lok Dal (B) MP. Mr Ram Advadhesh Singh, sought vacation of the stay saying that "we are affected by the non-implementation of the report". He said the five-judge Constitution Bench on 1 October granted stay without going into the merits of the case. One of the judges, Justice K.N. Singh, then remarked that "stay was granted after the Court had heard all the parties on both the sides." Today's hearing started amid tight security around the Court complex where a strong police bandobust had been made to stop anti-reservation students from entering the court compound. Several students carrying anti-Mandal placards staged a day-long *dharna* outside the Court, all the gates of which had been closed for general entry. In the high-domed Court room of the chief Justice, lawyers, litigants and a few students who are petitioners, rubbed their shoulders to have their say. They shouted from one corner of another their own names and the petitions they were interested in. It took some time for the chief Justice to write down the names of the petitioners or their counsel.

The key attraction of the day was eminent jurist. N.A. Palkhivala, who yesterday flew in here from Bombay to argue for quashing of the notification for implementation of the Mandal report. A galaxy of lawyers, including K.K., Venugopal, G. Ramaswamy, P.P. Rao, Shyamala Pappu and Gopal Subramaniam, were among 37 counsel who would be arguing against the Mandal Commission report, while the attorney-general. Soil Sorabjee, Ram Jethmalani, P.N. Lekhi, and R.K. Garg, would plead for the dismissal of the petitions.

Appearing for "Commission Cause", Palkhivala, warned that the consequence of the government's decision to implement the report would be to allow the administration to run without efficiency. He said the constitutional provision providing reservation for the "weakest among the weak" (the scheduled castes and scheduled tribes) do not create an absolute right on them at the altar of "efficiency of administration". Reading Articles 14 and 335 together, it would be evident that if efficiency of the administration could not be sacrificed even to favour SC and ST candidates, it could never be sacrificed for the OBCs, counsel argued. Deploring the Mandal Commission report, Palkhivala said the report had completely "ignored" the constitutional provision for efficiency in administration. It appeared as if efficiency was irrelevant for the Mandal Commission. Its recommendations were aimed at providing sub-standard services. On this, Justice K.N. Singh, remarked. "It is always the case wherever there is reservation."

During his day-long arguments which may continue till the end of next week, counsel submitted that if the Mandal Commission report was implemented, as much as 74.5 per cent jobs would be reserved for the SCs, STs and OBCs. He wondered how the government could create a "privileged class" (OBCs) and oppress the "minority" (non-reserved category). Describing the Mandal Commission recommendations as "caste-based", Palkhivala referred to the basic structure of Constitution which envisages the creation of a cohesive and unified society obliterating casteism. The founding fathers of the Constitution considered casteism an anthems and like a cancer cell in the body politic. He pleaded for putting casteism on the dust heap of Indian history. Palkhivala also mentioned various constitutional provision including Articles 15 and 16 to demonstrate that these were meant to obliterate "obnoxious casteism". The Constitution, he said, however provides protection to any socially and educationally backward class. It was not the time to "settle old scores" as we were not ordained by the God to settle such scores, Palkhivala submitted while referring to the government's affidavit that the decision to implement the report would uplift a section of society which had been backward for decades. The late Mandal, who headed the commission, was himself a backward class member but a rich landlord, Palkhivala said. Similarly, one of the famous business houses of India, the Mafatlals, were also entitled to all the privileges available to the reserved category persons, he added. But, millions of poor Brahmins in the country were denied the right to equality merely because they belonged to an upper caste, Palkhivala pointed out. On this, Justice K.N. Singh, remarked that it was a "hard reality" that a vast majority in the country is known by caste even after 40 years of freedom and despite the Constitution. Counsel, however, pleaded that reservation, if at all, should be based on economic backwardness. Emotions ran high when Palkhivala, while referring to the recent self-immolation cases said, "No wonder burning of youths is taking place." He said that perhaps he would have asked himself (if he was young) whether it was a country worth living in. Reacting sharply, Lekhi said such were "street arguments". "Emotional, populist and destructive", said Jethmalani seeking the Court's indulgence in restraining Mr Palkhivala from making such submissions. Later, Palkhivala "apologised" to the Court for making certain emotional submissions. He never meant it, counsel added. Picking up from where he had been interrupted, Palkhivala said these days it was a "status symbol" to belong to a backward caste. "Backward caste" is a privileged caste. He said caste or backwardness was not a permanent feature of the constitution. Counsel said the Constitution was not "compatible" with the apparent "compartmentalisation" of the country. The basic fallacy in the Mandal

Commission report was that it worked on the unstatable assumption that it was entitled to make recommendation for reservation in public services on the paramount ground of caste or social backwardness, counsel pointed out. He also referred to the Prime Minister's statements in which it had been reiterated that the government was determined to implement the report in toto without dilution and "in phases". Palkhivala cautioned that the Mandal Commission was implemented on the armed forces, the security and safety of the country would be in the hands of inefficient people, counsel added. Earlier, Sorabjee, objected to certain averments made by counsel saying these were not based on facts. As the hearing started in the morning, Jethmalani, appearing for the Bihar and the Tamil Nadu governments, sought issuance of notices of all the political parties, especially the Bahujan Samaj Party, since a large population of the country was interested in the matter. He said the political parties be asked to tell the court about their stand on the Mandal Commission report. This would help in exposing these parties' "hypocrisy", Jethmalani said adding that "no one should be allowed to shoot through someone else's shoulder".

The Court reminded counsel that it was seized of a constitutional matter and not a political parties were free to approach the Court. The judge said the political parties were not necessary parties in the case. The court decided to take up later a petition by an advocate, Bhim Singh, seeking contempt of court action against V.P. Singh, Ram Vilas Paswan and Sharad Yadav, for their provocative utterances despite the country's order. Besides the chief Justice the other judges on the Constitution Bench were Justice K.N. Singh, Justice M.H. Kania, Justice Kuldip Singh and Justice P.B. Sawant. The hearing will continue tomorrow.

NOVEMBER 1990

1 November 1990

— Teachers in Delhi take out a procession demanding that the Mandal Report be kept in abeyance till a national consensus is reached.

2 November 1990

— Dissidence within the ruling Janata Dal is increasing.

3 November 1990

— Rift in the ruling Janata Dal widens.
A demand for a National government is made by Orissa chief minister Biju Patnaik.

4 November 1990

— A rift in the Janata Dal seems imminent. Devi Lal wants V.P. Singh to resign from the Prime Ministership.

5 November 1990

— The rebels in the ruling Janata Dal elect Chandra Shekhar as leader, thereby confirming a vertical split in the Party. At the same time, Prime Minister V.P. Singh demonstrated his supremacy over the Janata Dal Parliamentary Party when 106 members of the 178-strong Parliamentary Party affirmed faith in him and authorised him to take all "necessary steps" to deal with the present situation.

— The Supreme Court of India held that Union Industries secretary A.N. Verma was guilty of contempt of the highest court in not complying with its directions concerning the filling in the posts of chairman and members of the Monopolies and Restrictive Trade Practices Commission. However, taking into account his unqualified apology to the Court and taking judicial notice of the fact that meanwhile the appointments had been made the Court did not impose any punishment on him.

— The need for raising productivity and profitability in the public sector enterprises was stressed by Arun Ghosh, member, Planning Commission.

6 November 1990

— Congress (I) promises to support Chandra Shekhar from outside.

— To escape provisions of the anti-defection law and to formalize the split in the Janata Dal, Chandra Shekhar today named his Party as Janata Dal (Socialist). He told newsmen that his party had formally requested Lok Sabha Speaker Rabi Ray to allot separate seats to its members in the House. It has also given a list to the Speaker containing signatures of 58 members.

— Janata Dal spokesman Jaipal Reddy said that the attempt of Chandra Shekhar to walk along with Congress(I) President Rajiv Gandhi was outrageously opportunistic and tantamount to total frustration of the anti-Congress(I) mandate of the people and pro-V.P. Singh mandate in the 1989 elections.

— President of India, R. Venkataraman, enlarged the scope of his discussions on the fluid political situation in the country with leaders of political parties who called on him by mooting the idea of formation of a national government or a national coalition after the anticipated fall of the V.P. Singh government on 8 November 1990.

— The 76-day-old anti-reservation agitation started by students was called off today.

— Lok Sabha Speaker Rabi Ray declares 25 members of the Lok Sabha belonging to the Janata Dal; as unattached. The Speaker had been sending letters to these individual members saying that since their leader in the Lok Sabha (V.P. Singh) had intimated to him (Ray) that they had been expelled from the party, the Speaker had declared them unattached.
It may be noted that the rebel Janata Dal MPs had informed the Speaker about the split in the Janata Dal and bad requested him to treat them as Janata Dal(S) members.
The position of political parties in the Lok Sabha was as follows as a result of the split:

Janata Dal	115
Janata Dal(S)	25
Congress(I)	195
BJP	86
CPI(M)	33
CPI	12
AIA (DMK)	11
RSP	4
Akali Dal (Mann)	5
Forward Bloc	3
National Conference	3
Jharkhand Mukti Morcha	3
BSP	3
Shiv Sena	3
Telugu Desam	2
Indian Union Muslim League	2

Independents	10
IPF	1
MGP	1
Marxist Coordination Group	1
Congress(S)	1
AIMEIM	1
Kerala Congress	1
Sikkim Sangram Parishad	1
ABHMS	1
GNLF	1
Vacancies	20

7 November 1990

— The 11-month-old V.P. Singh government was voted out in the Lok Sabha by an overwhelming majority after an 11-hour acrimonious debate during which Opposition leaders severely criticised Prime Minister V.P. Singh for allegedly bringing the country to the brink of disaster in all spheres. V.P. Singh could muster only 142 votes in his support while the combined Opposition got 346 votes. There were 8 abstentions and the total attendance was 496. V.P. Singh immediately tendered the resignation of his ministry. Making a comment, Chandra Shekhar said that a dark chapter of Indian politics had ended.

— Anti-Mandal agitation continues.

8 November 1990

— Breakaway Janata Dal (Socialist) leader Chandra Shekhar is being invited by President R. Venkataraman tomorrow to discuss the question of forming a viable government at the centre.

— The Congress(I) today sent a letter to the President conveying the Party's decision to extend support to Chandra Shekhar, leader of the Janata Dal breakaway group, to form a new government at the centre.

— The Congress(I) Parliamentary Board took a decision to decline the President's offer to the party to form the government. Instead, the CPB, decided to endorse its earlier decision to support Chandra Shekhar from outside.
The President then invited L.K. Advani, leader of the second largest Party, the Bhartiya Janata Party, to form the government. This was part of the on-going process of finding an alternative in place of V.P. Singh government. L.K. Advani declined the offer.

9 November 1990

— Chandra Shekhar, 63, will be the new Prime Minister of India. He will be sworn in tomorrow at 11 a.m. along with his council of ministers.

— The BJP feels that the Chandra Shekhar government would not last long and the country is in for an early snap poll to the Lok Sabha.

— The price situation is "extremely disturbing" and the current trends indicate that the inflation rate may be a double digit figure in 1990, according to a "Mid-year review of the economy 1990-91" prepared by Malcalm S. Adiseshiah.

10 November 1990

— Janata Dal (Socialist) leader Chander Shekhar was sworn in Prime Minister today by President R. Venkataraman. Chandra Shekhar and Devi lal took oath of office and secrecy in Hindi. In a chat with the Press after he took oath, Chandra Shekhar said that his government had come to power at a time when the country was facing many challenges and each one must come forward "in our endeavours to overcome them". He said the first task for him was to end the prevailing strife and bring about peace and harmony.
Chandra Shekhar is the eighth Prime Minister of India and seventh from U.P. Devi Lal staged a comeback when he was also sworn in a Cabinet Minister with the rank of Deputy Prime Minister. As he did last time. Devi Lal today again took oath as "Uppradhan mantri" although in the warrant of the appointment as Cabinet Minister there was no mention of "Uppradhan mantri".

— The Information Adviser to the Prime Minister, Prem Shankar Jha, resigned on V.P. Singh ceasing to be the Prime Minister. Jha was appointed by V.P. Singh.

11 November 1990

— Anxiety on the part of former Prime Minister V.P. Singh to go for a mid-term poll to consolidate his party's position and his determination to "teach the Bhartiya Janata Party a lesson" after L.K. Advani's "rath yatra" could not be stopped precipitated the crisis in the National Front government, according to well-placed sources in the party.

12 November 1990

— Chief Minister of U.P., Mulayam Singh Yadav, announced an increase in the reservations for the backwards from the existing 15 per cent to 27 per cent in all categories of government jobs. U.P. has identified 55 backward classes. Reservations will be 27 per cent in all the four classes in the government jobs. The reservations in government jobs go up to 62 per cent in class I and II and 53 per cent in Class III and IV.

— All the full-time members of the Planning Commission resigned. The Planning Commission consists of 8 members.

13 November 1990

— The task of ministry making by Chandra Shekhar was by no means easy or simple. First, he had to choose ministers from amongst 60 or 80 MPs who left the Janata Dal to constitute the splinter group.

— A motion seeking confidence in the Chandra Shekhar Ministry will be discussed on 16 November 1990.

— A confidential report of the World Bank has criticised the Indian banking system and has called for reforms. Since the 20 public sector banks under the direct control of the Finance Ministry account for more than 90 per cent assets of the entire banking in the country, the World Bank strictures are directed against the government's sloppy management of these banks: "these banks are uncompetitive, over-stretched, over-staffed and provide poor service".

— With the change in the government, the process of reshuffle in the bureaucratic set-up has begun.

14 November 1990

— V.P. Singh, the former Prime Minister, was quoted as saying that there had been many complaints from MPs loyal to him about offers of money from businessmen seeking to broaden the support for Chandra Shekhar. On the question how long the Chandra Shekhar would last, V.P. Singh said, "The Congress Party would decide that".

— National celebrates the 101st birth anniversary of Pandit Jawaharlal Nehru.

15 November 1990

— The Janata Dal(S) today claimed that its strength in the Lok Sabha had risen to 69 with four more MPs reportedly crossing over from the Janata Dal.

— The Congress(I) decided to support the Mulayam Singh government (Janata Dal-Socialist) in U.P., a minority government.
The support of the Congress(I) and its allies would ensure the Chandra Shekhar government getting the confidence of the Lok Sabha on 16 November. The JD(S) had at least 58 members while the Congress and its allied 211.

— Prices increased sharply rising by as much as 9.7 per cent during the tenure of the National Front government, an analysis of the official figures show.

— Chief Election Commissioner, R.V.S. Peri Sastri has proceeded on three

months' leave. Mrs. V.S. Rama Devi, secretary, Legislative Department, will officiate in his place.
This is for the second time that the CEC has proceeded on leave and someone else has been asked to officiate. It was in 1962 for the first time when K.V.K. Sundaram, the then CEC, had gone on leave and his deputy, Subramaniam, was appointed to officiate in his place.

16 November 1990

— The seven-day-old Janata Dal(S) government headed by Chandra Shekhar won the confidence of the Lok Sabha by 269 votes to 204.

— The Delhi Development Authority (DDA) has agreed in principle to extend pensionary benefits to its 22,000 work charge employees.

— The Central Administrative Tribunal today set aside the government order divesting Shiv Sharma, Director-General of Doordarshan, of his duties and functions.
Shiv Sharma was appointed in October-November 1989. In the mean time, the change in government came, and the V.P. Singh government did not appoint him on a regular basis but continued his ad hoc appointment. The government removed him from the post on 20 September 1990.

17 November 1990

— The Janata Dal admits that seven of its MPs voted for Chandra Shekhar.

— The expansion of the Union Cabinet has been postponed. The reasons were fluid political situation in Mulayam Singh Yadav's ruling Janata Dal(S) in U.P., lack of agreement between Chandra Shekhar and Devi Lal on sharing of power, inadequate support base of the party, etc. There was also disagreement over names suggested by the Congress(I).

— The Janata Dal(S) had 61 MPs in it.

— There are serious allegations of excessive use of force at Ayodhya on Ram Janamabhoomi pilgrims on and before 30 October 1990.

18 November 1990

— "Cabinet formation is, for me, a difficult job . . . very few people are available. . . they are junior people. I want some people to come forward and say that "we want to be in the cabinet", said Chandra Shekhar on expansion of his Council of Ministers.

— Faced with strong opposition by India the South Asian Association for Regional Cooperation (SAARC) has dropped the idea of inviting external funds for SAARC activities and decided to mobilize resources internally in keeping with the fundamental objective of self-reliance and prevent outside interference in the region.

19 November 1990

— The BJP ends support to the Laloo Prasad Yadav government in Bihar.

20 November 1990

— Mulayam Singh Yadav won the vote of confidence in the state Assembly in a surcharged atmosphere of fury tempers and scuffles between legislators of rival Janata Dal factions.

— An international seminar on Time (Kal) began at the Indira Gandhi National Centre for the Arts with recitations on Time in different languages.

21 November 1990

— Eleven days after he was sworn in, Prime Minister Chandra Shekhar expanded his council of ministers by inducting 13 cabinet ministers, 3 ministers of state holding independent charge, 12 ministers of state and 4 deputy ministers. A few features of the Chandra Shekhar Ministry may be noted:

1. The ruling Janata Dal (Socialist) is a minority government having a group of 61 MPs, supported from outside by the Congress(I) and its allies.
2. The council of ministers betrays an element of incompleteness.
3. The unprecedented delay in forming the council of ministers confirms the Congress(I) pressures on Chandra Shekhar.
4. The ministry now has 34 members, which means that every other member is in the government.
5. Because Chandra Shekhar had to choose from 61 MPs belonging to his Janata Dal(S) there is considerable unevenness of calibre of the council of ministers.
6. The Prime Minister is at present burdened with a heavy load of work.
7. The council of ministers virtually leaves the entire south India and north-eastern India unrepresented.

24 November 1990

— The new Industrial Policy would be finalised soon and fresh steps taken to hold the price line to provide relief to the millions of the poor reeling under the burden of high taxation.

— The BJP alleged that money played a role in the cross-voting by its legislators in Bihar during the confidence vote and nine of the 10 BJP members who did so would be expelled for six years.

25 November 1990

— Chief Election Commissioner, R.V.S. Peri Sastri died today.

— The Congress(I) today demanded a full-scale investigation into what it called the "wholesale corruption" by former Industry Minister Ajit Singh, particularly the last ten days of the V.P. Singh government.

26 November 1990

— The Uttar Pradesh Janata Dal split. The chief minister Mulayam Singh Yadav constituted the Janata Dal (Socialist).

— Prime Minister Chandra Shekhar has asked B.G. Deshmukh, Principal secretary to Prime Minister, to continue.

— Following an agreement reached between the Jammu-Kashmir state government Employees Coordination Committee and the State Governor the indefinite strike by nearly 150,000 employees, which started on 15 September 1990, was called off.

27 November 1990

— The chief of the Central Bureau of Investigation is being transferred.

— The Chandra Shekhar government decided to review all major decisions taken by the V.P. Singh National Front government after the withdrawal of support by the Bhartiya Janata Party.

28 November 1990

— The centre puts Assam under President's Rule.

— DAMS pollute the environment, says an environment experts Dr (Mrs) G. Howells.

29 November 1990

— The Assam government, which is under President's Rule, reinstated H.N. Das as the chief secretary soon after the state was brought under President's Rule. On Monday (November 26) Das was shifted from the post of chief secretary and appointed Director-General of Assam Administrative Staff College.

— The Central Bureau of Investigation has registered 21 cases against public servants including officials of public sector undertakings and nationalised banks for possessing assets disproportionate to the known source of income.

DECEMBER 1990

1 December 1990

— The BJP chief L.K. Advani said here today that a fresh election was the only solution to the present political uncertainty arising out of the installation of a "spineless" government at the centre.

— Vijayalakshmi Pandit died in Dehra Dun.

— The unprecedented bench-bar dispute in the Calcutta High Court took a new turn today, with Justice Dilip Kumar Basu going on an idefinite fast demanding settlement of the matter, even as an agreement formula was reached at another marathon meeting.

The Bar Council, meanwhile, reiterated its decision to observe a state-wide cease-work by lawyers in all courts on Monday to express solidarity with the agitating lawyers of Calcutta High Court. The dispute has risen owing to the en bloc dismissal of cases in the absence of lawyers. High Court registrar (appellate side), N.K. Bhattacharya, said deliberations at the bench-bar meeting today concluded "amicably", but the decisions "are subject to approval of the full court and of the three representative bodies of the High Court bar".

Justice Basu, in a letter to the Chief Justice, said he was constrained to observe that "we have failed to bring about a solution to resolve a deadlock in the mechanism of delivery system of justice". "If we have right to dismiss any case, we have also right to recall our dismissal order. I do not find any reason why we could not arrive at a settlement in the joint meeting of the bar and the bench held on 30 November 1990".

— Rajendra Singh Bismil, the Congress(I) MLC in Bihar state assembly, has urged Prime Minister Chandra Shekhar to "sack all bureaucrats and heads of public undertakings appointed by the V.P. Singh government".

— There are over 10,000 beggars in the Capital and their number continues to increase due to several socio-economic reasons, besides police laxity to arrest the beggars.

Begging is a cognizable offence in Delhi and the police are responsible for arresting the beggars and taking them to the court.

2 December 1990

— Lt Governor of Delhi Arjan Singh has asked all land-owning agencies to strengthen watch and ward arrangements in respect of their lands so that unauthorised constructions and encroachments in Delhi do not come up. In a notification today the Delhi Administration said it had the responsibility to safeguard public lands and to maintain the norms laid down in the Master Plan and municipal regulations. Instructions have been issued to civic authorities and local police to prevent putting up of *jhuggis* and construction of houses on public lands. In case the administration noticed such fresh encroachments and unauthorised constructions, responsibility would be fixed on concerned officials or agencies, the release said.

— The 1991 census operation would attempt to portray a genuine picture of women's economic activity, bringing out aspects which generally remain "invisible" in such statistical exercises. Census data on women's employment often did not take into account the work done by women engaged as seasonal agricultural labour, those working in home-based industries or in the unorganised sector. The last census conducted in 1981, for example, had showed that women formed a mere 16.5 per cent of the work force, a figure which was countered by women's organisations and other developmental agencies as being too low.

The office of the Registrar General and Census Commissioner, India (RGI), responsible for carrying out a headcount of the country's population, is attempting to set right this anomaly by directing census enumerators to ask more "probing questions" about the economic activities of the female members of each household. According to deputy Registrar-General N. Rama Rao the enumerators, who would be going door-to-door conducting the census, have been told to treat as economic activity any service or work which is productive, even it does not have a direct monetary value. Thus, the census enumerators' of annual work on the family farm, and of home-made dairy products, rearing of poultry and sale of the products, sale of fruits and vegetables, making of cowdung cakes or collection of fuel, fodder, grass or other forest produce, weaving, spinning, bee-keeping, sericulture, rope-making and making of leather products, pottery and block printing as economic activity, which women may carry out in the home. Other work done by women may include making agarbatties, match boxes, rolling bidis, laundry, making or finishing garments or making jams, pickles, papad, masala, snacks or other food products at home. Giving tuitions and running cookery, dance, music or arts and crafts classes at home all fall under the head of work done by women which need to be quantified.

Another problem contributing to women's work remaining unaccounted for is that of social conditioning. "In many sections of social taboos against women's work and often the male head of the household, who is being questioned, would be reluctant to reveal that the women contribute to the family income even though the woman's earnings may form a major part of the family budget", said Madhubala Nath of the United Nations Fund for Women (UNIFEM).

The census of India 1991, slated to be the world's biggest administrative exercise, will be conducted between 9 and 28 February with a reference date as at sunrise of 1 March 1991. The instructions manual, brought out by the RGI for census enumerators and supervisors, who are being trained for the task, has an additional set of "probing questions" to elicit information about the kind of work done by the women in the household.

These questions have been framed after prolonged discussions spread over the past one year between experts from the Department of Women and Child Development, SNDT Women's University, Bombay, Centre for Women's Development Studies, Delhi, the National Council of Applied Economic Research and the National Institute for Public Cooperation and Child Development among others. Part of the training would attempt to make the census enumerator more sensitive and perceptive about the nature of women's work and the need to include it as gainful economic activity. Census data itself forms a vital input in policy making. "Once the different occupations and occupational mobility are known, it simplifies the task of planning and taking remedial measures based on these figures", Rama Rao said. The RGI has also embarked on a programme of publicity regarding census and the need for people to cooperate with the enumerator. According to Rama Rao, the role of women's groups, especially at the grassroot level in increasing women's awareness about the importance of census cannot be underestimated.

The UNIFEM, with a 40,000 grant from the United Nations Fund for Population Activities (UNFPA) has nearly completed a one-minute audio-visual clip describing different kind of work done by women and the need to recognise economic activity.

"We hope the film, which would have noted playback singer, Asha Bhonsle, singing the theme song set to music by R.D. Burman, will be telecast every day before the census, so that people will not view the census enumerator with suspicion and will cooperate in giving information", said Ms Nath. The RGI has also appended to the instructions manual an illustrative poster describing different types of work done by women. The poster shows women at various jobs with the question, "do you still think she does not work". The UNIFEM film is pending clearance from Doordarshan, but if cleared it would be shown in the slot before the women's programme and Krishi Darshan to reach rural audiences. Even if the real impact of the media blitz is only evident in the next census in the year 2001, it would not be an effort gone waste.

— Orissa chief minister Biju Patnaik called upon the people particularly the youth to beat up corrupt officials. This, according to him, was the only effective way of combating corruption.

— The central government is looking for new incumbents of Raj Bhawans in various states in the wake of recent political changes.

— The central government today appointed G. Ramaswamy as the new Attorney-General of India for a period of three years with immediate effect. He succeeds Soli Sorabjee who resigned consequent on the change of government. The new appointee is sponsored by the Congress (I).

3 December 1990

— Prime Minister V.P. Singh's government never consulted

Attorney-General Soli Sorabjee, whose resignation was accepted by the Janata Dal (S) government on 2 December, on key legal issues like the imposition of President's Rule in Karnataka, the Mandal office memo reserving 27 per cent jobs in the union government and public undertakings the ordinance issued on the Babri Masjid - Ram Janambhoomi dispute and the Prasar Bharati Bill.

— The Central Reserve Police Force is developing its own intelligence network in the strife-torn Jammu and Kashmir.

— Haryana government is to give a bonus of 27 days salary to its employees for the year 1989-90. This would cost Rs. 19.25 crores to the state.

— There is a perceptible increase in the use of Punjabi in most government offices, the principal reason being the directive issue by the Panthic Committee, which is a policy-making body of some militant organisations.

5 December 1990

— Bihar chief minister Laloo Prasad Yadav today created history by adding 65 members to his ten-month-old Ministry, making it a 76-persons strong team.

6 December 1990

— The New Delhi Municipal Committee is likely to seal the four floors built on a high-rise building in 10 Bhagwan Das Road without permission. The building owner had been given the permission to construct a basement and seven floors. But under the refuge of a High Court stay, the owner added another four floors without permission.

— The Lok Mazdoor Sangh (LMS), a new trade union enjoying the patronage of Janata Dal (S) leader Om Prakash Chautala and of the local administration, is on the offensive in Faridabad.

Apprehensive about the motives of the newly formed trade union (LMS), which is trying to make its presence felt in the Thompson Press owned by the *India Today* group of publications, the dominant Hind Mazdoor Sangh (HMS) is getting ready for a showdown to prevent entry of a proxy union sponsored by Chautala in this industrial town's trade union circles. Chautala is keen to settle scores with the management of *India Today* which exposed his doings during the Meham elections through its video news magazine.

— The Tiger population in Andhra Pradesh has gone up to 275 in 1989 from a mere 36 in 1972, according to the latest census.

— Nine senior IAS officers of secretary and commissioner rank have been transferred in Haryana.

7 December 1990

— The chief minister of U.P. Mulayam Singh Yadav announced at Lucknow yesterday that a Rs. 10 crore project has been prepared for Ambedkar University in Lucknow.

— An I.P.S. officer, S.S. Warvade, (1973 batch), promoted as deputy Inspector General of Police in October 1990, has not been given any posting so far.

— The strength of the council of ministers in Bihar rose to 71 with one more joining the Laloo cabinet.

— Chief electoral officers of all the states and union territories unanimously recommended the use of the electronic voting machines in all future elections. They also favoured the introduction of multi-purpose identity cards to all voters.
The Election Commission has already acquired 1.50 lakh electronic voting machines at a cost of Rs. 75 crores.

— Manmohan Singh has been appointed Advisor to the Prime Minister on Economic Affairs.

8 December 1990

— The Chandra Shekhar government is working on a major package in the country for NRI (Non-Resident Indians) investment in the country which will be able to attract a minimum of $ 5 billion.

— The ULFA hardcore have gone underground even as the counter-insurgency operation of the Army — 'Operation Bajrang' — completed its first phase of flushing out armed militants from their jungle hideouts.

— The Supreme Court today allowed all those candidates to sit for the Civil Services Examination of 1990 who have been allocated to the Indian Police Service or to the Central Service Group A. Such candidates do not have to resign from respective services and will not lose the seniority in their service because they have not taken training with their batch.

— The strength of Laloo Prasad Yadav's ministry in Bihar went up to 72 with the appointment of yet another minister.

10 December 1990

— The new Chandra Shekhar government initiates the familiar process of transfers and appointments.

— The Janata Dal (S) government tonight announced major reshuffle of secretaries including appointment of a new deputy chairman of the Planning Commission, Mohan Dharia, an old associate of Chandra Shekhar.

The major change in the bureaucratic echelon was upgrading of the present home secretary Naresh Chandra as the new cabinet secretary in place of Vinod Pande. The agriculture secretary S.K. Mishra will be the new principal secretary to the Prime Minister in place of B.G. Deshmukh.

— 'They (the Chander Shekhar government) want to put their own man. I was nobody's man' said the Lt-Governor of Delhi, Arjan Singh. Arjan Singh submitted his resignation to President R. Venkataraman last night.

11 December 1990

— T.N. Seshan, Planning Commission member was appointed as Chief Election Commissioner. He supersedes Rama Devi who is officiating as the CEC.

— The Hindi news bulletin and commercial programmes on All India Radio, Jalandhar and Chandigarh Stations, remained suspended.

— Governors of a few states are expected to be replaced by this week-end.

— The Congress (I) today accused the previous V.P. Singh government of making "huge amount of illegal money" when it issued three Commerce Ministry notifications withdrawing quality central and preshipment inspection procedures exempting exports of higher quality cashew, engineering products and footwear components.

12 December 1990

— The well-known Bharatnatyam dancer Swapna Sundary lashed out at the Sangeet Natak Akademi for discriminating against established dancers and for "consistently and blatantly" propogating two or three classical dancers. She demanded an inquiry into such cases of nepotism and favouritism. "Can a public organisation be allowed to get away with complete impunity when it acts as a postal address for certain artists?"

— Three new secretaries to the government including a new secretary for Agriculture and Cooperation were appointed today as a part of the move to reshuffle the top bureaucrats. P.V. Krishnaswamy will be the new secretary in the Ministry of Fisheries. R.L. Mishra has been shifted as officer on special duty in the Department of Health.

— The Planning Commission was reconstituted with the appointment of six new members. They are G.S. Bhalla, S.R. Hashim, C.N.R. Rao, Sher Singh, D. Subramaniam and Jyotsnaben Shah. Mohan Dharia has assumed office as the new deputy chairman. A.N. Verma has joined today as member-secretary.

The Commission would now start work for finalising the Eighth Five Year Plan.

— The Janata Dal criticised the appointment of T.N. Seshan as the Chief Election Commissioner and alleged that he was a "politically pliable" person and was "privy to the process of cover-up" of the HDW submarine and the Bofors scandals.

— The Reserve Bank of India Governor R.N. Malhotra is currently at logger-heads with the Chandra Shekhar government. Differences on two major issues — incentives for NRI investment and deposits and the setting up of the proposed London based International Banking Corporation to lookafter foreign branches of the Indian commercial banks — have led to such a situation that the official sources do not rule out Malhotra's exit from the R.B.I.

— Arun Bhagat will assume the charge of Commissioner of Police, Delhi, tomorrow.

— Despite the abhorrence of the law of preventive detention and the threat it poses to human rights, there is a necessity for it in certain extreme situations. This view was expressed by Justice H.R. Khanna at a session of the World Congress on Human Rights. "This law was an anathema, no doubt, to all those who love personal liberty because it makes deep inroads in to the basic human freedoms which we all cherish and which occupy an important position among the higher values of life."

13 December 1990

— There is resentment in the bureaucracy at the manner in which the post of the Chief Election Commissioners was denied to Mrs. V.S. Rama Devi, who had been officiating for the past three weeks and who, according to well informed sources in the government had been assured that she would be continuing in office. The assurance had come from the Prime Minister and her papers had been processed for final assent by the President. The change has been a last-minute affair.

The T.N. Sheshan versus Rama Devi episode is seen as a part of the continuing tussle between the Indian Administrative Service and the Indian Legal Service. CECs have come from both the services in the past. The latter service has been held to be more suitable in view of the legal and constitutional aspects involved in the CEC's job.

— The Central Bureau of Investigation today received secret Swiss Bank documents relating to the Bofors case and these will be submitted in a Delhi Special Court.

14 December 1990

— The Andhra Pradesh chief minister Chenna Reddy's offer of resignation was accepted by the Congress (I) High Command.

— President's Rule has been imposed in Goa and the State Assembly kept in suspended animation.

— The CBI was allowed to retain the crucial papers relating to the Bofors case which it had received from the Swiss Bank for further investigation.

— General O.P. Malhotra (Retd.) is the new Governor of Punjab.

— Virendra Verma (Punjab Governor) shifts to Himachal Pradesh as its Governor.

— Markandey Singh is the Lt-Governor of Delhi in place of Air Marshal Arjan Singh (Retd.).

Dr Har Swarup Singh is the Lt-Governor of Gujarat.

B. Racjoaj is the Governor of Kerala.

Some appointments are new while others have been transferred. The transferred Governors would remain in office until the expiry of their term.

— S.P. Shukla is the new finance secretary, P.K. Lahiri is the Revenue secretary. Montek Singh Ahluwalia took charge as the commerce secretary.

The former cabinet secretary Vinod Pandey is the secretary of the Inter-State Council. Pandey would hold the rank of cabinet secretary.

15 December 1990

— The Chandra Shekhar government today announced the formation of a joint committee comprising representatives from the government and the industry which would meet regularly to sort out problems being faced by the industry in maintaining the tempo of industrial growth and increasing the country's exports.

— Prime Minister Chandra Shekhar has said that the Bofors documents do not reveal much as regards the names of the kickback recipients.

— Maharaja Sawai Madho Singh, a king of the Jaipur dynasty and great grandfather of Lt-Governor Bhawani Singh, was the first telephone subscriber of Jaipur.

— The Chief Justice of India, Rangnath Mishra, exhorted the Chief Justices of all High Courts to decide at least 50 per cent of the cases through Lok Adalats even if they had to devote extra time for the purpose. Justice Mishra said that about one lakh cases were decided every month by mutual consent through Lok Adalats.

16 December 1990

— N. Janardhan Reddy was unanimously elected leader of the Congress(I) Legislative Party.

— Making right to work a fundamental right at the moment will prove to be a disaster unless and until a proper strategy of generating employment opportunities is evolved. This was observed by the deputy chairman of the Planning Commission, Mohan Dharia.

— Illiteracy in rural India is more than twice that in the urban areas and its level is even higher than the poverty level in the country. Fifty-seven per cent of the adults (15 years plus) in the country are illiterates and the situation is even worse in the Hindi belt where over 80 per cent of the adults are illiterate.

These are the findings of the Operation Research Group, a marketing research group.

17 December 1990

— Faced with the prospect of a budget deficit of about Rs. 14,000 crore by the end of the current fiscal as against the projected deficit of Rs. 7206 crore, the government through a notification on December 15 undertoll this wide-ranging resource mobilisation drive which had all the features of a mini-budget.

And official announcement said this evening that the government had also decided to launch a campaign to ensure collection of all tax dues without delay or administrative slackness. The government said that goods now attracting auxiliary duty of 30 or 45 per cent would henceforth attract 50 per cent duty with some exceptions. Goods chareable to auxiliary duty at five per cent hitherto would in general attract auxiliary duty of 25 per cent. Goods at present fully exempted from auxiliary duty would with a few exceptions continue to be exempted. Import duty basic plus auxiliary had been doubled on carpet grade wool from 5 per cent to 10 per cent. On other raw wool it has been raised by 20 per cent from the present 5 per cent to 25 per cent. On other wood pulp auxiliary duty has been raised from per cent to 10 per cent. Auxiliary duty on crude oil remained unchanged. The basic excise duty on soda ash has been raised to 50 paise from the present 26 paise per bottle of 200 ml. Soft drinks other than soda would now attract 75 paise for a bottle of 200 ml as against 53 paise. The duty on bottles of higher capacity has also been adjusted suitably. Basic excise duty on acrylic fibre has been raised to Rs. 9.24 kg from Rs. 7.50 per kg, viscose fibre to Rs. 10.50 per kg from Rs. 8.50 polyester fibre from Rs. 6.50 to Rs. 10 a kg, polyester filament to Rs. 70 from Rs. 55, nylon filament yarn to Rs. 63 from Rs. 50 and viscose filament yarn to Rs. 12 from Rs. 9.

The announcement said that a review of the budgetary situation by the Finance Minister Yashwant Sinha showed that in spite of strict monitoring of expenditure there was an increase in Budget deficit and this deficit was alregerly attributable to the shortfall in revenues during April to November this year in relation to budget estimates. The several steps initiated by the Finance Minister in this regard included restraints on expenditure reinforced by austerity in all government activities. Regarding campaign for increasing tax collection, the Finance Minister proposed to visit major centres from which a large proportion of the revenue was realised. To start with, he had just visited Calcutta and now he would be visiting other centres, mainly Bombay. It is recalled that in a statement on the trends in 1990-91 Budget deficit, the former Finance Minister, Madhu Dandavate, told the Parliament in 28 August this year that the actual budget deficit as on 31 July 1990 to Rs. 11,390 crore in the four month period of the preceding year and the technical note presented by him projected that the deficit at the end of the current fiscal would be at the level of Rs. 8,931 crore as against Rs. 7206 crore estimated in the 1990-91 Budget. However, this trend analysis went haywrite due to the Gulf crisis which began on 2 August this year and since then, the Budget deficit had only been burgeoning as a result of higher prices being paid by India to import crude oil and petroleum products and its consequent impact on the other items. In the second four monthly report covering August t November months, the Budget deficit figure reportedly touched Rs. 14,000 and this gave a warning signal to the new government that drastic steps had become necessary to reduce the extent of Budget deficit during the current fiscal. The impact of this all round hike in duties will be doubtlessly inflationary and this is taking place at a time when the rate of inflation has already crossed 10 per cent. But the government had to take this decision sine, it was felt by the Finance Ministry officials that otherwise, the budgetary situation would be going totally out of control.

As regard the duty hike on man-made fibres, an analysis shows that a total of Rs. 553 crore will be realised in a full year and all the big houses have been affected as a result of this hike in duties and the Chandra Shekhar government is out to give the impression that it is not really friendly to big business. In fact, Reliance Industries Ltd. will be affected to the extent of Rs. 200 crore out of this Rs. 553 crore additional mobilisation in a full year. And others affected include JK group, B K Birla and Aditya Birla and RPG Enterprises. The public sector IPCL will also be affected. Industry sources tonight pointed out that as regards man-made fibres, which raising revenue from higher excise duties the government has virtually given encouragement to increasing imports as many users will like to import PFY which is in OGL since the international price will be lower than the domestic price. One source said that the net result would be heavy import outgo of foreign exchange resulting in negative indigenous production and less realisation of volume of duty.

In fact Prime Minister Chandra Shekhar soon after taking over the reins of the government said that the country would have to be prepared for austerity in true sense of the term and he told the senior officials of the government at his first meeting with the that the government could not continue with such high level of deficit. The exercises for such duties hike were started during Madhu Dandavate's tenure and Bimal Jalan prepared a paper for additional resource mobilisation. The latest hike in duties took effect ... e basis of that exercise.

18 December 1990

— "No one should ask for bringing in forces from abroad to control the prevailing law and order situation in the country", said Prime Minister Chandra Shekhar in an obvious reference to Shahi Imam Abdullah Bukhari's call for U.N. Forces at a function in New Delhi today.

— "There are many areas of serious human rights violation in India, and they are of political nature. One of the human rights violation common to many parts of India is tortures in police custody, deaths in police custody and also custodial rape," said Amnesty International Secretary-General Ian Martin. "Our most recent report published relates to the arbitrary arrests, detention and torture in Oinam village in Manipur state."

19 December 1990

— Supreme Court M.V. Ramaswami who was kept away from judicial work has been asked to resume work as the three judges of the Supreme Court Committee concluded that the allegations made against him pertaining to his tenure as Chief Justice of Punjab and Haryana "do not relate to any lapses of propriety in his judicial conduct". Justice Ramaswamy thus returns to the Supreme Court after a period of five months.

— About 5,000 New Delhi Municipal employees, mostly class III and class IV workers as well as the sanitary staff, struck work this morning to press for higher wages and better service conditions.

— A call for world-wide effort to put an end to mass child deaths and child malnutrition by the turn of the century has made in the 1991 state of the World's Children Report of the United Nations Children's Fund (UNICEF).

21 December 1990

— The world's biggest administrative exercise — the 1991 Indian Census — is expected to cost Rs. 130 crores, up by more than three times the amount spent on the last head count. This does not include the cost of processing the information collected during the "massive exercise" which was likely to be many times more than the "field cost" and was expected to run into another hundred crores.

— The top administrative changes being undertaken in Jammu and Kashmir are understood to be part of the "package" suggested by the former chief minister Farooq Abdullah to the new government at the centre to retrieve the situation in the valley.

— Prime Minister Chandra Shekhar took the captains of industry to task for failing to meet their export obligations and called upon them to shoulder more responsibilities.

22 December 1990

— Chaos prevailed in the U.P. Vidhan Bhawan this morning as several officers and their staff found themselves thrown out of the rooms in the secretariat lobbies. The rooms had been vacated for the new ministers.

It is after decades in U.P. that such a large Ministry would govern the state. Following induction of 46 ministers in a three-tier set-up, the strength of the Mulayam Singh Yadav council of ministers has gone up to 55. There are 27 cabinet ministers. With a view to accommodating 46 new ministers, an equal number of rooms were required and overnight various set-ups were disturbed.

The victims included the special secretaries, joint secretaries and under secretaries of the Finance Department, who in the morning found their belonging removed to the corridors.

— Chandra Shekhar rules out Plan holiday.

— With the government reinstating four members of the Advisory Panel of the Central Board of Film Certification (CBFC), dropped by the board chairman B.P. Singhal after protests over the passing of "College Girl" in October, the controversy over film censorship has come to an end.

23 December 1990

— The Bharatiya Janata Party (BJP) expelled nine more MLAs of Bihar from the Party for defying the whip in the Bihar Assembly on 22 November 1990; one of its members had already been expelled. The 22 November, Assembly meeting was held to pass a vote of confidence in favour or Laloo Prasad Yadav.

— Environment education is increasingly becoming a part of the school curriculum in the Capital, says a government spokesman.

24 December 1990

— The reconstituted Planning Commission authorised the Prime Minister, Chandra Shekhar, the deputy chairman, Mohan Dharia and the finance minister, Yashwant Sinha to sit and discuss by 26 December and determine the size of the Annual Plan for 1990-91 as well as the over-all size of the Eighth Five Year Plan "taking" into account the realities posed by the Gulf crisis. The meeting favoured gradual decentralisation of centrally sponsored schemes.

— V.P. Singh, the former Prime Minister, is all set to consolidate minorities and backward class votes in favour of his Janata Dal.

25 December 1990

— Indian scientists using data from satellites have prepared the country's first atlas containing detented districtwise maps of group water resources. This atlas runs to 18 volumes.

— The All India Muslim Backward Classes Federation today appealed to Chandra Shekhar that reservation be made for these classes in educational institutions and their children be proved modern training in their traditional vocations to improve their lot.

— In a far-reaching judgment, the Supreme Court has directed that temporary employees of the Railways be paid pension on retirement.

26 December 1990

— The warring Akalis, who decided to unite today under the leadership of Simranjit Singh Mann, responded positively to Prime Minister Chandra Shekhar's invitation for talks to sort out the Punjab imbroglio.

— The Supreme Court has ruled that public sector employees must be given alternative employment within the corporation in which they are working if they have lost their job due to a "widespread risk which those in that job are exposed to". If no alternative employment can be given then they are entitled to a compensation packet over and above the retirement benefits given to them on the termination of their service due to the occupational disease which does not totally disable them from doing all jobs but only the particular job in which they are engaged.

— Biju Patnaik, the Orissa chief minister, has supported the idea of a national government at the centre.

— The Ramamurti Committee which had been reviewing the 1986 National Education Policy submitted its final report today.

The Report containing 15 chapters covers all sectors of education. It consists of three parts, Part I being the main report consisting of 408 pages.

27 December 1990

— The government today announced two new direct tax proposals to mobilize an additional Rs. 810 crores the remaining period of the financial year. This is contrary to the Prime Minister's assurance given on 21 December that there would be no further taxation efforts in the current year. These relate to income-tax and depreciation rates allowed.

— "Today I come as a disappointed man", said J.R.D. Tata, as the "country has failed" in the essential and important task of population control.

— The Lok Sabha was told that the Delhi Transport Corporation had incurred a loss of about Rs. 1.02 crores on account of damage to about 3,290 buses during the anti-Mandal Commission agitation.

— The D. Ramachandran ministry in Pondicherry resigns: it was reduced to a minority.

— Rampant corruption prevailed in the public sector banks, alleged Gurudas Dasgupta, the CPI leader.

— The Comptroller and Auditor-General has noticed several deficiencies in the implementation of the Integrated Child Development Schemes. In his report presented to the Lok Sabha today, it has been pointed out that during the Seventh Five Year Plan period (1985-90), an expenditure of Rs. 660 crore was incurred outstripping the Plan outlay of rs. 520 crore. In sharp contrast, the physical progress of 2,236 projects by March 1990 was way behind the plan target of 3,019 projects. Out of the 2236 projects sanctioned, only 1617 projects were operational and of these 215 projects were interrupted. The focal point of ICDS services is an 'anganwadi. Anganwadis had not been set up in accordance with the norms. Most of the projects and anganwadis, in some of the state, had no safe and potable water supply, which was essential for improvement of health status of the target group. The implementation of the scheme was adversely affected on account of delays in supply and or non-supply of the essential equipment like first aid boxes, medicine kits, weighing scales etc. to the projects. Consequently the benefits failed to reach the target group. Under supplementary nutrition, shortfalls up to 80 per cent occurred in coverage of women and children and in some cases supplementary nutrition was not at all provided. Feeding suffered from frequent interruptions, for periods exceeding two years in some cases, and was provided for 28 days only against the norms of 300 days in some of the states test-checked. The quality of supplementary nutrition was below the prescribed norms; therapeutic food, rich in calories and proteins, required to be supplied to severely malnourished children, had not been supplied in several states. In nine state, cases of supply of substandard and infected food were noticed. Although the necessity for development of a system of cheap and hygeinically prepared ready-to-eat food had been recognised, no action in the matter had been taken. As a result of inadequate, interrupted and sub-standard quality of supplementary nutrition, the desired effect of raising the health status of beneficiaries could not be achieved.

28 December 1990

— The Congress(I) today demanded a judicial inquiry into the case of a file concerning the excise duty scandal which was earlier missing.

29 December 1990

— The 12-day strike by the employees of the New Delhi Municipal Committee was called off following an agreement between the NDMC Workers Federation and the committee. As a result, the employees up to grade B would be given an *ad hoc* payment of Rs. 100 per month from March 1990, and another committee would be set up to examine the recommendation of the Shiv Shankaran Committee as well as other demands of the employees. Also, temporary employees who had served for 240 days in a year would be recognised as regular muster roll employees.

30 December 1990

— The latest report on the country's population trends has emphasised the persistent gulf between the urban and rural areas and has called for a thorough review of the situation in most states. The rural birth rates were higher than urban rates by 28 per cent in 1989. The decline in the birth rate from 31.5 to 30.5 is largely an urban affairs.

7

DOMINANT THEMES AND CONCERNS OF THE YEAR 1990

I

THE MINORITY GOVERNMENT

A minority government refers to the government supported by fewer than half the total number of members of the legislature (or the Lower House in a bi-cameral legislature) and is a variety exclusive to parliamentary democracy only. By the very definition, a minority government is a party government: it may be one-party government or may be a coalition. A feature of a minority government is the assurance, tacit or implicit, of legislative support by parties outside it.

In the parliamentary election held in November 1989, no single political party emerged with an absolute majority. In a house of 525 members, the Congress (I) got 192 seats, the Janata Dal 141, the Bharatiya Janata Party 36, the CPI(M) 32 and the CPI 13, the remaining 61 seats going to other smaller, regional political parties. Sensing that the electorate rejected it even though it emerged as the single largest party in the new Lok Sabha, the Congress (I) laid no claims to form the government. A coalition, called the National Front, led by the Janata Dal, its other members being parties such as the Telugu Desam, the Assam Gana Parishad, the DMK, the Congress (S), staked its claim to constitute the government. Lacking a clear majority in the Lok Sabha, the National Front could form the government only when it was extended support by the Leftist Parties comprising the CPI(M), CPI, Forward Block, Revolutionary Socialist Party on the one hand and the Bharatiya Janata Party (BJP) on the other.

Minority governments are not an unfamiliar political phenomena in the parliamentary political system of the world. Indeed, such governments were a marked feature of Germany under the Weimar Republic (1910-33) and of France during the Fourth Republic (1946-1958). More recently, countries like Canada, Italy, Ireland, Denmark and Scandinavia have had minority governments.

The Constitution of India is absolutely silent on the statistical attribute of the government. It expresses neither any liking for, nor any aversion to, the numerical strength of the government. It may thus accommodate a national government, a majority government and a minority government. What it says is that the Council of Ministers shall be collectively responsible to the Lok Sabha and that a minister, if already not a member of either House of Parliament, should become a member within six months.

When the election results for the Ninth Lok Sabha came out in 1989, there was a mention about India constituting what was called the National Government. Leaders like A.B. Vajpayee indeed mooted the proposal for this government — which would be a government of national unity and national consensus. The idea did not travel much for it was felt that parties which are poles apart — the BJP and the Leftist parties — cannot function together, even though the apparent ideological incompatibility did not preclude the old Jana Sangh and Communists from working together in 1957 in the coalition governments of Punjab, Bihar and Uttar Pradesh. The picture which ultimately emerged was the swearing in of the National Front — a coalition with the Janata Dal (141 members) providing anchorage to it — supported, from outside, by the Bharatiya Janata Party and the Leftist parties.

Let it also be known that India has experimented with this form of government in the past, both at the centre and in the states. After the Congress split of 1967, Indira Gandhi continued to be the country's Prime Minister even though her party had lost its majority in the Lok Sabha. From 1967 till 1971, India had a minority government, receiving support, based on an informal understanding, from outside by the Communists and the DMK. Even Charan Singh, who became the Prime Minister in 1979 after Morarji Desai's resignation on the split in the ruling Janata Party, headed a minority government. At the state level, West Bengal, Punjab and Bihar had minority governments during the late sixties — a period of intense political fluidity in the country. The P.C. Ghosh government in West Bengal (21 November 1967 — 20 February 1968), the Lachman Singh Gill government in Punjab (27 November 1967 — 23 August 1968) and the B.P. Mandal government in Bihar (1 February 1968 — 18 March 1968) bore a minority character, each supported by the Congress (I) from outside. No such government, however, was very durable — nor did any of them command any popular respect being perceived as but a manifestation of defectors' power hunger.

It would be utterly immature to indulge in any glorification of a minority government. Basically, it lacks stability and durability, more so when the party in power itself suffers from a high measure of internal contradictions and inconsistencies. Moreover, such a government's options are necessarily limited. The numerical weakness itself imposes limitations and restricts its choice-making. What is more, the fact of the present National Front government under V.P. Singh was supported from outside by the Bharatiya Janata Party and the Leftists with little ideological affinity with each other also contributed to its vulnerability.

Yet the prospects of the National Front government continuing in power appear to be modestly good. First, despite its internal personality clashes and ideological heterogeneity, it enjoyed popular goodwill, which was its real saviour. To move to the other side of the spectrum, fortunately or unfortunately, there were not many alternatives avail- able to the political actors — at least for some time to come. All politicians including those in the BJP and the CPM were acutely aware of the limits to their manoeuvrability: all knew of the dangers inherent in the return of the Congress. The fact, therefore, of no one gaining from rocking the boat was itself an assurance of the continuance of the National Front government.

Prerequisites for the Success of Minority Government

A minority government, by its very definition, is a fragile government, its continuance in power depending on the continued support of political parties which have not joined it to share power, and bear responsibility and instead stay outside. The durability of this type of government demands the fulfilment of certain conditions. First and foremost, a minority government must enjoy a large measure of popular goodwill not only at the time of its assuming power but throughout its tenure. Indeed, popular goodwill is its single largest asset, which it must not lose. This must be underlined because there are instances of minority government foisted on the people even though the latter felt totally alienated. Secondly, the objective of a minority governments should be to serve the society and not to merely remain in office to enjoy its perks. Not enjoying the majority support in the legislature, it necessarily depends upon outside party/parties) for its continuance. A result is its high level of susceptibilities which makes it subject to heavy pressures. Therefore a minority government must learn to stay clear of such pressures. It must be ready to resign but must not yield on fundamental questions of state building, nation-making and development: it has been observed that a minority government, which just goes on surrendering to demands mounted on it, does not last long, but meanwhile bequeath only thorny problems for the future government by its short-range, pupulist appeasement measures. Also, a minority government which is given to easy surrendering does not last long: it dies under the weight of its own conflicts and contradictions. Thirdly, the political party or parties constituting the minority government must not suffer from any high measure of internal factionalism disturbing its functional harmony. A faction-ridden minority government is a notoriously short-living entity. Fourthly, the outside parties extending support to the minority government from outside must possess a certain amount of mutual goodwill and understanding among themselves. It has been seen that such outside parties may not stay together in their support if they have traditions of adverse relationship.

A minority government may be perceived as a sort of anomaly in the sense that it negates that basic of parliamentary democracy, which is the control of the executive by the legislature. This form of government is liable to legislative defeat, even resignation when confronted by a united opposition. Even otherwise, its policies may not gain the approval of the legislature. All these features tend to make minority governments unstable and less durable. But minority governments are not necessarily less effective than the majority governments. Some of them do perform reasonably well: they are permeated by an urge to show results as early as possible — a minority government's time-horizon being short.

II

COALITION GOVERNMENT

The *Oxford Dictionary* defines coalition as a temporary combination for special ends between parties that retain distinctive principles. A coalition government is combination of two or more different political parties in order to achieve some goal which is mutually shared. The goal generally is to secure a working majority to enable the members of the coalition to form the government. But in times of crises a coalition may be formed to reduce partisan politics. There may be some other reasons also for forming a coalition. A coalition government is generally formed only when no one party is able to secure a majority of seats in the legislature. If a party gets a majority in the legislature it would constitute the government on its own, thus taking full responsibility of implementing its election promises and being accountable to the people for it. This keeps in tact the clear-cut division of responsibility in a parliamentary democracy — one party forming the government the others remaining in opposition. In short, a coalition government, it is argued, is a device for special occasions — when no party is in majority or when there is a national emergency calling for united efforts. It is, thus, a sub-ideal. Some political analysts seem, however, to commend coalitionalism even for normal times, their argument being that this government would be more broad-based thus reducing discord and disharmony in the society.

Coalition Government in the West

The Indian perception of coalition is unconsciously shaped by the British orientations and political culture. Indians recall with jubilation that observation made by Disraeli, namely 'England does not love coalitions'. Harold Wilson has also commented:

> 'Peace time coalitions invariably produce fudged decisions where words mean more than actions, and the achievement of the lowest common denominator is regarded the highest act of coalition statesmanship. Moreover, an inter-party coalition produces — is sometimes designed to produce — a paralysis of opposition. And when an important and self-conscious section of the country is denied effective parliamentary representation, frustration leads to extra-parliamentary action'.

But one must note that Britain was coalitional more than once. Coalition government is much more widespread in West European countries. France, Belgium, West Germany, Holland, Denmark, Italy etc., have multiparty systems and a coalition government is a norm rather than an exception in them. Switzerland, of course, is the most outstanding example of coalition government; since 1959 it has had coalition government uninterruptedly. All these governments have been second to none in providing political stability to the people no less than economic prosperity.

History of Coalition Governments

Coalition government acquires a relevance only in a parliamentary democracy. It is, therefore, understandable that this question could arise only when India was firmly put on the path of parliamentarism. Though a sort of parliamentary democracy in India began with the Government of India Act, 1919 the pattern of governance — called dyarchy — did not leave any room for coalitional inter-play. It was under the Government of India Act, 1935 that the concept of parliamentary democracy as it is understood took root and was put into operation at the provincial level. It is politically significant that in the election held in 1937 no single party could win a majority in Punjab and Sindh and both these provinces were ruled by coalitions.

In 1946 the Interim Government under the prime ministership of Jawaharlal Nehru was itself a coalition consisting of the Congress, the Muslim League, the Hindu Mahasabha, etc. A coalition government dominated the party scenario in the year under review.

The credit of having the first-ever coalition under the present constitution goes to what was originally a class 'B' state, namely 'Pepsu'. As no party could muster a majority in the state assembly in the first general election of 1952 a coalition consisting of non-Congress parties (i.e., Akali Dal and others) was formed in April 1952. Lacking any ideological or programmatic homogeneity, the coalition barely lasted for eleven months and broke up in March 1952, followed by a spell of President's rule. The other states having coalition governments were Orissa, Andhra and Kerala. Significantly, all these coalitions were non-Congress ones. The Congress party was the pre-eminent party dominating the political scene, commanding an absolute majority of seats in the legislatures. Where a few exceptions occurred they were all coalitions (leaving aside Kerala in 1957-59): perhaps, a necessary stage in party building in developing democracies.

The fourth general elections (1967) inaugurated an era of coalition governments in India in a big way though the centre still escaped this phenomenon and continued to be ruled by a single party enjoying majority support, namely the Congress. As many as eight states — Punjab, Haryana, U.P., Bihar, West Bengal, M.P., Orissa and Kerala — had coalition governments as a result of no party obtaining a majority of seats in the state legislatures. What should be further noted is that these states had coalition governments in quick succession: when one coalition fell another took over with marginal or substantial change in composition, depending on the local exigencies. It was a period of extreme political fluidity in the country. The monolith Congress party failed to secure popular mandate, but no party emerged strong enough singly to replace it. In the event there occurred an apparently mindless rush for power, and the coalitions of this phase were generally in the nature of getting together of strange bed-fellows with the sole motivation of spiting the Congress and retaining political power in their hands. The mortality rate of such coalitions was bound to be very high.

The image of India being ruled by a single party has thus concealed the real dimensions of its coalitional politics. Since the inauguration of the Constitution in 1950 the country has witnessed no less than thirty coalitional governments in various states; besides, the central government had a minority ministry during 1969-71 and coalition one during 1977-79 and again during 1989-90. The split of 1969 in the Congress reduced the majority of Indira Gandhi's Congress which depended on the support of the DMK and the Communists. The Janata government, in power from 1977 to 1979, was a coalition in a double sense. Though the party was formed by the merger of the Congress (O), the BLD, the Jana Sangh, the Socialists party and the Congress for Democracy, the coalitituent units never mentally ceased to exist within it, and influence its functioning. Indeed, in practically all matters including allocation of party tickets for election and seats in the ministry each constituent unit commended a quota proportionate to its strength in the national and state level elected bodies prior to merger. Besides, it included the Akali Dal, thus fulfilling the criteria of a formal coalition. Thee year 1990 have seen two governments at the centre, both being coalition ones. The states experiencing coalition since 1952 are Punjab, Haryana, U.P., Bihar, West Bengal, Orissa, M.P., Gujarat, Maharashtra, Karnataka, Tripura and Kerala. West Bengal, Kerala and, to an extent, Tripura have by now imbibed the coalitional culture, and a coalition in these states has come to be viewed as a normal political arrangement rather than an aberration. It is no small achievement that the successive ministries in both West bengal and Kerala are enjoying a higher degree of political and ministerial stability than do states under the Congress rule. Even in 1990, Kerala and West Bengal have each a coalition government — like the centre.

Typology of Coalition Government

The coalition governments may be classified in many ways. This is because there are several variables which have a bearing on coalition meaning. A coalition may be a (1) dyadic coalition, (2) tridic coalition, or (3) polyadic coalition. A dyadic coalition is an alignment of two separate groups of parties. The triadic and polyadic coalitions are alignments of three separate groups and more than two groups respectively. Coalitions may also be classified on the basis of the following criteria:

1. What is the timing of the coalition making?
2. What is the number of members in the coalition?
3. What is the membership strength of the coalition members in relation to the total legislative membership?
4. What are the ideologies of the members of coalition?

While discussing the timing of the coalition partners, a coalition may be either a pre-poll electoral alliance turning into a coalition government or a mere post-election coalition. From the point of view of number of members, a coalition may be dyadic, triadic or polyadic. On the basis of the legislative strength of the coalition embars there may be a majority government coalition or a minority government coalition. Both the V.P. Singh government and the subsequent Chandra Shekhar government of 1990 have been minority and as well as coalition ones. Ideologically viewed a coalition may be homogeneous or heterogeneous. Further, even an ideologically homogeneous coalition may be: (a) leftist, (b) rightist, (c) centrist or (d) neutral or pragmatic.

Multiplicity of Parties

Coalition making becomes inescapable when there is a multiplicity of political parties contesting election. A multi-party system may broadly be a result of two factors. Where the electoral system is based on proportional representation or list system, there is apt to be, as already indicated, a multiplicity of parties. France and Germany are the oft-quoted examples of such an electoral system producing a multi-party system. The second factor could be the pluralistic character of the society itself. The more the interests and viewpoints in the society competing for articulation, the more parties there are bound to be. Politics, broadly speaking, is a reflection of the society and a plural society seeks its reproduction in a multi-party system. Indian society shows continental diversities and differences with people living at varying levels of social, economic and cultural development. They, therefore, belong to different political groupings depending upon their own aspirations no less than their perception of interest. Thus viewed, the country is likely to have for a long time to come some five substantial parties. The biggest party may be a centrist party and there may be two parties to the left and two to the right. One group of the left parties may consist of socialist parties and another the communist ones. One party on the right may accept democracy and secularism fully but may believe in free enterprise and more individual freedom in economic and fiscal matters. The other group of parties on the right may be traditionalist and believe in religious or cultural revivalism.

The multiplicity of parties has thus been viewed as a permanent feature of the political landscape of India, but this hardly posed any problem or concern in the system of governance. The Congress — which steered the country to Independence — was winning a majority of seats even though the votes polled in its favour never rose above 47.8 per cent for Lok Sabha and 42 per cent for State Assemblies except in the general election of 1984 after Indira Gandhi's death.

The above pattern of voting discloses how close the country could be to a system of alliance governance. A negative swing of a small margin is enough to knock the ruling party out of power. This apart, the traditional opposition parties are increasingly seeking alliances and thus preventing the splitting of votes as against the Congress. But no other party seems to be in a immediate position singly to fill the space left by the Leviathan Congress thereby making a coalition government an invitability. Indeed, the one party dominant system appears to be on its way out, and its alternative, today, is necessarily an alliance system of governance. It may be safe to speculate that India will have to learn to live with coalitional arrangements for some time — atleast before transiting into a two party system, even if this ever materialises. The coalition government is thus more than a political probability in India — at the centre, and in the states. Kerala and West Bengal are already accustomed to this form. Punjab with Sikh as constituting 51 per cent of the population and Hindu 49 per cent would find in it the key to its political harmony.

Requisites for Success of Coalition

The year 1990 was an year of coalitional governments in India, both the National Front and its successor being alliance ones. Coalition governments in India have lasted for a few days but examples also exist of such alliances completing the full term of five years. This serves to prove that a coalition is not necessarily a vulnerable form of government even though it has shown the highest propensity for President's rule. The question then arises. What factors make for the coalition longeveity? A coalition made up of parties with a programme compatible with their ideologies is more durable the one which is unprincipled and formed purely for the sake of power. The coalition in Kerala is more stable precisely for this reason. So is the case with the United Front government in West Bengal. Ideological homogeneity is thus a prerequisite for the stability of a coalition. This gets further deepened if the coalition becomes an extension of the pre-election poll alliance as in West Bengal. The National Front is now a famous example. On the other hand, when parties with differing political persuasions come together to form the government, the prospects of their staying together become reduced. This may be illustrated by the case of Pepsu In the general election of 1952 the party position in the Pepsu assembly was: Congress 16, Akali Dal 22, Jana Sangh 1, Communist party 3, KMPP 1 and Independents 7, its total strength being 60. A coalition government of all the non-Congress parties was formed on 22 April 1962. The government consisted of highly disparate and divergent elements that they could not stay together for long, and it broke part in less than a year. Similarly, an ideologically incompatible coalition consisting of parties like SSP, PSP, Jana Kranti Dal (later merged with BKD), and CPI was formed in Bihar in 1967 under the chief ministership of Mahamaya Prasad Sinha. It took office in March 1967 but fall in January 968. The B.P. Mandal coalition in Bihar formed in February 1968 fell after 47 days precisely for this reason.

Another factor contributing to coalition stability is that it must find anchorage in a party which enjoys considerable strength in the legislature. An example is the National Front. Other parties under the National Front government discovered such an achorage in the Janata Dal in 1990. Moreover, various parties in a coalition must have a fair distribution of power and patronage to deepen their sense of involvement in the government. But an excessive decentralisation too entails dangers for the coalition. In the north-eastern state a coalition cabinet of three regional parties functioned, in effect, as three sub-cabinets which destroyed the principle of joint responsibility and made adoption of a common policy or integrated administration impossible. The coalition collapsed very soon. Fourthly, a coalitional which is at the same time a minority is very vulnerable especially when it gets support of party or parties preferring to stay out and not formally joining it, thus refusing to share the responsibility of governance. The Chandra Shekhar government, formed in the later half of 1990, did not have even sixty MPs depending on the support of the Congress (I) and its allies with over 200 MPs. Such a government is plainly incongruous and is not to work for long.

A coalition government thus requires certain requisites for its success, but the role of the human factor is no less important. The human component of a coalition must be cultured and civilized; and imbued with a sense of purposeful service to the state.

III

INTER-STATE COUNCIL

Need for a body which remains seized of possible disagreements and disputes between the centre and the state is well understood in all federal systems. Inter-state disputes in them are inevitable and occasionally do arise even in the best of the Constitution.

To be sure, there is the Supreme Court of India which is empowered to examine the centre-state and inter-state disputes, but not all the problems faced in the field of centre-state relations can be referred to the judiciary with its legalistic and rigid procedures of working. One must not miss the fact that federal problems are, in the ultimate analysis, political problems, and for resolving them political solutions should be sought. also, there are in operation some mechanisms which may discuss such matters. One easily recalls forums like the National Development Council, the chief ministers' conference, the Central Council of Health, the Central Council of Local Self-Government, and other functional conferences of ministers convened by the central ministers corresponding to those functions. An analysis of their functioning, however, seems to suggest some shortcomings and limitations which should not be surprising. In the first place, the existing bodies, including even the National Development Council and the chief ministers' conference, partake of the nature of *ad hoc* ones, convened at the will and convenience of the central government. Secondly, they lack even a statutory base where as a body ideally suited for such purposes must as a rule be embedded in the Constitution so that it comes to command universal respect and attention. Thirdly, the existing forums suffer from a conspicuous lack of interest on the part of the states, which tend to regard them a central contrivances to make them dutifully fall in line with New Delhi's pre-determined policies, programmes, and wishes.

The very creation of such numerous forums indicates that the country's political system was experiencing for a long time problems and issues in the field of centre-state relationship, but they were generally taken on centre-determined paths. One must also not overlook the fact of single party dominance in the country, the Congress party being in office both at the centre and in all or most states. In this larger context, the centre's relationship with the states tend to acquire the spirit and style of intra-party functioning, and when differences arose or problems were felt, they as a rule used to be tackled along the party network, thereby bypassing the Constitution. The politically serenity was abruptly broken with the general election held in 1967 which ushered into power non-Congress government in many states. From then onwards the centre-state relationship acquired a new dimension, in the sense that it ceased to be the house affair of the Congress party, and, furthermore, as different political parties came into power in the states, federalism in India began to disclose new areas to tension and conflict.

It was within this larger politically plemical climate that the Administrative

Reforms Commission (1966-70) under H. Humanthaiyya found itself working. In its report on centre-state relationships submitted in 1969, the ARC recommended the setting up of inter-state council in India. No action, however, followed.

The Sarkaria Commission

The latest commission to recommend the setting up of such inter-state council has been the Commission on Centre-State Relations which the central government under Indira Gandhi appointed in 1983 under chairmanship of Justice R.S. Sarkaria. The Sarkaria Commission which submitted its report in 1987 strongly recommended the creation of such a body for resolving inter-state or central-state problems. This forum according to the Sarkaria Commission, should be utilised for discussing matters which do not pertain to planning and development and which are mostly administrative in character. All proposed legislation in the Constitution's concurrent list would be very apt matter to referred to the inter-state council. It suggested: 'A forum where free and fair discussion could take place on issues affecting inter-state and union (i.e. central) state relations is not only useful but is also necessary. It shall be a noble constitutional devise for discussing the nation's problems generally before those problems become intractable but particularly to maintain fair and just harmonious constitutional relations between the union and the states or between state and state.'[1] This body is to be called the Inter-Government Council (IGC) and is to be set up such article 263 of the Constitution. The 'Inter-Government Council' to use Sarkaria's nomenclature, will evolve guidelines for identification and selection of issues to be brought before it and will take care to ensure that only such matters of national importance relating to subjects of common interest are brought up before it as would fall within the ambit of clauses (b) and (c) of article 263. The Council will consist of a general body assisted by a smaller standing committee. The General Body will consist of:

1. Prime Minister - Chairman
2. All chief ministers - Members
3. All central cabinet ministers (or central ministers dealing with subjects of common interest to the centre and states) - Members

The standing committee will consist of:

1. Prime Minister - Chairman
2. Six chief ministers, one from each zone selected annually - Members
3. Six central cabinet ministers to be nominated by the Prime Minister - Members

The general body of the IGC will meet at least twice a year and the standing committee least four times. Every meeting of the general body will be held in camera and its proceedings will be conducted as in central cabinet meetings. Practices and procedures laid down for cabinet meetings may be followed by the general body. Matters proposed to be referred to the general body will first be discussed in the standing committee. Normally, such matters only as are referred by the standing committee will be taken up for discussion in the general body. All other matters will normally be considered and disposed of at the level of standing committee. Meetings of the standing committee will held in camera. Any member of the general body may attend a standing committee meeting with permission of the chairman of the committee. The Prime Minister may nominate any other central cabinet minister to preside over the standing committee meetings when he (i.e. the Prime Minister) is not present. The Inter-Governmental Council and its standing committee should be able to set up *ad hoc* sub-committees to investigate special matters. Procedure adopted for the standing committee meetings will, as nearly as may be, be the same as for cabinet sub-committee meetings. There should be a permanent secretariat to the Council.

The Sarkaria Commission submitted its report in 1987 but the central government was dragging its feet on its demand for the setting up of an inter-state council. To a parliamentary question asked by an M.P. belonging to AIADMK about the government's decision about this body, the Home Minister replied saying that the centre will decide after it had received the options of the chief ministers and the matter had been discussed in Parliament. The Member of Parliament (Kolandaivelu) had said that Article 263 of the Constitution provides for setting up of an inter-state council. He asked why it had not been set up even 40 years after Independence. The minister extolled the virtues of the Zonal Councils and inter-state disputes were getting resolved effectively in them.[2] This was rebutted some time later by Kerala chief minister E.K. Nayanar who on 6 June 1988 said, they served no 'useful purpose' and should be replaced with an inter-state council.

The political scenario changed before the year 1989 was wearing out. The National Front was in powers. On 7 March 1990, central government decided to set up the inter-state council as recommended under article 263 of the Constitution to inquire into inter-state disputes and investigate subject of inter-state or centre-state interest. The duties and functions of the council will be as enumerated under the constitutional provision other than socio-economic planning and development which will continue to be the National Development Council. The Sarkaria Commission had recommended the setting up of such a council to be called Inter-Governmental Council. It recommended that the council should consist of a general body assisted by a smaller standing committee. The general body will consist of the Prime Minister, the chief ministers of all the states and six other members. The central government did not agree to change the name of the Inter-State Council.

NOTES

1. *Report of the Commission on Centre-State Relations* (Chairman: R.S. Sarkaria), New Delhi, Government of India, 1987.
2. See *The Times of India*, 25 February 1988, p. 5.

IV

THE MANDALISATION OF THE PUBLIC SERVICES

The year 1990 will be remembered for a very, very long time to come for its resurrection of the Report of the Second Backward Classes Commission submitted in 1980, popularly known as the Mandal Commission Report after the name of its chairman B.P. Mandal. The Report is, today, the revered manifesto for the protagonists of job reservation for the backward classes of the Indian society.

The reservation of jobs in the country's public services for what are called the backward classes has acquired top-level national importance in view of the National Front government's decision to reserve 27 per cent of posts for them. Earlier, in its election manifesto of 1989, the Front publicly supported 'substantial reservations in employment, education and public offices to backward classes', observing at the same time that 'the recommendations of the Mandal (Backward Classes) Commission will be implemented expeditiously'.

The Constitution is, of course, loudly solicitous about the welfare of the backward classes, and while expressly providing for the reservation of posts in the public administration for two such classes — namely, the scheduled castes and scheduled tribes — it makes a general mention of similar promotional measures for what it calls 'other backward classes' (OBCs).

Obligation

Job reservation for the scheduled castes and scheduled tribes is a specific constitutional obligation, but it is not exactly so for the 'other backward classes'. Historically, the government has set aside, right since the inception of the present Constitution, positions only for the scheduled castes and scheduled tribes, and extension of these benefits to 'other backward classes' did not win the centre's approval until V. P. Singh government's 'momentous' decision.

What the Constitution says on OBCs is about the state's obligation to set up a commission to investigate the conditions of socially and educationally backward classes — and the difficulties under which they labour, and to make recommendations as to the steps that should be taken to remove such difficulties and to improve their condition. The commission's report is to be presented to the President and is to be laid, along with a memorandum explaining the executive action, before Parliament. Two backward classes commissions have been set up since the Constitution was adopted, one under Kaka Kalelkar in 1953 and another under B.P. Mandal in 1978, reporting in 1955 and 1980 respectively.

The Kaka Kalelkar Commission had a broadbased composition. It included members even from non-backward communities, which made for a wider perspective within which it viewed the problem. As the Constitution wanted the amelioration measures for these communities to be consistent with the need for administrative efficiency, the commission failed to produce a unanimous report. Five out of 11 members submitted separate notes of dissent.

But the majority report recommended a system of reservation in the civil service — 25 per cent in Class I, 33.5 per cent in Class II, and 40 per cent in Class III and IV — at the same time urging that the best candidates should, as a rule, be recruited by means of a competitive examination without any regard to caste considerations. In his forwarding letter, Kaka Kalelkar, the chairman, set his face firmly and resolutely against caste being made the basis of reservation in the public services. He wrote: 'I am definitely against reservation in government services for any community for the simple reason that the services are not meant for the servants but they are meant for the service of society as a whole.' Kaka Kalelkar recognised the central role of public administration in society and favoured the recruitment of only the best men available in the land. He ridiculed the practice of reservation by categorically declaring: 'Reservation of posts for certain backward communities would be as strange as reservation of patients for particular doctors. The patients are not meant to supply adequate or proportionate clientele to all the doctors whatever their qualifications.' He recommended the principle of 'no reservation' but 'generous preference', firmly believing that backwardness could be tackled on a basis other than that of caste.

The Kalelkar Commission failed to formulate any objective criterion for identifying 'backward classes', and this was why the government rejected its recommendations. The commission had classified a very large section of the population as backward, and if special assistance had to be given to such large numbers, the government argued, the 'really needy will be swamped by the multitude'. The government preferred economic criterion for the definition of 'backward class'.

The Second Backward Classes Commission was set up in 1978 by the Janata government, its chairman being B.P. Mandal. The commission had five members four drawn from the backward castes and one from the scheduled castes. Unlike the first Backward Classes Commission which was broadbased, the second's membership was from the backward castes, except one who was from the scheduled caste a partisanship that was reflected itself in its radicalism. As against 2399 backward classes identified by the first commission, the Mandal Commission spread itself much more widely listing over 3,000 castes as backward.

It is to be noted that between 1953 and 1978 the number of backward castes should have shown a decline to reflect the impact on backwardness, however marginal, of successive programmes of development. The Mandal Commission, however, was apparently unmindful of such inconsistencies. It boldly concluded that 52 per cent of all posts under the central government ought to be reserved for the backward castes. But since this recommendation could go against the earlier Supreme Court judgment stipulating that reservation had to be below 50 per cent, the commission proposed a figure which, when added to the 22.5 per cent for the scheduled castes and scheduled tribes, remained below 50 per cent. 'In view of this legal constraint the commission is obliged to recommend a reservation of 27 per cent only, even though their population is almost twice this figure.

Though the Mandal Commission was called a "Backward Classes Commission", its report does not define the term "class" and assumes, quite innocently, that class means caste. It would thus be more correct to call it the "Backward Castes Commission" which it became for all practical purposes. "class" is a socio-economic phenomenon and admits of mobility, while "caste" is static and is determined by an ascriptive factor like birth. It is also not unusual to find poor people even amongst the upper castes. Similarly, certain individuals belonging to the backward castes have worked their way up the social hierarchy to become very affluent.

In other words, the historically determined caste system has not remained completely immune to the impulses and energies released by the process of democracy and development. The doctrine of reservation in the public service based on caste shuts its an eye to the charges taking place since the inception of the Constitution. This makes it a fallible document.

Several consequences flow from the reservation system in the public services. One is its impact on efficiency, the widely prevalent view being that those who enter the civil service through deliberately lowered standards bring rather lower levels of efficiency in administration. Secondly, the "soft corridor" of recruitment deprives society of the services of the most competent people who would otherwise get into public administration. Thirdly, India is formally committed to abolition of the caste system, but the reservation system perpetuates its.

Today, instead of caste being on the decline it is tending to become part of the Indian psyche even in metropolitan cities. As a result of reservation, many remain deprived of the chance to improve their economic status because jobs have already been allotted to other through lower recruitment standards. This creates resentment threatening to tear apart the social fabric, and the Mandal Commission, report is a potentially explosive threat to social cohesion.

The reservation policy may be criticised on the grounds that it exhibits precisely the kind of injustice (favouring some one on grounds irrelevant to the purpose) that it is supposed to overcome. Indeed, caste has emerged as an unusually powerful force in many parts of India, with positive discrimination unintentionally fragmenting the country along caste lines. All political parties exploit caste sentiments during elections, and in several parts of the country, caste-based organisations have already started to spring up, striking deeproots in states like Tamil Nadu. They act as pressure groups to extract more concessions for themselves or safeguard what they have already gained — all in the name of social justice.

Mandalisation vs Indianisation

It would have been prudent for the national policy-makers to have first obtained the feedback from the already operating reservation system for scheduled castes and scheduled tribes and ploughed it in before its extension to other groups of people. This unfortunately has not been done.

It is common knowledge that the benefits of reservation made available since Independence have not percolated to all the levels and sectors of the target groups, which explains the deficiency of these arrangements. Indeed, the bulk of the benefits have been cornered by a few select castes and the remaining ones have largely or substantially remained where they were. To be more correct, even in these benefit-scoring castes, an elite group has emerged and the benefits of reservation mostly circulate among its members. The same skewed pattern is liable to be reflected in the case of backward castes also. The 3,700 and odd castes enumerated by the Mandal Commission are not internally homogeneous, being at different levels of development, social, economic, cultural and educational. In such a context, the reserved posts would get cornered, in a substantial number, by the forward among the backward castes. Thus the reservation for backward castes would result in the emergence of a few enclaves of affluence among them without serving the intended purpose.

Besides, the reservation for SC/STs was, wisely, a time-bound concession made for a period of ten years only. But powerful vested interests have emerged and it has in practice become self-perpetuating, being extended every time. It is also to be noted that reservation at the stage of recruitment is itself perceived as an injustice to the larger society, but its extension to the area of promotion has proved to be extremely harmful to inter-personnel relationship and to organisational harmony.

Warrants Scrutiny

These mistakes must not be repeated when extending the benefits and concessions to new groups. The caste system is peculiar to Hindus, no other religion suffers from such an encumbrance. Under V.P. Singh government's decision, caste-based benefits have been extended to other religions also. The Mandal Report is a lobbyist's report, its composition being what it was, making it an unreliable documents: indeed, it is a model of how a public report should to be written. Its list of no fewer than 3,774 backward castes is exaggerated and thus warrants closer scrutiny. Several professional or occupational groups have been included as backward castes, which is untenable.

Poverty, it must be noted, is becoming a less and less respector of the caste hierarchy, and one cannot rule out the emergence of affluence among sections of the backward castes. Such people who are economically well off must be kept excluded from the category of beneficiaries. This suggests adoption of a suitable 'means' test before the benefits of reservation become available.

To drive home the point, individuals who are in the category of income tax-payers may be kept out of the benefits. This will ensure that the really needy get the concessions. Further, the number of chances of getting the caste-based concession including concessions to SC/STs should be restricted so that there is a proper spread of the beneficiaries. Chance restriction is absolutely necessary. Finally, the duration of the concessions should be fixed at ten years and must not be extended. One should also utter a word of warning at this stage. Many more groups have already started mounting demands on the government for extending reservation benefits to them. This must be firmly resisted.

One more word, so long as caste remains on the national cognitive map of India the unity and cohesion of the country would remain drastically impaired. In other words, the nation-making process is liable to remain impeded as long as caste remains recognised, even indirectly, as the basis of state action. Rather, the purpose of ameliorating the lot of the backward communities would be better served by strengthening the country's educational system and providing quality education to all in society including the members of what are called backward castes. Everyone in the society should attend the same system of education regardless of the earning capacity or economic status. This will produce a society which would be psychologically and emotionally homogeneous and well-knit. After 1947, the challenge in India has been to make Indians out of us, who are basically Punjabis, Bengalis, Gujaratis or Brahmins, Thakurs, Jats, Yadavs, Reddys, Khammas, etc. Mandalisation and Indianisation cannot go together: one is centrifugal and the other is centripetal.

Curse

Caste has been India's historic curse, and it is this which is becoming the focus of loyalty under the policy of reservation. It is a dangerous trend which must be firmly discouraged by our national policy planners. The present reservation arrangements have led to the development of powerful vested interests which may thwart reform measures. In fact, so grave is the threat that it would be appropriate to have the entire philosophy and practice of protective discrimination reviewed in a comprehensive and objective way, keeping in mind the tasks of nation-making, state-building and development.

V

THE HIGHER CIVIL SERVICE ENTRY AGE

In India as in many other countries developed as well as developing, the higher civil service offers the most attractive career in society, and the brightest university graduates strive hard to compete for positions in it. The recruitment through a competitive examination in which the best alone hope to be selected is itself a societal recognition. Naturally, the governmental decision to raise the age of entry and the number of chances has evoked deep public interest. The Government of India's decision, announced early in January 1990, to raise the upper age for the higher civil service competitive examination from 26 to 28 years and, later, to 31 for one year only, has made this topic of great interest and significance for society, no less than for the bureaucracy. From the 1990 examination onwards, moreover, the candidates appearing at the civil services competitive examination shall be allowed four chances instead of the hitherto three. As a result of these two concessions, the number of candidates is likely to jump from the present 150,000 to nearly 300,000.

It has been a practice in India — as in other countries — to prescribe both the lower and the upper age for public service recruitment examinations. These have varied from time to time but the basic governing norm has been retained. The lower entry age is so fixed as to correspond broadly with the university graduation age. Naturally, the graduation age has to be interpreted flexibly. It is no less fair to give a reasonable number of chances to the aspiring candidates to take the examination — to offset the whims and caprices which every written examination inevitably entails.

The history of fixation of both lower and upper age is as old as that of the competitive examination itself. When the first competitive examination to the Indian Civil Service, the predecessor of the present Indian Administrative Service, was held in 1855, the candidates admitted to it were to be above 18 and under 23. This was in accordance with the recommendation of the committee on Consideration of the Subject of the Examination of Candidates for the Civil Service of the East India Committee, popularly known as the committee on the Indian Civil Service, or the Macaulay Committee after the name of its chairman.

The lower age of 18, one must note, was a purely notional one with little meaning in real life. In the words of the committee: ". . . except in very rare and extraordinary cases, it is not desirable that a lad should be admitted as early as 18. But we are convinced that, except in very rare and extraordinary cases, no lad of 18 will have any chance of being admitted. . . ."

Five years later, in 1860, the maximum age for admission to the competitive examination was lowered to 22 and in 1865 to 21. In 1866, the minimum age was also reduced from 18 to 17. The committee on the Selection and Training of Candidates for the Indian Civil Service under the chairmanship of Liddell, reporting in 1876, held the view that a competitive examination was better suited to a younger age and accordingly the maximum age was fixed at 19 and minimum age at 17.

By this time, many Indians also started learning English and, quite expectedly, aspiring for positions in the country's civil service. A lowering of age was bound to adversely affect their interests and was universally resented by Indians. Reporting in 1887, the Aitchison Commission, called the Public Service Commission, urged the maximum age to be re-fixed at 23, which was done.

From 1887 till 1905, the age limit for entry into the Indian Civil Service was 21 to 23. In 1906 both the lower age and the upper one were increased by one year. In 1922 the lower age was brought back, to the chagrin of the Indian aspirants, to 21 but the upper age remained unchanged at 24. In 1925, the upper age was reduced to 23, to be restored to 24 after an interval. The age group 21-24 enjoyed the qualification to sit at the competitive examination until India's Independence.

From 1947 until 1971 the candidates could appear at the higher civil service examination between 21 and 24 years of age. In 1972 the upper age was raised to 26 which, in 1979, was further raised by two years. In 1985 the upper age was reduced by two years, and until 1989 it remained fixed at 26 years.

In 1990, the upper age allowed to candidates for the higher civil service examination was again raised to 28 and the number of chances to four. However, for the candidates appearing at the 1990 competitive examination the upper age was even more liberal and fixed at 31 years. Furthermore, as candidates belonging to the scheduled castes and scheduled tribes have been getting a relaxation of five years, the upper age for these categories now stands at 33. One may also note that the upper age for candidates belonging to north eastern states in India is 44 years.

Many advantages are claimed in favour of fixing a higher upper age. Raising the age is to favour the "late starters" in society who generally come from rural areas and the lower classes. A bright child from a lower class or rural area goes to school late and, what is more, gets schooling of no conspicuous quality. These deficiencies can be made up, among others, by age allowance. A higher age is thus an egalitarian measure as it broadens the social base of the country's higher civil service. Other advantages, too, may be claimed for putting the upper age higher — a higher age enables candidates with higher specialised education to enter the higher civil service. The civil service is thus enabled to induct wide-ranging talent available in society which would have the effect of developing the much-needed capabilities in various sectors of administration. Also the higher age would bring into public administration persons possessing a measure of work experience and a number of them would necessarily come from the private sector, which would create a larger perspective in the selected personnel. They would also have fostered wider social affiliations, which would provide, at least in part, an answer to the public criticism of the country's administrators being aloof, arrogant and domineering.

These possible social advantages do not appeal to those in favour of a lower age of entry into the public service. Indeed, the classical British thinking on the question was to keep the age of entry as low as possible, and to have in the syllabus only those subjects which are commonly taught in the universities and for which thus no special preparation is necessary. This was defended on the ground that the competition being very stiff the losers, who would inevitably be far numerous in the society, should not have any regrets for having wasted their precious years in providing themselves with special education which ultimately yielded them no fruits. The number of civil service positions, moreover, being limited to 600 or so, there is little practical wisdom in arousing expectations which just cannot be fulfilled and thus causing them to degenerate into spiralling frustrations. Any liberalisation in age is thus a spurious measure, and counter- productive. It has also been claimed that even during 1978-1986 when the upper age was 28, the age-group 21-24 produced most of the successful candidates, showing that any higher age claims little practical utility. Many other disadvantages are also associated with a higher age for entry. The work experience would in practice mean that the newly recruited have already been exposed to the rather unsavoury life-style prevalent in many sectors of society, which they would later induct into the public service. The talk of wider social affiliations is likely to vitiate the civil service. Besides, a higher age-group does not generally leave in the successful candidates that propensity to receive training which the government provides at institutions like the Lal Bahadur Shastri National Academy of Administration. It was discovered, for instance, that a large number of those in the higher age group entering the civil service during 1978-86 were already married and had children, which prevented full attention to training at the Institute at Mussoorie. Of course, the higher age-group would demand a measure of re-structuring of these training institutions including the teaching faculty and training methodology.

Evaluation

Historically, the argument for a lower age for entry to the civil service was advanced by the British rulers though, it is noteworthy, the Indian public opinion firmly opposed it on the ground that Indian students suffered from many handicaps in preparing for it which higher age could overcome. After independence heralding the exit of the British, it is the Indian bureaucracy which has taken up the British viewpoint and has been opposed to any raising of age. The fact is that the lower age favours the elite sections of society fully aware of the need for planning the career of their offspring and who, moreover, enjoy early and easy access to expensive quality education. It must be noted that the Indian society is not homogeneous economically, socially, educationally and otherwise; and thus viewed, a lower age of entry is bound to affect different segments differently, most disadvantageously placed on this scale being people in rural areas and the lower classes in society. To bring them on a par a higher age seems inevitable at the present stage of the country's development.

The argument that the higher age group implying persons with work experience would induct questionable habits and practices within the public bureaucracy may not be wholly accepted. In India, who has corrupted whom is a moot point; at any rate it is universally acknowledged that the country's civil service is inadequately prepared to carry out responsibilities entrusted to it by society; and its radical restructuring is called for. The higher age may explore a wider social base to draw the civil servants from and these civil servants may bring with them wider social sympathies and less aloofness and arrogance. Moreover, to argue that the candidates recruited under the raised age would not be able to reach the highest level of secretaries to the government as they may retire earlier does not seem to be very logical. The raised age does not imply that all the successful candidates would be near 28. At any rate, a thinking man analyses the strengths and limitations of his prospective career before opting for it. What is more, even now not all members of the IAS are lucky enough to retire from the post of secretary to the government.

A risk, therefore, is worth taking. The present policy of fixing the higher age should be afforded a fair trial and must not be sabotaged by the career bureaucracy. It is also necessary that the recruiters to the higher civil service should not exhibit any bias against the older candidates at the stage of interview. To say that the interview has at best a modificatory role, and not decisive one may not be fully tenable; the maturity of the older group and wider range of its mental faculties may not find as good a reflection in the written papers as in the interviews.

One thing more, from 1978 till 1986 the upper age, as already mentioned, was 28. From 1990 it is again 28 years. One hopes, this is to stay regardless of change of government. What is equally important, frequent change in the age limit introduces an element of uncertainty in the minds of students and makes a nonsense of career planning on their part.

A comment is warranted on increasing the number of chances from three to four. On this issue also, views have differed. The Ramaswami Mudaliar Committee to determine the qualifications for recruitment (1956) preferred a span of two years between the minimum and the maximum limits. The National Front Government has, on the other hand, decided in favour of four chances to the aspiring candidates. The "fourth attempter" gains the benefit of experience of the examinations and acquires the techniques thereof, which may help him in sailing into the list of the successful candidates but he may not be of the stuff the civil service looks for. The innate mental and analytical qualities can quite satisfactorily be tested in the first three examinations.

VI

POSTINGS AND TRANSFERS OF SENIOR PERSONNEL

The year 1990 is unusually memorable in India's recent political history as it is marked by the coming into power by two successive governments other than the Congress — the first lasting for nearly a year and the other one is not even two months' old, both being minority ones. The second one though supported from outside is having only 56 MPs in its Party, depending for its survival on the much bigger party, the Congress (I). The year may rightly be viewed as the year of the National Front, a loose coalition consisting of the Janata Dal, Lok Dal, Telugu Desam, CPI, CPI(M), Assam Gana Parishad, etc.

The period preceding the general election and the taking over of government by the victorious party is generally characterised by an administrative lull, that is, nearly complete inaction in public administration. Policy decisions almost as a rule remain suspended and no civil servant, however mighty, avoids taking initiative. Among the first tasks which the new National Front government under the Prime Ministership of Vishwanath Pratap Singh took up was to initiate a process of transfer of civil servants. This is not constitutionally or statutorily mandated, but the custom has made it so. Civil servants, as one knows, are recruited on the basis of merit and ordained to be neutral and impartial and to serve political parties of all ideological hues with professionalism and devotion. In practice, parties, even individual ministers, choose their own men from the world of the career bureaucracy in whom they have trust and confidence. This is the practice of late, and it is not necessarily restricted to the top layer of the bureaucracy alone though it begins with that. Several secretaries' heads rolled with the coming into power of the National Front government consequent on the defeat of the Congress Party in November 1989, election. Chief among such vulnerable offices were the cabinet secretary and the secretary to the Prime Minister. Gopi Arora, a top-ranking civil servant who had allowed himself to come too close to the former Prime Minister, Rajiv Gandhi, was also included. There were some others too. M.K. Narayanan, Director, Central Intelligence Bureau had kept his organisation above controversy but on the eve of the general election in 1989 let his name be spoiled when he permitted his Bureau to get mixed up with the selection of the Congress candidates for the election. A not too small number of civil servants had moved very close to the politicians in the previous Congress government and thus they appeared to allow themselves to become politicised. Not unnaturally, they became suspects in the eyes of the National Front which was induced to transfer them. Gopi Arora was among the first to be shifted — from the office of the secretary in the Ministry of Finance to the Washington based International Monetary Fund. Bimal Jain, who was personally known to the new Prime Minister, was appointed as Finance secretary on 12 December 1989.

Suresh Mathur, a senior IAS officer, was appointed as secretary of the Ministry of Information and Broadcasting and V.P. Sawhney, additional secretary, banking, took over as secretary, Labour. Anand Ram, who had headed the Special Investigation Team (SIT) which probed the conspiracy to kill Indira Gandhi, was rewarded by Rajiv Gandhi, on the eve of going out of power, with a diplomatic assignment to North Korea. This patently politically-motivated appointment was set at naught by the V.P. Singh government. Similarly, the chairman of the Central Board of Direct Taxes, who had superseded several officers in his hierarchy, was shunted out and thus apparently a previous wrong was righted.

With the change of government it is customary for the members of the Planning Commission to resign to facilitate reconstitution. All the six members resigned early in October 1989. In the spoils fall posts of managing directors of Air-India and Indian Airlines. So are the posts of solicitor-general and advocate-general.

The second major shake-up in the bureaucracy took place on 25 December 1989, when four secretaries were shifted. These were:

Name	*Appointed as:*
S.R. Sankaran	Secretary, Department of Rural Development
M.D. Godbole	Secretary, Department of Petroleum and Natural Gas
R.L. Misra	Secretary, Revenue Department
S.K. Misra	Secretary, Department of Agriculture and Cooperation

On 2 January 1990, the government ordered the reshuffle of several senior-ranking civil servants (secretaries) at the centre, this being the third one since the V.P. Singh government came into power in November 1989. In this reshuffle 16 top officials were given new appointments, the details of more important among them are given below:

Sl. No.	*Name*	*Present Post*	*Shifted as*
1.	Nitish Sengupta	Revenue Secretary	Secretary in the Department of Supply
2.	R.K. Tikku		Secretary (Coordination) in the Cabinet Secretariat
3.	P.H. Vaishnav	Secretary (Coordination) Cabinet Secretariat	Chairman, Public Enterprises Selection Board

4.	Manish Bahal	Secretary, Personnel	Secretary, Tourism
5.	A.V. Ganeshan	Special Secretary, Ministry of Commerce	Civil Aviation Secretary Personnel Secretary
6.	K.N. Ardha-nareswaran		Special Secretary, Ministry of Commerce
7.	R.K. Dhar	Principal Secretary, Hill Areas Development, U.P.	Secretary Department of Textiles
8.	J.C. Jetli		Secretary, Department of Family Welfare
9.	M.M.S. Sri-vastava	Special Secretary, Planning Commission	Secretary, Programme Implementation
10.	K.V.R. Nair		Special Secretary, Planning Commission
11.	R.C. Kapila	Special Commissioner, Scheduled Castes and Tribes, Ministry of Welfare	Additional Secretary, Department of Supply
12.	M.R. Shiva-raman		Additional Secretary, Ministry of Commerce
13.	I.K. Barthakur (Mrs.)	Adviser, Planning Commission	Adviser (of Cabinet rank) Planning Commission

The month of June 1990, saw another spate of bureaucratic transfers, the fourth large-scale reshuffle by V.P. Singh, most affected being the IAS, the new appointments being from its cadre of the 1960 batch:

Sl.No.	*Name*	*New Appointment*
1.	Ramakant Rath	Secretary, Department of Food
2.	L. Ranganathan	Special Secretary, Department of Insurance
3.	Bhaskar Ghosh	Secretary, Department of Culture and Arts
4.	S.V. Giri	Special Secretary, Department of Agriculture
5.	K.K. Mathur	Special Secretary, Department of Power
6.	N. Vithal	Secretary, Department of Electronics

7.	Rajamani	Chairman, Council for Advancement of People's Action and Rural Technology.
8.	A.K. Saikia	Secretary, Planning Commission
9.	Usha Vohra	Secretary, Women's Commission
10.	V. Krishnan	Secretary, Special Commission on Scheduled Castes and Scheduled Tribes
11.	B.K. Goswami	Secretary, Department of Official Languages
12.	R.C. Kapila	Secretary, Sharad Joshi Committee on Agricultural Prices

In November 1990, the V.P. Singh government fell, after remaining in power for nearly one year. It was replaced by an even more vulnerable minority government run by a breakaway group of defectors now constituting the Janata Party(S) with a slender party strength of 56 MPs. For Chandra Sekhar, the new Prime Minister, it was the fulfilment of a dream: he was all these years waiting in the wings to reach the top position in the government. Unlike his immediate predecessors, Chandra Sekhar publicly promised not to effect a major shake-up in the bureaucracy. But, on becoming the Prime Minister, his first major act was to appoint his special secretary, Mr Gautam. Soon after becoming the Prime Minister, Chandra Shekhar is reported to have said at his meeting with the senior civil servants:

> I think Indian bureaucracy is one of the finest one. They should and they would run the administration in close cooperation with their ministerial heads. Only those who are politically affiliated and have personal projudices should be worried.[1]

The Chandra Shekhar government was going slow particularly in the case of political offices like Governors, members of Planning Commission, etc. This was because it was trying hard to convince those still in the parent Janata Dal and to lure them to switch sides. Also, the Janata Dal(S) was at the time unviable, not having enough people of competence and trust.

When a new government takes over, a change in the upper echelons of the bureaucracy is seen in practice to take place. The posts most vulnerable to change are the principal secretary to the Prime Minister and the cabinet secretary. Other positions though are not totally immune, much depending on the disposition of the political chief executive. The individual ministers too show interest its degree depending on their political stature in stalling individual officers who enjoy their confidence and pressurise the power that be. Even state chief ministers lobby for civil servants from their states for postings at the centre. If it is a minority government, the supporting party too exerts pressures, sometimes too heavy to be ignored. T.N. Seshan's appointment as the Chief Election Commissioner under the Chandra Shekhar government is generally explained by Rajiv Gandhi's pleadings on his behalf. Even commercial and industrial houses are known to show interest in bureaucratic postings in especially economic ministries where they have necessarily their dealings. Timing may also be important in matters of postings. It may perhaps be ventured that it may be difficult to transfer the Finance secretary and the revenue secretary when the budget preparation has reached an advanced stage, say, in December and around.

A retaliatory motivation too shapes the transfer practices. As the V.P. Singh government had earlier nominated his own set of officers in critical governmental positions to fit into his own policy directions and ideological orientation, the old group of civil servants may not be the right instruments to implement the policies of the Chandra Shekhar ministry. In other words, the new government was motivated to purge the bureaucracy of the earlier regime's loyalists. The CBI the IB and the Research and Analysis Wing (RAW) must also enjoy the confidence of the political executive and the Chandra Shekhar government brought their own officers to herd them as their existing chiefs had been inducted by the previous regime. Chandra Shekhar's reshuffle of the upper echelons of the bureaucracy had an added feature. It was not only in line with what his immediate predecessors began to do routinely but it had an added dimension of the Congress (I) interests being taken care in postings and transfers. This point has already been referred to but needs to be emphasised.

On 7 December 1990, Chandra Shekhar appointed Surendra Mohan Singh as Adviser to the Prime Minister on Economic Affairs. As regards T.N. Seshan's appointment, the story goes that his appointment as the Chief Election Commissioner was made in the teeth of opposition from the civil service. Even the principal secretary to Prime Minister, B.G., Deshmukh, recommended the name of Mrs Rama Devi to this post: she was already officiating as the CEC. The Law Ministry also recommended her name. T.N. Seshan's appointment was all the more controversial as it was made after withdrawing the recommendation to the President of India in favour of confirming Mrs Rama Devi who, as said earlier, had been officiating in that position. One must note that T.N. Seshan was cabinet secretary under Rajiv Gandhi. Completely forgetting his assurance given in his earlier address to the secretaries, Chandra Shekhar was in the midst of the old shifting game.

On 12 December 1990, the second organised reshuffle in the bureaucracy took place. Three new secretaries were appointed by the Chandra Shekhar government. They were:

Sl. No.	*Name*	*Existing Post*	*Appointed as*
1.	R.C. Kapila	Secretary, Official Language	Secretary, Agriculture and Cooperation
2.	P.V. Krishnaswamy	Secretary, Planning Commission	Secretary, Ministry of Fertilizers
3.	R.L. Misra	Secretary, Revenue	OSD in Department of Health

Chandra Shekhar even changed the CBI chief, apparently to de-emphasise, if not scuttle, the investigations in the Bofors case and the Syed Modi Murder case. Changes were made in the key departments like Home and Economic

Affairs. S.K. Misra, a civil servant very close to Devi Lal, replaced B.G. Deshmukh as the principal secretary to the Prime Minister.

But a major change was yet to come, and it materialised within a week. On 17 December 1990, as many as 15 secretaries to the central government were reshuffled:

Sl.No.	*Name*	*Existing Post*	*New Post Appointed*
1.	Suresh Mathur	Secretary, Ministry of Information and Broad-casting	Secretary, Industrial Development
2.	A.N. Verma	Secretary, Industrial Development	Member Secretary, Planning Commission
3.	Mahesh Prasad	Secretary, Ministry of Environment & Forests	Secretary, Ministry of Information and Broadcasting
4.	R. Rajamani	Director-General, CAPART	Secretary, Ministry of Forest and Environments
5.	R.K. Rath	Secretary, Department of Food and Civil Supplies	Director General, CAPART
6.	P. Tripathi	Secretary, Department of Civil Supplies	Secretary, Depart-ment of Food
7.	B.K. Goswami	Director-General, Tourism	Secretary, Department of Civil Supplies
8.	M. Gobbole	Secretary, Petroleum andNatural Gas	Secretary, Depart-ment of Food Processing Industry
9.	Ashok Chandra	Secretary, Food Processing Industry	Secretary, Petroleum and Natural Gas
10.	K. Ardhanaree-swaran	Special Secretary, Ministry of Commerce	Secretary, Ministry of Textiles
11.	Sovan Kanungo	Additional Secretary, Department of economic ment of Economic Affairs	Secretary, Ministry of Commerce
12.	J.C. Lynn	Establishment Officer	Chairman, Food Corporation of India (Secretary rank)
13.	J.N. Kureshi	Adviser to Governor of J&K	Secretary, Ministry of Welfare
14.	R.K. Dang	Additional Secretary, Ministryof Programme Implementation	Secretary Department of Mines
15.	P.K. Lahiri	Secretary, Ministry of Mines	Secretary Revenue

Contd.

Contd.

Sl.No.	*Name*	*Existing Post*	*New Post Appointed*
16.	Usha Vohra	OSD, National Commission on Women	Special Secretary, Programme Implementation
17.	Mozza Raza	Chairman, Trade Fair Authority	Chairman, TFA (Secretary rank)
18.	P.S. Bhinder	Director-General, CRPF	Director General, Central Industrial Security Force.

All these transfers, one may note, were made by a government which did not receive a direct mandate from the voters, comprising as it was of persons elected on a party ticket different from the one to which they now professed loyalty. What is more, it was a minority government, much more vulnerable than the previous minority ministry and thus had a very fragile base. The breakaway Janata Dal(S) had a pathetically small number of MPs in it — just 54 — which barely crossed the 10 per cent mark — the minimum needed to recognition as a legislative group. As already mentioned, the party had difficulty even in finding enough competent people for appointment to ministerial positions. It had thus to invoke caste, religion, region, etc., as the base for luring people. The exercise of transfers thus seemed to lack legitimacy and often appeared to be in the nature of distribution of loaves and fishes of offices on considerations substantially or largely unrelated to merit. One should not conclude that the transfer game was over only in the above three waves. There were individual transfers from time to time. To give an example, the much-talked about Bhure Lal, a trusted civil servant of V.P. Singh, and working in the Prime Minister's office since 1989 handling Bofors and some other sensitive cases was, on 4 February 1991, shifted to the Ministry of Finance as Financial Adviser in the Department of Expenditure.

Today, transfer of civil servants no longer evokes surprise, as the purists of the Westminster system would imagine. Repetitiveness of the game has worn out its novelty. The stay of an officer is becoming shorter and shorter. Indeed, the higher the level of an officer, more uncertain becomes his stay in his post. The situation in the states is generally even worse: there transfers are effected with almost undisguised aggressiveness and with an obvious fury especially prior to elections. This is despite the fact that the Election Commission of India has not failed to direct the states not to transfer, shortly before and during polling, officers who are directly involved in the polling work. Not very inappropriately did the retiring secretary to the Prime Minister B.G. Deshmukh recently remind that moving bureaucrats "like pawns in a chess board" raises serious questions. This hastens and is a consequence of the politicisation of the higher civil service in the country.

A spoils system, today, prevails in India's personnel administration system, but it is different from the first generation spoils system which prevailed in the earlier phase of personnel evolution in the West. The present spoils system does not make one lose his job altogether: he only gets reshuffled and may thus get a less attractive job with reduced ego value. His security of tenure and salary is constitutionally protected in India. Secondly, the present spoils system operates within the civil service only; in other words, the game is restricted to the higher civil servants only, mostly belonging to the IAS and IPS cadres of diverse states although other services are not immune.

Thirdly, a measure of vindictiveness is not always absent in its operation. At any rate, grace has departed from India's civil service. There are instances of shifting of full-fledged secretaries days or weeks before their retirement. Finally, unlike many countries, where technical qualifications are becoming more and more important criteria in matters of appointment, the grounds motivating spoils in India are different — being ascriptive. In India, loyalty certificates are at a high premium.

Concluding Observation

Transfers and postings, it is well conceded, are a normal process of a modern personnel administration, even a prerequisite of its soundness. A national transfer policy is thus an integral part of human resource development. Transfers are inevitable also. Officials retire or leave and some may even die, thus creating vacancies which are inevitably filled up by moving, vertically as well as horizontally, the already serving civil servants. Promotion, an integral part of a career civil service, does entail change of location. But transfers must be regulated by prudent policies and must be well planned. Too frequent and unrelated changes may have a demoralising impact on the civil services; and it is precisely this which is presently happening in India, causing widespread concern and anxiety to the reformers of the administrative system.

To sum up, the principal factors motivating the present bureaucratic changes are:

1. The age-group of bureaucrats at the top levels of administration gets already high, leaving reduced years of service. Retrements are thus inevitable, necessitating filling up of resultants vacancies.
2. Civil servants are also seen not to respect the divide between politics and civil service, become too close to the previous regime and thus reduce their acceptability to the political successors.
3. Some civil servants manage coveted posts in the government and, not unnaturally, this leads to retaliatory changes in the bureaucracy by the successor government.
4. Those civil servants who acquire an image of getting cold-shouldered by the previous government tend to be treated warmly and befriended by the successor politicians.
5. The personnel practices are tending to become much more aggressive and even normless as one goes down to the state level. Transfers and postings thus tend to degenerate and are recklessly indulged in.

NOTE

1. Quoted in *The Tribune*, 14 November 1989.

VII

THE HIGH-POWER COMMITTEE ON ELECTORAL REFORMS

Changes in the anti-defection law, delimitation of constituencies, rotation of reserved seats and lowering the eligibility age for candidates are among the major proposals put forth by the high-power committee on electoral reforms, headed by Law Minister Dinesh Goswami. The committee, which submitted its report in May 1990, was formed in February 1990.

The committee recommended that the disqualification of a member should be limited to contravention of the party whip in respect of vote of confidence, motion of no-confidence, money bill and vote of thanks to the President (or Governor in the case of state assemblies). Nominated members joining a political party should also be disqualified. Presently this provision is applicable to independent members, but not to nominated members. As a result, several nominated members in the recent past have joined the Congress-I.

On one or two major aspects, the committee has not been able to break any ground. Prior to the constitution of the committee in February, there had been some talk of changing the present election system itself and replacing it by some form of proportional representation, whose advocates included the BJP, CPI-M and a section of the Janata Dal.

Considering the sharp divergence of views among the committee members, a suggestion has been made to leave this matter to an expert committee. At the committee's deliberations, the idea of proportional representation was strongly supported by two independent experts, former Chief Election Commissioner S.L. Shakdhar and retired civil servant L.P. Singh, besides the BJP and CPI-M representatives.

Another important area on which the committee has not been able to make much headway is the issue of state funding of elections. Considering the difficult resource position, the committee has apparently concluded that the time is not ripe for this. It has, however, recommended a small beginning by way of 'state assistance in kind'.

The state assistance, to start with, could be provided in four areas, it has suggested. These could include provision of petrol or diesel for a prescribed number of vehicles for each candidate, making available additional copies of electoral rolls, meeting the hire charges for microphones, and issuing of voters' identity slips by the election machinery itself.

Of the various recommendations made by the committee, at least three will require amendments to the Constitution if they are to be implemented by the government. These include delimitation of constituencies, effecting changes in the anti-defection law and lowering the eligibility age for candidates from 25 to 21 years.

Delimitation of constituencies has been strongly pleaded by the Election Commission for a long time. This is because a good number of constituencies, notably in the urban centre, have become far too large and unwieldy in terms of population because of the steady influx in towns and cities.

There is, however, a constitutional bar to take up delimitation right now. Under one of the earlier statutory amendments, no delimitation is to be taken up until the holding of the census of 2001. The number of seats in Parliament is also to remain frozen until then. The Election Commission's plea has been that while the number of seats could be kept at the same level. The constituencies could be delimited to achieve a fair degree of uniformity in terms of the population represented. A Delimitation Commission will have to be set up if the government is able to come up with the suitable enactment.

A similar long-pending plea of the Election Commission, now upheld by the committee, concerns rotations of reserved seats. There have been representations from many aspiring candidates that they have to go outside their home constituencies to be able to contest.

The suggestion for lowering the age for candidates from 25 to 21 is said to a logical corollary of the earlier action in lowering the voting age from 21 to 18. The suggestion, if accepted, will enable a large number of youths to enter the electoral contest.

The committee's other recommendations include a statutory backing for the Election Commission's model code of conduct, a statutory ban on transfer of officers connected with the election work once the announcement is made, a time-bound programme to issue multipurpose identity cards for all voters and more stringent provisions for booth-capturing. It has been suggested that the Election Commission should be able to order total repoll in respect of booth-capturing malpractices on the basis of reports by its own teams and observers appointed by it, instead of going only by the report of the returning officer.

Definition of booth-capturing, it has said, should be sufficiently broadened to include coercion, intimidation and any form of threat, Booth-capturing itself should be made a cognizable offence. As for by election, the committee has said the Election Commission should hold them within six months of a vacancy arising.

The Congress-I's nominee on the committee, however, has made it clear that his party would not agree with at least some of the recommendations. H.K.L. Bhagat, the party's representative, gave a notice that he would submit a note of dissent on a number of issues dealt with by the committee. One such issue concerns the changes proposed in the anti-defection law. This law had been enacted in 1985 soon after the Congress-I's landslide victory in the general elections under Rajiv Gandhi's leadership. The party is apparently opposed to the dilution of its provisions now. As per the committee's proposal, the present jurisdiction of the Speaker or the chairman to determine defections should be taken away and vested in the President (or in Governor in the case of state legislatures) and the Election Commission.

The committee's recommendations was to be forwarded to the cabinet for necessary approval after which the government was to come up with the package. The Law Minister indicated that the necessary Bill was to be introduced in the current session of Parliament itself. No action followed.

It must be said at the end that no tangible result flowed from this exercise. It was an abortive effort.

VIII

OPEN GOVERNMENT

India is a democracy where sovereignty has been made explicitly to vest in 'we, the people of India', but the citizens do not enjoy free, unhindered access to governmental information, nearly the whole functioning of the government remaining hidden from the people. The government today invades practically every sphere of human endeavour. Yet its working has become increasingly shrouded in mystery. Equally true, information is power; and it has not been uncommon on the part of the government to restrict and suppress information, control it and even manipulate it. Never was citizens' need — and the resultant demand — for information thus more pressing. The demand goes under the name of right to information, right to know, openness in government, transparency in government, etc. The flow of information to the larger society in India is governed by a statute known as the Official Secrets Act of 1923.

The Official Secrects Act

The Official Secrets Act enacted by the colonial rulers to protect their imperial interests, severely restricts the flow of information from the government to the people and has thus the effect of removing a vital base for public discussion of issues and matters on which citizens must remain well-informed or which affect the national interest. Today, a democracy becomes meaningless without an unhindered flow of information on happenings within the public bureaucracy.

Passed on 2 April 1923, the Act consists of 15 sections, of which at least three are critically important — sections 3, 5, and 7. Section 3 defines penalties for spying and has raised not much murmur, being accepted for the country's security. Section 5 deals with wrongful communication etc. of information, it for example, states that if a person who is in possession of a secret information which relates to or is used in a prohibited place or is likely to assist an enemy or the disclosure of which is likely to assist an enemy, prejudice the security of the country or affect adversely our relations with a friendly country, passes on the information to unauthorised persons, he will be guilty of offence punishable with three years imprisonment or fine or both. This, in the whole Act, is the most obnoxious section, and a demand is made to repeal it as forcefully emphasised by the Second Press Commission set up after the internal emergency in the country. Section 7 which deals with people interfering with officers or members of the armed forces says: 'No person in the vicinity of any prohibited place shall obstruct or interfere with any police officer' engaged in guard duty or prohibited place'.

The Government of Independent India thus regulates its communication system with 'we the people of India' along the network of the colonial Official Secrets Act of 1923. What is more, instead of liberalising the Act, after the attainment of Independence, it has been made stiffer as a result of an amendment introduced in 1967. In the process, Parliament not only further sanctified official secrecy but also weakened itself as well as the society *vis-a-vis* the executive.

The Official Secrets Act, 1923 as amended in 1967 provides against two sets of events. First, it is directed against espionage and in this respect has practically left nothing to chance. The provisions covering espionage are made extremely favourable to the state, and an individual can be punished even on the faintest of evidence. For instance, the Act says that it shall not be necessary to show that the accused person was guilty of any particular act prejudicial to the safety or interests of the state; he may be convicted if, from the circumstances of the case or his conduct or his known character as proved, it appeared that his purpose was prejudicial to the safety or interests of the state. What is more, the Act says that a person may be presumed to have been in communication with a foreign agent if he has, either within or without (India), visited a foreign agent or either within or without India, the name or address of, or any other information regarding, a foreign agent has been found in his possession.

The second set of events covered by the Act relates to communication of official information to outsiders. The Act makes it a penal offence for any person holding office under the government wilfully to communicate any official information to any person other than a person to whom he is authorised to communicate it. What is more, it is equally an offence for any person to receive such information. In other words, the statute sets out to punish both 'the thief' and the 'receiver of the stolen goods'. This is contained in section 5 of the Official Secrets Act, 1923 which, as already referred to, is a catch all and there is hardly anything which can escape its staggering provisions.

It has been said that over 2,000 differently worded charges can be framed under section 5. This section, moreover, covers all that happens within the government; all information which a civil servant happens to learn in the course of his duty is official, and is thus covered under it. Even more important, the Act makes a mere receipt of official information an offence. The fact that the information might have been communicated to a person contrary to his desire is irrelevant and does not immunise him even in the least! Furthermore, section 5 relates not only to a civil servant but to other persons also — for instance, contractors having dealings with the government.

It appears rulers are rulers, and even the Government of Independent India does not appear to be ashamed of the Official Secrets Act of 1923. From the Report of the Press Laws inquiry committee it appears that the secrecy law has been invoked on quite a few occasions.

The Janata government (1977-79), which replaced the Congress rule, initially showed inclination towards relaxation of restrictions on the flow of administrative information and to this end it even set up in 1977 a working group consisting of senior secretaries to find out if the Official Secrets Act, 1923 could be modified so as to enable greater dissemination of official information to the public. After labouring for give months, the group came to the conclusion that there was nothing in the Official Secrets Act 1923 which could be said to stand in the way of flow of 'legitimate' information to the people.

This recommendation was not surprising. The very composition of the group ordained the kind of the verdict which ultimately emanated from it.

From the above, the 'catch-all' scope of the Official Secrets Act throttling information, is obvious. It effectively removes the base for public discussion of issues of general interest so vital for healthy democracy. Thus viewed, 'right to know' is being increasingly viewed as an integral component of democracy.

National Front and Right to Know

The National Front which swung into prominence around 1989 promised to the people the right to information in its election manifesto. It declared its intention to include this right as a fundamental right in the Constitution. Its election manifesto said: 'The National Front commits itself to full freedom of the media, autonomous corporations for television and radio and elimination of practices that lead to direcct and indirect arm-twisting of the Press, people's right to information shall be guaranteed through constitutional provisions'. That it was not an empty promise was reiterated by V.P. Singh. In his first address to the nation on radio and television on 3 January 1990, V.P. Singh, the Prime Minister, said: 'For increasing people's control and to curb corruption, if the government functions in full public view, wrong-doing will be greatly minimised. The Official Secrets Act will be amended and we will make the functioning of the government more transparent. Secrecy will be maintained only where the interests of national security and foreign relations so warrant. Free flow of information is a perquisite for democracy. The right to information will be enshrined in our Constitution'. Later, on 20 December 1989, R. Venkataraman, President of India, told a joint session of Parliament among other things that the Official Secrets Act would be suitably amended to ensure citizens' right to information.

At the same time, wind was flowing in favour of transparency in government, several western nations already provide statutorily protected public access to information. The USA passed the Freedom of Information Act in 1964, amending it extensively in 1974. The Scandinavian countries, Austria, France, Holland, Australia, Canada, New Zealand etc. have similar legislation thereby ensuring open government to their respective citizens. Even Great Britain has liberalised its Official Secrets Act, enacted in 1911.

Nor completely insignificant is the development in India. It was in 1981 that the people's insistence on the right to know found itself raised to the status of a constitutional right in the celebrated *S.P. Gupta* vs. *Union of India* case, popularly known as the *Judges' case*. The Supreme Court gave it a some unexpectedly generous interpretation of a fundamental right to freedom of speech, on the principle that certain inarticulated right are immanent and implicit in the enumerated guarantees in the Constitution. The Supreme Court observed: 'The concept of an open government is the direct emanation from the right to know which seems to be implicit in the right to free speech and expression guaranteed under article 19(1)(9)'.

The National Front government which rule in the better part of 1990 exuded a large measure of enthusiasm in taking action on its electoral pledge. A few seminars were organised, of course, hurriedly without much prior preparation and a lot of emphoria was generated on openness in government. Soon after coming into power the National Front government set up a committee on right to information comprising Mufti Mohammed Sayeed (Home Minister), I.K. Gujral

(External Affairs Minister), P. Upendra (Information and Broadcasting Minister), K.P. Unnikrishnan (Surface Transport Minister), George Fernandes (Railway Minister) and R.K. Hedge (deputy chairman of the Planning Commission). An inter-departmental study group to suggest concrete proposals on the proposed right to know even prepared an approach paper suggesting appropriate amendments to the Official Secrets Act. The approach paper is reported to have been even considered by the committee of secretaries.

But the subsequent steps are not encouraging. In the past too, the government under the Janata Party (1977-79) did show its willingness to liberalise the stringent Act of 1923. But it soon backtracked and we are where we were. The government should not take shelter under the view, as some jurists do, that article 19 of the Constitution concerning freedom of expression is a sufficient safeguard against hindering of free flow of the information to the people. It would be sad if India were to remain content with such a complacent view. It is equally necessary that the existing rule that all government information should be held secret for thirty years should be amended.

India thus continues to be stubborn in sharing its information with the citizens. A number of key reports thus remain hidden from the public knowledge. These include the Henderson-Brooks report on the 1962 north-east military defeat during the Chinese aggression, the L.P. Singh Report on reforming the Intelligence Bureau and the Central Bureau of Investigation, the Intelligence Bureau's report to the Home Minister on the flow of foreign money to political parties, the Thakkar Commission report on the Indira Gandhi's assassination (only sections of it were later published), etc.

It is high time to scrap the Official Secrets Act, and replace it by a new Right to Information Act which should clearly demarcate the fields in which official secrecy would be permissible. But a mere statutory measure is not enough. The right to know must be enshrined in the Constitution itself as a fundamental right. At the same time, while openness in government is an unassailable need, areas like defence, national security, commercial secrecy, citizens' privacy shall have to remain protected.

IX

PRASAR BHARATI

That the All-India (AIR) Radio should be released from the government's direct control and its management instead should vest in a corporation autonomous of the government is a long standing demand, dating back to the colonial days when broadcasting first began in India. Asoka Chanda examining the question of management in the early sixties had recommended a corporation form of organisation for running the radio. Later, television system emerged. This demonstrated the awesome power of the government — that is party in power — in controlling the minds of the people. Demand for autonomy of the radio and television became a crying need. But no action ensued. When the Janata government came into power in 1977 a committee on Mass Media under Verghese was appointed. The Verghese Committee on Mass Media recommended a public corporation for running the mass media. Commenting on the Verghese Report, the then Information and Broadcasting Minister, L.K. Advani, observed: 'The Verghese Committee had recommended the creation of an independent, constitutional entity, parallel to the judiciary on which the legislature has no control. No, we cannot accept it'. He continued: 'We had conceived of autonomy, while the committee conceived of independence'.

The Prasar Bharati Bill which was unanimously passed by the Lok Sabha in August 1990 provides for an autonomous corporation — to be known is the Broadcasting Corporation of India to run the electronic media of radio and television in the country. The present Bill is broadly based on the Prasar Bharati Bill of 1979 first introduced by the Janata Party. The enactment of the statute is fulfilment of the pledge made by the National Front in its election manifesto of 1989. Being a minority government, the National Front had necessarily to depend on the support of other parties. For the Bill the National Front secured approval of Congress-I, the Leftist Parties, and the Bharatiya Janata Party. It certainly was not an easy task. In the course of the Bill's discussion in the Lok Sabha over 400 amendments were moved out of which the government adopted 65 of them.

As the Act postulates, the All India Radio and the Doordarshan are to be run by a fifteen member-board of governors whose even part-time members will include representatives of the artistic, academic and professional worlds. They are to be appointed for a term of six years.

The chairman as well as members of the board of governors shall be appointed by the President of India on the recommendations of a committee consisting of the chairman of the council of states (upper house of Parliament), the chairman of the Press Council of India and a nominee of the President. The procedure to remove them before the expiry of their term will follow that required for removal of the chairman and the members of the UPSC. The board is to be answerable to a 22-member parliamentary committee which is to monitor whether it functions within the ambit of the Act's provisions. Also, there is to be an 11-member Broadcasting Council, appointed by the President of India which, like the Press Council, is to examine complaints against the corporation. Should the government seek information it considers necessary and this includes the sources of broadcasting journalists, the board of governors will have to provide it. In case it does not give such information or persistently defaults in complying with such directives which the government is empowered to issue, the government can ask Parliament to approve punitive action including supersession of the board. But the period of supersession is not to exceed six months. Likewise, if the parliamentary committee finds the corporation transgressing its powers, it may take its complaint to Parliament about the board's behaviour and recommend its supersession by the President of India. These provisions are calculated to make the corporation accountable both to Parliament and the government. This is necessary in national interest.

The reach of the electronic media today is of an unprecedented scale: the radio at present reaches 97 per cent of the population and the television 76 per cent. A government has every temptation to retain a strangle hold on them. In this respect the track record of all political parties is more or less dismal. Thus all the rulers look alike so far as the use — or misuse — of electronic media is concerned. They have manipulated the media ruthlessly to promote their own partisan even personal ends. The Prasar Bharati Act delinks Doordarshan and radio from the executive in day-to-day functioning leaving the media to professionals in these two wings of the corporation free to decide the contents without interference.

The Prasar Bharati Act (Annexure A) has the making of inaugurating to inaugurate a new information order in the country. It certainly releases the radio and the Doordarshan from the clutches of the executive, which is a distinct gain. But one is not sure if the Corporation will be able to function with autonomy, released from executive's day-to-day control over the electronic media. Much depends on the character and calibre of the governors to be appointed by the government. The balance between autonomy and governmental control is always uneasy. The Act has not yet become operative as the government has not notified the date of its commencement. Significant in this respect is the change in government at the centre. The succeeding Chandra Shekhar government has not yet give indication of how much priority it attaches to the Act.

It was after a great deal of debate and drama that the Prasar Bharati Bill was passed on 6 September 1990 and soon after the President's assent was given. By 1 April 1991 the Prasar Bharati Corporation was to begin functioning. Since the Chandra Shekhar government took over, all work on setting up the Corporation came to a standstill. Even the special call set up in the Ministry of Information and Broadcasting for the Prasar Bharati has for all practical purposes would up. The director who was dealing with it in the Ministry has gone on study leave and the deputy secretary of the cell is working as officer on special duty to the minister. The statute as said earlier had not yet come into force.

The Act is to come into force when notified by the government. Before the exit of the V.P. Singh regime, P. Upendra, the Minister for Information and Broadcasting, had worked out a time frame for the formalities to be completed. Since the collapse of that government, the fate of the Act is rather uncertain. It is to be noted that the Congress never really favoured the setting up of the Corporation. It was brought around by P. Upendra, by accepting all its amendments even though this has led to a rather watered down law. The Congress (I) never approved of an independent entity for the electronic media though it supports the concept of functional autonomy whatever it may mean. The concept of a board of professional media persons is ridiculed in many quarters. 'No one is apolitical', it is said. Even foreign agencies can control the board through the multinationals' advertising on the electronic media.

Another major problem to confront the government will be of accommodation of the 38,000 staff of Doordarshan and AIR in the Corporation. On the date when the Corporation is formed, all the employee will be considered on deputation to it. After the service rules are spelt out by the Corporation these employees will be given the option of staying with the Corporation or reverting to the government. For most people in radio and television this is a notional option. If they want not to stay with the Corporation their names are to be forwarded to a 'surplus cell' of the government from there they are to be picked by other government departments. But those in AIR and Doordarshan may not find too many takers because they have acquired special skills that not everybody has use for. Half of those in the central information Service, recruited through the Union Public Service Commission (UPSC), are working with AIR and Doordarshan. There are not enough posts to absorb them should they opt to come back to their parent cadre. Several government servants, especially those in the engineering department of AIR and Doordarshan, are reluctant to lose the benefits of government service. The engineers in particular have been suggesting that the government create a structure whereby the hardware and the engineers continue to remain with the government. They further say that the Corporation, as envisaged, would be unwieldy so there should be two or three separate corporations working under a common broadcasting authority.

ANNEXURRE A

THE PRASAR BHARATI (BROADCASTING CORPORATION OF INDIA) ACT, 1990

An Act to provide for the establishment of a Broadcasting Corporation of India, to be known as Prasar Bharati, to define its composition, functions and powers and to provide for matters connected therewith or incidental thereto.

BE it enacted by Parliament in the Forty-first Year of the Republic of India as follows:

CHAPTER I

PRELIMINARY

1. *Short title, extent and commencement:* (1) This Act may be called the Prasar Bharati (Broadcasting Corporation of India) Act, 1990.

(2) It extends to the whole of India.

(3) It shall come into force on such date as the central government may, by notification, appoint.

2. *Definitions:* In this Act, unless the context otherwise requires —

(a) "Akashvani" means the offices, stations and other establishments, by whatever name called, which, immediately before the appointed day formed part of or were under the Director-General, All India Radio of the Union Ministry of Information and Broadcasting;

(b) "appointed day" means the date appointed under section 3;

(c) "broadcasting" means the dissemination of any form of communication like signs, signals, writing, pictures, images and sounds of all kinds by transmission of electro-magnetic waves through space or through cables intended to be received by the general public either directly or indirectly through the medium of relay stations and all its grammatical variations and cognate expressions shall be construed accordingly.

(d) "Board" means the Prasar Bharati Board;

(e) "Broadcasting Council" means the Council established under section 14;

(f) "Chairman" means the chairman of the Corporation appointed under section 4;

(g) "Corporation" means the Prasar Bharati (Broadcasting Corporation of India) established under section 3;

(h) "Doordarshan" means the offices, kendras and other establishments, by whatever name called, which, immediately before the appointed day, formed part of or were under the Directorate-General, Doordarshan of the Union Ministry of Information and Broadcasting;

(i) "Elected Member" means a member elected under section 3;

(j) "Executive Member" means the executive member appointed under section 4;

(k) "Kendra" means by telecasting centre with studios or transmitters or both and includes a relay station;

(l) "Member" means a member of the Board;

(m) "Member (Finance)" means the Member (Finance) appointed under section 4;

(n) "Member (Personnel)" means the Member (Personnel) appointed under section 4;

(o) "Nominated Member" means the member nominated by the Union Ministry of Information and Broadcasting under section 3;

(p) "Non-lapsable Fund" means the Fund created from the commercial revenues of Akashvani and Doordarshan to meet expenditure on certain schemes;

(q) "Notification" means a notification published in the Official Gazette;

(r) "Part-time Member" means a part-time member of the Board appointed under section 4, but does not include an *ex officio* member, the nominated member or an elected member;

(s) "Prescribed" means prescribed by rules made under this Act;

(t) "Recruitment Board" means a board established under sub-section (1) of section 10;

(u) "Regulations" means regulations made by the Corporation under this Act;

(v) "Station" means any broadcasting station with studios or transmitters or both and includes a relay station;

(w) "Whole-time Member" means the executive member, Member (Finance) or Member (Personnel);

(x) "Year" means the financial year.

CHAPTER II

PRASAR BHARATI (Broadcasting Corporation of India)

3. *Establishment and composition of Corporation:* (1) With effect from such date as the central government may by notification appoint in this behalf, there shall be established for the purposes of this Act a Corporation, to be known as the Prasar Bharati (Broadcasting Corporation of India).

(2) The Corporation shall be a body corporate by the name aforesaid, having perpetual succession and a common seal with power to acquire, hold and dispose of property, both movable and immovable, and to contract, and shall by the said name sue and be sued.

(3) The headquarters of the Corporation shall be at New Delhi and the Corporation may establish offices, kendras or stations at other places in India and, with the previous approval of the central government, outside India.

(4) The general superintendence, direction and management of the affairs

of the Corporation shall vest in the Prasar Bharati Board which may exercise all such powers and do all such acts and things as may be exercised or done by the Corporation under this Act.

(5) The Board shall consist of—

(a) a chairman;
(b) one executive member;
(c) one Member (Finance);
(d) one Member (Personnel);
(e) six part-time members;
(f) Director-General (Akashvani) *ex officio*;
(g) Director-General (Doordarshan), *ex officio*;
(h) one representative of the Union Ministry of Information and Broadcasting, to be nominated by that Ministry; and
(i) two representatives of the employees of the Corporation, of whom one shall be elected by the engineering staff from amongst themselves and one shall be elected by the other employees from amongst themselves.

(6) The Corporation may appoint such committees as may be necessary for the efficient performance, exercise and discharge of its functions, powers and duties:

Provided that all or a majority of the members of each committee shall be members and a member of any such committee who is not a member shall have only the right to attend meetings of the committee and take part in the proceedings thereof, but shall not have the right to vote.

(7) The Corporation may associate with itself, in such manner and for such purposes as may be provided by regulations, any person whose assistance or advice it may need in complying with any of the provisions of this Act and a person so associated shall have the right to take part in the discussions of the Board relevant to the purposes for which he has been associated, but shall not have the right to vote.

(8) No act or proceeding of the Board or of any committee appointed by it under sub-section (6) shall be invalidated merely by reason of—

(a) any vacancy in, or any defect in the constitution of, the Board or such committee; or
(b) any defect in the appointment of a person acting as a member or a member of such committee; or
(c) any irregularity in the procedure of the Board or such committee not affecting the merits of the case.

4. *Appointment of Chairman and other Members:* (1) The chairman and the other members except the *ex officio* members, the nominated member and the elected members shall be appointed by the President of India on the recommendation of a committee consisting of—

(a) the chairman of the Council of states, who shall be the chairman of the committee;

(b) the chairman of the Press Council of India established under section 4 of the Press Council Act, 1978; and

(c) one nominee of the President of India.

(2) No appointment, of a member shall be invalidated merely by reason of any vacancy in, or any defect in the constitution of, the committee appointed under sub-section (1).

(3) The chairman and the part-time members shall be persons of eminence in public life; the executive member shall be a person having special knowledge or practical experience in respect of such matters as administration, management, broadcasting, education, literature, culture, arts, music, dramatics or journalism; the member (Finance) shall be a person having special knowledge or practical experience in respect of financial matters and the Member (Personnel) shall be a person having special knowledge or practical experience in respect of personnel management and administration.

(4) The recommendations made by the committee constituted under sub-section (1) shall be binding for the purposes of appointments under this section.

5. *Powers and functions of Executive Member:* The executive member shall be the chief executive of the Corporation and shall, subject to the control and supervision of the board, exercise such powers and discharge such functions of the Board as it may delegate to him.

6. *Term of office, conditions of service, etc., of Chairman and other members:* (1) The chairman shall be part-time member and shall hold office for a term of six years from the date on which he enters upon his office.

(2) The executive member, the Member (Finance) and the Member (Personnel) shall be whole-time members and every such member shall hold office for a term of six years from the date on which he enters upon his office or until he attains the age of sixty-two years, whichever is earlier.

(3) The term of office of part-time members shall be six years, but one-third of such members shall retire on the expiration of every second year.

(4) The term of office of an elected member shall be two years or till he ceases to be an employee of the Corporation, whichever is earlier.

(5) As soon as may be after the establishment of the Corporation, the President of India may, be order, make such provision as he thinks fit for curtailing the term of office of some of the part-time members then appointed in order that one-third of the members holding office as such part-time members shall retire in every second year thereafter.

(6) Where before the expiry of the term of the office of a person holding the office of chairman, or any other member, a vacancy arises, for any reason whatsoever, such vacancy shall be deemed to be a casual vacancy and the person appointed or elected to fill such vacancy shall hold office for the unexpired period of the term for which his predecessor in office would have held office if such vacancy had not arisen.

(7) The whole-time members shall be the employees of the Corporation and as such shall be entitled to such salaries and allowances and shall be subject to such conditions of service in respect of leave, pension (if any),

provident fund and other matters as may be prescribed:

Provided that the salaries and allowances and the conditions of service shall not be varied to their disadvantage after their appointment.

(8) The chairman and part-time members shall be entitled to such allowances as may be prescribed.

7. *Removal and suspension of Chairman and Members:* (1) Subject to the Provisions of sub-section (3), the chairman or any other members, except an *ex officio* member, the nominated member, and an elected member, shall only be removed from his office by order of the President of India on the ground of misbehaviour after the Supreme Court, on a reference being made to it by the President has, on inquiry held in accordance with such procedure as the Supreme Court may by rules provide, reported that the chairman or such other member, as the case may be, ought, on such ground, be removed.

(2) The President may suspend from office the chairman or other member, except an *ex officio* member, the nominated member or an elected member, in respect of whom a reference has been made to the Supreme Court under sub-section (1) until the President has, passed orders on receipt of the report of the Supreme Court on such reference.

(3) Notwithstanding anything contained in sub-section (1), the President may, by order, remove the chairman or any whole-time member from his office if such chairman or such whole-time member—

(a) ceases to be a citizen of India; or
(b) is adjudged an insolvent; or
(c) engages during his term of office in any paid employment outside the duties of his office; or
(d) is convicted of any offence involving moral turpitude; or
(e) is, in the opinion of the President, unfit to continue in office by reason of infirmity of body or mind:
Provided that the President may, be order, remove any part-time member from his office if he is adjudged an insolvent or is convicted of any offence involving moral turpitude or where he is in the opinion of the President unfit to continue in office by reason of infirmity of body or mind.

(4) If the chairman or any whole-time member except any *ex officio* member the nominated member, or any elected member is, or becomes in any way concerned or interested in any contract or agreement made by or on behalf of the Corporation or the Government of India or the government of a state or, participates in any way in the profit thereof, or in any benefit or emolument arising therefrom than as a member, and in common with other members of an incorporated company, he shall, for the purposes of sub-section (1), be deemed to be guilty of misbehaviour.

(5) If a part-time member is, or becomes in any way concerned, or interested in any contract or agreement made by or on behalf of the Corporation, he shall for the purposes of sub-section (1), be deemed to be guilty of misbehaviour.

(6) The chairman or any other member may resign his office by giving

notice thereof in writing to the President of India and on such resignation being accepted, the chairman or other member shall be deemed to have vacated his office.

8. *Meetings of Board:* (1) The Board shall meet at such times and places and shall observe such rules of procedure in regard to the transaction of business at its meeting (including the quorum at meetings) as may be provided by regulations:

Provided that there shall not be less than six meetings every year but three months shall not intervene between one meeting and the next meeting.

(2) A member shall be deemed to have vacated his office if he absents himself for three consecutive meetings of the Board without the leave of the chairman.

(3) The chairman shall preside at the meetings of the Board and if for any reason he is unable to attend any meeting, the executive member and in the absence of both, any other member elected by the members present at such meeting, shall preside at the meeting.

(4) All questions which come up before any meeting of the Board shall be decided by a majority of the votes of the members present and voting and, in the event of an equality of votes, the chairman, or in his absence, the person presiding shall have and exercise a second or casting vote.

9. *Officers and other employees of Corporation:* (1) Subject to such control, restrictions and conditions as may be prescribed, the Corporation may appoint, after consultation with the Recruitment Board, the Director-General (Akashvani), The Director General (Doordarshan) and such other officers and other employees as may be necessary.

(2) The method of recruitment of such officers and employees and all others matters connected therewith and the conditions of service of such officers and other employees shall be such as may be provided by regulations.

10. *Establishment of Recruitment Board:* (1) The Corporation shall, as soon as may be, after the appointed day and in such manner and subject to such conditions and restrictions as may be prescribed, establish for the purposes of section 9, one or more Recruitment Board consisting wholly of persons other than the members, officers and other employees of the Corporation:

Provided that for the purposes of appointment to the posts carrying scales of pay which are not less than that of a joint secretary to the central government, the Recruitment Board shall consist of the chairman, other members, the *ex officio* members, the nominated member and the elected members.

(2) The qualifications and other conditions of service of the members constituting the Recruitment Board and the period for which such members shall hold office, shall be such as may be prescribed.

11. *Transfer of service of existing employees to Corporation:* (1) Where the central government has ceased to perform any functions which under section 12 are the functions of the Corporation, it shall be lawful for the central government to transfer, by order and with effect from such date or dates as may be specified

in the order, to the Corporation any of the officers or other employees serving in the Akashvani or Doordarshan and engaged in the performance of those functions:

Provided that no order under this sub-section shall be made in relation to any officer or other employee in the Akashvani or Doordarshan who has, in respect of the proposal of the central government to transfer such officer or other employee to the Corporation, intimated within such time as may be specified in this behalf by the central government, his intention of not becoming an employee of the Corporation.

(2) The provisions of sub-section (1) shall also apply to the members of the Indian Information Service, the central Secretariat Service or any other service or to persons borne on cadres outside Akashvani and Doordarshan who have been working in Akashvani or Doordarshan immediately before the appointed day:

Provided that where any such member intimates, within the time specified in sub-section (1) his intention of not becoming an employee of the Corporation but to continue on deputation, he may be allowed to continue on deputation in accordance with such terms and conditions as may be prescribed.

(3) In making an order under sub-section (1), the central government shall, as far as may be, take into consideration the functions which the Akashvani or as the case may be, Doordarshan has ceased or ceases to perform and the area in which such functions have been or are performed.

(4) An officer or other employee transferred by an order under sub-section (1) shall, on and from the date of transfer, cease to be an employee of the central government and become an employee of the Corporation with such designation as the Corporation may determine and shall, subject to the provisions of sub-sections (5) and (6) be governed by such regulations as may be made as respects remuneration and other conditions of service including pension leave and provident fund and shall continue to be an officer or other employee of the Corporation unless and until his employment is terminated by the Corporation.

(5) Every officer or other employee transferred by an order made under sub-section (1) shall, within six months from the date of transfer, exercise his option, in writing, to be governed—

(a) by the scale of pay applicable to the post held by him in the Akashvani or Doordarshan immediately before the date of transfer or by the scale applicable to the post under the Corporation to which he is transferred;

(b) by the leave, provident fund, retirement or other terminal benefits admissible to employees of the central government in accordance with the rules or orders of the central government, as amended from time to time, or the leave, provident fund or other terminal benefit admissible to the employees of the Corporation under the regulations, and such option once exercised under this Act shall be final:

Provided that the option exercised under clause (a) by an officer or other employee shall be applicable only in respect of the post under the Corporation to which such officer or other employee is transferred and on appointment to a higher post under the Corporation he shall be eligible only for the scale of pay applicable to such higher post:

Provided further that if immediately before the date of his transfer any such officer or other employee is officiating in a higher post under the government either in a leave vacancy or any other vacancy of a specified duration, his pay on transfer shall be protected for the unexpired period of such vacancy and thereafter he shall be entitled to the scale of pay applicable to the post under the government to which he would have reverted or to the scale of pay applicable to the post under the Corporation to which he is transferred, whichever he may opt:

Provided also that when an officer or other employee serving in the Union Ministry of Information and Broadcasting or in any of its attached or subordinate offices is promoted to officiate in a higher post in the ministry or office subsequent to the transfer to the Corporation of any other officer or employee senior to him in that ministry or office before such transfer, the officer or other employee who is promoted to officiate in such higher post shall, on transfer to the Corporation, be entitled only to the, scale of pay applicable to the post he would have held but for such promotion or the scale of pay applicable to the post under the Corporation to which he is transferred, whichever he may opt.

(6) No officer or other employee transferred by an order made under sub-section (1) or sub-section (2)—

(a) shall be dismissed or removed by an authority subordinate to that competent to make a similar of equivalent appointment under the Corporation as may be specified in the regulations;

(b) shall be dismissed or removed or reduced in rank except after an inquiry in which he has been informed of the charges against him and given a reasonable opportunity of being heard in respect of those charges:

Provided that where it is proposed after such inquiry to impose upon him any such penalty, such penalty may be imposed on the basis of evidence adduced during such inquiry and it shall not be necessary to give such person an opportunity of making representation on the proposed penalty:

Provided further that clause (b) shall not apply where an officer or other employee is dismissed or removed or reduced in rank on the ground of conduct which has led to his conviction on a criminal charge.

12. *Function and powers of Corporation:* (1) Subject to the provisions of this Act, it shall be the primary duty of the Corporation to organise and conduct public broadcasting services to inform, educate and entertain the public and to ensure a balanced development of broadcasting on radio and television.

Explanation — For the removal of doubts, it is hereby declared that the provisions of this section shall be in addition to, and not in derogation of, the provisions of the Indian Telegraph Act, 1885.

(2) The Corporation shall, in the discharge of its functions, be guided by, the following objectives, namely—

(a) upholding the unity and integrity of the country and the values enshrined in the Constitution;
(b) safeguarding the citizen's right to be informed freely, truthfully and objectively on all matters of public interest, national or international, and presenting a fair and balanced flow of information including contrasting view without advocating any opinion or ideology of its own;
(c) paying special attention to the fields of education and spread of literacy, agriculture, rural development, environment, health and family welfare and science and technology;
(d) providing adequate coverage to the diverse cultures and languages of the various regions of the country by broadcasting appropriate programmes;
(e) providing adequate coverage to sports and games so as to encourage healthy competition and the spirit of sportsmanship;
(f) providing appropriate programmes keeping in view the special needs of the youth;
(g) informing and stimulating the national consciousness in regard to the status and problems of women and paying special attention to the upliftment of women;
(h) promoting social justice and combating exploitation, inequality and such evils as untouchability and advancing the welfare of the weaker sections of the society;
(i) safeguarding the rights of the working classes and advancing their welfare;
(j) serving the rural and weaker sections of the people and those residing in border regions, backward or remote areas;
(k) providing suitable programmes keeping in view the special needs of the minorities and tribal communities;
(l) taking special steps to protect the interests of children, the blind, the aged, the handicapped and other vulnerable sections of the people;
(m) promoting national integration by broadcasting in a manner that facilitates communication in the languages in India; and facilitating the distribution of regional broadcasting services in every state in the languages of that state;
(n) providing comprehensive broadcast coverage through the choice of appropriate technology and the best utilisation of the broadcast frequencies available and ensuring high equality reception;
(o) promoting research and development activities in order to ensure that radio and television broadcast technology are constantly updated; and
(p) expanding broadcasting facilities by establishing additional channels of transmission at various levels.

(3) In particular, and without prejudice to the generality of the foregoing provisions, the Corporation may take such steps as it thinks fit

(a) to ensure that broadcasting is conducted as a public service to provide and produce programmes;

(b) to establish a system for the gathering of news for radio and television;

(c) to negotiate for purchase of, or otherwise acquire, programmes and rights of privileges in respect of sports and other events, films, serials occasions, meetings, functions or incidents of public interest, for broadcasting and to establish procedures for the allocation of such programmes, rights or privileges to the services;

(d) to establish and maintain a library or libraries of radio, television and other materials.

(e) to conduct or commission from time to time, programmes, audience research, market or technical service, which may be released to such persons and in such manner and subject to such terms and conditions as the Corporation may think fit;

(f) to provide such other services as may be specified by regulations.

(4) Nothing in sub-sections (2) and (3) shall prevent the Corporation from managing on behalf of the central government and in accordance with such terms and conditions as may be specified by that government the broadcasting of External Services and monitoring of broadcasts made by organisations outside India on the basis of arrangements made for reimbursement of expenses by the central government.

(5) For the purposes of ensuring that adequate time is made available for the promotion of the objectives set out in this section, the central government shall have the power to determine the maximum limit of broadcast time in respect of the advertisement.

(6) The Corporation shall be subject to no civil on the ground merely that it failed to comply with any of the provisions of this section.

(7) The Corporation shall have power to determine and levy fees and other service charges for or in respect of the advertisements and such programmes as may be specified by regulations:

Provide that the fees and other service charges levied and collected under this sub-section shall not exceed such limits as may be determined by the central government, from time to time.

13. *Parliamentary Committee:* (1) There shall be constituted a committee consisting of twenty-two members of Parliament, of whom fifteen from the House of the People to be elected by the members thereof and seven from the Council of States to be elected by the members thereof in accordance with the system of proportional representation by means of the single transferable vote, to oversee that the Corporation discharges its functions in accordance with the provisions of this Act and, in particular, the objectives set out in section 12 and submit a report thereon to Parliament.

(2) The committee shall function in accordance with such rules as may be made by the Speaker of the House of the People.

14. *Establishment of Broadcasting Council, term of office and removal etc., of members thereof:* (1) There shall be established, by notification, as soon as may be after the appointed day, a Council, to be known as the Broadcasting

Council, to receive and consider complaints referred to in section 15 and to advise the Corporation in the discharge of its functions in accordance with the objectives set out in section 12.

(2) The Broadcasting Council shall consist of—

(i) a President and ten other members to be appointed by the President of India from amongst persons of eminence in public life;

(ii) four members of Parliament, of whom two from the House of the People to be nominated by the Speaker thereof and two from the Council of States to be nominated by the chairman thereof.

(3) The President of the Broadcasting Council shall be a whole-time member and every other member shall be a part-time member and the President or the part-time member shall hold office as such for a term of three years from the date on which he enters upon his office.

(4) The Broadcasting Council may constitute such number of Regional Councils as it may deem necessary to aid and assist the Council in the discharge of its functions.

(5) The President of the Broadcasting Council shall be entitled to such salary and allowances and shall be subject to such conditions of service in respect of leave pension (if any), provident fund and other matters as may by prescribed:

Provided that the salary and allowances and the conditions of service shall not be varied to the disadvantage of the President of the Broadcasting Council after his appointment.

(6) The other members of the Broadcasting Council and the members of the Regional Council constitute under sub-section (4) shall be entitled to such allowances as may be prescribed.

15. *Jurisdiction of and the procedure to be followed by, Broadcasting Council:* (1) The Broadcasting Council shall receive and consider complaints from—

(i) any person or group of persons alleging that a certain programme or broadcast or the functioning of the Corporation in specific cases or in general is not in accordance with the objectives for which the Corporation is established;

(ii) any person (other than an officer or employees of the Corporation) claiming himself to have been treaded unjustly or unfairly in any manner (including unwarranted invasion of privacy, misrepresentation, distortion or lack of objectivity) in connection with any programme broadcast by the Corporation.

(2) A complaint under sub-section (1) shall be made in such manner and with in such period as may be specified by regulations.

(3) The Broadcasting Council shall follow such procedure as it thinks fit for the disposal of complaints received by it

(4) If the complaint is found to be justified either wholly or in part, the Broadcasting Council shall advise the executive member to take appropriate action.

(5) If the executive member is unable to accept the recommendation of the Broadcasting Council, he shall place such recommendation before the Board for its decision thereon.

(6) If the Board is also unable to accept the recommendation of the Broadcasting Council, it shall record its reasons therefore and inform the Broadcasting Council accordingly.

(7) Notwithstanding anything contained in sub-sections (5) and (6), where the Broadcasting Council deems it appropriate, it may, for reasons to be recorded in writing, required the Corporation to broadcast its recommendations with respect to a complaint in such manner as the Council may deem fit.

CHAPTER III

ASSETS, FINANCES AND ACCOUNTS

16. *Transfer of certain assets, liabilities, etc. of central government to Corporation:* As from the appointed day—

(a) all property and assets (including the Non-lapsable Fund) which immediately before that day vested in the central government for the purpose of Akashvani or Doordarshan or both shall stand transferred to the Corporation on such terms and conditions as may be determined by the central government and the book value of all such property and assets shall be treated as the capital provided by the central government to the Corporation;

(b) all debts, obligations and liabilities incurred, all contracts entered into and all matters and things engaged to be done by, with or for the central government immediately before such day for or in connection with the purposes of Akashvani or Doordarshan or both shall be deemed to have been incurred, entered into and engaged to be done by, with or for the Corporation;

(c) all sums of money due to the central government in relation to the Akashvani or Doordarshan or both immediately before such day shall be demanded to be due to the Corporation;

(d) all suits and other legal proceedings instituted or which could have been instituted by or against the central government immediately before such day for any matter in relation to the Akashvani or Doordarshan or both may be continued or instituted by or against the Corporation.

17. *Grants, etc., by central government:* For the purposes of enabling the Corporation to discharge its functions efficiently under this Act, the central government may, after due appropriation made by Parliament by law in this behalf, pay to the Corporation in each financial year—

(i) the proceeds of the broadcast receiver licence fees, it any, as reduced by the collection charges; and

(ii) such other sums of money as that government considers necessary, by way of equity, grant-in-aid or loan.

18. *Fund of Corporation:* (1) The Corporation shall have its own fund all the receipts of the Corporation (including the amounts which stand transferred to the Corporation under section 16) shall be credited to the Fund and all payments by the Corporation shall be made therefrom.

(2) All moneys belonging to the Fund shall be deposited in one or more nationalised banks in such manner as the Corporation may decide.

(3) The Corporation may spend such sums as it thinks fit for performing its functions under this Act and such sums shall be treated as expenditure payable out of the Fund of the Corporation.

Explanation — For the purposes of this section, "nationalised bank" means a corresponding new bank specified in the First Schedule to the Banking Companies (Acquisition and Transfer of Undertakings) Act, 1970 or a corresponding new bank specified in the First Schedule to the Banking Companies (Acquisition and Transfer of Undertaking) Act, 1980.

19. *Investment of moneys:* The Corporation may invest its moneys in the securities of the central government or any state government or in such other manner as may be prescribed.

20. *Annual Financial Statement of the Corporation:* (1) The Corporation shall prepare, in each financial year, an Annual Financial Statement for the next financial year showing separately—

(a) the expenditure which is proposed to be met from the internal resources of the Corporation; and
(b) the sums required from the central government to meet other expenses and distinguishing—

(i) revenue expenditure from other expenditure; and
(ii) non-plan expenditure from plan expenditure.

(2) The Annual Financial Statement shall be prepared in such form and forwarded at such time to the central government for its approval as may be agreed to by that government and the Corporation.

21. *Accounts and audit of Corporation:* (1) The Corporation shall maintain proper accounts and other relevant records and prepare an annual statement of accounts in such form and in such manner as may be prescribed.

(2) The accounts of the Corporation shall be audited by the Comptroller and Auditor-General of India at such intervals as may be specified by him and any expenditure incurred in connection with such audit shall be payable by the Corporation to the Comptroller and Auditor-General.

(3) The Comptroller and Auditor-General and any person appointed by him in connection with the audit of the accounts of the Corporation shall have the same rights and privileges and authority in connection with such audit as the Comptroller and Auditor-General has in connection with the audit of government accounts and, in particular, shall have the right to demand the production of books, accounts, connected vouchers and other documents and papers and to inspect any of the offices of the Corporation.

(4) The accounts of the Corporation as certified by the Comptroller and Auditor-General of India or any other person appointed by him in this behalf together with the audit report thereon shall be forwarded annually to the central government and that government shall cause the same to be laid before each House of Parliament.

22. *Corporation not liable to be taxed:* Notwithstanding anything contained in the Income-tax Act, 1961, or any other enactment for the time being in force relating to income-tax or any other tax on income, profits or gains the Corporation shall not be liable to pay any income-tax or any other tax in respect of—

(a) any income, profits of gains, accruing or arising out of the Funds of the Corporation or any amount received in that Fund; and
(b) any income, profits or gains, derived in any amount received, by the Corporation.

CHAPTER IV

MISCELLANEOUS

23. *Power of central government to give directions:* (1) The central government may, from time to time as and when occasion arises, issue to the Corporation such directions as it may think necessary in the interests of the sovereignty, unity and integrity of India or the security of the state or preservation of public order required it not to make a broadcast on a matter specified in the direction or to make a broadcast on any matter of public importance specified in the direction.

(2) Where the Corporation makes a broadcast in pursuance of the direction issued under sub-section (1), the fact that such broadcast has been made in pursuance of such direction may also be announced along with such broadcast, if the Corporation so desires.

(3) A copy of every direction issued under sub-section (1) shall be laid before each House of Parliament.

24. *Power of central government to obtain information:* The central government may require the Corporation to furnish such information as that government may consider necessary.

25. *Report to Parliament in certain matters and recommendations as to action against the Board:* (1) Where the Board persistently makes default in complying with any directions issued under section 23 or fails to supply the information required under section 24, the central government may prepare a report thereof and lay it before each House of Parliament of any recommendation thereof as to any action (including supersession of the Board) which may be taken against the Board.

(2) On the recommendation of the Parliament, the President may by notification supersede the Board for such period not exceeding six months as may be specified in the notification:

Provided that before issuing the notification under this sub-section the President shall give a reasonable opportunity to the Board to show cause as to why it should not be superseded and shall consider the explanations and objections, if any, of the Board.

(3) Upon the publication of the notification under sub-section (2)—

(a) all the members shall, as from the date of supersession, vacate their offices as such;
(b) all the powers, functions and duties which may, by or under the provisions of this Act be exercised or discharged by or on behalf of the Board, shall, until the Board is reconstituted under this Act, be exercised and discharged by such person or persons as the President may direct.

(4) On the expiration of the period of supersession specified in the notification issued under sub-section (2), the President may reconstitute the Board by fresh appointments, and in such a case any person who had vacated his office under clause (a) of sub-section (3) shall not be disqualified for appointment:

Provided that the President may, at any time before the expiration of the period of supersession, take action under this sub-section.

(5) The central government shall cause the notification issued under sub-section (2) and a full report of the action taken under this section to be laid before each House of Parliament.

26. *Office of member not to disqualify a Member of Parliament:* It is hereby declared that the office of the member of the Broadcasting Council or of the committee constituted under section 13 shall not disqualify its holder for being chosen as, or for being, a member of either House of Parliament.

27. *Chairman, Members, etc., to be public servants:* The chairman and every other member, every officer or other employee of the Corporation and every member of a committee thereof, the President and every member of the Broadcasting Council or every member of a Regional Council or a Recruitment Board shall be deemed to be a public servant within the meaning of section 21 of the Indian Penal Code.

28. *Protection of action taken in good faith:* No suit or other legal proceeding shall lie against the Corporation, the chairman or any member or officer or other employees thereof or the President or member of the Broadcasting Council or a member of a Regional Council or a Recruitment Board for anything which is in good faith done or intended to be done in pursuance of this Act of any rules or regulations made thereunder.

29. *Authentication of orders and other instruments of Corporation:* All order and decisions of the Corporation shall be authenticated by the signature of the chairman or any other member authorised by the Corporation in this behalf and all other instruments executed by the Corporation shall be authenticated by the signature of the executive member or by any officer of the Corporation

authorised by him in this behalf.

30. *Delegation of powers:* The Corporation may, by general or special order, delegate to the chairman or any other member or to any officer of the Corporation, subject to such conditions and limitations, if any, as may be specified therein, such of its powers and duties under this Act as it may deem fit.

31. *Annual report:* (1) The Corporation shall prepare once in every calendar year, in such form and within such time as may be prescribed, an annual report giving a full account of its activities (including th recommendations and suggestions made by the Broadcasting Council and the action taken thereon) during the previous year and copies thereof shall be forwarded to the central government and that government shall cause the same to be laid before each House of Parliament.

(2) The Broadcasting Council shall prepare once in every calendar year, in such form and within such time as may be prescribed, an annual report giving a full account of its activities during the previous year and copies thereof shall be forwarded to the central government and that government shall cause the same to be laid before each House of Parliament.

32. *Power to make Rules:* (1) The central government may, by notification, make rules for carrying out the provisions of this Act.

(2) In particular, and without prejudice to the generally of the foregoing power; such rules may provide for all or any of the following matters, namely—

(a) the salaries and allowances and conditions of service in respect of leave, pension (if any), provident fund and other matters in relation to the whole-time members under sub-section (7) of section 6;
(b) the allowances payable to the chairman and part-time members under sub-section (8) of section 6;
(c) the control restrictions and conditions subject to which the Corporation may appoint officers and other employees under sub-section (1) of section 9;
(d) the manner in which and the conditions and restrictions subject to which a Recruitment Board may be established under sub-section (1) of section 10;
(e) the qualifications and other conditions of service of the members of a Recruitment Board and their period of office under sub-section (2) of section 10;
(f) the term and conditions in accordance with which the deputation may be regulated under sub-section (2) of section 11;
(g) the salary and allowances and conditions of service in respect of leave, pension (if any), provident fund and other matters in relation to the President of the Broadcasting Council under sub-section (5) of section 14;
(h) the allowances payable to other members of the Broadcasting Council and the members of the Regional Councils, under sub-section (6) of section 14:

(i) the manner in which the Corporation may invest its moneys under sections 19;

(j) the form and the manner in which the annual statement of accounts shall be prepared under sub-section (1) of section 21;

(k) the form in which, and the time within which, the Corporation and the Broadcasting Council prepare their annual report under section 31;

(l) any other matter which is required to be, or may be, prescribed.

33. *Power to make regulations:* (1) The Corporation may, by notification, make regulations not inconsistent with this Act and the rules made thereunder for enabling it to perform its functions under this Act.

(2) Without prejudice to the generality of the foregoing power such regulations may provide for all or any of the following matters, namel—

(a) the manner in which and the purposes for which the Corporation may associate with itself any person under sub-section (7) of section 3;

(b) the times and places at which meetings of the Board shall be held and, the procedure to be followed thereat, and the quorum necessary for the transaction of the business at a meeting of the Board under sub-section (1) of section 8;

(c) the methods of recruitment and conditions of service of officers and other employees of the Corporation under sub-section (2) of section 9;

(d) the remuneration and other conditions of service, including pension, leave and provident fund in relation to an officer or other employee of the Corporation under sub-section (4) of section 11;

(e) the authority competent to make certain appointments referred to in clause (a) of sub-section (6) of section 11;

(f) the services which may be provided by the Corporation under clause (f) of sub-section (3) of section 12;

(g) the determination and levy of fees and other service charges in respect of advertisements and other programmes under sub-section (7) of section 12;

(h) the manner in which and the period within which complaints may be made under sub-section (2) of section 15;

(i) any other matter in respect of which provision is, in the opinion of the Corporation, necessary for the performance of its functions under this Act:

Provided that the regulations under clause (c) or clause (d) shall be made only with the prior approval of the central government.

34. *Rules and regulations to be laid before Parliament:* Every rule and every regulation made under this Act shall be laid, as soon as may be after it is made, before each House of Parliament, while it is in session for a total period of thirty days which may be comprised in one session or in two or more successive sessions, and if, before the expiry of the session immediately following the session or the successive sessions aforesaid, both Houses agree in making any modification in the rule or regulation, or both Houses agree that the rule or regulation should not be made, the rule or regulation shall thereafter have effect only in such modified form or be of no effect, as the case may be; so, however,

that any such modification or annulment shall be without prejudice to the validity of anything done under that rule or regulation.

35. *Power to remove difficulties:* If any difficulty arises in giving effect to the provisions of this Act, the central government may, by order, published in the Official Gazette, make such provisions, not inconsistent with the provisions of this Act, as it may deem necessary, for the removal of the difficulty:

Provided that no such order shall be made after the expiry of a period of three years from the appointed day.

X

RIGHT TO WORK

Constitutional provision regarding gainful employment to the people has for some time acquired nearly front-ranking importance in the eyes of many national planners, and programmes like the Nátional Rural Employment Programme (NREP) and the Rural Landless Guarantee Programme (RLGP) bear testimony to the high priority the country has been attaching to the problem especially in the agricultural and allied sector. One is aware of the Nehru Rojgar Yojana, which is to provide jobs to the rural poor. The urban space, however, remained vacant. In 1989 the Jawahar Rojgar Yojana was designed as the urban flip of the rural-based Nehru Rojgar Yojana.

Political parties of the land have been according increasing importance to plans and programmes of combating unemployment. In India, employment has failed to keep pace with the growth of population with the result that unemployment has been growing year after year. Today, the number of the unemployed in the country is staggering: nearly eighteen per cent of the country's employment-seeking population (one is hesitant to use the term 'employables' for them, which in view of their level and quality of skills and motivations is doubtful in many cases) is estimated to suffer from unemployment or, severe under-employment. Which is a cause for national concern. A demand is thus being made of guaranteeing to the citizens the 'right to work'. Indeed, it was in June 1986 that a voluntary forum like the Citizens for Democracy launched for the first time the right to work movement in the country. The National Front went further in its commitment by promising to make the 'right to work' a fundamental constitutional right. Its election manifesto loudly promised, 'Right to Work' will be included in the fundamental right guaranteed by the Constitution. Elaborating this, the manifesto argued in favour of a citizen's right to productive and gainful work in order to live meaningfully and with dignity. To this end are to be directed the nation's social and economic policies: the latter are to be directly and boldly geared to the realisation of the right to work as a fundamental right. The National Front promised productive work at need-based wages, which is entirely possible. It promised to introduce a new Employment Guarantee Scheme all over the country. Also, to realise conditions of full employment, an alternative strategy of development is to be followed. This would mean primacy to development of agriculture and allied occupations and strengthening of social and physical infra-structure in rural and semi-urban areas. Cottage and small industries are to be augmented.

With such a commitment to 'right to work' to be enshrined in the Constitution, the National Front was bound to accord it high priority in the event of its coming into power. And when it was in power, it moved swiftly in this direction. It addressed itself to the task of making the Eighth Five Year Plan, under preparation at the time heavily job-oriented. A shift, too, was sought to be given from the capital- intensive national economic orientation to the setting up of employment generating activities. Indeed, one of the earliest tasks of the National Front government under V.P. Singh was to initiate action on its electoral pledge. The first step in concretising 'right to work' was taken early in February 1990 when it constituted a cabinet sub-committee to examine how it could be included as a fundamental right in the Constitution.

The cabinet sub-committee on right to work met several times. It first (13 February 1990) decided to prepare a 'conceptual' paper which it discussed on 1 March 1990, the sub-committee's second meeting. Finance Minister Madhu Dandavate was the chairman of the committee which had Railway Minister George Fernandes, Textiles Minister Sharad Yadav, Labour Minister Ram Vilas Paswan and Urban Development Minister M. Muran as members. Little did eventually emerge out of these confabulations and the whole effort was finally given up.

Evaluation

'Right to work' sounds very attractive but is very difficult to achieve. It, in the first place, pre-supposes the availability of sufficient work to absorb the burgeoning population. The feasibility of such a large-scale employment-generation in India is very doubtful at the present stage of its development, to put it mildly. Secondly, as a counterpart to the proposed right, a social security net will become unavoidable. This raises the question of availability of resources. Indeed, the 'right to work' would require tremendous resource mobilisation effort beyond India's capacity, the country's track record being what it is.

Ultimately, 'right to work' proved to be V.P. Singh's Achielles' heel. Indeed, very few in political parties even cared to apply their mind to what could a slogan like the right to work imply. Even, it is difficult to define the term 'right to work'. Is it the same as the right to life and freedom of expression? What does threaten the right to work as these other rights are threatened during the emergency? Does it mean right to government employment? It is also to be considered whether the realisation of this right would presuppose a level of regimentation of the economic system of the country, indeed of the society. Theoretically, right to work postulates the State's right to send an employment-seeking youth to a far-off place which he may not like, and give him a wage-earning job which he may dislike. In other words, the government's obligation and a citizen's freedom of choice may not necessarily be harmoniously blended. The really practically sound solution lies in India making its national planning employment-oriented and even more important, in expanding the avenues of self-employment. This in turn demands, among others, less of governmental control and regulation presently strangling the economy.

XI

THE NATIONAL COMMISSION FOR WOMEN

Need for upliftment of women in India hardly needs elaboration, there being total unanimity on it in the country. Women constitute nearly half of the society — the silent half comprising 331 million of the total population according to 1981 census. About 150 million of them live in visible material poverty and many are close to it. They are a historically neglected section of the society, denied the basic right to human dignity. In India, culture, caste and class all have tended to discriminate against gender.

Independent India has been consistently giving attention to the amelioration of social and economic conditions of women, and some gains have been achieved in the society despite the slowness and unevenness of progress. The expectation of female life at birth has improved from 44.7 years in 1961-71 to 52.9 during 1971-81. Gains have been registered in other spheres too. Currently, the central government has more than 27 schemes for women, some women-specific while others are common and are thus for both the male and female population. These schemes are run by different departments and ministries of the government. The total outlay on the women-specific schemes in the Seventh Five-Year Plan (1985-90) was 2.4 per cent of the total outlay. Since 1985, the Government of India has a separate Department in the Ministry of Human Resource Development, namely the Department of Women and Child Development to direct its concentrated attention to ameliorate the condition of this retarded section.

Yet, women constitute the neglected half of the Indian society. Education among them is low and the percentage of illiteracy is very high. In 1981, women formed a mere 16.5 per cent of the country's work force, which is evidently very inadequate. Only 994 women hold senior administrative positions in the central government as against 15,993 men in similar jobs in the all-India services, thus constituting only 5.8 per cent. The Indian Administrative Service had 339 women against 5209 (7.5%) while the Indian Police Service had 21 women officers as against 2418 men (0.99%). These figures relate to the year 1988 and a miracle has not occurred since then. Crimes against women continue almost unabated. In 1987, there were 6668 reported victims of rape and 1517 dowry deaths. That women constitute the critical inputs for national development should be well recognised by national planners.

The National Front comprising the Janata Dal and other parties expressed its concern for women's advancement and welfare right since the beginning. Its manifesto of 1989 reiterated this concern in no ambiguous terms: out of 36 pages into which the National Front manifesto runs nearly two are devoted exclusively to women advancement, and makes mention of them at least at two places. The manifesto promises self-respect to women. Women are to lead life free from oppression and indignity. They are to enjoy equality with men before law. Social equality of the sexes shall be guaranteed. India will become the signatory to the U.N. Convention on Women's Rights to ensure that its policies and programmes for women flow from its charter. Women are to fully participate in the development processes underway in the country. Jobs for them will be planned on a massive scale particularly in the agrarian sector mainly through agro-industries. Vocational training institutes are to be set up to encourage self-employment among women as well as to make them eligible for employment in industrial enterprises and offices. Thirty per cent reservation for women will be provided in government jobs. The private sector will be encouraged to employ more women. Sectors especially conducive to female employment will be encouraged. A maternity fund is to be set up to benefit pregnant women. Social legislation concerning marriage, divorce, maintenance custody, inheritance will be reviewed, with a view to remove their disadvantageous position, if any. Women are to be given preference in allotment of houses.

What is more, a statutory national commission on women is to be set up to monitor and accelerate the process of their equal representation to enforce legislation for women's rights including labour laws, and to check gender discrimination in all spheres of life.

National Commission for Women Act

Of all the electoral promises made by the National Front in its manifesto, that relating to the National Commission for Women (NCW) is of key importance. The proposed NCW is to act as the nation's watchdog to protect and promote women's welfare. When the National Front government came into power it began to be widely believed that the new government will swiftly unfold action on its recommendations. The V.P. Singh government lost little time in drafting a special legislation and steering it through Parliament. The outcome is the National Commission for Women Act, enacted by Parliament in March 1990 (Annexure B).

The National Commission for Women is a statutory body set up under a specific law of the national legislature. It is to consist of a chairperson and five members out of whom one is to be from the scheduled caste and one from the scheduled tribe. Members including the chairperson would all be appointed by the central government for a term not exceeding three years. The commission is to be assisted by a member secretary who is to be drawn from the world of civil service — central or all-India — and is, like others, to be appointed by the central government. Qualifications for the members including chairperson are of general nature. The chairperson should be a person committed to the cause of women whatever that may mean while the members must be from amongst persons of ability, integrity and standing who have had experience in law or legislation, trade unionism, management of an organisation and industry committed to increasing the employment potential of women, women's voluntary organisations, administration, economic development, health education or social welfare. The salaries and terms and conditions of service of the chairperson and members are to be prescribed by the central government. This will be the case with regard to other employees of the Commission.

The commission, as the statue postulates, is to function as the government's conscience-keeper, and its philosopher and guide on all policy matters affecting women. The Act defines the functions of the National Commission for Women. These are:

1. To investigate and examine all matters relating to the safeguards for women under the Constitution and the laws.
2. to make recommendations for implementation of safeguards for women for improving their conditions by the centre or any state.
3. to review, from time to time, the existing provisions of the Constitution and other laws affecting women and make appropriate recommendations to improve them.
4. to take up the cases of violation of the provisions of the Constitution and other laws relating to women.
5. to fund litigation involving issues affecting a large body of women.
6. to undertake promotional and educational research relating to women and their advancement.
7. to recommend action to the government for promotion of women welfare.

To help build-up public and political opinion in favour of the NCW and the women's cause, its reports to the government are required to be laid before each House of Parliament along with a memorandum which puts the executive under an obligation to explain the action taken or proposed to be taken on the recommendations. To meet the NCW's expenditure, the commission is to get its grants from the central government. Its accounts are to be audited by the Comptroller and Auditor-General of India.

The National Commission for Women has not yet come into force. The government has to notify the date in the official gazette.

ANNEXURE B

THE NATIONAL COMMISSION FOR WOMEN ACT, 1990

An Act to constitute a National Commission for Women and to provide for matters connected therewith or incidental thereto.

BE it enacted by Parliament in the Forty-first Year of the Republic of India as follows:

CHAPTER I

PRELIMINARY

1. *Short title, extent and commencement*: (1) This Act may by called the National Commission for Women Act, 1990.

(2) It extends to the whole of India except the State of Jammu and Kashmir.

(3) It shall come into force on such date as the central government may, by notification in the Official Gazette, appoint.

2. *Definitions:* In this Act, unless the context otherwise requires,—

(a) "Commission" means the National Commission for Women constituted under section 3;
(b) "Member" means a member of the Commission and includes the member-secretary;
(c) "prescribed" means prescribed by rules made under this Act.

CHAPTER II

THE NATIONAL COMMISSION FOR WOMEN

3. *Constitution of the National Commission for Women:* (1) The central government shall constitute a body to be known as the National Commission or Women to exercise the powers conferred on, and to perform the functions assigned to, it under this Act.

(2) The Commission shall consist of—

(a) a chairperson, committed to the cause of women, to be nominated by the central government;
(b) five members to be nominated by the central government from amongst persons of ability, integrity and standing who have had experience in law or legislation, trade unionism, management of an industry or organisation committed to increasing the employment

potential of women, women's voluntary organisations (including women activists), administration, economic development, health, education or social welfare:

Provided that at least one member each shall be from amongst persons belonging to the Scheduled Castes and Scheduled Tribes respectively.

(c) one member-secretary to be nominated by the central government who shall be—

(i) an expert in the field of management, organisational structure or sociological movement, or

(ii) an officer who is a member of a civil service of the Union or of an all-India service or holds a civil post under the Union with appropriate experience.

4. *Terms of office and conditions of service of Chairperson and Members:* (1) The chairperson and every member shall hold office for such period, not exceeding three years, as may be specified by the central government in this behalf.

(2) The chairperson or a member (other than the member-secretary who is a member of a civil service of the Union or of an all-India service or holds a civil post under the Union) may, by writing and addressed to the central government, resign from the office of chairperson or, as the case may be, of the member at any time.

(3) The central government shall remove a person from the office of chairperson or a member referred to in sub-section (2) if that person—

(a) becomes an undischarged insolvent;

(b) gets convicted and sentenced to imprisonment for an offence which in the opinion of the central government involves moral turpitude;

(c) becomes of unsound mind and stands so declared by a competent court;

(d) refuses to act or becomes incapable of acting;

(e) is, without obtaining leave of absence from the Commission, absent from three consecutive meetings of the Commission; or

(f) in the opinion of the central government has so abused the position of chairperson or member as to render that person's continuance in office detrimental to the public interest:

Provided that no persons shall be removed under this clause until that person has been given a reasonable opportunity of being heard in the matter.

(4) A vacancy caused under sub-section (2) or otherwise shall be filled by fresh nomination.

(5) The salaries and allowances payable to, and the other terms and conditions of service of, the chairperson and members shall be such as may be prescribed.

5. *Officers and other employees of the Commission:* (1)The central government shall provide the Commission with such officers and employees as

may be necessary for the efficient performance of the functions of the commission under this Act.

(2) The salaries and allowances payable to, and the other terms and conditions of service of, the officers and other employees appointed for the purpose of the Commission shall be such as may be prescribed.

6. *Salaries and allowance to be paid out of grants:* The salaries and allowances payable to the chairperson and members and the administrative expenses, including salaries, allowances and pensions payable to the officers and other employees referred to in section 5, shall be paid out of the grants referred to in sub-section (1) of section 11.

7. *Vacancies, etc., not to invalidate proceedings of the Commission:* No act or proceeding of the Commission shall be questioned or shall be invalid on the ground merely of the existence of any vacancy or defect in the constitution of the Commission.

8. *Committees of the Commission:* (1) The Commission may appoint such committees as may be necessary for dealing with such special issue as may be taken up by the Commission from time to time.

(2) The Commission shall have the power to co-opt members of any committee appointed under sub-section (1) such number of persons, who are not members of the Commission, as it may think fit and the persons so co-opted shall have the right to attend the meetings of the committee and take art in its proceedings but shall not have the right to vote.

(3) The persons so co-opted shall be entitled to receive such allowances for attending the meetings of the committee as may be prescribed.

9. *Procedure to be regulated by the Commission:* (1) The Commission or a committee thereof shall meet as and when necessary and shall meet at such time and place as he chairperson may think fit.

(2) The Commission shall regulate its own procedure and the procedure of the committees thereof.

(3) All orders and decisions of the Commission shall be authenticated by the member-secretary of any other officer of the Commission duly authorised by the member-secretary in this behalf.

CHAPTER III

FUNCTION OF THE COMMISSION

10 *Functions of the Commission:* (1) The Commission shall perform all or any of the following functions, namely:

(a) investigate and examine all matters relating to the safeguards provided for women under the Constitution and other laws;
(b) present to the central government, annually and at such other times as the Commission may deem fit reports upon the working of those safeguards;

(c) make in such reports recommendations for the effective implementation of those safeguards for improving the conditions of women by the Union of any state;

(d) review, from time to time, the existing provisions of the Constitution and other laws affecting women and recommend amendments thereto so as to suggest remedial legislative measures to meet any lacunae, inadequacies or shortcomings in such legislations;

(e) take up the cases of violation of the provisions of the Constitution and of other laws relating to women will the appropriate authorities;

(f) look into complaints and take *suo moto* notice of matters relating to—

(i) deprivation of women's rights;

(ii) non-implementation of laws enacted to provide protection to women and also to achieve the objective of equality and development;

(iii) non-compliance of policy decisions, guidelines or instructions aimed at mitigating hardships and ensuring welfare and providing relief to women,

and take up the issues arising out of such matters with appropriate authorities;

(g) call for special studies or investigations into specific problems or situations arising out of discrimination and atrocities against women and identify the constraints so as to recommend strategies for their removal;

(h) undertaken promotional and educational research so as to suggest ways of ensuring due representation of women in all spheres and identify factors responsible for impeding their advancement, such as, lack of access to housing and basic services, inadequate support services and technologies for reducing drudgery and occupational health hazards and for increasing their productivity;

(i) participate and advise on the planning process of socio-economic development of women;

(j) evaluate the progress of the development of women under the Union and any state;

(k) inspect of cause to be inspected a jail, remand home, women's institution or other place or custody where women are kept as prisoners or otherwise, and take up with the concerned authorities for remedial action, if found necessary;

(l) fund litigation involving issues affecting a large body of women;

(m) make periodical reports to the government on any matter pertaining to women and in particular various difficulties under which women toil;

(n) any other matter which may be referred to it by the central government.

(2) The central government shall cause all the reports referred to in clause (b) of sub-section (1) to be laid before each House of Parliament along with a memorandum explaining the action taken or proposed to be taken on the recommendations relating to the Union and the reasons for the non-acceptance, if any, of any of such recommendations.

(3) Where any such report or any part thereof relates to any matter with

which any state government is concerned, the Commission shall toward a copy of such report or part to such state government who shall cause it to be laid before the Legislature of the state along with a memorandum explaining the action taken or proposed to be taken on the recommendations relating to the state and the reasons for the non-acceptance, if any, of any of such recommendations.

(4) The Commission shall, while investigating any matter referred to in clause (a) or sub-clause (i) of clause (f) of sub-section, (1) have all the powers of a civil trying a suit and in particular, in respect of the following matters, namely:-

(a) summoning and enforcing the attendance of any person from any part of India and examining him on oath;
(b) requiring the discovery and production of any document;
(c) receiving evidence on affidavits;
(d) requisitioning any public record or copy thereof from any court of office;
(e) issuing commissions for the examination of witnesses and documents; and
(f) any other matter which may be prescribed.

CHAPTER IV

FINANCE, ACCOUNTS AND AUDIT

11. *Grants by the Central Government:* (1) The central government shall, after due appropriation made by Parliament by law in this behalf, pay to the Commission by way of grants such sums of money as the central government may think fit for being utilised for the purposes of this Act.

(2) The Commission may spend such sums as it thinks fit for performing the functions under this Act, and such sums shall be treated as expenditure payable out of the grants referred to in sub-section (1).

12. *Account and audit:* (1) The Commission shall maintain proper accounts and other relevant records and prepare an annual statement of accounts in such form as may be prescribed by the central government in consultation with the Comptroller and Auditor-General of India.

(2) The accounts of the Commission shall be audited by the Comptroller and Auditor-General at such intervals as may be specified by him and any expenditure incurred in connection with such audit shall be payable by the Commission to the Comptroller and Auditor-General.

(3) The Comptroller and Auditor-General and any person appointed by him in connection with the audit of the accounts of the Commission under this act shall have the rights and privileges and the authority in connection with such audit as the Comptroller and Auditor-General generally has in connection with the auditor of government accounts and, in particular, shall have the right to demand the production of books, accounts, connected vouchers and other documents and papers and to inspect any of the offices of the Commission.

(4) The accounts of the Commission, as certified by the Comptroller and

Auditor-General or any other person appointed by him in this behalf, together with the audit report thereon shall be forwarded annually to the central government by the Commission.

13. *Annual report:* The Commission shall prepare, in such form and at such time, for each financial year, as may be prescribed, its annual report, giving a full accounts of its activities during the previous financial year and forward a copy thereof to the central government.

14. *Annual report and audit report to be laid before Parliament:* The central government shall cause the annual report together with a memorandum of action taken on the recommendations contained therein, insofar as they relate to the central government, and the reasons for the non-acceptance, if any, of any of such recommendations and the audit report to be laid as soon as may be after the reports are received, before each House of Parliament.

CHAPTER V

MISCELLANEOUS

15. *Chairperson, Members and Staff of the Commission to be Public Servants:* The chairperson, the members, officers and other employees of the Commission shall be deemed to be public servants within the meaning of section 21 of the Indian Penal Code.

16. *Central Government to consult Commission:* The central government shall consult the Commission on all major policy matters affecting women.

17. *Power to make Rules:* (1) The central government may, by notification in the Official Gazette, make rules for carrying out the provisions of this Act.

(2) In particular, and without prejudice to the generality of the foregoing power, such rules may provide for all or any of the following matters namely:-

(a) salaries and allowances payable to, and the other terms and conditions of service of, the chairperson and members under sub-section (5) of section 4 and of officers and other employees under sub-section (2) of section 5;
(b) allowances for attending the meetings of the committee by the co-opted persons under sub-section (3) of section 8;
(c) other matters under clause (f) of sub-section (4) of section 10;
(d) the form in which the annual statement of accounts shall be maintained under sub-section (1) of section 12;
(e) the form in, and the time, at which the annual report shall be prepared under section 13;
(f) any other matter which is required to be, or may, be prescribed.

(3) Every rule made under this Act shall be laid, as soon as may be after it is made, before each House of Parliament, while it is in session, for a total period of thirty days which may be comprised in one session or in two or more successive sessions, and if, before the expiry of the session immediately

following the session or the successive sessions aforesaid, both Houses agree in making any modification in the rule or both Houses agree that the rule should not be made, the rule shall thereafter have effect only in such modified form or be of no effect, as the case may be; so, however, that any such modification or annulment shall be without prejudice to the validity of anything previously done under that rule.

8

MAJOR REPORTS BY THE COMPTROLLER AND AUDITOR-GENERAL OF INDIA

CAG's REPORT ON CENTRAL GOVERNMENT — CIVIL

I

PREFATORY REMARKS

This report for the year ended 31 March 1989, has been prepared for submission to the President under article 151 of the Constitution. It has been submitted in 1990. It relates mainly to matters arising from the Appropriation Accounts of the Union Government (Civil) for 1988-89 prepared (with a few exceptions) by the Controller General of Accounts and test-checked in audit and other points arising from test audit of the financial transactions of some of the civil departments of the union government.

Certain points of interest arising from the union government finance accounts for 1988-89 as consolidated by the controller general of accounts and based on the statements of Finance Accounts furnished by the Controller General of Accounts/Controllers of Accounts are included in chapter I of this Report.

This Report includes, among others, the following reviews:

(a) Jawahar Rozgar Yojana; and
(b) Purchase and construction of properties for Indian missions abroad.

The cases mentioned in this Report are among those which came to notice in the course of audit during 1988-89 as well as those which came to notice in earlier years but could not be dealt with in previous Reports; matters relating to the period subsequent to 1988-89 have also been included, wherever considered necessary.

OVERVIEW

The Audit Report for the year ended 31 March 1989, contains 35 paragraphs including two reviews. The points highlighted in the Report are given below:

I. **Accounts of the Central Government**

The total revenue expenditure during 1988-89 was Rs. 63,485 crores against total revenue receipts of Rs. 52,971 crores. This resulted in revenue deficit of Rs. 10,514 crores as against Rs. 9,137 crores in 1987-88. The overall deficit during 1988-89 was Rs. 5,642 crores as against Rs. 5,816 crores in the previous year.

The internal debt increased to Rs. 1,14,498 crores at the end of March 1989 as against Rs. 98,646 crores at the end of March, 1988. The external debt had also increased to Rs. 25,746 crores as against Rs. 23,223 crores in the previous year. The total liabilities including internal debt, external debt and small savings, provident funds, etc., registered an increase of 17 per cent over the previous year and stood at Rs. 2,29,772 crores at the end of March, 1989. The net outgo on interest and debt service obligations increased from Rs. 5,497 crores in 1987-88 to Rs. 7,297 crores in 1988-89.

The receipt on account of profit from nationalised banks declined from Rs. 45.65 crores in 1987-88 to Rs. 0.62 crore in 1988-89. The dividend received during the year from investment of Rs. 30,750 crores in statutory corporations, government companies, other joint stock companies, etc. (excluding those under construction) was Rs. 141.05 crores representing only 0.45 per cent return on investments.

II. **Ministry of Agriculture**

Jawahar Rozgar Yojana: Jawahar Rozgar Yojana was launched from 1 April 1989, merging the National Rural Employment Programme and Rural Landless Employment Guarantee Programme with the main objective of generating additional gainful employment for the unemployed and underemployed in rural areas. Expenditure on the programme was to be shared between the centre and states on 80 : 20 basis.

The funds provided for the programme were inadequate to achieve the objectives of the programme. Total resources of Rs. 2,623.08 crores provided for the programme for 1989-90 could sustain provision of employment for hardly 21 days on an average to one member of each rural family living below the poverty line.

The prescribed criteria for release of central assistance to the states/union territories on the basis of rural poverty was not strictly adhered to.

Central assistance to 12 states/union territories was released in excess of their entitlement and in the cases of 19 states and one union territory, the assistance was less. Even though the overall utilisation was hardly 24 per cent of available funds, the second instalment of central assistance totalling Rs. 1,112.60 crores was released prematurely to the districts in September 1989. The prescribed conditions of 50 per cent utilisation of the available resources had been satisfied in only tow states and one union territory. Release of second instalment of central assistance despite substantial underutilisation of funds already available with the implementing agencies only contributed to increased accumulation of unutilised balances with them.

Unutilised resources of the National Rural Employment Programme and Rural Landless Employment Guarantee Programme totalling Rs. 422.48 crores available with the states/union territories were not reckoned for fixing employment generation targets for 1989-90.

Due to launching of the new programme without adequate preparatory work, employment generated during the first four months of 1989-90 under the Jawahar Rozgar Yojana was less as compared to the average employment generation in the corresponding period of the last three year under the National Rural Employment Programme and Rural Landless Employment Guarantee Programme. This was despite availability of more resources for the programme. Targets set for generation of employment were not achieved. Employment generation was nil during the first quarter of 1989 in three of the four districts test-checked in Uttar Pradesh. In Karnataka, achievement was only 36 per cent in the districts test-checked. In Andhra Pradesh, only about 11 per cent of the target was achieved.

Identification of the targeted beneficiary families, essential for proper implementation of the programme, was not done in Andhra Pradesh, Bihar, Uttar Pradesh, while in Karnataka and Rajasthan, the work was stated to be in progress. Annual plans for district rural development agencies/zila parishads and panchayats were not prepared in any of the states. Training workshops/programmes to provide necessary orientation to officers handling Jawahar Rozgar Yojana work at various levels had not been arranged. Prescribed monitoring arrangements for the implementation of the programme did not exist.

III. **Ministry of Commerce**

Cash Compensatory Support Scheme: Under the scheme of cash compensatory support, also called cash assistance, government pays cash compensation to exporters of different specified product groups at rates prescribed for the various export items. Payment of cash assistance is to be regulated in accordance with the instructions contained in the Import/Export Trade Central Policy and procedures and the Cash Assistance Manual. Due to non-observance of the instructions contained in the guidelines for fixing the rates of cash assistance and the regulations for payment of cash assistance, irregular/excess/inadmissible and avoidable payments of cash assistance amounting to Rs. 5.31 crores were noticed by Audit.

IV. **Ministry of Commerce — Department of Supply**

Purchase of Tent Stores-fly Inner: Notwithstanding the departmental instructions that the entire quantity against operational indents should be covered on registered/past suppliers, 640 tents (store-fly inner) valued at Rs. 26.31 lakhs were covered by the Director General, Supplies and Disposals, on un-registered/untried firms which failed to execute the acceptance of tender. For coverage of cancelled quantity limited tender inquiry was issued *inter alia* to un-registered/untried firms thereby frustrating the chances of a valid risk purchase. Consequently, the extra expenditure of Rs. 14.43 lakhs incurred in the re-purchase could not be recovered from the defaulting firm. General damages had also not been assessed till October 1989.

Purchase of Ingot Leaded Bronze: The Director General, Supplies and

Disposals, ignored the lower offer of a firm for the supply of ingot-leaded bronze resulting in extra expenditure of Rs. 8.15 lakhs on grounds of unsatisfactory past performance which was not proved from departmental records. It also ignored the lower offer on the unsubstantiated ground of malpractice despite the fact that in a similar case mentioned in paragraph 43 of the Report of the Comptroller and Auditor-General of India for the year 1982-83 : Central Government (Civil), the Department of Supply has stated that a firm's offer could not be ignored simply on the ground of alleged offence against it.

V. Ministry of Defence

Audit on Pension Payment Accounts: During a test check of pension payment accounts, it was noticed that a sum of Rs. 47.56 lakhs overpaid in 1981 to pensioners was yet to be recovered. 909 monthly accounts for the period 1973-88 were yet to be received in the office of the Chief Controller of Defence Accounts (Pensions), Allahabad, from the various pension disbursing officers. 79,780 monthly accounts pertaining to the period 1978-89 were yet to be scrutinised by the internal audit of that organisation.

VI. Ministry of Energy — Department of Power

Infructuous Expenditure on Purchase of Equipment: Northern Regional Electricity Board imported 13 pieces of facsimile telecopying equipment at a cost of Rs. 9.03 lakhs in November 1982, for installation in various regional and state load despatch centres in the country. The equipment received was inspected after 28 months of its receipt by which time the guarantee period was over and many of the pieces were found badly rusted. There was no likelihood of the equipment being put to use because of non-availability of spares rendering the expenditure infructuous.

VII. Ministry of External Affairs

Purchase and Construction of Properties for Indian Missions Abroad: There was absence of technical expertise in the ministry to scrutinise/analyse competently proposals received from missions abroad for purchase and construction of properties. The CPWD consultancy services were not fully utilised and only in five cases, the services were availed of. The progress of work *vis-a-vis* expenditure incurred on construction of buildings which was important and crucial to avoid time and cost overrun was not monitored.

The prescribed space norms for purchase of properties for residences were contravened resulting in excess expenditure of Rs. 62.04 lakhs. Absence of a clear-cut policy, co-ordinated planning and avoidable delays in the finalisation of construction proposals and taking prompt decisions led to non-utilisation of properties resulting in additional rental liability of Rs. 1,095.41 lakhs till 1988-89 and subsequent recurring liability of Rs. 412.23 lakhs per annum. Besides there was escalation in cost of construction to the extent of Rs. 2,606.64 lakhs. The ministry failed to evolve plans for construction of plots of land acquired at a cost of Rs. 109.41 lakhs in Bangkok, Kabul, Lilongwe, New York and Sri Lanka and plots gifted free of cost on reciprocal basis in Abu Dhabi, Aden, Brasilia, Doha and Dubai leading to blocking of funds for periods ranging from 5 to 26 years.

Adoption of wrong measurements, purchase in excess of evaluated price, abandonment of construction plans and payment of taxes on vacant plots resulted in avoidable expenditure of Rs. 79.83 lakhs.

A consolidated up-to-date record of properties purchased/ constructed was not maintained.

VIII. **Ministry of Finance**

Under-utilisation of Modernised Plant: The installed capacity of 6,000 tonnes per annum had not been achieved and the actual production was short by 31 to 47 per cent. One of the reasons for low production given to the department was the problem with the Union. Though the mill paid incentive bonus and overtime allowance amounting to Rs. 5.23 crores, there was shortfall in production of 9,963 tonnes of paper valued at Rs. 5.76 crores.

CAG's REPORT ON CENTRAL GOVERNMENT
(Other Autonomous Bodies)

II

PREFATORY REMARKS

This Report for the year ended 31 March 1989, has been prepared for submission to the President under article 151 of the Constitution.

The results of test audit of the Central Autonomous Bodies (other than those under Scientific Departments included in Report No. 2 of 1990) under the various provisions of the Comptroller and Auditor-General's (Duties, Powers and Conditions of Service) Act, 1971, are set out in this Report.

2. This Report includes, among others, reviews on:

(a) Trade Development Authority,
(b) Indian Institute of Management, Bangalore,
(c) National Institute of Educational Planning and Administration, New Delhi,
(d) Indian Council of Philosophical Research, New Delhi,
(e) Panjab University, Chandigarh,
(f) Kendriya Hindi Shikshan Mandal, Agra,
(g) Stores and Material Management, Bombay Port Trust, and
(h) Dry Dock System, Calcutta Port Trust.

3. The audited organisations are varied and different in character and discipline but since these are autonomous bodies the audit observations on all figure in this Report.

4. The cases mentioned in this Report are among those which came to notice in the course of audit during the year 1988-89 as well as those which had come to notice in earlier years but could not be dealt with in previous Reports;

matters relating to the period subsequent to 1988-89 have also been included, wherever considered necessary.

OVERVIEW

The Audit Report for the year ended March 31 1989, contains 44 paragraphs including eight reviews. The points highlighted in the Report are summarised below:

I. General

The accounts of autonomous bodies which receive financial assistance from the government are audited by the Comptroller and Auditor General of India.

The Government of India paid Rs. 1,096.05 crores as grants and Rs. 117.86 crores as loans to various autonomous bodies during 1988-89. In addition, nine universities received Rs. 150.97 crores as grants from the University Grants Commission/central government. The annual accounts of 69 out of 87 bodies (other than those under the Scientific Departments) whose accounts were to be audited under sections 14(1) and 14(2) of the Comptroller and Auditor General's (Duties, Powers & Conditions of Service) Act, 1971, had not been received. Further, for the year 1987-88, out of 175 central autonomous bodies whose accounts together with Audit Reports thereon were required to be placed before Parliament, accounts of 85 bodies were received late beyond the prescribed time limit of three months by a period ranging up to six months and above and accounts of three bodies were not received.

Utilisation Certificates totalling 13,600 amounting to Rs. 1,263.74 crores were outstanding in March 1989, in respect of grants released to various bodies during 1976-77 to 1985-86. This indicated that the authorities releasing the grants had not exercised proper control over the receipt of utilisation certificates.

II. Trade Development Authority

The Trade Development Authority (TDA), a registered society, is one of the export promotion institutions set up by the Ministry of Commerce. Its primary objective is to induce and organise entrepreneurs to develop their export capabilities and also to provide package of assistance including export intelligence to its members (clients) with a view to securing and implementing export orders.

Enrolment of entrepreneurs, etc., as its members, declined from 353 in 1984-85 to 167 in 1987-88 while de-enrolment increased from 104 in 1984-85 to 182 in 1987-88. The TDA had no reliable data base in respect of export performance of its members (clients). Out of 17 products under its engineering group and 12 under consumer goods, eight products of the former and seven of the latter group registered a decline in foreign exchange earnings in U.S. dollar terms in 1986-87 compared to exports in 1983-84. During the same period, although total exports from the country increased over the years, the share of exports of the TDA products to TDA markets showed a decline in 10 engineering products and five consumer goods. The extent to which the exports were augmented on the basis of development and adaptation of samples imported by the TDa was not known.

An integrated Nationai Centre for Trade information for export promotion, for which a proposal was mooted by the TDA in 1976, had not been established.

Excess government grant of Rs. 73.61 lakhs was held by the TDA up to the year 1987-88 according to the annual accounts. A deficit of Rs. 120.87 lakhs had accumulated up to 1985-86. The grant accounts after the year 1985-86 had not been finalised by the government. The grants from the government to the India Trade Centre, Brussels, were routed through the TDA. The final accounts for the centre for the year 1983-84 and onwards were not prepared.

III. Indian Council for Cultural Relations

Overpayment to a Visiting Professor: An Associate Professor of Jawaharlal Nehru University sponsored by the Indian Council for Cultural Relations for appointment as a visiting professor of Hindi in a University in the German Democratic Republic during September 1985 to August 1988, was paid pay and allowances as per the Council's rules by the indian Mission as well as GDR DM 1,250 per month by the University. As the Professor was not entitled to receive salary from two sources for the same work, this resulted in excess payment of GDR DM 46,050 (Rs. 3.26 lakhs) which had not been recovered so far.

Further, due to payment of salary to the Professor at the preferential rate of exchange and its recovery from the Council at the current commercial rates of exchange, the Mission suffered a loss of Rs. 1.35 lakhs. The amount recoverable from the Council had also not been recovered.

IV. All India Institute of Medical Sciences

Encroachment on Land: The All-India Institute of Medical Sciences did not make proper arrangement like fencing, etc., for 87 acres of land acquired by it from the Delhi Development Authority at a cost of Rs. 31.03 lakhs. Consequently, a number of unauthorised *jhuggis* were put up over the years covering an area of 31 to 33 acres. For the removal of the *jhuggis*, the AIIMS paid Rs. 1.30 crores to the DDA in March 1987, at the rate of Rs. 10,000 per *jhuggi* which had been put up prior to June 1977. However, there was no authentic record of *jhuggis* which had come into existence prior to June 1977. A survey done by the DDA, in December 1986, revealed that the number of *jhuggis* had increased by 1,067 and the DDA demanded additional payment of Rs. 1.07 crores. Further, despite the payment of Rs. 1.30 crores, in March 1987, only about 700 *jhuggis* had been removed so far, and Rs. 60 lakhs already paid remained blocked with the DDA. The AIIMS had planned to construct, *inter alia*, nurses' hostel in the Masjid Moth area. The estimated cost of construction of the hostel was revised from Rs. 2.52 crores in July 1984 to Rs. 4.04 crores in September 1987. The major portion of increase in the estimated cost amounting to Rs. 97 lakhs was attributed to price escalation. According to the AIIMS, some delay in taking up this project was due to procedural delay such as preparation of detailed drawings including plans, elevations, sections and other details and obtaining approval from the DDA, Delhi Urban Arts Commissions, etc.

V. **Delhi Library Board**

Blocking of Funds: Delhi Library Board spent expenditure of Rs. 11.36 lakhs in February-March 1986, on the purchase of six chassis for augmenting the existing facilities. Four of these chassis purchased at a cost of Rs. 7.91 lakhs were oversised and hence could not be used. While two oversised chassis could be sold for Rs. 4.33 lakhs in July and September 1988, the remaining two chassis could not be disposed of so far. Delay of two years in the utilisation of the remaining two chassis was also noticed.

VI. **Indian Institute of Management, Bangalore**

Against the intake capacity of 180 students for the two-year post-graduate programme of the Institute, the actual enrolment ranged between 109 and 125 during 1983-88. The Institute had attributed the shortfall to a decision of its Board of Governors, in March 1983, to limit the intake to 120 students till the availability of dormitory facilities in the campus. Audit scrutiny, however, revealed that stay in hostel was optional, and that in any case till 1986-87, the available hostel accommodation was more than the number of students on roll. In view of the fact that the course, in question, is extremely popular, much sought after and prestigious in nature, the shortfall in the intake of students was not merely unjustified but also an avoidable underutilisation of scarce national resource.

In the fellow programme in management, recognised as equivalent to a Doctorate in Management, only 30 students were enrolled during 1983-89 against the sanctioned intake of 72, and of these, only two students completed the programme. Sixteen out of 30 students dropped out; expenditure of Rs. 1.12 lakhs incurred on payment of stipends and contingent grants to these students proved infructuous.

The Institute conducted only 188 out of 290 short-term management development programmes originally planned by it during 1983-89. The number of participants was less than the prescribed minimum in 43 cases; last-minute cancellation resulted in infructuous expenditure of Rs. 3.47 lakhs in 81 cases and fees amounting to Rs. 3.33 lakhs were irregularly refunded in 79 cases of withdrawals/cancellation of nominations. Test check also showed that only 23 per cent of the programmes covered the area as specified in the Institute's brochure.

The number of organisation-based programmes declined from 35 in 1985-86 to 20 in 1988-89 and was as low as 11 in 1987-88. Six out of 47 internally funded projects awarded during 1983-89 were not taken up, no report detailing results of research was submitted in the case of 34 projects and there was delay of more than 30 months in 10 out of 34 projects completed. Four out of 33 externally funded research projects were closed without completion after incurring an expenditure of Rs. 1.42 lakhs, there were delays up to seven years in 11 out of 12 completed projects and out of 17 projects still in progress, the delay was more than seven years in one case. Expenditure of Rs. 8.17 lakhs incurred on a project on bullock-cart design proved unfruitful. Out of 84 consultancy programmes awarded to the Institute during 1983-89, there were delays ranging from one to three years in respect of 10 completed programmes and five ongoing projects had not been completed even after one to four years of delay.

Forty-nine faculty members had not taken any teaching assignment during the academic years 1983-84 to 1988-89. Out of these, one member had not conducted any class for five years, 12 members had not conducted any class for one year. On the other hand 58 per cent of the faculty members had received consultancy fees exceeding 14 per cent of their gross salary income during 1983-89. Consultancy rules framed by the Institute were not in conformity with the government instructions and also did not provide for recovery of cost of services of faculty members from outside agencies for whom their services were spared.

Ex-gratia payment on account of escalation charges amounting to Rs. 9 lakhs was paid to two contractors. A further commitment of Rs. 4.84 lakhs was also accepted although this was not provided in the original contract.

As a result of delay in completion of the second portion of a work, the building completed in February 1986, at a cost of Rs. 21.97 lakhs remained unused for more than three years.

VII. National Institute of Educational Planning and Administration

The National Institute of Educational Planning and Administration, a registered society, was established mainly to organise training programmes, undertake research and provide consultancy in the field of educational planning and administration. The total number of calendar days of the faculty of the Institute utilised for training programmes progressively declined from 862 in 1985-86 to 376 in 1988-89. Although the Institute attributed this to a deliberate decision in order to keep a proper balance between research, training, extension and consultancy services, it did not furnish details of utilisation of mandays of the faculty separately for each activity.

Out of 287 training programmes organised by the Institute during 1984-85 to 1988-89, the duration of 72 programmes was from one to three days. The number of participants was fewer than six in 19 programmes and ranged from 6 to 10 in 36 programmes. The Institute did not have any scientific system to study the impact of training programmes organised by it.

The first ever Review Committee for reviewing the work of the Institute which had been in existence for nearly two decades was appointed only in March 1989. The Review Committee on the basis of response to questionnaires sent by the participants reported that the participants had stressed the need for follow-up action with a view to improving the quality of training programmes. The committee suggested that the clientele and programmes should be chosen where the Institute had competencies, where the clients needed the programme and where there was scope for making an impact.

Out of 38 projects/studies due for completion up to March 1989, 28 projects/studies had been completed of which 12 were completed after delays of up to 32 months. In respect of other 36 sponsored projects/studies due for completion by 1988-89, only 10 projects/studies were completed within the prescribed time and 24 project/studies were completed in extended time which ranged from 6 to 13 months. In 14 out of 16 cases checked in Audit, there was time gap ranging up to 6 to 22 months between the approval and commencement of study. The reports were also not submitted within the prescribed period of three months of completion. There was no system to ascertain whether the studies had been of any use to policy makers, planners and administrators. No unit-wise and consolidated record was maintained showing the projects approved from year-to-year, sanctioned budget of the projects, time for completion and the actuals against all these. According to the Review Committee, the research studies undertaken lacked management thrust and hence the result. The study reports enthused people only to a limited extent. The committee, therefore, recommended that more experimental and path-breaking studies should be undertaken by the Institute.

The Institute had deposited a total sum of Rs. 17.85 lakhs with the central Public Works Department in March 1988, and January 1989, for construction of staff quarters even though the building plans had not been approved. The construction work had not started till November 1989.

The Review Committee while observing that the Institute had by and large fulfilled its objectives suggested that the Institute should develop as a National Centre for excellence in educational planning and administration and evolve a long-term perspective plan for the next 10 to 15 years. The committee further suggested that the programmes undertaken by the Institute should be a good mix of training, research, advisory and dissemination activities and the faculty members and the group should plan and review their activities annually under various fields and there should be a system of performance appraisal for all faculty and research staff.

VII. **Indian Council of Philosophical Research, New Delhi**

The Indian Council of Philosophical Research started functioning in July 1981, and received grants aggregating Rs. 370.53 lakhs from the Government of India up to March 1989. The administrative expenditure exceeded the ceiling of 30 per cent year after year except during 1983-84. The expenditure on academic schemes was actually less than the administrative expenditure during 1981-82, 1982-83, 1987-88 and 1988-89.

The academic activities of the Council include award of fellowships and travel grants, seminars and workshops, research projects, international conferences and collaborations, exhibitions and publications. Contrary to the rules and regulations of the Council, the Chairman sanctioned 68 cases of extension of fellowships, seminars, travel grants, etc., involving Rs. 14.44 lakhs during 1983-84 to 1988-89 without prior scrutiny of the Research Project Committee. Utilisation certificates had not been received for Rs. 13.20 lakhs from 1981-82 onwards out of Rs. 47.27 lakhs paid by the Council to individuals and organisations on account of seminars, and fellowships.

Against the target of 199 fellowship the Council had sanctioned 64 fellowships involving Rs. 48.98 lakhs during 1982-83 to 1988-89. Fellowships were awarded in 20 cases without the fellows being affiliated to an approved university or an institution. This involved a total fellowship amount to the extent of Rs. 11.94 lakhs. In 10 cases, the scholars had resigned without completing the fellowships. This involved a total amount of Rs. 3.18 lakhs. There was no systematic reporting of the academic activities by the national fellows; two of the six national fellows did not submit the prescribed reports of their academic activities to the Council.

The Council did not publish the proceedings of any of the three major seminars held by it during 1986-89. The proceedings/reports in respect of 66 seminars, conferences, workshops for which the Council released Rs. 17.67 lakhs were also not received.

No time schedule of completion of projects was prescribed by the Council. Out of 16 projects approved by the Council during 1984-85 to 1988-89, only one project approved in 1986-87 was completed, five projects approved in 1986-87 were not taken up at all and the remaining 10 projects were in progress.

The Council did not prepare any report of the first international conference held in October 1984, with an expenditure of Rs. 8.94 lakhs. A sum of Rs. 2.04 lakhs was spent on items not included in the tentative estimates. Out of this, Rs. 0.40 lakh were paid as honorarium by the Council to its own staff. The Council did not fully observe the financial rules and regulations while incurring expenditure of Rs. 29.73 lakhs on holding five special exhibitions during 1981-82 to 1984-85.

In contravention of government orders, the Council spent Rs. 2.44 lakhs on appointment of a Consultant for its publications from February 1984, to July 1989, and brought out 15 priced publications costing Rs. 7.30 lakhs. Thus, the amount paid to the Consultant was 33 per cent of the total cost of publications. The Council's journal was not published as per the prescribed periodicity and there were delays of 6 to 8 months in its publication. The Council incurred an expenditure of Rs. 0.89 lakh on the visit of its Chairman and Director (Plan and Research) to the United Kingdom and the United States of America for the purchase of books of the value of Rs. 0.40 lakh. One micro-film reader and computer acquired by the Council for Rs. 7.02 lakhs during 1986-89 remained unutilised till June 1989.

The Council had paid Rs. 3.16 lakhs to 41 scholars for participating in international conferences who had not submitted their papers through their departments. Fifteen scholars who were paid amounts totalling Rs. 1.16 lakhs did not submit reports of their visits abroad.

The Council had not covered some of its major objectives as per its Memorandum of Association and the Council had no effective monitoring regarding its academic activities, and implementation of its various objectives set forth in the Memorandum of Association.

XI. Panjab University, Chandigarh

The enrolment of students in Panjab University declined by more than 25 per cent from 0.86 lakh in 1983 to only 0.52 lakh in 1988. Specific purpose grants aggregating Rs. 78.80 lakhs out of total grants of Rs. 1,071,02 lakhs received during 1983-88 had remained unutilised. The University spent only Rs. 0.46 lakh out of Rs. 2.10 lakhs received from the Council of Scientific and Industrial Research in 1985-86 for a sponsored scheme, but neither completed the scheme nor refunded the unspent balance. The University suffered loss of interest of Rs. 3.92 lakhs due to injudicious investment of its surplus cash balances.

Equipment worth Rs. 20 lakhs imported by the University in October 1982 was installed only in April 1989, and had not been put to use as the technicians had not been trained. Improper assessment of demand resulted in unsold publications valued at Rs. 2.65 lakhs, unutilised lesson scripts costing Rs. 2.36 lakhs were disposed of as waste paper for Rs. 0.17 lakh and periodicals/journals worth Rs. 2.37 lakhs for which advance payments had been made had not been received.

The University had neither renewed the lease deeds of various shops in its commercial complex leased for a period of one year prior to March 1966, nor revised the rents. The University paid Rs. 88.37 lakhs for water charges during 1981-88 but recovered only a sum of Rs. 72.47 lakhs from the consumers resulting in short realisation of Rs. 15.90 lakhs.

X. Kendriya Hindi Shikshan Mandal, Agra

The Mandal had neither determined the intake capacity for its various courses/centres, nor fixed any targets. The number of persons trained under various courses had been very small. The expenditure on pay and allowances of the administrative staff, rent, etc., was more than one-third of the total revenue expenditure.

Textbooks and video teaching lessons prepared for the states and erstwhile union territories in the North-Eastern region in 1984-85 at a cost of Rs. 4.36 lakhs had remained unpublished (May 1989). Priced publications of the Mandal remained unsold for long.

The survey and research work on functional Hindi and socio-linguistic unit project on Pan Indian Hindi was suspended after incurring an expenditure of Rs. 1.86 lakhs.

A generator costing Rs. 1.78 lakhs and installed, in October 1988, remained uncommissioned till July 1989. An intercom-system costing Rs. 1.65 lakhs installed in 1982-83 had not been in operation since its installation.

XI. Banaras Hindu University

Idle Equipment: The Banaras Hindu University imported 10 items of equipment costing Rs. 62.82 lakhs, between 1976 and 1987, for intensive research and development programmes and for strengthening infrastructure of various wings, of which, 8 items costing Rs. 44.41 lakhs had not been installed/commissioned till July 1989. The remaining two items costing Rs. 18.41 lakhs were used partially for routine works. Thus, the amount spent in foreign exchange remained largely unfruitful.

XII. University of Delhi

Blocking of Funds: On receipt of intimation, in April 1983, from the Municipal Corporation of Delhi (MCD) for payment of property tax including general tax amounting to Rs. 90 lakhs, the University of Delhi obtained additional grants of Rs. 45 lakhs and Rs. 22.50 lakhs from the University Grants Commission (UGC) in March 1984, and during 1984-85 respectively. The University paid Rs. 10 lakhs to the MCD, in March 1984, towards property tax. The demand for general tax had been received for the first time, and on a petition filed by the University in the High Court of Delhi in October 1983, its recovery was stayed in November 1984. Consequently no money was paid to the MCD. Despite this, the amount of Rs. 57.50 lakhs was not refunded to the UGC and was retained in a separate account with the State Bank of India from March 1985. This resulted in the blocking of funds amounting to Rs. 57.50 lakhs, i.e., Rs. 35 lakhs from March 1984, and Rs. 22.50 lakhs from March 1985, onwards.

XIII. **National Book Trust**

Blocking of Funds: The Department of education decided to allot a plot in the campus of the National Council of Educational Research and Training to the National Book Trust in November 1980, to enable the latter to construct its own office building. The NBT paid Rs. 6 lakhs to the NCERT towards the cost of land in March 1983, and a further amount of Rs. 20.46 lakhs in two instalments to the CPWD, in March 1985, and May 1986. However, the NCERT neither handed over possession of the plot of land to the NBT nor refunded the amount of Rs. 6 lakhs received from it. Consequently, the construction could not start and funds to the extent of Rs. 26.46 lakhs remained blocked. Approval of the Cabinet Committee on Accommodation to the location of the office of the NBT in Delhi had also not been obtained. In the meantime the NBT continued to function from residential areas because of which it had to pay Rs. 7.78 lakhs to the Delhi Development Authority towards composition fee during 1981-89.

XIV. **University Grants Commission**

Construction of Second Phase of Ram Lal Anand College Building, New Delhi: Ram Lal Anand College awarded the work of construction of the second phase of its building to a contractor, in February 1979, for Rs. 5.57 lakhs as per the plans and estimates approved by the University Grants Commission (UGC), in December 1977. However, the UGC did not release any grant to the College for this purpose till September 1980, and in the meantime, the contractor abandoned the work, in January 1979, after executing the work worth Rs. 0.56 lakh. The central Public Works Department (CPWD) which was approached in October 1981, to execute the remaining work, submitted estimates for Rs. 32.50 lakhs in March 1985, which were approved by the UGC, in February 1986, for Rs. 26.75 lakhs. However, the UGC did not release any funds to the College and in September 1986, the CPWD revised the estimates to Rs. 40.07 lakhs. The estimates were again revised to Rs. 32.27 lakhs in November 1988, excluding certain additional items, which were finally approved by the UGC. The work was actually started in November 1989.

Thus, delays in the release of funds by the UGC, abandonment of work by the original contractor and further delay in making alternative arrangements for execution of work resulted in escalation in cost by Rs. 27.26 lakhs besides denial of intended facilities to the students for over 10 years. The estimates for additional items concerning development of site and other services for Rs. 10.93 lakhs submitted by the College were not approved till November 1989.

XV. **Regional Engineering College, Durgapur**

Underutilisation of Facility: Against the total intake capacity of 248 students for the post-graduate engineering courses of the Regional Engineering College,

Durgapur, the number of students actually enrolled during 1984-89 was 88, of whom 59 dropped out. The initial intake of students was less than 50 per cent of the capacity year after year, and the extent of dropouts were more than 50 per cent each year. Rs. 2.02 lakhs were paid as scholarships to the students who dropped out; this expenditure proved infructuous and the additional faculty provided for the post-graduate courses also remained largely unutilised.

XVI. **Bombay Port Trust**

(i) *Stores and Material Management:* In the Stores Department of the Bombay Port Trust, there was inordinate delay in processing of indents received from various departments and the issue of goods received and accepted notes after receipt of materials. The materials were stocked in excess of the requirement for immediate use. No reconciliation had been done between the balances as per bin cards and priced stores ledger. Physical verification was not conducted as per prescribed periodicity.

Materials worth Rs. 4.55 lakhs procured during 1964 to 1976 and spare parts for fork lifts amounting to Rs. 2.93 lakhs purchased during 1943 and 1953 remained unutilised. The fork lifts had earlier been disposed of. Excess quantity of stitched uniforms costing Rs. 2 lakhs had remained undisposed of since 1981 and cotton *dosuti* cloth costing Rs. 10.27 lakhs remained unissued due to change in the policy for issue of cloth to certain categories of employees.

As at the end of March 1989, advance payments of Rs. 125.99 lakhs and Rs. 36.80 lakhs were outstanding from private and government parties respectively. Rs. 0.60 lakh deposited with the suppliers of gas cylinders since 1982 had not been recovered even after the return of empty cylinders.

Cases of avoidable expenditure of Rs. 1.87 lakhs due to non-acceptance of the lowest tender and delay in issue in purchase order were also noticed.

(ii) *Unauthorised Subletting of Lease-hold Premises:* A plot at Frera land estate was leased out by the Bombay Port Trust to a lessee from December 1925, to January 1974, which was further renewed up to 1990. In September 1985, the lessee informed the Port Trust their intention to effect a change in the use of shops, office godowns, etc., for storage of non-hazardous goods and also for subletting a portion of the premises. No decision was taken on the proposal submitted to Chairman of the Port Trust for granting the permission of subletting to the lessee with additional rent recovery in accordance with the accepted guidelines. Premises admeasuring 28,301 square feet were nevertheless sublet by the lessee in July 1985, by charging Rs. 3.11 lakhs at the rate of Rs. 11 per square feet without the permission of the Port Trust. This came to the notice of the Port Trust only in 1987. A suit for eviction and other relief as admissible under the law was filed in October 1989, as per the proposal submitted by the Estate Manager in January 1986: A total sum of Rs. 43.14 lakhs towards lease rent and additional deposit was recoverable from the lessee up to September 1989.

(iii) *Infructuous Expenditure on Computerisation:* The Port Trust incurred an expenditure of Rs. 10.91 lakhs up to March 1987, on computerisation for the centralised billing system in respect of the vessel-related services. Additional equipment and accessories worth Rs. 3.43 lakhs were also procured in March 1987. However, in July 1987, the Port Trust decided not to pursue the computerisation of operations as no agreement could be reached with unions. This resulted in an unfruitful expenditure of Rs. 10.91 lakhs. The equipment and accessories procured at the cost of Rs. 3.43 lakhs have also been lying idle for over two years.

XVII. **Calcutta Port Trust**

(i) *Dry Dock System:* The percentage occupancy of dry docks for commercial vessels declined from 64 in 1982-83 to 39 in 1987-88. The three dry docks earmarked for commercial vessels remained unoccupied for 527 days during 1982-83 resulting in a potential loss of revenue of about Rs. 105.40 lakhs.

Underutilisation of dry docks was traced to poor conditions of infrastructure involving longer servicing time. In order to improve the services and to make the dry docks more attractive, a modernisation programme sanctioned in September 1984, was to be completed by December 1986, at the total cost of Rs. 475.76 lakhs. Against this, a total amount of Rs. 179.05 lakhs could only be spent up to March 1989. Forty-nine per cent of the work had so far been completed. Out of 15 tender packages for modernisation, only eight could be finalised up to January 1989, and out of these, procurement could be completed only in four cases.

A crane procured in October 1984, was found unsuitable resulting in a loss of revenue of Rs. 42.10 lakhs during October 1984, to November 1987.

Trimmer blocks, high-pressure jet pumps and spray applicators procured at a cost of Rs. 114.96 lakhs between September 1986, and March 1987, remained unutilised till January 1989.

Mechanised hull cleaning equipment and pressure jet pumps purchased at a cost of Rs. 22.17 lakhs in October 1986, could not be used resulting in blocking of funds.

(ii) *Non-recovery of Dues:* Calcutta Port Trust had been operating and maintaining "Mechanical grain unloading equipment" owned by the Food Corporation of India since 1966 on "cost plus basis" without settling the terms and conditions with the latter. Audit noticed that bills amounting to Rs. 134.56 lakhs on payment of maintenance charges incurred by the Port Trust during the period of non-operation of equipment as a result of suspension of import of foodgrains in various spells during September 1978, to March 1989, were not paid by the Corporation. According to the Corporation, staff of only 55 was justified for maintenance of the equipment during idle period against 66 and 108 entertained by the Port Trust. Thus, non-settlement of terms and conditions led to non-recovery of Rs. 134.56 lakhs from the Food Corporation of India.

(iii) *Loss Due to Non-availing of Exemption from Payment of Customs Duty:* According to the Ministry of Finance notification issued in July 1983, capital goods, components, raw materials and consumables are exempted from payment of Customs duty when imported for repair of ocean-going vessels by a ship repair unit registered with the Director General of Shipping. Although the Port Trust was registered in November 1986, for this very purpose up to

November 1987, with the Director General of Shipping, it did not avail of exemption of Customs duty amounting to Rs. 47.59 lakhs. The Port Trust also did not get its registration renewed after November 1987, and consequently could not avail exemption from payment of Customs duty amounting to Rs. 16 lakhs paid after the expiry of registration till March 1989. Thus, the Port Trust incurred a total loss of Rs. 63.59 lakhs due to failure to avail exemption from payment of Customs duty.

(iv) *Irregular Payment of Interest on Arrears of ad hoc/interim Relief:* In October 1987, the government sanctioned *ad hoc*/interim relief to the employees of the major Port Trusts from January 1986. In consultation with the various staff federations, the Calcutta Port Trust decided to make payment of arrears of *ad hoc*/interim relief only in the next financial year 1988-89, i.e., with interest at the rate 10.8 per cent from January to March 1988. An amount of Rs. 23.72 lakhs was accordingly paid as interest by the Port Trust to the employees of Calcutta Dock System and Haldia Dock System and debited under the head "salaries". No interest is normally allowed due to delay in disbursement of pay and allowances. The Port Trust had also not obtained government sanction to the payment as required under the Major Port Trusts Act, 1963. The payment of interest on deferred disbursement of arrears of *ad hoc*/interim relief was, therefore, irregular.

(v) *Loss Due to Non-revision of Rates of Electricity Charges:* The Calcutta Port Trust supplies electricity in low voltage to its employees for domestic use and also to contractors, market stall-holders, banks, etc., for commercial consumers through inner distribution lines on "no loss, no profit basis". Although the rates at which electricity was procured by the Port Trust were enhanced several times between February 1983, and February 1988, the recovery rates fixed by the Port Trust in June 1975, and October 1981, for domestic and commercial consumers separately were not revised. This resulted in a loss of Rs. 8.77 lakhs to the Port Trust.

(vi) *Procurement of Cutter Suction Dredger:* Calcutta Port Trust incurred an expenditure of Rs. 22.38 lakhs on the purchase of a dredger in October 1974, from Garden Reach Workshop Limited. The dredger was accepted and entire payment made without demonstration of successful operation. Although the supply was received late, liquidated damages amounting to Rs. 1.15 lakhs were also not recovered. Expenditure of Rs. 15.22 lakhs was incurred by the Port Trust on the repair of the dredger and the dredger could be put to use only from March 1983. The dredger was rendered idle from August 1985, consequent upon a decision to discontinue silting operations. The Port Trust incurred expenditure of Rs. 18.60 lakhs on the manning, maintenance and repair of the dredger from August 1985, to March 1989, when it remained idle. No decision had been communicated by the government for the disposal of the dredger proposed by the Port Trust in 1989.

(vii) *Blocking of Funds and Avoidable Expenditure:* Calcutta Port Trust purchased one set of rerailing equipment in October 1977, from a foreign firm for Rs. 5.13 lakhs for providing adequate rerailment facilities for its railway system. The equipment could not be put to operation due to a dispute between the Union and the Port Trust till April 1986. In the meantime, the equipment became unserviceable due to its prolonged non-use and the Port Trust had to approach the Director General of Technical Development in April 1989, for clearance for import of accessories and spares worth Rs. 5.43 lakhs. Thus non-use of the equipment for about 11 years resulted in blocking up of funds of Rs. 5.13 lakhs. In addition, the Port Trust incurred an avoidable expenditure of Rs. 12.20 lakhs on hiring of accident relief vans from the Eastern Railway.

(viii) *Procurement of Gear Boxes:* Against an order placed by the Calcutta Port Trust on a firm in April 1985, for manufacture and supply of seven gear boxes for Rs. 25.91 lakhs plus taxes, duties, etc., by August 1986 only five gear boxes were received by December 1986. Out of the five gear boxes two gear boxes found defective were returned in July 1987, to the firm for repairs. These had not been received back. One gear box could not be put to use as it was not according to required specifications. The remaining two had not been supplied by the firm so far.

Despite poor performance of the firm, the Port Trust placed a further order in August 1986, for supply of 10 gear boxes at a cost of Rs. 49.49 lakhs plus taxes and duties to be completed by August 1987. The firm could supply only six gear boxes by October 1988, out of which four gear boxes were without necessary accessories and were consequently lying idle.

XVIII. **Cochin Port Trust**

Unfruitful Expenditure: The Cochin Port Trust awarded a contract for closing a gap of 456 metres in a reclamation bund at an estimated cost of Rs. 27.29 lakhs to a contractor in June 1984. The work required construction of a wall of 2-1 metres above water level and was to be completed in one year. The work was partially completed up to November 1985.

Instead of filling up the reach area by dredging, 5,200 cubic metres of rubble worth Rs. 9.10 lakhs was dumped in the reach, which would have been washed away from the alignment of the proposed wall in view of heavy sinkage and erosion caused by heavy water current and tidal waves. As the chances of retrieving or making use of the rubble are apparently remote, the expenditure of Rs. 9.10 lakhs was rendered infructuous, besides the reclamation project remaining unfinished so far.

XIX. **Jawaharlal Nehru Port Trust**

Extra and Avoidable Expenditure on Filling Work: The Jawahar Lal Nehru Port Trust entrusted the work of filling in the township and container freight station areas to the Gujarat State Construction Corporation Limited for Rs. 12 crores in March 1986. During execution the quantities of grade I fill increased from 9.40 lakh cums to 30.18 lakh cums, which necessitated revision in rate for this item from Rs. 45 to Rs. 67.25 per cum resulting in an extra expenditure of Rs. 4.21 crores. The Port Trust had got the work of preparation of estimates done by a consultant. No action was, however, contemplated against the consultant for its failure in drawing up a reasonably accurate bill of quantities.

XX. Kandla Port Trust

Underutilisation of Container Handling Equipment: Kandla Port Trust purchased container handling equipment worth Rs. 60.79 lakhs from 1980 to 1986 in order to handle five lakh tonnes cargo per annum. The equipment remained underutilised due to various reasons and was declared surplus in September 1987. Out of the total, equipment costing Rs. 11.49 lakhs was sold for Rs. 6 lakhs; and the remaining equipment costing Rs. 49.30 lakhs declared surplus was still to be disposed to.

XXI. Indian Jute Industries Research Association, Calcutta

Blocking of Funds: The Indian Jute Industries Research Association, Calcutta, incurred an expenditure of Rs. 7.91 lakhs (including Rs. 7.50 lakhs in foreign exchange) on purchase of Fade-O-Meter-cum- Weather-O-Meter and refrigeration unit. The machine had, however, remained uninstalled even after lapse of more than two and a half years. This resulted not only in blocking of funds of Rs. 7.91 lakhs but also defeated the purpose of procurement. The warranty period of the equipment had also expired.

XXII. Institute of Hotel Management, Catering Technology and Applied Nutrition, Bombay

Infructuous Expenditure on Water-proofing Treatment: A leakage in the terrace was noticed for the first time during 1977-78 in the building of the Institute of Hotel Management, Catering Technology and Applied Nutrition, Bombay, constructed in 1965-66. Although an expenditure of Rs. 3.68 lakhs was incurred on water-proofing work of the terrace, through the Central Public Works Department (CPWD), the work was left incomplete by the CPWD in September 1989, and the leakage continued to persist. This had damaged the building as well as electric installations besides rendering the expenditure of Rs. 3.68 lakhs infructuous.

XXIII. Institute of Physically Handicapped, New Delhi

Purchase of Flats from Delhi Development Authority: The Institute of Physically Handicapped, New Delhi, acquired 30 flats under the Janata category at Nand Nagri from the Delhi Development Authority at a cost of Rs. 6.30 lakhs in June 1982, with a view to providing alternative accommodation on rent to employees both handicapped and others who had been squatting in the premises. Contrary to the general policy of providing residential accommodation to the employees on lease for the period of their service, the Institute arranged transfer of flats on ownership basis, thereby adversely affecting the interest of the remaining present and future employees. Further, both the government and the DDA had communicated their approval to the transfer of flats only to the physically handicapped employees of the Institute, but 16 out of 30 employees to whom flats were allotted were not physically handicapped.

The Institute also failed to get the refund of Rs. 6.30 lakhs deposited with the DDA while surrendering these flats to the DDA in October 1987.

CAG's REPORT ON CENTRAL GOVERNMENT — CIVIL

PREFATORY REMARKS

This Report for the year ended 31 March 1989, has been prepared for submission to the President under article 151 of the Constitution. It relates mainly to matters arising from test audit of the financial transactions of some of the Civil Departments of the union government.

2. This Report includes, among others, reviews on

(a) Guarantees given by the government for external loans,
(b) Central Government Health Scheme,
(c) National Malaria Eradication Programme,
(d) Doordarshan commercial service, and
(e) Directorate of Estates.

3. The cases mentioned in this Report are among those which came to notice in the course of audit during the year 1988-89 as well as those which had come to notice in earlier years but could not be dealt with in the previous Reports; matters relating to the period subsequent to 1988-89 have also been included, wherever considered necessary.

OVERVIEW

The Audit Report for the year ended 31 March 1989, contains 32 paragraphs including five reviews. The points highlighted in the Report are given below:

I. Ministry of Finance — Department of Economic Affairs

Guarantees given by Government for External Loans: Internal and external loans raised by public sector undertakings, private companies, institutions, etc., are guaranteed by the central government for repayment of principal and payment of interest. These guarantees constitute contingent liabilities of the government.

The amount of guarantees given by the government for raising external loans increased by 81 per cent between 1984 and 1988 and stood at Rs. 6,850 crores. Audit scrutiny, however, showed that the amount as per budget documents was not correct as it did not include the amount of accrued interest, where the loans were interest, bearing and the government had given guarantee for principal as well as interest. The amount also did not include the guarantees given by the Ministry of Railways. The amounts of guarantees had not been adjusted for fluctuations in the rate of exchange. There was no regular procedure in converting the amount of guarantee into Indian rupees; different ministries followed different procedures and even the same ministry followed different procedures in respect of the amount of guarantees provided in favour of different institutions. Where historical rate of conversion was adopted, the actual liability in terms of rupees was much more due to the depreciation of Indian currency.

The amount of guarantees shown in different budget documents for the same year did not mutually agree and there were several discrepancies. The payment of Rs. 17 crores made on account of invoking of guarantee in the 1987-89 by creditors was not reported in budget documents.

There was no centralised control exercised by the Ministry of Finance to watch that the loans and interest were paid as per the terms of the agreements. Other ministries which had stood guarantee also did not intimate whether any such monitoring was done. Although the Ministry of Finance had issued instructions for a consolidated review of all government guarantees, it was observed that even the Ministry of Finance (Department of Economic Affairs) had not undertaken such a review.

In most of the cases, no guarantee fee was charged and by not charging proper guarantee fee, the government had paid hidden subsidy amounting to Rs. 718 crores.

No provision existed in the agreements with the institutions for recovery of interest/penalty for delay in payment of guarantee fee.

II. **Ministry of Health and Family Welfare**

Central Government Health Scheme: The central Government Health Scheme covers 16 cities through 221 allopathic units, 13 allopathic polyclinics and 71 units of the Indian systems of medicines. It covers a beneficiary population of 37.59 lakhs.

The annual expenditure of the scheme had increased from Rs. 29.63 crores in 1984-85 to Rs. 55.20 crores in 1988-89 and the average cost per card holder had increased from Rs. 375 to Rs. 650. While the expenditure had increased over the years, the amount spent on medicines was proportionately less. The average cost per card holder varied widely from station to station. Despite the recommendations of the Estimates Committee, the government did not compile and publish the dispensary-wise information on cost per card holder. Audit analysis of expenditure in respect of selected dispensaries showed that the cost per beneficiary in high income areas was relatively more. In Delhi, the average annual expenditure on medicines per beneficiary was Rs. 9 in Srinivaspuri and Rs. 65 in North Avenue.

The contribution from the beneficiaries covered just 13 per cent of the recurring expenditure. Despite the recommendations of the Fourth Central Pay Commission, the rates of contribution from government servants prescribed in 1954 had not been revised.

The Seventh Five Year Plan targets of opening of new units were not likely to be achieved.

Several shortcomings were noticed in the working of dispensaries. The criteria for opening dispensaries were not observed. In Delhi, the number of families attached to a dispensary varied from 1,547 (President's Estate) to 17,432 (Kingsway Camp). The dispensaries were working on a single shift of six hours' duration though it had resulted in inconvenience to the beneficiaries. The deployment of medical and para-medical staff conformed neither to the sanctioned strength nor to the recommended norms, resulting in uneven workload. Fifty per cent of the doctors whose work was test-checked attended to 50 patients against the norm of 75 patients per day.

The family folder system which would include the total history of a patient, at a glance, and put a restraint on malpractices had not been introduced though recommended by the Estimates Committee.

The expenditure on specialist services had increased from 9.5 to 11.3 per cent of total expenditure between 1984-85 and 1988-89. Though the attendance in dispensaries had declined the number of cases referred for specialist treatment had increased. There were no facilities for emergency beds, requisite number of specialists were not provided, X-ray, ECG equipment were not functioning or remained closed for want of films, etc.

Dental clinics at Ahmedabad, Allahabad and Kanpur did not function for long periods up to five years for want of dental surgeons.

In the procurement and supply of medicines, several irregularities in provisioning resulting in excessive stocking, short supply necessitating local purchases at extra cost, receipt and supply of substandard medicines and non-disposal of expired medicines were notice. In Delhi alone, the additional expenditure on local purchase of medicines was about Rs. 33.1 lakhs during 1987-88 and 1988-89.

There was no analytical system of quality control in the purchase of Ayurvedic and Unani medicines. Procurement of Unani medicines fell short of the requirement due to delay in finalisation of contracts. Cases of non-availability of homeopathic medicines for long periods were also noticed.

In Delhi, 75 out of 111 units did not have proper accommodation. In other cities also, 95 out of 194 units were housed in private accommodation. Despite an adverse notice by the Estimates Committee in 1981-82, no targets were fixed for construction of CGHS buildings during the Sixth and Seventh Five Year Plan.

The reporting system and monitoring by the Director, CGHS, showed that though several returns had been prescribed, the compilation of statistical data was in arrears for over two years, and the data published/compiled were inaccurate. The scheduled inspections of the dispensaries were not conducted and complaints were not monitored.

National Malaria Eradication Programme: The National Malaria Eradication Programme in 1958 aimed at total eradication of malaria within six to seven years. In April 1977, this objective was abandoned, the Modified Plan of Operation was directed towards controlling and containing malaria and preventing deaths due to malaria.

However, these limited objectives had also not been achieved. According to the information furnished by the Directorate of National Malaria Eradication Programme, the incidence of malaria actually increased in Andhra Pradesh, Goa, Gujarat, Kerala, Mizoram, Rajasthan, Tamil Nadu, West Bengal and Dadra and Nagar Haveli between 1981 and 1988. The increase was 64 per cent in Andhra Pradesh and 4,358 per cent in Goa. The total number of deaths due to malaria in the country also increased from 170 to 209 between 1981 and 1988. In four states (Assam, Madhya Pradesh, Mizoram and Orissa), the number of deaths increased from 70 to 580 per cent during 1986 over 1985.

Audit scrutiny of figures of incidence of malaria as well as deaths due to malaria showed that these statistics were not reliable. The incidence of malaria was understated due to under-reporting, shortfalls in collection of blood smears and unexamined blood smear slides, etc. The number of deaths due to malaria was also understated. The Indepth Evaluation Committee consisting of National and International experts had also observed in October 1985, that the official records were extremely unreliable and there were no guidelines and parameters to monitor whether the objective of arresting the deaths was achieved. The committee had observed that the actual number of deaths due to malaria was considerably higher and many times more than officially recorded.

Under the Modified Plan of Operation, the main activities were selective spray operations, fortnightly collection of blood smears from fever cases and their examination and treatment with anti-malaria drugs. Health education, public cooperation, distribution of drugs, establishment of fever treatment depots were other important components of the Modified Plan of Operation. For designated urban areas, the Urban Malaria Scheme was launched in November 1971.

While the major thrust of the programme was on spraying activity, substantial population areas requiring regular spray were left unsprayed each year; the shortfall in spraying ranged from 33 to 53 per cent during 1980-88. Shortfalls in spraying occurred up to 90 per cent in Gujarat, up to 86 per cent in Madhya Pradesh, up to 88 per cent in Meghalaya and 100 per cent in Sikkim. Mopping up operations and focal sprays were also not carried out in many states.

Some of the states had attributed shortfalls in spraying operations to resource constraints. Test check, however, showed that in many states, the quantity of insecticides used in spraying operations was far in excess of requirement as per the prescribed norms. This resulted in avoidable extra expenditure of Rs. 908.58 lakhs and improper utilisation of scarce insecticides in Bihar, Goa, Gujarat, Karnataka, Madhya Pradesh, Meghalaya, Mizoram and Uttar Pradesh. In Karnataka, avoidable extra expenditure of Rs. 33.84 lakhs was incurred in conducting spray operations in areas where the state governments had recommended discontinuance of such operations.

Cases of excess supply of insecticides to Bihar, Meghalaya, Punjab and Rajasthan were noticed in Audit. In Gujarat, Haryana, Karnataka, Manipur, Dadra and Nagar Haveli, excessive procurement of insecticides and their retention beyond the date of expiry resulted in avoidable expenditure of Rs. 144.63 lakhs during 1982 to 1988.

Entomological surveys were the basic requirement in the selection of the right type of insecticides and the effectiveness of the spray operations depended upon the susceptibility of the vector mosquito to the insecticides sprayed. Such entomological surveys had not been carried out in several states. In Madhya Pradesh, an expenditure of Rs. 17,710 lakhs was incurred on spray of insecticides to which the resistance of vector was indicated. In Andhra Pradesh, Malathion which is the costliest of insecticides was used for spray in several places incurring an extra expenditure of Rs. 88 lakhs; the use of Malathion did not result in control of incidence of malaria which actually increased.

Insecticides testing laboratories had not started functioning in seven out of nine states where the establishment of such laboratories was recommended by the Public Accounts Committee in 1985-86.

Under the Modified Plan of Operation, fortnightly surveillance by enumerating all the families in village register had not been carried out in several states properly. In terms of blood smears, 10 per cent of the population was required to be screened every year. Targets of blood smear collection were not met; the shortfall in collection ranged from 15 to 76 per cent in four states of Bihar, Punjab, Tamil Nadu and Uttar Pradesh.

The incidence of un-examined blood slides was particularly high in two malaria-infested states, viz. Kerala and Madhya Pradesh. Consequently, an estimated expenditure of Rs. 23.28 lakhs on their collection was rendered unfruitful and positive cases were denied the benefit of treatment.

Radical treatment of administering prescribed dosage of primaquine tablets for five days was required to be given to all cases found malaria positive. In Bihar, Madhya Pradesh, Rajasthan, Tamil Nadu and West Bengal, shortfalls ranging from 13 to 23 per cent were noticed in administering radical treatment.

In Assam, Bihar, Meghalaya, Mizoram and West Bengal, excessive use of anti-malaria drugs worth Rs. 132.39 lakhs was noticed. Cases of administering time-barred anti-malarial drugs were noticed in Bihar, Karnataka, Madhya Pradesh, Rajasthan and Tamil Nadu. Several states had huge stocks of time-barred drugs.

The urban malaria scheme sanctioned for 133 towns was actually in operation only in 126 towns. Except in Bombay, the implementation of bye-laws of mosquito control was very tardy or non-existent.

The multi-purpose worker is at the core of operational efficiency of the programme and the success of the programme depends upon active case detection through routine collection of blood smears by the multi-purpose worker from individuals presently suffering from or reporting recent spell of fever. Vacancies against the posts of multi-purpose workers were common. The Indepth Evaluation Committee had also observed that the converting of a vertical unipurpose malaria worker scheme into a horizontal multi-purpose worker scheme proved too heavy a drag on the frontline worker. Emphasis on other activities particularly family welfare was stated to be responsible for poor performance of multi-purpose worker in malaria eradication.

Key posts of officers responsible for implementation of the programme remained vacant for long periods in a very large number of states. In Nagaland, an extra expenditure of Rs. 108 lakhs was incurred due to over-staffing. In West Bengal excessive deployment of gangs of field workers resulted in an extra expenditure of Rs. 112.49 lakhs.

One of the major objectives of the Modified Plan of Operation was to make available anti-malaria drugs to fever cases in remote inaccessible areas through voluntary institutions like Fever Treatment Depots and Drug Distribution Centres. These institutions had either not been established or were not functioning properly.

Health education is the basic means of enlightening the masses for control of malaria. This area remained largely neglected. The funds provided for publicity were not utilised; the extent of saving ranged from 51 to 92 per cent in seven out of nine years up to 1988-89.

The various records and reports and returns as prescribed for monitoring and assessing the performance of the programme were either not maintained or not submitted to the designated authorities.

There had been no follow-up on the recommendations of the Indepth Evaluation Committee (1985) which included malariogenic stratification of the country, professionalisation of health education, strengthening of community participation and inter- and intra-sector co-ordination.

Construction of Nurses Hostel in Safdarjung Hospital: The construction of a new nurses hostel in Safdarjung Hospital sanctioned in November 1970, was commenced in March 1980, and completed after 18 years in July 1988, at a cost of Rs. 2.29 crores. The hostel was constructed for unmarried nurses though it was known that the requirement of accommodation was more for married nurses. The hostel with 543 rooms taken over by the hospital had not been put to use. Even the existing hostel with 222 rooms for nurses was not fully occupied. Out of the 706 nurses, 520 nurses were married, 120 nurses were unmarried and 66 student nurses. Consequently, while on the one hand, the constructed accommodation remains unoccupied, there is, on the other, denial of quarters to married nurses whose requirements remain unfulfilled. The investment of Rs. 2.29 crores on the building will remain substantially blocked.

Construction of a Sterilisation Ward: Under the All India Hospital *Post Partum* Scheme sanctioned by the government in 1969 as part of the programme of family welfare, separate sterilisation wards were to be constructed in various medical institutions. The construction for the building for one such centre in the All-India Institute of Medical Sciences, New Delhi, could not start as funds amounting to Rs. 5.33 lakhs provided to it in March 1981, were inadequate. Although grants aggregating Rs. 20.17 lakhs were again paid to AIIMS in November 1985, and September 1986, for construction of the ward, the construction could not be taken up initially because of non-receipt of permission from the New Delhi Municipal Committee and, subsequently, because of certain difficulties expressed by AIIMS on construction at the proposed location. AIIMS had not been able to decide upon an alternative site for construction of the ward. Thus the benefit of the facilities envisaged under the family welfare programme could not be provided even after a period of 20 years.

Establishment of a Drug De-addiction Ward at Safdarjung Hospital: Since treatment of drug addiction cases was not possible in general wards, it was decided to set up a drug de-addiction ward in Safdarjung Hospital, New Delhi. The ward was to start functioning in the hospital by October 1986. An expenditure of Rs. 9.79 lakhs was incurred on the ward during 1987-89. Information regarding the installation of equipment; number of patients admitted in the ward during 1987-89 was not furnished by the hospital. The hospital incurred further expenditure of Rs. 2.91 lakhs on staff during 1989-90. In July 1989, the ministry ordered the establishment of the centre at Lady Hardinge Medical College and Smt. Sucheta Kripalani Hospital. The 11 members of the staff ordered to be transferred to the college in September 1989, did not join. Only a limited in-patient service was being provided by the college for drug de-addicts as the nursing staff and house-surgeon were not in position. Thus the total expenditure of Rs. 12.70 lakhs incurred in the Safdarjung Hospital did not prove fruitful and the benefit of de-addiction services could also not be provided to drug addicts.

III. **Ministry of Information and Broadcasting**

Doordarshan Commercial Service: The receipts from commercials are credited to a non-lapsable fund. The fund was to be utilised primarily on expenditure for improvement of the software and hardware and for experimentation in the new fields of development of electronics and programming in Doordarshan and Akashwani, implementing schemes, which would increase the commercial revenues, payment of financial assistance to artists, etc. A sum of Rs. 445.59 crores was deposited in the fund by Doordarshan during 1976-77 to 1988-89. Against this, a sum of Rs. 298.10 crores (revenue expenditure: Rs. 95.33 crores; capital expenditure: Rs. 202.77 crores) was utilised till 1988-89. The earnings of Doordarshan from advertisements increased from Rs. 31.43 crores in 1984-85 to Rs. 161.26 crores in 1988-89.

The time allotted for commercials prescribed in the Doordarshan Manual was 10 per cent, later reduced to 5 per cent. The actual utilisation of time was only two and a half per cent; substantial efforts were not made to market more time. Further, there was no fixed periodicity for review and revision of rate structure. Doordarshan did not revise the rate at any time between February 1980, and September 1983, despite the increase of 76 per cent and 141 per cent in the number of television sets and transmitters.

Doordarshan paid 15 per cent commission to the agencies booking advertisements; no commission was payable for advertisements booked directly (direct business constituted less than 1 per cent of the total business). Nearly one quarter of the business was accounted for by three agencies during 1987-88 and 1988-89. The agency commission had increased from Rs. 4.84 crores in 1984-85 to Rs. 24.19 crores in 1988-89; however, the rate of commission which stood at 15 per cent had not been revised.

Doordarshan did not maintain record of time demanded for commercials, time available and sold and advertisers waiting for time. The prescribed agents' ledger was also not maintained. No record showed the outstanding dues from the parties. According to the information furnished by Doordarshan in June 1989, bills amounting to Rs. 444.93 lakhs and interest amounting to Rs. 41.09 lakhs were outstanding from 142 agencies. An internal team decided to be set up in April 1989, to tackle the outstanding bills had not started functioning so far. There were delays of more than 90 days in raising the bills against the agencies. In 3,303 cases, the payment of bills by the agencies was delayed, but Doordarshan did not recover interest amounting to Rs. 61.06 lakhs from the parties concerned for delayed payments. Sixteen agencies which owed Rs. 54.57 lakhs to Doordarshan up to March 1987, were granted fresh accreditation from January 1988. A sum of Rs. 56.17 lakhs was also due from these agencies in September 1989, for bills raised up to January 1989. The non-accredited agencies were required to deposit the telecast charges, at least 15 days in advance. Cases were noticed where the charges were not paid even up to October 1989, for telecasts made during 1988-89.

Doordarshan suffered loss of revenue amounting to Rs. 25.49 lakhs due to reduction in prescribed rates, improper categorisation of telecasts, make good sports, telecasting advertisements not contracted, allowing extra time, underbilling, etc. This included concession of Rs. 4.50 lakhs allowed to an agency in connection with the telecast of the highlights of the programme "Freedom Run" at reduced rates for which Doordarshan had no authority. Although Doordarshan admitted having given similar concession in other cases as well, it did not furnish details of these cases.

IV. **Ministry of Steel and Mines**

Avoidable Expenditure on Payment of Terminal Charges: The Controller of Stores, Geological Survey of India, Calcutta, paid Rs. 10.30 lakhs as terminal charges in 47 cases between August 1984, and November 1988, due to delay in clearing consignments which had arrived at Calcutta Airport from abroad. These charges were being paid in a routine manner due to lack of control over such expenditure.

V. **Ministry of Surface Transport**

Purchase of Racons: Twenty-four solid state radar transponder beacons (Racons) for providing navigational aid to mariners ordered in November 1986, at a cost of Rs. 36.53 lakhs failed during field trials even though these had been inspected by the DGSD in association with the department. Only two Racons could be rectified and made functional by the end of August 1988, resulting in an expenditure of Rs. 33 lakhs towards the cost of 22 non-functional Racons remaining unfruitful. Besides the intended improved navigational facilities to the mariners could also not be provided.

VI. **Ministry of Textiles**

Implementation of Handloom Project: In September 1986, the Ministry of Textiles sanctioned a pilot project costing Rs. 39.72 lakhs as there was an urgent need to make the handloom industry adept in the use of blended yarns. Against the sanction, a sum of Rs. 20 lakhs was released to the Silk and Art Silk Mills Research Association (SASMIRA). The ministry, however, did not lay down the physical and financial targets and instead stipulated that the targets would be worked out by SASMIRA who also failed to do so. This contributed to the slow pace of the project. The pilot project which was to be completed within a period of one and a half years had been languishing and only Rs. 7.33 lakhs were utilised by SASMIRA till March 1988.

VII. **Ministry of Urban Development**

Working of Directorate of Estates, New Delhi: Due to acute shortage of residential accommodation, a government employee could not ordinarily get allotment of accommodation before he renders service ranging between 17 and 27 years. A large number of *ad hoc* allotments are being made and 48 per cent of the total allotments in Type V in 1988 were on out-of-turn basis. This further delayed the availability of accommodation to those entitled to regular allotment.

Only 2,525 additional residential units became available for allotment during 1986 to 1988 as compared to 3,119 units during 1983 to 1985 and 12,814 units during 1981 to 1982.

While on the one hand, there was a long waiting period for government servants to get allotment of accommodation, on the other instances of considerable delays ranging up to 62 months in allotment of units vacated by earlier occupants and up to 17 months for newly constructed units were noticed in test check.

Due to ineffective monitoring and control, cancellation of allotment in many cases of unauthorised occupation was unduly delayed. Delay in cancellation was more than 60 months in 26 cases. Procedure for getting unauthorised occupation vacated was also not effective with the result that as on 31 March 1989 1,739 quarters were under unauthorised occupation out of which in 116 cases, the period of unauthorised occupation ranged from 60 to 165 months. Out of 437 cases in which eviction orders were passed, the accommodation was got vacated only in 37 cases.

Steps taken for realisation of dues were not adequate. Arrears of licence fee increased from year-to-year. Extent of realisation with reference to total outstandings at the end of each year declined from 75 per cent in 1984-85 to 64 per cent in 1988-89. Assessment of recovery dues was not made in a number of cases.

Out of 150 flats purchased from the DDA at a cost of Rs. 10.20 crores for allotment for special allocation within the general pool, 77 flats remained unallotted from December 1986, to July 1988, resulting in blocking of capital of approximately Rs. 5.24 crores.

Abnormal Delay in Construction of Quarters: The work of construction of 128 Type III quarters at Saltlake, Calcutta, awarded to a contractor in December 1977, could not be completed by him by May 1979. The contract was rescinded in January 1984. The balance work was awarded to another contractor in March 1985, which was completed in January 1987. This resulted in an extra expenditure of Rs. 11.02 lakhs which was to be recovered from the defaulting contractor. This has not been recovered. Another contract for the work, namely, construction of 96 Type III quarters at Saltlake awarded to a contractor in January 1979, was rescinded in September 1983. The remaining work was awarded to another contractor in November 1984, which was completed in December 1988. This resulted in an extra expenditure of Rs. 11.09 lakhs.

The quarters completed in January 1987, and December 1988, could not be handed over for allotment (August 1989) owing to non-completion of internal work and external electric supply connection. This resulted not only in blocking of funds but also payment of house rent allowance in lieu of these quarters. Besides, the beneficiaries were deprived of the facilities for about 14 years.

Infructuous Expenditure Due to Idle Printing Machines: Out of two rotary printing machines of Government of India Press, Calcutta, one remained totally idle from April 1987, to February 1988, and the other for two months in January and February 1988, for want of 43 cms wide reel papers. Consequently, the workers attached to these two machines remained idle and the expenditure of Rs. 21.26 lakhs incurred on these workers was rendered infructuous.

Disposal of Metal Dross Residue: Government of India Press, Minto Road, New Delhi, offered 1,100 quintals of metal dross (residue) for disposal. The acceptance of valid tender at Rs. 1,541 per quintal was conveyed to the tenderer after the expiry of extended validity period. Further extension of time for lifting the material requested for by this tenderer was not granted and the tenders were re-invited. The offer at Rs. 856 per quintal was accepted permitting the tenderer to lift the material in 139 days against 30 days provided in the tender. Non-acceptance of the earlier tender within the validity period resulted in short realisation of Rs. 7.38 lakhs.

VIII. **Ministry of Water Resources**

Delay in Execution of a Work: For restoring vehicular traffic and pedestrian movements, the government accorded sanction, in November 1973, for construction of an additional bridge at the feeder canal of Farakka barrage. After four years, the project authority awarded the work for Rs. 82.52 lakhs to a state government undertaking of West Bengal for completing the work by April 1980. The work could not be started due to failure of the department to supply soil boring data for the canal soil and on the part of the undertaking to submit the design in time. The undertaking after completing 77 per cent work stopped the work. Till May 1986, Rs. 63.98 lakhs had been paid. In January 1988, the contract was rescinded. In addition, a total expenditure of Rs. 36.39 lakhs was also incurred on free ferry services from April 1988 to July 1989. Thus work sanctioned in 1973 has not yet been completed.

IX. **Andaman and Nicobar Administration**

Delay in Fabrication of Bus Bodies: For augmenting the road transport service in the union territory, the administration purchased 12 bus chassis for Rs. 20.99 lakhs. A firm at Jamshedpur was allowed to take delivery of the chassis in March 1976, for fabrication of bus bodies without furnishing any indemnity bond for the value of chassis delivered in violation of the terms of the agreement executed with it. The Director of Transport could not trace the chassis or the proprietor of the firm. For all 12 chassis, action had not been initiated for their fabrication. The failure of the administration to evaluate and assess the capacity of the firm not only resulted in blocking of funds to the extent of Rs. 20.99 lakhs but also the objective for putting more buses on the road was not achieved.

Injudicious Procurement of Spares: The administration purchased spares of the value of Rs. 41 lakhs during June 1970, to August 1977, for use in two Komatsu bulldozers purchased in February 1969, at a cost of Rs. 8.60 lakhs. As per norms prescribed in the *Central Water Commission Guide Book,* spares could be purchased to the extent of 240 per cent of the cost of equipment at the estimated life of 10 years of the equipment. Accordingly, spares worth Rs. 20.64 lakhs could be purchased during 1969-78 instead of Rs. 41 lakhs.

The bulldozers were condemned in 1985 and auctioned for Rs. 1.26 lakhs in January 1988.

No action had been taken for the disposal of spares. Thus injudicious procurement of spares contrary to the norms resulted in procurement of surplus spares.

Abnormal Delay in Execution of Work: For construction of a 5-km long rural road from Millangram to Radhanagar, administrative sanction of Rs. 4.04 lakhs was accorded in May 1970, which was revised to Rs. 9.61 lakhs for extension of road up to 6.65 kms in March 1971. Again in March 1974, the specifications were further revised for the work which was completed in March 1986. Up to July 1987, a sum of Rs. 72.67 lakhs had been incurred. Thus delay in the execution of work resulted in an abnormal increase in expenditure and the objective of linking isolated settlements of the locality remained unfulfilled for 14 years.

CAG's REPORT — DEFENCE SERVICES
(Army and Ordance Factories)

OVERVIEW

The Audit Report for the year ended 31 March 1989 contains 128 paragraphs including three reviews. The points highlighted in the Report are given below:

I. **General**

Instances of failure on the part of executive authorities, shortcomings in induction, purchase and maintenance of weaponary and allied equipment, deficiencies in procurement of ordnance stores, ration articles, transport and workshop equipment, lacunae in inspection procedures, etc. resulting in avoidable or wasteful expenditure have been pointed out. It also contains observation on development and production of arms, ammunitions and other equipment by ordnance factories. While commenting on several cases involving injudicious purchase, low capacity utilisation, defective contracts, non-fulfilment of targets and shortcomings in execution of works, the Report highlights the inadequacies in management systems and the delays in execution leading to escalation of costs and set-back to production programmes. The Report underscores the need for stricter financial control, in-depth planning, timely action and close monitoring at every sage of operation.

II. **Budgetary Control**

The total grant for the Defence Services as a whole for the year 1988-89 was Rs. 13,812.24 crores. The actual expenditure was Rs. 13,714.17 crores as against Rs. 12,378.75 crore in 1987-88. the supplementary grant of Rs. 241.10 crores obtained for the Army proved inadequate to the extent of Rs. 103.65 crores. Though supplementary grant of Rs. 57.87 crores was obtained for Air Force, Rs. 51.26 crores remained unutilised. Similarly, against the supplementary grant of Rs. 26.75 crores for ordnance factories, the amount remaining unutilised was Rs. 67.87 crores. Despite obtaining supplementary grants, re-appropriations were made and they were in a few cases wholly or partially unnecessary.

Ministry of Defence

III. **Contracts with Bofors for (a) purchase and licence production of 155 mm gun system and (b) counter trade**

The agreement with Bofors for supply of 155 mm towed gun system etc. contained a provision for counter trade to facilitate buy back of goods from India. Appropriate mechanisms for ensuring implementation of the provisions of the counter trade were not conceptualised. In the mechanisms it could not be ensured that counter trade resulted in additionality and product market diversification in India's or STC's exports and that there was no diversion of traditional exports.

Out of exports of over Rs. 207 cores during April 1987 to June 1989 under counter trade, exports of traditional items constituted 59 per cent. Commodities like cashew kernels, meat, etc. which re not qualified were reckoned against counter trade.

Additional exports from India to Sweden, as envisaged, not only did not materialise but also exports to that country declined in 1989-89 from 1987-88.

Government have decided (February 1990) not to operationalise the licence agreement for indigenous manufacture of guns and ammunition till Bofors furnish full details about the persons/parties to whom payments of commission had been made. Meanwhile Rs. 1.67 cores have been paid on account of commitment fee on unutilised credit in respect of licence production.

A test check of he records with reference to delivery schedule indicated that there were delays in issue of items of gun system to the regiments. One of the systems costing Rs. 34.51 crores had not been issued at it did not conform to the prescribed specifications.

Fuze 'A' costing Rs. 13.24 crores was awaiting check proof with shell 'N' as supplies of shell 'N' costing Rs. 26.29 crores were rejected. Stock of another defective fuze valuing Rs. 3.27 crores was being back loaded to suppliers for replacement/rectifications involving avoidable expenditure on its transportation in India.

An amount of Rs. 21 crores on account of liquidated damages as of December 1989 was still to be recovered from Bofors (February 1990).

Acceptance of liability for repayment of a portion of credit in Deutsche Mark was likely to result in an uncertain liability due to fluctuations in foreign exchange rates.

No claims for damaged ammunition costing Rs. 96.43 lakhs received during January-February 1989, were raised against carriers as marine survey report was not received.

Segregation of ammunition which was damaged by fire and which arrived in India during September 1987 was yet to be completed and out of a claim of Rs. 6.60 crores raised therefore, an amount of Rs. 1 crore only has been realised so far.

IV. Induction and De-induction of a Gun System

The reinduction of a gun, earlier in use, was justified in 1975 and after approval by government in 1982, a contract for import and licence production was concluded in January 1983. The indigenous version of the gun was found to be superior in performance and part of the order was placed on ordnance factories. A contract for ammunition was concluded in February/March 1984 at a cost of Rs. 33.62 crores and the ammunition was imported during 1984 to 1988. The order for guns on the foreign firm could not be performed by the latter due to export restrictions leading to cancellation of the order in June 1983. The indigenous guns, initially found superior in performance, were later on not acceptable to the users in August 1984. The order placed for guns on the ordnance factories was consequently closed in August 1985. It was decided in September 1986 not to induct the guns due to changes in operational requirements. The imported ammunition remained unutilised.

V. **Canteen Stores Department**

The report underlines the need for a review of the pricing policy by the Canteen Stores Department, better inventory management and appropriate changes in the pattern of allocation of profits to secure better consumer-demand-satisfaction and capital growth for the enlargement of the activities to attain the prime objectives of this venture.

The customers were over-charged by CSD by way of incidental expenses of the extent of Rs. 59.91 crores and by levying profit margin on excise duty to the extent of RS. 23.34 crores during 1984-89. While the allocation of profit as a percentage of the surplus for grants-in-aid was increasing, that for capital growth was decreasing. The payment of quantitative discount to unit run canteens and retail outlets rose from two per cent (Rs. 1.52 crores) in 1977-78 to 3.5 per cent (Rs. 20.30 crores) in 1988-89. The benefit on account of quantitative discount was not passed on to the consumers but was utilised for welfare of troops notwithstanding that CSD is paying grants-in-aid separately for this purpose.

Computerisation of data for better demand projections, improved turn-over, and better inventory management at an expenditure of Rs. 36.68 lakhs did not prove effective. While procurement of certain goods was far in excess of requirement, 27 per cent of consumer demands for other goods could not be met. Of stocks worth Rs. 40.26 crores held on 31st March 1989, Rs. 19.40 crores were in excess of the norms. There was accumulation of newly introduced goods due to failure to return the unsold items as per understanding with the suppliers.

VI. **Provisioning of NCC Uniforms**

The Director General, Ordnance Factories, who was supplying uniforms to NCC, started according low priority to NCC supply from 1983-84 because of large Army requirements. Failure to make alternative arrangements led to local purchases at higher rates. On purchase of uniforms of Rs. 122.57 lakhs, made in 1986-88, the excess expenditure, based on the rates at which the purchases were made by the Director General Supplies and disposals was Rs. 52.30 lakhs. Thus, there has been a failure to make suitable arrangement for centralised procurement of a relatively simple item like NCC uniforms.

VII. **Disposal of Surplus Stores**

Security stores valued at Rs. 82 crores had accumulated over a period of eleven years occupying not only valuable storage space but resulting in expenditure on their safeguarding. Successive committees appointed since 1980 had failed to find a solution for their disposal.

ARMY

VIII. **Weaponry and Allied Equipments**

A certain number of weapon system to provide air defence cover to Army formations and installations was imported during 1973-74 for Rs. 27.25 crores. Eight years were taken in finalising the necessary arrangement with the foreign supplier for setting up of repairs and overhauling facilities and in obtaining approval of Cabinet Committee on Political Affairs. The project was ultimately approved by government in 1981, but its execution was further delayed as the sanction for civil works was accorded only in November 1984. the overhauls required for the weapon system in 1981 and 1989 could not be carried out, even once, due to delay in establishing the facilities and non-procurement of spares. The infrastructure for the purpose had been created at a cost of Rs. 13.50 crores, but Army Headquarters stated that it remained under-utilised and, consequently, the weapon system remained in the poor fitness state. Further the firing range for the project was still under planning.

Fitment of a passive night vision device on a certain number of tanks, under a modernisation scheme, was approved during the Sixth Army Plan (1980-85). After procurement action was initiated, Army Headquarters envisaged fitment of the devices on more number of tanks and, accordingly, indents for the devices costing Rs. 6.22 crores were placed over and above the quantity cleared in the Sixth Plan. As a consequence of a review carried out in July 1988, orders for a certain number were short-closed involving a loss of Rs. 18.35 lakhs. It was also noticed that the devices costing Rs. 9.28 crores had been procured in excess of requirements.

A contract was concluded in February 1981 with a foreign firm for 70 sets of tank fire control system without a fresh evaluation, notwithstanding that the system, earlier supplied by the firm, had failed in trials during 1977-78. Sixty-nine sets costing Rs. 8.58 crores received during April 1983 to March 1985 were found defective and had been lying unutilised for four to six years awaiting rectification/modification.

There was a high incidence of premature failure of engines of a tank. During 1984 to 1988, 256 overhauled engines of a tank failed prematurely. 73 failed before achieving 500 km including nine which failed even before completing 100 km after overhaul. Premature failure worked out to 30 per cent of the engines overhauled. Action was stated to be in hand to find an alternative engine and to introduce improved technological measures for ensuring enhanced reliability of overhauled engines.

Two contracts concluded in May 1980 and August 1982 did not provided for inspection by the purchaser of the ammunition imported or the date of manufacture of the ammunition resulting in supply with a short shelf-life. Out of 12,856 rounds costing Rs. 184.12 lakhs declared defective, 3307 rounds costing Rs. 47.05 lakhs, had been issued to users units. Disposal of balance quantity of 9549 rounds, costing Rs. 137.07 lakhs, was not intimated to Audit.

A tank simulator was imported in June 1984 at a cost of Rs. 18.50 lakhs. However, it was installed in May 1986 after which defects in the hydraulic system were noticed. The defects had not been rectified so far. One of the two cabins in the simulator could be used sub-optimally thereby adversely affecting the training programme. Spares and special maintenance tools could not procured in sufficient quantity as the simulator had gone out of production.

IX. **Logistics and Transport**

Even though the necessary for procurement of coaching stock was approved in August 1986 and funds were made available in December 1986 sanction for purchase was issued in August 1987, after the offer of the Bharat Earth Movers Limited had expired in May 1987. The firm revised its rate in June 1987 which resulted in extra expenditure of Rs. 1.74 cores. Training and relief movements also suffered in the meantime due to inadequate coaching stock.

To expedite manufacture of wagons by about eight months, it was decided to import bearings for wagons at a higher cost by Rs. 1 crore approximately though the required bearings were indigenously available. Although extra expenditure was incurred in foreign exchange, the objective of expediting the supply could not be achieved due to slippages in delivery.

Risk purchases within the stipulated period of six months from the date of breach of the terms of supply orders for camouflage equipment were not made resulting in extra expenditure of Rs. 44.78 lakhs. Claim for general damages of Rs. 8.29 lakhs had been initiated.

Department of Defence Production and Supplies had procured steel water tanks without water sprinklers at a cost of Rs. 17.11 lakhs and these were lying idle since May 1987 for want for water sprinklers.

Motor boat workshops were authorised for the Army in 1972 to repair service vessels mid-stream. A contract was concluded in July 1981 with a firm for supply of workshops by September 1985. The firm failed to supply them, even though extensions for delivery were given up to December 1986. Even after a lapse of over four years the Department of Defence Production and Supplies had neither cancelled the contract nor encashed the bank guarantees obtained for payment of Rs. 8.28 lakhs. Servicing countries on shore locations which was not considered desirable in an operational situation.

171 mules purchased during August 1987 to November 1988 for Rs. 20 lakhs were found to be sub-standard though these had been inspected before purchase by a Board of officers. The mules could not be deployed for the purpose for which they had been purchased. An expenditure of Rs. 4.13 lakhs was incurred on their ration during December 1988 to September 1989.

X. **Workshop Equipment**

Out of two electronic gear testing machines imported for the purpose of securing optimum accuracy of the gears, one machine costing Rs. 28.74 lakhs received in June 1986 by an Army Workshop, was lying in a defective condition. Due to non-finalisation of the proceedings of a Court of Inquiry, the repair to the machine had been delayed.

Despite the advice given in July 1984 by an Army Base Workshop not to procure a type of dynamometer because of its inherent design deficiency, three sets for Rs. 18.37 lakhs were procured in 1986-1987. These did not prove useful to the Workshop.

XI. **Ordnance Stores**

Failure of Army Headquarters in realistically assessing the requirement of packing paper and a recolouring compound resulted in excess procurement valued at Rs. 285.36 lakhs. These had been lying in stock for over two to five years for want of demands from the users.

A fire broke out in the storage hanger of Central Ordnance Depot, Kanpur destroying boots worth Rs. 1.53 cross on the night of 28th/29th May 1986. Investigations revealed that no stock taking was carried out after August 1984. Further 30 per cent of the 5764 boots salvaged from fire were without the inspection stamp suggesting that the inspection standards were not rigorous. The loss was awaiting regularisation.

XII. **Inspection**

Instructions issued in October 1985 provide for inspection and check-proofing of imported stores immediately on their receipt in India. Nevertheless, inspection of ammunition, valuing Rs. 13.72 crores, imported in April 1986, was delayed and carried out during February-June 1987. The entire consignment being affected with ingress of moisture was sentenced unserviceable. A claim for free replacement was rejected in August 1987 by the foreign supplier as it was preferred after expiry of the warranty period. On a further cent per cent inspection, ammunition costing Rs. 12.22 crores was found moisture affected and the balance valued at Rs. 1.50 crores was again being check-proofed for assessing its residual shelf-life.

Defects arising out of old components in 655 missiles, supplied by Bharat Dynamics Limited, could not be noticed by the inspecting authorities there by underscoring the need for revising inspection procedures for detecting substandard components. 542 defective missiles were repaired at a cost of Rs. 9.13 lakhs. Besides, 113 defective missiles costing Rs. 107.35 lakhs were held in repairable condition and in the process of being phased out as obsolescent.

XIII. **Ration Articles**

Offers of firms for procurement of ration articles like skimmed milk powder, fresh meat, tinned butter and tinned meat could not be accepted within their validity period awaiting sanction of the ministry. Consequently the contracts had to be concluded at higher rates and local purchases resorted to, to meet urgent requirements resulting in avoidable extra expenditure of Rs. 1.87 crores. This calls for a review of systems and procedures and delegation of powers to formations.

In pursuance of policy directive, tenders were floated on state co-operative federations without assessing their capability for supply of *dal*. The federations failed to supply. As a result, 697.75 tonnes of *dal* had to be purchased from other sources incurring an additional expenditure of Rs. 95.19 lakhs.

ORDNANCE AND CLOTHING FACTORIES

XIV. **General Performance of Ordnance Factories**

Working of the ordnance factories in terms of capacity utilisation, as assessed by the Ordnance Factory Board was above 60 per cent in 32 factories and below 40 per cent in one. Verification of the correctness of the computation by Audit on a sample basis in respect of one factory, however, showed that the statistical basis of computation was not correct. In terms of production performance, 10 out of 66 special items of weapons and ammunition registered significant short-fall owing to failure in accuracy proof, non-availability of components and diversion of capacity. A comprehensive review of the outstanding indents from 1950-51 to 1985-86 showed that 5659 indents were outstanding at the end of 1987-88. The value of abnormal rejections in 1987-88 increased by 85 per cent approximately over the preceding year. Most of the rejections were on account of defective materials and defective castings.

XV. **Material Management in Ordnance and Ordnance Equipment Factories**

Stores worth Rs. 182.42 crores in 14 factories were not accounted for in stock as at the end of March 1988. Further, stores valued at Rs. 426.48 crores, for which payments had already been made, could not be linked to the receipts. In one factory there was a discrepancy of Rs. 59.43 crores as on 31 March 1986 between the computerised accounting figures and manually compiled figures in the store balance. Physical verification of all items of stock, once during each financial year, had not been carried out during 1986-87 and 1987-88 in 7 out of 14 factories. Stock holding had been in excess of authorised limits in some factories.

Discrepancy in stores amounting to Rs. 84.38 lakhs receive in a factory from a sister factory had been treated as loss in transit without sanction by the competent authority. Discrepancy vouchers for deficiencies in stores valuing Rs. 78.35 lakhs raised by a factory in 1984-85 had not been adjusted. Loss on rejection of empty shell bodies valuing Rs. 1.30 crores during 1984-87 had not yet been regularised.

Materials valuing Rs. 53.62 lakhs had been drawn by one factory over and above the authorised quantity.

XVI. **Ordnance Factory, Muradnagar**

In Ordnance Factory, Muradnagar, capacity of the foundries, was never fully utilised during the last five years. Utilisation of machining capacity was at a low level. Rejections during the last five years ranged from 69 to 74 per cent. Total value of abnormal rejections was Rs. 312.49 lakhs.

A plant costing Rs. 1 crore, procured in March 1982, to provide washed and graded sand to the foundries had been utilised only to the extent of 17 to 18 per cent of capacity.

Items produced had been under valued as pricing had not reflected the cost of production.

XVII. **Development and Production**

There were instances of lack of clarity in the choice of technical specifications and purposiveness in execution affecting the development and production of arms, ammunition and equipment.

A mortar and its ammunition could not be developed through Rs. 41.50

lakhs had been incurred on developmental efforts in the last 16 years, for the reasons that quality parameters and user's trial had not been specified.

Notwithstanding that an appropriate fuze had not been developed even after years of work, bulk production had been ventured in leading to rejection of components and filled fuzes valued at Rs. 173.45 lakhs.

In the development of a naval ammunition, the estimated rose from Rs. 15 lakhs in 1978 to Rs. 55 lakhs in 1988. The capacities created in the ordnance factories a Rs. 258.57 lakhs had remained un-utilised since February 1988. Due to delay, the Navy had imported ammunition worth Rs. 158.82 during 1986 to 1988.

The Army gave the clearance for development of light tank without properly assessing the availability of BMP vehicles for productionisation. This resulted in an infructuous expenditure of Rs. 26.79 lakhs for modifying a BMP vehicle for mounting 90 mm turret. The expenditure being incurred on development of light taken with 105 mm turret would also prove infructuous as the Army do not have any requirement for this tank.

The selection of an improved version of a search light at a later stage, had rendered the expenditure of Rs. 12.28 lakhs incurred on the development of an earlier version, wasteful.

A project for productionisation of aviation gun sanctioned in December 1983 mainly on self-reliance and strategic considerations and which was to be completed by December 1987, had not been completed. The project productionisation of the ammunition sanctioned in January 1977 was completed in October 1985 but the bulk production of ammunition had not commenced till March 1989. Due to delay, complete ammunition rounds and components costing Rs. 5.20 crores were imported during May 1983 to October 1987.

Sanctioning of a project for self-reliance and on strategic consideration took 37 months. The project scheduled to be completed in December 1987 was expected to be completed by September 1989 mainly due to delay in completion of civil works. The anticipated completion cost was Rs. 5.24 crores against Rs. 4.58 crores sanctioned. Due to delay in completion of the project, practices ammunition had to be imported at a cost of Rs. 8.73 lakhs.

There was a mismatch between the design data and the actual design requirement rendering an investment of Rs. 8.91 crores in the creation of production capacity for ammunition in a factory idle.

There was a mismatch in the production of different quantities of the components of an ammunition. This resulted in the production failing to meet the specified target. As a consequence an investment of Rs. 370.57 lakhs for augmenting the production capacity of the factory failed to yield the desired return. Further, shortfall in production exceeded Rs. 12.12 crores in four years. Ammunition worth Rs. 55.74 lakhs were rejected and imports were to be resorted to.

Production of an adapter required for fitment of a fuze to the shell body of an ammunition was undertaken before the suitability of the fuze to the shell body was assessed leading to wasteful production of adapters costing Rs. 86.56 lakhs.

A new pyrotechnic factory sanctioned at a cost of Rs. 15.59 crores to produce 29 different items for ammunition could produce only 14 items. Short-fall in the production of two of the fourteen was so large that items costing

Rs. 11.80 crores had to be imported.

A project for strip-making was sanctioned even before the technological parameters were known. This resulted in cost and time overrun. Other adverse consequences were market dependence for Rs. 233.14 lakhs worth of cold rolled strips, import of brass cups worth Rs. 182.48 lakhs and additional cost of Rs. 9.94 crores on conversion of scraps into strips.

Delay in the completion of a project for the production of shell bodies and cartridge cases for a type of ammunition led to procurement of forgings for shell bodies from trade at a higher cost of Rs. 111.07 lakhs. Another project sanctioned to create facilities for the production of three other types of the same ammunition scheduled to be completed by July 1987 had not been completed.

Empty bodies for an ammunition supplied by a firm were cleared by the authorised Inspectorate but were found defective during production. Defective empty bodies and rejected filled bodies valuing Rs. 12.24 lakhs had been lying in a factory without any prospective use.

XVIII. **Provisioning**

There were instances of lack of co-ordination, delays in processing, deficiencies in contracts, etc. Due to lack of co-ordination, items indigenously developed and available were needlessly imported at a cost of Rs. 52.09 lakhs.

Terrywool cloth costing Rs. 27.61 lakhs had been lying unutilised in a factory for the last three years due to the indentor not providing the specifications for the uniform.

An instance of procurement without assessing the requirement showed that forgings valued at Rs. 88 lakhs had become surplus with the discontinuance of the production of an ammunition.

Aluminium rods had been purchased at higher rates from a firm involving an extra expenditure of Rs. 42.21 lakhs, ignoring the fact that the sale price of the rod of similar specification, manufactured by the same firm, had been much less.

Despite a track record of unsatisfactory performance, orders had been placed on a supplier who again failed to perform and the on-account payment of Rs. 43.13 lakhs eventually became irrecoverable.

XIX. **Plant and Machinery**

A purchase contract was concluded, based on incorrect specification, for high-capacity presses for Rs. 1.31 crores. The presses failed to provide the envisaged advantage of an improved mechanical process.

XX. **Other Cases**

Instances of losses detected in audit were related to accidents, uneconomical disposals, abnormal rejections, purchase of defective materials, short-closures and abandoned claims. Successive explosions in the nitroglycerine plant in a factory occurred due to selection of the plant of obsolescent technology involving the risk of explosion. A loss of Rs. 26.04 lakhs was incurred.

Losses due to abnormal rejections in one factory amounted to Rs. 322.48

lakhs during the period 1975 1985 and were written off long after their occurence as to special cases. A further loss of Rs. 140.05 lakhs was yet to be regularised. There was no system for regular investigation of cases of abnormal rejections.

In another case under-pricing resulted in the disposal of a material valuing Rs. 25 lakhs at Rs. 0.52 lakh.

XXI. Works and Military Engineer Services

Military Engineer Services constructed additional accommodation for the Chief Engineer, Jabalpur un-authorisedly, by utilising funds of Rs. 19.13 lakhs from contingencies of five projects though necessity for construction of a new building was neither accepted nor sanctioned by the competent authority.

The work of air-conditioning at certain installations at Gorakhpur sanctioned in December 1979 and due for completion in July 1982 was still incomplete after incurring an expenditure of Rs. 17.11 lakhs. Another work of air-conditioning at Jabalpur was pending for more that 15 years without any benefit though a sum of Rs. 4.46 lakhs had been spent. Yet another air-conditioning plant costing Rs. 3.84 lakhs installed in November 1983 had been lying without any use for more than five years as the requisite test and rectification of defects by the firm had not been carried out.

A work relating to residential accommodation had been executed despite change in deployment of Army units. Another work relating to installation of sewage pumps had not been executed so as to synchronise it with the main work of sewage plant. This resulted in non-utilisation of assets costing Rs. 197 lakhs for over two years.

Military Engineer Services (MES) failed to apprise suppliers of electricity about the Constitutional provision with regard to non-imposition of electricity duty/tax on the consumption of electricity by the central government departments. MES also failed to get the approval for upward revision of maximum demand of electricity and also to disclose the excess connected load under voluntary disclosure scheme. This resulted in avoidable payment of Rs. 99.12 lakhs.

Surplus spares worth Rs. 41 lakhs approved for disposal as early as in 1978 had been lying in an Engineer Stores Depot un-disposed. An expenditure of Rs. 1.73 lakhs had been incurred up to March 1986 on their maintenance and preservation.

XXII. Non-collection of Sales Tax

There was failure to recover sales tax on goods disposed of in auction sales between April 1976 and October 1981 resulting in a loss Rs. 81.45 lakhs.

CAG's REPORT ON CENTRAL GOVERNMENT
(Defence Services — Air Force and Navy)

OVERVIEW

The Audit Report for the year ended 31 March 1989 contains 57 paragraphs including 9 reviews. The points highlighted in the Report are given below:

I. Flight Safety

The flight safety programme of the Indian Air Force covers both the determination of causes of aircraft accidents and incidents, and the timely introduction of preventive measures together with their implementation. A review by Audit of certain aspects of flight safety management revealed that a significantly high number of major accidents that occurred during 1983-84 to 1987-88 were due to human error (35 to 42.85% of the total) and technical failure or malfunctioning of components (25 to 50%).

Accidents caused by bird hits ranged between 7.5 and 14.28 per cent out of the major accidents. The fighter aircraft accident rate ranged between 68.25 and 59.31 per cent in respect of major accidents and minor accidents/incidents respectively. For trainer aircraft and helicopters this figure of major accidents was 13.27 and 12.32 per cent respectively. Cases of total loss of aircraft in respect of fighters ranged between 52.63 and 83.33 per cent, 3.84 and 26.31 per cent for trainer aircraft and 7.14 and 17.14 per cent for the helicopter element out of all cases of this nature during 1983-84 to 1987-88. Similarly, fatal accidents were to the extent of 62.96, 18.52 and 12.96 per cent in respect of the fighter, trainer and helicopter respectively.

The factors responsible for human error accidents and incidents were lack of knowledge or skill and experience and attitudinal faults besides inadequacy in training processes.

Monitoring of post-accident activities with reference to the recommendations made by the courts of enquiry on operational, technical or administrative aspects was not very effective in Air Headquarters till April 1988. The unsuitability of existing trainer aircraft and the absence of an advanced jet trainer and simulators were the factors which handicapped the learning process to attain the required standards of operational skills and competence.

An important equipment (cockpit voice recorder) has not been incorporated in the transport fleet so far though its necessity was accepted as early as 1979. Its absence in a large number of aircraft imposed constraints on the proper investigation of accidents and in preventive measures being initiated to control accidents.

The quantum of loss was assessed only to the extent of 30 per cent of the accidents (major and minor) over the five year period which worked out to Rs. 419 crores. The loss in respect of the remaining 70 per cent was still to be assessed. The total loss, when assessed, would be substantial.

II. Light Transport Aircraft

The process of induction into the Air Force of a light transport aircraft was reviewed in Audit. There was a delay in identification and selection of the aircraft besides the inability of the Air Headquarters to firm up their requirement even after the project was launched in 1983 and the contract for manufacture signed. Even the four aircraft ordered and procured against the requirement of 50 up to 1988-89 had shown poor serviceability. This requirement of 50 aircraft was reduced to 41 in March 1987 and increased to 45 in May 1987 and again reduced to 43 in July 1987. In the case of supply for the Navy, due to the standards of preparation not being finalised until July 1988 and the equipment fit not being finalised as well, the delivery could not be made. Due to delay in induction of these aircraft, heavy transport aircraft have been mobilised for communication duties, resulting in an avoidable expenditure of Rs. 9.67 crores during 1986 to 1988.

III. **Acquisition of Weapons for an Aircraft**

There was a mismatch between the induction of the aircraft into squadron service and that of the weapons required for it. While the contract for the aircraft was concluded in October 1982, the contracts for weapons were concluded after two to three and a half years resulting in inordinate delay in the availability of the weapons. Owing to the delay in the availability of the weapons required for training and instructional purposes, the IAF depended largely upon simulation methods and dummy modes. A single supplier situation prevailed throughout in respect of all weapons.

Price escalation amounting to Rs. 57.39 lakhs in foreign currency had to be paid due to delay in finalisation of contracts. An incorrect assessment of the quantitative requirement of a weapon initially and the procurement of an additional quantity subsequently at a higher rate led to an avoidable extra expenditure of Rs. 1.12 crores. Owing to the absence of a specific clause in the agreement regarding the period for which the aircraft will be kept with the manufacturer, four aircraft remained with the manufacturer for weapon integration and clearance for long periods leading to deficiency of aircraft in the squadrons.

IV. **Base Repair Depots**

Maintenance support for the Indian Air Force is mainly provided by the base repair depots which undertake the repair/overhaul of various types of aircraft and associated equipment.

It was seen that the repair work in the base repair depots was carried out without cost considerations. There was extra expenditure on account of uneconomical repairs which worked out to Rs. 42.51 lakhs in respect of diesel generating sets and airconditioners in one of the depots. The position of repair work relating to rotables at some depots have not been satisfactory. There have been delays in the setting up of repair facilities at two depots resulting in an expenditure of Rs. 48.25 crores on repair jobs abroad. At the same time installed capacity at four depots remained underutilised. Formulation of tasks by Air Headquarters lacked accuracy and realism and restricted the utilisation of available resources in the depots. There were considerable premature failures of repaired items warranting their repair again which involves avoidable expenditure.

There was no monitoring system to analyse the failure pattern of the products by which the situation can be improved upon. No effective monitoring and control over the utilisation of manpower in the depots was being exercised. Consequently, there were unproductive man hours estimated cost of which was Rs. 30.37 crores in respect of six depots during 1983-84. 13.71 lakh hours costing Rs. 2.40 crores were consumed in excess of the standard labour element fixed for various jobs by Air Headquarters at four depots during the five years ending 1987-88.

The provisioning of materials to meet the production requirements of various depots has not been effective. Inventory control measures were not being implemented effectively. Resultantly, inactive inventory costing about Rs. 180 crores had accumulated over the years which involves an avoidable expenditure of approximately Rs. 18 crores per annum as its carrying cost.

V. Procurement, Manufacture, Operation and Maintenance of an Aircraft

The review reveals poor planning, project management and implementation. Though government sanctioned placement of orders on Hindustan Aeronautics Limited (HAL) for the manufacture of aircraft 'B' in October 1982, the order on HAL was placed only in September 1984. This resulted in a delay of over one year in achieving the established rate of production by HAL.

The cost of the project had increased by Rs. 237.48 crores and the anticipated savings of Rs. 233.86 crores negated. Poor aircraft serviceability affected the utilisation rate and consequential flying efforts. There was considerable shortfall in the flying efforts achieved.

There was a mismatch in the induction of the aircraft and procurement of weapons and training aids. Although the aircraft was inducted in December 1985, the weapons started arriving from the end of 1985 onwards and continued till January 1989. The squadron was without trained personnel to use the specialist weapons till December 1986.

No facilities for repair of aeroengines fitted on a class of aircraft have been set up so far owing to the possibility of HAL taking up the task. Ambiguity on this point had led to delay in initiating action for setting up of overhaul facilities and even the protocol had not been signed with the manufacturers till March 1989, even though expected overhaul arisings of engines commenced from July 1988. Consequently indents worth Rs. 8.96 crores for overhaul of engines and Rs. 22.78 lakhs for overhaul of aggregates have been placed with the manufacturers.

VI. Commissioning of a Training Simulator

Due to the non-availability of technical instructions and operating manuals, a simulator imported in December 1983 at a cost of Rs. 11.81 lakhs remained non-operational for over five years, after its purchase. The matter was, however, taken up with the supplier only 42 months after the receipt of the simulator. This requires investigation and enforcement of accountability.

VII. Delay in Completion of a Training Project

A training equipment worth Rs. 4.32 crores was received by an Air Force establishment in 1979. As civil works to house the equipment had to be constructed, a payment of Rs. 10.40 lakhs was made towards land acquisition in March 1985. The land had not been acquired. Consequently, the equipment had not been used effectively.

VIII. **Procurement of Cables for Air-field Lighting**

Non-acceptance by Air Headquarters of the technical advice given in September 1983 led to extra expenditure of Rs. 9.40 lakhs and delay in procurement of cables required for air field lighting. This also led to inability of units to maintain the serviceability of air field lighting which restricted optimum utilisation of the air field, till supply of cables materialised (September 1988).

IX. **Procurement of Air Defence Equipment**

The inadequate appreciation of the total needs of the Air Force resulted in import of only part of the requirement. The system required for optimising the equipment purchased has not been procured so far. This resulted in a sub-optimal utilisation of an investment of Rs. 63.25 crores.

X. **Damage to a Tower Crane**

Serious lapses occurred in the inspection and acceptance of a tower crane procured in 1987 at a cost of Rs. 25.11 lakhs. Precautionary measures were not provided by the supplier and were not pointed out during the inspection. This resulted in extensive damage to the crane, soon after its purchase. The supplier had already been made full payment and his bank guarantee was also released. Meanwhile, the tasks at the station were being managed by obtaining a crane on loan and by hiring a crane at a cost of Rs. 10.50 lakhs. Consequently, the radar installation programme at the station had also slipped seriously and the case revealed laxity in inspection.

XI. **Procurement of Night Vision Goggles**

To enhance night operational capability of the helicopter fleet, Ministry of Defence sanctioned in May 1985 import of 25 sets of night vision goggles at a cost of Rs. 65.08 lakhs through a Defence laboratory and indigenous development of 35 sets at a cost of Rs. 64.5 lakhs. The goggles were procured between July 1986 and September 1988 but could not be put to use till April 1989 due to delays in carrying out the modification in cockpit lighting and lack of training to the crew. The night operation role of helicopter could not, therefore, be practised.

XII. **Brake System of Ajeet Aircraft**

The brake system for the Ajeet aircraft inducted into the Indian Air Force in April 1978 was developed by a public sector undertaking and accepted by Air Headquarters. The failure to detect defects in the design of the brake system during the extensive trials prior to the introduction of Ajeet aircraft in April 1978 and the delay of ten years in carrying out modifications resulted in losses worth Rs. 2.90 crores and extra expenditure of Rs. 31.55 lakhs to the state.

XIII. **Induction of a Helicopter**

In November 1985, government approved the procurement of the MI-17 helicopter as a replacement for its ageing MI-8 fleet. Although the performance characteristics of the MI-17 were distinct when compared to the MI-8, no Air Staff Requirement was framed and the MI-17 was treated as an improved version of the MI-8.

It was noticed that there were obvious weaknesses in induction planning ranging from a delayed maintenance arrangement to a mismatch between the setting up of the helicopter units, associated civil works and the arrival of the helicopters. The evaluation team of Air Headquarters had omitted to inform the negotiating team that the new helicopter would have to be wired for weapon delivery like the MI-8. As a result an extra expenditure of Rs. 2.62 crores was incurred on the modification of the 37 aircraft. Also, two separate contracts for spares had to be concluded at an additional cost of Rs. 26.23 lakhs. Training aids not originally provided for had to be procured at an extra cost of Rs. 16.65 lakhs.

XIV. **Induction of Heavy Transport Aircraft**

In March 1983, government approved the induction of IL-76 aircraft in the Indian Air Force for its heavy transport requirements. Due to delay in concluding the contract for two aircraft during 1987 an extra expenditure of Rs. 2.94 crores had been incurred. Engines were withdrawn for overhaul after completing only 9.05 to 38.15 per cent of their prescribed overhaul life. As a result, the aircraft utilisation rate ranged from 15.35 to 28.26 hours only against the sanctioned utilisation rate of 66 hours per aircraft per month. Consequently, the IAF had to import three additional engines at a cost of Rs. 6.36 crores to maintain the operational status of the fleet.

There were also instances of other components such as rotables, gear boxes etc., being withdrawn for overhaul before their prescribed time and cases where components were withdrawn and sent abroad for repairs. Some of these have not been received back.

Although a need for a fleet of 20 aircraft had been planned during the 1985-90 Plan no cost benefit evaluation was done for setting up of indigenous maintenance facility. The expenditure on repair abroad of ten engines prematurely withdrawn for overhaul was Rs. 5.71 crores. Ten more engines have further failed which require urgent repairs. Thus, there would appear to be considerable scope for improved induction planning including a strong maintenance element.

XV. **Operation and Maintenance of an Aircraft**

Aircraft 'A' was procured and inducted into service between April 1981 and May 1983 through two contracts concluded in May 1980 and February 1981. Aircraft 'C' contracted for in September 1981 was also inducted into service between May 1982 and July 1983. Thirtyfive trainer aircraft to be used for both 'A' and 'C' were procured through the May 1980 and September 1981 contracts.

It was seen that there were shortfalls in the authorised flying task of these three aircraft which ranged between 17.87 to 77.97 per cent for 'A' 25.37 to 80.10 per cent for 'C' and 53.86 to 72.86 per cent for the trainer aircraft. The average utilisation rate per aircraft *vis-a-vis* the authorised utilisation rate was also low ranging from 15.22 to 52.89 per cent for 'A', 22.45 to 78.89 per cent for 'C' and 46.42 to 70.08 per cent for the trainer. The shortfall in respect of the trainers would have adverse impact on pilot training. The expected serviceability percentage of the aircraft was 70. Against this, the achievement was sub-optimal while the aircraft on ground percentage was high ranging from 11.4 to 38.4 per cent. Even this was achieved by resorting to heavy cannibalisation which was due to the unsatisfactory level of production support by the supplier.

Although the setting up of repair and overhaul facilities had been contracted for in 1983, delays occurred in the preparation of detailed project report for these facilities and the associated civil works. The overhaul of aircraft scheduled to commence from May 1984 could not be undertaken. Due to the delayed setting up of these facilities an avoidable expenditure of Rs. 38.35 crores was incurred during 1984 to 1988 on repairs abroad.

XVI. **Procurement, Operation and Maintenance of an Aircraft**

The government approved in 1947, procurement of an aircraft from abroad for a dedicated role for the Navy. The basis on which the purchase of used and overhauled aircraft was considered economical and advantageous could not be ascertained as the ministry stated that the file was misplaced.

Flying efforts and utilisation of the aircraft were affected considerably due to poor availability of the aircraft to the squadron, thereby not achieving the full flying task including training. Additional expenditure of Rs. 89.39 lakhs (approximately) had to be incurred in the deputation of foreign specialists as a result of delay in completion of civil works. Manhours prescribed for the scheduled maintenance of the aircraft have never been adhered to and the excess manhours utilised for each maintenance ranged from 110 to 123 per cent. Certain systems and communication sets originally fitted in the aircraft were considered inadequate for operational role. These were replaced at a cost of Rs. 3.61 crores. Airconditioning plants and chassis procured at a cost of Rs. 38.37 lakhs were found to be technically unsuitable for operational use and had to be replaced at a cost of Rs. 19.31 lakhs.

There was delay in the setting up of maintenance facilities. This in turn led to an expenditure of Rs. 3.34 crores on repair of aircraft components abroad. The repair facilities likely to be ready by March 1991 at a cost of Rs. 6.13 crores will finally be under-utilised as the aircraft are due for phasing out between September 1992 and January 1998.

XVII. **Induction of SSK Submarines**

During 1987, a review was made by Audit on the acquisition of two submarines, two material packages and torpedoes. This was commented upon in Para 55 of the Report of the Comptroller and Auditor General of India for the year ended March 1987. A further study by Audit during 1989 of the indigenous construction of the two submarines and the utilisation of the infrastructure created specially for this construction revealed that the time assessed for construction was grossly underestimated. Delay in taking a decision regarding the future construction of submarines has led to the under-utilisation of the special facilities created at a cost of Rs. 44.7 crores for the production of indigenous submarines. There was a mismatch between the receipt of materials and creation of storage facilities. The induction of submarines was not co-ordinated with the commissioning of related training simulators. An incorrect assessment of spares at the contract finalisation stage resulted in the procurement of Base and Depot spares at a higher cost of Rs. 91 crores against the original provision of Rs. 32 crores.

XVIII. **Crash Local Purchase of Stores by a Project Team**

A project team was appointed by the Controllerate of Procurement in Bombay for accelerating the process of liquidating pending material demands of the Indian Navy. A review by Audit revealed that the team paid scant regard to the laid down principles of local purchase and the powers vested in them. It either did not maintain proper records or manipulated them and favoured certain suppliers.

In the purchase of stores worth Rs. 98.89 lakhs, an avoidable expenditure of Rs. 47.06 lakhs was revealed. Orders worth Rs. 2.75 crores were placed on firms which were not on the approved list. It was noticed during test check that in 50 cases worth Rs. 6.36 lakhs, the requirement regarding quotations from a minimum number of firms was not observed. Incomplete tender inquiries were issued in 227 cases. In 48 cases the supplies were accepted even before placement of the purchase order. 216 orders worth Rs. 25.48 lakhs were placed on unregistered firms for items not under the purview of the team. Failures to quote demand/authority were noticed in 100 local purchase orders worth Rs. 12.77 lakhs.

The local purchase order register showed that 5664 orders were placed by the team. However, the numbers reported by the Controllerate of Procurement were only 5469. Only 5069 including 378 cancelled orders were produced for audit.

No assessment was made by either Naval Headquarters or the Ministry of Defence of the extent to which the team's objectives had been met and at what cost. No orders were issued to ensure that such cases do not recur. The role of Controller of Defence Accounts (Navy) in making the payments by neglecting some of the glaring irregularities committed by the team while making the purchases was also questionable.

XIX. **Sanctions for Works Services**

Sanctions issued between 1981-82 and 1986-87 for works services costing Rs. 33 crores, though required the sanction of higher authorities, were split up and sanctioned piece-meal to bring the value of sanctions within the financial powers of lower authorities. Certain works services which were specifically prohibited were sanctioned in disregard of government orders. Works costing Rs. 0.65 crore which were not sanctioned in accordance with the regulations and orders, were subsequently cancelled at the instance of Audit.

Non-observance of regulations, orders and instructions by Naval authorities while sanctioning various works were also noticed.

XX. Training of Naval Pilot

In 1986-87, eight aircraft were acquired at a cost of Rs. 7.60 crores to provide necessary training and experience in aerobatics to Naval pilots. The first line servicing facilities were also set up at a cost of Rs. 1 crore. Only 13 pilot were trained in 1987. Due to lack of volunteers, no training has been imparted thereafter. As a result, the investment of more than Rs. 8.5 crores has remained largely infructuous.

XXI. Construction of Residential Accommodation in Bombay

Accommodation was constructed in Bombay for officers and sailors of the Indian Navy in 1987-88. However, the accommodation could not be put to use. This was due to the Navy not obtaining prior clearance form the Municipal authorities. As a consequence, the officers and sailors had to be accommodated in hired buildings and additional expenditure had to be incurred on hire charges, house rent allowance etc., apart from the accommodation constructed at a cost of Rs 3.37 crores remaining unutilised.

XXII. Designing a Dry Dock

Extension of the submarine compartment in a Naval dry dock from a length of 100 to 240 metres was completed in March 1985. This included construction of a monolith at a cost of Rs. 16.03 lakhs which functioned as a headwall. This monolith had to be demolished at a cost of Rs. 11.21 lakhs to further extend the compartment to 272 metres to accommodate the needs of a special project. Since the detailed project report for the special project was already under preparation at that point of time, the construction and subsequent demolition of the monolith has resulted in an avoidable expenditure of Rs. 27.24 lakhs. This indicates the need for instituting better planning processes to avoid recurrence of such cases.

XXIII. Setting up of a Naval Aviation Enclave at Meenambakkam

While the development of the Naval Air Station at Arkonam was in progress, the Navy planned in 1981 to set up a Naval aviation enclave at Meenambakkam close to Arkonam, when the Arkonam station itself would have been able to provide all the required facilities. An investment of Rs. 152 lakhs will, therefore, have doubtful utility. Additionally, there will be a recurring avoidable expenditure of Rs. 8.32 lakhs per annum towards lease charges payable to International Airports Authority of India. The planning deficiencies together with the absence of the ministry's administrative approval to the works even after a lapse of above six years requires investigation.

XXIV. Construction of VVIP Accommodation in Violation of Delegated Powers

In the Headquarters of a Naval Command the top two floors of a six storey building, sanctioned for construction in December 1980 at a cost of Rs. 46.10 lakhs, were converted to VVIP and VIP accommodation by additions and alterations at a cost of Rs. 17 lakhs. As the basic requirement of security and fire hazards were not looked into at the time of conversion, this accommodation could not be utilised for VVIPs. This led to the construction of another set of VVIP accommodation at a cost of Rs. 19.06 lakhs, which was in contravention of powers delegated to the Command.

XXV. Purchase of Blowers for a Ship

As an urgent operational requirement for undertaking the refit of a Naval ship, offers were obtained from a firm abroad for two forced draught blowers in August 1984. The offers were valid up to January 1985. Due to failure to pursue the offer effectively within the validity period, the Navy had to incur an extra expenditure of Rs. 13.99 lakhs on procuring the blowers through fresh offers in September 1985.

XXVI. Procurement and Utilisation of Hydrographic Survey Equipment

For drawing of accurate and high resolution charts for navigation purposes, the Naval Headquarters required the installation of imported geodetic satellite survey systems in its survey ships under construction. The requirement was stated to be urgent as the installation was to be completed before the commissioning of the ships.

The equipment was acquired between May 1980 and March 1989 at a cost of Rs. 208.87 lakhs. In these purchases, an Indian agent of a foreign firm was paid a commission of Rs. 19.54 lakhs against the maximum permissible commission of Rs. 1.09 lakhs. Delays in commissioning the ships resulted in delays in installation of the systems. Meanwhile, the Central Processing Units of the computers were returned to the supplier, for obtaining updated version, in October 1980. Delay in obtaining government sanction for procurement of the updated Central Processing Units resulted in an extra expenditure of Rs. 17.10 lakhs exclusive of transportation cost. Meanwhile, the survey systems installed in the ships could not be fully exploited without these computing systems.

XXVII. Procurement of Rocket Launchers

In April 1974, government had approved the procurement of a certain type of rocket launchers for fitment on a certain class of ships. A contract was concluded in April 1975 for the launchers and spares and test equipment. Although the firm had quoted for supply of ammunition as well, the contract did not provide for this. Consequently, a separate contract had to be concluded with the same firm in March 1977 for the supply of ammunition at an additional cost of Rs. 1.09 crores. A second test equipment was procured in February 1986 at a cost of Rs. 29.48 lakhs although the volume of work did not justify the purchase.

XXVIII. **Receipt of a Damaged Machine**

A machine ordered in October 1984 at a cost of Rs. 7 lakhs was received in July 1985 in a damaged condition. Even four years after its receipt, the machine was not repaired nor was the insurance claim settled. In the absence of the machine, the Naval Dockyard had to undertake urgent operational jobs by makeshift arrangements.

XXIX. **Engine Modification on Kamorta Class Ships**

There was absence of timely review arrangements in the procurement process of modification kits for upgrading the ships' engines. This resulted in an avoidable expenditure Rs. 42.07 lakhs in the procurement of modification kits although the ships themselves for which these were being acquired, were in the process of being phased out.

XXX. **Development of an Integrated Air Defence System**

Based on the firm requirements of the Air Force and Navy in early 1983 the Defence Research and Development Organisation took up the work in March 1985 for a project definition, leading to the preparation of a detailed project report for an integrated air defence system without adequate appreciation of the full financial and technical implications. This included the setting up of 43 schemes to establish the data-base for the required technology. Out of the 43 schemes only 17 had been completed until June 1989 and the remaining 26 schemes were scheduled to be completed by March 1990. The detailed project report for the whole project was not prepared and cabinet approval for continuance of the project was not forthcoming. The expenditure of Rs. 14.82 crores so far incurred on the 43 schemes would, therefore, be largely unproductive.

EXCERPTS OF REPORT OF THE COMPTROLLER AND AUDITOR-GENERAL OF INDIA ON CENTRAL GOVERNMENT (RAILWAYS)

This Report of the year ended 31 March 1989 has been prepared for submission to the President under article 151 of the Constitution. It relates mainly to matters arising from the Appropriation Accounts of Indian Railways for 1988-89 together with other points arising from test audit of the financial transactions of the Railways.

The report includes audit reviews on the following:

(a) Inventory Control;
(b) Passenger Amenities;
(c) Human Resource Planning in the Indian Railways;
(d) Working of the Personnel Department;
(e) Review of Efficiency, Workstudy and Staff Inspection studies; and
(f) Constitution of new Broad Gauge line between Wani-Pimpalkutti.

Included in this report are also comments on topics related to purchases, stores, works, establishment, other expenditure and earnings.

The cases included in this Report are from among those which came to notice in the course of audit during 1988-89 as well as from among those which had come to notice in earlier years but could not be dealt with in previous reports. Some matters relating to the period subsequent to 1988-89 have also been included, wherever considered necessary.

OVERVIEW

Audit Report for the year ended 31 March 1989 contains 75 paragraphs including six reviews. The points highlighted in the Report are:

1. Financial Results

The net surplus of the Railways for 1988-89 was Rs. 21.67 crores against Rs. 28 crores anticipated in the Budget Estimates. If contribution to the Pension Fund had been made commensurate with liabilities on this account, the working results would have ended with a deficit of Rs. 133.45 crores. The contribution to the Pension Fund was Rs. 550 crores against withdrawals of Rs. 744.15 crores from the fund.

The declining trend in the effective rate of dividend on the capital-at-charge continued during 1988-89. This represented 3.91 per cent of the capital-at-charge as against 4 per cent in 1987-88 and 4.19 per cent in 1986-87. The amount of dividend paid was Rs. 715.66 crores. The Railways received a subsidy of Rs. 207.40 crores from the General Revenues.

Indebtedness of Railways to General Revenues at the end of 1988-89 was Rs. 1018.44 crores which comprised loans from General Revenues (Rs. 529.29 crores) and deferred dividend (Rs. 489.15 crores) kept outside the Railway Accounts.

The percentage of working expenses to earnings representing the operating ratio showed a marginal improvement over the previous year. This is, however, to be viewed in the context of insufficient contribution to the Pension Fund. Further, the operating ratio rose from 88.3 in 1982 to 92.5 in 1987-88 due to faster growth of expenditure as compared to that of Revenue Receipts.

Against Rs. 1759.39 crores raised by Indian Railway Finance Corporation (IRFC) during 1987-88 and 1988-89 Railways utilised a sum of Rs. 1,630 crores leaving a balance of Rs. 129.39 crores as unutilised.

The average life of various items of rolling stock ranges between 30 and 36 years. As against this, the existing arrangement of payment of lease rental to IRFC, which seeks to redeem the cost of acquisition of rolling stock over a period of 10 years, results in inflating the operating expenses and reducing the net surplus available to Railways. The maintaining of the revenue surplus at levels not affected by the disturbance caused by the excessive burden of lease charges may call for steps to augment revenues.

While operating expenses of the Railways would go up as indicated above, there would be relief to General Revenues which is not to bear the burden of interest and other charges on raising resources for Railways and, in return, getting only a dividend on General Revenues.

The lease rental of 16 per cent includes 6 per cent towards redemption of capital cost over a period of 10 years. For the next 20 years of the life of rolling stock, the burden on the operating expenses of Railways would be negligible. Operating expenses of the Railways would not, therefore, be bearing an uniform charge over the life span of the rolling stock. Further, as the value of the rolling stock is not reflected in the Block Account and the Balance Sheet of the Railways as ownership thereof vests with IRFC, the accounts of the Railways would not be portraying a true and fair picture.

2. **Inventory Control**

The percentage of stores balances at the end of the year of the total issues during the year represents the turn over ratio on inventory. The ratio achieved was 32 at the end of 1987-88 against the target of 27 which itself has to be viewed as high representing nearly three and half months balance in terms of consumption. The ratio varied significantly from zone-to-zone; from 79 and 45 in Northeast Frontier and North Eastern Railways to 26 and 25 in the Central and Southern Railways.

Inventory norms were yet to be fixed for production units.

There was a tendency to overstate issues at the end of the financial year to exhibit a low turn over ratio vitiating the true state of affairs.

There were considerable delays in taking procurement action after receipt of requisitions. Delays in finalisation of tenders ranged from three to twenty-four months in some of the cases test checked.

Due to lack of co-ordination and delay in procurement action, the Railways suffered a loss of Rs. 142.16 lakhs.

The percentage of imported stores had been increasing over the years with a markedly sharp increase in the three production units.

Unplanned excess production of steam loco components by CLW resulted in inactive inventory of Rs. 1.25 crore.

There were 2749 stock sheets pointing out exesses (Rs. 6.84 crores) and shortages (Rs. 9.78 crores) awaiting clearance in three Railways and two production units.

Effective steps were not taken for speedy disposal of scrap resulting in its accumulation.

Computerisation of inventory has not been comprehensive covering all aspects of inventory management.

3. **Passenger Amenities**

Expenditure on passenger amenities remained static at an average of Rs. 5 crores per annum during the Sixth Five Year Plan. While earnings during the first four years of the Seventh Plan increased by 41.3 per cent over total passenger earnings of the previous plan, there was only a meagre increase of 0.2 per cent in the ratio of expenditure on passenger amenities over earnings.

The proposed scale of acquisition of new coaches would not be adequate to replace even the overaged coaching stock. Against 12914 coaches and 1390 EMUs to be replaced acquisition of only 6900 coaches and 950 EMUs had been planned.

Instead of augmenting lower class services like second class 3-tier mail/express coaches and AC chair cars on long distance trains, the number of AC sleeper coaches is being disproportionately increased.

Compensation is paid only for train accidents and not for dacoities and stabbings that take place in trains. The desirability of ensuring timely compensation to victims now excluded deserves consideration.

Items that constitute 'Passenger Amenities' had not been laid down in clear terms despite the recommendations of the Railway Convention Committee and Estimates Committee.

A test check in three Railways revealed that basic amenities had not been provided in -

366 out of 693 on Central,
378 out of 796 on Eastern, and
258 out of 851 stations on South Eastern Railways.

On the above Railways, there were as many as 875 stations without arrangements for drinking water, 718 stations without latrines and 604 stations without waiting sheds/halls.

There were delays of two to eight years in completing passenger amenity works on some Railways. In a test check, Audit noticed extra expenditure of Rs. 2.02 crores in this regard.

A large number of halt stations sanctioned for public conveyance long ago had not yet been opened.

4. Human Resource Planning in the Indian Railways

A definite approach and application of the concept of human resource planning was not taken till 1985.

Staff cost as a percentage to working expenses has been increasing steadily and in 1987-88 it constituted 46 per cent of total working expenses.

Staff productivity varied significantly from one Zonal Railway to the other. The average productivity of Indian Railways, as a whole, was 218 thousand traffic units per employee in 1986-87 as against 289, achieved by the Central Railway.

Non-surrender of surplus gangs due to non-implementation of the recommendations of the special committee resulted in an avoidable expenditure of Rs. 14.76 crores on Western, Central and Northern Railways during 1986-89. Not only gang strengths were not reduced, casual labour was engaged over permanent gangs and the avoidable expenditure on Central and Northern Railways during 1984-85 to 1988-89 was Rs. 140.05 crores. The required quantum of reduction of gang strength on uneconomic branch lines was not given effect to resulting in avoidable expenditure of Rs. 0.21 crore.

Despite a marked reduction in the work relating to maintenance of steam locomotives and closure of steam sheds, there was no corresponding reduction in staff in loco sheds leading to avoidable expenditure estimated at Rs. 1.39 crore during 1982-89.

Non-surrender of surplus posts based on the recommendations of Staff Inspection Unit, resulted in non-realisation of savings of Rs.5.35 crores during

1985-86 to 1988-89.

Training facilities to improve the skills of staff were not fully utilised and shortfall in training ranged from 25 to 66 per cent.

The payment of Productivity Linked Bonus (PLB) in terms of number of days wages is measured on the basis of revenue earnings net tonne kilometres (NTKMs). The output value of one bonus day had declined in successive revisions from 6400 million NTKMs in 1979 to 5502 million NTKMs in 1986.

5. Working of the Personnel Department

A well organised Personnel Department, supported by an internal audit system provided by the Financial Adviser and Chief Accounts Officer is expected to ensure that administration of personal claims is managed well and that recoveries due from employees are effected promptly. The results of an audit review, based on a test check on a limited sample, revealed deficiencies in the system as enumerated below:

Leave accounts were not maintained properly which resulted in excess payment of leave salary of Rs. 43.99 lakhs.

Failure to undertake periodical revision of assessed rent of railway quarters on time led to arrears of rent of Rs. 267.90 lakhs remaining outstanding.

The amount on account of non-recovery/short recovery of rent/penal rent for unauthorised occupation of railway quarters, loss of rent due to delay in allotment of railway quarters and payment of house rent allowance to the employees occupying railways quarters was Rs. 95.06 lakhs.

Non-maintenance of relevant records and failure of internal checking units in not ensuring proper maintenance of the records resulted in the short recovery of electricity charges amounting to Rs. 252.69 lakhs during 1970-1989.

Arrears in recovery in respect of scooter advance, advance of pay on transfer/tour, flood advance, bicycle and other advances amounted to Rs. 647.83 lakhs. Even after expiry of the permissible period of instalments for recoveries, an amount of Rs. 505.64 lakhs was outstanding for more than three years on Central, Eastern, Northern, Northeast Frontier, South Central and South Eastern Railways.

6. Efficiency, Workstudy and Staff Inspection Studies

Work studies on various topics are undertaken for bringing about economy, rationalisation of deployment of staff, efficient methods of operation for effecting savings and, above all, improvement of the image of the Railways. A review by Audit revealed that there were delays in undertaking studies and in processing them. There were instances where the recommendations were not implemented. In some cases, the recommendations were implemented after considerable delays leading to additional expenditure. These instances are mentioned below:

Delay in surrendering 42 posts identified as surplus in goods office, New

Delhi led to extra expenditure of Rs. 0.21 crore. Recommendation for surrender of 100 posts of clerks following computerisation of documentation was not implemented.

A recommendation to revise the existing ratio of engine kilometre/day/engine in use and wagon kilometre/day was not implemented. The study undertaken had identified a saving of Rs. 40.77 crores.

Delays in surrendering surplus staff as recommended by various workstudy teams resulted in extra expenditure of Rs. 0.51 crore.

There is recurring loss in operating services in the Kalka-Shimla section: in 1987-88 the loss amounted to Rs. 4.42 crores. A study carried out to reduce operating costs in this section did not prove effective as most of the recommendations were found to be not acceptable and, hence, not implemented.

Similarly, work study team conducted techno-economic studies in respect of uneconomic branch lines incurring losses in excess of Rs. 20 lakhs and recommended measures, the implementation of which was expected to yield saving. The measures, however, did not prove effective and the losses increased from Rs. 4.06 crores in 1985-86 to Rs. 8.38 crores in 1986-87 and Rs. 10.67 crores in 1987-88.

7. **Construction of new Broad Gauge Line between Wani-Pimpalkutti**

Indecision of the Railway to go ahead with the project led to an inordinate delay of ten years in the completion of the project after it was conceived and to a cost overrun of Rs. 12.26 crores.

The project, though financially not viable, was taken up at the instance of a state government. The branch line costing Rs. 17.56 crores had become unremunerative entailing a total deferred dividend liability to General Revenues of Rs. 7.73 crores up to 1987-88, adding yet another uneconomic line to the network. The project cost would have been less by Rs. 98 lakhs if, instead of first class CST-9 sleepers, second class sleepers as provided in the estimates had been used.

8. A Project was set up at Ponmalai for reclamation of cylinder blocks at a cost of Rs. 5.35 crores in 1988 although the capacity available with DLW was adequate to meet the requirements of all Zonal railways. Delay in the completion of the Project resulted in a cost overrun of Rs. 2.65 crores.

9. A third bridge across the river Krishna near Vijayawada, though taken up on an urgency certificate in December 1978, and planned for completion by December 1984, was completed and commissioned in July 1989. There were delays in awarding the contract and supply of steel by the Railway. This led to avoidable escalation in cost by Rs. 2.37 crores.

10. Major modifications to the original design in the construction of two parallel tunnels by the Metro Railway, Calcutta seven years after the award of the contract led to changes in method of operation contributing to delays and consequential additional payment to contractor for claims as under:

on account of losses	Rs. 2.70 crores
compensation	Rs. 0.56 crore
escalation	Rs. 0.93 crore

11. Despite having been cautioned by RDSO and the Railway Board, ballastless track was provided by Metro Railway for the whole length in the expectation of low maintenance cost. These expectations were belied in view of large expenditure of Rs. 1.18 crores on maintenance and upkeep of track during the first three years after opening.

12. Development of a continuous automatic train protection type of signalling system for the underground Metro Railway entrusted to Electronic Corporation of India Limited (ECIL) was foreclosed after the prototype was developed and found to meet the fail-safe requirements. Specifications were upscaled later from fail-safe tests of single component to that of multiple component tests. The foreclosure of the contract with ECIL resulted in the investment of Rs. 1.93 crores including grants-in-aid and value of equipments supplied going idle. Further, this had the effect of virtual abandonment of indigenous research in this area.

13. An incorrect projection of requirements of wheelsets without a fresh review of the production in the Wheel and Axle Plant and the stock and dues position led to avoidable import of 4000 wheelsets costing Rs. 5 crores.

14. There was failure on the part of a Zonal Railway to collect sales tax in respect of auctions though it was obligatory on its part to do so in terms of notifications/amendments issued under the state's Sales Tax Act. This resulted in a loss of Rs. 82.97 lakhs.

15. Delay in the disposal of an abandoned track resulted in a loss of Rs. 90.42 lakhs. Scrap worth Rs. 0.15 lakh could be salvaged.

16. Failure to transport a camshaft grinding machine after it was imported in Calcutta Port for as long as seven months resulted in extra expenditure of Rs. 24.22 lakhs due to damage to the machine and a further delay of five years in its installation. On account of the delayed installation of the imported machine, camshafts had to be arranged through imports for Rs. 1.01 crores and through indigenous sources for Rs. 0.58 crore.

17. Instructions are issued form time-to-time for carriage and freighting of traffic by specified routes for securing rational movement aimed at optimising utilisation of available routes.

A review by Audit revealed routing of traffic other than by the rationalised routes resulting in loss of revenue of Rs. 72.76 lakhs on the South Central (Rs. 35 lakhs), Northern (Rs. 10.03 lakhs) and Western (Rs. 27.73 lakhs) Railways.

18. Instances were also noticed of cargo being carried by a longer route though charged for by a shorter route.

Foodgrains traffic, booked from Broad Gauge stations on Northern Railway to Broad Gauge/Metric Gauge destinations on the North-east Frontier Railway continued to be routed via longer route by transhipment at Garhara instead of via Malda for transhipment at New Bongaigaon resulting in loss of revenue of Rs. 4.80 crores.

19. Train load consignments of coal and cement, on the South Central Railway, and diesel traffic on the South Eastern Railway, though booked by shorter routes, were carried by longer routes involving loss of earnings of Rs. 4.31 crores.

20. Concession was granted on freight rates for carriage of rock phosphate in open wagons although concession was admissible only to such cargo which were transported in closed wagons. Grant of concession in freight on rock phosphate traffic traditionally carried in open wagons on Western Railway, resulted in loss of Rs. 43.29 lakhs.

21. North Eastern and South Eastern Railways realised freight charges of Rs. 4.74 crores 6 to 182 days after loading and despatch of goods instead of at the time of booking thereby granting financial accommodation to consignors.

22. Consignments booked 'To Pay' to private sidings served by Raniganj, Japla and Shyamnagar stations on Eastern Railway were delivered to siding owners without realisation of freight and other charges amounting to Rs. 48.36 lakhs. Instructions were also not issued to originating stations not to book cargo 'To Pay' to these sidings.

9

IMPORTANT JUDICIAL JUDGEMENTS

J.C. Jetli, a senior officer belonging to the Indian Administrative Service, went to the Supreme Court to challenge his supersession by a junior officer of the same service for appointment to the position of secretary to government. The Supreme Court upheld his claim of seniority and directed that he appointed as secretary.

Jetli had a grievance against the central government when he was superseded by Anil Bordia, a batch junior to him, who was preferred as secretary overlooking Jetli's both brilliant academic and service record. He decided to hit back. Jetli first sent a representation to the then cabinet secretary B.G. Deshmukh, and even sought an appointment with the then Prime Minister Rajiv Gandhi. When he was told that he should revert to his cadre state of Bihar at the end of his tenure, Jetli took his petition to the Central Administrative Tribunal (CAT).

Jetli observed that the government rules laid down that the cabinet secretary assesses the various claims and makes his recommendation directly to the cabinet committee for appointments for orders, but no guidelines have been prescribed to govern the cabinet secretary's recommendation. In the absence of explicitly laid down criteria such decisions are liable to be often arbitrary. The government replied by saying that since the post of secretary was a sensitive one, the selection could not be regulated by any fixed norms; it had to be based on various relevant considerations like suitability to the particular post. It justified Jetli's supersession by pointing out that even a person who did not belong to the regular hierarchy of the bureaucracy could be appointed secretary if he was found suitable and was a man of confidence. The government further insisted that the procedure for selection of secretaries was just and did not leave room for discrimination.

But the Central Administrative Tribunal found the government's argument weak and without substance. In what appeared to be a historic judgement, it ordered that norms and guidelines for the selection of a secretary be laid down instead of leaving it to the discretion of the cabinet secretary. It found that the government had not only been not just in the case of Jetli but several other bureaucrats also. One such case was that of C.S. Sastry, an IAS officer, who was made secretary, Ministry of Agriculture in 1986 superseding two of his seniors. When P. Murari was appointed secretary, he superseded twelve others. Similarly, Gopi Arora jumped ahead of seven seniors when he was appointed as secretary to the government. The CAT felt that rules authorising the cabinet secretary to take the final decision suffered from a vice of unfettered discretion. It ordered the government to review all the forty-two cases including that of

Jetli's after laying down the selection criteria.

The government refused to accept the CAT's direction and filed a special leave petition in the Supreme Court of India. The scene of the legal battle now shifted to the highest judiciary of the land.

Jetli, who had in the meantime returned to Bihar as chairman of the Bihar State Electricity Board, had to cool his feet for two years. Ironically, the state government equated this post to the level of secretary. But the central government continued to maintain that despite Jetli's brilliance he was not suitable. In February 1990, a three judge bench of the Supreme Court rejected the government's objections about his seniority. But the Attorney General Soli Sorabjee's argument that it would be difficult for the government to lay down selection norms was accepted by the Court. Justice Thakkar made the famous remarks that the governments have the right to appoint their own 'cooks' (Quoted by Sunil Sethi in *The Times of India*, 24 December, 1989).

Although Jetli had been personally vindicated, the question of criteria for selection for the post of secretary remains unanswered. So the problem of supersession will continue to plague the civil service.

The two judgements are reproduced in what follows:

IN THE SUPREME COURT OF INDIA

CIVIL APPELLATE JURISDICTION
CIVIL APPEAL NO. 3860 OF 1984

Vinod Krishna Kaul ... Appellant

versus

The Union of India & Ors. ... Respondents

JUDGEMENT

Kasliwal, J.

This appeal by special leave is directed against the order of Delhi High Court dated 13 January, 1983 in Civil Writ No. 1297 of 1980.

The petitioner was selected for the Indian Police Service in the open competitive examination held in 1955. He was given Rajasthan Cadre. He joined government service on 25 October 1956 and his All India seniority in the combined list of 1956 IPS batch is at No. 3. After initial service in the Rajasthan State Police and Delhi Police, the petitioner was inducted into the Intelligence Bureau, Ministry of Home Affairs, Government of India, New Delhi in 1960. He continued to serve in the Intelligence Bureau on posts outside and within Delhi. He got the selection grade of the I.P.S. on 24 June 1972. On 23 January 1973, the petitioner got the grade of joint deputy director/deputy director, Intelligence Bureau (equivalent to Deputy Inspector General of Police — a selection post). According to the petitioner his service record has always been extremely bright and there is no adverse remark against him in his service record. In the year 1977, the petitioner was selected for the prestigious National Defence College, New Delhi and he successfully obtained the graduateship from the aforesaid college. According to the petitioner he was given another prestigious assignment in 1979, details of which he is not free to disclose.

The case of the petitioner is that there were 336 posts of joint secretaries under the Government of India as on 1 June 1980. These posts are in the pay scale of Rs. 2500-125/2-2750. The posts of joint secretaries are ex-cadre posts and appointments to the posts of joint secretaries are made from different sources, out of a panel of officers belonging to the Indian Administrative Service, Indian Police Service and other central services. According to the petitioner two posts of joint secretaries were to be filled in the Police Commission in 1980. The petitioner was empanelled in 1978 for appointment to the posts of joint secretaries. Respondent No. 4, Sri Ved Prakash Marwah member of I.P.S. and Respondent No. 5 Sri Kailash Prakash member of Indian Postal Service were also put in the above panel. According to the petitioner both these officers were junior to the petitioner. It has been alleged that the above two posts of joint secretaries in the Police Commission were given to respondent Numbers 4 and 5 totally ignoring the claim of the petitioner. It has been alleged that the petitioner who was placed higher in merit and seniority throughout in comparison to respondent Numbers 4 and 5, was discriminated and was not considered for a higher post of joint secretary and appointments to such post was given to respondent Numbers 4 and 5 in violation of articles 14 and 16 of the Constitution. It has thus been contended by the petitioner that he was put to financial loss as well as in rank and status in comparison to respondent Numbers 4 and 5 who were junior to him.

The petitioner challenged the above action of the respondents by filing a writ petition under article 226 of the Constitution before the Delhi High Court. The respondents submitted counter affidavits. In an affidavit sworn by Sri D.B. Ailawadi, under secretary to the Government of India in the Ministry of Home Affairs on 10 April 1981, it was stated *inter alia* that the contention of the petitioner that the respondent Number 4 was appointed to the joint secretary level post by passing the claim of the petitioner was wrong and denied. The empanelment of an officer as joint secretary does not give him any absolute legal right for appointment as a joint secretary as has been assumed by the petitioner. Joint secretary's panel is only an eligibility list of such suitable officers who could be considered for appointment to the posts of joint secretary to the Government of India and this list is clearly not an entitlement list nor does it give any legal right to the petitioner or to the other officers, concerned for the actual appointment as joint secretary. The selection for the posts of joint secretary has to be made by the concerned administrative ministry/department from amongst the names of suitable officers suggested by the Establishment Officer. The appointments to these posts have to be made on the basis of relative suitability of eligible officers as well as keeping in view the job requirements of the post and such senior posts, like this could not be filled up only on the basis of the individual seniority of the officers alone. The High Court apart from the above affidavit also called for the record and then observed as under:

> "We are satisfied both on the basis of the record shown to us and on a reading of the pleadings that unfortunately for the petitioner his assignment was such at the relevant point of time that he was not available for being considered for the post of a joint secretary. In other words, in the exigencies of public service he could not be spared. The averments in Shri Ailawadi's affidavit are correct. If that is the position we fail to understand how the petitioner can put forward any claim of hostile discrimination or arbitrariness. Since he was not available to be considered and the posts to which respondents 4 and 5 were appointed were ex-cadre posts, to which petitioner as such did not have a right, he can have no cause for complaint."

The High Court in these circumstances dismissed the petition filed by the petitioner.

It was contended by the learned counsel for the appellant before us that once the name of the petitioner was included in the panel for appointment to the post of joint secretary, it was incumbent upon the respondents to appoint the petitioner on such post of joint secretary prior to respondent Number 4 who was admittedly junior to the petitioner in the Indian Police Service. It was contended that the respondents cannot take the plea that the petitioner was not available for such post due to exigencies of public service. The respondents ought to have spared the petitioner for such appointment as it was within the competence of the government itself to post the petitioner in a place from where he could be spared. It was also contended that the scale of joint secretary goes up to Rs. 2,750 while the post of deputy Inspector General went up to Rs. 2,250. It was thus submitted that the petitioner was not only put to financial loss but was also deprived of being considered and appointed for other higher posts of additional secretary and secretary under the central government.

On the other hand a counter affidavit on behalf of the respondents has been filed before the Court by Sri K.V. Sampath Kumar, under secretary to the Deptartment of Personnel and Administrative Reforms. In the counter affidavit it has been stated that the system of appointments to the posts in the secretariat the Government of India in general and to the posts of joint secretary in particular is done in the following manner.

At the outset, the establishment officer to the Government of India addresses a letter to the controlling officers of the various cadres, eligible for consideration for appointments to the posts of under secretary and above, inviting names of officers in their respective cadres who, according to the controlling authority of the cadre are, suitable for consideration for these posts. The suitability of officers eligible for the posts of joint secretary and equivalent posts is, thereafter, assessed by a committee of secretaries, specially constituted for the purpose in accordance with the prescribed guidelines. The assessments of this committee are then considered by the senior selection board and such of them as are finally considered suitable for appointments in the posts of joint secretaries or equivalent posts are included in a list called the 'joint secretaries suitability list'. The officers in the 'joint secretaries suitability list' are not necessarily arranged in the order of seniority or in order of merit. At the beginning of each calendar year, the various cadre authorities of the feeder services are addressed by the Establishment Officer to find out the names of the officers of the respective services who would be available during that calendar year for being considered for posts under the senior staffing scheme. The list of such officers is *inter alia* known as the 'offer list' and the officers are 'said to be available' during that calendar year. Although no limit on the number of such officers has been prescribed in respect of any service, the respective cadre authorities are expected to offer only such officers who could be released during that calendar year with due regard to the cadre position viz. the total sanctioned strength of the various grades, deputation reserve and the extent to which it is utilised etc. It has been further stated in the counter affidavit that when any vacancy in the post of joint secretary or equivalent post is invited by a ministry/department, the Establishment Officer, acting on behalf of the senior selection board, considers the claims, merits and availability of all officers within the field of choice and recommends to the ministry/department a panel of names, keeping in view educational qualifications, service, experience and special training required for effective performance of the job. It is then for the ministry or department to accept or not to accept any officer from the said panel after considering the suitability of each officer for the particular job. It has thus been alleged that the procedure which is set out above clearly indicated that an officer borne on the 'joint secretaries suitability list' has no absolute legal right to be appointed to the post of a joint secretary or to any equivalent post. The list merely contains the names of officers who are considered generally suitable for appointment to the posts of joint secretaries, and equivalent posts and is not an entitlement list. For specific vacancies only such of the officers in the general suitability list are considered who are comparatively more suitable than others in the list, keeping in view the job requirements of the vacancy in question. Availability of the officer from his parent cadre is also taken into account. It was further stated in the counter affidavit that at the time when respondent numbers 4 and 5 were appointed to the posts in the National Police Commission, the petitioner was not available for consideration for such post. According to the respondents, the crucial point at issue revolved around availability of the petitioner for being considered for appointment to the posts to which the respondents numbers 4 and 5 were appointed. It was conclusively proved to the satisfaction of the High Court that the petitioner was not available for appointment to the post at the relevant time.

The petitioner filed a rejoinder affidavit in which *inter alia* it was stated that the factum of empanelment of the officer concerned denotes his availability unless and until the same is negatived by a subsequent specific withdrawal in the case of such officer. Mere omission to submit his name from year to year does not *ipso facto* affect his availability. The petitioner fulfilled all the requirements on merits, seniority, suitability etc. to the hilt and yet he was not considered for the post of joint secretary. It has been stated that the purported non-inclusion of the petitioner in the list of officers sent by the Ministry of Home Affairs as available for appointment to the post of joint secretary during that year is arbitrary and illegal and had offended articles 14 and 16 of the Constitution.

This Court on 23 July 1984 gave a further direction that the reply of the state respondents on the specific point about the non-availability of the petitioner for being considered for appointment to the post of joint secretary to which respondents numbers 4 and 5 were appointed may be further clarified with specific reference to whether such conclusion was arrived at by the state respondent with due regard to all facts and after applying its mind to all relevant factors. In pursuance of the above direction further affidavit of K.V. Sampath Kumar above-named was filed by the respondents. In this affidavit it was again reiterated that the petitioner was not available for consideration for appointment as joint secretary, since the Ministry of Home Affairs which is the cadre authority in respect of the I.P.S. to which the petitioner belongs, were unable to spare his services during the relevant year for good and valid administrative consideration and in public interest, which are amplified as under.

That the petitioner was appointed in April 1960 in the Intelligence Bureau, a central police organisation to which the tenure position detailed in the preceding paragraphs apply, and had continued in the said organisation since then till he was repatriated to his state cadre in 1983. In other words, the petitioner had already served 20 years in a central police organisation which was much beyond the normal tenure of 5 years allowed and this exception was made in the petitioner's case, only because his services were continued to be required in the sensitive central police organisation in which he was working at the relevant time. If his services could be spared by the central police organisation for appointment elsewhere, there was no justification in making an exception in the petitioner's case in retaining him far beyond the prescribed tenure of 5 years in the central police organisation.

That as long as the Ministry of Home Affairs was not in a position to offer the petitioner's name for deputation to the central secretariat at the relevant time on account of the considerations indicated above, he had to be considered as non-available by the Establishment Officer for appointment to tenure posts in the central secretariat, and that the statement/conclusion made in the averments of this respondent both before the Hon'ble High Court and in the counter affidavit filed by this respondent in reply to the special leave petition were so made on sound and valid grounds and after applying his mind to all the facts and circumstances of the case.

Even so, a mention was made during the hearing of the writ petition of the High Court that, if the Hon'ble Court so directed, the petitioner's name would also be circulated. Although no such specific direction was given by the Hon'ble Court, it was decided to retain the petitioner's name 'on offer' during 1981 and sponsor his name against suitable vacancies of joint secretaries in the central secretariat. The petitioner was not, however, select by any of the ministries/department to whom his name had been sponsored.

The petitioner submitted a rejoinder affidavit to the above- mentioned counter affidavit of the respondents. The petitioner has further asserted that the contention of the state respondents indicating non-availability of the petitioner was totally misleading and incorrect. The respondents numbers 4 and 5 were respectively promoted to the post of joint secretary in the National Police Commission on 8 May 1980 and 4 December 1979 (in this case retrospectively) in the grade of Rs. 2500-125/2-2750. On the other hand the petitioner was promoted as joint director, Intelligence Bureau on 8 December 1982 in the same grade i.e. after 3 years. Thus the two respondents were drawing Rs. 2,750 per month as their basic salary, whereas the petitioner was drawing a mere Rs. 2,500 per month. The respondents have also been drawing enhanced dearness allowance, travelling allowance etc. on the basis of their higher salaries, apart from enjoying various other perquisites of office. Respondents 4 and 5 were also entitled to higher death-cum-retirement benefits they are also eligible to be appointed as additional secretary to the government. All this has been denied to the petitioner as he was given current promotion belatedly in December 1982.

We have considered the arguments advanced by learned counsel for both the parties and have perused the entire record. We do not think it necessary or proper to go into the larger questions of the manner of preparation of 'select list' for the appointment of joint secretaries as it may have larger ramifications, because this case can be disposed of on the basis of its own facts. The name of the petitioner was included in the panel in the year 1978. The question of appointment on the post of joint secretary in the National Police Commission arose in the year 1980. The petitioner was continuing in the department of Intelligence Bureau at that time and according to his own saying he was assigned a prestigious appointment in 1979 which according to him cannot be disclosed. The respondents have come out with a categorical and consistent stand taken before the High Court as well as before us that at the relevant time the petitioner was not available due to exigencies of public service for being considered and appointed on the post of joint secretary in the National Police Commission. The High Court after examining the original record and the pleadings of the parties has also recorded a finding that the petitioner was not available at the relevant time for being considered for the post on which respondents numbers 4 and 5 were appointed. We find no reason to take a different view in this regard. We are not prepared to accept the contention of the petitioner in this regard that the claim of the petitioner was ignored or he was not considered on account of any malafide intention. Admittedly the post of joint secretary is outside the cadre and is not a promotion post of Indian Police Service to which the petitioner belongs. There is no question of consideration of any seniority of the petitioner *qua* respondent number 5 Sri Kailash Prakash who admittedly belongs to Indian Postal Service and not Indian Police Service. So far as the claim of seniority of the petitioner *qua* respondent number 4 Sri Ved Prakash Marwah is concerned, it would remain according to their position in the parent cadre in IPS and the same cannot be disturbed merely because respondent number 4 worked as joint secretary in the National Police Commission for some period. In the circumstances mentioned above, there is no question of any violation of articles 14 and 16 of the Constitution as contended on behalf of the petitioner.

In the result we find no force in this appeal and it is accordingly dismissed with no order as to costs.

Sd/-
(N.M. Kasliwal, J.)

New Delhi:
12 September 1990

Sd/-
(M. Fathima Beevi, J.)

IN THE CENTRAL ADMINISTRATIVE TRIBUNAL PRINCIPAL BENCH

Regn. No. OA 653/87 Date of Decision: 19-11-1987

Shri Jagdish Chander Jetli . . . Petitioner

versus

Union of India and another . . . Respondents

For Petitioner: In person.
For Respondents: Shri G. Ramaswamy, Addl. Solicitor General of India with Mr P.P. Khurana, Advocate

CORAM: HON'BLE MR. JUSTICE J.D. JAIN, Vice-Chairman
HON'BLE MR. BIRBAL NATH, Administrative Member

JUDGEMENT

By this application under section 19 of the Administrative Tribunals Act, 1985 (hereinafter referred to as "the Act"), the petitioner, who is a member of Indian Administrative Service, seeks to challenge the Order dated 19 March 1987 of the Government of India (Ministry of Human Resources and Development), Department of Education (copy Annexure I), whereby Shri Anil Bordia, respondent number 2, who is also a member of Indian Administrative Service has been appointed as secretary, Department of Education in the Ministry of Human Resource Development with effect from the forenoon of the date of the said order. The contention of the petitioner is that Shri Anil Bordia was junior to him in the cadre of IAS officers. The petitioner has also challenged the order dated 20 April 1987 of the Union of India, Department of Personnel and Training informing him that his extended tenure as additional secretary, Rural Development, Government of India, would expire on 31 May 1987 when his services would stand replaced at the disposal of the state government (copy Annexure II).

2. The case of the applicant succinctly is that he is an I.A.S. officer of 1957 batch. He belongs to state cadre of Bihar and came on deputation to the Government of India as joint secretary in the Ministry of Social Welfare on 16 June 1980. He was later transferred as joint secretary to the Ministry of Rural Development now redesignated as Department of Rural Development under the Ministry of Agriculture. He was placed on the panel of additional secretaries in 1984 and was promoted as such on 21 March 1984, Shri Anil Bordia, respondent number 2 belongs to Rajasthan Cadre of Indian Administrative Service; although he too belongs to the same batch of 1957, but the petitioner was promoted earlier to him as additional secretary in the first instance and not on review etc. He considers that his performance in the service must have been

rated to be very good/outstanding before he was appointed as additional secretary to the Government of India and likewise, he was always praised by his secretaries and ministers under whom he had occasions to work as additional secretary. So, he asserts that in the background of his proven record and performance, merit and seniority, he ought to have been promoted before Shri Anil Bordia. Feeling aggrieved by order dated 19 March 1987, he made a representation to the cabinet secretary, Government of India, on 30 March 1987. He, *inter alia*, invited the attention of the cabinet secretary to the fact that his normal tenure under the Government of India was due to end on 20 March 1987 and he was likely to revert to his parent state of Bihar on 31 May 1987 on the completion of his extended tenure. So, he prayed for an early decision of his representation in view of his pending reversion to the state cadre. However, on 20 April 1987, he received a communication from the Establishment Officer, Department of Personnel and Training, Government of India through the secretary, Department of Rural Development intimating him that his services would stand replaced at the disposal of the state government with effect from 31 May 1987. He was also required to intimate his leave intention, if any, so that the state government could be informed. The said communication, according to him, amounts to rejection of his representation to the Government of India against his unwarranted supersession and therefore, he was left with no alternative but to seek redressal of his grievance from this Tribunal.

3. The petitioner has made a frontal attack on the procedure for selection and appointment of officers to the secretariat posts of and above the rank of under secretary to the Government of India as prescribed in office memorandum number F.No.33(1)-EO/70 dated 27-10-70 (Annexure IV) which according to him suffers from intrinsic procedural infirmities and has led to arbitrary decisions in the selection of officers to the aforesaid posts. In order to bring out the enormity of the injustice which is being done in senior appointments of special secretary/secretary, Government of India in general and in his case, in particular, he has highlighted certain infirmities in the procedure laid down in the aforesaid O.M. We shall however dwell on the same at length at a later stage. He has also cited instances of various senior I.A.S. officers who had been passed over earlier, but were appointed later on to the post of secretary without there being any explanation for their having been passed over earlier.

4. The application is vehemently resisted by the respondents especially the Union of India who contend that the posts of special secretary/secretary in the central government secretariat are not cadre posts and appointment thereto is not made by way of promotion from any hierarchy in lower rungs, but it is really an appointment made by the President pursuant to the decision of the Appointments Committee of the cabinet. They explain that since the post of a secretary is a very sensitive post where he has to carry out the policies of the government etc. the selection to a post of secretary cannot be regulated by any fixed norms and it has to be on various relevant considerations, like suitability to the particular post etc. According to them under the scheme for staffing senior administrative posts of and above the rank of deputy secretaries, systematic arrangement for manning senior administrative posts at the centre have been framed and that the said posts in the central government secretariat are not traceable to any statutory rules as such, but appointments are made thereto by borrowing services from state cadres or otherwise. They assert that taking into

consideration the special position of secretary to the Government of India in the administration of the union government and the administrative history of India in regard to appointment of secretaries to the government in the centre, the redress which is normally available in regard to promotion in the strict sense of the term from a lower cadre is not available for appointment to the posts of secretaries. They submit that since appointments to the sensitive posts of secretaries are made by the Appointments Committee of the cabinet such appointments are not amenable to judicial scrutiny at all. As for order dated 20 April 1987, the stand taken by the respondents is that it was made in due course because the normal tenure of the petitioner had expired on 20 March 1987 and his extended tenure was to expire on 31 May 1987. So, by letter dated 20 April 1987, he was simply informed that his extended tenure would come to an end on 31 May 1987 when his services would stand replaced at the state cadre of Bihar. Thus, according to them, the said letter had no connection whatsoever with the so-called supersession of the petitioner or the representation made by him in regard to his non-appointment as secretary to the Government of India. It is averred that once an IAS officer comes to the centre from the state he must revert to his state cadre on completion of his tenure and he has no right nor claim statutory or otherwise to continue beyond the period of his tenure. Thus, the application made by the petitioner to this Tribunal is wholly misconceived is liable to be rejected being devoid of any merit. They deny that the claim of Shri Anil Bordia, respondent No. 2 for appointment as secretary to the Government of India is in any way inferior to that of the applicant as alleged. They admit that the O.M. dated 27-10-70 has been modified by O.M. dated 8-4-87 which supersedes the senior selection board by the civil services board but the amendment does not affect the procedure that is being followed in respect of appointments to the posts of additional secretary, special secretary/secretary to the Government of India. It is further contended that the applicant has approached this Tribunal even before the representation made by him had been replied to by the competent Authority and therefore, the application is liable to be rejected on the short ground of its being premature. On merits, their stand is that the competent authority found that the applicant is not suitable for appointment to the post of secretary. They reiterate that the appointments are made to the posts of special secretary/secretary to the Government of India keeping in view the job requirements of each post and the qualifications and experience of the officers in the field of choice and the procedure followed is equitable, just and fair and does not leave any room for discrimination. So the question of violation of the provisions of articles 14 and 16(1) of the Constitution does not arise.

5. The very first question which falls for determination therefore is whether the post of a special secretary/secretary is one of the posts to which the petitioner cannot lay claim as of right by promotion. In other words, the point for consideration is whether the said post can be said to be a post on the cadre Strength of I.A.S. officer, if not a cadre post, as contended by the petitioner or it is just a civil post in the central government to which senior officers from various categories of services are appointed at the discretion of the Government of India having regard to their suitability for a particular post on tenure basis. The submission of the learned additional Solicitor General succinctly is that no statutory rule exists to govern the appointment of persons to these posts; none

can hold these posts substantively and the posts do not constitute promotional avenue of any civil service. According to him, persons are appointed to the said post in accordance with the scheme of staffing senior administrative posts of and above the rank of deputy secretary framed in 1957 and then modified vide O.M. dated I1 August 1958 which was subsequently superseded vide Officer Memorandum of 1970 referred to by the petitioner himself in this application.

6. Historically speaking, all India services have been constituted on the pattern of erstwhile secretary of State Services when India was a British colony. As pointed out by their Lordship in *Debesh Chandra Das* vs. *Union of India and others:* AIR 1970 SC 77, prior to 1946, the members of the Indian Civil Service were in a Civil Service of the secretary of state. As a result of a conference between Chief Ministers and the Government of India an All India Administrative Service was constituted in October 1946. This agreement was entered into under section 263 of the Government of India Act, 1935. The Indian Administrative Service was common to the centre and the provinces. On 25 January 1950 rules were framed under sections 241(2) and 247 of the Government of India Act, 1935. The said rules were known as the Indian Civil Administrative (Cadre) Rules, 1950. Subsequently, article 312(1) of the Constitution of India provided for creation of all India services common to the Union and the States, if it was considered necessary or expedient in the national interest so to do and under article 312(2) the services known at the commencement of this Constitution as the Indian Administrative Service and the Indian Police Service were deemed to be the services created by the Parliament under the said article. So the all India services Act, 1951 was enacted to, as its preamble states, regulate the recruitment and the conditions of service of persons appointed to the all India services common to the Union and the States. By its very definition as given in section 2 thereof 'An All India Service' means the service known as the Indian Administrative Service; besides, of course, the Indian Police Service or any other service specified in section 2-A of the said Act. section 3 thereof empowers the central government to make rules after consultation with the government of the state concerned and by notification in the official gazette, for regulation of recruitment and the conditions of service of persons appointed to an all India service. Thus, there is no room for doubt that Indian Administrative Service is a service common to the Union and the States. It is in this context that the various categories of rules framed by the central government in exercise of authority conferred upon it by section 3 of the said Act have to be read and construed unless, of course, any provision expressly points to the contrary. Under the Indian Administrative Service (Cadre) Rules, 1954, a cadre officer means a member of the Indian Administrative Service and a 'cadre post' means any of the post specified under Item No. 1 of each cadre in the Schedule to the Indian Administrative Service (Fixation of Cadre Strength) Regulations, 1955. Rule 3 lays down that there shall be constituted for each state or group of states an Indian Administrative Service Cadre. Rule 4 provides that the strength and composition of each of the cadres constituted under rule 3 shall be as determined by regulations made by the central government in consultation with the state governments in this behalf. The word 'Cadre' however has not been defined in the said Rules, but as defined in Fundamental Rule 9(4) the cadre means the strength of a service or a part of service sanctioned at separate unit. Under the Indian Administrative Service (Fixation of

Cadre Strength) Regulations, 1955, the posts borne on, and the strength and composition of the cadre of Indian Administrative Service of various states shall be as specified in the Schedule to the said Regulations. A perusal of the Schedules would show that senior posts under various state governments have been specified. These *inter alia* include the chief secretary to the government of the state, financial commissioner, member board of Revenue and additional chief secretary etc. In the case of state of Bihar, the total authorised strength of the Cadre of the IAS is given as 301. Of these 147 posts have been enumerated as senior posts under the state government. Fifty-nine posts have been described as central deputation reserve at 40 per cent of the above and 39 posts have been shown as deputation reserve while rest of the posts belong to other categories like leave reserve etc. Similar is the position with regard to the composition of the cadre strength of I.A.S. of other states. It is thus abundantly clear that the cadre strength of various states has been fixed keeping in view not only the requirement of the concerned state, but also of the central government which has been prescribed as 40 per cent of the senior posts under the state government.

7. A question would naturally arise whether the central deputation reserve which as stated above is 40 per cent of the senior posts of the state government *inter alia*, comprises post of secretary to the Government of India or not. The answer to the said question in our view is to be found in the Indian Administrative Service (Pay) Rules, 1954. Rule 3 thereof prescribes the time-scales of pay admissible to a member of the service and the dates with effect from which the said time-scales would be deemed to have come into force. These comprise junior scale and senior scale. The senior scale is further sub-divided into time-scale and selection grade. This Rule has now been amended by I.A.S. (Pay) Second Amendment Rules, 1987 by, *inter alia*, insertion of "super time scale" and "above super-time scale" with effect from 1-1-86. Further, sub-rule (2A) of rule 3 lays down that, "appointment to the selection grade and to posts carrying pay above the time-scale of pay in the Indian Administrative Service shall be made by selection on merit with due regard to seniority". Conflicting interpretations are sought to be put on this provision. The petitioner submits that this sub-rule specifically lays down how the appointment to the selection grade and the posts carrying pay above the time-scale of an All India Administrative Service have to be made, viz., by selection on merit with due regard to seniority. However, the submission of learned Additional Solicitor General is that this sub-rule occurs in the I.A.S. (Pay) Rules and as such it only prescribes the scales of pay and is not designed to lay down any rule for appointment to super time-scale posts and the post of secretary to the Government of India etc. He has vigorously urged that the phrase "and to post carrying pay above the time-scale of pay" refers to some post which may be in between a post in the selection grade and a post carrying ordinary time-scale of pay but not post above the selection grade. At first flush we felt impressed by the force of this argument, on a careful consideration of the whole matter especially keeping in view the other provisions bearing on the subject, we find no merit in this contention.

8. Rule 8 of the said rules provides that any member of the service appointed to hold a post specified in Schedule III shall for so long as he holds that post, be entitled to draw the pay indicated for the post in the said Schedule.

Rule 9(1) enjoins that no member of the Service shall be appointed to a post other than a post specified in Schedule III, unless the state government concerned in respect of posts under its control, or the central government in respect of posts under its control as the case may be, make a declaration that the said post is equivalent in status and responsibility to a post specified in the said Schedule. Therefore, a member of Indian Administrative Service has per force to be appointed to a post specified in Schedule III, unless, of course, the other requirements regarding declaration etc. are satisfied. A look at Schedule III to the said Rules would reveal that it consists of three parts, viz., namely, Schedules III-A, III-B and III-C. Schedule III-A relates to posts carrying the pay above the time-scale in the Indian Administrative Service under various state governments. Schedule III-B pertains to post carrying pay in the senior time-scale of the I.A.S. Service under various state governments including posts carrying special pay, in addition to the pay in the time-scale and Schedule III-C enumerates the post carrying pay above the time-scale or special pay in addition to pay in the time-scale under the central government when held by members of I.A.S. This Schedule includes the posts of secretaries to the Government of India, additional secretaries to the Government of India etc. The learned counsel for the respondents have not been able to show if there are any other posts which carry the pay above the time-scale under the central government. So on a conjoint reading of sub-rule (2A) of Rule 3 with Schedule III-C it becomes crystal clear that the post of secretary to the Government of India is covered by sub-rule (2A) as being a post carrying pay above the time-scale of pay. For this obvious reason this sub-rule does not talk of post carrying pay above the selection grade. The terminology used in sub-rule (2A) and Schedules III-A and III-C is identical whereas Schedule III-B specifically refers to posts which carry pay in the senior time-scale of the I.A.S. We may also advert in this context with advantage to the I.A.S. (Regulations of Seniority) Rules, 1954. Rule 2(g) thereof defines a "senior post" as meaning a post included and specified under Item No. 1 of the cadre of each state in the Schedule to the I.A.S. (Fixation of Cadre Strength) Regulations, 1955 and includes a post included in the number of posts in Items 2 and 5 of the said cadre. Reverting to cadre strength of various states it may be noticed that Item No. 1 of the cadre strength of various states enumerates senior posts under the state government while Item No. 2 refers to central deputation reserve at 40 per cent of Item No. 1. There can thus be no shadow of doubt that the central deputation reserve comprises only senior posts within the meaning of Rule 2(g) of I.A.S. (Regulation of Seniority) Rules, 1954 and as a necessary corollary it would follow that the posts of secretary to the Government of India are not only senior posts, but are posts carrying pay above the time-scale when held by members of the Service. The sum up, therefore, we are of the considered view that even if the post of secretary to the Government of India is not a cadre post it is certainly a post borne on cadre strength of various states. Indeed the learned Additional Solicitor General candidly conceded that 40 per cent central deputation reserve is *inter alia* comprised of the post of the secretary to the Government of India when held by the members of the I.A.S. This conclusion is further fortified by clarification made by the Government of India, Department of Personnel and Administrative Reforms in their letter No. 11031/19/75-AIS(II) dated 16 April 1975, which bears on the subject "Cadre Schedule — all India service deputation Reserve-Officers to be counted against the". Item No. 2 pertains to central deputation reserve which reads as under:

> "All ex-cadre posts held by cadre officers under the control of the central government, all posts under a Company, . . . under the control of the Central government when held by a cadre officer not belonging to the Union Territories cadre. . . .

Lastly, copies of two tables prepared by National Informatics Centre showing (a) distribution of officers of various all India services serving at the centre by service and level and (b) distribution of officers I.A.S. at centre by cadre and level have also been placed on record. These tables indicate the number of secretary level appointments held by various I.A.S. officers of different states, the total number being 57 which include 12 officers in posts of equivalent status.

9. The upshot of the whole discussion therefore is that the post cabinet secretary to the Government of India constitutes a promotional avenue for members of Indian Administrative Service of various states to the extent such posts are held by them. At the fagend of the arguments, the learned Additional Solicitor General filed an affidavit dated 18-9-87 of Shri B.C. Deshmukh, cabinet secretary to the Government of India to the effect that the officers of the organised Group 'A' Services who were found eligible and I.A.S. officer batchwise are assessed for the suitability by a special committee of secretaries comprising of cabinet secretary, secretary to the Prime Minister, home minister and secretary, Department of Personnel. Hence, we entertain no doubt in our mind that the posts of secretary to the Government of India, although tenure posts, do provide promotional avenue to the members of I.A.S to the extent they are earmarked for them. The following observations of the Supreme Court in Debesh Chandra Das (supra) are very pertinent to note:

> "The position that emerges is that the cadres for the Indian Administrative Services are to be found in the states only. There is no cadres in the Government of India. A few of these persons are, however, intended to serve at the centre. When they do so they enjoy better emolument and status. They rank higher in the service and even in the warrant of precedence of the President. In the states they cannot get same salary in any post as secretaries are entitled to in the centre. The appointments to the centre are not in any sense a deputation. They mean promotion to a higher post. The only safeguard is that many of the posts at the centre are tenure posts. Those of secretaries and equivalent posts are for five years. . . ."

As for the contention of the learned Additional Solicitor General that since sub-rule 2A of rule 3 occurs in I.A.S. (Pay) rules it is not designed to lay down any rule for appointment to Super time-scale posts, Suffice it to say that it stands totally demolished by letter No. 11030/20/75-AIS(II) dated 27-12-75 of the Government of India to the chief secretaries to various state governments on the subject of "I.A.S.-promotion to the senior scale and super time-scale guidelines regarding". It lays down the following method the selection:

(i) Selection should be based on merit with due regard to seniority as provided in sub-rule 2A of rule 3 of the IAS (Pay) Rules, 1954.

(ii) Suitability of officers to hold super-time scale posts may be judged by evaluating their *character roll* record as a whole *and general assessment of their work.*

10. That brings us to the second and perhaps most crucial question in this case, namely, whether the scheme of Staffing senior administrative posts in the central government especially the posts of secretary level is just, fair and valid or whether it suffers from the vice of arbitrariness on account of very wide discretionary power which vests in the cabinet secretary to the Government of India in the matter of selection of suitable officers for appointment to such posts. It is common ground between the parties that no statutory rule or regulation exists for regulation of appointments to the posts of secretary to the government. Even consultation with the Union Public Service Commission under article 320 of the Constitution of India has been dispensed with vide Union Public Service Commission (Consultation) Regulations, 1958 which, *inter alia,* provide that it shall not be necessary to consult the Commission in regard to selection for appointment to a post included in an all India service of any officer who is already a member of all India service. However, the Government of India in consultation with the state governments and other concerned authorities passed a resolution dated 17-10-57 vide which a scheme for staffing senior administrative posts of and above the rank of deputy secretary under the Government of India was formulated, with the object of providing for systematic arrangements for manning senior administrative posts at the centre of and above the rank of deputy secretary. A perusal of the said scheme would show that such posts were to be ordinarily manned by officers of one or other of various categories enumerated therein. These sources included officers borrowed from the state cadres of the all India services and from other Class-I Services of the states (other than the State Civil Service) on tenure deputation. The scheme further envisaged setting up of a central establishment board headed by and comprising cabinet secretary, (ex-officio), home secretary as member (ex-officio) a finance secretary and three other secretaries. It stipulated that appointments of individual officers from any of the sources mentioned therein to posts covered by the scheme would be made on the advice of the central establishment board with the approval of the Appointments Committee of the cabinet. The scheme also prescribed the periods of tenure for the officers, viz., 4 years in the case of those appointed to the posts of or equivalent to deputy secretary and 5 years for posts of or equivalent to joint secretary and secretary and they were to revert to their parent state cadres on the expiry of their respective periods of tenure.

11. Later vide another office memorandum dated 11 August 1958 modified procedure for the selection and appointments of officers of secretariat posts of and above the rank of under secretary to the Government of India and certain important non-secretariat posts was prescribed. The said notification superseded all orders which were in force till then on the said subject. It postulated the creation of Appointments Committee of the cabinet (referred to as "the Appointments Committee") consisting of the Prime Minister, the minister of Home Affairs and the minister or ministers concerned with a particular appointment in question. It also provided for the setting up of the central

establishment board in accordance with paragraph 4 of the scheme for Staffing senior administrative posts of and above the rank of deputy secretary under the Government of India in accordance with the Ministry of Home Affairs Resolution dated 17 October 1957 (supra), under the chairmanship of cabinet secretary (ex-officio) and home secretary as member (ex-officio), besides, of course, other members. The functions and duties of the board, *inter alia,* consisted of making recommendations for the selection and appointments to all posts of and above the rank of under secretary to the Government of India in the secretariat, having regard to the *merits, claims* and *availability* of officers in the field of choice for any particular vacancy (emphasis ours). Subsequently, vide office memo dated 2-11-63, the posts of additional secretary special secretary and the secretary to the Government of India were excluded from the purview of selection by the central establishment board, and it was specifically laid down in paragraph 4(2) of the office memo that:

> "The central establishment board shall not be concerned with recommendations for appointments to posts of additional secretary, special secretary and secretary to the Government of India. In all such cases, the chairman of the board shall after considering the claims of various officers, whether serving in the Government of India or in the states, submit his recommendations direct for the orders of the Appointments Committee."

It is thus manifest that the selection of officers for appointments to the posts of additional secretary, special secretary and secretary to the Government of India became the exclusive prerogative of the cabinet secretary and other members of the central establishment board had no longer any voice in the matter of their selection. Of course, the final decision in this respect rested with the Appointments Committee.

12. Still later, the aforesaid office memo of 11 August 1958 was superseded by office memo dated 27 October 1970 issued by the cabinet secretariat, Government of India in respect of the procedure for the selection and appointments of officers to secretariat posts of and above the rank of under secretaries to the Government of India and certain important non-secretariat posts. This office memo superseded not only O.M. dated 11 August 1958 as amended from time to time but also all other orders hitherto in force on the subject. The new scheme for taffing enior administrative posts in the Government of India envisaged constitution of two high-powered boards instead of one to advise the Department of Personnel. One of them called The senior selection board was entrusted with the task of making recommendations having regard to the *merits, claims* and *availability* of all officers in the field of choice for appointment to the posts of joint secretary to the Government of India and all other non-secretariat posts which carried a pay-scale the maximum of which exceeded Rs. 25,000 but did not exceed Rs. 3,000 when it was proposed to appoint thereto officers of the all India services/Central secretariat Service etc. The second board called the central establishment board which retained its original nomenclature was entrusted with the duty of making recommendations for the selection and appointments to all posts of and above the rank of under secretary, but below the rank of joint secretary to the Government of India in the secretariat and all other non-secretariat posts which carried the pay scale the

minimum of which was Rs. 1,200 or more and the maximum of which was Rs. 2,500 or less when it was proposed to appoint thereto officers belonging to all India services/central secretariat service etc. having regarding to the *merits, claims* and *availability* of all officers in the field of choice for any particular vacancy (emphises ours). As for appointments to the posts at the level of additional secretary, special secretary and secretary to the Government of India the following specific rule was framed:

4. (1) ....

(2) The senior selection board or the central establishment board shall not be concerned with recommendations for appointment to posts at the level of additional secretary, special secretary and secretary to the Government of India.

(3) In respect of cases referred to at (2) above, the cabinet secretary shall, after considering the claims of various officers, whether serving in the Government of India or in the states, submit his recommendations directly to the Appointments Committee for orders. In the discharge of his special responsibility for management tasks concerning senior management, the cabinet secretary shall be assisted by the secretary, Department of Personnel.

13. The submission of the petitioner precisely is that while definite guidelines/criteria have been prescribed in the staffing scheme of 1970 for selection of eligible officers to the post of joint secretary, deputy secretary and under secretary, namely, "having regard to the merits, claims and availability of all officers in the field of choice", the only requirement in the case of selection of officers for appointment to the posts at the level of additional secretary, special secretary and secretary to the Government of India is that cabinet secretary has to consider the claims of various officers whether serving in the Government of India or in the states and submit his recommendations directly to the Appointments Committee for orders. In the discharge of his duties, he is to be assisted by the secretary, Department of Personnel. However, the criteria of merit and availability are totally conspicuous by their absence in para 4(3) of the staffing scheme which deals with appointments to the posts at the level of additional secretary, special secretary and secretary to the Government of India. Thus, according to him, the deliberate deletion of the words "merits" and "availability" in the later provision confers absolute discretion on the cabinet secretary to select and recommend the names of any officers at his sweet will to the Appointments Committee of the cabinet for appointment. As would be clear from the phraseology of sub-rule (3) of Rule 4 even the secretary, Department of Personnel would have no voice in the matter as he is simply to assist the cabinet secretary. However, that is not so, in the case of members of the senior selection board and the central establishment board members whereof will naturally have full voice in the matter. It is urged that even if the cabinet secretary being a high dignitary may be presumed to discharge his official duties in this respect faithfully and diligently, the possibility of his being swayed by purely subjective predilection, bias and prejudice cannot be altogether ruled out. It was therefore absolutely necessary that proper safeguards were provided to ensure impartial, objective and fair assessment of the service profile of each

eligible officer for the said posts.

14. The learned Additional Solicitor General has canvassed with considerable vehemence that the post of secretary to the Government of India being a highly sensitive one carrying as it does enormous degree of responsibility requires special considerations. The secretary is directly answerable to the minister Incharge of a particular Ministry and he is supposed to keep a certain wave length with him. Moreover being bureaucratic head of the ministry he has to display not only abundant measure of knowledge of relevant laws, rules and regulations, but also a high degree of tact and experience of public administration. Therefore, the cabinet secretary while scanning the service dossiers of various officers who happen to be in the field of choice at a given time has to virtually examine the entire horoscope of the concerned officer and assess his capability and suitability for the post on an overall view of his personality on the basis of various factors including his meritorious performance in the past, the type of experience gained by him and his rectitude etc. In particular, he has to ensure that the concerned officer is best suited for the particular post to which he is sought to be appointed. Thus, there is hardly any scope of misuse of power or authority by the cabinet secretary who is the senior most bureaucrat in the central secretariat hierarchy and knows his job fully well. Moreover he is directly answerable to the Appointments Committee of the cabinet who is the ultimate authority for approving or disapproving the candidates recommended by the cabinet secretary.

15. The learned Additional Solicitor General has laid special stress on the fact that as per the affidavit dated 18-9-87 of the cabinet secretary Shri B.G. Deshmukh the officers of the Organised Group 'A' Services who are found eligible, and in the case of Indian Administrative Service officers batchwise, are assessed for their suitability by a special committee of secretaries, comprising the cabinet secretary, secretary to the Prime Minister. Home secretary and the secretary, Department of Personnel. The I.A.S. officers of 1957 batch including the applicant were considered by the said special committee of secretaries and the recommendation of the committee, together with the C.R. dossiers of all the officers considered by it were submitted to the competent authority, i.e., the Appointments Committee of the cabinet which finally approves the names of those to be included in the suitability list for holding secretary level appointments. So, according to him, the process involves firstly empanellment of various officers for appointment to the post of secretary etc. and then actual appointment of a particular officer having regard to his special qualification/suitability for a particular post.

16. No doubt, it would appear from the affidavit of the cabinet secretary that he had associated with him a number of secretaries mentioned in the affidavit in the task of selecting the suitable candidates. However, the above mentioned rule of the staffing scheme only talks of cabinet secretary as the sole authority to consider the claims of various officers while secretary, Department of Personnel is required to assist him in the task. There is no mention of any other secretary being associated in this job in the said rule. It is not, therefore, comprehensible how and under whose authority whether written or verbal were the other secretaries associated by the cabinet secretary to constitute what has been called "special committee of secretaries". No such nomenclature exists in the Rule 4(3) of the staffing scheme. Further, it is not quite clear what precise

role was played by the said secretaries in the process of selection. One is left guessing whether the final recommendations were made on the basis of consensus or unanimous decision. That apart, there is no indication in the affidavit as to what was the criterion adopted by the special committee for selecting the best officers from amongst those who happened to be in the field of choice. Was it seniority or merit or rectitude or special type of experience or exceptional brilliance or a combination of all or some of these high sounding virtues? Surely, it would have been better if the respondents and for that matter the cabinet secretary had thrown some light on this aspect of the matter. Of course, it may be well said that it is implicit in the very nature of the functions to be performed by the cabinet secretary in this respect that he must have been guided by considerations of merit, rectitude and suitability etc. even though the word "Claim" appearing in Rule 4(3) may not signify anything specific and leave it to the subjective discretion of the cabinet secretary to consider whatever facts he may think best for determining the suitability of a particular candidate for the appointment to the post of secretary.

17. The learned Additional Solicitor General has contended on the strength of the observations made by a Constitution Bench of the Supreme Court in *Matajog Dobey* vs. *H.C. Bhari* (AIR 1956 SC 44) that a discretionary power is not necessarily a discriminatory power and abuse of power is not to be easily assumed where the discretion is vested in the government and not in a minor official. These observations were repeated by another Constitution Bench of the Supreme Court in *M/s. Pannalal Biniraj and others* vs. *Union of India and others*: (AIR 1957 SC 397). That was a case for grating/withholding of sanction to prosecute a public servant under section 197, Criminal Procedure Code. It is well settled that the observations made even by the highest court have to be primarily construed in the context of the case in which the same were made. But that apart such a presumption even though not altogether unfounded is difficult to be drawn in a case like the present where service careers of a large number of very senior officers belonging to all India services etc. are at stake. It is indeed an uphill task to assess fairly and impartially the competing claims of various officers who happen to be in the field of choice especially when no criteria or guidelines are prescribed.

18. In the second case, the question of possibility of discriminatory treatment of persons falling within the same group or category with regard to the transfer of cases from the jurisdiction of one Income-tax officer to that of another was under consideration. So, we do not see how the aforesaid observations of their Lordships can be aptly applied to the facts of the instant case.

19. That apart, one cannot be oblivious to the fact that much water has flown down the bridges during the last 30 years when the aforesaid observations were made by their Lordships. Generally speaking, standards of merit rectitude and of uprighteousness have considerably fallen all round. So what might have been true way back in 1956 or 1957 need not necessarily be true today. Surely, one cannot loose sight of falling standards even at the highest level. In *Organo Chemical Industries and another* vs. *Union of India and others*: (1979) 4 SCC 573, the question for determination was whether section 14-B of Employees' Provident Fund and Miscellaneous Provisions Act, 1952 was *ultra vires* the Constitution because it conferred unguided, uncontrolled and arbitrary power on the concerned authority. Krishna Iyer, J., sounded the following note of caution:

> "The bogie of absence of guidelines in the provision and consequential possibility of the authority running berserk or acting bubristically does not frighten. *Of course, the more bereft of explicit guidelines a statutory power is, the more searching must be the judicial invigilation to discover hidden injustice and masked malafides.* Even so, let us examine the ground that, absent detailed guidelines, the law is void. What is not explicit may still be implicit. What is not articulated at length may be spun out from a single phrase. (emphasis ours)

His Lordship further observed that:

> "Although our democratic ethos is incongruous with the assumption that highly paid officials are more responsible than low-paid minions, the jurisprudence of power must be applied workably and not untouched by reality."

On a consideration of the built-in safeguards in the aforesaid Act itself it was held that the aforesaid section was not violative of article 14 the Constitution.

20. However, in *Central Inland Water Transport Corporation Limited and another* vs. *Brojo Nath Ganguly and another* (1986) 3 SCC 156, where the question arose whether Rule 9(1) the Central Inland Water Transport Corporation (Service, Discipline and Appeal) Rules, 1979, which provided that the services of a permanent employee could be terminated on three months' notice on either side or on payment of three months' pay plus DA to the employee or on deduction of a like amount from his salary as the case may be in lieu of notice without assigning any reason was void or unconstitutional or not, one of the arguments advanced was that the discretion for termination of service under the said provision vested in the board of Directors who were high dignitaries. The Supreme Court repelled this contention with the following observations:

> "There are no guidelines whatever laid down to indicate in what circumstances the power given by rule 9(1) is to be exercised by the Corporation. . . . It was urged that the board of Directiors would not exercise this power arbitrarily or capriciously as it consists of responsible and highly placed persons. *The submission ignores the fact that however highly placed a person may be, he must necessarily process human frailties.* It also overlooks the well-known saying of Lord Acton, which has now almost become a maxim, in the appendix to his "Historical Essays and Studies", that "power tends to corrupt, and absolute power corrupts absolutely." (emphasis ours).

21. More recently, in *R.S. Dass* vs. *Union of India and others*: (1987) 2 Administrative Tribunals Cases 628, the question arose whether the criterion of merit alone as the sole basis for selection to higher post would justify any apprehension that in the absence of reasons there would be no objectivity and the members of the State Civil Service would not receive discriminatory treatment by the selection committee. While K.N. Singh, J., expressed the view

consistent with the view adverted to above "that the machinery designed for preparation of select list under the regulations for promotion to all India service secures the objective sought to be achieved. The selection committee is constituted by high ranking responsible officers presided over by chairman or a member of the Union Public Service Commission. There is no reason to hold that they would not act in fair and impartial manner in making selection. The recommendations of the selection committee are scrutinised by the state government and if it finds any discrimination in the selection it has power to refer the matter to the Commission with its recommendations. . . . Where power is vested in high authority there is a presumption that the same would be exercised in a reasonable manner and if the selection is made on extraneous considerations, in arbitrary manner the courts have ample power to strike down the same and that is an adequate safeguard against the arbitrary exercise of power." However, Mukharji, J. had his own reservations in this respect. While observing that if promotion is made on merit alone the senior officer per se has no legal right to promotion and if promotion is on merit, it cannot be said that a senior officer has been superseded, his Lordship sounded a note of caution saying -

> "I have my reservations on this aspect though I accede to the position that in the absence of any other practicable solution this is perhaps a sufficient safeguard and perhaps a practical way of facing a rather delicate task. *It cannot be said nowadays if one is aware of the facts and currents of life that simply because categorisation* and judgement of the service record of officers are in the hands of senior officers it is sufficient safeguard. *There has been considerable erosion in the intrinsic sense of fairness and justice n the senior officers by all concerned* from the instances of conduct of many, some of senior officers and men to high position, it cannot be said that such erosion is not only unjustified." (emphasis ours)

It is significant to note here that in the aforesaid case Amended Regulations 5(4) and 5(5) of the I.A.S. (Appointment by Promotion) Regulations, 1955 were under consideration. It was provided under the said regulations that the selection committee should classify eligible officers as "Outstanding", "Very Good", "Good" or "Unfit" as the case might be, on an overall relative assessment of service record of the officers. There is however absolutely no such requirement in para 4(3) of the staffing scheme, the only requirement being that the cabinet secretary has to consider "claims" of all officers who happen to be in the field of choice.

22. *Sudhir Chandra Sarkar* vs. *Tata Iron and Steel Co. Ltd. and others*: (1984) 3 S.C.C. 369, is yet another case in which exercise of unfettered discretionary power came up for consideration. The Rules of the respondent Company therein provided for payment of gratuity etc. However, rule 10 thereof reserved to the Company absolute discretion in the matter of grant of gratuity irrespective of whether an employee had or had not satisfied all or any of the conditions prescribed in the rules for payment of gratuity and no employee howsoever otherwise eligible could be deemed to be entitled as of right to any payment under the said rules. It was observed by the Supreme Court that:

"Our Constitution envisages a society governed by rule of law. Absolute discretion uncontrolled by guidelines which may permit denial of equality before law is the anti-thesis of rule of law. *Absolute discretion not judicially reviewable inheres the pernicious tendency to be arbitrary and is therefore violative of article 14.* Equality before law and absolute discretion to grant or deny benefit of the law are diametrically opposed to each other and cannot co-exist. Therefore, also the conferment of absolute discretion by Rule 10 of the Gratuity Rules to give or deny the benefit of the rules cannot be upheld and must be rejected as unenforceable" (emphasis ours).

Reference may also be made in this context to *The State of Mysore* vs. *S.R. Jayaram*, reported as AIR 1968 SC 346 in which the last part of rule 9(2) of Mysore Recruitment of Gazetted Probationers' Rules, 1959 was struck down as being *ultra vires* the Constitution. The said rule reserved to the government the right of appointing to any particular cadre any candidate whom it considered more suitable for such cadre. The rules were silent on the question as to how the government was to find out the suitability for a particular cadre. It was held that:

"It follows that under the last part of R.9(2) it is open to the government to say at its sweet will that a candidate is more suitable for a particular cadre and to deprive him of his opportunity to join the cadre for which he indicated his preference. . . . The last part of Rule 9(2) subverts and destroys the basic objectives of the preceding rules. It vests in the government an arbitrary power of patronage".

23. That apart it is now well settled that while wisdom of the legislative policy may not be open to judicial review but when the wisdom takes the concrete form of law, the same must stand the test of being in tune with the fundamental rights and if it trenches upon any of the fundamental rights, it is void as ordained by article 13. The scope and ambit of article 14 have been the subject-matter of a catena of decisions. One facet of article 14 which has been noticed in *E.P. Royappa* vs. *Sate of Tamil Nadu* (1974 (4) SCC 3) deserves special mention because that effectively answers the contention of the learned Additional Solicitor General. The Constitution Bench speaking through Bhagwati, J. in a concurring judgement in *E.P. Royappa's* case observed as under:

"The basic principle which, therefore, informs both articles 14 and 16 is equality and inhibition against discrimination. . . . Equality is a dynamic concept with many aspects and dimensions and it cannot be "cribbed, cabined and confined" within traditional and doctrinaire limits. From a positivistic point of view, equality is antithetic to arbitrariness. In fact equality and arbitrariness are sworn enemies; one belongs to the rule of law in a republic while the other, to the whim and caprice of an absolute monarch.

Articles . . . 14 and 16 strikes at arbitrariness in state action and ensures fairness and equality of treatment."

(See also in this context *Ajay Hasia* vs. *Khalid Mujib* AIR 1981 SC 467). In *A.L. Kalra* vs. *Project and Equipment Corporation*: (1984) 3 S.C.C. 316, it was held that:

> "It thus appears well-settled that article 14 strikes at arbitrariness in executive/administrative action because any action that is arbitrary must necessarily involve the negation of equality. One need not confine the denial of equality to a comparative evaluation between two persons to arrive at a conclusion of discriminatory treatment. An action *per se* arbitrary itself denies equality of protection by law."

In *Maneka Gandhi* vs. *Union of India* (AIR 1978 SC 597), too it was observed that article 14 strikes at arbitrariness in state action and ensures fairness and equality of treatment. It is thus too late in the date to contend that an executive action shown to be arbitrary is not either judicially reviewable or within the sweep of article 14.

24. It is thus manifest that vesting of absolute discretion in an executive functionary howsoever highly placed he may be is likely to lead to arbitrariness/capriciousness in action. It, therefore, falls for consideration whether the staffing scheme adverted to above so far as it relates to the appointments to the post of additional secretary, special secretary and secretary to the Government of India and confers very wide powers, if not absolute power, on the cabinet secretary to select and recommend the names of various officers after considering their claims for appointment directly to the Appointments Committee for orders, suffers from the vice of arbitrariness or not. Of course, it bears repetition that final orders have to be emanated from the Appointments Committee. As already pointed out, the senior selection board is required to make recommendations having regard to the merits, claims and availability of all officers in the field of choice for appointment to the posts of joint secretary to the Government of India etc., but the words "merits and availability" do not find place in sub-para (3) of para 4 of the staffing scheme. The dictionary meaning of the word "claim" simply is "a demand for something as due; an assertion of a right to something, right or title to something or to have or be or do something" (See: *The Oxford English Dictionary*). Likewise, in the *Concise Oxford Dictionary* the meaning assigned to the word "claim" is "demand for something as due, right, title to thing, right to make demand on person". In the *Chambers Twentieth Century Dictionary*, the meaning of the word "claim" is given as "a demand for something due; right or ground for demanding; lay claim to, assert a right". Thus, there can be no room for doubt that a person may found his claim on various grounds. In the case of officers who are eligible and are within the zone of consideration for promotion to a higher post the word "claim" signifies various facets, for instance, seniority, expertise and experience in some special field of service, meritorious service rendered in the past may be during the whole of his service career or during a short spell of his service just preceding his expected promotion and special suitability for a particular job/post. Of course, it would be difficult to exhaust all the grounds on which the claim of an officer to be considered for selection may be founded. Thus, the word "claim" may signify everything or anything because it leaves to the absolute discretion of the selecting functionary what particular aspect of his claim will tilt the balance in his favour or against him. The words "merits and availability" as a consideration for selection to the post of joint secretary etc. were not mere surplusage. Certainly the intention of the makers of the staffing scheme was to

ensure that merit of an individual officer will be the predominant factor while considering his suitability for the higher post having regard to other aspects of his claim. We are at a loss to understand why these two words have been deleted for consideration of the eligible officers to the posts of additional secretary, special secretary or secretary to the Government of India. Does it mean that the merit of the officer is relegated to the background that is, it looses its predominant position *vis-a-vis* other factors to be considered. If the answer to this question is in the negative, it is not intelligible what was the rationale behind dropping this word when it is conceded even by the learned Additional Solicitor General that merit will still be the principal factor in the choice and selection of the concerned officer. However, he has tried to canvass rather vehemently that the principal reason for dropping this word is that the cabinet secretary must adjudge and assess the suitability of every officer for a particular post. We are, however, not impressed with the logic of this argument because even though the post of secretary to the Government of India is a highly responsible assignment demanding tremendous responsibilities, talent and wide experience of administration, but all the same there seems to be neither any basis or justification for dropping the word "merit" and the only plausible explanation which may be offered is that the intendment was to confer wider discretion on the cabinet secretary in the matter of selection. So, he may make his recommendation uninhibited even by consideration of merits if he feels that a particular officer is otherwise suitable atleast according to his judgement for a particular assignment of the level of the secretary to the Government of India.

25. It is now well settled that while article 14 forbids class legislation, it does not forbid classification for the purpose of legislation. However, in order to meet the test of article 14, the classification must be based on intelligible differentia which distinguishes persons or things that are grouped together from those that are left out of the group and the differentia must have a rational nexus to the objects sought to be achieved by the legislative or executive action under challenge. In other words, legislative and executive action may be sustained if it satisfies the twin test of reasonable classification and rational principle co-related to the object sought to be achieved. We are unable to comprehend in this case as to what was the rational principle in dropping the word "merit" while considering the selection of officers for appointment to the posts of secretary to the Government of India. The mere fact that such a post carries a very high degree of responsibility and is very sensitive in nature would hardly justify the differentiation made in the criteria for selection to the post of joint secretary and that of the additional secretary/secretary to the Government of India. In the absence of any safety valve designed to prevent arbitrary cobourable exercise of power, therefore, it is rather difficult to sustain the staffing scheme as it stands today. Needless to say that naked and arbitrary exercise of powers is bad in law, being violative of the mandate of equality enshrined in articles 14 and 16. It may well be said that in the discretionary power conferred on a high dignitary it is implicit that he will take all relevant factors into consideration while selecting some out of many IAS officers for the post of secretary to the Government of India, but in our considered view what is implicit, if at all, ought to be made explicit so as to obviate any apprehension which may assail the minds of the concerned officers that they will not be meted out justice and fair play in action. Looked at from this angle, there is no escape from the conclusion

that rule 4(3) of the staffing scheme suffers from the vice of unfettered, uncontrolled and unguided discretion. It is high time, indeed imperative, that some criteria/guidelines are laid down in this respect. Of course, we may hasten to add that the staffing scheme having been operative for more than a decade by now, scores of appointments to the posts of additional secretary, special secretary and secretary to the Government of India must have been made during the period of its operation. Hence, in all fairness, the question of setting aside the selection and appointments already made at this juncture would not arise. All the same the question still survives whether the petitioner's claim for promotion can be said to have been considered justly and fairly by the cabinet secretary.

26. We have already adverted to the affidavit date 18-9-87 sworn by the cabinet secretary Shri B.G. Deshmukh. While it is heartening to note that the officers of the Organised Group 'A' services who are found eligible, and in the case of Indian Administrative Service officers batchwise, are assessed for their suitability by a special committee of secretaries, comprising the cabinet secretary, secretary to the Prime Minister, home secretary and the secretary, Department of Personnel. Apparently it seems that the selection and recommendations were made by the special committee and not the cabinet secretary as is contemplated in para 4(3) of the staffing scheme. All the same the said affidavit is totally bereft of necessary details. It does not shed any light as to what were the factors/criteria on the basis of which the claims of various officers of 1957 batch including the applicant were considered by the special committee of the secretaries. So, we are just left to guess and imagine for ourselves what might have been the criteria adopted by the special committee for this purpose. Of course, from the recital "The recommendation of the committee, together which the C.R. dossiers of all the officers considered by it is submitted to the Competent Authority (Appointments Committee of the cabinet. . . .)" in the affidavit it would appear that C.R. Dossiers of all officers were considered. Surely, that can hardly satisfy the judicial conscience when examining the case of an aggrieved officer who contends that he had not been meted out justice and fairplay in action and he has been passedover/superseded arbitrarily despite his having a very good record of service.

27. Since the affidavit of cabinet secretary is absolutely silent on this aspect sport of the matter we are left with no option but to see for ourselves whether the selection of officers and recommendations for their appointment to the posts of secretary to the Government of India were based on relevant considerations or not, and it is not a case where some officers have been just picked up out of the whole lot without considering the just and rightful claims of all of them. This will naturally necessitate looking into the proceedings and the report submitted by the special committee to the Appointments Committee to ascertain the methodology and criteria for selection adopted by the special committee.

The cabinet secretary has filed an affidavit claiming privilege against disclosure of the contents by virtue of protection afforded by sections 123 and 124 of the Indian Evidence Act on the ground that the relevant file Dy. No. 2292/Cs(A)/86 dealing with the preparation of suitability list of officers for holding secretary level posts at the centre comprises unpublished official records relating to the affairs of the state and are as such privileged. He has further sworn that the disclosure of the details pertaining to the preparation and finalisation of the secretary level suitability list contained in the said documents would affect the free and frank expression of opinion or advice before decision-making and therefore, the public interest would suffer by the disclosure of the said document.

28. Provisions of sections 123 and 124 of the Evidence Act which afford protection to certain categories of documents on the ground of public interest immunity have been expounded and considered in a catena of cases by the highest court of the country, *S.P. Gupta* vs. *Union of India* [1981 (suppl) SCC 87] commonly known as 'High Court Judges case' being the latest and most elaborate on the subject. We can do no better than to advert to some of the observations made by Bhagwati, J. (as his Lordship then was) who spoke for the majority of the Constitution Bench. While recognising that there may be a class of documents which public interest requires should not be disclosed irrespective of what they contain, for instance, cabinet papers, minutes of discussion of the heads of departments and high level document relating to the inner working of the government machine or concerned with the framing of the government policies, His Lordship observed that:

> "There is nothing sacrosanct about the immunity which is granted to documents because they belong to a certain class. Class immunity is not absolute or inviolable in all circumstances. It is not a rule of law to be applied mechanically in all cases. The principle upon which class immunity is founded is that it would contrary to public interest to disclose documents belonging to that class, because such disclosure would impair the proper functioning of the public service and this aspect of public interest which requires that justice shall not be denied to anyone by withholding relevant evidence. This is a balancing task which has to be performed by the court in all cases."

His Lordship further observed that:

> "Whenever an objection to the disclosure of a document under section 123 is raised two questions fall for the determination of the court, namely, whether the document relates to affairs of state and whether its disclosure would, in the particular case before the court, be injurious to public interest. The court in reaching its decision on these two questions has to balance two competing aspects of public interest, because the document being one relating to affairs of state, its disclosure would cause some injury to the interest of the state or the proper functioning of the public service and on the other hand if it is not disclosed, the non-disclosure would thwart the administration of justice by keeping back from the court a material document. There are two aspects of public interest clasing with each other out of which the court has to decide which predominates."

His Lordship then adverted to certain observations of Lord Reid in *Conway* vs. *Rimmer*. 1968 A.C. 910 and concluded as under:

> "The court has to balance the detriment to the public interest on the

> administrative of executive side which would result from the disclosure of the document against the detriment to the public interest on the judicial side which would result from non-disclosure of the document though relevant to the proceeding. . . . The court has thus to perform a balancing exercise and after weighing the one competing aspects of public interest against the other decide where the balance lies. If the court comes to the conclusion that, on the balance, the disclosure of the document would cause greater injury to public interest than its non-disclosure, the court would uphold the objection and not allow the document to be disclosed but if, on the other hand, the court finds that the balance between competing public interests lies the other way, the court would order the disclosure of the document."

His Lordship also adverted to the following observations of Mathew, J., which are in the same strain in *State of U.P.* vs. *Raj Narain* (AIR 1975 SC 865):

> "In a government of responsibility like ours, where all the agents of the pubic must be responsible for their conduct, there can be but few secrets. The people of this country have a right to knew every public act, everything that is done in a public way, by their public functionaries. They are entitled to know the particulars of every public transaction in all its bearing. The right to know, which is derived from the concept of freedom of speech, though not absolute, is a factor which should make one way, when secrecy is claimed for transactions which can, at any rate, have no repercussion on public security, see *New York Times Co.* vs. *United States*, (1971) 29 Law Ed.822-403 U.S. 713. To cover with veil of secrecy, the common routine business, is not in the interest of the public. Such secrecy can seldom be legitimately desired. It is generally desired for the purpose of parties and politics or personal self-interest or bureaucratic routine. The responsibility of officials to explain and to justify their acts is the chief safeguard against oppression and corruption."

Lastly the learned Additional Solicitor General canvassed with considerable ferver that the disclosure of the details pertaining to the preparation of and finalisation of the secretary level suitability list, would affect the free and frank expression of opinion or advice before decision-making and therefore the public interest would suffer by the disclosure of the said document. The "candour argument" was examined by Bhagwati, J. in depth and adverting to observation of Lord Reid and some other Law Lords in *Conway* vs. *Rimmer* (supra) *Glasgo Corporation* vs. *Central Land board* 1956 S.C.1(HL)20 and *Reg.* vs. *Lewes Justices exparte Secretary of State for Home Deptt.* 1973 AC 388, His Lordship observed that the need for candour and frankness cannot satisfy granting of complete immunity against disclosure of document of this class. The need for candour and frankness must however be regarded as a factor to be taken into account in determining whether, on balance, the public interest is in favour of disclosure or against it. The object of granting immunity to documents of this kind is to ensure the proper working of the government and not to protect the ministers and other government servants from criticism, however, intemperate and unfairly based.

29. It is in the light of the foregoing observations in relation to the provisions

of section 123 of the Indian Evidence Act that we have to see whether we can and if so, to what extent, look into the proceedings of the special committee and the recommendations made by them for empanelling certain officers of 1957 batch of the I.A.S. to be eventually appointed to the post of secretary to the Government of India. The right of the court to peruse this file itself has not been disputed by the learned Additional Solicitor General and it is for obvious reasons, namely, that the court has to decide the claim of privilege and can do so only after perusing the same. Accordingly, we opened the sealed cover relating to empanelment of I.A.S. officers for secretary level posts. We notice that it consists of three parts. The first part relates to the methodology adopted by the special committee in preparing the panal out of 1957 I.A.S. officers considered suitable for appointment to the post of secretaries (level) to the Government of India. It *inter alia* comprises the names of 19 officers who were actually recommended for empanelment. The second part consists of the advice tendered by the Hon'ble Minister of State for Home Affairs, Department of Personnel and the Hon'ble Minister of Home Affairs and the third part comprises the approval of empanelment of 17 officers of 1957 batch of the I.A.S. for inclusion in the panel for secretary level posts by the Hon'ble Prime Minister. There can be no room for doubt that the disclosure of names of the officers of 1957 batch who were actually selected and recommended for empanelment, that is, for inclusion in the panel for promotion as secretary to the Government of India would not be in public interest. It is for two obvious reasons. In the first instance, it would appear that the said pannel is still current and has not been fully exhausted. Disclosure of the names of all of them would be virtually stirring the harnets' nest and it will open the floodgates of fresh litigation from the officers who have not been recommended for empanelment. Secondly this court is not supposed to sit in appeal and undertake the task of reassessment/reevaluation of the relative merit of each candidate unless of course *mala fide* or colourable exercise of power is alleged. Thus, we consider that interests of justice would be well served if only the methodology and the criteria adopted by the special committee of secretaries/Hon'ble Ministers for selection and empanelment of I.A.S. officers of 1957 batch are disclosed. Needless to state that partial disclosure of a document, i.e., the innocuous part or the part disclosure of which would not injure public interest in comparison to the public interest in due administration of justice is quite permissible. So the court is free to disclose that part and uphold the objection as regards the rest, provided that this will not give a misleading impression. (See Speech of Lord Pearce in *Conway* vs. *Rimmer* (supra) (1968) 1 A11. E.R.874 at page 911). The criteria may be summarised as under:

(1) All IAS officers are considered batch-wise as a whole and the criterion of minimum of 3 years service in a post carrying a basic pay of Rs. 3,000 and above applicable for empanelment of officers of the Central Services was not applied in the case of I.A.S. officers on the ground that no such condition had been adhered to in the past in their case as affirmed from the records.

(2) The officers who had less than 2 years service before their superannuation were left out of consideration by the committee. By excluding 9 officers, who had either less than 2 years service left before

officer has been superseded. All the same in order to rule out any grievance actual or fancied, some objective basis for the categorisation of various officers considered for selection should be indicated. In the instant case, as already observed, no such criteria or guidelines have been spelt out in the Staffing Science and even to special committee has given no inkling as to how relative assessment with regard to the merit and suitability of the various officers was made. It is trite that justice need not only, be done but it also must seem to have been done, however, we have looked in vain for any governing considerations for relative assessment of the various officers considered by the special committee except that they just recommended 19 out 61 officers considered by them. To our mind that does not ensure justice and fairplay to those who have been passed over seemingly unceremoniously. Of course, we say this with all deference to cabinet secretary and his companion members of the special committee. In contradistinction to the report of the special committee, the Hon'ble Minister of State for Home Affairs, did take pains to examine the service dossiers of 9 officers included in the list of officers recommended by the special committee and made his own comments. The Hon'ble Minister observed:

> "In my view we should look for officers with leadership qualities, conceptual skills and ability in policy formulation. Officers with varied experience and who have been consistenal graded as Very Good/Outstanding by a number of superiors and whose record contains mention of noteworthy performance, would possess the qualities that we are looking for. I have examined the CR dossiers in this background."

To say the least the approach of the Hon'ble Minister is extremely laudable. However, unfortunately, the staffing scheme does not even remotely refer to the guidelines/criteria adopted by the Hon'ble Minister. It is high time that the proper criteria/guidelines for the selection of officers for appointment to the posts of secretary to the Government of India etc. are duly incorporated in the staffing scheme so as to minimise the chances of capricious/colourful exercise of power by the concerned selection committee.

32. It is further noticed that the Hon'ble Minister made a critical appraisal of the service performance of the 9 officers about whom he had his own reservations. We wish that the special committee should have adopted the same approach and articulated the same in recording concise service profile of each officer mentioning both their plus and minus points in order to give an overall picture of their merit and suitability. So even though we are disinclined to quash the empanelment of 17 officers as finally approved by the Hon'ble Prime Minister for appointment to the posts of secretary level, we feel persuaded to hold that the possiblity of some of the officers who have been passed over without a proper fair appraisal of their service record cannot be altogether ruled out. As already observed, one need not confine the equal of quality to a comparative evaluation between two persons to arrive at a conclusion of discriminatory treatment. An action *per se* arbitrary itself denies equal protection of law. Undoubtedly, the must look with respect upon the performance of duties by experts committee, but the task of ushering in a society based on rule of law is entrusted to the court and it cannot abdicate its functions.

33. To sum up, therefore, we allow this application and direct the respondents

to suitably amend the senior staffing scheme of 1970 as also O.M. dated 8-4-87 by laying down and incorporating therein in express terms the requisite criteria for selection of officers who happen to be in the field of choice so as to ensure just and fair treatment to all of them and minimise the chances of arbitrary/capricious/colourful exercise of power by the concerned authorities. After the needful is done, the respondents shall review the cases of the remaining 42 officers including the petitioner, it still available, for selection and empanelment of those found suitable for promotion as secretary to the Government of India. Their service dossiers etc. shall be considered as on the date on which the special committee had considered their cases earlier, viz., 18-12-86 and those found suitable and selected shall be promoted forthwith with all consequential benefits. These orders shall be implemented by the respondents within six months from today. It is further clarified that if any appointments are made to the posts of secretary to the Government of India or posts equivalent thereto from out of later batch of I.A.S., the same shall be subject to the final selection from amongst all the remaining I.A.S. officers of 1957 batch.

34. As regards the second relief with regard to the extension of the tenure of the petitioner, suffice is to say that his deputation tenure has already expired. Surely, it cannot be extended on the bare expectation that he may be eventually selected and empanelled pursuant to the orders of this court. Hence, no relief with regard to the extension of his tenure can be granted.

35. Lastly, we also make it clear that the petitioner was permitted to continue his occupation of official residence under the orders of this court from time to time. Hence, he shall be liable to pay licence fee under the rules as if he were still posted at Delhi till today and shall not be liable to pay the penal rent.

sd/-
J.D. Jain, Vice Chairman

I agree. However, in order to arrive at a correct and just conclusion in this case, one has also to traverse some segments of historical/sociological landscape relevant to the issues raised herein.

2. The learned Additional Solicitor-General of India, appearing for the respondent-Government of India, argued at length that the appointments to the post of secretary to the Government of India were extremely sensitive and they could not be covered by the usual norms and further that the orders of the Appointment Committee of the cabinet could not be open to review. According to him, the appointments to the posts of additional secretary and above in Government of India could not be confined to the straitjacket of normative procedure. The argument put forth on behalf of the Government of India has wider implications which can be better studied against a historical/sociological perspective. Justice Oliver W. Holmes has observed "the law requires the help of history in clearing away subbish."[1] Similarly, Justice V.R. Krishna Iyer in the course of his judgement in the case of *State of Kerala and other* vs. *Thomas and others* has observed as follows:

"131. Law, including constitutional law, can no longer 'to it alone', but must be illumined in the interpretative process by sociology and fields of knowledge."

Aid of history and sociology has to be invoked in determining the merits of the issue raised in this case since it encompasses not only the right of the application but also the question of ultimate control over the civil servants and the manner of exercising the same. Such issues are not truly amenable to a facit one-dimensional analysis/treatment.

3. The structure of Civil Services in India is based upon what is called 'the merit system' which simply means selection of the best available persons regardless of any other extraneous considerations. This system prevails, at present, in almost all the countries in he world with varying degrees of autonomy granted to the Services and control over the Services vesting in the political apparatus of the state. To the modern man, if appears that merit-based system of administration is a natural one and as if it has always been there. It is not so. The original system by which the feudal state administrated was the system of patronage and which, later on, came to be called "spoils system" in the U.S.A. It is only recently, that is, in the 19th Century, that the Civil administration based on merit system was evolved. Earlier, the posts both in civil administration and in the military establishment went to the members of the privileged classes of known lineage and loyalty.

4. Ralph P. Hummel, in this book 'The Bureaucratic Experience' observes as follows on the pre-modern system of administrations:

"In contrast, the precursors of modern bureaucracy are patriachal and patrimonial systems. Pre-modern organisations that survive today include the family, especially the extended family of some ethnic groups, political machines and the Mafia. In such pre-modern organisations, the law is what the father-rule says it is, within the confines of tradition. Areas of responsibility may be delegated, but not systematically and they are subject to the arbitrary will of the father as sovereign. . . .

(Page 77).

"In contrast, under pre-modern rule, authority is centralised in the paternal rulers and either not clearly distributed, if delegated, or not distributed at all. A contemporary example is the unstable fate of a White House staffer whose authority not only may overlap with others, but who has no permanence since the President may relieve him at any time; nor are his functions usually clearly delineated or clearly understood by others. Contrast this with authority distribution in any of the permanent cabinet departments."

(Page 78)

The above extracts bring out the arbitrariness of the earlier system — the pattern which still persists in some areas of the U.S. administration.

5. In the U.S.A., with the inauguration of the Presidency in 1789, the civil administration was packed with political appointees. It is a misreading of history that the spoils system was ushered in by the seventh President, Andrew Jackson. Andrew Jackson was an outspoken advocate of this system, but the political appointments to civil services were made by all the earlier Presidents

including the first President, George Washington and even the third President, Thomas Jefferson though he is known for his enlightened views. The patronage pressures of the spoils system continued to plague the administration in the U.S.A. till Woodrow Wilson, who having done his law from the Princeton, had emerged as an ardent proponent of an apolitical civil service. Though he hedged on certain points, he was successful to impress the distinction in politics and administration and secure a measure of acceptance for merit based civil service. Later, Max Weber's model of the apolitical type of bureaucracy came to command wider acceptance.

6. In our country, the posts in the Government were offered under patronage system as this system was prevalent in the ruling country, i.e. the Great Britain till 1854 when a switch-over was made to a merit-based civil service on the basis of Northcote Travleyian report. The Indian Civil Service operated in a feudal and agricultural hinterland where the main tasks were largely confined to collection of land revenue and maintenance of law and order. These civil servants not only comprised an elitist class but were so well paid off in the prevailing backwardness of the economy that they came to be called to constitute a "Rolls-Royce administration in a bullock-cart country".[2] The prize of I.C.S. posts was glittering and attracted the best of the talents. I.C.S. officers came to be looked upon with a measure of admiration and tried to emulate the ideal of Plato's philosopher administrators and a sympathetic vignette of their working lives is available in some books — one of the most well-known being 'The Guardian (The Men who ruled India)' by Phillip Woodroff.

7. We may now note the evolution of all India services in our country, after Independence in 1947, because this has a bearing on the problem thrown up in this case. The provisions for the constitutional safeguards for the services were evolved after long deliberations among the Home Ministry and the provinces and were debated in the Constituent Assembly on 7th and 8th September, 1949: Only article 314 was moved in the Assembly on 10th October, 1949. Preceding the debate, the case for provision of Constitutional safeguards for these Services was put forth in the following words by the then deputy Prime Minister Sardar Vallabhai Patel, in his letter of April 17, 1948 addressed to the Prime Minister:

> "In consultation with, and with the unanimous support of, provincial governments, we have evolved two new services to take the place of the Indian Civil Service and the Indian Police viz., the Indian Administrative Service and the Indian Police Service. We have made recruitments, have issued rules of recruitment, discipline, control et., and have entered into agreements with candidates for these services. . . I need hardly emphasise that an efficient, disciplined and contended service assured of its prospects as a result of diligent and honest work, is a sine qua non of sound administration under a democratic regime even more than under an authoritarian rule. The service must be above party and we should ensure that political considerations, either in its recruitment or in its discipline and control, are reduced to the minimum, if not eliminated altogether. . . .[3]

During the debate in the constituent Assembly on the Constitutional safeguards for the Services, the then deputy Prime Minister answering the critics of the proposals said:

> "When the Indian Independence Act was to be passed in Parliament the draft was sent here. The leaders of the nation were called for; the cabinet was there, the Congress President was there, your President was there and your leader today was there. Mahatma Gandhi was also present. Every section was scrutinised and the draft was approved. After that it was passed in Parliament. Now, these guarantees were circulated before that to be provinces. All provinces agreed. It was also agreed to incorporate these into the Constituent Assembly's new Constitution. That is one part of the guarantee. . . ."
>
> ". . . as a man of experience, I tell you, do not quarrel with the instruments with which you want to work. It is a bad workman who quarrels with his instruments. Take work from them. . . . If you have done with it and decide not to have this service at all, even in spite of my pledge word, I will take the services with me and go. . . .[4]

8. With the above Constitutional provisions, security of tenure became available to the administrators. However, security of tenure can also breed a sense of complacency in some individuals. Intensive and extensive research has been carried out by social scientists into the structure and behaviour of administrators and they have dealt at length with a number of problems generated by the administrative culture. It is no place to go into the myriad facets researched. Suffice to say that the services received praise from only a few of the perceptive researchers and leaders of public opinion but they have come in generally for criticism. Here, notice has to be taken of two deficiencies which affect their relationship with the elected rulers in a democracy. First is the alleged 'non performance' or 'non administration' or being not sufficiently achievement-oriented to secure the results promised to the electorate and secondly, their not being accountable to the people whereas the elected representatives are. This problem is best illustrated in the following words of President Truman when he was to hand-over U.S. Presidency to his successor General Eisenhower:

> "He will sit here and he will say 'do this, do that' and nothing will happen. Poor Ike — It will not be a bit like the Army. He will find it very frustrating."

Same exasperation is facetiously brought out in 'Yes Minister' where the authors Jonathan Lynn and Antony Jay put forth that political opposition to the ruling party is opposition in exile whereas civil service is the real opposition in residence. Observers have found not only occasional mistrust between the elected rulers and permanent servants but also a measure of antipathy between them which is highly dysfunctional. Government is an organisation and in all human organisations, hierarchy provides the mechanism for achieving results. According to Dr. Laurence J. Peter (of Peter Principle) each new hierarchy provides considerable competence but eventually matures into a bureaucracy of ineptitude.[5] Thus meritocracy degenerates, in time, to mediocracy, according to him. The so-called bureaucratic inertia has accordingly attracted adverse notice both from elected rulers and researchers. This problem is confronted in the third world countries too which are working hard to overcome problems of backwardness of stagerring proportions. Having been bye-passed by the industrial revolution and now the technological as well as hi-tech revolution, there are pressure in these countries to find instant solutions to complex problems. Thus, their leaders sometimes lose patience and feel that merit-based system should be scrapped. Prime Minister Z.A. Bhutto lost patience with rule-based administration in his country and denounced the same by saying that it had created a class of 'Brahmins or mandarins unrivalled in its snobbery and arrogance, insulted from the life of the people and incapable of identifying itself with them. . . .'[6] Then he proceeded to radars the situation by placing political appointees in all the establishments and invitaed consequences which by now are well-known, but also bequeathed a legacy whose full impact has yet to unfold. Some of the problems which the U.S. Administration faces and which periodically surface attracting media attention (viz. Watergate, Irancontra etc.) are also ascribed by some of the experts due to the compromising of merit-based system of administration by allocating posts to the political appointees in some sensitive areas.

9. The second problem in this connection is that of contract and accountability. The leviathan character and ceaseless expansion of bureaucracy are universally commented along with the difficulty of controlling this runway machine. At the same time, the problem of accountability in modern times has emerged as one of serious proportions. The civil servant remains independent of the electoral control though as shares governing power with the elected representatives and is thus not accountable to the electorate. John A. Rohr observes that the 'combination of these two ingredients — governing power and independence from the electorate — presents a significant problem for a democratic society. . . ."[7] This problem was debated fiercely and passionately in early days of U.S. revolution and still reges in some countries. The problem is of extension of democratic principle requiring accountability to the people from those who seek to govern them. Different polities have been evolving different instruments of accountability for their civil servants. One of the most favoured coping strategy is of greater publicity of decisions and reasons thereafter. This has been taken to such an extant in Canada and Sweden that in the latter, it has been said that the administration works 'in a gold fish bowl'. Whether it is the Presidential America, the Politbureau USSR, or the Parliamentary England, the difficulty is being encountered in enforcing the achievement norm and accountability. In all these countries, elected leaders of the government have come to exercise considerable discretion in choosing their senior civil servants; in U.K. also such selections have recently come to be made by the Prime Minister — a clear departure from pastpractice.[8]

10. The argument addressed on behalf of the Goverhment of India has to be examined in this overall context. So far as the primacy of the elected representatives in the government is concerned, the same cannot be disputed. Paul M. Appleby, the American export on administration, has brought out this feature in the following words:

> "Hallmark of democracy is dominance of government by politicians of popularly oriented, chosen and accountable."[9]
>
> ". . . . The civil servant exists for the government and the government for

the sake of the people. The politician is the special formal embodiment of that popular dedication".[10]

He distinguishes the political and parties in character of the government as follows:

"All administration and all policy making within the government are political, being governmental, but only a small part of either, by mass, has identifiable partisan character".[11]

Thus, in democracy, the control of the administration must vest in the elected representatives but such political control is not to be equated with procurement of partisan ends. It is, therefore, but right that the final authority to make senior appointments vests in the Appointments Committee of the cabinet. From the foregoing brief historical background, it will also be clear that there can be no challenge to such a power of the cabinet. All the suggestions of any selection committees can thus be only recommendatory, and not mandatory, for consideration of the Appointments Committee of the cabinet. It would imply that the cabinet or its committee need not affix seal of approval on names recommended. It also postulates that the committee can incorporate names of officers according to its own selection. The argument advanced by the applicant that such control is not in the best interests of justice or administration lacks a legal foundation as well as ignorance of evolution of a democratic polity.

11. However, all control is to emanate from the powers conferred by the Constitution. In this regard, the rights given by the Constitution to the civil servants have also to be ensured. Now, the only question to be determined is how the ultimate power of the cabinet for selection of civil servants to higher posts is given effect to. It was strenuously urged on behalf of the Government of India that the selection made by the Appointments Committee of the cabinet could not be reviewed. This argument would prevail only if the civil servants had no right. Only 'a slave can have no right against his master . . . rightlessness is a condition of slavery'[12] — an atavistic situation which will be the antithesis of democracy and a negation of all human dignity and progress. The Indian Constitution enshrines an elaborate network of rights for all its citizens including civil servants. The rights conferred by the Constitution cannot be denied by a mere assertion that the purported decision was taken by a committee of the cabinet. Thus the method of selection has to be such which protects the rights of civil servants as well as leaves control of the process in the hands of the cabinet committee.

12. The method for selection for the post of additional secretary and secretary is provided in the scheme contained in the cabinet secretariat office memorandum F.No.33(1)-EO/70 dated 27 October 1970. Paragraphs 2 and 3 of the said office memorandum read as under:

"(2) The senior selection board of the central establishment board shall not be concerned with recommendations for appointment to posts at the level of additional secretary, special secretary and secretary to the Government of India.

(3) In respect of cases referred to at (2) above, the cabinet secretary

> shall after considering the claims of various officers, whether serving in the Government of India or in the states, submit his recommendations directly to the Appointments Committee for orders. In the discharge of his official responsibility for management tasks concerning senior management, the cabinet secretary shall be assisted by the secretary, Department of Personnel."

Whereas a structural matrix of selection is provided herein, there is, however, nothing contained in these instructions to show how the cabinet secretary will engage himself in the process of selection. The only criterion laid is that the cabinet secretary shall consider the 'claims of various officers'. The mechanics for evaluating the claims has not been spelt out. Though the cabinet secretary may take into consideration the sensitive nature of the duties of secretary to the Government of India, nonetheless the method of selection has to be articulated to exclude any element of caprice.

13. It is observed that detailed guidelines exist for selection of I.A.S. officers to the super-time scale posts. These guidelines were circulated by the Government of India vide their No. 11030/4/82-AIS (11) dated 28 March 1983 in continuation of the instruction of 27 December 1975. These guidelines not only provide for the composition of the Screening Committee etc, but also lay down the method of selection. Relevant portion of para (3) of these guidelines is reproduced below:

> "3 *Method of selection*
>
> (i) selection should be based on merit with due regard to seniority as provides in sub-rule 2(A) of rule 3 of the Indian Administrative Service (Pay) Rules, 1954.
>
> (ii) Suitability of officers to hold super-time scale posts may be judged by evaluating their *character roll* record as a whole, *and general assessment of their work.*
>
> (iii) An officer against whom a vigilance or departmental inquiry has been started should also be assessed and the assessment placed in a sealed cover. The question of including him in the panel should be considered when the rule of the inquiry is known.
>
> (iv) The reasons for supersession may be indicated in the case of officers who are not included in the panel. . . ."

Here, it may be mentioned that in view of these guidelines, the argument advanced on behalf of the Government of India-respondent at the bar that sub-rule 2(A) of rule 3 of the Indian Administrative (Pay) Rules, 1954 does not provide for method of selection beyond selection grade, would collapse. Once the Government of India issues guidelines based on this sub-rule, it cannot be argued on their behalf that this sub-rule is to regulate pay and has no part to play in selections.

Again, these instructions are being carried out by the state governments. It is rather strange that there should be such guidelines for the posts in super-time scale but no such guidelines should exist for selection of posts above super-time scale, i.e. additional secretary and secretary to the Government of India. It is true that in view of enormously complex tasks which a modern